Contemporary Debates in Philosophy of Mind

Contemporary Debates in Philosophy

In teaching and research, philosophy makes progress through argumentation and debate. *Contemporary Debates in Philosophy* presents a forum for students and their teachers to follow and participate in the debates that animate philosophy today in the western world. Each volume presents pairs of opposing viewpoints on contested themes and topics in the central subfields of philosophy. Each volume is edited and introduced by an expert in the field, and also includes an index, bibliography, and suggestions for further reading. The opposing essays, commissioned especially for the volumes in the series, are thorough but accessible presentations of opposing points of view.

Contemporary Debates in Philosophy of Mind

Edited by

Brian P. McLaughlin and Jonathan Cohen

Blackwell
Publishing

BLACKWELL PUBLISHING
350 Main Street, Malden, MA 02148-5020, USA
9600 Garsington Road, Oxford OX4 2DQ, UK
550 Swanston Street, Carlton, Victoria 3053, Australia

First published 2007 by Blackwell Publishing Ltd

1   2007

Library of Congress Cataloging-in-Publication Data

Contemporary debates in philosophy of mind / edited by Brian McLaughlin and
Johnathan Cohen.
        p.   cm. – (Contemporary debates in philosophy)
    Includes bibliographical references and index.
    ISBN 978-1-4051-1760-9 (hardcover : alk. paper)
    ISBN 978-1-4051-1761-6 (pbk. : alk. paper)
    1. Philosophy of mind.   I. McLaughlin, Brian P.   II. Cohen, Jonathan.

    BD418.3.C656 2007
    128′.2–dc22

                                                              2007010201

A catalogue record for this title is available from the British Library.

Set in 10 on12.5 pt Rotis Serif
by SNP Best-set Typesetter Ltd, Hong Kong

For further information on
Blackwell Publishing, visit our website:
www.blackwellpublishing.com

We dedicate this volume to Judy H. McLaughlin
and Liza Perkins-Cohen.

Contents

Notes on Contributors

Louise Antony is Professor of Philosophy at the University of Massachusetts, Amherst. In her research she attempts to develop naturalistic accounts of meaning, knowledge, and agency that square with our scientific understanding of the mind. She is the author of numerous articles in the philosophy of mind, epistemology, and feminist theory, and has co-edited two collections of original essays, *Chomsky and His Critics* (with Norbert Hornstein) and *A Mind of One's Own: Feminist Essays on Reason and Objectivity* (with Charlotte Witt).

David Braddon-Mitchell is Reader in Philosophy at the University of Sydney. He has published papers in the philosophy of mind and metaphysics in *Noûs*, the *Journal of Philosophy*, *Mind*, the *Australasian Journal of Philosophy*, *Philosophical Studies*, the *British Journal for the Philosophy of Science*, *Erkenntnis*, *Synthese*, and various others. He is author, with Frank Jackson, of *The Philosophy of Mind and Cognition*.

Anthony Brueckner is Professor of Philosophy at the University of California, Santa Barbara. He has written articles about skepticism, transcendental arguments, content externalism, self-knowledge, theories of justification, anti-realism, personal identity, and the metaphysics of death.

Paul M. Churchland is Professor of Philosophy and holds the Valtz Chair at the University of California, San Diego. He is the author of *Scientific Realism and the Plasticity of Mind*, *Matter and Consciousness*, and *Neurophilosophy at Work* (forthcoming). His research lies at the intersection of cognitive neuroscience, epistemology, and the philosophy of mind.

Jonathan Cohen is Associate Professor of Philosophy at the University of California, San Diego. He works on topics in philosophy of mind, language, and perception, particularly as these are informed by the cognitive sciences. Many of his articles in recent years have concerned the metaphysics of color.

Jerry Fodor shares an appointment between the Philosophy Department at Rutgers and the Rutgers Center for Cognitive Science. He is currently at work on a book about the language of thought.

Richard G. Heck Jr is Professor of Philosophy at Brown University. He works primarily on philosophy of language, logic, and mathematics, and has written extensively about the work of Gottlob Frege.

Frank Jackson is Distinguished Professor of Philosophy at the Australian National University.

Jaegwon Kim is the William Perry Faunce Professor of Philosophy at Brown University. Among his recent publications are *Physicalism, or Something Near Enough* (2005) and *Philosophy of Mind* (2nd edn., 2006).

Barry Loewer is Professor at Rutgers, Director of the Rutgers Center for Philosophy and the Sciences, and fellow at the Collegium Budapest. He is the author of many articles in the philosophy of physics, the philosophy of mind, metaphysics, and logic. He is finishing a book on the metaphysics of laws, causation, and chance.

Michael McKinsey is Professor of Philosophy at Wayne State University. He is the author of many articles in the philosophy of language, the philosophy of mind, and ethics. His work has primarily concerned the semantics of natural language, especially the meaning and reference of proper names, indexicals, and natural kind terms, as well as the meaning and logical form of cognitive ascriptions.

Brian P. McLaughlin is Professor of Philosophy at Rutgers University. He is the author of numerous articles in the philosophy of mind.

Martine Nida-Rümelin is Professor at the Department of Philosophy, University of Fribourg, Switzerland. Her published work focuses on issues related to the debate about the ontological status of consciousness, especially on phenomenal consciousness (phenomenal concepts, anti-materialist arguments) and on transtemporal identity of conscious individuals (first person thought and identity across time). She is at present directing a research project on the philosophy of color vision. In her more recent research she has worked on the phenomenology of agency and the problem of free will.

Christopher Peacocke is Professor of Philosophy at Columbia University and a Fellow of the British Academy. He is currently working on a book on reference, understanding, and reasons.

Jesse Prinz is Associate Professor of Philosophy at the University of North Carolina, Chapel Hill. His books and articles concern various aspects of the mind, including consciousness, concepts, emotion, moral psychology, and cultural cognition.

Georges Rey is Professor of Philosophy at the University of Maryland at College Park. He works primarily in the philosophy of psychology, particularly the foundations of cognitive science, and has written extensively on the nature of concepts, images, qualia, and consciousness. He is the author of *Contemporary Philosophy of Mind* (Blackwell, 1997), and the editor of the cognitive science entries for the *Routledge Encyclopedia of Philosophy* and (with Barry Loewer) of *Meaning in Mind: Fodor and His Critics* (Blackwell, 1991). He is at present working on a book on the role of intentionality and intentional inexistents in early visual and linguistic processing.

Sarah Sawyer is Associate Professor of Philosophy at the University of Sussex. Her research is in the philosophy of mind, epistemology, and the philosophy of language.

Gabriel Segal is Professor of Philosophy at King's College, London. He is author of *A Slim Book about Narrow Content* (MIT Press, 2000) and co-author, with Richard Larson, of *Knowledge of Meaning* (MIT Press, 1995).

Sydney Shoemaker is Susan Linn Sage Professor of Philosophy Emeritus at Cornell University. He is the author of *Self-Knowledge and Self-Identity, Identity, Cause and Mind*, and *The First-Person Perspective and Other Essays*.

Michael Tye is Professor of Philosophy at the University of Texas at Austin. He is the author of several books on consciousness, including *Ten Problems of Consciousness*.

Ralph Wedgwood is Lecturer in Philosophy at the University of Oxford and a Fellow of Merton College, Oxford. He has published several articles on metaethics, epistemology, and related areas in metaphysics and the philosophy of mind. In 2007 he will publish a book, *The Nature of Normativity*, that will give a unified presentation of some of his thinking about these subjects.

Introduction

Jonathan Cohen

Philosophy of mind today is a sprawling behemoth whose tentacles reach into virtually every area of philosophy, as well as many subjects outside of philosophy. Of
course, none of us would have it any other way. Nonetheless, this state of affairs
poses obvious organizational challenges for anthology editors. Brian McLaughlin and
I have attempted to meet these challenges in the present volume by focusing on ten
controversial and fundamental topics in philosophy of mind. "Controversial" is clear
enough: we have chosen topics about which there is not a settled consensus among
philosophers. By "fundamental" we don't mean that the issues are easy or that the
approaches taken toward them are introductory. Rather, we mean that (i) the resolu-
tion of these topics has implications for other issues inside and outside philosophy of
mind, and (ii) past rounds of debate have revealed these topics as underlying broader
disagreements. We asked leading philosophers of mind to defend one side or another
on these topics. The result is what you now have in your hands.

In the remainder of this introduction I'll say something by way of explanation of
the topics covered and attempt to say how the topics relate to one another.

Content

A first cluster of topics concerns the nature of mental content. To say that mental
states have content is to say that they can be *about* other things: for example, my
current belief that there is a coffee cup on my desk is about the coffee cup and the
desk. That mental states can be about things is a striking fact about them, and one
that distinguishes them from most entities in the world (e.g., atoms, rocks, tables,
numbers, properties). Moreover, insofar as things other than mental states (e.g., words,
some paintings, scientific models) can have content, many philosophers have followed
Grice (1957) in maintaining that they do so only by deriving their content from that

of the mental states of the makers or users of these other things; thus, while a painting might also be about the coffee cup, the Grice-inspired thought is that it has this content only by virtue of the content of the painter's intentions (e.g., her intention to produce a painting that is about that particular coffee cup), which are of course mental states. If this general picture is right, then mental content is more fundamental than other sorts of content. But what sort of a thing is mental content? And how is it constituted? What makes it the case, for example, that my current thought is about a coffee cup rather than a palm tree or nothing at all? These and related questions lie at the heart of the first cluster of topics in this volume.

Our first topic in this cluster is best appreciated against the backdrop of work starting in the mid-1970s (e.g., Putnam, 1975; Burge, 1979) arguing that the content of a thought is not wholly determined by the internal state of the thinker's brain. On the contrary, these writers argued for what has come to be called *content externalism* – the view that what a thought is about is partially determined by factors outside the head of the thinker, such as the thinker's physical and social environment. In Chapter 1, Gabriel Segal argues against content externalism. More specifically, he argues that what he calls "cognitive content" – the kind of content invoked in psychological explanations and propositional attitude ascriptions – is not fixed externalistically. His claim is that, even if externalists are right that the *extensions* of public language words (e.g., "water") are determined by factors outside the thinker's brain, nonetheless the cognitive content expressed by such terms is (i) idiosyncratic to individuals (or even time-slices of individuals), and (ii) determined by factors inside their heads. If so, then cognitive content is best understood as a kind of narrow or individualist (as opposed to externalist/anti-individualist) content. Sarah Sawyer argues against this approach in Chapter 2. She argues that if cognitive contents were to float free from the shared meanings and extensions of the public language words we use to attribute contents, as Segal holds, then it would be a rare miracle if any verbal attribution ever succeeded in capturing anyone's cognitive contents. And this, she claims, would make a mystery of the utility and ubiquity of our practice of making verbal ascriptions of psychological contents to others. Ultimately, she contends, proponents of narrow content have failed to appreciate the significance, force, and scope of extant arguments for content externalism.

A second issue connected with content externalism comes up in Chapters 3 and 4, and concerns privileged access about the content of our mental states. It seems deeply plausible that our access to the content of at least some of our thoughts has some sort of epistemic privilege. For example, it seems deeply plausible that if I take myself to be thinking about water, it is truly *water* (not coffee, not a palm tree, and not some clear, tasteless liquid other than water) that is the subject of my thought. However, in recent years philosophers have argued that content externalism poses a serious threat to this plausible idea. The thought here is that if, as per externalism, the contents of my thoughts depend on factors outside my head (including contingent facts about the existence of particular elements of my physical and social environment), then I won't know what those contents are whenever I am ignorant about the relevant external factors. In Chapter 4, Michael McKinsey argues that privileged access and content externalism are indeed incompatible, and that we should respond to the incompatibility by giving up the former. Anthony Brueckner holds, in Chapter 3, that the alleged incompatibility is merely apparent. He argues that, although content externalism entails that the content of my thought depends on contingent facts about my environment, it does not entail that my *knowing* the content of my thought requires *knowing* contingent facts about my environment: consequently, Brueckner holds, it is consistent with content externalism that I can know the content of my thoughts without having knowledge of contingent facts about my environment. Their debate raises important issues about exactly how to understand the entailments content externalism has about thinkers' environments, and about how we should individuate thoughts.

The volume also contains debates on two other foundational debates about content: one about the alleged normativity of content and one about how best to think about non-conceptual content.

The debate about the normativity of content is joined in Chapters 5 and 6 by Ralph Wedgwood and Georges Rey. The issue here is whether intentional (/contentful) mental states, such as beliefs, desires, the acceptance of inferences, and so on, are constitutively tied to "normative" properties such as value, goodness, and, in particular, rationality. Such normative properties are traditionally contrasted against the "descriptive" properties one finds invoked in the natural sciences. Thus, this debate has important implications for the question of whether the standard explanatory apparatus of the natural sciences can provide a complete account of contentful mental states.

Wedgwood argues that the intentional is essentially normative. He holds that intentional states are constituted by concepts, and he argues that the best theory of concepts has them constitutively linked to the normative. In particular, Wedgwood is attracted by a two-factor theory of concepts according to which each concept is constituted by (i) its correctness condition together with (ii) "certain basic principles of rationality that specify certain ways of using the concept as rational (or specify certain other ways of using the concept as irrational)" (p. 86). Thus, for example, on this account, we might understand the concept of logical conjunction as constituted by (i) the systematic contribution made by AND to the truth conditions of the complex contents in which it appears (its correctness condition) together with (ii) a principle specifying that (*inter alia*) the inference from (P AND Q) to P is rational while the inference from P to (P AND Q) is not. Insofar as this conception of the constitution of concepts ineliminably invokes notions of rationality, it results in an essentially normative view of the intentional; but Wedgwood argues that his is the most plausible view of concepts, so we should embrace the latter result.

Rey argues against Wedgwood's view in Chapter 5, and urges that our best scientific and philosophical accounts of mentality support a non-normative ("merely" descriptive) understanding of the intentional. Among the many complaints he levels against normative theories of the intentional, Rey worries (i) that there is no serious account of just which norms characterize particular concepts; (ii) that normative accounts of concepts don't do justice to the portions of our mental lives that don't seem to be governed by rational norms at all; and (iii) that even where applicable, such accounts give at best a superficial account of our mental lives. Rey suggests that Wedgwood and other proponents of an essentially normative account of the intentional base their view largely on intuitions about which rational inferences they are disposed to make involving particular concepts; but, while allowing that these intuitions are often widely and deeply held, he echoes Quine (1951) in worrying that their wide and deep support may show only that these inferences are deeply ingrained (as opposed to concept-constitutive, as Wedgwood claims). If so, Rey points out, then such intuitions (despite being widely and deeply held) should not be taken as revealing the nature of our concepts; but if taking these intuitions to be concept-constitutive really is the source of the view that concepts are normative, then Rey's worry threatens the case for the essentially normative character of the intentional.

In Chapters 7 and 8, Jerry Fodor and Richard Heck take on the topic of non-conceptual content. Discussion of this issue has centered in part on issues about perceptual justification. Many writers have thought that the best way to understand how perception justifies belief is by attributing content to perceptual states – thus, for example, my belief that there is a coffee cup on the desk would receive its justification from being appropriately related to a perceptual state with the very same content (that there is a coffee cup on the desk). But (a suitably generalized version of) this picture threatens to impose high cognitive demands on perception: it seems to require that our perceptual contents, in order to play any justificatory role, must be fully conceptualizeable (see Sellars, 1956, for a famous articulation of this worry). But many philosophers have felt that this demand is unreasonable – for example, because it threatens the idea of a preconceptual "given" that could justify belief, or because it threatens to rob the possibility of perceptual justification from non-human animals and human infants.

Some philosophers of mind have maintained that the best response to these threats is to credit perceptual states with a special kind of "non-conceptual content" – content whose tokening is both (i) suited to justify the conceptual content of beliefs, and (ii) not dependent on sophisticated conceptual capacities of the perceiver. The problem for theorists sympathetic to this move is to provide an informative characterization of this hypothesized non-conceptual content, and then to give reasons for believing there is any mental content satisfying that characterization.

This is where both Fodor and Heck begin in their essays for the present volume. Both accept the existence of non-conceptual content (in this sense they are both giving kinds of "yes" answers to the question "is there non-conceptual content?"); but they differ in how they understand what it is, and how to distinguish non-conceptual content from conceptual content. In his contribution, Fodor spends most of his effort massaging the philosophical question "is there non-conceptual content?" into a form that makes it susceptible to answers by empirical psychology. In particular, Fodor holds that a mental state is conceptual if and only if it is an instance of representation-as, and he takes it that such states count as bearing content in virtue of the information they carry about the world. Thus, for Fodor, the existence of non-conceptual content hinges on the evidence in favor of mental states that are contentful (in the informational sense) but not instances of representation-as. But, Fodor argues, there is ample psychological evidence of states of this kind, so we have reason to accept the existence of non-conceptual content. Heck also spends much of his essay trying to get clear on what sort of a thing non-conceptual content might be. According to Heck, it is structural features of a contentful state that make it conceptual or non-conceptual: the state will count as conceptual if it has constituent structure, and non-conceptual if not. This criterion allows Heck (unlike Fodor) to accept that instances of representation-as could be non-conceptual – namely, by lacking the right sort of constituent structure. Indeed, Heck argues that, on this way of making the distinction, the best accounts of perceptual content entail that it is non-conceptual.

Physicalism

A second, more ontological, cluster of topics taken up in this anthology concerns the relationship of mental states to the physical. Discussion of these topics is often organized around the physicalist/materialist hypothesis that everything (a fortiori, everything mental) is physical. With a few notable exceptions, contemporary philosophers of mind are generally sympathetic to some version of this hypothesis. But there is a startling lack of consensus about the details.

One way in which consensus is left behind is over the question of whether the best version of physicalism is reductive, non-reductive, or eliminativist – an issue taken up by Paul Churchland and Louise Antony in Chapters 9 and 10. Eliminative materialism, which is defended by Churchland in Chapter 10, is the view that our mental lives can be fully characterized by the (physical) kinds of neuroscience, and that putative psychological kinds such as belief, pain, and desire should be discarded as posits of a failed and outdated explanatory framework. Antony, in contrast, sees an important scientific role for such psychological kinds. Indeed, she wants to insist on a non-reductive materialism that preserves a place for these kinds without reducing them to (/identifying them with) physical kinds. The best-worked-out version of non-reductive materialism, endorsed by Antony in Chapter 9, is the so-called functionalist view according to which mental types are understood in terms of their causal profiles; on this view, for example, a state might count as a pain if it is caused by damage to its host organism and causes "ouch" -utterances and avoidance behavior (as it might be), no matter what its physical realization. Antony argues that this kind of non-reductive materialism is not only viable, but preferable to reductive or eliminative materialism in that it better respects the reality and causal/explanatory centrality of psychological state types (Antony calls this "psychological realism"), and the distinctness of the phenomena and explanations of psychology from lower level (e.g., neuroscientific) phenomena and explanations (she calls this "the autonomy of psychology"). Churchland defends eliminative materialism in Chapter 10 by claiming that non-reductive materialism has been oversold. In particular, he urges that the most popular functionalist versions of the view have failed to meet the promises made on their behalf, while eliminativist materialism turns out to be more plausible than many have allowed.

A second way in which consensus about physicalism is left behind turns on a contrast between a priori and a posteriori versions of the thesis. It is widely accepted that if physicalism is true, then the physical determines the mental. In contrast, it is deeply controversial whether the determination of the mental by the physical is a priori or a posteriori. What is in dispute here is not the epistemic status of physicalism itself (all sides agree that if physicalism is true then it is a posteriori), but instead the epistemic status of the determination of the mental by the physical that is implied by physicalism.

In Chapter 11, Frank Jackson defends a priori physicalism on epistemological and semantic grounds. In particular, he alleges that, if a posteriori physicalism were true, then this would undercut our warrant for adopting physicalism in the first place, and would also leave ordinary users of mental predicates without an understanding of what we are saying in ascribing such predicates (e.g., pains and beliefs) to each other. In Chapter 12, Brian McLaughlin first tries to cast doubt on the a priori physicalist thesis that the totality of truths of ultimate physics (in conjunction with a certain minimality thesis) will imply a priori all the truths couched in our everyday, vernacular physical vocabulary (e.g., the truth that water freezes at 32 °F). He maintains that it is an open question whether the concepts expressed by terms in our ordinary physical vocabulary will bear the kinds of a priori links to the concepts expressed in the vocabulary of ultimate physics that would be needed to underwrite such a priori implications. He then appeals to the conceivability of certain absent and inverted qualia cases – cases that have traditionally been used against physicalism itself – to argue that the links between our phenomenal concepts and physical/functional concepts are likewise non-a-priori. He holds that the phenomenal is indeed determined by the physical since phenomenal state types are identical with (broadly) physical/functional state types; but he contends that such type identity claims are warranted on a posteriori grounds of overall coherence and theoretical simplicity, and that they are not a priori implied by the totality of physical truths (and the minimality thesis).

One reason that the debate about a priori physicalism is so important is that it is intimately connected with the question of how far (certain kinds of) conceivability can be taken to reveal what is possible, which in turn bears directly on the modal commitments of physicalism. For we seem to be able to conceive of our world as one in which the physical facts fail to determine the mental facts. Now, if the determination required by physicalism comes with a priori knowability, then we should presumably be able to know a priori whether there is such necessary determination or not. But we have said that a priori reflection seems to leave open the possibility that there is no determination of the mental by the physical, which is to say that it tells against the claim that such determination is a priori. Thus, if we regard physicalism as requiring a priori determination, then what we can conceive poses a prima facie threat to its truth – a threat that has been regarded as fatal by at least some prominent philosophers of mind (e.g., Chalmers, 1996). On the other hand, if we regard the determination entailed by physicalism as a posteriori determination, we won't regard the conceivability of differences in mental facts without differences in physical facts as a decisive objection to physicalism.

Another ontological dispute connected with physicalism concerns mental causation – causation by mental states. Ordinary action explanations (e.g., the explanation of why I drained the glass of water that cites my desire for liquid) bring out our pretheoretical commitment to the idea of causation by mental states. Unfortunately, it is unclear how to understand what this commitment amounts to. Part of the difficulty has its source in a more general controversy over the nature of causation (for example, between counterfactual, nomological, and productive approaches to causation). But there are difficulties particular to mental (or at least higher-level) causation as well. Perhaps the most widely discussed of these is the problem of explanatory exclusion, pressed at the end of Chapter 13 by Jaegwon Kim. Kim worries that if every physical event has a sufficient physical cause, then there is no causal work left over for the mental to do. Kim takes this to show that either the mental is without causal efficacy (mental events would then be entirely epiphenomenal) or that the mental must be reductively identified with the physical. In Chapter 14, Barry Loewer disagrees with Kim's assessment. He argues that we have the materials we need for understanding mental causation, unless we insist on a "productive" understanding of causation that he thinks is eschewed in science. Thus, he responds to Kim's exclusion concerns by arguing that it is based on mistaken metaphysical presuppositions about causation. The upshot of Loewer's chapter is that, while there may be unresolved problems about causation itself, there are no further outstanding problems about mental causation in particular.

The Place of Consciousness in Nature

The ontological debates surveyed so far are directed at issues about mental states, generally speaking. But in the last decade or so philosophy of mind has seen a renewed focus on ontological issues about consciousness in particular. Many philosophers have found consciousness to be especially resistant to explanation in physicalist terms, and this has raised profound concerns about its place in nature.

For example, some thinkers have thought that consciousness, unlike the rest of mentality, is ontologically emergent from the physical – that it is something fundamentally new and different from the physical. Thus, in Chapter 15, Martine Nida-Rümelin argues that at some point in the historical evolution of life, certain bits of matter got arranged in a way that marked a fundamental break with what had come before (viz., mere physical stuff): new individuals that are conscious came into being where none had been previously. Nida-Rümelin's motivation for this view is a sense of puzzlement that she shares with many other philosophers, and that Levine (1984) famously dubbed "the explanatory gap": it seems extremely hard to see how or why a certain complex physically organized system should enjoy any conscious phenomenology rather than none, or should enjoy the particular conscious phenomenology it does rather than some other. Some have argued that the existence of this gap reveals more about our kinds of minds and the concepts they deploy than it does about the relationship of consciousness to the physical; for these thinkers, the explanatory gap is not evidence of the ontological emergence or non-physical status of consciousness. Nida-Rümelin, however, is unimpressed by this treatment of the explanatory gap. She suggests, instead, that we should take the gap, and our natural "astonishment" about consciousness seriously – and that the best explanation of why we are astonished is that the relation between consciousness and the physical is, after all, just as deeply astonishing as emergentism says that it is.

David Braddon-Mitchell opposes this and other forms of emergentism about consciousness, in Chapter 16. As he sees it, the appeal of emergentism is the hope of securing what is attractive about both physicalism (its integration of consciousness with the physical) and dualism (its recognition of the distinctiveness of consciousness vis-à-vis the physical). Thus, the emergentist claims that consciousness is a novel, hence genuinely emergent, feature of the world (this is the dualist ingredient) that emerges from a physical basis (this is the physicalist ingredient). However, Braddon-Mitchell argues, the emergentist's two opposing poles of attraction ultimately make her position unstable. For if the emergentist insists on the dualist-inspired claim that consciousness is distinct from the physical, she thereby loses the ability to explain the causal relations between the base and what emerges, and consequently is stuck with an unattractive epiphenomenalism. On the other hand, if she emphasizes the connections between consciousness and the physical base from which it emerges sufficiently to avoid charges of epiphenomenalism, it will turn out that consciousness is straightforwardly physical. Thus, Braddon-Mitchell claims, there is no coherent way for emergentists to have their cake and eat it.

Questions about the place of consciousness in nature come up again in a related debate between Michael Tye and Sydney Shoemaker in Chapters 17–18. Tye and Shoemaker would agree that when you consciously see a ripe tomato, or taste a chocolate soufflé, your experience represents the world in some particular way. Moreover, picking up on the content-externalist themes discussed in connection with Chapters 1–4, both these authors would agree that the representational properties of your experience are determined at least partly by factors outside your head. What divides Tye and Shoemaker is the question whether there is a further aspect of your experience – its phenomenal character (or, as it is sometimes glossed, the what-it's-like-to-have-it aspect) – that is distinct from its representational properties and is determined entirely by factors inside the head. Shoemaker argues that there is such a further, internalist, aspect of experiences, and concludes that the representational and phenomenal properties of experiences are distinct. Tye, in contrast, argues that the phenomenal character of an experience is identical to that experience's (externally determined) representational content. More particularly, he argues against the view that phenomenal character is entirely determined by factors inside the head, and against the view that phenomenal character is nonrepresentational.

This debate will, of course, interest anyone who wonders what an adequate characterization of conscious experience will look like. Moreover, in asking how far philosophical ideas about content can be pressed in the service of explaining consciousness, it bears on the question whether we can reduce one philosophical problem to another. This last point is especially important because, as remarked above, many philosophers have been baffled by the problem of how to integrate consciousness into a physicalist ontology; and while there has by no means been a convergence on a single physicalist theory of content, it has seemed to many that the outstanding problems about content are (at least, by comparison to those about consciousness) solvable matters of detail.

A final debate about consciousness in this volume concerns conscious awareness of our own thought – the kind of awareness we have of what we are doing when we consciously deliberate, wonder, imagine, judge, and so on. In Chapter 20, Christopher Peacocke argues that we should conceive of our awareness of our own thought as a special form of action-awareness. Peacocke takes his inspiration from the (widely held) idea that subjects have a special, non-perceptual awareness of their own physical actions (say, the action of sitting, of kicking, etc.). Building on this idea, he maintains that subjects have a special, non-perceptual awareness of their own mental actions (say, the action of deliberating, of wondering, etc.), and takes this to motivate the view that awareness of thought is a species of action-awareness. Peacocke maintains that this conception of conscious thought not only provides the right way to think about the metaphysics, phenomenology, and epistemology of an important species of awareness, but also sheds light on related questions about self-knowledge and the first person. Jesse Prinz defends a sharply contrasting picture of conscious thought in Chapter 19 that gives a far more important role to perception. As his title suggests, Prinz holds the view that all consciousness, including consciousness of our mental acts, is perceptual consciousness. He defends this view by arguing that many of the putatively non-perceptual elements of our conscious mental lives are, on the best psychological and neuroscientific accounts, plausibly construed as perceptual after all. Moreover, since the existence of perceptual consciousness is accepted by all sides, he argues that parsimony should incline us against accepting a separate, non-perceptual form of consciousness to account for awareness of our own thoughts.

Conclusion

It would be impossible for an anthology like this one to touch on every topic, or even every important topic, or even every important and hotly disputed topic, in contemporary philosophy of mind. But the debates in this volume do, I think, give a fair sense of the current state of play with respect to many of the most fundamental and controversial issues in the subject. If they whet readers' appetites for more of the subject, they will have served their purpose.

References

Burge, T. (1979). Individualism and the mental. In P. French, T. Euhling, and H. Wettstein (eds.), *Studies in Epistemology*, Midwest Studies in Philosophy, 4. Minneapolis: University of Minnesota Press.

Chalmers, D. (1996). *The Conscious Mind: In Search of a Fundamental Theory*. New York: Oxford University Press.

Grice, H. P. (1957). Meaning. *Philosophical Review*, 66, 337–88.

Levine, J. (1984). Materialism and qualia: the explanatory gap. *Pacific Philosophical Quarterly*, 64, 354–61.

Putnam, H. (1975). The meaning of "meaning." In K. Gunderson (ed.), *Language, Mind, and Knowledge*. Minneapolis: University of Minnesota Press, 131–93.

Quine, W. V. O. (1951). Two dogmas of empiricism. *Philosophical Review*, 60, 20–43. Reprinted in W. V. O. Quine (ed.), *From a Logical Point of View*. New York: Harper and Row, 1953.

Sellars, W. (1956). Empiricism and the philosophy of mind. In H. Feigl and M. Scriven (eds.), *Minnesota Studies in the Philosophy of Science*, vol. 1. Minneapolis: University of Minnesota Press, 253–329.

PART I
MENTAL CONTENT

IS THERE A VIABLE NOTION OF NARROW MENTAL CONTENT?

Cognitive Content and Propositional Attitude Attributions

Gabriel Segal

1 Background

Tyler Burge (Burge, 1979) has developed a very influential line of anti-individualistic thought. He argued that the cognitive content[1] of a person's concepts depends in part on their socio-linguistic environment. The argument of that paper centered around the example of a subject, now often called "Alf," who does not know that by definition "arthritis" applies only to conditions of the joints. We are to imagine that Alf has many typical, mundane beliefs about arthritis: he believes that arthritis is a painful condition, that he himself has suffered from arthritis for years, that his arthritis in his wrist and fingers is worse than his arthritis in his ankles, and so on. One day he wakes up with a new pain and fears that his arthritis has spread to his thigh. On a twin Earth,[2] the term "arthritis" is used more liberally than it is here, and applies to various rheumatoid conditions of bones and other sorts of tissue, and indeed is true of the condition that Alf has in his thigh. Twin Alf, being an inhabitant of this Twin Earth, has no concept of arthritis and so does not believe that his arthritis has spread to his thigh.

Burge would argue that (1) is true and (2) false:

1   Alf thinks that he has developed arthritis in his thigh
2   Twin Alf thinks that he has developed arthritis in his thigh

He would argue, more particularly, that (1) is true, and (2) false, on *de dicto* readings, where the content sentences specify the cognitive content of the attributed attitudes. Thus the cognitive contents of Alf's and Twin Alf's "arthritis" concepts[3] differ. The difference is due to a difference between Earth and Twin-Earth experts' opinion as to the meaning of the word-form "arthritis" in their respective languages. In particular, the opinions of Earth and Twin Earth experts fix different extension conditions for the Earth and Twin Earth terms "arthritis." This means that Alf's "arthritis" concept is true of arthritis and arthritis only, while Twin Alf's "arthritis" concept has a different extension condition.

And a difference of extension conditions entails a difference of cognitive content.

Burge's articulation of the argument actually appears to involve commitment to a view that is significantly stronger than is required to establish the conclusion. The view is that, in typical cases, the words that a speaker uses are words of public language. A word of public language has a public meaning that is available to its different users. Speakers who are minimally competent with a word get to use the word with this public meaning. So, for example, if both Alf and a consultant rheumatologist say "Mr Jones has arthritis," the words they utter express the same meaning – even though the expert believes that by definition "arthritis" applies only to swelling of the joints, while Alf does not believe this. Moreover, what is true of meaning is true of the content of propositional attitudes. When Alf and the doctor say "Mr Jones has arthritis" they express beliefs with the same cognitive content: what they both believe is that Mr Jones has arthritis.

Roughly following the terminology of Segal (2000), who was roughly following the terminology of Kaplan (1990) and Mercier (1994), we can label the two theses "weak consumerism" and "strong consumerism." The idea behind "consumerism" is that a speaker is a consumer of public words with public contents: it is not for the speaker to produce his own meaning or content. I stipulatively use the terms as follows.

> *Weak consumerism* is the (conjunctive) thesis that: (a) in typical cases, the extension conditions of the concept that a subject expresses by a term are partly determined by expert opinion, and (b) the cognitive content of a concept determines its extension conditions.

> *Strong consumerism* is the thesis that: in typical cases, each term of public language[4] has a unique cognitive content associated with it, and when a speaker uses the term, that is the cognitive content they express by it.[5]

The two theses could come apart. It would be prima facie perfectly reasonable to endorse weak consumerism while rejecting strong consumerism. One might hold, for example, that Alf does not associate the very same cognitive content with "arthritis" as does the expert, thus rejecting strong consumerism. But one might still hold that (1) is true and (2) is false on *de dicto* readings, because Alf has and Twin Alf lacks an "arthritis" concept that extends over arthritis and arthritis only.

The idea of adopting weak consumerism while rejecting strong consumerism receives some support from a natural response to the famous puzzle cases of Kripke (1979), of which the following is typical.

Ignacy Jan Paderewski (1860–1941, Polish) was both a great pianist and a renowned statesman. One can easily imagine a subject, call him "Barney," who has heard of Paderewski the statesman and of Paderewski the musician, but who does not believe that they are one and the same person. Barney happens to believe that politicians typically lack musical talent. He is thus disposed sincerely to assent to both (3) and (4):

3   Paderewski had musical talent
4   Paderewski did not have musical talent.

Thus (5) and (6) both appear to be true:

5   Barney believes that Paderewski had musical talent
6   Barney believes that Paderewski did not have musical talent.

One might sensibly conclude that the classical, Fregean account of *de dicto* propositional attitude attribution has to be given up. On the classical account, (5) and (6) entail that Barney believes contradictory Fregean thoughts. But, since Barney is being completely rational, this does not depict the situation correctly. One might, however, want to retain a fundamental aspect of Frege's philosophy of mind. In particular, one might want to maintain that Barney's dispositions in relation to (3) and (4) show that he associates different cognitive contents with his different uses of the name "Paderewski." And that means that strong consumerism is false. There is at most one public-language term "Paderewski" (naming the musician and statesman), with at most one public content. But Barney uses different occurrences of the term to express different cognitive contents.

Now imagine a twin Earth with a twin Barney and a twin Paderewski. Twin Barney has beliefs about twin Paderewski that correspond to Barney's belief about our Paderewski. But of course Twin Barney has no beliefs about Paderewski. And there is no interpretation under which (7) is true:

7   Both Barney and Twin Barney believe that Paderewski had musical talent.

And so, one might think, Barney's and Twin Barney's "Paderewski" beliefs do not have identical cognitive contents. So, one might conclude, extension is fixed by social facts, and cognitive content determines extension.

I will return later to the question of how we are to understand (5) and (6). I return now to Alf and arthritis. In Segal (2000) I articulated individualist responses to both strong and weak consumerism in relation to Alf. Allow me briefly to summarize.

The argument against strong consumerism, originally formulated in Loar (1987), works simply by turning the arthritis case into a Paderewski case. Suppose that Alf goes to France and there becomes competent with the term "arthrite." He fails to realize that "arthrite" translates "arthritis." He becomes disposed sincerely to assent to (8) and dissent from (9), a normal translation of (8) into French:

8   I have arthritis in my thigh
9   J'ai de l'arthrite a la cuisse.

These linguistic dispositions show us that Alf has two different concepts with different cognitive contents that he expresses by the two terms "arthrite" and "arthritis." But their public contents are the same. So, strong consumerism is false. The argument is defended in depth and detail in Segal (2000), and, in my opinion, can be made almost as irrefragable as an informal argument can get in philosophy.

Cognitive Content and Propositional Attitudes   7

My argument against weak consumerism (which is not almost as irrefragable as an informal argument can get in philosophy) went roughly as follows. When Alf says "arthritis" he does not mean *arthritis*.[6] After all, that's what he means when he says "arthrite." Given this, there is no good reason to suppose that the concept he expresses by "arthritis" extends over arthritis and arthritis alone. And, given that, there is no compelling reason to suppose that Alf's and Twin Alf's concepts have different cognitive contents. Moreover, given that the concepts play identical roles in the two Alfs' cognitive economies, there are good grounds for supposing that their concepts have the same cognitive content after all.

What I shall do now is consider a different, though closely related, argument of Burge's that centers around a different but related type of example. The motivations for this consideration are: to show that the individualist responses to Alf are robust, to develop further the response to weak consumerism, and to explore some interesting issues that come to the fore in connection with the latter argument and example. After that, I will deal briefly with an objection to my approach.

2 Doubting Definitions

Burge (Burge, 1986) asks us to consider the case of a man, whom Burge calls "A" and whom I shall call "Arthur," who has an iconoclastic theory about sofas. Arthur is competent in the use of the term "sofa," having acquired it in a normal way. He is aware of what are considered to be standard truisms about sofas, such as that they are designed to be sat upon.

> At some point, however, [Arthur] doubts the truisms and hypothesizes that sofas function not as furnishings to be sat upon, but as works of art or religious artifacts. He believes that the usual remarks about the function of sofas conceal, or represent a delusion about, an entirely different practice. [Arthur] admits that some sofas have been sat upon, but thinks that most sofas would collapse under any considerable weight and denies that sitting is what sofas are preeminently *for*. (p. 707)

We now imagine that a twin of Arthur's, Twin Arthur, inhabits a twin Earth where the objects that he standardly calls "sofas" in fact are works of art or religious artifacts and are not made for sitting on. Most of them would collapse under any considerable weight. What Twin Arthur and his fellows call "sofas" are thus not sofas. Burge suggests that we call them "safos."[7] According to Burge, while Arthur has numerous propositional attitudes involving the concept of a sofa (Burge, 1986, p. 708) – such as that sofas are works of art or religious artifacts – Twin Arthur does not. Rather, Twin Arthur's corresponding attitudes involve the concept of a safo. So, the contents of the subjects' concepts depend in part on the natures of the artifact kinds in their local environment.

One obvious difference between this case and the "arthritis" case is that in this one it is not just expert opinion that varies across the twins' environments, but also the nature of the artifact kinds involved. This will not be hugely important in what follows. But for bookkeeping purposes it requires another formulation of weak consumerism. I will call it "weak consumerism[A]," "[A]" for "artifact":

Weak consumerism[A] is the (conjunctive) thesis that (a) in typical cases, the extension conditions of the concept that a subject expresses by an artifact term are partly determined by expert opinion and by the nature of the artifacts to which the term is actually applied; (b) the cognitive content of a concept determines its extension conditions.

A second major difference between the "sofa" and the "arthritis" case – a difference that Burge focuses on – is that Arthur is aware of the relevant definition, where Alf is not. While Alf just doesn't know that, by definition, "arthritis" applies only to swellings of the joints, Arthur is aware that, at least according to some people, "sofa" is supposed to apply, by definition, only to objects made for sitting upon. But Arthur takes it that what are put forward as definitional remarks – such as "sofas are made for sitting on" – are incorrect. These remarks, he thinks, "conceal, or represent delusions about, a completely different practice."

3 Paderewski Variations

I now deploy the Loarish argument against strong consumerism, in relation to Arthur. Let us indulge ourselves in another story. Arthur lives in London, England. He shares a flat with young man, Ban, who comes from a country in the far east called "Vantong." Arthur and Ban become friends and spend much time in discussion of a multitude of topics. Arthur confides his views about sofas to Ban. Ban is at first skeptical. But he gradually becomes more open-minded in respect of Arthur's iconoclastic views. Ban's position is that he is quite certain that in his part of the world, sofas are really sofas. But he gradually becomes more and more sympathetic to Arthur's views about sofas in the western world, until he is eventually convinced by them. However, Ban's reasons for thinking that in Vantong sofas really are sofas are very convincing. His uncle is in the furniture business, he has visited a sofa factory, and so on. Arthur himself is at first skeptical about Ban's claims. But after a while Ban convinces him. Thus they both arrive at the view that while the vast majority of sofas in the western world are religious artifacts or works of art, all the sofas in Vantong are genuine sofas.

Let us suppose that Arthur becomes reasonably competent in Vantong. The Vantong word for sofa, an exact translation of the English "sofa," is "navid." Arthur and Ban are agreed "navid" by definition applies only to items of furniture made for sitting upon and that anything that is not an item of furniture made for sitting on is automatically not a navid. They are both disposed sincerely to assent to the Vantong (10), which is an exact translation of (11) in normal English:

10   Navid yan-tse han saksak
11   All sofas are made for sitting on.

However they are of course happy to apply "sofa" to works of art or religious artifacts. And they are both disposed sincerely to dissent from (11).

If we were overhasty in our deployment of standard heuristics for attributing beliefs, we would conclude on the basis of their dispositions to assent to (10) that our protagonists believe that all sofas are made for sitting on. And we would conclude from their disposition to dissent from (11) that they believe that it is not the case that all sofas are made for sitting on. We might then conclude that they are completely insane. A more charitable conclusion would be that they associate two different concepts, with two different cognitive contents, with the terms "sofa" and "navid." Hence strong consumerism is false.

Moreover it looks as though, if there is such thing as *the* concept of a sofa, then it is the one they express by "navid" rather than the one they express by "sofa." In that case, when Arthur says "sofa" he does not express the concept of a sofa. And if that is right, then it is not true that when Arthur uses "sofa," he expresses propositional attitudes involving the concept of a sofa. Let us look into the matter in more detail.

4 *De Re* and *de Dicto*

What exactly does Arthur believe? Let us return to the time before he met Ban and focus on the attitude attribution (12):

12   Arthur believes that sofas are works of art or religious artifacts.

Two propositions are crucial to Burge's argument for weak consumerism[A]. The first is some utterances of (12) would be true on a *de dicto* reading, and the second is that, in such utterances, the word "sofa" extends over sofas and sofas alone. Further reflection casts doubt on these propositions. Utterances of (12) can be true on a *de re* reading. But a true *de dicto* reading is available only if "sofa" is being used in an idiosyncratic way. So let us further reflect.

When we are given the story of iconoclastic Arthur, we find it easy enough to accept (12). But that is on a *de re* reading like (13) or (14), which we also find unproblematic:

13   Arthur believes that long, upholstered seats are works of art or religious artifacts.
14   Arthur believes that sofas are not sofas.

I think that there is a significant difference here between this case and the case of Alf. It is not natural to give (1) ("Alf thinks that he has developed arthritis in his thigh") a *de re* interpretation. We are not thinking that Alf thinks of arthritis that he has developed it in his thigh. Part of the reason for this contrast is that it is very plausible that Arthur has various concepts of sofas that verify *de re* (de sofa) attributions. For example, he could think of sofas as *instances of the same sort of artifact as that* with *that* demonstrating a specific sofa. By contrast, Alf couldn't think of arthritis as *the same sort of disease as that*, with *that* demonstrating the swelling of some joint. One reason for this is that "disease" doesn't fix a principle of individuation that will collect the right extension: if the description fixes an extension at all, then it will be the disease that causes the arthritis – Paget's disease, say (which can cause both arthritis and symptoms in the thigh) – rather than arthritis itself, which is a symptom of the disease. Relatedly, it would be hard to construct a plausible example of a subject who had an iconoclastic theory according to which arthritis might affect the thigh. What would you make of a subject who insisted that "in spite of what the medical dictionaries say, arthritis is really a condition that frequently occurs outside the joints"?

Arthur of course would not express any of his beliefs using the embedded clauses in (13) and (14). But he might well express himself by saying (15):

15   Sofas are works of art or religious artifacts.

Does this mean that an utterance of (12) could be true *de dicto*? That depends on what Arthur means by "sofa." Obviously, if, when he says "sofa," he doesn't mean *sofa*, then his saying (15) doesn't support a true *de dicto* reading of (12). So what does he mean by "sofa"?

Here's something that might help us find out. Suppose we were to ask Arthur whether a long, upholstered seat – an item of furniture that was definitely made for sitting on, and had no other purpose – would be a sofa.

It would not be surprising if he were to say "no." It is quite possible that what he believes entails (16):

16   [Necessarily, all sofas are works of art] or [necessarily, all sofas are religious artifacts].

In this case, he thinks of sofas as objects created for a specific purpose and he thinks of this purpose as essential to the items being what they are. It is just that he doesn't know which of two candidate purposes actually plays the individuating role.

So he might well say "no" in answer to our question. The items might look a lot like sofas. Perhaps the original inspiration for them came from sofas. But they aren't really sofas, since they are simply practical pieces of furniture and not works of art or religious artifacts.

It is pretty clear that if that is how Arthur uses the term "sofa," then he doesn't mean *sofa* by "sofa." And if that is the case, then his saying (15) doesn't support a true *de dicto* reading of (12), with "sofa" used in its normal sense.

Notice also that when we are talking about Arthur we can use the term "sofa" in the same nonstandard way, to match Arthur's own use. We too can use it so that by definition it fails to apply to long, upholstered seats. I just did so in the last sentence of the paragraph before last. I will use "sofa$_D$" for "sofa" interpreted in that unusual manner, so that it entails (16) ("D" for "disjunctive").

So, then, if we are inclined to accept a *de dicto* reading of (12), it may well not be one under which "sofa" means *sofa*. Rather, it might be interpreted as (17):

17   Arthur believes that sofa$_D$s are works of art or religious artifacts.

Suppose, on the other hand, he says "yes, a long, upholstered seat would be a sofa – though of a very unusual sort." Then what concept is he expressing by "sofa"? I'd like to invite you to engage in a thought experiment that might help us answer that question. Let us put ourselves in Arthur's shoes. Please join me in the following simulation.

For centuries, many aspects of human society have been run by the secret religious order of Sofaism. Although the order is secret, a large contingent of the more powerful individuals in western society are members. Secrecy is of the utmost importance to Sofaists, partly because they do not wish to become involved in debate. In particular, they do not want to enter into intellectual discussions with scientists or philosophers, who might undermine their religious beliefs and shake the faith of many of the less committed members of the order.

Perfectly in line with Arthur's suspicions, most sofas are in fact the creations of the secret order of Sofaists. These sofas are religious artifacts, objects of worship, manufactured according to strict rules, under the aegis of anointed sofa masters. Many Sofaists like to keep such sofas in their houses, as symbols of their faith.

In spite of the best efforts of the leaders of the order, a small but significant number of members have lost their faith. They have formed their own secret society, which functions as a self-help group. They have all agreed not to reveal themselves to society at large, for they wish to avoid the large-scale conflict with religious Sofaists that would inevitably ensue. There is a strong artistic movement amongst the lapsed Sofaists. And some of the sofas that you have seen in showrooms and certain other venues are in fact works of art created by lapsed Sofaists.

The vast majority of sofas are creations of Sofaists and lapsed Sofaists: they are religious artifacts or works of art. And, as Arthur suspects, most of them would not be suitable for sitting on, but would break under the weight of the average human. Nevertheless, some sofas are what we always thought they were. They were made by ordinary people, who know nothing of the secret order. They are mere items of furniture: long, upholstered seats, quite suitable for bearing the weight of one or more reposing humans.

Now please try hard to suppose that the story I have been telling you is true. Picture a secret place of worship, perhaps disguised as an exclusive health club in the Alps. Inside the grand building is a great hall. And within this great hall, many fine sofas are available for worship. They are the most delicate and fragile of sofas, and worshippers must take care not place any weight upon them, lest they break.

If you are happy to imagine what I have just asked you to, then you have interpreted my word "sofa" in a liberal sense, so that it might truly apply to an object no purpose of which has anything to do with sitting. You have interpreted it so that it includes non-sofas in its (modal) extension. This is an unusual sense, since the normal English sense relates "sofa" to sitting by definition. In normal English (in the idiolects of most of those who call themselves "English-speakers," including myself) "some sofas are not meant for sitting on" is analytically false. I will use "sofa$_L$" for "sofa" in the unusual, liberal sense. In the world we have been imagining, the world according to Arthur, most sofa$_L$s are not sofas at all.

With all this in place, we can now perhaps work toward another true *de dicto* reading of (12). We have (18):

18   We supposed, and Arthur believes, that most sofas are religious artifacts or works of art.

And, indeed, we even have (19):

19   We supposed, and Arthur believes, that most sofas are not sofas, but are religious artifacts or works of art.

There are unproblematic *de re* readings of (18) and (19) under which they are true. But we can also get true *de dicto* readings, if we interpret them as (18′) and (19′) respectively:

18′   We supposed, and Arthur believes, that most sofa$_L$s are religious artifacts or works of art.
19′   We supposed, and Arthur believes, that most sofa$_L$s are not sofas, but are religious artifacts or works of art.

And if that's right, then we can get the analogous true *de dicto* reading of (12).

I think that the concept expressed by "sofa$_L$" comes under the heading of what Burge terms a "'reduced' notion of a sofa, like one an anthropologist might employ on coming into a society that uses a term for objects that he or she can recognize, but whose use he or she has not yet determined" (p. 711). Burge briefly considers a couple of ways of elaborating on the nature of the "reduced" concept. On one elaboration, the reduced notion is "tied to perceptual aspects of sofas." The other proposal is that the reduced notion is "*thing of a kind relevant to understanding what these things are* (where some sofas are indicated)." Burge points out that the first proposal might well not capture Arthur's notion, and that the second at best confuses reference-fixing with a meaning-given description.

I concur that *sofa$_L$* is perhaps not a perceptual notion. Maybe a sofa$_L$ has to be an artifact. Or maybe it has to have at least some kind of unobservable unifying essence. There are a variety of different types of notion that "sofa$_L$" might express. You can ask yourself which one you deployed during our little imaginative game. I concur also that the description that Burge mentions is no good. But there is no reason why an individualist account of the reduced notion should be descriptive. Given certain ways of fleshing out Arthur's character, there are "reduced" notions that would capture his way of thinking.

What then of weak consumerism[A]? According to weak consumerism[A], when Arthur says "sofa" he expresses a concept the extension of which is fixed by the local experts and the nature of the local items they call "sofas," so his "sofa" concept differs in extension from Twin Arthur's. Once it is conceded that when Arthur says "sofa" he doesn't mean *sofa*, there is very little to be said for this view. For one thing, Arthur does not defer when it comes to the extension of his word. His behavior is different in this respect from Alf's. When Alf's doctor tells him that by definition arthritis afflicts only the joints, Alf immediately accepts correction. Arthur, according to the way Burge describes him, has been confronted by expert opinion about what it is for something to be a sofa. But Arthur disagreed, taking the view that the standard "conceal[s], or represent[s] a delusion about, an entirely different practice."

We have looked at two ways of fleshing out the Arthur story, and we have seen that in neither of those does his "sofa" concept extend over sofas and sofas alone. *Sofa$_D$* is constrained by its very nature not to extend over sofas at all. (Sofa$_D$s, recall, aren't really sofas, since these are simply practical pieces of furniture and not works of art or religious artifacts.) And *sofa_L*, although it is true of sofas, is true of non-sofas as well. (Recall the Alpine temple, with its most delicate and fragile of sofa_Ls.) And we would get the same result on any fleshing out of the Arthur story. If his linguistic and other dispositions are coherent enough to be interpretable at all, then there will be an account of his concept under which it includes non-sofas in its modal extension.

We should, then, abstract away from the differences between Arthur's and Twin Arthur's environments and see their concepts as having the same cognitive content.[8]

5 Attitude Attributions, Neologisms, and Generalizations

Sawyer (THERE IS NO VIABLE NOTION OF NARROW CONTENT) objects to my strategy of introducing neologisms to express idiosyncratic concepts on the grounds that it "threatens ... both the ordinary practice of ascribing psychological states by means of standard terms and a scientific psychology that appeals to concepts expressed by standard terms." There is a prima facie threat to ordinary practice and scientific psychology that arises in relation to neologisms. But the prima facie threat arises because there is a lot of conceptual variation across individuals, not because one might usefully introduce neologisms to help describe what is going on. I will discuss ordinary practice first, then say a word about scientific psychology.

The prima facie threat arises because there are more individual concepts than there are public words. This is apparent already in the Paderewski case. Rather than revisiting that, let us switch to a new example. Sonia is a native of England. She is averagely competent with the term "blackbird," as it is typically used in England. She is even able, on occasion, to recognize blackbirds. Sonia spends a few moths visiting Australia. There she sees some birds with brown plumage and brown beaks, which the locals call "blackbirds." In fact, these are females of the same species as English blackbirds, *Turdus merula*. But Sonia does not know this, and, reasonably enough, she assumes that Australian blackbirds belong to a different family from English ones. When Sonia is in Australia, addressing someone whom she takes to be a speaker of Australian English, she is disposed sincerely to assent to (20):

20   Blackbirds typically have brown feathers.

But when she is in England, addressing someone whom she takes to a speaker of British English, she is disposed sincerely to dissent from it.

Ordinary practice then legitimates both (21) and (22):

21   Sonia believes that blackbirds typically have brown feathers
22   Sonia believes that blackbirds typically do not have brown feathers.

(20) and (21) can both be true *de dicto*. Hence the prima facie threat to ordinary practice: it appears to commit us to attributing contradictory thoughts to Sonia, when she doesn't have any. The introduction of neologisms helps to dispel this appearance.

14   **Gabriel Segal**

What motivates the introduction of neologisms has nothing to with individualism, nor some manic desire to generalize over possible but non-actual twins. Rather, it is a Fregean approach to propositional attitudes. It is the recognition that (i) when a subject associates different attitudes with two expressions, as Sonia does with her two "blackbirds," she expresses different cognitive contents by them, and (ii) propositional attitude attributions attribute cognitive contents. Neologisms help to show how the Fregean approach is consistent with Paderewski cases. Sonia has two words that share the orthographical form "blackbird" that I can represent as "blackbirds$_A$" (for her Australian version) and "blackbirds$_E$" (for her English one). Having introduced these neologisms, I can now write (21') and (22'):

21' Sonia believes that blackbirds$_A$ typically have brown feathers
22' Sonia believes that blackbirds$_E$ typically do not have brown feathers.

(21') and (22') can serve two purposes. First, they can serve as partial depictions of the logical forms of utterances of (21) and (22), which help show us how they could be true, *de dicto*. Second, they could be used as the orthographical forms of propositional attitude attributions that make explicit those logical forms.

Sawyer observes correctly that, if my view is right, then conceptual variation is rife. She appears to worry that then the "introduction of neologisms would be rife." It would be a worry if my view entailed that usually when speakers offer propositional attitude reports using what appear to be familiar terms they should be interpreted as using neologisms – so, if they were to express themselves clearly they should really be using novel orthographical or phonological forms. That would be implausibly revisionary. But my view does not entail that at all. Neologisms are only necessary when small conceptual variations matter. Such cases are very rare.

Moreover it does seem to me that when speakers are confronted with Paderewski cases, they often do endeavor to introduce neologisms. A speaker confronted with the Sonia case and asked "Does she or does she not believe that blackbirds have brown feathers?" might well feel some discomfort. (It's the same discomfort you might feel when I tell you that I live in London, England, and not London, Ontario. Do I live in London, or do I not? Answer me!) The speaker might well react by trying to do the same sort of thing that I did by introducing subscripts. They might try saying "blackbirds" with an Australian accent when saying (21). Or they might put quotation marks round it (perhaps by waggling four of their fingers). Or they might say: "She believes that Australian blackbirds typically have brown feathers, but that English blackbirds do not."

As I said, though, cases where small conceptual variations matter are rare. Usually they can be ignored, even in *de dicto* attributions. Here is a very rough summary of what I take to be the best account of the semantics of attitude attributions in natural language. The core of the idea is to be found in Davidson (1969).[9] In a standard propositional attribution, the reporter uses a sentence of their own language, with its own particular meaning in the context of utterance, to talk of a content that is attributed to the reportee. In the case of belief, the idea might be roughly formulated as in (P) (adapted from Segal, 2000, p. 81):[10]

P   A report of the form "a believes that s" as uttered by b, in conversational context c, is true iff the content of s in b's mouth, in c, is similar enough, by the standards of c, to that of some belief of a's.

The similarity clause affords plenty of flexibility.[11] All kinds of pragmatic factors enter into determining what counts as "similar enough" in a given context. They determine whether the attribution is *de re* or *de dicto*. And, if the attribution is *de dicto*, they determine whether the similarity should be at the level of Kaplanian character (Kaplan, 1989) or something more like Fregean sense. (23) and (24) are examples where the former is at issue:

23   Every boy wants his mother to love him
24   Chief Vitalstatistix was forever afraid that the sky would fall on his head tomorrow.[12]

Moreover, where an attribution is *de dicto* and something more like sense than character is at issue, required standards of similarity may still vary along a dimension of strictness. Sometimes standards are very strict. The reportee has to have a belief the cognitive content of which is really very similar to that of the content sentence, for the attribution to be true. But often the standards are more relaxed. The reportee just has to have belief the cognitive content of which is reasonably similar to that which the speaker expresses by the content sentence. Suppose, for example, that Sonia has observed blackbird chicks in Australia, and on that basis has formed the view that blackbird$_A$ chicks are mottled, with a rufous hue. Then (25) may be true, *de dicto*:

25   Sonia and you and I all believe that blackbird chicks are mottled, with a rufous hue.

In this case, we abstract away from the variation in cognitive content between Sonia's concept *blackbird$_A$* and your and my "blackbird" concepts, to formulate a true *de dicto* generalization.[13]

Notice that in Sonia's case, as in the Paderewski case, the protagonist has neither a mistaken nor an incomplete understanding of the focal concept.[14] It might be slightly unusual for someone to think that blackbirds are brown. But it does not involve any mistakes about or ignorance of a truth of meaning. Thus the term "blackbird" is used in (25) in a normal sense. This contrasts with, for example, the use of "sofa" in a *de dicto* version of (12). In cases like that, when we are using words in aberrant senses, the motivation for deploying neologisms is greater than in Paderewski cases.

I conclude now with a brief word about scientific psychology. Sawyer points out that, according to my view, we need to deploy neologisms when we need to be precise and explicit, and that I also hold that psychology is concerned with concepts that "are common across the whole species or some significant population within it." She objects that imprecision "ought not to be tolerated within scientific practice" and continues: "If conceptual variation is rife, there will be few concepts that are common either across the whole species or across some significant population within it. Consequently, the concepts available for scientific psychology to study would, on the face of it, be too few for the practice to be scientifically viable."

I disagree that imprecision ought not to be tolerated within scientific practice. The sort of imprecision in question is simply a matter of selecting the right level of grain for the type of generalization sought. For example, astronomers sometimes regard the planets as spherical. This sort of imprecision is necessary, harmless (when care is taken) and rife in science. Psychology is no different.[15]

Those (many) areas of scientific psychology that deal in concepts and cognitive content standardly use ordinary-language *de dicto* propositional attitude attributions to generalize over large populations.[16] These are best interpreted on the model of (P) – where the "conversational context" normally is academia.

Acknowledgments

Many thanks for comments and discussion to Mat Carmody, Keith Hossack, Christian Nimtz, Guy Longworth, Brian McLaughlin, David Papineau, Richard Samuels, and Mark Textor.

Notes

1 By "cognitive content" I mean roughly: content that is relevant to psychological explanation. For the purposes of this paper, I will assume that cognitive content is distinct from reference and that it is relevant to the truth conditions of opaque propositional attitude attributions.

2 Burge presents a counterfactual scenario involving Alf, which I recast in standard twin-Earth format.

3 Schematically: I use "x's 'w' concept" for "the concept x expresses by the word w."

4 Strong consumerism is committed to the idea that words and their meanings are shared, public property but need not be committed to the view that there are such things as public languages, i.e. whole languages that are shared by communities.

5 Assume that cognitive content is partly determined by expert opinion and that cognitive content determines extension conditions. Then, subject to obvious clarifications, strong consumerism entails weak consumerism.

6 I italicize to write about concepts: "*arthritis*" applies to "arthritis" concepts.

7 A note on the individuation of artifacts. The individuation of artifacts is a complex and subtle matter, of which there is as yet no satisfactory account. (See Wiggins, 2001, and Keil, 1989, respectively, for important philosophical and psychological discussion.) Here's part of the story. Artifacts are individuated in terms of purpose: e.g., sofas are for sitting on. Hence safos are not sofas: if a particular safo happens to be intrinsically physically identical to a particular sofa, it still fails to be a sofa because it lacks the right sort of purpose. Having a purpose is often a matter of manufacturer's design. But it needn't be (see Matan and Carey, 2001). Further, a sculptor might make an ice sofa which was not meant for sitting on. Someone might make a giant sofa out of balloons, for a children's party. I think that in these cases the artifact term has a sort of secondary usage, parasitic on its primary one. These objects are sofas because their purpose is related to sofas in the primary sense. They are intended to be sofas. Notice also that while one might naturally call the ice- or balloon- object a "sofa," one might also say "Don't sit on that: it's not a real sofa."

8   So, for example, it might be true that Arthur and Twin Arthur both believe that sofa$_L$s are not usually made for sitting on. There is no analogous way of using an attitude attribution to generalize over Barney's and Twin Barney's "Paderewski" beliefs. The relevant difference is that between general and singular concepts. For extensive discussion see Segal (2004).

9   It goes back at least to Bello and Cuervo (1874).

10 (P) is an informal summary of how attitude attributions work, which brushes over important details concerning the different contributions of semantics and various pragmatic and other non-semantic factors. See Larson and Segal (1995).

11 Kripke is concerned that in Paderewski cases, "our normal practices of interpretation and attribution of belief are subjected to the greatest possible strain, perhaps to the point of breakdown" (1979, pp. 268–9). The flexibility allows them easily to take the strain.

12 From Goscinny and Uderzo (e.g., 1961).

13 Why *de dicto*? Suppose that she knows that English blackbirds belong to the species *Turdus merula*. Then, consistently with the truth of (25), she might not believe that *Turdus merula* chicks are mottled with a rufous hue.

14 Cases like this can be deployed on a variation of the Loarish argument to show that cognitive content is holistic. See Segal (2003).

15 It would be a worthwhile enterprise to compare and contrast *de dicto* psychological generalizations, as the holist sees them, with idealizations in other sciences. My claim here is just that the imprecision involved is comparable.

16 Many psychologists more or less explicitly hold a theory of concepts that is consistent with the idea that cognitive content is holistic and that psychological generalizations generalize over concepts that are suitably similar in cognitive content. For references and discussion see section IV of Laurence and Margolis (1999).

References

Bello, A. and Cuervo, R. (1874). *Gramatica de la lengua castellana*. Madrid: Arco/Libros.

Burge, T. (1979). Individualism and the mental. *Midwest Studies in Philosophy*, 4, 73–121.

—— (1986). Intellectual norms and the foundations of mind. *Journal of Philosophy*, 83, 679–720.

Davidson, D. (1969). On saying that. In D. Davison and J. Hintikka (eds.), *Words and Objections: Essays on the Work of W. v. Quine*. Dordrecht: D. Reidel.

Goscinny, R. and Uderzo, A. (1961). *Astérix le Gaulois*. Paris: Hachette.

Kaplan., D. (1989). Demonstratives. In J. Almog, J. Perry, and H. Wettstein (eds.), *Themes from Kaplan*. Oxford: Oxford University Press.

—— (1990). Words. *Proceedings of the Aristotelian Society*, 64 (supp.), 93–119.

Keil., F. (1989). *Concepts, Kinds and Cognitive Development*. Cambridge, MA: MIT Press.

Kripke, S. (1979). A puzzle about belief. In A. Margalit (ed.), *Meaning and Use*. Dordrecht: D. Reidel.

Larson, R. and Segal G. (1995). *Knowledge of Meaning*. Cambridge, MA: The MIT Press.

Laurence, S. and Margolis, E. (1999). Concepts in cognitive science. In E. Margolis and S. Laurence (eds.), *Concepts: Core Readings*. Cambridge, MA: MIT Press.

Loar, B. (1987). Social content and psychological content. In R. Grimm and D. Merrill (eds.), *Contents of Thought: Proceedings of the 1985 Oberlin Colloquium on Philosophy*. Tucson: University of Arizona Press, 99–139.

Matan, A. and Carey, S. (2001). Developmental cages within the core of artifact concepts. *Cognition*, 78, 1–26.

Mercier, A. (1994). Consumerism and language acquisition. *Linguistics and Philosophy*, 17, 499–519.

Segal, G. (2000). *A Slim Book about Narrow Content*. Cambridge, MA: MIT Press.

— (2003). Ignorance of meaning. In A. Barber (ed.), *The Epistemology of Language*. Oxford: Oxford University Press.

— (2004). Reference, causal powers, externalist intuitions and unicorns. In R. Schantz (ed.), *The Externalist Challenge: Studies on Cognition and Intentionality*. Berlin and New York: de Gruyter.

Wiggins, D. (2001). *Sameness and Substance*. Cambridge: Cambridge University Press.

There Is No Viable Notion of Narrow Content

Sarah Sawyer

1 Narrow and Broad Content

A property is *anti-individualistic* if its specification makes essential reference to the environment of the individuals in which it is instantiated and *individualistic* if its specification does not make such essential reference.[1] Thus the property of standing astride the equator is anti-individualistic, whereas the property of having folded arms is individualistic. Intrinsic physical duplicates may well have different anti-individualistic properties – one may be astride the equator, the other astride the meridian – but they could not differ with respect to properties that are individualistic: if one has folded arms, so must the other. To put the same point in different terms, individualistic properties are those that *supervene locally* on the intrinsic physical properties of the individuals that instantiate them; anti-individualistic properties are those that do not.

Psychological properties such as the property of believing that the value of silver will rise, the property of desiring that good ale be available in Nebraska, and the property of fearing that terrorism is on the increase have associated contents.[2] When I believe that the value of silver will rise I am in a psychological state the content of which is that the value of silver will rise. If a psychological property is individualistic, the associated content is narrow: *narrow content* is content that is locally supervenient, hence preserved across intrinsic physical duplicates. The associated content of an anti-individualistic psychological property is *broad*. The question before us is whether there is a viable notion of narrow content – whether there is a viable sense in which psychological properties are individualistic.

Why would anyone think otherwise?[3] The first and most widely recognized set of considerations in favor of broad content emerges from reflection on counterfactual scenarios in which a subject's intrinsic physical makeup is hypothesized to remain constant, while the broader physical environment in which she is embedded is hypothesized to differ. Such an environmental difference, it is urged, would affect the subject's psychological states precisely because non-intentional, fundamentally causal relations to objective properties in one's environment partially determine what one can represent in thought. For example, a subject S, related in the right kind of non-intentional way to silver, may think various thoughts involving the concept *silver*, such as the thought that the value of silver will rise. She may be unable to distinguish various other actual or possible metals from silver – either practically or theoretically – and may well acknowledge this. Nevertheless, it is silver she represents in thought, and *as* silver. Now suppose S had lived in different circumstances, and had been related neither to silver nor to anyone else who could think about silver. In such a scenario, S would be unable to think about silver herself. There would be nothing to ground her possession of the concept *silver*. Suppose instead that she had been related to one of the actual or possible metals she is unable to distinguish from silver. Call this metal "twilver." In such circumstances, where S thinks that the value of silver will rise, counterfactual S thinks instead that the value of twilver will rise. The difference in representational content between the belief S has and the belief S would have lies in the difference between the objective properties to which she is and would be related and which her psychological states consequently represent or would represent respectively. What determines the representational content of the respective beliefs goes beyond her intrinsic physical nature and her discriminative capacities – which are identical in the two circumstances – and is anchored instead by the objective properties. The content of her psychological state, then – that the value of silver will rise – is broad.

Since there is nothing obviously special about the concept *silver*, one may be forgiven for assuming that the line of thought generalizes and that all content is broad. However, it is widely thought that there is a significant difference between natural kind concepts – concepts that "carve nature at her joints" – and other concepts. *Silver* falls into the former category along with *quark, electron, acid*, and *water*, and examples of the latter include *ale, terrorism, sofa, arthritis*, and *game*.[4] That the content of thoughts involving natural kind concepts is broad is more widely accepted than that the content of thoughts involving other concepts is. But there are reasons in favor of the generalization. The conventional linguistic meaning of a term (roughly, its dictionary definition) is a complex abstraction from communal rather than individual use. It is determined by possible and actual agreement among the most competent users, where the most competent users are those to whom others do and would defer if a question about an individual's use were to arise. Correct use is consequently use that accords with that of the most competent, and hence the norm for linguistic understanding lies outside the individual. We do not all count as amongst the most competent. The extent to which an individual understands the linguistic meaning of an expression varies in accord with her theoretical and empirical knowledge.

Reflection on a second kind of counterfactual scenario shows how the possibility of incomplete linguistic understanding grounds the anti-individualistic nature of thought more generally. First suppose that a subject S has a wide range of ordinary beliefs attributable by means of the term "game": she believes that games are typically enjoyable, that football is a game, and so on. But she believes in addition and mistakenly that games must involve at least two people. Nevertheless she would readily accept correction on this point if her error were pointed out. Next consider a counterfactual scenario in which her intrinsic physical properties are hypothesized to remain constant, but in which the word "game" is defined and standardly used to apply to activities of a certain sort that involve at least two people. The word-form "game" has a different linguistic meaning and expresses a different concept in the two circumstances. In the actual situation the word expresses the concept *game*, which includes in its extension such activities as solitaire; in the counterfactual situation the word expresses a concept that does not include in its extension such activities as solitaire, and hence is not the concept *game*. The extensions of the two terms overlap to a significant degree, but they are not identical. Consequently, S may in fact believe that snakes and ladders is a game, but had she been in the counterfactual scenario she would not have had that thought since she would not have possessed the concept *game* that is a constituent of it. S's intrinsic physical properties are identical in the two scenarios, as are her classificatory dispositions. The difference in representational content again lies outside the subject's intrinsic physical nature, and this time lies in the classificatory practices of the wider linguistic community of which she is and takes herself to be a part. And here again the content of S's belief – this time that snakes and ladders is a game – is broad.

But the anti-individualistic nature of thought need not turn on a subject's incomplete linguistic understanding either. An individual who has a complete understanding of the conventional linguistic meaning of a term can nonetheless raise doubts about whether the entities characterized by the definition have been characterized correctly. (Are sofas really pieces of furniture meant for sitting, or are they religious artifacts?)[5] It is this possibility of nonstandard theory that forms the basis of a third kind of counterfactual scenario in favor of broad content. All we need do is imagine a situation in which a subject proposes a false nonstandard theory about a class of entities, and then hypothesize a counterfactual situation in which the nonstandard theory is standard and true of a different and yet superficially indistinguishable class of entities. The linguistic meaning of the relevant term will differ as a result, as will the concept expressed.[6] If a proposed characterization, originating as a challenge to a standard definitional characterization, comes to be accepted by the community, the linguistic meaning of the term will change accordingly. And this brings in a distinction between linguistic meaning and concept expressed, a distinction that is often overlooked. While the linguistic meaning of a term will change as communal use does – as the received view about the entities changes – the concept expressed by that term may well remain unaltered. This will happen, for instance, in cases where entities of a given kind are identified demonstratively through perception and then characterized. The concept will be anchored to the entities by the perceptual demonstrations, whereas the linguistic meaning will reflect received views about the entities thus demonstrated. Linguistic meaning is thus tied to an agreed characterization of a class of entities, but agreement does not entail truth. In contrast, a complete grasp of a given concept is not independent of a true understanding of the nature of the very entities that fall under that concept. Linguistic meaning and concept must be distinguished. It is precisely the fact that we can be mistaken about the nature of things in the world that legitimizes the possibility of nonstandard theory and indicates that

Sarah Sawyer

the norm for thought lies not only outside the individual but outside the collective current capacities of the community at large.

While many have been persuaded that a wide range of psychological properties is anti-individualistic, and hence that the content of a wide range of psychological states is broad, few have been willing to give up the thesis that there is some form of narrow content that all representational psychological states possess. There are both metaphysical and epistemological reasons for this reluctance. The current era is marked by the felt need to relate such putatively nonphysical properties as psychological properties to "lower-level" properties and ultimately to physical properties – those of interest to the physical sciences. A neat identity of the psychological and the physical first came under pressure when it was suggested that subjects need not be intrinsic physical duplicates in order to instantiate the same psychological properties – in short, that psychological properties are multiply realizable. That physically diverse individuals could have psychological states in common is something people have typically come to accept, although there remain differences of opinion as to how to accommodate multiple realizability in a materialist, broadly physical worldview. But the suggestion that psychological properties are anti-individualistic – that subjects who instantiate all and only the same intrinsic physical properties could nevertheless differ psychologically – would mean not only that no intrinsic physical state of an individual is necessary for the instantiation of a given psychological property, the lesson of multiple realizability, but in addition that no such state is sufficient. If this were so, the tie between a subject's intrinsic physical states and her psychological states would be severed in both directions. It is widely assumed that such a severance would render psychological properties naturalistically problematic and would render apparently commonplace causal connections between psychological states and actions naturalistically inexplicable. I deal with this worry in more depth in Section 2.[7]

The epistemological motivation for holding onto the claim that intrinsic physical duplicates must share a significant range of psychological properties is less theoretically driven and more intuitive. How things seem to one has traditionally been thought of as the core of one's perspective on the world and hence the core of the psychological. But there is a generally acknowledged sense in which how things seem to one is determined by one's physical makeup. In each of the scenarios outlined above, for example, it is assumed that S would be unable to distinguish the actual from the counterfactual situation. There is a near incoherence in the idea that one's perspective on the world could differ unnoticeably, hence the idea that the psychological states that in part constitute one's perspective could differ unnoticeably has seemed problematic. If psychological properties are anti-individualistic such unnoticeable differences are possible.

In the face of this problematic – both metaphysical and epistemological – attempts have been made to mitigate the force of the claim that psychological properties are anti-individualistic. Such attempts range from arguing on the one hand that the broadness of content applies only to a certain subclass of (relatively unimportant) psychological states, or only to psychological states conceived in a certain (non-fundamental) way – both instances of a limitation strategy – to arguing on the other that there is no reason to accept the claim that content is broad at all, a strategy of denial.

In this paper I examine what I take to be the three primary attempts to salvage the claim that psychological properties are individualistic and argue that none of them is successful.[8] Underlying the desire to retain a notion of narrow content is a failure to acknowledge the range of considerations in favor of the broadness of content and a set of mistaken assumptions about the metaphysical and epistemological implications of broad content. The structure of the paper is as follows. In Section 2 I examine the standard two-factor theory of psychological content, as latterly proposed by Jerry Fodor. In Section 3 I examine David Chalmers's recent attempt to ground a notion of narrow content in the notion of epistemic possibility. Each of these two views is an instance of the limitation strategy, since each acknowledges that there is a sense in which psychological content is broad. The motivation in the former case is metaphysical, the motivation in the latter epistemological. In Section 4 I examine the claim, championed by Gabriel Segal, that all psychological content is narrow – that intrinsic physical duplicates are psychological duplicates *simpliciter*. This is a strategy of denial. I conclude briefly in Section 5.

2 Narrow Narrow Content

One response to the relevant counterfactual scenarios has been to grant that psychological content as ordinarily conceived is broad, but to insist that a scientific psychology cannot concern itself with such anti-individualistic properties, and that there must in addition be a form of psychological content that is narrow and scientifically legitimate.[9] What, then, is the new, narrow, supposed scientifically respectable counterpart to the more ordinary kind of content? The new notion of narrow content is defined as a function from contexts to broad content. On this view, intrinsic physical duplicates necessarily have the same narrow psychological properties, but have the same broad psychological properties only if their surrounding environments are relevantly similar; if intrinsic physical duplicates are in relevantly different contexts, though, they will have different broad psychological properties – as consideration of counterfactual scenarios such as those detailed in the previous section illustrates.

There are several problems with the view. First, narrow content thus conceived is arguably not a form of content at all. It is plausibly essential to content that it represent the world as being a certain way. Beliefs have truth-conditions: if the way a belief represents the world as being is the way the world is, then the belief is true – otherwise it is false. Similarly, desires have satisfaction conditions, fears have realization conditions, and so on. But narrow content does not represent the world as being any given way: the narrow content of a belief is not truth-conditional; the narrow content of a desire does not have satisfaction conditions; the narrow content of a fear does not have realization conditions. Narrow content is, instead, a theoretical abstraction from representational content. Moreover, narrow content is explicitly and essentially defined in terms of broad content. Consequently, broad content is the more fundamental notion: there is no psychological specification of narrow content available other than as a function from contexts to broad content.[10] But the fact that narrow content thus conceived is not definable independently of broad content would render a scientific psychology that restricted its focus to individualistic properties unworkable. The only purchase there would be on such properties would be via anti-individualistic properties, appeal to which is presumed illegitimate: the notion of narrow content would then be inaccessible from within the discipline. The notion of narrow content proposed, then, fails to serve the very function for which it was introduced.[11]

More fundamentally, the underlying assumption that the properties of interest to a scientific psychology must be individualistic rests on confusion. Cognitive psychology appeals extensively to psychological properties as ordinarily construed, and such properties are anti-individualistic – as are the properties of many other of the so-called "special sciences." Consequently, there is reason to think that scientific inquiry should concern itself with properties that are other than individualistic. Three primary confusions can be discerned.[12] The first amounts to a conflation between the kinds of a given science – in this case psychology – and the properties relevant to the individuation of those kinds.[13] As Burge says, "not every relation between individual and environment that is necessary, sufficient, or importantly contributory to the individuation of mental kinds is itself a candidate for a scientifically useful kind or relation. It is one thing to presuppose a property or relation in one's typology. It is another to use it in one's explanations" (p. 313). Thus the fact (if it is a fact) that cognitive psychology is not interested in the relations between individuals and their environment has no bearing on the claim that psychological properties are anti-individualistic. Bearing certain non-intentional relations to silver is essential to the individuation of the psychological kind *possessing the concept silver*, but this does not mean that a cognitive psychology that appeals to that property must itself be concerned either with an individual's non-intentional relations to silver, or even with the question whether such a relation obtains.

The second confusion amounts to a conflation between causation, which is a relation between particular events or states, and individuation, which is based on patterns among causal relations.[14] Psychological properties are causal properties, typed by their causes and effects. For example, it is S's belief that the value of silver will rise that in part causes her to invest in silver on the stock market. But there could be no such causal chains between psychological states and pieces of behavior without causal chains between brain states and subsequent bodily movements: psychological causation depends on neurophysiological causation. Given this, it is tempting to conclude that people with the same brain states could not have psychological states with different causal powers. If psychological properties are anti-individualistic, however, people with the same brain states *could* have psychological states with different causal powers:[15] in the counterfactual situation S's belief that the value of twilver will rise causes her to invest in twilver – a different action from investing in silver. But to think this problematic is to confuse particular causal chains with types of causal relations. As Burge has pointed out, "the question whether causal chains of events that run from the environment to behaviour necessarily run 'via' neural chains of events" is independent of "the question whether *patterns* of causal relation between the environment and the individual could bear on the *individuation* of psychological kinds in a different way from the way they bear on the individuation of neural kinds" (p. 309). That psychological properties are anti-individualistic does not render psychological causation mysterious.

Special sciences study patterns of causation involving entities in their normal environment, and the properties to which they appeal in causal explanations are individuated in a way that presupposes such relations between the entities and their environment. To borrow examples from Burge, "astronomy studies the motions of the planets; geology studies land masses on the surface of the Earth; physiology studies hearts or optic fibres in the environment of a larger organism; psychology studies activity involving intentional states in an environment about which those states carry information; the social sciences study patterns of activity among persons" (p. 317). Because such properties are individuated with reference to patterns in a normal environment that extends beyond the surfaces of the individuals that instantiate those properties, the properties do not in general supervene on the constituents of those individuals. Consequently, the causal powers relevant to individuating the properties of one such science need not supervene on the causal powers of the properties of a lower-level science. Further, two individuals with the same causal powers as recognized by the lower-level science may have different causal powers when assessed from within the higher-level science. This is the case for S and counterfactual S with respect to their distinct psychological and identical neurophysiological properties. This leads on to the third confusion – the assumption that there is a way to individuate causal powers, and hence to assess contexts as "the same" or "different" independently of a particular scientific endeavor. Contexts appropriate to the individuation of properties in a given science are sensitive to the science in hand rather than independent of it, and are not immediately sensitive to sciences at lower levels.

Broad psychological properties, then, are an apt subject matter for scientific study. The felt need for a notion of narrow content to accord with good scientific practice is unwarranted.

3 Epistemic Narrow Content[16]

Chalmers (2003)[17] has recently suggested that a viable notion of narrow content can be grounded in the notion of epistemic possibility, which corresponds, he says, to "rational coherence, on idealized a priori reflection" (p. 47). Consider the thought that silver is Jk, where "Jk" is shorthand for the chemical formula of twilver, one of the possible metals that is distinct from silver but that S cannot distinguish from it. The thought is false – indeed its content states a metaphysical impossibility, given that silver is necessarily Ag. Nevertheless, the content of the thought states an *epistemic* possibility, since no amount of a priori reasoning can reveal the chemical formula of silver and hence no amount of a priori reasoning can reveal that silver is not Jk. When a thought is epistemically possible it endorses certain epistemically possible scenarios and excludes others. Thus the thought that silver is Jk endorses scenarios in which Jk is used to make jewelry and high-grade cutlery, is a constituent in batteries and in photographic paper, and so on, and excludes scenarios in which jewelry and cutlery are made from Ag. Now consider the thought that twilver is Jk. The thought is, of course, a different broad thought with different broad truth-conditions. Indeed, the thought is necessarily true. But, Chalmers wants to say, it nonetheless endorses and excludes the very same scenarios as the thought that silver is Jk.

Sarah Sawyer

In Chalmers's terms, the thoughts "divide epistemic space" in the same way. For two thoughts to share a narrow content just is for them to divide epistemic space in the same way. The thought that silver is Jk and the thought that twilver is Jk do this. Consequently, they share a narrow content even though they are different broad thoughts.

Central to the view is the notion of a scenario, and more specifically that of considering a scenario as actual. Scenarios can be characterized either in metaphysical terms or in epistemic terms, but neither is adequate to the task of grounding a viable notion of narrow content – or so I shall argue. Let us look at each characterization in turn. On the metaphysical construal, a scenario is a possible world.[18] When I consider a world W as actual, I consider that my world is qualitatively just like W. So, when I consider the hypothesis that the Jk-world is actual, I consider the hypothesis that my world is qualitatively just like the Jk-world (that is, just like the actual world) and that batteries and photographic paper contain Jk. In considering this hypothesis, the thought that silver is Jk is verified: if I accept that the Jk-world is my world, I should rationally accept that silver is Jk. More specifically, to consider a world as actual is to consider the hypothesis that a certain description is true, which description must be a description of a world given purely qualitatively. Consequently, the description has to be given in what Chalmers calls "semantically neutral" terms, where a term is semantically neutral just in case it is not susceptible to the kinds of counterfactual scenarios that motivate the anti-individualistic individuation of psychological properties. And this is where the problem for Chalmers's notion of epistemic content arises. To assume that there is a semantically neutral vocabulary rich enough to divide epistemic space in the way required is to assume that there is a wide range of terms that express concepts that are individualistic. Chalmers maintains that names, natural kind terms, and demonstratives are not semantically neutral, and hence does not allow their occurrence in the canonical descriptions of possible worlds that he claims yield the scenarios relevant to epistemic possibility: but he does not take seriously the thought that the vast majority of terms are anti-individualistic and hence that the purely qualitative canonical descriptions of possible worlds he requires are unavailable. For Chalmers's project to be viable the qualitative properties of every natural kind must be specifiable in a semantically neutral way.[19]

But even if we grant that the only anti-individualistic terms are names, natural kind terms, and demonstratives, Chalmers's project is still problematic. To see this, reflect on the following two ways in which a semantically neutral vocabulary might be sought. First, anti-individualistic terms such as "silver" might be replaced by descriptions such as "shiny metallic element . . . that is a constituent of batteries and photographic paper." The constituents of such descriptions must all be semantically neutral if the descriptions as a whole are to be semantically neutral: but terms such as "metallic" and "element" are plausibly natural kind terms and hence anti-individualistic even on the restricted view of broad content Chalmers accepts. Similar problems are likely to arise for any alternative description proposed. It might be objected that in any given case it is only the specific anti-individualistic term relevant to the possibility under consideration that need be eliminated – in this case "silver" – and that other anti-individualistic terms can remain. But this will not do: the epistemic content of a thought, if it is to be narrow, must be shared by *all* intrinsic physical duplicates, which includes those whose term "metallic" is semantically different from ours, those whose term "element" is semantically different from ours, and so on. The second way in which one might seek a semantically neutral vocabulary is by replacing anti-individualistic terms such as "silver" with adjectival counterparts such as "silvery stuff." This second option will not yield a semantically neutral vocabulary either, however, since the adjectival counterpart of an anti-individualistic term is dependent for its meaning on the original term, and hence is not semantically neutral. The term "silvery" means (roughly) "like silver in relevant respect." The first, metaphysical construal of scenarios as possible worlds, then, fails to yield the required epistemic notion of narrow content.

The second construal of scenarios is as equivalence classes of epistemically complete sentences in an idealized language. Here are the basics. A sentence S is epistemically necessary just in case it is a priori; S and T are epistemically equivalent just when the biconditional $S \equiv T$ is epistemically necessary; S leaves a sentence T open just when both S & T and S & ~T are epistemically possible; and S is epistemically complete when it leaves no sentence open. To consider a world W as actual on this understanding is to consider any of the epistemically complete sentences in W's equivalence class. But the same problem arises here as arises with the metaphysical construction of scenarios: the epistemically complete sentences that form the equivalence class for any given world must contain what Chalmers calls "epistemically invariant" terms if they are to do the work required. But an epistemically invariant term is the epistemic equivalent of a semantically neutral term, and as we saw above, there is good reason to think the range of such terms will not be wide enough to yield an appropriate specification. This second, epistemic construal of scenarios as equivalence classes of epistemically complete sentences in an idealized language also fails to yield the required epistemic notion of narrow content.

Chalmers's notion of narrow content, then, depends upon the availability of a semantically neutral or epistemically invariant language, which there is no reason to think available.[20]

4 Thoroughly Narrow Content

The final position I will examine is an instance of what I referred to in Section 1 as a strategy of denial: it rejects the considerations in favor of broad content altogether, providing instead an alternative understanding of the relevant counterfactual scenarios to which they give rise. The view has been articulated and defended most notably by Segal, and I shall concentrate on his work in what follows.[21]

Segal accepts that psychological content drives both common-sense psychological explanation and explanation in those branches of scientific psychology that recognize intentional states. What he maintains, however, is that "psychology as it is practised by the folk and by the scientists, is already, at root, [individualist]" (p. 122). The view thus avoids one of the worries faced by the two-factor theorist's notion of narrow content: narrow content is representational and can be specified by standard terms. As Segal says: "The narrow content of my belief that tigers can be playful is simply this: *tigers can be playful*" (p. 122). However, certain ascriptions do need to be revised.

Our subject S does not possess the concept *silver*, since her concept applies also to twilver, which the concept *silver* does not; and she does not possess the concept *game*, since her concept does not include solitaire in its extension, which the concept *game* does. If we are "correctly, precisely and explicitly" to describe S's state of mind we should, according to Segal, adopt neologisms. We should say, for instance, not that S believes that the value of silver will rise, or that snakes and ladders is a game, but rather that she believes that the value of n-silver will rise, and that snakes and ladders is an n-game. These beliefs S shares with counterfactual S and all other intrinsic physical duplicates, and hence their contents are narrow. It is not that the concepts expressed by "silver" and "game" are broad, on this view, with the concepts expressed by "n-silver" and "n-game" being narrow counterparts; it is just that S does not possess the standard (narrow) concepts that are expressed by the standard terms. Nor are the neologisms shorthand for complex descriptions of qualitative properties. The view thus also avoids the kind of objection raised against the epistemic notion of narrow content in Section 3.

The primary objection to the view is that the introduction of neologisms to express idiosyncratic concepts threatens to undermine both the ordinary practice of ascribing psychological states by means of standard terms and a scientific psychology that appeals to concepts expressed by standard terms.[22] Segal recognizes this but maintains that despite the fact that neologisms will sometimes be required to capture a person's state of mind "correctly, precisely and explicitly," no sweeping revision of either common-sense or scientific practice would follow. This is for two reasons. First, according to Segal, many subjects do possess the standard concepts and hence their states of mind can be captured by standard terms and without the introduction of neologisms. Second, even in those cases where the subject possesses an idiosyncratic concept, there may be no need to introduce a neologism to mark this fact since the standard term is close enough for the purposes in hand (p. 142). To back the first claim Segal points out that the kinds of counterfactual scenarios that motivate the acceptance of broad content cannot be marshaled when the subject is theoretically and practically competent. But while this may be true it does not help Segal's case. People are not in the main either theoretically or practically competent over a wide range of subject matters. For any given word there will typically be numerous subjects each of whom would apply that word in slightly different ways in non-central cases, and each of whom has slightly different beliefs about the relevant entities. Given the wide range of abilities and knowledge throughout a linguistic community, cases that would require the introduction of neologisms would be rife. More importantly, even if people were in the main competent, this would not undermine the considerations in favor of broad content since the anti-individualistic nature of thought rests on the mere possibility rather than the actuality of ignorance, incomplete linguistic understanding, and nonstandard theory.

Turning to his second claim, Segal acknowledges that conceptual variation may be rife, but claims "it does not follow that we are doomed to any manic introduction of neologisms. In ordinary practice, we can get by perfectly well without being precise and explicit"; moreover, scientific psychology "does not, by and large, study the idiosyncrasies of particular individuals. . . . Its concern is with the general, not the particular. . . . Particular concepts will be of interest to the extent that they are not idiosyncratic, but common across the whole species or some significant population within it" (pp. 146–7). But again, while this may be true it does not support Segal's position. We may well be able to get by in ordinary practice without being precise, but such imprecision ought not be tolerated within a scientific practice that emerges from the ordinary practice. If conceptual variation is rife, there will be few concepts that are common either across the species or across some significant population within it. Consequently, the concepts available for scientific psychology to study would, on the face of it, be too few for the practice to be scientifically viable: the idiosyncrasies would dominate. It might be objected that a general, perhaps ideal, concept could be constructed by an abstraction from sets of particular idiosyncratic concepts possessed by individuals, but this would render the idiosyncrasies primary and would not allow scientific psychology to proceed without appeal to them. In contrast, if concepts are anti-individualistic the idiosyncrasies fall out quite naturally as differences in empirical knowledge and linguistic and conceptual understanding. The fact that scientific psychology is concerned with "the general, not the particular" favors broad rather than narrow content. Broad concepts remain stable across idiosyncratic variations, where narrow concepts, in contrast, are anchored to those variations. Anti-individualistic concepts are anchored in part by the nature of the things to which they refer, and not solely by the beliefs of people who employ them in thought.[23]

A distinction drawn by Burge between concept and conceptual explication is pertinent here.[24] Concepts are communally available and possessed by individuals to differing degrees. Conceptual explications, by contrast, may be specific to individuals. A subject's conceptual explication of a given concept C is, roughly, her theory of what Cs are. Segal's position allows no slack such as that between concept and conceptual explication, and hence no distinction between common reference to kinds of things and subjects' individual views about things of those kinds. With the distinction in place, the distinction between the communal and the idiosyncratic is theoretically marked. It is this distinction between concept and conceptual explication that allows for constancy of reference in thought through change in belief – one advantage of the anti-individualistic outlook. As noted above, the linguistic meaning of a term may vary as the changes in belief are accepted across the community, but the concept expressed can remain the same. The ancient Greeks may have been mistaken in believing that stars were holes in the sky, but it is surely stars about which they were thinking. This can only be so if concepts are anti-individualistic.

It is worth noting that the anti-individualist can accept that the introduction of neologisms is sometimes appropriate. Segal states that in child psychology it has been argued that young children possess concepts that differ from those possessed by adults and older children: a single concept that later matures into the concept of belief and the concept of pretense, a single concept that differentiates into weight and density, a concept expressed by the term "alive" that contrasts with being dead rather than with being inanimate, and so on. For each of these a neologism would be useful to scientific psychology – and in the first case the term "prelief" has already been introduced.[25] But such examples do not favor Segal's position over that of the anti-individualist unless the concepts introduced by such neologisms are themselves narrow, and this has not been shown.

Segal's view is in part motivated by certain of the considerations that motivate the standard two-factor theorist's notion of narrow content and that were criticized in Section 2. For instance, Segal places weight on the fact that the actual and the counterfactual situations are plausibly indistinguishable from S's point of view, and the fact that S and counterfactual S mark out the same trajectories through space, exhibit the same speech patterns (non-intentionally described), possess the same discriminatory capacities (again, non-intentionally described), and so on. He says: "There is no reason to suppose that the best overall interpretation would distinguish twins, and some reason to suppose that it would not. For the relevant account of the subjects' behaviour would probably be the same for twins" (p. 154). But to think that the twins should not be distinguished at one level – in this case the behavioral level – provides no support for the claim that they should not be distinguished at a different level – the psychological level. The generalizations that capture the similarities in movement, speech patterns, discriminatory capacities, and so on between S and counterfactual S are plausibly neurophysiological generalizations that appeal to neurophysiological properties, but, as argued above, psychological properties cannot be assumed to supervene on neurophysiological properties. The individuation of explanatory properties of interest to a given science is responsive to causal patterns discerned from within that science, and hence the properties of interest to one science may be more or less dependent on the environment than those of interest to another.

I have not here addressed the many arguments Segal offers against the anti-individualistic nature of psychological properties. This is unfortunate given that part of the motivation for his positive view is based on these arguments. Addressing them is the topic for another occasion. Despite this, I hope to have shown that Segal's account of thoroughly narrow content is not viable.

5 Conclusion

I have discussed what I take to be the three primary attempts to define a notion of narrow content and have found none to be viable. Given the multiple realizability of the psychological and the fact that psychological properties are anti-individualistic, no intrinsic physical state is either necessary or sufficient for the instantiation of a psychological state. This renders psychological properties in one very good sense independent of physical properties. It does not, however, render the psychological naturalistically problematic. Psychology – like astronomy, geology, physiology, sociology, and so on – makes reference to properties whose specifications make essential reference to the environment of the individuals that instantiate them.

Acknowledgments

Thanks to Joe Mendola for comments. As will be clear, the paper is very much indebted to the work of Tyler Burge.

Notes

1   Properties have more than one specification. A property is individualistic if there is some specification of it that makes no reference to the environment, and anti-individualistic if there is no specification of it that does not. This is captured in the body of the text by the term "essential."

2   There are likely psychological properties that do not have associated contents, such as the property of being in pain. The focus of the paper is on those psychological properties that do have associated contents, and the term "psychological property" should henceforth be understood as thus restricted, artificial though the restriction may be.

3   What follows is not intended as an argument for the broadness of content so much as a statement of the view together with considerations that favor it. For a precursor to the first kind of consideration offered in the text see Putnam (1975). See also Kripke (1972). For the four primary original arguments for the anti-individualistic individuation of psychological properties together with extensive discussion, see Burge (1979, 1982, 1986a, and 1986b). The first of these trades on the possibility of understanding the conventional linguistic meaning of a term incompletely; the second on the possibility of ignorance of expert knowledge; the third on the possibility of perceptual error; and the fourth on the possibility of doubting necessary truths, specifically those truths that state meanings. I touch on all but the third of these in the text. For further, epistemological considerations in favor of broad content see Burge (2003) and Sawyer and Majors (2005 and 2007).

4   Whether and to what extent choice plays a role in natural kind taxonomy is a difficult issue, but it need not affect the question whether there is a substantive distinction between natural kinds and non-natural kinds.

5   The example is from Burge (1986b).

6   For discussion see Wikforss (2001) and Sawyer (2003).

7   In brief, the perceived problem is not that the entities to which one must be related in order to possess certain concepts are naturalistically problematic, but that properties that fail to supervene on the intrinsic properties of the individuals that instantiate them are problematic.

8   While anti-individualism is now orthodox, one or another attempt to retain a notion of narrow content convinces the majority of philosophers, either explicitly or implicitly.

9   For example see Fodor (1980), McGinn (1982), and Stich (1983). Fodor (1994) renounces this form of narrow content but holds onto the underlying motivations.

10   Stalnaker (1990) makes the point that narrow content presupposes rather than explains broad content. He goes on to say that in this sense it differs from Kaplan's notion of character, which, while a function from contexts to truth-conditional content, is explanatorily prior to that content. See Kaplan (1977).

11   There is a further potential worry here. What one can represent in thought is a product of a complex, temporally extended and ongoing interaction with objects, properties, and fellow thinkers. In contrast, according to the standard two-factor theory, narrow content is a function from current context to broad content, which means that one's ordinary, broad psychological states could change in an instant if one were switched from one environment to another. It may be that a two-factor theory can be adapted to accommodate this particular concern, but as it stands the reasons in favor of the broadness of content are acknowledged at most superficially.

12   The points that follow are documented in detail in Burge (1989). References in this part of the text are to that paper. See also Burge (1986a).

13   This conflation is evident in Block (1986), Fodor (1987, ch. 2), and Segal (2000, p. 47).

14 This conflation is evident in Fodor (1987, ch. 2, and 1991).

15 As Burge notes, this claim rests upon the assumption that brain states are individualistic, which is, while not disputed, a separate assumption.

16 The view considered in this section is similar in motivation and in substance to certain functional role and conceptual role theories of narrow content. There are also similarities to the view proposed in Dennett (1982) and Loar (1985), both of which talk of a belief's realizations conditions. I do not discuss such theories here because of limitations of space, but see Segal (2000, ch. 4) for apt criticisms.

17 Page references in this section are to that paper.

18 In fact, the worlds must be *centered* possible worlds, as Chalmers explains. I leave this complication to one side since nothing here turns on it.

19 See Mendola (1997, pp. 23–165) for an attempt to develop a semantically neutral specification of qualitative properties.

20 At a minimum there is an obligation on the part of the proponent of this epistemic notion of narrow content to provide a more detailed account of what such a semantically neutral language might look like. The worry with the proposal is reminiscent of the problems faced by sense-datum theorists attempting to provide a sense-datum language that does not presuppose objective reference. But see n. 19.

21 See Segal (2000). Page references in this section are to that book. See also Loar (1985) and Fodor (1994).

22 Burge (1979, section III) has argued at length against a wide variety of reinterpretation strategies, together with the apparent motivations for each. See also Burge (1986b).

23 There is a further objection in the offing here. Segal's view shares with conceptual role theories the individuation of concepts by beliefs in which those concepts feature. To the extent that this is so, Segal needs to provide an account of stability of concept through change in belief. The anti-individualist position is well placed to do this, but it is unclear how Segal's position could.

24 See Burge (1990).

25 See Perner (1991).

References

Block, N. (1986). Advertisement for a semantics for psychology. In P. French, T. Uehling, and H. Wettstein (eds.), *Midwest Studies in Philosophy*. Minneapolis: University of Minnesota Press.

Burge, T. (1979). Individualism and the mental. In P. French, T. Uehling, and H. Wettstein (eds.), *Midwest Studies in Philosophy*. Minneapolis: University of Minnesota Press.

—— (1982). Other bodies. In A. Woodfield (ed.), *Thought and Object: Essays on Intentionality*. Oxford: Oxford University Press.

—— (1986a). Individualism and psychology. *Philosophical Review*, 95, 3–45.

—— (1986b). Intellectual norms and foundations of mind. *Journal of Philosophy*, 83, 697–720.

—— (1989). Individuation and causation in psychology. *Pacific Philosophical Quarterly*, 70, 303–22.

—— (1990). Frege on sense and linguistic meaning. In D. Bell and N. Cooper (eds.), *The Analytic Tradition*. Oxford: Blackwell.

—— (2003). Perceptual entitlement. *Philosophy and Phenomenological Research*, 67, 503–48.

Chalmers, D. (2003). The nature of narrow content. *Philosophical Issues*, 13, 46–66.

Dennett, D. (1982). Beyond belief. In A. Woodfield (ed.), *Thought and Object: Essays on Intentionality*. Oxford: Oxford University Press.

Fodor, J. (1980). Methodological solipsism considered as a research strategy in cognitive psychology. *Behavioral and Brain Sciences*, 3, 63–73.

— (1987). *Psychosemantics: The Problem of Meaning in the Philosophy of Mind*. Cambridge, MA: MIT Press.

— (1991). A modal argument for narrow content. *Journal of Philosophy*, 88, 5–26.

— (1994). *The Elm and the Expert*. Cambridge, MA: MIT Press.

Kaplan, D. (1977). Demonstratives. In J. Almog, J. Perry, and H. Wettstein (eds., 1989), *Themes from Kaplan*. Oxford: Oxford University Press.

Kripke, S. (1972). *Naming and Necessity*. Oxford: Blackwell.

Loar, B. (1985). Social content and psychological content. In H. Grimm and D. Merrill (eds.), *Contents of Thought*. Arizona: University of Arizona Press.

McGinn, C. (1982). The structure of content. In A. Woodfield (ed.), *Thought and Object: Essays on Intentionality*. Oxford: Oxford University Press.

Mendola, J. (1997). *Human Thought*. Dordrecht: D. Reidel.

Perner, J. (1991). *Understanding the Representational Mind*. Cambridge, MA: MIT Press.

Putnam, H. (1975). The meaning of "meaning." In *Mind, Language and Reality*. Cambridge: Cambridge University Press.

Sawyer, S. (2003). Conceptual errors and social externalism. *Philosophical Quarterly*, 53, 265–73.

Sawyer, S. and Majors, B. (2005). The epistemological argument for content externalism. *Philosophical Perspectives*, 257–80.

— and — (2007). Entitlement, opacity and connection. In S. Goldberg (ed.), *Internalism and Externalism in Semantics and Epistemology*. Oxford: Oxford University Press.

Segal, G. (2000). *A Slim Book about Narrow Content*. Cambridge, MA: MIT Press.

Stalnaker, R. (1990). Narrow content. In N. Salmon and S. Soames (eds.), *Propositional Attitudes*. Oxford: Oxford University Press.

Stich, S. (1983). *From Folk Psychology to Cognitive Science: The Case against Belief*. Cambridge, MA: MIT Press.

Wikforss, A. M. (2001). Social externalism and conceptual errors. *Philosophical Quarterly*, 51, 217–31.

IS EXTERNALISM ABOUT MENTAL CONTENT COMPATIBLE WITH PRIVILEGED ACCESS?

Externalism and Privileged Access Are Consistent

Anthony Brueckner

1 Anti-individualism

In Hilary Putnam's well-known thought experiment, we consider earthling Oscar and his twin Toscar, who inhabits Twin Earth, where there is no H_2O but instead a super-ficially indistinguishable liquid composed of XYZ molecules.[1] This liquid is not water, given its strange chemical structure. Call the liquid *twater*. When Toscar says, "I swim in water," his sentence does not express the mistaken belief that he swims in water (the belief expressed by Oscar's use of the sentence). Instead, Toscar's sentence expresses the correct belief that he swims in twater. We can suppose that Oscar and Toscar are indistinguishable in respect of their *individualistic properties*: those that concern their qualitative perceptual experience and stream of consciousness, their behavior and behavioral dispositions, and their functional states. Even so, their uses of the sentence "I swim in water" express beliefs that differ in their intentional content.[2]

This thought experiment illustrates the thesis of *anti-individualism*. This thesis can be seen as the denial of a supervenience claim: the *content properties* of a thinker (such as *thinking that water is wet*) do *not* supervene upon his individualistic proper-ties. Oscar and Toscar are indistinguishable in respect of their individualistic properties though they differ in their content properties.

It is tempting to characterize anti-individualism as the thesis that content depends upon features of the thinker's external, causal environment (e.g., whether it contains water or twater). It is tempting, further, to think that this dependence involves an entailment of some sort – an entailment between the proposition that John thinks that some masts are made of aluminum and the proposition that John's external environment is a certain way (e.g., containing aluminum rather than twaluminum).

2 The McKinsey Problem

In an ingenious and provocative paper, Michael McKinsey launched a literature concerning a problem in what we might call the *epistemology of anti-individualism*.[3] McKinsey presented what he claimed to be an inconsistent triad of propositions:

1   Oscar knows a priori that he is thinking that water is wet.
2   The proposition that Oscar is thinking that water is wet conceptually implies E.
3   The proposition E cannot be known a priori, but only by empirical investigation.

E is some "external proposition" describing "the relations that Oscar bears to other speakers or objects in his external environment" (McKinsey, 1991, p. 1). By "a priori knowledge," McKinsey means "knowledge obtained independently of empirical investigation" of the external world. (1) expresses the view that Oscar has *privileged access* to his thought that water is wet. (2), according to McKinsey, expresses the core idea of anti-individualism as it applies to Oscar's thought about water. (2) is McKinsey's way of expressing the idea that according to the anti-individualist, the contents of Oscar's thoughts involving the concept of water *depend upon* Oscar's environment. This is knowable a priori by Oscar, if anti-individualism is true and knowable a priori by Oscar.

According to McKinsey, our triad can be seen to be inconsistent in the following way.

> Suppose (1) that Oscar knows a priori that he is thinking that water is wet. Then by . . . [(2)], Oscar can simply *deduce* E, using only premises that are knowable a priori, including the premise that he is thinking that water is wet. Since Oscar can deduce E from premises that are knowable a priori, Oscar can know E itself a priori. But this contradicts (3), the assumption that E *cannot* be known a priori. Hence (1), . . . [(2)], and (3) are inconsistent. And so in general, it seems, anti-individualism is inconsistent with privileged access (McKinsey, 1991, p. 15).

So: if (1) and (2) are true, then (3) is false – an inconsistent triad.

This reasoning depends upon McKinsey's understanding of the notion of *conceptual implication* (which in recent work he also calls *logical implication*). He says:

> a proposition p *conceptually implies* a proposition q if and only if there is a correct deduction of q from p, a deduction whose only premises other than p are necessary or conceptual truths that are knowable a priori, and each of whose steps follows from previous lines by a self-evident rule of some adequate system of natural deduction. (McKinsey, 1991, p. 14)

Insofar as the members of our triad (1)–(3) seem plausible, we have a puzzle on our hands, since, according to the reasoning quoted earlier from McKinsey, (1)–(3) cannot all be true. I will call this *the McKinsey problem*.

3 Types of Response to the McKinsey Problem

In the literature generated by the McKinsey problem, most writers (including me) incorrectly assumed that in presenting the apparently inconsistent triad, McKinsey intended to be presenting a *reductio ad absurdum* of anti-individualism. But in his seminal article, McKinsey in fact took no stand regarding the truth values of (1)–(3). We will look at his considered view of the matter later in this paper.

As far as I can tell, there are four types of response to the puzzle presented by the triad.

Type I: You deny that the triad is inconsistent. This is the strategy of Martin Davies and Crispin Wright.[4] They consider various *limitation principles* according to which justification, or warrant, is not transmitted via the deduction that yields E as its conclusion. Thus Oscar cannot come to know E via the deduction, and, a fortiori, cannot come to know E in an a priori manner via the deduction. So (1) and (2) are seen to be *consistent* with (3).[5]

On the other types of response to our triad, the inconsistency of the triad is granted while some member of it is rejected as false. *Type II*: there are two versions. *Type IIa* is the type of response commonly attributed to McKinsey and endorsed by Paul Boghossian: you maintain that anti-individualism is false and therefore unavailable to provide the basis for (2).[6] (2) is thus rejected as false, allowing us to hold on to privileged access and (1), as well as the intuitively plausible (3).

Type IIb: (2) is again held to be the culprit. But on this type of response, anti-individualism is not rejected. Rather, it is held that (2) does not follow from anti-individualism. (2) is false, according to response type IIb, but anti-individualism is true. This is the response I favor, and I will explain it in detail below.

Type III: You deny the privileged access thesis and its instance (1). Few accept this response, though it turns out that McKinsey himself is a proponent of it (this only emerged in his recent work).

Type IV: You deny (3). In Sarah Sawyer's phrase, we have *privileged access to the world* (or, as Ted Warfield calls it, *a priori knowledge of the world*).[7] Sawyer thinks that some concepts (such as *water* and other natural kind concepts) are like photographs, in that in possessing such concepts, you are in a position to glean information about those aspects of the world that are required for your possession of the concept. Warfield is a bit of a wolf in sheep's clothing: he argues that you can know a priori that *you are not a brain in a vat in a waterless world*. However, his argument for this admirably anti-skeptical conclusion proceeds via the claim that you know a priori that thinking that water is wet requires the existence of water. So in the end, Warfield is arguing that you can know a proposition E about the external world a priori, where E = *Water exists*.

I find every response other than type IIb to be unattractive. Denying transmission of warrant via deduction, denying anti-individualism, embracing privileged access to the world – these all seem to be rather desperate measures. Surely type IIb is the most attractive option (if it works), enabling us to have it all: transmission, anti-individualism, privileged access, and a sanely conservative view of the scope of a priori knowledge. I will now begin to explain why IIb is right: you just can't get (2) out of anti-individualism.

4 Anti-individualism Does Not Imply (2)

McKinsey does not say what the proposition E is, beyond saying that it is an "external proposition" concerning relations between Oscar and other speakers or objects in his environment. So in order to see whether the anti-individualist is committed to (2), we must consider various interpretations of E. (2) is false, according to the anti-individualist, if E is interpreted as

E1   Oscar inhabits an environment containing H_2O and not XYZ.

For the Burgean anti-individualist, there is no conceptual/logical connection between (a) Oscar's thinking that water is wet, and (b) the existence of H_2O. Consider the conditional

4   If Oscar is thinking that water is wet, then E1.

(4), if true, expresses a *metaphysical necessity* that is knowable only a posteriori, since its truth would depend upon the a posteriori necessity that water is H_2O. Thus, if E in (2) is interpreted as E1, then (2) is false. The anti-individualist can hold on to the privileged access thesis asserted in (1) while affirming (3) and rejecting (2).

Further, according to the Burgean anti-individualist, it is possible for Oscar to think that water is wet in a world lacking H_2O. So (4) does not even express an a posteriori, metaphysical necessity in the first place, much less an a priori truth. There is thus all the more reason to reject (2) if E is interpreted as E1. But how is it possible, according to Burge, for Oscar to think that water is wet in an H_2O-free world?

To see this, note that Burge does seem to commit himself to the view that the following is a metaphysical necessity:

N   If Oscar is thinking that water is wet, then either (i) H_2O exists, or (ii) Oscar theorizes that H_2O exists, or (iii) Oscar is part of a community of speakers some of whom theorize that H_2O exists.

Oscar can think that water is wet in a world lacking H_2O in virtue of the holding of either (ii) or (iii) in such a world.[8] (2) is once again false if E is interpreted as the disjunctive consequent of (N) (call this *E2*). Even if (N) is a metaphysical necessity, it is not knowable a priori, since its truth would depend upon the a posteriori metaphysical necessity that water is H_2O. The anti-individualist can again affirm both (1) and (3) while rejecting (2), on this interpretation of E as E2.

Though the matter is controversial, (2) may be true if E is interpreted as

E3   An external world of physical objects exists.

In this case, though, (3) would, arguably, be false. There might well be a transcendental argument, whose premises are knowable a priori, that connects thinking that water is wet with the existence of a physical world.[9] On this interpretation of E as E3, then, the anti-individualist can affirm (1) and (2) while rejecting (3) – he would hold that one *can* know E3 a priori.

This is a version of the type IV response to the McKinsey problem. On this version, we do have *unproblematic* privileged access to the world, in the sense that we can know a priori that there is a physical world, without knowing a priori about its details (such as its containing H_2O). I will return to this position at the end of the paper.[10]

5 Reconsideration of McKinsey's Position

I have been assuming that if p conceptually/logically implies q, then the conditional

> If p, then q

is knowable a priori. Since the conditionals (4) and

> 5   If Oscar is thinking that water is wet, then E2[11]

are *not* knowable a priori, it would follow that the antecedent of the conditionals does not conceptually/logically imply the consequents. (2), then, would come out false on the pertinent interpretations of E, allowing the anti-individualist to hold on to privileged access in the form of (1) while affirming (3).

In recent work on these issues, McKinsey maintains that his original position has been misinterpreted by various writers in the literature (including me).[12] Critics, and supporters as well, have made a crucial, unwarranted assumption about McKinsey's view of the connection between apriority and conceptual/logical implication. Before describing the misinterpretation in question, I will discuss McKinsey's overall strategy in his recent paper "Forms of Externalism and Privileged Access." Whereas his original paper has often been seen in the literature as an attempted *reductio* of anti-individualism, McKinsey (2002a) points out that there he in fact argued *only* for the inconsistency of (1)–(3), without taking a stand on which member of the triad is to be rejected. In the new paper, he maintains that *semantic externalism,* his version of anti-individualism, is true, and that it entails (2):

> SE   There are many sentences of the form "S thinks that p" whose truth logically or conceptually implies the existence of contingent objects external to S (McKinsey, 2002a, p. 200).

Given the inconsistency of our triad and the plausibility of (3) and (SE), McKinsey says, (1) is seen to be the false member of the triad. More generally, the following principle ("Privileged Access to Content") is shown to be false:

> PAC   It is necessarily true that if a person x is thinking that p, then x can in principle know a priori that he himself, or she herself, is thinking that p (McKinsey, 2002a, p. 199).

McKinsey maintains that

> 6   Dave is thinking that Larry is a janitor

is true only if Larry exists. McKinsey puts this point by saying that (6) is *singular with respect to Larry.* The idea is that the proposition that Dave thinks is a *singular proposition,* that is, a proposition that contains Larry himself as a constituent. McKinsey thinks that (6) is, in a key respect, on a par with

6'   Dave is holding the painting that Larry wants to buy.

(6') is true only if said painting exists. On McKinsey's view, (6) *logically implies* the existence of Larry, just as (6') logically implies the existence of the painting held by Dave. So this example illustrates the truth of (SE).

Let us return to the question of how exactly the inconsistency of the triad (1)–(3) is supposed to be established. Both supporters of McKinsey's position and critics as well have interpreted him in the following way. Assume that (1) is true: Oscar knows a priori that he is thinking that water is wet. Assume that (2) is true: the proposition that Oscar is thinking that water is wet conceptually/logically implies E. Then Oscar can know a priori a *corresponding conditional*:

2*   If Oscar is thinking that water is wet, then E.

The following principle ("Closure under A Priori Knowable Implication") is very plausible:

CAK   Necessarily, for any person x and any propositions P and Q, if x can know a priori that P and x can know a priori that if P then Q, then x can know a priori that Q (McKinsey, 2002a, p. 207).

From (1), (CAK), and the a priori knowability of (2*), it follows that

not-(3)   The proposition E can be known a priori (by Oscar).

As I said earlier, one way of reacting to McKinsey's triad is to hold that (2) can be rejected by the anti-individualist. This is the type IIb response to the McKinsey problem that I favor. The reasoning behind this response is as follows. If (2) is true, then it must be the case that the corresponding conditional (2*) is knowable a priori. That is, if the logical implication asserted in (2) held – if the proposition that Oscar is thinking that water is wet logically implied E – then the corresponding conditional (2*) would have to be knowable a priori: it would have to be knowable a priori that if Oscar is thinking that water is wet, then E. But since that conditional is *not* knowable a priori, (2) is false.

In response, McKinsey, in the new paper, correctly points out that he never committed himself to the a priori knowability of (2*) in his original paper. In the new paper, he explicitly denies that (2*) is knowable a priori, even given the truth of (2). He affirms the truth of (CAK), while maintaining, though, that it does not apply in the present case, since the conditional (2*) is not knowable a priori. This means that the foregoing way of arguing for the inconsistency of the triad using CAK is not *McKinsey's* way. So how is the inconsistency supposed to be established without using CAK?

According to McKinsey, the pertinent closure principle is not (CAK) but rather the principle of "Closure of Apriority under Logical Implication":

CA   Necessarily, for any person x, and any propositions P and Q, if x can know a priori that P, and P logically implies Q, then x can know a priori that Q (McKinsey, 2002a, p. 207).

Given (1) and (2), (CA) yields not-(3) without appeal to the a priori knowability of (2*). Since (2) and (3) are both true, says McKinsey, (1) must be false. If Oscar *could* know a priori that he is thinking that water is wet, he would, given (CA) and (2), be able to know E a priori. But this he cannot do.

Thus, according to McKinsey, one cannot fairly reject (2) by denying the a priori knowability of (2*), the corresponding conditional, as I tried to do.

6 Problems for McKinsey

One would have thought, however, that if p conceptually/logically implies q, the corresponding conditional

> If p, then q

is going to be knowable a priori. If p logically/conceptually implies q, then given McKinsey's understanding of such implication, it would seem that we can construct a correct conditional derivation of q from p, each of whose steps consists in an a priori knowable deduction from previous lines (which may contain additional a priori knowable premises other than p itself). The existence of such a derivation appears to be guaranteed by the assumed conceptual/logical implication (given McKinsey's understanding of such implication), and knowledge of the derivation would yield a priori knowledge of the conditional.

According to McKinsey (2002a), however, "externalist claims like (2) constitute an important class of exceptions to the assumption that logical relations are knowable a priori" (p. 208). In order to illustrate this point, McKinsey returns to his claim:

> 7   The proposition that Dave is thinking that Larry is a janitor logically implies that Larry exists.

I quote McKinsey (2002a) at length:

> Now ... [(7)] is *not* knowable a priori. For even though ... [(7)] is a meta-proposition about the logical implication of one proposition by another, it is also a proposition that is singular with respect to Larry. ... the meta-proposition expressed by ... [(7)] is itself a singular proposition that does not exist unless Larry does, and hence its truth cannot be known a priori. Similarly, the conditional proposition that if Dave is thinking that Larry is a janitor then Larry exists, is also singular with respect to Larry, and so it too cannot be known a priori. (p. 208)

McKinsey goes on to say that for the same reason, the conceptual/logical implication asserted in our triad's (2) does not imply that the corresponding conditional

> 2*   If Oscar is thinking that water is wet, then E.

is knowable a priori. Neither (2) nor (2*) is knowable a priori, on McKinsey's view.

There are a number of problems with McKinsey's reasoning in the foregoing passage. It is not perfectly clear why McKinsey holds that (7) is not knowable a priori (and similarly for (2) and (2*)). It seems that McKinsey believes that no singular proposition about contingent, external objects is knowable a priori. It seems that he holds that since such propositions exist only if their constituent objects exist, and since one cannot know a priori that these constituent objects exist, it follows that one cannot know the singular propositions in an a priori manner. This reasoning seems to rest upon the principle that if one knows a priori that p, then one knows a priori that the proposition that p exists. But this assumption is problematic for two reasons. First, it implies that one cannot have a priori knowledge that p if one lacks the concepts required for having higher-order knowledge regarding *the existence of the proposition that p*. Second, the assumption generates a problematic regress. In order to know a priori that p, one needs to know a priori that p* = *the proposition that p exists*. But by the assumption in order to know a priori that p*, one needs to know a priori that p** = *the proposition that p* exists*. And so on without end.

Let us now return to McKinsey's claims about the holding of the alleged conceptual/logical implications expressed in (2) and (7). According to McKinsey's (7), there is a correct deduction of

8   Larry exists

from

6   Dave is thinking that Larry is a janitor

such that (a) each step in the deduction follows from a previous line by a self-evident rule of inference, and (b) any premises other than (6) are knowable a priori. According to McKinsey (2002a), since the proposition that, according to (6), Dave thinks is a singular proposition, (6) ascribes to Dave and Larry that relation "which an object x bears to an object y just in case x has a thought about y to the effect that y is a janitor" (p. 204). If we symbolize this relation by the two-place predicate "R(xy)" and we let "D" denote Dave and "L" denote Larry, then we can represent (6)'s logical form by

6*   R(DL).

From (6*) and

9   L = L

we can deduce

10   R(DL) & L = L.

From (10), we can deduce

11 [∃] x[R(Dx) & x = L].

That is, there exists something that is Larry and is R-related to Dave. Larry exists! So we have made a case for the conceptual/logical implication of (8) by (6).

We cannot, however, in an analogous fashion correctly deduce

12 Pegasus exists

from

13 Dave is thinking that Pegasus flies.

This is because (13) does not have a relational logical form analogous to that given in (6*). Indeed, given McKinsey's remarks about why the conditional

14 If Dave is thinking that Larry is a janitor, then Larry exists.

is not knowable a priori, his view is presumably that (13) fails to express a proposition. That is, according to McKinsey, one cannot know (14) a priori, because one cannot know a priori whether or not there exists a proposition that is expressed by (14). One cannot know a priori whether or not Larry exists, and if he does not, then neither the antecedent nor the consequent of (14) expresses a proposition. Similarly, for McKinsey, (13) presumably fails to express a proposition, in virtue of the nonexistence of Pegasus.

Let us now return to the question whether McKinsey is right in holding that our triad's (2) is true. If (2) is true, then there must be a correct deduction of E (whatever "external proposition" this turns out to be) from

15 Oscar is thinking that water is wet.

Presumably McKinsey believes that the deduction of E from (15) parallels the deduction of (8) from (6). Thus, where "R*(xy)" symbolizes a relation between a thinker and the set of external objects whose existence is asserted by E, "O" denotes Oscar, and "W" denotes the set of external objects in question, the logical form of (15) is, for McKinsey, presumably given by

15* R*(OW).

As before, from (15*) and

16 W = W

we can deduce

17 R*(OW) & W = W.

From (17) we can deduce

18   [∃] x[R*(Ox) & x = W].

E follows from (18), since "W" denotes the set of external objects whose existence is asserted by E.

Even granting this view of (15)'s logical form and the concomitant deduction of E from (15), McKinsey's defense of the inconsistency of (1)–(3) in the end runs into an insuperable difficulty. Recall that that defense hinged on the principle (CA). I will now argue that (CA) is false given McKinsey's apparent view of the deduction of E from (15), whose existence is required by the conceptual/logical implication asserted in (2).

We treated the deduction starting from (15) as being on a par with the deduction starting from

6   Dave is thinking that Larry is a janitor.

Recall that the existence of Pegasus is not deducible from the premise

13   Dave is thinking that Pegasus flies.

Similarly, there is no proposition E* concerning external objects such as phlogiston that is deducible from the premise

19   Oscar is thinking that phlogiston is plentiful.

Let us grant that there is a correct deduction of E from (15) that flows from the logical form of (15), as McKinsey claims. One can know a priori that E is deducible from (15) only if one can know a priori that (15) has the relational logical form given in (15*). Now, one cannot know a priori that (6) has the logical form given in (6*). For all one knows a priori, (6) might be on a par with (13), which, on McKinsey's view, fails to express a proposition at all.

Similarly, for all one knows a priori, (15) is on a par with (19). In that case, (15) lacks the relational logical form given in (15*) and fails to express a proposition. Even if (15) *in fact* has the logical form given in (15*), which would allow for the deduction of E, this is something that one cannot know a priori. To put the point in a different way: One cannot know a priori whether or not "water" is a *successful* natural kind term, rather than a term that merely *purports* to denote an existing natural kind but fails to so denote. For all one knows a priori, "water" is like "phlogiston" and fails to pick out an existing natural kind. For all one knows a priori, then, (15) does not have the relational logical form given in (15*), which is required for the deduction of E.

These points show that given McKinsey's apparent conception of how (15) conceptually/logically implies E, he is barred from embracing

CA   Necessarily, for any person x, and any propositions P and Q, if x can know a priori that P, and P logically implies Q, then x can know a priori that Q.

In some cases in which a proposition p conceptually/logically implies q, one cannot know a priori that this implication holds. In such cases, then, given that one knows a priori that p, it does not follow that one can know a priori that q. For this to follow, one would have to be able to *recognize* the conceptual/logical implication of q by p in an a priori manner. Thus, McKinsey cannot appeal to (CA), as he does, in arguing for the inconsistency of the triad (1)–(3).

The point is similar to a familiar one that arises in connection with deductive closure principles for knowledge. This closure principle is clearly false:

CL   If S knows that p, and p logically implies q, then S knows that q.

If S fails to know that the implication holds, his knowledge that p will not ensure that he knows that q. The following plausible closure principle avoids this problem:

CL*   If S knows that p, knows that p logically implies q, and deduces q from p, then S knows that q.

Oddly enough, McKinsey himself makes the foregoing point upon which my objection to (CA) relies, viz. that some conceptual/logical implications are not knowable a priori. As we saw, he makes this point in connection with

7   The proposition that Dave is thinking that Larry is a janitor logically implies that Larry exists.

His justification for the point seemed to involve the dubious assumption discussed above (that knowing a priori that p requires knowing a priori that the proposition that p exists). The point, though, can be seen to hold by examining, as we have done, McKinsey's rationale for the deducibility of (8) from (6) and his apparent rationale for the deducibility of E from (15).

Given the existence of counterexamples to (CA), McKinsey is left in an untenable position with respect to our triad (1)–(3). In order to show that (1) and (2) imply

not-(3)   The proposition E can be known a priori (by Oscar).

McKinsey in the end needs to maintain that (2) implies the a priori knowability of the corresponding conditional

2*   If Oscar is thinking that water is wet, then E.

Then (CAK), which McKinsey accepts, would yield not-(3), given (1):

CAK   Necessarily, for any person x and any propositions P and Q, if x can know a priori that P and x can know a priori that if P then q, then x can know a priori that Q.

Since (CA) is false, McKinsey is forced to depend upon (CAK) in order to demonstrate the inconsistency of (1)–(3). However, I have argued that there is no interpretation of

E on which the corresponding conditional (2*) is knowable a priori and on which (3) is true. McKinsey has nowhere countered these claims about the a posterioricity of (2*). Indeed, his main thrust in his new work has been aimed at establishing the inconsistency of the triad (1)–(3) *without* challenging the claims in the literature regarding the a posterioricity of (2*).

I conclude that the considerations that McKinsey has brought forward in his recent work do not vindicate his position on the triad (1)–(3). The type IIb response to the McKinsey problem stands. The anti-individualist can affirm privileged access while rejecting the interpretations of (2) on which (3) is true. For all that McKinsey has shown, anti-individualism is compatible with privileged access.

7 Unproblematic Privileged Access to the World?

I have said in passing that it is intuitively problematic to hold that we have privileged access to the existence of water and other natural kinds. I have argued, further, that the existence of such privileged access does not follow from the truth of anti-individualism: I cannot know a priori that water exists by deducing this from my a priori knowledge of the abstract philosophical doctrine of anti-individualism (and its consequences) together with my a priori knowledge of what I am thinking. One of the main problems for such a deduction is that I cannot know a priori whether or not my concept of water is an *empty concept* like my concept of phlogiston, that is, a concept that has no actual instances, a concept with an empty extension in the actual world. However, as I in effect suggested earlier, it might be thought that I can know a priori that the following Cartesian skeptical possibility is *not actual*, is *not the case*:

> SK   I have thoughts with determinate contents involving concepts that appear to apply to actually existing physical natural kinds, as well as to other actually existing physical objects external to my mind. However, these concepts are all *empty*. Nothing physical exists at all. All that exists is my mind and that of a nonphysical, deceiving Evil Genius who causes my systematically misleading experiences.

In order to show that SK is not the case via a transcendental argument, we might try to follow Descartes's lead in Meditation I. In examining the scope of the Dream Argument, Descartes says:

> although these general things, to wit, [a body], eyes, a head, hands and such like, may be imaginary, we are bound at the same time to confess that there are at least some other objects yet more simple and more universal, which are real and true; and of these just in the same way as with certain real colors, all these images of things that dwell in our thoughts, whether true and real or false and fantastic, are formed.[13]

In a similar vein, Leora Weitzman represents Burge's anti-individualism as generating the following anti-skeptical result: "Some of the concepts which we apply to perceivable objects may be derived from others, but . . . there must be some that are basic and not derived. . . . our perceptual beliefs of the form *there are X's* cannot mislead us when the X position is occupied by a basic concept; for our basic concepts cannot have empty extensions."[14] If Weitzman's Meditation-I-style claim is correct, then SK is not the case: it is not the case that *all* my concepts that appear to apply to physical natural kinds, and to physical objects generally, are empty. So: I know a priori that I think thoughts involving physical object concepts, I know a priori that anti-individualism is true and entails the Meditation-I-style claim, and thus I can know a priori, by deduction, that *not all of my physical object concepts are empty*. Privileged access to the world, but of a wonderful, unproblematic sort – an a priori rejection of the skeptic's possibility SK!

Let us call Weitzman's Meditation-I-style claim the *basic concept theory*:

BC   Genuine, contentful empty concepts must be constructible out of basic concepts that are non-empty.

I will argue that contrary to Weitzman's suggestion, BC does not follow from anti-individualism in any obvious way. Weitzman's justification for asserting this connection is that on anti-individualism, our basic concepts of perceivable objects "have their extensions determined in a directly causal way" (Weitzman, 1996, p. 301). Weitzman focuses upon Burge's discussion of the crack and shadow worlds.[15] Suppose that in the shadow world, S's perceptual states of a given (individualistically individuated) neural type t are normally caused by shadows (and there are very few cracks). In the crack world, S also has perceptual states of type t, but they are normally caused by cracks (and there are very few shadows). According to Burge (1986), "it makes no sense to attribute systematic perceptual error" to S by attributing to him the concept *crack* in the shadow world and *shadow* in the crack world (p. 131). Instead, the right way to ascribe content to S is to attribute mostly correct *shadow*-thoughts in the shadow world and mostly correct *crack*-thoughts in the crack world. Similarly, Burge finds it incredible to suppose that a thinker who has always lived in an XYZ-filled world possesses the concept *water* and uses it to make systematically mistaken judgments about the twater around him. Burge (1982) wonders how such a thinker could have acquired the concept *water* in his waterless world (pp. 114–18).

But these anti-individualist points do not establish that among my concepts there must be some basic ones that are non-empty. Granted, if our problem is to attribute one or the other of a pair of concepts to a thinker, one of which is empty (in his world) and the other of which is not, then Burge's solution seems right: attribute the non-empty concept and interpret the thinker as making correct judgments about the instances of the concept in his causal environment. But this is compatible with the emptiness of all one's basic concepts. Suppose that God were to attempt to attribute concepts and thoughts to some thinker S. He would not attribute *crack* to S if S is in a shadow world. However, for all that has been said, God might find S in a world in which no method of attributing physical object and natural kind concepts served to make S's judgments about objects largely true. In this empty world, God would have no choice but to attribute nothing but empty physical object concepts to S, if he attributes physical object concepts to S at all. Alternatively, God might properly *withhold* attribution of thoughts and concepts with determinate content. We will return to this possibility below.

I have just tried to argue that anti-individualist principles of concept attribution do not force the acceptance of BC. But suppose that BC is thought to be independently plausible, knowable on a priori philosophical grounds. Then the a priori rejection of SK could be defended. However, even assuming that BC is true, there are still difficulties in the attempted vindication of unproblematic privileged access to the physical world.

First, as Weitzman herself points out, BC is silent on the question of which of my concepts are basic (and hence non-empty). Why assume that concepts of physical objects are basic (and hence non-empty)? Perhaps my concepts of experiences and other mental states are the basic ones. If physical object concepts are non-basic, then BC is compatible with their emptiness. As against this, the BC theorist could point to the failure of phenomenalist constructions, maintaining that the following picture cannot be right: concepts of experiences are basic (and hence non-empty), while physical object concepts are non-basic and plausibly constructible out of the basic experiential concepts.

A second problem for the BC theorist arises as follows. According to BC, if I possess a genuine, contentful, but empty concept c, then c must be constructible from basic, non-empty concepts. It certainly *seems* to me that I use terms that express genuine, contentful physical object concepts, concepts that, I think, successfully apply to things in my world. If these concepts are basic (given the failure of phenomenalistic constructions), then, by BC they are non-empty. But maybe my terms "water," "tree," "block," and so on fail to express genuine contentful concepts. Then I cannot bring BC to bear in the envisaged manner, since BC governs only genuine, contentful concepts.

However, this suggestion stands in tension with the view that I have a priori knowledge of my own mind, a view that I have not challenged here. I believe that, in the absence of empirical investigation of the external world, I can know that I think certain thoughts with determinate contents involving genuine concepts that either apply to things in my world or fail to so apply. According to the foregoing suggestion that, say, my term "water" may fail to express a genuine concept, I *lack* the a priori knowledge of my mind just described.

Perhaps a priori knowledge of BC and the a priori knowledge of my mind in question will yield unproblematic privileged access to the physical world. But we have seen no argument from anti-individualism to BC and no argument for BC itself (which theory seems to be doing all the work in the attempt to establish privileged access to the world).

8 Conclusion

Anti-individualism is compatible with privileged access to one's own thoughts and their contents. Anti-individualism by itself does not in any obvious way allow us to establish unproblematic, wonderful privileged access to the existence of a physical world. BC, the basic concept theory, might undergird such privileged access. But BC is independent of anti-individualism and is far from being clearly knowable a priori.

Anthony Brueckner

Acknowledgment

Thanks to Jessica Brown for helpful comments.

Notes

1 See Putnam (1975).
2 See Burge (1979, 1982).
3 See McKinsey (1991). Some of the papers in the ensuing literature are listed in the references.
4 See the papers Davies (1993, 1998, 2000, 2003) and Wright (2000, 2003).
5 This is a bit of an oversimplification of Wright's view. He holds that (1) and (2) are do not entail that Oscar can know E a priori *as a result of deducing E from the a priori known proposition that he is thinking that water is wet*. So he holds that (1) and (2) are consistent with a version of (3) in which it is held that Oscar cannot know E a priori *as a result of the deduction in question*. This leaves open the question of whether Oscar knows E a priori by some other means.
6 See Boghossian (1997).
7 See Sawyer (1998) and Warfield (1999). See also Brewer (2000) and Brueckner (2004).
8 See Burge (1982).
9 See Brueckner (1992, 1999) for discussion of this issue. The second paper makes a case against the existence of such a transcendental argument.
10 See Brueckner (1992) for discussion of the points in this section. This article was the first response to McKinsey (1991).
11 This is just (N) rewritten.
12 See McKinsey (2002a, 2002b).
13 See Descartes (1996).
14 See Weitzman (1996).
15 See Burge (1986).

References

Boghossian, P. (1997). What the externalist can know a priori. In C. MacDonald, B. Smith, and C. Wright (eds.), *Knowing Our Own Minds*. Oxford: Oxford University Press.

Brewer, B. (2000). Externalism and a priori knowledge of empirical facts. In P. Boghossian and C. Peacocke (eds.), *New Essays on the A Priori*. Oxford: Oxford University Press.

Brown, J. (1995). The incompatibility of anti-individualism and privileged access. *Analysis*, 55, 149–56.

Brueckner, A. (1992). What an anti-individualist knows a priori. *Analysis*, 52, 111–18.

— (1995). The characteristic thesis of anti-individualism. *Analysis*, 55, 146–8.

— (1999). Transcendental arguments from content externalism. In R. Stern (ed.), *Transcendental Arguments: Problems and Prospects*. Oxford: Oxford University Press, 229–50.

— (2004). Brewer on the McKinsey problem. *Analysis*, 64, 41–3.

Burge, T. (1979). Individualism and the mental. *Midwest Studies in Philosophy*, 4, 73–121.

— (1982). Other bodies. In A. Woodfield (ed.), *Thought and Object: Essays on Intentionality*. Oxford: Clarendon.

— (1986). Cartesian error and the objectivity of perception. In P. Pettit and J. McDowell (eds.), *Subject, Thought and Context.* Oxford: Oxford University Press.

Davies, M. (1993). Aims and claims of externalist arguments. *Philosophical Issues,* 4, 227–49.

— (1998). Externalism, architecturalism, and epistemic warrant. In C. MacDonald, B. Smith, and C. Wright (eds.), *Knowing Our Own Minds.* Oxford: Oxford University Press.

— (2000). Externalism and armchair knowledge. In P. Boghossian and C. Peacocke (eds.), *New Essays on the A Priori.* Oxford: Clarendon.

— (2003). The problem of armchair knowledge. In S. Nuccetelli (ed.), *New Essays on Semantic Externalism and Self-Knowledge.* Cambridge, MA: MIT Press.

Descartes, R. (1996). *Meditations on First Philosophy,* trans. J. Cottingham. Cambridge: Cambridge University Press.

McKinsey, M. (1991). Anti-individualism and privileged access. *Analysis,* 51, 9–16.

— (2002a). Forms of externalism and privileged access. *Philosophical Perspectives,* 16, 199–224.

— (2002b). Review of *Knowing Our Own Minds. Philosophical Quarterly,* 52, 107–16.

Putnam, H. (1975). The meaning of "meaning." In K. Gunderson (ed.), *Language, Mind, and Knowledge.* Minneapolis: University of Minnesota Press.

Sawyer, S. (1998). Privileged access to the world. *Australasian Journal of Philosophy,* 76, 523–33.

Warfield, T. A. (1999). A priori knowledge of the world. In K. DeRose and T. A. Warfield (eds.), *Skepticism: A Contemporary Reader.* Oxford: Oxford University Press.

Weitzman, L. (1996). What makes a causal theory of content anti-skeptical? *Philosophy and Phenomenological Research,* 56, 299–318.

Wright, C. (2000). Cogency and question-begging: some reflections on McKinsey's paradox and Putnam's proof. *Philosophical Issues,* 10, 140–63.

— (2003). Some reflections on the acquisition of warrant by inference. In S. Nuccetelli (ed.), *New Essays on Semantic Externalism and Self-Knowledge.* Cambridge, MA: MIT Press.

Externalism and Privileged Access Are Inconsistent

Michael McKinsey

In my paper "Anti-Individualism and Privileged Access" (1991a), I argued that an externalist, or anti-individualist, view about cognitive properties is inconsistent with the traditional Cartesian view that we all have a privileged non-empirical way of knowing about our own thoughts and other cognitive acts and states. In this paper, I want to clarify both my argument and the specific principles of privileged access and externalism to which the argument does and does not apply. I also want to discuss the main response that has been made to my argument, and defend my view of what the correct response should be.

1 The *Reductio* Argument for Incompatibilism

The externalist principle about cognitive properties that I argued is inconsistent with privileged access can be stated as follows:

Semantic Externalism (SE)

Many *de dicto*-structured predicates of the form "is thinking that p" express properties that are wide, in the sense that possession of such a property by an agent *logically implies* the existence of contingent objects or substances of a certain sort that are external to the agent.[1]

Here, I mean "logically implies" in a broad sense that includes what I have elsewhere called "conceptual implication" (see McKinsey, 1991a, p. 14, and 1991b, p. 152). For simplicity, I have stated SE by use of one specific form of cognitive predicate "is thinking that p," but defenders of SE would endorse a similar principle for all other cognitive predicates of the form "Cs that p," where C is any cognitive operator.

The traditional Cartesian principle of privileged access that I argued is inconsistent with SE is a principle to the effect that we have privileged access, not just to our thoughts, but to our thoughts as having certain *contents*:

Privileged Access to Content (PAC)

It is necessarily true that if a person x is thinking that p, then x can in principle come to know a priori that he himself, or she herself, is thinking that p.[2]

Here, by "a priori" knowledge I mean knowledge that is obtained "just by thinking," and not on the basis of empirical investigation or perceptual observation. Thus under a priori knowledge I include knowledge that is obtained from introspection of one's own cognitive and sensory states, acts, and experiences, as well as knowledge of the truths of logic and mathematics that is obtained by pure reason.[3] Again, as with SE, I have stated PAC for the special case of occurrent thought, but defenders of PAC might also wish to endorse similar principles for other cognitive states and acts such as belief, intention, and desire.

My argument that PAC and SE are inconsistent was a simple *reductio ad absurdum*. As an instance of the form "is thinking that p," I chose a predicate that contains a natural kind term such as "water," since such predicates are generally assumed to express wide psychological properties. So suppose that a given person, Oscar, say, is thinking that water is wet. Then it follows by PAC that

1   Oscar can know a priori that he's thinking that water is wet.

And given that the predicate "is thinking that water is wet" expresses a logically wide psychological property, it is also true that

2   The proposition that Oscar is thinking that water is wet logically implies E,

where E is some "external" proposition that asserts or logically implies the existence of contingent objects or substances of a certain sort that are external to Oscar. Depending on the form of externalism in question, E might for instance be the proposition that water exists, or the proposition that Oscar has experienced samples of water, or the proposition that members of Oscar's linguistic community have experienced samples of water.

But whatever external proposition we take E to be, the conjunction of (1) and (2) is clearly absurd. For if Oscar can know a priori that he's thinking that water is wet, and the proposition that he's thinking that water is wet logically implies E, then Oscar could correctly deduce E from something he knows a priori, and so Oscar could also know E itself a priori. But this consequence is absurd. For E is an external proposition such as the proposition that water exists, a proposition that asserts or logically implies the existence of contingent external things, and so Oscar could not possibly know E a priori. Thus if the property of thinking that water is wet is logically wide, then contrary to PAC, no one could know a priori that he or she is thinking that water is wet. Of course the same *reductio* can be given for any logically wide property

Michael McKinsey

expressed by a predicate of the form "is thinking that p," and so in general SE is inconsistent with PAC.

It is worth noting that the *reductio* just given assumes only one premise. This premise is a principle to the effect that the capacity for a priori knowledge is closed under logical implication:

Closure of Apriority under Logical Implication (CA)

Necessarily, for any person x and any propositions P and Q, if x can know a priori that P, and P logically implies Q, then x can know a priori that Q.

Given CA alone, the absurd conclusion that Oscar can know E a priori follows from the conjunction of (1) and (2).[4]

2 The Proper Response to the *Reductio*

Of course, the first response to a correct *reductio* (whose only premise is a necessary truth) should be to note that the assumptions reduced to absurdity, being inconsistent, cannot all be true. In the present case, this means that at least one, perhaps both, of SE and PAC must be false, and so the question arises as to which of these principles is false, and as to whether one or both of the principles can be plausibly revised so as to achieve a consistent view.

Oddly enough, however, no one who has responded critically to my argument has discussed these additional questions that the argument raises.[5] Instead, the main response has been that of *evading* the argument by insisting that semantic externalism regarding cognitive properties should not be understood, as it is understood in SE, in terms of logical implication. Rather, this response goes, semantic externalism should be understood in terms of some weaker dependency relation such as *metaphysical* entailment, or even *counterfactual* implication.[6]

I am myself partly responsible for turning the discussion in this direction, since in the paper (1991a) where I first gave the *reductio* I was also concerned to counter the attempt by Burge (1988) to defend the consistency of anti-individualism and privileged access. Burge endorsed a form of anti-individualism or externalism on which a person's possession of cognitive properties such as those expressed by predicates of the form "is thinking that p" may "necessarily depend on" or "presuppose" the bearing of relations by the person to things in the person's physical or social environment. (See Burge, 1988, pp. 650, 653, 654.) Burge never tells us what sort of necessary dependency relation he has in mind, nor what the term "presuppose" is supposed to mean in this context. However, Burge does clearly insist that one can directly and non-empirically know one's own mental states without being able to know a priori the facts about the external world on which those states "depend" (Burge, 1988, p. 651). So I suggested on Burge's behalf that he might be tacitly endorsing a form of externalism that is based on the relation of metaphysical dependency, rather than logical implication (McKinsey, 1991a, pp. 12–13). We might call this view

Many *de dicto*-structured predicates of the form "is thinking that p" express properties that are wide, in the sense that possession of such a property by an agent *metaphysically entails* the existence of contingent objects or substances of a certain sort that are external to the agent.[7]

Unlike SE, MSE is clearly consistent with unrestricted privileged access in the form of PAC (as I pointed out in the original paper, 1991a, p. 13). This is because, as Kripke (1972) showed, there are some metaphysical dependencies that can only be known a posteriori and that cannot form the basis of a priori knowledge. In short, in contrast to logical implication, the capacity for a priori knowledge is obviously *not* closed under metaphysical entailment. However, as I argued in the original paper, MSE is a trivial, uninteresting form of semantic externalism. For given certain commonly accepted materialist assumptions, it turns out that probably *every* psychological property is "wide" in the metaphysical sense invoked by MSE. (For details, see McKinsey, 1991a, 1994b, 2002a.)

I will return to more detailed discussion of "metaphysical" forms of externalism below. Right now, I want to evaluate the move to MSE simply as a response to my *reductio*. Those who make this move seem to be primarily motivated by the desire to avoid inconsistency with privileged access in the form of PAC. These philosophers thus want to hold on to PAC while (tacitly) giving up the strong form of externalism SE, replacing SE by the weaker principle MSE. But this way of responding to my *reductio* is precisely the *opposite* of the correct response. For there is strong, well-known semantic evidence that shows that SE is in fact *true* and hence that PAC is *false*. So we should hold on to SE and replace PAC with a weaker, restricted principle that is consistent with SE.

3 Why Semantic Externalism (SE) is True

Defenders of externalism such as Burge (1988), Brueckner (1992), McLaughlin and Tye (1998), and others who advocate the metaphysical evasion, are committed to the conjunction of MSE and PAC. But as these metaphysical externalists all seem to concede, my *reductio* argument shows that SE is incompatible with PAC. Hence, these "externalists" are all committed to the *denial* of the strong externalist principle SE.

Yet the semantic facts about proper names and indexical pronouns provide strong evidence that SE is in fact true. Consider the case of Laura, who upon hearing George use the word "disassemble" when he means "dissemble" exclaims "Incredible!" Hearing Laura's exclamation, Karl then says

3 Laura is thinking that George is inarticulate.

It seems intuitively clear that in uttering (3), Karl would be using the name "George" simply to refer to George and would be saying that Laura is having a thought about him to the effect that he is inarticulate. If ordinary names like "George" had some sort of descriptive meaning in English, then perhaps a cognitive ascription like (3), in which "George" is assumed to have smallest scope, could be used to say something about Laura's way of thinking about George.[8] However, for various reasons, including

Kripke's (1972) famous argument based on his "Gödel/Schmidt" example, I am convinced that most ordinary names have no descriptive meanings of any sort.[9]

Thus in a case like (3), since the name "George" lacks any descriptive meaning, the only semantic contribution that the small-scope occurrence of this name could make to the proposition expressed by (3) is simply the name's *referent*. Thus the cognitive predicate contained in (3), "is thinking that George is inarticulate," must express a property that is relational with respect to George. In effect, then, the cognitive predicate in question, while it is *de dicto* in structure, is semantically *de re*.

Cognitive predicates that contain small-scope indexical and demonstrative pronouns are even more obviously relational in meaning. Consider:

4   Laura is thinking that *he* (or: *that man*) is inarticulate.
5   Laura is thinking that *you* are inarticulate.
6   Laura is thinking that *I* am inarticulate.

Given that the small-scope terms in (3)–(6) all refer to George, the cognitive predicates in (3)–(6) all express the same relational property, namely the property that any object x has just in case x is having a thought about George to the effect that he is inarticulate. Since the property in question is relational with respect to George, possession of this property by an agent *logically implies* that George exists. Hence the *de dicto*-structured cognitive predicates contained in (3)–(6) all express logically wide properties, and thus sentences of this kind show that semantic externalism (SE) is true.

Of course, since SE is inconsistent with PAC, these same kinds of sentence also provide straightforward counterexamples to PAC. Thus suppose that (3) is true, so that Laura is thinking that George is inarticulate. By PAC it follows that Laura can know a priori that she is thinking that George is inarticulate. But this is just false. Since what Laura allegedly knows a priori logically implies that George exists, it follows that Laura could also know a priori that George exists, and this of course is absurd.

Thus the semantic facts about proper names and indexical pronouns show both that SE is true and that PAC is false.

4 The Retreat to MSE Is Unmotivated

Of course, since SE is true and SE implies the weaker principle MSE, MSE is also true. But the fact that PAC is false eliminates what appears to be the primary motivation behind the "metaphysical" externalists' retreat to the weaker principle MSE and their tacit rejection of SE. For given that PAC is false, the retreat to MSE is just pointless: consistency with a false principle is no advantage.

Another reason that the "metaphysical" externalists might have for their retreat to MSE is their plausible assumption that externalist dependency theses are not knowable a priori.[10] I agree with this assumption. (See McKinsey, 2002a and 2002c.) In general, externalist dependency theses are true because certain cognitive properties are relational with respect to certain external contingent objects or substances. But one cannot know a priori that such relational properties exist, since one cannot know a priori that the relevant contingent objects or substances exist. Now the fact that externalist dependency theses cannot be known a priori might easily lead one to infer that such theses must assert the obtaining of metaphysical but *not* logical relations. For, so the inference goes, if these theses asserted the obtaining of logical relations, then they *would* be knowable a priori.[11]

But this inference is seriously defective. Consider the following (true) externalist dependency thesis:

> 7 The proposition that Laura is thinking that George is inarticulate logically implies the proposition that George exists.

Even though (7) truly ascribes a logical relation between propositions, (7) is *not* knowable a priori. This is because (7) itself, though a meta-proposition about the logical implication of one proposition by another, is also a proposition that is singular with respect to the referents of the names "Laura" and "George." Since the truth of (7) logically requires the existence of these objects, one cannot know that (7) is true without knowing that both Laura and George exist, and the latter knowledge is not in general obtainable a priori. What *is* knowable a priori is not (7), but rather the general formal principle of which (7) is an instance, namely

> 8 For any objects x and y, and any relation R, the proposition that xRy logically implies the proposition that y exists.

So *part* of the basis of one's knowledge that (7) is true is knowable a priori. But (7) itself is not knowable a priori. Hence it simply does not follow from the assumption that externalist theses are not knowable a priori that such theses must ascribe the obtaining of metaphysical but *not* logical dependency relations. Thus the fact that externalist theses are not knowable a priori provides no reasonable basis for assuming that only some weak "metaphysical" form of externalism such as MSE could be correct.

Many of those who have discussed my *reductio* argument in the literature have assumed that the argument requires as a premise the (false) assumption that externalist dependency theses are all knowable a priori.[12] But this is simply wrong. Again, the only premise that my argument requires is the principle CA, that the capacity for a priori knowledge is closed under logical implication.[13]

5 Individuating Thoughts

Since PAC is false, it is an incorrect expression of the traditional idea that we have privileged access to the fundamental features of our thoughts. I have proposed elsewhere (McKinsey, 1994a) that the correct principle would restrict the properties of a thought to which one has privileged access to those fundamental semantic properties that *individuate* the thought, in the following sense:

> I A thought that a person x has in a possible world w is *individuated* by a property F just in case in any other possible world w* a person y would have the very same thought if and only if in w* y also has a thought that has F.

Then the correct principle of privileged access would be

Privileged Access to Individuating Properties (PAI)

It is necessarily true that if a person's thought is individuated by a property F, then that person can in principle come to know a priori that he or she has a thought that has the property F.

We have seen that no one ever has privileged access to one's having any logically wide psychological property, and so PAI implies an important metaphysical principle to the effect that our thoughts are individuated only by logically *narrow* properties (where a property is logically narrow if and only if it is not logically wide). I will call this principle

Logical Internalism (LI)

It is necessarily true that if a person's thought is individuated by a given property F, then F is logically narrow.

I endorse both PAI and LI.

I indicated earlier that I also endorse semantic externalism, the thesis SE that many *de dicto*-structured cognitive predicates express logically wide properties. But of course SE is perfectly consistent with both PAI and LI. For being merely a *semantic* thesis, SE is silent on the metaphysical question of which kinds of properties *individuate* our thoughts.

Those who like me restrict their externalism to the semantics of cognitive predicates are thus free to endorse the principle PAI, that we have privileged access to the fundamental properties that individuate our thoughts. But it seems to me that many philosophers have wanted to endorse externalism as a *metaphysical* (not just semantic) view about the *nature* of thought. And many of these externalists, I suggest, can most plausibly be understood as claiming that certain kinds of thoughts are individuated, in the sense I've defined, by their logically wide contents, or by the logically wide property of having such a content. (For details, see McKinsey, 1994a. By a "logically wide" content, I mean an abstract semantic entity, like a singular proposition, whose very existence logically implies the existence of some contingent object or substance.) We might call this view

Logical Externalism (LE)

In some cases, a person is thinking that p, the content that p is logically wide, and the person's thought is individuated by the property of being a thought that has the content that p.

LE is the sort of view that is endorsed by those who follow Gareth Evans (1982) in holding that there are "object-dependent" thoughts. These are thoughts like Laura's thought that George is inarticulate, which are based on direct or demonstrative reference and which have Russellian singular propositions as contents. According to LE, such thoughts would not be the thoughts they are – the thoughts would not exist – independently of their singular contents and the objects that are constituents of those contents. However, my original *reductio* shows that we can have no privileged access to the logically wide properties of our thoughts, and so PAI implies that our thoughts cannot be individuated by such properties, contrary to LE.

Being inconsistent with the most plausible principle of privileged access, LE is thus false.[14] But the devotee of metaphysically but not logically wide cognitive properties might want to endorse a different externalist view of individuating properties, which we can call

Metaphysical Externalism (ME)

In some cases, a person is thinking that p, the content that p is metaphysically but not logically wide, and the person's thought is individuated by the property of being a thought that has the content that p.

Now ME has a distinct advantage over LE, in that ME, like logical internalism (LI), is perfectly consistent with the principle PAI, that we have privileged access to the properties that individuate our thoughts. So we need to consider whether, in addition to logical internalism (LI), ME might also be true. That is, we need to consider whether, in some cases, the logically narrow property that individuates a thought might also be the metaphysically wide property of being a thought that has a specific metaphysically – but *not* logically – wide content.

6 What's Wrong with Metaphysical Externalism (ME)

I believe that ME is false, and my reason is that I can see no way to make sense of the claim that the contents of some thoughts depend metaphysically but not logically for their existence upon contingent objects or substances external to the agent.[15] We can at the outset eliminate *singular propositions* as being the relevant sort of content, since, as we've seen, the existence of such propositions that are singular with respect to contingent things *logically* (not just metaphysically) implies the existence of the contingent things in question. The main kind of example considered by the metaphysical externalists is that of cognitive predicates containing natural kind terms, such as "is thinking that water is wet." But here again, the imbedded sentence expresses a singular proposition, in this case a proposition about the natural kind W to which water belongs, a proposition to the effect that all stuff that belongs to W is wet.[16] In this case again, the propositional content ascribed to a thought would be *logically* wide, since the existence of the content logically (and so metaphysically) implies the existence of the contingent kind W. So again, this type of content will not serve the metaphysical externalists' purposes.

Apparently, then, these externalists must assume that sentences containing natural kind terms must have a *second* type of content in addition to the proposition expressed. And they must also assume that contents of this second type can be metaphysically but not logically wide, and that contents of this type can somehow be ascribed to thoughts by use of such predicates as "is thinking that water is wet."

It is not uncommon for philosophers of language and mind to suggest that some kinds of words and the sentences that contain them can have two types of meaning or content, and that persons' cognitive attitudes can be characterized in terms of both kinds of content.[17] I have myself proposed this type of view for natural kind terms

(McKinsey 1987, 1994a). On my view, the *propositional* meaning of such a term, the contribution made by the term to the propositions expressed by use of it, is simply the relational property of belonging to a given natural kind K. By contrast, such a term also has a *linguistic* meaning. This is the term's meaning in the language in question, and on my view, it determines the term's propositional meaning. We might call a term's linguistic meaning its *conceptual* meaning or content, or simply the concept that the term expresses.

Since metaphysical externalists must rely on this second type of content, they must be committed to the thesis that, in addition to their propositional contributions, natural kind terms express conceptual meanings that are somehow metaphysically, but *not* logically, wide.[18] But oddly enough, no externalist who has emphasized the importance of metaphysically but not logically wide contents has stated, or even suggested, any actual *view* or *account* that would explain, or at least help us understand, what these allegedly wide concepts or meanings are, or what makes these concepts or meanings metaphysically but not logically related to external things.

In my opinion, these alleged metaphysically but not logically wide conceptual contents are just an unintelligible philosophers' fiction, like the idealists' absolute or the vitalists' *élan vitale*. Kripke's (1972) important discovery that there are a posteriori metaphysical dependencies, like the dependency of water's existence upon the existence of H_2O, makes sense because such dependencies are due to the *nature* or *essence* of some sort of object or substance, and the truth about such natures can only be known by empirical investigation. But surely the suggestion that some *concepts* or *meanings* could also have "hidden" natures or essences discoverable only by science (neurophysiology, perhaps?), natures that somehow necessarily (but not logically) relate these concepts to external objects or substances, is a suggestion that is quite unintelligible and that should not be taken seriously by analytic philosophers. After all, concepts and meanings, like numbers, properties, and relations, are *abstract entities*. Unlike material substances such as water and gold, these abstract entities simply do not *have* hidden natures or essences that are discoverable only by scientific investigation.

By contrast, it is fairly easy to state a clear, intelligible view on which the conceptual meanings of natural kind terms are *logically* wide, and thus are also metaphysically wide for this reason. On the sort of view I've proposed, the linguistic or conceptual meaning of a natural kind term is provided by a semantic rule whose specification requires direct reference to some contingent object or substance. (See McKinsey, 1987, 1991b, 1994a.) The linguistic meaning of "water," for instance, is captured by a rule of the following sort:

W   For any token φ of "is water" and any property F, φ is to predicate F if and only if there is just one natural kind K such that (in the actual world) the watery stuff found in *our* environment belongs to K, and F = the property of belonging to K.

Here, "watery stuff" is a euphemism for a conjunction of surface qualities that ordinary speakers associate with "water." Use of the indexical expression "*our* environment" allows me to distinguish the meaning that "water" has in the English spoken by *us*, the inhabitants of Earth, from the meaning of "water" in the English spoken by our counterparts on the Twin Earth of Putnam's (1975) famous example. (For details, see McKinsey 1987.)

On my view, the conceptual contents of natural kind terms are logically (and hence metaphysically) wide in a manner analogous to the logical wideness of singular propositions. Thus the rule (W) is singular with respect to the referent of the indexical "*our*," namely, the class of human inhabitants of Earth, and so the existence of this rule logically requires the existence of the human race, a contingent entity. As a result, the conceptual content ascribed to a thought by use of a predicate such as "is thinking that water is wet" is also logically wide, requiring for its existence the existence of the contingent object that is an essential component of the linguistic meaning of "water" (for details, see McKinsey 1991b, 1994a, and 1999). Given my original *reductio* argument, no one can have a priori privileged access to the fact that one's thought has a logically wide content of the sort that is expressed by use of natural kind terms. Thus by PAI, cognitive predicates containing these terms ascribe properties that do not succeed in individuating persons' thoughts or other attitudes.

The main competitor to my semantic account of the wideness of natural kind terms is the so-called "causal theory," according to which the referents of both proper names and natural kind terms are somehow determined by some as yet unspecified kind of causal relation between the terms and their referents. Proponents of metaphysically but not logically wide conceptual contents all seem to endorse the causal theory. But as far as I can see, the causal theory is a semantic dead-end.[19] In particular, and in contrast to my account, the causal theory provides no suggestion whatever as to what the conceptual meaning of a natural kind term might be like, and it yields no clue at all as to why, or in what respect, such terms' conceptual meanings would be either logically or metaphysically wide.

Given that no actual account has been suggested as to how some conceptual meanings might be metaphysically but not logically wide, given that this idea is in fact at least prima facie unintelligible, and in light of the fact that I have proposed and defended a clear, intelligible account on which the wideness of both propositional and conceptual meanings are given explanations in terms of *logical* implication, the metaphysical externalist's principle of individuation ME should not be taken seriously. Thus the clearest and most plausible metaphysical principle of individuation for thoughts is my principle of logical internalism (LI).

In this paper, I have tried to clarify my *reductio* argument for the inconsistency of semantic externalism (SE) and the unrestricted principle of privileged access to content (PAC). I argued that the most common response to my argument, which is to endorse a weaker "metaphysical" form of semantic externalism (MSE), is both inappropriate and based on mistaken assumptions. Instead, we should respond to the *reductio* by simply accepting the true principle SE and replace the false PAC by a restricted principle of privileged access to the properties that *individuate* our thoughts, my principle PAI. This principle has important metaphysical consequences, since it implies that our thoughts are individuated only by logically *narrow* properties (LI), and hence it implies that there are no "object-dependent" thoughts. Finally, I argued against a form of metaphysical externalism (ME) on which some thoughts are individuated by metaphysically but not logically wide conceptual contents. I contended that this idea is

Michael McKinsey

unintelligible and should not be taken seriously, especially given the existence of my clear alternative account of conceptual wideness.

Notes

1 The brief explanation here of a "wide" mental property is inadequate, but it should serve my purposes here. For clear definitions of the concepts of "wide" and "narrow" psychological properties, and for detailed discussion of the difficulties in providing such definitions, see McKinsey (1991b and 2002a).

2 This principle is quite similar to the principle of privileged access discussed and endorsed by McLaughlin and Tye (1998, p. 286).

3 See McKinsey (1987), where I introduced and discussed this notion of the a priori. In adopting a conception that allows a priori knowledge of some contingent truths, I was following Plantinga (1974, pp. 1–9).

4 In my original statement of the *reductio* in 1991a (p. 15), I implicitly appealed to CA, which I still believe is a correct closure principle. More recently, I have shown that CA is derivable from two other closure principles for apriority, principles that may be even more obviously correct than CA. For details, see McKinsey (2002a, pp. 206–10).

5 Although I have myself discussed these questions. See McKinsey (1994a and 2002a).

6 Brueckner (1992) appears to make *both* of these suggestions, the first on p. 116 and the second on pp. 113 and 114. I replied to Brueckner in McKinsey (1994b). Burge (1988) was the first to suggest something like the metaphysical evasion, but it has been suggested by many others as a response to my *reductio*. See for instance Nuccetelli (2003, pp. 183–4, n. 7) and Goldberg (2003). McLaughlin and Tye (1998) at least implicitly endorsed the same sort of response. I replied at length to their criticisms in McKinsey (2002b).

7 A proposition p metaphysically entails a proposition q just in case it is metaphysically necessary that if p then q, that is, it is true in every possible world that if p then q. Since all logical necessities are metaphysical necessities (but not vice versa), all logical implications are also metaphysical entailments, but not vice versa. Hence SE implies MSE, but not vice versa. Similarly, all forms of logical wideness, whether of properties, contents, or concepts are forms of metaphysical wideness, but not vice versa.

8 I have argued elsewhere (McKinsey, 1999) that there are in fact names with descriptive meanings in natural languages such as English, though such names are rare. I have also explained and defended an account of cognitive ascriptions on which such descriptive names could be used to ascribe thoughts involving particular ways of thinking of objects. See McKinsey (1986, 1994a, 1999).

9 For detailed discussions of what Kripke's famous example does and does not show, see McKinsey (1978a, 1978b, and 1984).

10 See, for instance, Gallois and O'Leary-Hawthorne (1996) and McLaughlin and Tye (1998).

11 McLaughlin and Tye (1998) apparently make just this inference. See p. 290, where they explicitly assume that all conceptual (logical) truths are knowable a priori.

12 See, for instance, Brown (1995), Gallois and O'Leary-Hawthorne (1996), Boghossian (1997), Davies (1998), and McLaughlin and Tye (1998).

13 For a thorough discussion of this topic, see McKinsey (2002a, pp. 206–10).

14 I have elsewhere provided strong additional evidence that our thoughts are in general not individuated by singular propositional contents or by the objects that the thoughts are about. See McKinsey (1994a).

15 I have discussed this topic in some detail in McKinsey (2002b).
16 For detailed discussion of this idea, see McKinsey (1987).
17 See for instance McGinn (1982), McLaughlin (1991), and McKinsey (1986, 1987, 1994a, and 1999).
18 McLaughlin and Tye (1998) seem to endorse such a thesis. For critical discussion, see McKinsey (2002c).
19 For critical discussion of the causal theory of names, see McKinsey (1978a, 1978b, and 1984).

References

Boghossian, P. A. (1997). What the externalist can know a priori. In C. MacDonald, B. Smith, and C. Wright (eds.), *Knowing Our Own Minds*. Oxford: Oxford University Press.

Brown, J. (1995). The incompatibility of anti-individualism and privileged access. *Analysis*, 55, 149–56.

Brueckner, A. (1992). What an anti-individualist knows a priori. *Analysis*, 52, 111–18.

Burge, T. (1988). Individualism and self-knowledge. *Journal of Philosophy*, 85, 649–63.

Davies, M. (1998). Externalism, architecturalism, and epistemic warrant. In C. MacDonald, B. Smith, and C. Wright (eds.), *Knowing Our Own Minds*. Oxford: Oxford University Press.

Evans, G. (1982). *Varieties of Reference*. Oxford: Clarendon.

Gallois, A. and O'Leary-Hawthorne, J. (1996). Externalism and scepticism. *Philosophical Studies*, 81, 1–26.

Goldberg, S. C. (2003). On our alleged a priori knowledge that water exists. *Analysis*, 63, 38–41.

Kripke, S. (1972). Naming and necessity. In D. Davidson and G. Harman (eds.), *Semantics of Natural Language*. Dordrecht: D. Reidel.

McGinn, C. (1982). The structure of content. In A. Woodfield (ed.), *Thought and Object*. Oxford: Oxford University Press.

McKinsey, M. (1978a). Kripke's objections to description theories of names. *Canadian Journal of Philosophy*, 8, 485–97.

— (1978b). Names and intentionality. *Philosophical Review*, 87, 171–200.

— (1984). Causality and the paradox of names. *Midwest Studies in Philosophy*, 9, 491–515.

— (1986). Mental anaphora. *Synthese*, 66, 159–75.

— (1987). Apriorism in the philosophy of language. *Philosophical Studies*, 52, 1–32.

— (1991a). Anti-individualism and privileged access. *Analysis*, 51, 9–16. Reprinted in A. Pessin and S. Goldberg (eds.), *The Twin Earth Chronicles*. Armonk, NY: M. E. Sharpe, 1996. Reprinted also in P. Ludlow and N. Martin (eds.), *Externalism and Self-Knowledge*. Stanford: CSLI, 1998.

— (1991b). The internal basis of meaning. *Pacific Philosophical Quarterly*, 72, 143–69.

— (1994a). Individuating beliefs. *Philosophical Perspectives*, 8, 303–30.

— (1994b). Accepting the consequences of anti-individualism. *Analysis*, 54, 124–8.

— (1999). The semantics of belief ascriptions. *Noûs*, 33, 519–57.

— (2002a). Forms of externalism and privileged access. *Philosophical Perspectives*, 16, 199–224.

— (2002b). The semantic basis of externalism. In J. Campbell, M. O'Rourke, and D. Shier (eds.), *Meaning and Truth*. New York: Seven Bridges, 34–52.

— (2002c). On knowing our own minds. *The Philosophical Quarterly*, 52, 107–16.

McLaughlin, B. P. (1991). Dretske on naturalizing content. In B. McLaughlin (ed.), *Dretske and his Critics*. Malden, MA: Blackwell.

McLaughlin, B. P. and Tye, M. (1998). Externalism, Twin Earth, and self-knowledge. In C. MacDonald, B. Smith and C. Wright (eds.), *Knowing Our Own Minds*. Oxford: Oxford University Press.

Nuccetelli, S. (2003). Knowing that one knows what one is talking about. In S. Nuccetelli (ed.), *New Essays on Semantic Externalism and Self-Knowledge*. Cambridge, MA: MIT Press.

Plantinga, A. (1974). *The Nature of Necessity*. Oxford: Oxford University Press.

Putnam, H. (1975). The meaning of "meaning." In K. Gundarson (ed.), *Minnesota Studies in the Philosophy of Science*, 7, 131–93.

IS THE INTENTIONAL ESSENTIALLY NORMATIVE?

Resisting Normativism in Psychology

Georges Rey

1 The Background Normativity Claims

"Intentional content," as I understand it, is whatever serves as the object of "propositional" attitude verbs, such as "think," "judge," "represent," "prefer" (whether or not these objects are "propositions"). These verbs are standardly used to pick out the intentional states invoked to explain the states and behavior of people and many animals. I shall take the "normativity of the intentional," or "Normativism," to be the claim that any adequate theory of intentional states involves considerations of *value* not essentially involved in the natural sciences. Thus, according to Normativism, whether or not someone *thinks* that fish sleep, or even can *represent* fish at all, depends upon making a judgment about the person's goodness or rationality, of a sort that would not be involved in merely determining whether or not fish in fact sleep.[1]

Normativism has influenced a great deal of philosophy of mind for at least the last 50 years, its roots stretching back even further. One source is a concern with the links between freedom, morality, and rationality that can be traced back at least to Kant. Another is the distinction many have felt between natural scientific ("erklären") and historical "empathic" ("verstehen") explanation, as it emerged in the work of Dilthey ([1894] 1977), Weber ([1913] 1981), and (for many) Wittgenstein (1953). Most importantly for purposes here, it was recruited by Quine (1960), as "the principle of charity," as a way of accounting for intentional ascription in the wake of his skepticism about the analytic/synthetic distinction, and his related thesis of the indeterminacy of translation. This latter thesis was the basis on which Davidson (1980, p. 222) claimed that, in ascribing propositional attitudes to someone:

> We must work out a theory of what he means, thus simultaneously giving content to his attitudes and to his words. In our need to make him make sense, we will try for a

theory that finds him consistent, a believer of truths, and a lover of the good. . . . the constitutive ideal of rationality partly controls each phase in the evolution of what must be an evolving theory. (pp. 222–3)

Davidson took these constraints to mark a fundamental difference between psychological and the physical sciences: "It is a feature of physical reality that physical change can be explained by laws that connect it with other changes and conditions physically described. It is a feature of the mental that the attribution of mental phenomena must be responsible to the background of reasons, beliefs, and intentions of the individual" (p. 222). In keeping with his sympathy with Quine, Davidson (1982, p. 301) goes on to claim that "these matters bear directly on the . . . question how scientific a science of the mental can be,"[2] a view echoed by Daniel Dennett: "deciding on the basis of available evidence that something is (or may be treated as) an intentional system permits predictions having a normative or logical basis rather than an empirical one . . . Intentional theory is vacuous as psychology because it presupposes and does not explain rationality or intelligence" (Dennett, 1978, pp. 13, 15).

In earlier work (Rey, 1994, 1997, 2002) I argued that these claims are unwarranted. They presuppose our enjoying a sufficiently adequate understanding of serious psychology – as well as of rational norms – to reasonably make them, but, even if they are restricted to ordinary "folk" psychology, they are based upon a small diet of examples that don't do justice to folk wisdom. I'll summarize some of these arguments in §2 of what follows, indicating how variable and probably indeterminate are existing conceptions of rational norms and their application to actual psychology (§2.1); how intentional explanation tolerates a great deal of irrationality and frequently doesn't involve "reason" at all (§2.2); and how, in any case, serious judgment about these matters is premature, based upon an implausible "superficialism" that would not be invoked in any other domain, and is in fact at odds with the folk psychology it tries to enshrine (§2.3).

In §3 I'll turn to Ralph Wedgwood's recent defenses of normativism. Although he has admirably resisted some of the less convincing arguments for it, his new arguments seem to me open to some of the same objections. Ironically enough, I'll argue in §4, they bring us back to the very issues about the analytic that led philosophers such as Quine to normativism in the first place. At any rate, Wedgwood's frequent appeals to mere intuitions about counterfactual cases would, I argue, be better served by a substantive theory of analytic conceptual connections, instead of an effort to base psychology upon norms that are ill-defined, open to subjective variation, and risk an invidious distinction between psychology and the natural sciences.

2 Norms and Psychology[3]

Normative reasons, of course, have their place in ethics, decision theory, and epistemology: what one *ought* to believe or do, given a set of values and evidence of how things are. The question is whether they are essential to *psychology*. There seem to me a number of reasons to think they aren't.

2.1 Which norms?

In the first place, there really isn't any serious agreement about what the relevant norms might be. To be sure, there has been considerable progress in understanding *deduction*, and, to a lesser extent, with respect to certain highly idealized theories of normative "decision." But the various problems of characterizing "good" inductions, abductions, *actual* decisions, and the rational "updating" of one's store of beliefs in the light of further actions and experience (the so-called "frame" problem) are notoriously more difficult. As things stand here, there are merely hosts of intuitions about particular cases – some good, some questionable – that have yet to admit of a general characterization, much less one that is uniform across different people and intelligent animals.

Moreover, as Gilbert Harman (1986, 1999) has repeatedly stressed, it is crucial to distinguish an interest in "logic" as a theory of rational *relations among propositions* from a theory of rational *inference* as a theory about what it is rational for someone to *believe*: the former enjoys a stability and objectivity that may never be available for the latter. Why, after all, should one person's high standard of confirmation (in a particular context?) be any more or less rational than another's lower one? Is it better to optimize than to satisfice? How are we to assess differences in people's attitudes toward risk, e.g., toward being exactly right in a few cases or approximately right in many; or toward making up their mind under the pressure of time? Is it more rational to undertake risk (however that is to be defined) by maximizing average expected utility or by minimizing the likelihood of a worst outcome? What is the role of second- (and *n*-) order reasonings (thoughts about one's thoughts) to the usual first-order ones? Reflection on the difficulties of understanding the world has led many to tolerate the likely falsehoods of idealized models or promising research programs, and sometimes even outright contradictions (think of the standard philosophical paradoxes).[4]

Even should there emerge a unified and determinate account of rational norms, the question would arise as to how it should be applied to intentional creatures. Should it be applied only to their "whole" minds, or also to the specialized modules that seem to underlie, e.g., speech, perception, navigation and motor control? In the case of people, is it really *the beliefs* they are willing to *avow on reflection* that are the appropriate domain of rationality, or is it rather their "gut" reactions? Or their underlying *judgments*, whether or not they can avow or are even remotely conscious of them?[5] Remembering the absent-minded, perhaps the norms should be applied only to what a person *notices* (consciously or unconsciously) in a sufficiently brief window of time. But then should our short-term memory and processing limitations be regarded as intrinsic to our reason, or should we nonetheless idealize ourselves as rational gods, closed under deduction – but then who would need any mental *processes*?[6] Even if there turn out to be facts of the matter about all these difficult issues, it is hard to see why someone whose psychology did not (or appeared not to) satisfy them in the right way would *ipso facto* fail to have the intentional states the theorist might otherwise have good reason to ascribe.

2.2 Non-rationality

Whatever norms do emerge, it is also hard to see that they play the crucial role on which normativists insist. While it is certainly true that we sometimes explain someone's action by citing reasons[7] that recommend it, as when we explain a good piece of reasoning or a successful bet, sometimes people's reasons are *terrible*, as, for example, when they persist in standard fallacies, e.g., expecting a coin to come up heads after a run of tails. In 2002 Daniel Kahneman was awarded a Nobel prize for his and Amos Tversky's extensive research on the surprisingly extensive range of errors of this sort to which humans seem naturally prone.[8] And philosophers themselves make their living discussing incoherencies that arise for our unreflective beliefs about truth, knowledge, motion, freedom, and the existence of the external world. In general, people fail to see some of the most immediate consequences of their thought, are often inconsistent, say the most bizarre things regarding logic, knowledge, statistics, religion, history, psychology, biology, cosmology, and physics; they want all sorts of things they don't need, have positively alarming views about the good, and regularly disregard it when even minor interests compete. Whatever the idealized norms of rationality turn out to be, they would seem to be only some among many of the determinants of those roles, alongside limitations on perception, memory, attention, the influence of tradition, habits and desires, the sway of charismatic authorities, and the sudden impulses of a moment. Awareness of these complexities doesn't in the slightest undermine intentional ascription: to the contrary, it regularly refines it.[9]

There is also a lot more to intentionality than reason alone. Wittgenstein and Austin emphasized how philosophy often suffers from too restricted a diet of examples, and this seems strikingly true of the normativist's standard examples. Again, while it is true that much human thought and action is explained "rationally," a lot of it is not: intending to wriggle a finger brings about its wriggling whether or not one has a good reason to do so. Some actions, what Kent Bach (1978, p. 363) has called "minimal actions," such as scratching an itch, doodling, or automatically tying a shoelace, don't involve rational deliberation, although they may still involve rich representations, full of intentional content (about the location of the itch, the position of the laces).

Even many fully intentional actions are often performed without reasons. Arguing against Davidson's (1982, p. 292) claim that an intentional action must be caused by a rationalizing belief–desire pair, Rosalind Hursthouse (1991) discusses a significant range of what she calls "arational actions," e.g., kicking a door in anger, jumping up and down in glee, "rumpling the hair of, or generally messing up the person or animal one loves" (p. 58). She reasonably argues that such actions are not ordinarily performed to achieve some *end*. Although they may in fact *express* one's feelings, they are typically not performed *in order* to do so – indeed, their being so performed can undermine their genuineness as actions of the relevant sort. She draws attention also to *symbolic* actions, such as gouging holes in the eyes of a photo of one's rival in love (pp. 59–60), which, again, seem not to involve any serious rational plan (or, if they did, would involve pretty irrational use/mention confusions!).

And, of course, in addition to all these cases, there are all sorts of effects of intentional states that are not *actions* at all: startle at the unexpected,[10] laughter at jokes, tears at bad news, ulcers due to stress, trembling at the thought of speaking in court. Again (cf. n. 7), the joke may be the *explanatory* "reason" for the laughter, the stress the "reason" for the ulcer, without a trace of normativity (it's not *irrational* to fail to laugh at a joke or develop an ulcer!).

Bearing the full range of ordinary cases in mind, it should be plain that intentional states are not invoked merely to rationalize actions, but to explain an extremely wide range of rational, irrational, arational, and brute physical actions and events simply by subsuming them in the standard way under conceptions about how people ordinarily work. The evidential situation seems the same as for the other sciences: any of the explicanda could serve as evidence of the underlying states. Someone's belief that a friend has died not only explains her making funeral arrangements, but also her tears, grief, exclamations, beating her breast, inattention, sleeping late, placing the friend's photo in a special box, etc., from each of which we might infer that belief. In this way, we would certainly appear to (in Davidson's phrase) "triangulate" onto such internal states as the common causes of these events, but in a way no different from how a doctor triangulates upon some malady from a set of symptoms, or a geologist upon some subterranean process from the age and shape of a rock. In view of the wide diversity of especially non-rational evidence, it is hard to see why rational norms need play any special role.

Well, it is argued, all these complexities and examples of non-rationality are supposed to be explained away by the fact that "disagreement and agreement alike are intelligible only against a background of massive agreement" (Davidson, 1984, p. 137), and that consequently the norms must hold on the whole: "to the extent that we fail to discover a coherent and plausible pattern in the attitudes and actions of others we simply forgo the chance of treating them as persons" (Davidson, 1980, pp. 221–2). But, especially in view of the diverse examples we have noted, why should we think so? The only argument of Davidson's that I can find is his appeal to the "holistic character of the mental":

> The meaning of a sentence . . . is not an item that can be attached to it in isolation from its fellows. We cannot intelligibly attribute the thought that a piece of ice is melting to someone who does not have many true beliefs about the nature of ice, its physical properties connected with water, cold, solidity, and so forth. . . . The clarity and cogency of our attributions of attitude, motive and belief are proportionate, then, to the extent to which we find others consistent and correct. (Davidson, 1982, pp. 302–3)[11]

But normativism hardly follows from or plausibly explains cases like that of attributing [ice]. Even if it were true that attributing a concept of x entails attributing "many" true beliefs about x (although didn't Kripke, 1980, famously refute such a claim?), still this doesn't entail a proportionate truth and consistency on the whole: maybe there are many true beliefs – and maybe *even more* false and inconsistent ones! After all, who's counting? And, again, with respect to precisely which of the diversity of belief-like attitudes (avowing, noticing, unconsciously judging at a time) that a typical human mind enjoys?

Resisting Normativism in Psychology | 73

2.3 Superficialism

One sometimes gets the impression that normativists presume our relation to psychology to be like the relation Einstein enjoyed in 1905 to physics, permitting sweeping claims about the character of an explanatory realm and the determinacy of certain parameters within it.[12] But surely, made explicit, the comparison is embarrassing. The physics of 1900 was a well-worked-out, well-confirmed (even if still mistaken) theory of the nomological structure of the world, on the basis of which Einstein could say with substantial empirical authority that certain distinctions had no basis in the world. There is nothing remotely approaching such a theory yet in psychology.

Of course, many think there is, in particular, that our "folk psychology" is really all one needs. I've discussed elsewhere what seems to me this "superficialism" that has dominated the philosophy of mind, not only in the form of overt behaviorism, but in more recent defenses of ordinary thought and talk.[13] Originally, it was a piece of the verificationist response to skepticism generally, but it oddly survives in the philosophy of mind in a way that would (at best) be found quaint in physics or biology. Thus, Dennett (1991, p. 461) defends an "Urbane Verificationism" according to which all psychological distinctions should be available in ordinary behavior; Colin McGinn (1991, pp. 132–3) "doubt[s] that our naive psychological classifications could be overturned . . . under pressure from any sort of scientific theory of the mental"; and Jennifer Hornsby (1997, pp. 3–4) writes that "we ought not to assume at the outset that the basis of our everyday understanding of one another is susceptible of correction and refinement by experts in some specialist field where empirical considerations of some non-commonsensical kind can be brought to bear." I suspect it is something like this sort of confidence in at least the *perspective* of our folk thought about mind that leads Davidson or Dennett to their sweeping pronouncements. Indeed, when Steve Stich (1983) marshals scientific evidence against Dennett's (1978) normativist claims ("a system's beliefs [and] . . . desires are those it ought to have given its biological needs": Dennett, 1987, pp. 48–9), Dennett simply replies: "I would insist, however, that all this empirically obtained lore is laid over a fundamental generative and normative framework that has the features I have described" (Dennett, 1987, p. 54). After all: "No other view of folk psychology . . . can explain the fact that we do so well explaining each other's behavior" (p. 51).

But I don't see that what success folk psychology enjoys remotely warrants such confidence. Although we are sometimes subtle and insightful, a moment's reflection reveals we know next to nothing about even such basic activities as perception, thinking, reasoning, language, decision making, motor control, not to mention consciousness, creativity, scientific insight, or morally responsible action. And, *pace* Dennett, Hornsby, and McGinn, we *know* we don't: many folk all the time presume that specialized knowledge may well cast light on all those issues, as well as on the nature of personality, intelligence, psychological development, supposed racial and gender differences, and so forth. It seems increasingly apparent that our relation to our minds is pretty much on a par with our relation to our bodies. More specifically, along the lines of present research, our understanding of the minds of people and animals seems like the understanding clever children have of their computers: they know a good deal about their *interaction* with them – they can play games, and get them to do various things – but with only the sketchiest ideas about their internal causal/computational structure.

Given our massive ignorance, normativism would require some pretty powerful, relatively *a priori* arguments. These are what Ralph Wedgwood tries to provide.

3 Wedgwood's Arguments

3.1 Wedgwood's claims

In a number of articles and a forthcoming book, Wedgwood has defended the claim that "intentional facts are partially constituted by normative facts" (Wedgwood, forthcoming-a, §1). Unlike the superficialists, he adds that he understands the thesis as a "metaphysical claim concerning the essence of intentional states . . . not a semantic thesis about the meaning of intentional terms or a conceptual thesis about what is built into our concepts of intentional states" (Wedgwood, forthcoming-a, §1; see also forthcoming-b, §7.3). As states of real spatiotemporal beings, of course, the crucial claim is that the agent of an intentional state have a *disposition* to accord with rational norms: "The sort of disposition that a thinker must have, if she is to possess these concepts or be capable of these sorts of attitude, is a disposition to use the concept in ways that the principle in question specifies as rational" (Wedgwood, forthcoming-b, §7.4). Thus, a *belief* is "correct if and only if the content of the belief is true," and it is "rational (in relation to a body of information *I*) just in case *I* makes it sufficiently likely that the content of the belief is true" (§7.4). A person actually enjoys the relevant state only if she possesses *ceteris paribus* dispositions to conform to these objective constraints. For example, someone has a belief with the content [yellow][14] iff she is "disposed to form a judgment applying the concept '. . . is yellow' to a perceptually presented object whenever she has a visual experience that represents an object in the relevant way" (§7.4). And she possesses the concept of a conditional, only if she has "the disposition for rationally accepting instances of inferences like *modus ponens*" (§7.6).

Of course, as merely *ceteris paribus* dispositions, these proposals are free of some of the implausible commitments of Davidson and Dennett I discussed in §2. Dispositions may persist even if *never* manifested. The force of Wedgwood's constraints is that "when we do not conform to these very basic requirements of rationality, then the situation was in some way abnormal (the *cetera* were not *paria*), and so there must be some special explanation of what went awry" (Wedgwood, forthcoming-b, §7.4). He claims (n. 16) that so construing the dispositions makes them invulnerable to the kinds of objections raised by Edward Stein (1996) regarding the standard evidence of human foibles in reasoning mentioned earlier.

Confidence regarding this latter issue, however, requires more discussion than Wedgwood provides. Appeals to *ceteris paribus* clauses are well and good, but only so long as there is *independent evidence* that *cetera* and are not *paria*. Specifically in the case of rationality, what would need to be shown is that deviations from rationality are "performance" errors, concealing an underlying competence. But, as Stein (1996, chs. 3, 8) is at pains to point out, it is far from obvious that they are. The *persistence* of many foibles despite correction and reflection suggests that some of them are built into at least some subsystems of the mind. Kahneman (2002) himself regards much of his own and others' recent work as supporting the hypothesis that humans work with at least two systems of reasoning, one "intuitive," fast and automatic, the other slow, deliberate and reflective, the second occasionally (although, alas, not reliably) correcting the errors of the first. In order to sustain his normativism, Wedgwood would need to show that the first system is essentially an interference with the workings of the second, and could not be understood without it. None of the evidence so far seems to me to suggest that this is so. To the contrary, the "intuitive" system may be, evolutionarily, a more primitive one, present without the slower one in many animals (see Wilson, 2002, pp. 44–45, who cites Reber, 1992).

Wedgwood himself (see forthcoming-a, §3) is also unconvinced by many of the standard arguments for normativism, and relies instead on two further arguments, which I will discuss in turn: an argument from asymmetry (§3.3) and one from defeasibility (§3.4). Before considering them, however, I want to examine an argument that both he and I reject, but is so easily suggested by the terms in which he and many others set up the discussion that it deserves explicit airing from the start.

3.2 The argument from (in)correctness

The usual discussion begins, as does Wedgwood, "with the assumption that the paradigmatic normative terms are 'ought,' 'should,' 'right,' 'wrong,' . . . 'correct,' 'incorrect,' 'rational,' and 'irrational'" (forthcoming-a, §1). If one combines this assumption with the (let us grant) independently plausible assumption that intentional ascription necessarily involves such concepts, then, of course, normativism would immediately follow.

But, of course, one trouble with so facile an argument is the starting assumption. Although all these quoted terms have a variety of normative uses, they also have non-normative ones (cf. note 7). Thus, one can say such things as, "given how long he was in the water, he ought to be dead by now," or "the planets should move in ellipses," meaning merely that these claims follow from, say, the truth of various laws of physiology and motion, without any serious normative implications. Moreover, as Wedgwood himself acknowledges, some philosophers might argue that "correct" applied to beliefs "is just a synonym for 'true'," and that "rationality" is merely a logical, not a normative concept (forthcoming-b, §7.2).

In any case, as Wedgwood (forthcoming-a, §3) notes Paul Horwich noted, normative implications by themselves don't make a concept itself normative: "killing is *prima facie* wrong; nonetheless one can presumably characterize 'x kills y' in entirely non-normative terms" (Horwich, 1998, p. 188). We need, that is, to distinguish properties, such as *moral* or *beautiful*, that are *intrinsically* or *constitutively* normative, from ones, such as *killing*, that are normative owing to some *further, extrinsic* normative theory. So the question raised by normativism is whether intentional notions are intrinsically normative. Wedgwood proceeds to provide two arguments that they are.

3.3 The asymmetry argument

Wedgwood rightly notes that intentional states cannot "float completely free of our dispositions" (forthcoming-b, §7.5), where I take him to mean *all* of a person's dispositions to deploy a concept, both internally in relation to other concepts and in relation to the external world (any more restrictive claim would require further argument). He then reasonably argues that, among the dispositions that fix the content of a concept, some must be *basic*, determining which concept it is, on which all the other dispositions depend (Wedgwood, forthcoming-a, §4). These basic dispositions could, let us suppose, be either rational or irrational. "However," Wedgwood writes: "it seems to me doubtful that one's possession of a concept can rest on an irrational disposition . . . The possession of a concept is a cognitive *power* or *ability* – not a cognitive defect or liability" (forthcoming-a, §4). He provides as an example the case of "if," in which "it seems plausible that it is the disposition for rationally accepting instances of inferences like *modus ponens* that is essential to possessing the concept, whereas the dispositions to make fallacious inferences is not" (forthcoming-b, §7.6).

One can certainly agree with the plausibility of the case. But I don't see how it begins to establish normativism. First of all, it does rather beg the question to suppose that concept possession must be the kind of "power" or "ability" that couldn't be a "defect" or "liability." The question is why we should think it is a power that needs *intrinsically* to be described in any normative terms at all.

Second, a doctrine as controversial as normativism needs to be supported by something more substantial than a seeming doubt. In a footnote supporting his doubt, Wedgwood (forthcoming-b, §7.6, n. 21) does cite Gareth Evans's (1982, p. 331) remark that "there can be no truth which it requires acceptance of a falsehood to appreciate." But this won't be enough. Perhaps possessing certain concepts requires having certain *conditional* "analytic" beliefs, e.g., that if something is a square it is four-sided, and, arguably, all such beliefs would perforce be true. However, this doesn't entail any claims about the believer's adherence to norms *generally* (I'll return to this point in §4).

Third, there are at least some cases that ought at least to give Wedgwood pause. Put aside concepts that can be *truly* applied, and consider many of the concepts that I mentioned earlier are routinely found problematic by philosophers, for example, [freedom]. As Peter Strawson (1968) vividly pointed out, it's a concept that plays a significant role in our moral thought, feelings, and interpersonal relations, and we may have little choice but to deploy it; but as Galen Strawson (1987) and others have also pointed out, it is a concept that may well be incoherent. Suppose this latter claim were true. Then, arguably someone wouldn't possess the concept unless they had the disposition to the incoherent ideas it implies. Similarly, one arguably doesn't have the traditional concept of [soul] if one doesn't feel the pull of a kind of personal identity, transcending memory, character, and bodily continuity that Hume and Parfit have plausibly shown to be unintelligible; or of [angel] if one weren't confused about the status of their "bodies"; or of [cause] if one doesn't feel at least the pull of the idea of a "necessary connection" that seems, well, at least problematic.[15]

Lastly, the same "asymmetry" conception of meaning to which Wedgwood is appealing is advocated (in different ways) by both Jerry Fodor (1987, 1990) and Paul Horwich (1998), the meaning constitutive "laws" or "uses" being the ones on which all other uses asymmetrically depend. Why does Wedgwood insist, unlike Fodor and Horwich, that the basic ones are normative?

Resisting Normativism in Psychology | 77

3.4 The defeasibility argument

I take Wedgwood's main argument to be the following:

> There is a reason for thinking that [the meaning constituting] dispositions cannot in fact be specified without mentioning normative properties or relations. . . . They are dispositions to engage in certain forms of *rational reasoning*. For example, one sort of rational reasoning might lead one from having visual experience that presents an object in a certain distinctive way (in the absence of any positive reason to believe one's experiences to be unreliable) to one's forming a belief that predicates the concept ". . . is yellow" of the object in question. A disposition for this sort of reasoning might be essential to mastering the basic rule of rationality that applies to the concept ". . . is yellow" and so also to possessing that concept (Wedgwood, forthcoming-a, §4).

Now, of course, this *might* be true; but what reason is there to insist that it *must* be? Wedgwood goes on to call attention to his proviso "in the absence of any *positive reason* to believe one's experiences to be unreliable" (forthcoming-a, §4; forthcoming-b, §7.6), which, he points out, is a normative condition. Indeed: "These sorts of reasoning . . . are *defeasible*. . . . [and] the nature of defeating conditions is precisely that they are those conditions that make it *irrational* for one to regard it as reliable in the circumstances to form the belief or intention in question in response to the relevant input conditions" (forthcoming-a, §4; forthcoming-b, §7.6). And he adds a little later that "the only *simple* way" of specifying what those defeasible conditions all have in common "is in normative terms – as conditions that make it irrational to reason in certain ways" (forthcoming-b, §7.6).

I find these claims puzzling. If Wedgwood is merely explaining, as a matter of *epistemology* in *abstraction* from psychology, what it is to *be* a reason for believing something, then of course, what he says is perfectly plausible. But normativism is an issue not about epistemology, but about psychology. And the question for psychology is whether people could possess a particular content and not be disposed to apply it appropriately, or to respond to defeaters. Of course they could. A person might have all sorts of patently *bad* reasons to withhold a concept – superstitions, silly theories, blind prejudice – or perhaps a holier-than-thou confirmation metric ("You call *that* confirming that something is – or even appears – yellow?!" he cries, worrying about all manner of wild deceptions); or he might apply it in the face of genuine defeaters, failing simply to appreciate them, or mistakenly thinking they in turn have been defeated. Moreover, entirely non-rational, brute physical interferences in the normal operation of the brain could block dispositions here as anywhere, without dissolving a specific content.[16] There may well be *some* necessary connection between a concept and its deployment, but it is not clear how it can be captured by overt dispositions to apply it, or by insisting on a person's appreciating genuinely defeating conditions. These latter are, indeed, a matter in part of a person's rationality – as of her overall psychology – but a rationality that is *additional* to conceptual competence, not *constitutive* of it.

4 General Qualms

In addition to the specific objections I've raised to Wedgwood's arguments, I want to raise some general qualms about his project as he construes it, and suggest a better way that he might try to capture what he is after.

4.1 Intuitions as evidence of concepts, not properties

As we noted in §3.1, Wedgwood claims to be interested not in claims about our *concepts* of intentional states, but in their real essences.[17] However, as Putnam (1975a, 1975b) so admirably stressed, claims about the real essences of phenomena that exist independently of our thoughts require empirical evidence about how the phenomena fit into the independently existing world.

Wedgwood nowhere appeals to any serious empirical psychology, which, on the face of it, doesn't seem remotely committed to normativism. To the contrary, as I already mentioned, Kahneman suggests that the fast, "intuitive" subsystems may be hopelessly disposed to error, and, quite independently of his work, theorists of vision and language comprehension argue that these tasks are performed by "informationally encapsulated modules" that produce illusions that they are constitutionally incapable of correcting (see Fodor, 1983). Indeed, discussing vision, Pylyshyn (2003) argues that the system doesn't engage in "inference" at all: "Although it might be possible to characterize the operation of the visual system in terms of 'rules,' these differ significantly from rules of inference since they only apply to representations arising directly from vision and not to those with a different provenance" (p. 39, n. 8). But note that this doesn't lead Fodor, Pylyshyn, or other vision theorists to doubt that the systems traffics in intentional representations of, e.g., edges, objects, surfaces, or spatial points.[18] This fact alone should lead one to wonder about supposed rational constraints on intentional ascription.

4.2 Diagnosis of intuitions

In the absence of any serious psychological theory about the real essences of the attitudes, it seems to me that Wedgwood's arguments for normativism must rest in the end on his conceptual intuitions. They seem to me perfectly *good* intuitions – I certainly feel the pull of his claims about [yellow] and [if]. The question that divides us is not the intuitions themselves, but their explanation. Wedgwood thinks they reveal the role of rational norms. I'm inclined to a simpler, more traditional account: they are simply the intuitions philosophers and many others have about "the meanings" of the relevant words.

However, although I share such intuitions, I also share the embarrassment many philosophers have come to feel about them since reading Quine (1953, 1976) and wondering what distinguishes them from merely deeply ingrained beliefs. It was because Quine despaired of drawing that distinction that he and Davidson turned to charity and normativism to stabilize ascriptions of content.[19] But, if normativism is problematic in the ways I have suggested, perhaps we ought to reconsider Quine's despair.

Such reconsideration is not without independent motivation. Many of us have been skeptical not only of normativism, but in general of Quinean efforts to explain away analytic intuitions. Rather than being particularly "central," which many of them patently are not,[20] they seem on a par with the sorts of intuitions about syntax that regularly inform fairly rich and well-supported theories of grammar (see, e.g., Katz, 1972; Chomsky, 2000). This is not to say that intuitions are infallible (cf. note 5). Nor is it to say that the theory of lexical semantics is anywhere near as developed and convincing as the theory of syntax. It is just that the epistemic situation seems so much the same: there are clear convergences in people's judgments, not only about what is rational and revisable, but about, e.g., intelligibility, possibility, synonymy, redundancy, antinomy, and "logical" entailment. To answer Quine, of course, any explanation will need to ground the distinction between these and other judgments, showing, for example, how it is part of a general distinction between a system for language and one for general thought; and what seems to be needed for that is a well-supported theory that goes beyond merely the superficial(ist) evidence of mere conceptual intuitions or dispositions to overt behavior. As the case of grammar has illustrated for the last 50 years, the theory needs to be informed by empirical theories about the structure of the mind.

Note that Wedgwood's own particular version of normativism itself requires analytic claims. Spelling it out, he writes: "the nature of each concept is given *both* by the principle that defines when beliefs involving that concept are correct, and *also* by certain basic principles of rationality that apply to the use of that concept – that is, basic principles that specify certain ways of using that concept as either rational or irrational" (forthcoming-b, §7.4). However, deciding which principles for a given concept are rational or irrational will involve precisely the defense of conceptual intuitions that would establish that these "principles" are analytic. But if they are analytic, then that might *by itself* plausibly explain why it would be irrational to deny them (it might not be irrational to apply "yellow" to blue things if "yellow" meant [blue]!). And, as we noted earlier, it might also accommodate Evans's (1982) claim on which Wedgwood relies, about how appreciation of truth cannot depend upon acceptance of a falsehood. Any further normativist principles of rationality would seem unnecessary and, given the other problems discussed earlier, unwelcome.

Notes

1   I join Rosen (2001, p. 611) in not trying to provide a general characterization of the normative, but merely relying on cases for the issues at hand. I shall not, though, discuss here the views of Brandom's that Rosen seems to me to adequately discuss along lines compatible with my discussion here.

2   Which is how Davidson is standardly understood. Jaegwon Kim (1993), for example, writes about how Davidson "joins a small but influential group of philosophers who have taken a dim view of the scientific prospects of psychology. . . . [His] argument has far-reaching implications regarding some basic issues about the nature of mind, . . . and points to a conception of the mental that I find both intriguing and appealing" (pp. 194–6).

3   Portions of this section have appeared previously in Rey (1997) and (2002).

4   See Slote (1989) regarding satisficing; Elster (1979, 1983) and even Davidson (1982, p. 305) himself regarding higher-order attitudes; Cartwright (1983) on the likely role of falsehoods in practicing science; and Pollock (1991), Nozick (1993), Harman (1999), and Frisch (2005) regarding at least provisional toleration of inconsistencies.

5   See Stich (1983), Rey (1988), and Moran (2001) for discussion of some of these complexities. Wilson (2002) discusses a variety of experimental data that suggest introspective reflection is often less reliable about revealing one's enduring attitudes than are spontaneous "gut" reactions (which rather gives one pause about the status of "philosophical intuitions").

6   See, e.g., Cherniak (1986) and Harman (1986, 1999) for discussion.

7   I leave aside the perfectly good use of "reason" that is just a paraphrase of "cause" or "causally explain," as in "the reason that Humpty Dumpty fell is that he was pushed." Throughout this discussion, one needs to be constantly alert to non-normative uses of normative terms, as in, e.g., "According to the *ideal* gas laws, the *right* temperature should have been higher; indeed, it *ought* to have risen quite rapidly." See Rey (1997, ch. 10) for further discussion.

8   See Stein (1996), Kahneman and Tversky (2000), and Kahneman (2002) for extensive discussion. One might also merely reflect on the standard fallacies cataloged in elementary logic books, which, of course, share little other than being common human errors.

9   In a nice reply to Dennett's insistence on optimal rationality, Fodor (1981) pointed out that in playing chess, for example, part and parcel of one's "intentional stance" may be the hypothesis that one's opponent is "a sucker for a knight fork" (p. 108).

10   Think of how much is now being learned about the intentional states of pre-linguistic infants from merely observing their involuntary startle responses: see Mehler and Depoux (1994).

11   Davidson no doubt is relying here on Quine's peculiar combination of confirmation holism and a verificationist theory of meaning (see Quine, 1969, pp. 80–1; 1986, p. 185) – peculiar, since a more likely response to confirmation holism might well be to abandon verificationism altogether. It is hard to see what else Davidson could summon on behalf of a thesis so extreme, one that, n.b., entails that people – even different stages of the same person – who differ about *any* content differ about *all* (see Fodor and LePore, 1992, and Devitt, 1996, for discussion)! I think what he really wants here is nothing quite so global, but just the standard intuitions about some claims being analytic, or true "by virtue of meaning," to which Quine forbade him to appeal. I'll return to this point in §4.2.

12   Dennett (1995, p. 532) is quite explicit about the comparison, and it is sometimes cited on behalf of Quine's indeterminacy and inscrutability theses (see, e.g., Quine, 1969, pp. 48–9).

13   See Rey (1994 and 1997, pp. 197–201, 275–80) for extended discussion. Note that Dennett (1995) cheerfully embraces superficialism, quoting with approval Quine's quotation of the motto of the Sherwin-Williams paint company, "Save the surface and you save all" (p. 530).

14   I refer to concepts by enclosing in square brackets the words that express them, properties by placing the words for them in italics. I would ordinarily distinguish concepts from the natural (or mental) language symbols that express them, but, since Wedgwood doesn't in his discussions, I won't do so here.

15   See Slote (1975) for interesting discussion of some of these and other what he calls "inapplicable concepts," such as [magic] and [miracle].

16   Indeed, in view of the indefiniteness of the conditions that could interfere, one might wonder whether it is even necessary to lasso together all the defeating conditions. As

Pietroski and I argued (Rey and Pietroski, 1995), *ceteris paribus* clauses are best regarded as checks written on the banks of independent theories, their acceptability turning on the explanatory merits of those theories, not on whether the clause can be replaced by some specification of the conditions under which the unqualified law would hold. So Wedgwood's *proviso* needn't involve *any* characterization, normative or otherwise.

17 He does allow that an *expressivist* about normativity might have to restrict the view to concepts (Wedgwood, forthcoming-a, §1), a restriction to which he himself curiously retreats in discussing the concept of a rational attitude (Wedgwood, forthcoming-b, §7.2).

18 This seem sometimes to be denied, as in Chomsky (2000, 2003); in Rey (2003a, 2003b) I argue it shouldn't be.

19 As we saw above (note 11), this seemed to be Davidson's tack. It is also Quine's (1970, p. 81; 1976, p. 109) in his treatment of the logical particles. Note that there can be another response to Quine's despair, viz., Fodor's (1987, 1990) "meaning atomism," by which he hopes to ground meaning independently of the analytic; but see Rey (2005) for skepticism about this approach.

20 To take the well-worn examples, "bachelors are male" and "pediatricians are doctors" are hardly *central* to anyone's belief system. The only reason people are tenacious about them – and why it seems "irrational" to give them up – is that people regard them as analytic! If someone wants to redefine "bachelor" to include women, fine. But that's just a redefinition, not an "empirical discovery" – much less a sudden fit of irrationality (see Rey, 2005, for further discussion).

References

Bach, K. (1981). An analysis of self-deception. *Philosophy and Phenomenological Research*, 41 (March), 351–70.

Cartwright, N. (1983). *How the Laws of Physics Lie*. Oxford: Oxford University Press.

Cherniak, C. (1986). *Minimal Rationality*. Cambridge, MA: MIT Press.

Chomsky, N. (2000). *New Horizons in the Study of Language*. Cambridge: Cambridge University Press.

Chomsky, N. (2003). Reply to Rey. In L. Antony and N. Hornstein (eds.), *Chomsky and His Critics*. Oxford: Blackwell, 274–87.

Davidson, D. (1980). Mental events. In *Essays on Actions and Events*. Oxford: Oxford University Press. Originally published 1970.

— (1982). Paradoxes of irrationality. In R. Wollheim and J. Hopkins (eds.), *Philosophical Essays on Freud*. New York: Cambridge University Press.

— (1984). Radical interpretation. *Inquiries into Truth and Interpretation*. Oxford: Oxford University Press. Originally published 1973.

Dennett, D. (1978). *Brainstorms*. Cambridge, MA: MIT Press.

— (1987). *The Intentional Stance*. Cambridge, MA: MIT Press.

— (1991). *Consciousness Explained*. Boston: Little, Brown.

— (1995). Superficialism vs. hysterical realism. *Philosophical Topics*, 22, 530–6.

Devitt, M. (1996). *Coming to Our Senses: A Naturalistic Program for Semantic Localism*. Cambridge: Cambridge University Press.

Dilthey, W. ([1894] 1977). Ideas concerning a descriptive and analytic psychology. *Descriptive Psychology and Historical Understanding*, trans. R. Zaner and K. Heiges. The Hague: Martinus Nijhoff.

Elster, J. (1979). *Ulysses and the Sirens: Studies in Rationality and Irrationality.* Cambridge: Cambridge University Press.

— (1983). *Sour Grapes: Studies in the Subversion of Rationality.* Cambridge: Cambridge University Press.

Evans, G. (1982). *The Varieties of Reference.* Oxford: Clarendon.

Fodor, J. (1981). *Representations.* Cambridge, MA: MIT Press.

— (1983). *The Modularity of Mind.* Cambridge, MA: MIT Press.

— (1987). *Psychosemantics.* Cambridge, MA: MIT Press.

— (1990). *A Theory of Content and Other Essays.* Cambridge, MA: MIT Press.

Fodor, J. and LePore, E. (1992). *Holism: A Shopper's Guide.* Oxford: Blackwell.

Frisch, M. (2005). *Inconsistency, Asymmetry, and Non-Locality: Philosophical Issues in Classical Electrodynamics.* Oxford: Oxford University Press.

Harman, G. (1986). *Change in View: Principles of Reasoning.* Cambridge, MA: MIT Press.

— (1999). Rationality. *Reasoning, Meaning and Mind.* Oxford: Oxford University Press. Originally published: 1995.

Hornsby, J. (1997). *Simple Mindedness: In Defense of Naive Naturalism.* Cambridge, MA: Harvard University Press.

Horwich, P. (1998). *Meaning.* Oxford: Oxford University Press.

Hursthouse, R. (1991). Arational action. *Journal of Philosophy*, 83, 291–5.

Kahneman, D. (2002). Maps of bounded rationality: a perspective on intuitive judgment and choice. Nobel Prize Lecture, 8 December. http://nobelprize.org/economics/laureates/2002/kahneman-lecture.html.

Kahneman, D. and Tversky, A. (eds.) (2000). *Choices, Values and Frames.* Cambridge: Cambridge University Press.

Katz, J. (1972). *Semantic Theory.* New York: Harper and Row.

Kim, J. (1993). Psychophysical laws. *Supervenience and Mind: Selected Philosophical Essays.* Cambridge: Cambridge University Press. Originally published 1985.

Kripke, S. (1980). *Naming and Necessity.* Cambridge, MA: Harvard University Press. Originally published 1972.

McGinn, C. (1991). *The Problem of Consciousness.* Oxford: Blackwell.

Mehler, J. and Depoux, E. (1994). *What Infants Know.* Oxford: Blackwell.

Moran, R. (2001). *Authority and Estrangement.* Princeton: Princeton University Press.

Nozick, R. (1993). *The Nature of Rationality.* Princeton: Princeton University Press.

Pollock, J. (1991). OSCAR: a general theory of rationality. In R. Cummins and J. Pollock (eds.), *Philosophy and AI: Essays at the Interface.* Cambridge, MA: MIT Press, 189–213.

Putnam, H. (1975a). Dreaming and "depth grammar." *Philosophical Papers*, vol. 2, *Mind, Language and Reality.* London: Cambridge University Press, 304–24. Originally published 1962.

— (1975b). The meaning of "meaning." *Philosophical Papers*, vol. 2, *Mind, Language and Reality.* London: Cambridge University Press, 215–71.

Pylyshyn, Z. (2003). *Seeing and Visualizing: It's Not What You Think.* Cambridge, MA: MIT Press.

Quine, W. (1953). Two dogmas of empiricism. *From a Logical Point of View.* New York: Harper and Row.

— (1960). *Word and Object.* Cambridge, MA: MIT Press.

— (1969). *Ontological Relativity and Other Essays.* New York: Columbia University Press.

— (1970). *Philosophy of Logic.* Englewood Cliffs, NJ: Prentice-Hall.

— (1976). Carnap and logical truth. *The Ways of Paradox and Other Essays*, rev. edn. Cambridge, MA: Harvard University Press. Originally published 1954.

— (1986). Reply to Vuillemin. In L. E. Hahn and P. A. Schilpp (eds.), *The Philosophy of W. V. Quine*. La Salle: Open Court.

Reber, A. S. (1992). The cognitive unconscious: an evolutionary perspective. *Consciousness and Cognition*, 1, 93–133.

Rey, G. (1988). Towards a computational account of akrasia and self-deception. In B. McLaughlin and A. Rorty (eds.), *Perspectives on Self-Deception*. Berkeley: University of California Press.

— (1994). Dennett's unrealistic psychology. *Philosophical Topics*, 22, 259–89.

— (1997). *Contemporary Philosophy of Mind: A Contentiously Classical Approach*. Oxford: Blackwell.

— (2002). Physicalism and psychology: a plea for substantive philosophy of mind. In C. Gillet and B. Loewer (eds.), *Physicalism and Its Discontents*. Cambridge: Cambridge University Press.

— (2003a). Chomsky, intentionality and a CRTT. In L. Antony and N. Hornstein (eds.), *Chomsky and His Critics*. Oxford: Blackwell, 105–39.

— (2003b). Intentional content and a Chomskyan linguistics. In A. Barber (ed.), *Epistemology of Language*. New York: Oxford University Press, 140–86.

— (2005). Philosophical analysis as cognitive psychology: the case of empty concepts. In H. Cohen and C. Lefebvre (eds.), *Handbook of Categorization in Cognitive Science*. Amsterdam: Elsevier, 71–89.

Rey, G. and Pietroski, P. (1995). When other things aren't equal: saving ceteris paribus. *British Journal for the Philosophy of Science*, 46, 81–110.

Rosen, G. (2001). Brandom on modality, normativity and intentionality. *Philosophy and Phenomenological Research*, 63, 611–23.

Slote, M. (1975). Inapplicable concepts. *Philosophical Studies*, 28, 265–71.

— (1989). *Beyond Optimizing: A Study of Rational Choice*. Cambridge, MA: Harvard University Press.

Stein, E. (1996). *Without Good Reason*. Oxford: Oxford University Press.

Stich, S. (1983). *From Folk Psychology to Cognitive Science: The Case Against Belief*. Cambridge, MA: MIT Press.

Strawson, P. (1968). Freedom and resentment. In P. Strawson (ed.), *Studies in the Philosophy of Thought and Action*. Oxford: Oxford University Press. Originally published 1962.

Strawson, G. (1987). *Freedom and Belief*. Oxford: Oxford University Press.

Weber, M. ([1913] 1981). Some categories of interpretive sociology, trans. E. Graber. *The Sociological Quarterly*, 22, 151–80.

Wedgwood, R. (forthcoming-a). The normativity of the intentional. http://users.ox.ac.uk/~mert1230/normativityofintentional.htm. Forthcoming in B. McLaughlin and A. Beckermann (eds.), *The Oxford Handbook of the Philosophy of Mind*. Oxford: Clarendon.

— (forthcoming-b). *The Nature of Normativity*. http://users.ox.ac.uk/~mert1230/book/contents.htm. Forthcoming from Oxford: Oxford University Press.

Wilson, T. (2002). *Strangers to Ourselves: Discovering the Adaptive Unconscious*. Cambridge, MA: Harvard University Press.

Wittgenstein, L. (1953). *Philosophical Investigations*, trans. G. E. M. Anscombe. New York: Macmillan.

Normativism Defended

Ralph Wedgwood

My aim in this chapter is to defend the claim that "the intentional is normative" against a number of objections, including those that Georges Rey presents in his contribution to this volume. In the first section of this chapter, I shall outline a specific version of this claim; and in the second section, I shall give a quick sketch of the principal argument that I have used to support this claim, and briefly comment on Rey's criticisms of this argument.

In the remaining sections of this chapter, I shall try to answer the main objections that have been raised against this claim. Broadly speaking, there are two main objections here (both of these objections are mentioned by Rey, but in one form or another they have been raised by many other philosophers as well). First, it may seem that the claim that "the intentional is normative" is just hopelessly *Panglossian*: this claim seems to imply that rationality is in some way essential to the capacity for intentional mental states as such; but doesn't this just willfully ignore all the mountains of evidence that we have for the sheer ubiquity and pervasiveness of human irrationality? Second, the claim that intentional mental states are essentially normative seems to be intended as a purely *philosophical, non-empirical* account of the nature of these mental states: but why should we think that purely philosophical reflection can tell us *anything* interesting about the nature of the mind – shouldn't we look to empirical psychology to enlighten us about such matters? I shall take these two objections in turn.

1 A Version of the Claim That "the Intentional Is Normative"

In general, the claim that "the intentional is normative" is the claim that any adequate account of the nature of intentional mental states must employ normative terms (or at least must mention the properties and relations that these normative terms stand for). But different versions of this claim will give very different accounts of the exact role that normative terms must play in adequate accounts of the nature of intentional mental states.[1] In this section, I shall briefly outline a specific version of this claim; it is this version of the claim, and not any others, that I shall try to defend here.

By an "intentional mental state" I mean a mental state that is *about* something, or in other words has some *content*. For example, beliefs, intentions, desires, suppositions, and the acceptance of inferences all seem to be intentional mental states in this sense.

It is clear on reflection that there are infinitely many types of intentional mental state. (For example, for every natural number n, there is the belief that there are at least n atoms in the universe.) Thus, there is no possibility of giving an account of all these intentional mental states one by one. Instead, any account of these mental states would have to proceed by giving an account of the *basic components* out of which these mental states are built up. I shall assume here that intentional states are built up out of the following components. First, they have some sort of *content*, which I shall assume here to be composed of *concepts*. Thus, the content of the belief that snow is white (and of the hope or the fear that snow is white) is the content "snow is white," which is composed by predicating the concept "white" of the concept "snow." Second, these intentional mental states involve a certain *mental relation* to that content; in many cases this mental relation could be called an *attitude* (such as the attitude of belief or hope or fear) toward that content.

As I am using the terms here, the term "correct" and the term "rational" both express normative concepts. That is, to say that an attitude is "incorrect" is to say that it is an attitude that – in a certain way – one *ought not* to have; and to say that a way of thinking is "irrational" is to say that it is a way of thinking that – in a somewhat different way – one *ought not* to engage in. The main difference between the concept of a "correct" attitude and the concept of a "rational" way of thinking is the following. Whether or not an attitude is *correct* is typically determined by some relation between that attitude and the external world. By contrast, whether or not a way of thinking is *rational*, for a thinker at a given time, is determined purely by the intrinsic features of that way of thinking and its relation to the antecedent mental states that the thinker has at that time.[2]

According to the version of the claim that "the intentional is normative" that I am outlining here, the nature of every concept is given both by the principle that specifies when beliefs involving that concept are correct, and also by certain basic principles of rationality that specify certain ways of using the concept as rational (or specify certain other ways of using the concept as irrational). Assuming that a belief is correct if and only if the content of the belief is true, the conditions under which beliefs involving a concept are correct would in effect define the concept's *semantic value* – the contribution that the concept makes to the truth conditions of contents in which it appears. On the other hand, the basic principles of rationality that feature in the account of the nature of the concept would determine what we could call – to adapt a term from Frege (1892, p. 25) – the concept's *cognitive significance*.

Thus, for example, the nature of logical concepts, like "if" and "not," might be given both by their semantic values – their contribution to the truth conditions of contents in which they appear – and also by the basic principle that it is rational (at least in the absence of any special reason for doubt) to accept instances of certain fundamental rules of inference for these logical concepts. The nature of the concept "yellow" might be given both by the concept's semantic value – the property of yellowness that the concept stands for – and also by the basic principle that it is rational to make a judgment applying this concept to some perceptually presented object if one has a visual experience that represents that object in a certain distinctive way (and one has no special reason for doubting the reliability of one's experiences in the circumstances).

According to the version of the idea that "the intentional is normative" that I am outlining here, it is not just *concepts* whose nature is given by the normative principles that apply to them: the same is true of the various *types of attitude* as well. Thus, for example, perhaps the nature of the attitude of *belief* is given both by the principle that a belief is correct if and only if the content of the belief is true, and by some related principle that specifies certain ways of revising beliefs as rational (or specifies certain other ways of revising beliefs as irrational). This approach could also be applied to other types of attitude. Thus, perhaps the nature of the attitude of *admiration* is given both by the principle that it is correct to admire something if and only if the object of one's admiration really is admirable, and also by some related principle that specifies certain ways of coming to have attitudes of admiration, or ways of responding to such attitudes of admiration, as rational.

This then, roughly, is the core of this normative theory of intentional mental states – an account of the nature of the various concepts, and of the various attitudes that we can have toward contents that are composed of such concepts, in terms of some of the normative principles that apply to mental states involving these concepts or attitudes. But this core will need to be surrounded by a shell that explains what it is for a *thinker* to *possess* those concepts, or to *be capable of* those attitudes. If this is the correct account of the nature of the concepts "or" and "yellow," and of the attitudes of belief or admiration, what has to be true of a thinker if she is to possess these concepts, or to be capable of having these attitudes?

One plausible answer to this question is that the thinker must have some *disposition* that amounts to an appropriate sort of sensitivity to the normative principles that give the nature of the concept or type of attitude in question.[3] In most cases, it will be more plausible to suppose that the thinker must have a disposition to conform to the principles of *rationality* that feature in the correct account of the nature of the relevant concept or attitude-type than that she must have a disposition to conform to the corresponding principles of *correctness*. As I explained above, whether a mental state is correct is typically determined by the relation between that mental state and the external world, and one's dispositions to have many sorts of mental states do not respond directly to the external world, but only to one's antecedent mental states.

Specifically, then, the sort of disposition that a thinker must have, if she is to possess a given concept, is a disposition to think in ways that the relevant basic principle of rationality specifies as rational. Such principles typically take the form of specifying some set of antecedent mental states such that – according to this principle – it is rational to respond to being in those antecedent mental states by forming a certain further mental state. Then, the disposition that one must have, in order to possess the concept, will be a disposition to respond to one's actually being in those antecedent mental states by forming that further mental state. So, for example, the thinker must be disposed to form a judgment applying the concept "yellow" to a perceptually presented object whenever she has a visual experience that represents the object in the relevant way (at least if the question of the object's color arises, and the thinker has no special reason for doubting the reliability of her experiences in the circumstances). According to this version of the claim that the "intentional is normative," this disposition is essential to possessing the concept "yellow."

Since this version of the claim that "the intentional is normative" crucially involves the notion of a *disposition*, it will be useful be say something about how I am understanding dispositions here. In general, a disposition can be specified by means of a function from stimulus conditions to corresponding response conditions. (For example, the function that specifies the disposition of fragility might be defined by means of a function from any stimulus condition like *being struck at time t* to the corresponding response condition *breaking shortly after t*.) To say that you have a certain disposition is not necessarily to say that if you were *ever* to be in any of the relevant stimulus conditions you would *invariably* go into the response condition onto which the function in question maps that stimulus condition. It is to say that *ceteris paribus*, or in any *normal* case, when you are in one of these stimulus conditions, you will also go into the corresponding response condition. In effect, each of these "stimulus conditions" and "response conditions" is a property that you might have, and to say that you have the disposition is in effect to say that you fall under a *ceteris paribus* law that connects one domain of properties (the stimulus conditions) with another domain of properties (the response conditions) according to the function that specifies the disposition.[4]

It follows from this conception of dispositions that even if you are in one of the relevant stimulus conditions, you may still fail to manifest the disposition – that is, you may fail to go into the corresponding response condition. This can happen when the case in question fails to be normal, and *cetera* fail to be *paria*. When this happens, there will in principle be some explanation of why the case in question failed to count as normal – for example, an explanation of the interfering factors that blocked or inhibited the manifestation of the disposition in this case. It is only when all such interfering factors are absent, and the case is normal in the relevant sense, that the disposition must be manifested.

It seems that the cases that count as "normal" for one domain of stimulus conditions may not be exactly the same as those that count as "normal" for another domain of stimulus conditions. Indeed, it may even be that certain cases that do not count as normal for one domain of stimulus conditions count as normal for a certain narrower domain of stimulus conditions that is properly included the first domain. This makes it possible for one to have a disposition with respect to a certain domain of stimulus conditions even if one does *not* have the corresponding disposition with respect to a certain narrower domain of stimulus conditions that is properly included in the first domain. For example, you might have a general disposition to accept *modus ponens* instances as such, even if you do *not* have a disposition to accept a certain special subcategory of *modus ponens* instances. Relative to the whole domain of *modus ponens* instances, none of the cases in which you consciously consider the inferences in this special subcategory counts as normal, and so the fact that you do not accept these special *modus ponens* instances in these cases does not count against the claim that you have a general disposition to accept *modus ponens* instances as such. However, relative to the narrower domain that consists of this special subcategory of *modus ponens* inferences, some of these cases *do* count as normal cases, and so the fact that you do not accept these inferences in these cases does count against the claim that you have a disposition to accept this special subcategory of *modus ponens* inferences.

Another important feature of dispositions, as I understand them, is that since dispositions are essentially like *ceteris paribus* laws, they will also be subject to essentially the same restrictions that apply to *ceteris paribus* laws. In particular, since any such law is in effect a connection between domains of properties, it seems plausible to require that these domains of properties must in a sense be "*natural* property domains," rather than gruesomely gerrymandered domains of properties.[5]

For example, suppose that you have a general disposition to accept instances of *modus ponens*. To say that you have this disposition is to say that *ceteris paribus*, or in any *normal* case, when you consciously consider an inference that is an instance of *modus ponens*, you accept that inference. There are two relevant domains of properties here: first, the domain of properties that for every *modus ponens* instance S includes the property *consciously considering S*; and second, the domain of properties that for every such *modus ponens* instance S includes the property *accepting S*. These domains of properties seem to be "natural property domains." They certainly seem much more natural than a domain that includes the property of consciously considering S_1, for every member S_1 of a completely random assortment of inferences, or the property of considering S_2 for all inferences S_2 that are instances of some very strange and gerrymandered "form," which coincides with *modus ponens* in all cases that any human being has actually considered, but diverges wildly from *modus ponens* in some of the less easily accessible cases. Those unnatural domains of properties are less apt to enter into *ceteris paribus* laws, and so they are less likely to be the domains of stimulus conditions that your disposition is responding to. So, when you manifest this disposition, it is plausible to say that you accept the inference in question precisely *because* it is an instance of modus ponens – not because it is an instance of the strange and gerrymandered "form" that coincides with *modus ponens* in some cases but diverges wildly from *modus ponens* in others.[6]

A final feature of dispositions that I should like to highlight here is that something's possession of a disposition may in a sense be "realized in" its possession of various other dispositions, or in the possession of various other dispositions by one or more of its parts. There is no requirement that the dispositions that realize a given disposition D should all be of the same kind, nor that these realizing dispositions should not play a role in realizing other dispositions besides D. For example, most of us are disposed to become annoyed when we are insulted. This disposition is itself realized in the following dispositions: our dispositions to perceive communicative actions of various kinds (such as spoken or written utterances); our disposition to understand these communicative actions correctly, and so to recognize insults for what they are; and our disposition to respond to the belief that one has been insulted with the emotion of annoyance. These realizing dispositions are themselves dispositions of many different kinds – including perceptual, cognitive, and emotional dispositions – and each of them is involved in the realization of many other dispositions besides our disposition to become annoyed when we are insulted. But this does not count against the claim that we have the general disposition to be annoyed when we are insulted.

2 An Argument for the Claim That "the Intentional Is Normative"

How might one argue for this claim about the nature of intentional mental states? I shall now give a quick sketch of an argument for this claim.[7]

The first step in this argument is to defend a sort of *dispositionalism* about concepts and types of attitude. What makes it the case that a concept that you possess in your conceptual repertoire is the concept "yellow"? According to this sort of dispositionalism, it is in virtue of some of your *dispositions* for *reasoning* with a certain concept in your repertoire that that concept counts as the concept "yellow." If this is right, then it is also plausible that these dispositions are *essential* to possessing the concept, so that two thinkers will count as sharing this concept only if they also share these dispositions for using the concept in reasoning.[8] We could also give a similar answer to the parallel question about attitude-types: What makes it the case that an attitude-type in your repertoire is the attitude of intention? According to this sort of dispositionalism, it in virtue of some of your dispositions with respect to an attitude-type in your repertoire that this attitude-type counts as the attitude of intention, and this disposition is essential to being capable of the attitude of intention.

Now there are reasons for thinking that the dispositions that are essential to possessing a concept (or to being capable of an attitude-type) must be *rational dispositions.* One of these reasons is that it seems that any concepts that you have could be shared by a perfectly rational being who had no irrational dispositions at all. (For example, the perfectly rational being would need to possess these concepts in order to ascribe attitudes to you accurately, and to diagnose the various confusions and irrationalities that mar your thinking.)

However, if it is in virtue of some of her dispositions that the perfectly rational being possesses these concepts, and the perfectly rational being has no irrational dispositions at all, then it must be in virtue of some rational disposition that she possesses the concept.[9] And if the dispositions in virtue of which a thinker possesses a concept are essential to possessing the concept, then it must also be in virtue of this rational disposition that *you* possess the concept in question. Moreover, this picture of what it is to possess concepts seems intuitively plausible. For example, take the concept "if." It is plausible that it is at least in part in virtue of your rational disposition to accept instances of *modus ponens* that you possess this concept. It wouldn't be correct to interpret any concept in your repertoire as the concept "if" unless you had this disposition with respect to the concept. On the other hand, it seems that you could still possess the concept if you lost all your irrational dispositions with respect to the concept. So it seems that the dispositions that are essential to possessing a concept must all be rational dispositions.

Ralph Wedgwood

Rey has a number of objections to this argument, which he labels my "asymmetry argument" (RESISTING NORMATIVISM IN PSYCHOLOGY, §3.3). First, he asks whether it really is impossible for one's possession of a concept to rest essentially on some irrational disposition. Perhaps there are some intrinsically irrational or incoherent or problematic concepts? Possible examples of such intrinsically irrational concepts might be the concept of "free will," the traditional concept of the "soul," and the concept of an "angel." I shall answer this objection in the next section, where I shall argue that such intrinsically irrational concepts are indeed impossible.

Second, Rey objects that the sort of intuition that my argument rests on "doesn't entail any claims about the believer's adherence to norms *generally*." Here, however, he seems to be misunderstanding what I am arguing for. I am not arguing that it is necessary that all believers must adhere to "norms *generally*." On the contrary, all that I am arguing for is that anyone who possesses a concept must have some disposition to reason in accordance with the *basic* principle of rationality that features in the correct account of the nature of the concept. For example, it is quite compatible with my argument that thinkers who possess this concept may have no disposition at all to comply with many of the valid rules of inference for the concept "if," such as *modus tollens* or contraposition. My argument implies only that all such thinkers must have at least some disposition to reason in accordance with the *basic* principle of rationality governing the concept: in the case of "if," presumably, they must have some disposition to accept *modus ponens* inferences. According to my argument, that is all that is required for possession of the concept "if," not a general adherence to *all* norms that apply to the use of this concept.

Finally, Rey presents the following objection: "Lastly, the same 'asymmetry' conception of meaning to which Wedgwood is appealing is advocated (in different ways) by both Jerry Fodor . . . and Paul Horwich . . . , the meaning-constitutive 'laws' or 'uses' being the ones on which all other uses asymmetrically depend. Why does Wedgwood insist, unlike Fodor and Horwich, that the basic ones are normative?" Rey is quite right that my account resembles the accounts of Fodor and Horwich by appealing to a basic disposition to use a concept on which all other uses of the concept asymmetrically depend. Of course, I have also argued for something that neither Fodor nor Horwich has argued for – that the "basic" or "meaning-constitutive" dispositions with respect to a concept must all be *rational dispositions*. Still, perhaps these rational dispositions can be adequately specified in wholly non-normative terms? If so, then we would not be able to infer that normative terms must be used in any adequate account of what it is to possess the concept, and so we would not be able to use this argument to support the claim that the intentional is normative.

It is precisely in order to answer this objection that I give the supplementary argument that Rey has labeled my "defeasibility argument" (RESISTING NORMATIVISM IN PSYCHOLOGY, §3.4). Rational dispositions are dispositions to engage in rational forms of reasoning. But whenever we specify a form of reasoning in wholly non-normative terms, it will turn out that the form of reasoning in question is *defeasible*, and so circumstances can arise in which it is not in fact rational to engage in that form of reasoning. Even forms of reasoning that involve basing a belief on utterly conclusive grounds – such as forming a belief in a mathematical theorem on the basis of a genuine proof of the theorem – can be defeated, if a sufficiently large number of experts testify, with apparent sincerity and confidence, to the incorrectness of one's belief.

So the only way to specify a form of reasoning that will always count as rational is for one's specification to include a proviso that requires the absence of such defeating conditions. For example, the most plausible way of specifying the basic rational form of reasoning with the concept "yellow" might be as the form of reasoning that leads from one's having a visual experience that presents an object in a certain distinctive way to one's forming a belief that predicates the concept "yellow" of the object in question – *provided that* one is not in any defeating conditions that give one a special reason to doubt the reliability of one's color experience in the circumstances. But the very notion of a "defeating condition" is a normative notion. So, contrary to Rey's objection to my "asymmetry argument," it is doubtful whether the relevant rational dispositions can be specified in wholly non-normative terms.

Against this "defeasibility argument," Rey objects as follows:

> The question for psychology is whether people could possess a particular content and not be disposed to apply it appropriately, or to respond to defeaters. Of course they could. A person might have all sorts of patently *bad* reasons to withhold a concept – superstitions, silly theories, blind prejudice ... ; or he might apply it in the face of genuine defeaters, failing simply to appreciate them, or mistakenly thinking they in turn have been defeated.

Again, Rey seems to be misinterpreting me as claiming that anyone who possesses a concept must have a *general* disposition "to apply it appropriately," and to respond to defeaters to *any* way of "applying" the concept. As I have already explained, I am claiming only that anyone who possesses a concept must have some disposition to reason in accordance with the *basic* principle of rationality that features in the account of the nature of the concept (in the case of the concept "if," this will presumably be a disposition to accept *modus ponens* inferences – not a disposition to accept *all* valid inferences involving "if").

What my "defeasibility argument" adds is the following point: Since the disposition that is essential to possessing the concept must be a rational disposition, it must be a disposition that tends not to be manifested in the presence of defeaters. This is not to say that this disposition will *never* be manifested in the presence of *any* defeaters – only that there is a range of defeaters in the presence of which the disposition will not be manifested. In saying that possessing the concept requires having a disposition to use the concept in a certain basically rational way, I need not claim that this disposition must be *perfectly* rational; I need only claim that this disposition must to a greater or lesser degree *approximate* to such perfect rationality.

However, I am still claiming that every thinker who possesses a given concept must have a rational disposition toward a certain basic form of rational reasoning involving the concept. Rey would presumably think that it is still far too Panglossian a view to suppose that all thinkers who possess the concept must have a rational disposition of this kind. Surely this view is incompatible with all the mountains of evidence that we have of how thoroughly and pervasively irrational human beings are? This is the objection that I shall try to answer in the next section.

3 A Hopelessly Panglossian Picture of the Mind?

On my picture, the possession of a concept is always a rational power or ability, and never a defect or liability. But some philosophers have toyed with the idea that some concepts – perhaps especially the concepts that are routinely found problematic by philosophers – might be essentially incoherent concepts; that is, they might be concepts that rest on irrational dispositions of some kind.[10]

In fact, however, it does not seem plausible to postulate incoherent concepts of this sort. The reason for this is similar to the reason against postulating concepts that essentially depend on mistaken beliefs. I am assuming here that the content of thoughts is composed of concepts; so when I deny the existence of witches or unicorns, I am surely using the very same concepts that were used by the medieval thinkers who believed in witches and unicorns. If I were not using the very same concepts, I would not really be *disagreeing* with these medieval thinkers, in the sense of denying the very thoughts that they affirmed. But of course I do not make the mistakes that characterized medieval thinking about witches and unicorns. So making these mistakes does not seem to be necessary in order to possess these concepts.

It seems to me that an essentially similar point applies to the concepts that Rey mentions, such as the concepts of an "angel" or of the "soul." Again, suppose that there were a perfectly rational being, who had no irrational dispositions of any kind. This perfectly rational being would have to possess these concepts in order to ascribe beliefs involving these concepts (for example, by thinking to herself "Many human beings believe that they have an immortal soul"), and also in order to reject the mistaken beliefs that many human beings have involving these concepts (for example, by thinking to herself "Human beings do not have immortal souls"). It seems possible that there could be a perfectly rational being who could do this. So it does not seem that it is *essential* to possessing these concepts that one should have any irrational dispositions. But it seems that any of the "problematic concepts" that appear to be deeply entwined in confused or irrational thoughts could be shared by a perfectly rational being who was capable of diagnosing and rejecting our mistaken and irrational thoughts. So in fact, these problematic concepts do not seem to be essentially irrational concepts. The concepts themselves are perfectly innocent: it is our *use* of those concepts that is defective.

However, even if I am right that there are no such intrinsically irrational concepts, it is an undoubted fact that our thought is riddled with fallacious thinking of many kinds. How can the claim that the intentional is essentially normative be reconciled with this undoubted fact?

First, my account implies only that any thinker who possesses a concept must have a *disposition* to conform to the basic principle of rationality that features in the correct account of the nature of the concept. But as I have already explained, the claim that a thinker has a disposition of this kind does not imply that this disposition will be manifested in every possible case. It is only in the relevantly *normal* cases, when *cetera* are *paria*, that the disposition is bound to be manifested.

Thus, this claim – that everyone who is capable of having a certain type of mental state must have a disposition toward a certain basic sort of rational thinking involving mental states of that type – does not imply that these rational dispositions are always manifested. It implies only that when we do not conform to these very basic requirements of rationality, the situation was abnormal (*cetera* were not *paria*), and so there must be some explanation of why the disposition was not manifested in this case – perhaps an explanation that appeals to certain interfering factors that blocked or inhibited the manifestation of the disposition in this case. Indeed, it seems possible, in extreme circumstances, for there to be an agent, or even an entire community of agents, for whom the circumstances are always abnormal, so that these dispositions are in fact *never* manifested.

Second, in addition to the ways in which one's dispositions toward these basic kinds of rational thinking can fail to be manifested in abnormal cases of various kinds, one may also have many *other* mental dispositions, which may be dispositions that it is irrational to manifest. This too is quite compatible with its being the case that in general, one *also* has dispositions toward certain basic kinds of rational thinking.

These two points must be taken together with the point (which I emphasized in the previous section, in discussing Rey's objections to my "asymmetry argument") that the claim that I am defending does not imply that all thinkers must have a disposition to adhere to *all* the norms of rationality that apply to them. Instead, it implies only that they must have a disposition to adhere to *those particularly basic* norms of rationality that feature in the correct accounts of the nature of the various concepts that they possess (and of the various attitude-types of which they are capable).

Taken together, these points help to show how my claim can be reconciled with the well-known evidence about how strikingly bad most humans are at even fairly elementary deductive reasoning.[11] In recent empirical studies of conditional reasoning,[12] for example, only 72 percent of subjects accepted instances of *modus tollens*. But this is compatible with my claims, since it is plausible that it is *modus ponens*, and not *modus tollens*, that is the basic form of rational inference for the concept "if." In addition to failing to accept certain valid forms of inference, many of the subjects in these experiments endorsed certain fallacious forms of inference: as many as 63 percent committed the fallacy of affirming the consequent, and 55 percent committed the fallacy of denying the antecedent. This too is compatible with my claims, since I have claimed only that we must have certain basic rational dispositions, not that we cannot *also* have many irrational dispositions as well. These studies do not undermine my claims about what is involved in possessing concepts, since 97 percent of the subjects in these experiments accepted instances of *modus ponens*, and in the case of the 3 percent who did not accept instances of *modus ponens*, we can either appeal to some slippage between language and thought (so that they were not genuinely entertaining the relevant inference in thought), or else to some other interfering factor that inhibited the manifestation of their general disposition to accept *modus ponens* inferences in those cases.[13]

At one point, Rey (2002, pp. 107–8) raises the issue of what Rosalind Hursthouse (1991) has called "arational actions" (such as jumping for joy, or rumpling one's lover's hair). But my version of the claim that the intentional is normative has no problem with these actions. These arational actions are indeed counterexamples to a certain well-known theory of action, according to which every action is done for a reason, and this reason consists of a desire for some goal, together with a belief

Ralph Wedgwood

that the action in question is a means toward that goal.[14] But my version of the claim that "the intentional is normative" does not imply that every single action is the manifestation of a rational disposition to act for reasons. At most, my version of this claim implies that if one is capable of making decisions about what to do at all, one must have at least some disposition to take account of reasons for action in deciding what to do, and some disposition to try to carry out one's decisions. But there certainly can be abnormal cases in which one fails to manifest this disposition, and one may also have many other irrational or non-rational dispositions, which will often influence how one acts. Moreover, as Joseph Raz (1999) has pointed out, these arational actions do not typically involve failing to take account of *all* reasons for action: in performing one of these arational actions, one is usually aware, as part of one's background beliefs, that there are no strong reasons against the action in question (one would not jump for joy on the edge of a precipice, for example). So these examples pose no problems for the claims that I am defending here.

Recently, Timothy Williamson (2003 and 2006) has emphasized the example of philosophers whose revisionary views lead them to reject some of the laws of logic. For example, Vann McGee (1985) believes that there are counterexamples to *modus ponens*, and a philosopher who agreed with P. F. Strawson (1952) in holding that the natural-language universal quantifier has existential import might (if she also denied the existence of sets) insist that the sentence "All sets are sets" is neither true nor false. As Williamson argues, it is highly implausible to say that these philosophers do not understand the sentences involved, or express different concepts with these sentences from those that we would be expressing by using them. But, Williamson maintains, these revisionary philosophers are not even *disposed* to accept the relevant instances of these logical laws; so how can a disposition to accept these logical laws be constitutive of possessing the concepts involved?

It is not clear exactly how to interpret these revisionary philosophers. Are these philosophers being *irrational* (albeit perhaps in a quite blameless way)? Or is it actually *rational* for them, given the unusual philosophical reflections that they have gone through, to take the view that they do? Whichever interpretation is correct, these examples create no problems for my claims. If it is *rational* for these revisionary philosophers to take the view that they do, then this must be because their philosophical reflections constitute a rather unusual *defeater* for the rationality of accepting the relevant instance of the logical law in question. In that case, these philosophers plainly are *not* counterexamples to my claims. The principle of rationality that features in the account of the nature of the concept "if" is, strictly speaking, the principle that it is rational to accept *modus ponens* inferences *unless one has sufficiently strong defeating reasons not to*, and, on this interpretation, Vann McGee *has* a disposition to comply with this principle.

On the other hand, if it is *irrational* for these philosophers to reject these instances of these logical laws, then we must say that the case in question is abnormal, perhaps because some interfering factor is inhibiting the manifestation of their rational disposition to accept instances of these laws. On this view, Vann McGee has a general disposition to accept *modus ponens* inferences, and the follower of Strawson has a general disposition to accept propositions of the form "All *F*s are *F*s"; their misleading philosophical reflections, and the false philosophical beliefs that they have acquired as a result, are operating as an interfering factor that inhibits the manifestation of this disposition in these cases.

Williamson (2006, pp. 15–20) considers this second response to his objection, and argues that it is not correct to ascribe these dispositions to these revisionary philosophers. There are, he suggests, two ways of taking the claim that they have these dispositions – as a "*personal* level account" and as a "*sub-personal* level account." According to Williamson (2006, pp. 16–17), if the claim that these philosophers have these dispositions is a "personal level account," it is refuted by the fact these philosophers would persist in their rejections of the relevant instance of *modus ponens*, and of "All sets are sets," even after the most careful and self-conscious reflection.

However, Williamson's argument is not a conclusive refutation of the "personal level" version of the claim that these revisionary philosophers have these dispositions. As it has recently been persuasively argued, disposition ascriptions are not in general equivalent to counterfactuals.[15] So the fact that the thinker would not manifest the disposition in this specific case is not enough to show that the thinker lacks the disposition altogether.

Moreover, as I explained in §1, even if we concede that Vann McGee does *not* have a *specific* disposition to accept *this particular instance* of *modus ponens*, it could still be the case that he does have a *general* disposition to accept *modus ponens* inferences as such. Relative to the wider domain of properties that includes the property of consciously considering S for every *modus ponens* instance S, the cases in which McGee considers these complicated instances of *modus ponens* in the course of philosophical reflections of the sort that he is pursuing do not count as "normal" cases in the relevant sense, and so the fact that McGee does not accept these special instances of *modus ponens* does not count against the claim that he has a disposition to accept *modus ponens* inferences in general. But we could still consistently concede that relative to the much narrower domain of properties that includes only the property of consciously considering this particular *modus ponens* inference, the case in question does count as normal, and so the fact that he does not accept the inference in this case does count against the claim that he has the more specific disposition.

It surely is highly plausible that Vann McGee does have this general disposition to accept *modus ponens* inferences. Like everyone else, he accepts the vast majority of such inferences that he consciously considers; in the cases in which he does not, there seems to be something distinctly abnormal going on, and there seems to be no more "natural" way of capturing all the cases in which he does accept such inferences in a general *ceteris paribus* law than by classifying them all as involving his consciously considering, and then accepting, an instance of *modus ponens*. Moreover, this disposition is clearly at the "personal level," in the sense that its manifestations consist in conscious events in the mental life of the whole person, rather than in the unconscious cognitive processes that realize our conscious thinking.

Williamson (2006, pp. 17–20) goes on to develop an objection to the second "way of filling out the dispositional story" – the interpretation of this dispositional story as a "sub-personal level account." Fundamentally, his objection is that philosophers should not attempt to develop such sub-personal level accounts without consulting the relevant empirical evidence, which may well not tell in favor of this account. This is only a specific instance of a more general objection that is often raised against the claim that "the intentional is normative." I shall consider this objection in the next section, the last section of this chapter.

4 Psychology, A Priori and Empirical

Some of the philosophers who have claimed that the intentional is normative have gone on to make some further claims to the effect that empirical psychology will never tell us anything interesting about the mind. Rey (2002) has criticized these further claims effectively, and I have no intention whatsoever of defending any such further claims myself.

Indeed, it seems to me that we have every reason to expect empirical psychology to reveal many crucial truths about how our minds work. The philosophical account that I have sketched above could at best reveal only what is *essential* to the various types of intentional mental states as such. Empirical psychology could tell us about all the numerous *contingent* truths about the nature of the *human* mind (or the minds of any of the other actually existing species). Thus, empirical psychology can be expected to give us a huge amount of information about the contingent psychological dispositions that we have, which are not essential to the capacity for having the various types of intentional mental states. For example, the contingent facts mentioned above about our dispositions to accept fallacious forms of reasoning are facts that we can know only by doing empirical psychology.

Moreover, the rational dispositions that this philosophical account appeals to are all dispositions at the "personal level." This philosophical account cannot tell us anything about the "sub-personal level" – that is, about the various unconscious mechanisms and processes that realize our conscious mental processes. Thus, we may also expect empirical psychology to give us much illuminating information about these "sub-personal" processes and mechanisms, including information about the "sub-personal" mechanisms that realize our possession of the dispositions that are essential to our being capable of the various types of intentional mental states. For example, empirical psychology may tell us that we actually have two reasoning systems – in the terms of Stanovich and West (2000), System 1 and System 2 – and it may also tell us, as Johnson-Laird and Byrne (1993) suggest, that System 1 does not involve any encoded rules of inference, but operates by means of other mechanisms. So far as I can see, it is quite compatible with my philosophical claim that possession of the concept "if" requires a rational disposition to accept *modus ponens* inferences (at least in the absence of defeaters) that this rational disposition itself is realized in a state of System 1, which does not itself involve any encoding of the rule of *modus ponens* itself.[16] In general, the claims that I have been defending here are not obviously inimical in any way to any such accounts of the sub-personal mechanisms that realize our reasoning capacities.

In general, my view of the relation between empirical psychology and the philosophy of mind is entirely in line with Rey's analogy (RESISTING NORMATIVISM IN PSYCHOLOGY, §2.2; compare 2002, p. 101): "our understanding of the minds of people and animals seems like the understanding clever children have of their computers: they know a good deal about their *interaction* with them – they can play games, and get them to do various things – but with only the sketchiest ideas about their internal causal/computational structure."

Philosophical, a priori psychology can at best give us a certain basic part of the sort of understanding that a skilled computer *user* has of his computer. Empirical psychology can ideally give us other sorts of understanding as well. Empirical cognitive science could ideally give us the sort of understanding that the computer *programmer* has of the computer's programming code, and empirical neuroscience can ideally enable us to achieve the sort of understanding that an *electrical engineer* has of the computer's internal electrical circuits. Still, it does not follow that the understanding of the mind that we can achieve through a priori psychology is worthless. After all, many skilled computer users are paid a decent wage to advise others on how to use their computers to do such things as the following: to import and manipulate sound and image files; to create spreadsheets, web pages, and other electronic documents; to root out viruses, and fix other software problems; and to install and configure the computer's programs in ways that will be most useful to the users. In many cases, these computer advisers need no more than the most rudimentary knowledge of the computer's electrical circuits or of its programming code in order to do their job perfectly well.

However, Rey and other philosophers of broadly "naturalist" sympathies may be tempted to make a stronger claim. According to this stronger claim, the various types of intentional mental states are like "natural kinds," in that the essential nature of these mental states *cannot* be known a priori, but can *only* be known empirically. Now, I am not denying that the essential nature of these mental states can be known empirically. At least, it is certainly possible to observe empirically what mental dispositions various thinkers have, and then further reflection on these empirical observations may lead one to understand which of these dispositions are essential to the various types of mental states and which are not. What I am claiming is that it is *also* possible to know the essential nature of these mental states a priori: even without observing the dispositions that thinkers actually have, one can simply try to consider more abstractly which dispositions it is possible to lack, and which it is not possible to lack, given the essential nature of the relevant mental states.

Admittedly, many objections could be raised against the idea of such a priori knowledge of the nature of our concepts and attitudes. I cannot discuss all these objections here. But prima facie, it would be surprising if the essential nature of the concepts that we possess could not be known a priori – that is, by relying not on any empirical observations, but simply on the resources that are already built into the mind itself. When one investigates what it is to possess a given concept, one's investigation itself involves an exercise of the very capacity that one is investigating. So it should be possible, at least under favorable circumstances, for this investigation to draw directly on the very phenomenon that is being investigated. Traditionally, many philosophers have worried about how one could know anything about *extra-mental* reality by purely a priori methods; but there was usually thought to be much less difficulty in knowing the nature of our *concepts* by methods that draw on what is already built into our possession of those very concepts. If the nature of our concepts can be known a priori, then it also seems plausible that the nature of the various types of attitude can be known a priori as well.

Moreover, the mental facts that can clearly be known only by the methods of empirical psychology – facts about the unconscious sub-personal mechanisms and processes that realize our perceptual, cognitive, and behavioral processes – do not seem to be essential to the intentional mental states in question. This is an old point, which Ned Block (1978, pp. 310–11) made in criticizing the view that he called "Psychofunctionalism." It seems intuitively possible for the very same type of conscious mental process to be realized in very different sub-personal mechanisms. To take Block's example, suppose that when we get to know the Martians, we develop extensive cultural interaction with them: we study each other's science and philosophy journals, read each other's novels, and so on. But it turns out that our sub-personal processing systems are very different. (Suppose, for example, that it is as if our brains had been designed to use as much memory capacity as necessary in order to minimize use of computation capacity, and their brains had been designed to use as much computation capacity as necessary in order to minimize use of memory capacity.) Still, it is intuitively possible for these Martians to have many of the same sorts of intentional mental states – beliefs, desires, plans, and so on – as we do. Thus, it seems possible for there to be creatures who share some of our intentional mental states but do not have the specific sorts of unconscious sub-personal mechanisms and processes that we have. Thus, these unconscious sub-personal mechanisms seem not to be essential to these intentional mental states.

So there is no obvious reason to think that knowledge of the sorts of facts that only empirical psychology can tell us is strictly necessary in order to understand the essential nature of these intentional mental states. It seems, prima facie, as though it should be possible, at least in principle, to know the essential nature of these types of intentional mental states a priori. The fact that my claim that the intentional is normative is based purely on philosophical a priori considerations is not in itself an objection to that claim.

Acknowledgments

I am very grateful to Georges Rey for taking the time to engage in this debate with me, and to Timothy Williamson for some very helpful comments on an earlier draft.

Notes

1   For some very different versions of the claim, see the works of Davidson (1980, essays 11 and 12, and 2001, essays 9 and 10), Morris (1992), and Brandom (1994); for a parallel normative theory of linguistic meaning, see Lance and Hawthorne (1997).
2   For more on my conception of normative concepts, see Wedgwood (2001 and 2006).
3   In effect, this is a principle of interpretive *charity* rather like the principle that was famously advocated by Davidson (2001, essay 9). A normative theory could invoke such a principle without accepting Davidson's full-blown "interpretivism." As Lewis (1974) suggests, the reference to interpretation could just be taken as a way of dramatizing what is objectively constitutive of the intentional states in question.
4   For an illuminating discussion of *ceteris paribus* laws, see Rey and Pietroski (1995).

5 For this notion of "natural properties," see especially Lewis (1999, essays 1 and 2).

6 It is this feature of my "dispositionalism" about concepts that I believe will enable me to escape the sort of indeterminacy worries that are inspired by Kripke (1982).

7 For a more detailed statement of this argument, see Wedgwood (forthcoming).

8 This conception of concepts has been disputed recently, e.g., by Timothy Williamson (2006). I reply to some of Williamson's arguments in §3, but unfortunately I shall not be able to offer a full defense of this conception of concepts here.

9 I am assuming that dispositions to use a concept in reasoning are all either rational dispositions or irrational dispositions. None of them is a purely non-rational disposition (like the disposition to sneeze when one inhales finely ground pepper). The norms of rationality cover the whole of reasoning, and so there are no processes of reasoning that are neither rational nor irrational in that way.

10 A subtle version of this idea has been defended recently by Matti Eklund (2002).

11 It was careless of me to suggest that the first point alone was enough to answer the objections of Stein (1996); Rey was quite right to criticize me on this score.

12 For these results, see Oaksford (2005, p. 427).

13 Williamson (2006, p. 18) points out that "in some cases, when a further premise of the form 'If r then q' is added to modus ponens only a minority endorse the inference (Byrne 1989)." But an inference with an extra premise of this form is simply not an instance of modus ponens. So these cases are simply irrelevant to my claim that people who possess the concept "if" have a suitable disposition to accept instances of modus ponens. (There is a difference between merely having a background belief, and consciously considering an inference that actually involves the content of that belief as a premise of the inference.)

14 This theory of action is often ascribed to Davidson (1980, essay 1). For the record, I would prefer simply to define an action as the execution of an intention or volition, but I obviously cannot defend this account of action here.

15 See especially Alexander Bird (1998) and Michael Fara (2005).

16 As I explained in §1, for a sub-personal mechanism to realize this personal-level rational disposition, it is not necessary that it should not realize any other personal-level dispositions as well. All that is necessary is that this sub-personal mechanism should make it *no accident* that normally, *ceteris paribus*, the thinker responds to the mental state of consciously considering an inference that is in fact an instance of *modus ponens* (in the absence of defeaters) with the mental state of accepting that inference.

References

Bird, A. (1998). Dispositions and antidotes. *Philosophical Quarterly*, 48, 227–34.

Block, N. (1978). Troubles with functionalism. In C. W. Savage (ed.), *Perception and Cognition: Issues in the Foundations of Psychology*. Minnesota Studies in the Philosophy of Science, 9. Minneapolis: University of Minnesota Press.

Brandom, R. (1994). *Making It Explicit*. Cambridge, MA: Harvard University Press.

Byrne, R. M. J. (1989). Suppressing valid inferences with conditionals. *Cognition*, 31, 1–21.

Davidson, D. (1980). *Essays on Actions and Events*. Oxford: Clarendon.

—— (2001). *Inquiries into Truth and Interpretation*, rev. edn. Oxford: Clarendon.

Eklund, M. (2002). Inconsistent languages. *Philosophy and Phenomenological Research*, 64, 251–75.

Fara, M. (2005). Dispositions and habituals. *Noûs*, 39, 43–82.

Frege, G. (1892). Über Sinn und Bedeutung. *Zeitschrift für Philosophie und philosophische Kritik*, NF 100, 25–50.

Hursthouse, R. (1991). Arational actions. *Journal of Philosophy*, 88, 57–68.

Johnson-Laird, P. N. and Byrne, R. M. J. (1993). Models and deductive rationality. In K. Manktelow and D. Over (eds.), *Rationality: Psychological and Philosophical Perspectives*. London: Routledge.

Kripke, S. (1982). *Wittgenstein on Rules and Private Language*. Cambridge, MA: Harvard University Press.

Lance, M. and Hawthorne, J. (1997). *The Grammar of Meaning*. Cambridge: Cambridge University Press.

Lewis, D. (1974). Radical interpretation. *Synthese*, 23, 331–44.

—— (1999). *Papers in Metaphysics and Epistemology*. Cambridge: Cambridge University Press.

McGee, V. (1985). A counterexample to modus ponens. *Journal of Philosophy*, 82, 462–71.

Morris, M. (1992). *The Good and the True*. Oxford: Clarendon.

Oaksford, M. (2005). Reasoning. In N. Braisby and M. Gellatly (eds.), *Cognitive Psychology*. Oxford: Oxford University Press.

Raz, J. (1999). Agency, reason, and the good. In J. Raz (ed.), *Engaging Reason*. Oxford: Clarendon.

Rey, G. (2002). Physicalism and psychology: a plea for substantive philosophy of mind. In C. Gillet and B. Loewer (eds.), *Physicalism and Its Discontents*. Cambridge: Cambridge University Press.

Rey, G. and Pietroski, P. (1995). When other things aren't equal: saving ceteris paribus. *British Journal for the Philosophy of Science*, 46, 81–110.

Stanovich, K. E. and West, R. F. (2000). Individual differences in reasoning: implications for the rationality debate? *Behavioral and Brain Sciences*, 23, 645–65.

Stein, E. (1996). *Without Good Reason*. Oxford: Oxford University Press.

Strawson, P. F. (1952). *Introduction to Logical Theory*. London: Methuen.

Wedgwood, R. (2001). Conceptual role semantics for moral terms. *Philosophical Review*, 110, 1–30.

—— (2006). The meaning of "ought." In R. Shafer-Landau (ed.), *Oxford Studies in Metaethics*. Oxford: Oxford University Press.

—— (forthcoming). The normativity of the intentional. In B. P. McLaughlin and A. Beckermann (eds.), *The Oxford Handbook of the Philosophy of Mind*. Oxford: Clarendon.

Williamson, T. (2003). Understanding and inference. *Proceedings of the Aristotelian Society*, 77, 249–93.

—— (2006). Conceptual truth. *Proceedings of the Aristotelian Society*, 80, 1–42.

IS THERE NON-CONCEPTUAL CONTENT?

The Revenge of the Given

Jerry Fodor

1 Introduction

Could there be unconceptualized mental representations? What would they be like? Where might one look for some? How would you know if you had found one? I think these questions are, in the long run, largely empirical. But limning the landscape that they occupy is a philosophical enterprise within the meaning of the act, and that I shall presently try to do. I also propose to push at them and prod at them until they are in a form where psychological data can be brought to bear, and to say something about how the relevant data have come out so far.

For present purposes, I assume without argument that there are *conceptualized* mental representations. This assumption is the backbone of the "Representational Theory of Mind," which is, of course, itself famously tendentious. But I'm too old to worry about what to do if RTM isn't true.

I shall also assume what is maybe less familiar: that *conceptualized representation* is *representation as* and vice versa. So, to represent (e.g., mentally) Mr James as a cat is to represent him as falling under the concept CAT; and to represent Mr James as falling under the concept CAT is to represent him as a cat; and thinking of Mr James as a cat requires applying the concept CAT to Mr James. This is, to be sure, just the sort of "intellectualist" kind of thinking about thinking that mid-century logical behaviorists (notably Ryle and Wittgenstein) said that psychology and the philosophy of mind could profitably do without. Well, they were wrong.

If that is all granted, it suggests a first move: we have the option of exchanging "can there be unconceptualized mental representation?" for "can there be mental representing without mental representing as?" This serves to locate the present concerns in relation to a family of others that are philosophically familiar: for example, "represents X" is transparent to substitution of coextensive terms at the X position; but "represents as X as F" is opaque to substitution of coextensive predicates at the

"F" position. If (a token of) "that cat" represents that cat, and if that cat is Granny's favorite cat, then that token of "that cat" represents Granny's favorite cat. But though a token of "that cat" represents that cat *as* that cat, it doesn't follow that "that cat" represents that cat as Granny's favorite, not even if that is the cat that Granny prefers to any other. In this respect the semantic distinction between *representing and representing as* works like the psychologist's distinction between *seeing* and *seeing as*. (You can see that cat without seeing it as that cat, but you can't see that cat *as* that cat without seeing it as a cat.) That's all implicit in RTM, according to which seeing X only requires mentally representing X somehow or other, but seeing X as F requires applying to X the mental representation that expresses the concept F. Seeing requires representation; seeing as requires representation as.

So, then: It is part of RTM that, if there is seeing without seeing as, then there is unconceptualized seeing. Piety recommends a more traditional formulation: If there is seeing without seeing as, then there is a "perceptual given." In what follows I will often put the matter the second way, but with a caveat: I assume, contrary to a main epistemological tradition, that the given may be both sub-personal and encapsulated; which is to say that it may be neither conscious nor (in Steven Stich's term) "inferentially promiscuous." This is, to be sure, the thin edge of a complicated tangle of issues. It is arguable, for example, that the content of a representation cannot be alienated from its accessibility to consciousness. That might be because (in the case of perceptual judgments or quite generally) the connection between content and first person justifications of beliefs is itself inalienable. And it is likewise arguable that the connection between content and inferential role is inalienable because content is, in fact, a construct out of inferential role. On that sort of view, the notion of a kind of mental representation that is given rather than inferred, and that is unconscious to boot, is doubly a contradiction in terms.

Discussions of unconceptualized content in the philosophical literature (like, come to think of it, discussions of practically everything else) routinely beg both the question whether the identity of a mental representation is dissociable from its role in inference and the question whether the intentionality of a mental state is dissociable from its accessibility to consciousness. Speaking just for myself, I see no reason why the very same mental content that is de facto proprietary to unconscious processes of (as it might be) visual-form recognition in one mind might not be available to (as it might be) mechanisms of conscious problem-solving in another mind (or in the same mind at a different time). In effect, the received philosophical view has it that conceptual atomists have failed to recognize that the content of a representation supervenes on its inferential role, and computational psychologists have failed to recognize that mental states are *ipso facto* epistemologically transparent. Well, maybe; but I wouldn't bet much on either, and I wouldn't be flustered if the given flouts both.

2 Kinds of Representations

For reasons I'll presently set out, I think that there probably are non-conceptual perceptual representations. The line of argument I'll have on offer goes like this: On one hand, it is (empirically) plausible that some perceptual representation is iconic and, on the other hand, it is in the nature of iconic representation to be non-conceptual. That being the proposed polemical strategy, I had better now say something about what I mean by "iconic" representation.

First, then, my usage is idiosyncratic. In the semantics/semiotics literature, "iconic" frequently comports with notions like, for example, "pictorial" and "continuous." But it isn't always clear just what any of these come to, or just what the connections between them are supposed to be. As often as not, they are made to take in one another's wash. For the moment, I propose to pretend the slate is blank and stipulate the following.

First, "iconic" and "discursive" are mutually exclusive modes of representation: that a representation is either entails that it is not the other. I leave it open that some kinds of representation are neither iconic nor discursive. Offhand, I cannot think of a good candidate but it doesn't matter for the present purposes.

Second, I assume, for familiar reasons, that all the kinds of representations we are concerned with are compositional. To a first approximation, a representation is compositional iff its syntactic structure and semantic content are both determined by the syntactic structure and semantic content of its parts. Compositionality is required by any serious theory of linguistic and/or mental representations because both thought and language are productive and systematic, and that is intelligible only on the assumption of their compositionality. I suppose everybody knows this story, so I won't elaborate.

2.1 Discursive representations

The sentences of natural languages are the paradigms: here again the outlines are familiar. Every expression is a finite arrangement of constituents that are themselves either primitive or complex. Each complex constituent is a finite arrangement of "lexical" primitives (words, near enough). Lexical primitives have their syntactic and semantic properties intrinsically. Roughly, a word is a triple consisting of a bundle of orthographical/phonological features, a bundle of syntactic features, and a bundle of semantic features: these are enumerated by the word's "entry" in the "lexicon" of the language. A discursive representation in L is *syntactically* compositional iff its syntactic analysis is exhaustively determined by the grammar of L together with the syntactic analysis of its lexical primitives. A discursive representation is *semantically* compositional iff its semantic interpretation is exhaustively determined by its syntax together with the semantic interpretations of its lexical primitives. Consider, for example sentence (1). Its syntactic structure is (more or less) as shown in (2), and its semantic interpretation is (more or less) *John loves Mary*:

1   John loves Mary
2   $(John)_{NP} ((loves)_V ((Mary_{NP}))_{VP})_S$

The syntax and semantics of the sentence are determined by such facts as that "John" is a noun and denotes *John*, that "loves" is a verb and denotes the relation *X loves Y*, and that "Mary" is a noun and denotes *Mary*. Further details are available upon application at your local department of linguistics.

What matters for us is this: the semantic interpretation of a sentence (*mutatis mutandis*, of any discursive representation) depends exhaustively on the way that properties of its lexical primitives interact with properties of its constituent structure, and *not every part of a discursive representation is ipso facto one of its constituents.* So, for example, "John," "Mary," and "loves Mary" are among the constituents of (1) according to the analysis (2). But "John loves" is not, and nor is "John . . . Mary." This is part and parcel of the fact that neither the semantic interpretation of "John loves" nor the semantic interpretation of "John . . . Mary" contributes to determining the semantic interpretation of "John loves Mary"; in fact, neither of them *has* a semantic interpretation in that sentence (though, of course, each of the lexical primitives they contain does). I'll say: The constituents of a discursive representation are those of its parts that are recognized by its *canonical decomposition.* According to me, it is *having a canonical decomposition* that distinguishes discursive representations from iconic ones.

2.2 Iconic representations

Pictures are paradigms (but see the caveats to follow). I suppose that pictures, like sentences, have a compositional semantics. Their principle of compositionality is this:

> *Picture Principle:* If P is a picture of X, then parts of P are pictures of parts of X.

But pictures and the like differ from sentences and the like in that icons don't have canonical decompositions; they have *interpretable parts*, but they don't have *constituents.* Or, if you prefer, all the parts of a picture are *ipso facto* among its constituents; icons are compositional according to the Picture Principle whichever way you carve them up. Take a picture of a person, cut it into parts however you like; still, each picture-part pictures a person-part. And the whole that you have if you reassemble all the picture's parts is a picture of the whole person that the parts are pictures of parts of.

So, then, in everything that follows, a representation that has no canonical decomposition is an icon. I will argue (quite soon now) that iconic representations lack a number of the characteristic features of conceptualizations, so the question we started with, "Could there be unconceptualized mental representations?", can be swapped for the question "Are any mental representations iconic?" And that, finally, is a question on which empirical evidence can be brought to bear.

2.3 Iconicity and individuation

So far, iconic representations are typically semantically evaluable (they are typically *of* this or that). But they have no canonical decompositions, which is to say, they have no constituent structure; which is to say that, however they are sliced, there is no distinction between their *canonical* parts and their *mere* parts. Here's another way to put this: an icon is a homogeneous kind of symbol from both the syntactic and the semantic point of view. Each of its parts *ipso facto* gets a semantic interpretation according to the same rule of interpretation that applies to each of the others (viz. according to the Picture Principle).

But none of that is true of discursive representations. Only a specifiable subset of the parts of a discursive symbol are syntactic or semantic constituents, and it is thus far open that the various constituents of a discursive representation may contribute in *different* ways to determining the semantics of their hosts. Our paradigms, the sentences of a natural language, are clearly structurally heterogeneous in this respect. Considered syntactically, they contain: nouns, verbs, adjectives, noun phrases, verb phrases, prepositional phrases, and so on. Considered semantically, they contain: singular terms, descriptions, predicates, and an apparatus of logical terms such as quantifiers, variables, and connectives, and so on once again. Correspondingly, both the rules that distinguish sentential constituents from mere sentential parts and the rules that compose the interpretation of sentential expressions from the interpretation of their constituents turn out to be disconcertingly complex and hard to state; linguists have thus far had only very partial success in formulating either. Compare the unarcane apparatus that sufficed to formulate the Picture Principle.

Because they decompose into syntactically and semantically heterogeneous constituents, discursive representations can have logical forms (maybe all discursive representations that can express truths have them). By contrast, because they decompose into syntactically and semantically homogeneous parts, iconic representations don't have logical forms. I take that to be truistic. The logical form of a symbol is supposed to make its compositional structure explicit, viz. to make explicit the contribution that each of the interpreted parts contributes to the interpretation of the whole symbol. But icons don't *have* logical forms: each part of an interpreted iconic symbol contributes to the interpretation in the same way as each of the others.

We are now about to see that discursive symbols have a galaxy of representational properties that icons don't: properties that are, in fact, the characteristic marks of conceptualization. That's largely *because*, discursive representations being semantically and syntactically heterogeneous, their various constituents can contribute in different ways to determining the content of their hosts: singular terms contribute in one way, predicates contribute in quite another way, and logical constants in still another. But the Picture Principle says that every part of an icon contributes to its interpretation in the same way: it pictures part of what the icon does. In consequence, icons can't express (for example) the distinction between negative propositions and affirmative ones which turns (*inter alia*) on distinctions among logical constants. Likewise, they can't express quantified propositions, or hypothetical propositions, or modal propositions. They can't even express predication, since that requires (*inter alia*) distinguishing terms that contribute individuals from terms that contribute sets (or properties, or whatever).

For reasons that are quite closely related, whereas discursive representations typically carry ontological commitments, iconic representations don't. In particular, discursive representations do, but iconic ones do not, impose *principles of individuation* on the domains in which they are interpreted. I don't want to talk about this at length because I'm scared to. So it would help enormously if you'll just let me assume that what individuals a system of representation is ontologically committed to depends on the apparatus of quantifiers, variables, singular terms, and sortal predicates to which it has access. To a first approximation, systems of representation are committed to the individuals over which they quantify; conversely, if the available representations don't include quantifiers (or classifiers or something of the sort), then there won't be principles of individuation for whatever it is that the representations are of. Since iconic representations lack that sort of apparatus, there is no right answer to the question "which things (how many things?) does this iconic symbol represent?" (Didn't Quine say something of that sort? I hope he did; I would so like to be in respectable company for a change.)

To be sure, a photograph may show three giraffes in the veldt, but it likewise shows: a family of giraffes; and an odd number of Granny's favorite creatures; and a number of Granny's favorite odd creatures; and a piece of veldt that is inhabited by any or all of these. No doubt, we usually can agree about how to interpret the ontology of such a photograph; we do so in light of whatever project we happen to have in hand. But that isn't the relevant consideration for present purposes: what matters to us is that the discursive symbol "three giraffes in the veldt" specifies a scene relative to such concepts as THREE, GIRAFFES, IN, and THE VELDT. A fortiori, a mind that lacks these concepts cannot use that symbol to represent the scene. Contrast iconic representation: you can, of course, *see* three giraffes in the veldt without having GIRAFFE, etc. Nor do you need those concepts to take make a picture of three giraffes in the veldt; a camera and film will suffice.

Equivalently (more or less): the context "iconically represents . . .", like the contexts "sees . . .," "describes . . .," "points at . . .," "and "photographs. . . ." All are transparent to the substitution of coextensive descriptions. But "discursively represents . . ." is like "sees as," and "describes as . . ." always has an opaque reading (which, in fact, it usually prefers). According to RTM, that's because *seeing as . . .* and *describing as . . .* , like other acts of conceptualization, operate by subsuming distal things under the concept that is expressed by the predicate of some mental representation. It is entirely in the spirit of RTM that "conceptualizing" and "predicating" are two ways of talking about much the same thing. So if conceptualization requires the apparatus of predication, and if iconic representations *ipso facto* lack such apparatus, then it follows that iconic representations are *ipso facto* non-conceptual. Which is just what I've been telling you for the last many pages.[1]

Brief review: We started with conceptualized v. unconceptualized representations. We swapped that for *representing as* v. *representing tout court*, which we then swapped for iconic v. discursive representation. This allowed us to swap the question whether there are unconceptualized mental representations (in particular, whether there is a perceptual given) for the question whether any mental representations are iconic. I then suggested that (because they lack logical form) iconic representations don't provide principles of individuation for their domains of interpretation. This suggests a final metamorphosis: "Are there unconceptualized representations?" becomes "are there mental phenomena in which representation and individuation are dissociated?" If there are, then that is prima facie evidence of non-conceptual mental representation.

Well, is there such evidence? To begin with, if you want to test a theory, you need (what used to be called) "correlating definitions." Here is one: It is a rule of thumb that, all else being equal, the "psychological complexity" of a discursive representation (for example, the amount of memory it takes to store it or to process it) is a function of the number of individuals whose properties it independently specifies. I shall call this the "item effect."

Consider, as it might be, phone books. They specify properties of individuals (their numbers and addresses), and they are explicit as to both the individuals and the properties. All sorts of things follow: the phone books of big cities are generally bigger than the phone books of small cities; and they take up more shelf space; and it takes longer to look up an arbitrary number in a big phone book than in a small one; and it is harder to memorize (or even to copy) the contents of a big phone book than those of a small one; and so forth. This is all because the representations in phone books are discursive, hence conceptualized; they presuppose the possession and employment of such concepts as X'S NAME IS "Y" and PHONE P HAS THE NUMBER N. Lists, like sentences, are paradigms of discursive representation. They exhibit effects of their content (it is the number that is listed for John that you proceed to dial in consequence of looking his number up), and they also exhibit an effect of the number of items they contain.

Compare photographs: A photograph of 60 giraffes takes no more space in your album (or on the screen) than a photograph of 6 giraffes. For that matter, it takes no more space than a photograph of no giraffes (the one that you made when you forgot to take the lens cap off). Photographs are time-sensitive (very old ones are generally more degraded than very new ones) but they aren't item-sensitive. This is hardly surprising in light of the preceding discussion: iconic representations don't individuate; they don't represent individuals *as* individuals. A fortiori, nothing about them depends on the number of individuals that they represent.

3 Some Data at Last

Can we find, in the perceptual psychology literature, indications of a mode of representation that exhibits typical effects of iconicity; in particular, a mode of representation that *fails* to yield an item effect? If we can, then it is in the cards that such representations are unconceptualized, hence that there is a perceptual given.

In fact, relevant examples are the stock in trade of intro-level cognitive science texts. The basic idea is that perceptual information undergoes several sorts of processes (typically in more or less serial order) in the course of its progress from representation on the surface of a transducer (e.g., on the retina) to representation in long-term memory. Some of the earliest of these processes operate on representations that are stored in an "echoic" buffer (EB) and these representations are widely believed to be iconic.

Two consequences of their presumed iconicity should be stressed, since both suggest possible experimental investigations.

First, since iconic representations are unconceptualized, they do not individuate items that they represent; so representations in EB ought not produce item effects. Second, qua unconceptualized, iconic representations can't express properties whose recognition requires perceptual inferences. So, in the case of vision, icons register the sorts of properties that photographs do (two-dimensional shape, shading, color, and so forth) but not "object" properties such as *being an animal* (or a fortiori, *being a cat belonging to Granny*).

Correspondingly, in the case of auditory perception, icons in the echoic buffer should register the sorts of properties that show in a spectrogram (frequency, amplitude, duration), but not whether the distal sound is a rendering of "Lillibullero." For present purposes, if you have turned up a mental representation that doesn't individuate and isn't inferred, that is good reason to think what you've turned up is an icon.

Bearing all that in mind, let's start with an anecdote by way of building intuitions. So: there I am, seated at the keyboard, working hard on a piece for *Mind and Language* (or whatever); at the moment, I vacillate between a semicolon and a comma. A clock begins to chime. "Chime, chime, chime," the clock says. At first I ignore this, but then it seizes my attention. "I wonder what it may be o'clock," I say to myself (it being my habit to address myself in a sort of pig Georgian). What happens next is the point of interest: I commence to count the chimes, including the ones that I hadn't previously noticed. Strikingly (so, anyhow, the phenomenology goes) it's not just that I say to my self "there have been three chimes so far"; rather it's that I *count* the chimes that I hadn't till now attended to: "one chime, two chimes, three chimes," I think, thereby subsuming each chime under the sortal concept A CHIME. Four more chimes follow and I duly add them to get the total. I think: "it must be 6:30" (the clock in the hall runs half an hour fast).

Notice that one's ability to do this trick is time-bound; it lasts only for perhaps a second or two, so you can't count the unattended chimes that you heard yesterday. A psychologist might well conclude: *There's a brief interval during which an iconic (hence unconceptualized) representation of the chiming is held in EB. Within this interval, you can conceptualize (hence individuate, hence count) the chimes more or less at will. After that the trace decays and you've lost your chance.* I think he'd probably be right to so conclude. And I think that, in so concluding, he would postulate a perceptual given.

Prima facie objection: But clearly there *is* an item limit on the buffer. You may be able to count 2 or 3 chimes retrospectively, but I'll bet you can't do 15.

First reply (in passing): Temporal effects can mimic item effects so they must be controlled for. Suppose representations in EB last 2 seconds and it takes the clock 60 seconds to chime 15 times. You will "lose" the last 11 chimes in such a sequence. This is not, however, an effect of the number of stimulus items that can be stored in EB; it's just an interaction between the temporal duration of the stimulus and the temporal capacities of the buffer.

Second reply (more interesting): It's not because the buffer is item-limited that you can't count up to 15 retrospectively. Rather (once you control for the rate of temporal decay) it seems that how much you can put in the buffer actually is relatively unconstrained. It's not *representing* many chimes that's hard, it's *counting* them. For counting requires individuation, and individuation requires conceptualization, and it's independently plausible that conceptualizing costs.

There are data that suggest that this is indeed the right diagnosis. Some of the most convincing come from a deservedly famous series of experiments by George Sperling (1960). These findings are richer than I have space to summarize, but they support a pervasive phenomenological intuition: "when complex stimuli consisting of a number of letters are tachistoscopically presented, observers enigmatically insist that they have seen more than they can remember afterwards, that is, [more than they can] report afterwards." In the experiment, "the observer behaves as though the physical stimulus were still present when it is not (that is, after it has been removed) and . . . his behavior in the absence of the stimulus remains a function of the same variables of visual stimulation as it is in its presence." The critical experimental finding was that, queried just after the stimulus was turned off, though the subject could report only three of the letters he'd seen, he could report *any* three of them. So it appears there is a very short-term visual memory of which the capacity is, at a minimum, considerably greater than what S is able to read out of it. Apparently it is the cost of conceptualizing information in this memory, rather than the number of items that the memory is able to register, that bounds the subject's performance.

Notice that, though the Sperling results argue that the content of representations in EB is unconceptualized, these representations must of course *have* content; in particular, they must contain a content from which the categorization of an unattended stimulus (for example, a count of the chimes) can be recovered. That they do is crucial to explaining why the subject is accurate more often than chance. But, equally, the content they contain must not be *conceptual* content since, if it were, then there ought to be an item effect; which, apparently, there isn't. The long and short is: if "a given" is what is unconceptualized but nonetheless semantically contentful, it is thus far plausible that the representations in EB qualify as given.

But I do want to emphasize the "thus far" part. The argument I have set out is empirical through and through; it rather suggests that there is iconic representation in perception, but it certainly doesn't demonstrate that there is. Demonstrations are ever so much nicer than suggestions, of course; their level of confidence is so much higher. But there isn't one either pro or con in the present sort of case. Nor will there be. Since the issue about what kinds of mental representations there are is empirical, so too are the considerations that resolve it.

But I also want to emphasize that Sperling's study, though particularly elegant, is only one of a plethora of straws in the wind, all of which appear to be blowing in much the same direction. Effects of content without item effects are quite easy to find when you know where to look. I wonder why so many philosophers are so resistant to looking there.

4 Conclusion

I think there is quite likely a perceptual given. In any case, it would seem that the issue is empirical, so whether there's a given is, to that extent, no philosopher's business. On the other hand, if in fact there is a given, that should be of professional concern to philosophers who argue a priori that there can't be, that all content has to be conceptualized. Those philosophers are now required to sketch an alternative explanation of the sorts of empirical findings I've been gesturing toward. I am not holding my breath.

But does it matter philosophically in any other way? Does it, in particular, matter to epistemology? I have two reflections, both of which return us to considerations I raised earlier in the paper.

First epistemological reflection: If the given is supposed to be what ultimately grounds explicit justifications of perceptual inferences, then it must be both non-inferential and introspectible (as, indeed, foundationalist epistemologies have generally assumed). But then the empirical evidence is very strongly that there is no given: it seems to be a sort of iron law, one that holds in just about every case I've heard of, that what can be introspected is *always* the product of inferences (though the inferences are typically sub-personal and encapsulated). Contrapositively, what is a plausible candidate for *not* being inferred is almost never available to introspection. In particular, all the perceptual representations that are accessible to consciousness exhibit constancy effects and, by pretty general consensus, constancy effects are the products of inferences. You cannot, for example, see the retinal color of a thing (i.e. the color of the light the thing actually reflects to the eye); inferences that correct for background, distance, illumination, and so forth are automatic, mandatory, and *prior* to introspective access. You see oranges as orange even when the light is dim; that's because what you see is the retinal color *as corrected for* the effects of the intensity of the ambient illumination. Such considerations suggest, pretty strongly I think, that the given doesn't do what foundational epistemology wants it to: it doesn't provide a kind of representation that is both insensitive to contextual bias and available for conscious report. Well, if what is given turns out not to support a certain kind of epistemology, that does not argue against there being a given; it just argues against that kind of epistemology.

I wonder, sometimes, whether our current epistemology has quite caught up with the Freudian revolution in psychology: there is every sort of evidence that a great deal of the reasoning involved in the fixation of quotidian perceptual beliefs is unconscious, hence unavailable for report by the reasoner. That being so, the residual options for epistemology are to say either that most of our perceptual beliefs are unjustified or that much of what justifies our perceptual judgments isn't conscious. I'm unclear that much turns on which of these epistemology chooses.

Second epistemological reflection: It is often suggested, especially by philosophers in the Sellars tradition (such as Brandom, McDowell, and Davidson in some of his moods) that unconceptualized representations *can't* be what ground perceptual judgments because justification is a relation among *contents*, and whatever is unconceptualized thereby *lacks* content. The (putative) consequences of this (putative) truth are horrific. They include the principled impossibility of a "naturalized" epistemology; indeed, the principled isolation of "the realm of causes" from the "realm of reasons" quite generally. Thus McDowell says that causal explanations of perceptual judgments of the kind that psychologists seek can at best provide "exculpations where we wanted justifications." This is, to be sure, a long question; but I do hate a priori arguments that such and such a kind of discourse can't be naturalized; and "realm"-talk makes my skin crawl. So I can't resist a couple of brief comments.

First, discussions about whether any representational content is given shouldn't just take for granted all content is *ipso facto* conceptualized. Not if, as I've been trying to convince you, there is a plausible case for preconceptual, iconic representation. On

Jerry Fodor

that assumption the (putative) truism that justification is a relation among the contents of representations does *not* entail that justification is a relation among *conceptualized* contents. Accordingly, the question that needs settling is whether the content of an unconceptualized representation might be the datum that grounds (i.e. makes rational) a perceptual judgment.

Well, I'm damned if I see why it can't be. A picture of three giraffes in the veldt carries information about there being three giraffes in the veldt. (Since "carries information about ..." is extensional, it carries information about all sorts of other things too, of course. But so what?) Somebody who has the concepts GIRAFFE, THREE, VELDT, and so on (and *only* somebody who does) is *ipso facto* in a position to see the picture *as* showing three giraffes in the veldt, and hence to recover that information from the picture. All that being so, his reason for believing that there are three giraffes may well be that the picture shows three of them. His *reason*, notice; not his mere exculpation. As far as I can see, none of this is under threat from the consideration that judgment requires conceptualization.

Judgment requires conceptualization even if (as I suppose) *representation* doesn't; and, of course, there's no conceptualization without concepts. The question *how* (for example, by what computational processes) iconic representations might get conceptualized is, of course, very hard and the answer is unknown for practically any of the interesting cases. On the way of looking at things of which I've been trying to convince you, that is a large part of what the psychology of perception is about.

But, so far as I can see, there is nothing to preclude a story about how iconically carried information might function to ground a perceptual judgment. *Ground*, not just *cause*. I note in passing that I know no reason to suppose that such a story must have to assume that the required concepts are *constituted*, even in part, by rules for their application to iconic representations; or, indeed, that they are constituted, even in part, by *any* rules for applying them. There aren't, I shouldn't think, any *criteria* for applying GIRAFFE to giraffes; which is to say that perceptual inferences about giraffes don't have to ground in a priori truths. I take this to be a virtue of the story I've been telling.

I'll end with a brief methodological homily. I don't see that the epistemology of perception can simply ignore the empirical question how perception works. Quite generally, justifying a belief cannot require a thinker to do such-and-such unless the thinker has the kind of mind that *can* do such-and-such. (It cannot require him to introspectively access the preconceptual grounds of his beliefs unless he has the kind of mind that *has* introspective access to the preconceptual grounds of belief.) I've heard it said that how perception works doesn't matter to epistemologists because theirs is a normative not a descriptive enterprise. But how could one be bound by norms that one is, in point of nomological necessity, unable to satisfy? And what is the conceivable interest, even to epistemologists, of norms that don't bind us?

Note

1   I can imagine a line of objection that runs like this: "You connect intentionality with conceptualization, and you say that iconic representation is *ipso facto* unconceptualized. So it

ought to follow that there is no such thing as iconic *representation as*. But that's wrong; a green picture of a tree represents the tree that it pictures as green. Doesn't it?" What is wanted here is a more extensive discussion of iconic representation than I have the time or talent for, but here is the short answer: A green picture of a tree is one thing; a picture of a green tree is another; and a picture that represents a tree as green is yet a third. None of the three entails any of the others, which is to say that iconic representation per se cannot distinguish among them. You need conceptualization for that; in particular, you need the concept GREEN TREE.

Reference

Sperling, G. (1960). The information available in brief visual presentations. *Psychological Monographs*, 74, 1–29.

Are There Different Kinds of Content?

Richard G. Heck Jr

The cup from which I am drinking water now is yellow, and I know that it is. Why does my belief that the cup is yellow count as knowledge? Presumably, the answer must involve some reference to my current perceptual experience: I see the cup, and I see that it is yellow. What is it for me to see *that* the cup is yellow? The obvious answer would seem to be that it is for me to stand in a certain relation – namely, the relation expressed by the verb "to see" – to a proposition, namely, the proposition that the cup is yellow: Perception, that is to say, is a kind of propositional attitude, like belief, though it is also different from belief in many ways. So my seeing that the cup is yellow, being a kind of propositional attitude I take toward that proposition, can count as my reason for believing that the cup is yellow. I've thus got a reason for that belief, and it is a good one. No sort of inference from a prior judgment about my experience is necessary. Rather, I need only import the content of my perceptual state into cognition to believe it.

If one could accept that much, then – though there would no doubt be many problems left to discuss – it would make the question how perceptual experience justifies perceptual beliefs significantly more tractable. But the problem, as I see it, is that accepting that much threatens to impose high costs. If the "importation" model of perceptual justification is to be extended to all perceptually justified beliefs, then every concept that figures in a belief that is perceptually justifiable for a given subject must also be able to figure in the content of her perceptual experience: Only what the subject can conceptualize can play any justificatory role for her. It does not, of course, follow that there is nothing in the content of one's current perceptual experience that one cannot now conceptualize. But even if there is, it can play no role in thought: it cannot so much as figure in thought. A fortiori, non-conceptual elements of experience, if such there be, can play no role in one's decisions about what to believe or, more generally, one might conjecture, in any rational process. Elements of one's current perceptual experience that cannot be conceptualized would be of no significance for the thinking subject. Or, as Kant put it, in a famous passage: "It must be possible for the 'I think' to accompany all my representations; for otherwise something would be represented in me which could not be thought at all, and that is equivalent to saying that the representation would be impossible, or at least would be nothing to me" (*Critique of Pure Reason*, B131–2). No verbal report, indeed, no rational act of any kind, could reflect the presence of unconceptualized elements of experience, if such there should be, because such elements of experience cannot figure in thought.

That the importation model makes non-conceptual content at best "nothing to me" was powerfully argued by John McDowell in *Mind and World* (McDowell, 1996). McDowell, of course, does not regard this consequence as a cost of the importation model, let alone a high cost. He regards it, rather, as a straightforward and welcome consequence of reasoning's essentially conceptual character. If reasons for belief must themselves be wholly conceptual, then no non-conceptual element there might be in perceptual experience can contribute to one's reasons for one's beliefs. Of course, there is a familiar way in which non-conceptual elements of experience could be *represented* in thought: we may regard the subject as thinking *about* the non-conceptual elements of her experience. In some cases – in particular, in cases involving qualitative aspects of experience – such a model seems to me appealing: If there is a purely qualitative aspect to, say, what a 15-year-old Laphroaig tastes like (and if there isn't, then I have wasted a lot of money), perhaps it can become an object of thought for me through a kind of ostension. So, although those who have wanted to defend views close to McDowell's have often also wanted to reject the claim that there are nonrepresentational aspects of experience, I do not see that there is any quick argument from the one view to the other.

On the other hand, I do agree with McDowell that this sort of maneuver is not generally viable. To suppose that non-conceptual elements of my experience can play a role in thought only by becoming objects of thought is to adopt a view sufficiently reminiscent of sense-datum theories to make me, anyway, dubious. If so, however, we are in a bind. As Gareth Evans famously remarked, one's experience seems to represent much that one cannot antecedently conceptualize (Evans, 1982, pp. 227ff.).

There are many ways out. One would be to deny that perception does give us reasons for belief. It need not follow that perceptual experience does not, in some sense, justify our perceptual beliefs: Perceptual states cause beliefs, and a suitably externalist epistemology – some form of reliabilism, say – could be invoked to explain under what circumstances perceptual beliefs count as knowledge. But I, anyway, do feel the pull of the intuition on which McDowell is relying: When I say that I believe that my cup is yellow because of how it looks to me, I do not mean to be reporting a merely causal relation between my belief and my perceptual experience; on the contrary, I mean to be giving my reason for taking the cup to be yellow, and I am, as McDowell emphasizes, able to reflect on the deliverances of perception in deciding what to believe. The puzzle, then, is how non-conceptual aspects of my experience, if such there are, could play any role in a rational process of this kind. And the solution to the puzzle, or so I have argued elsewhere, is to reject the claim that all psychological states that may figure in something rightly described as "reasoning" must

Richard G. Heck Jr

be conceptual: There can be rational relations between states with conceptual content, such as beliefs, and states whose content is not conceptual, such as perceptions (Heck, 2000).[1]

In his contribution, Jerry Fodor has argued that there is good empirical evidence that there are representational states of the visual system whose content is non-conceptual. Whether that is so is an empirical question, one on which I am not competent to pronounce, so for present purposes I shall assume Fodor is right that there are both iconic and discursive representations. The relevance of this claim to the literature whose central concerns I have just summarized is not obvious, however. It is tempting to dismiss it with the remark that those who have wanted to defend the view that perceptual content is wholly conceptual – whatever their own personal inclination may be – need not deny that *sub-personal* states have non-conceptual content. Their motivations are, after all, broadly epistemological,[2] so the question of interest is what kind of content *conscious* perceptual states have, that is, perceptual states that can figure as reasons for belief.[3] But such a reaction would be too quick. If the experiments Fodor discusses involved something like MRI scans of subjects' brains, that would be one thing. But they do not. They involve the investigation of subjects' *beliefs*, for example, their beliefs about what letters are present in a given array. The belief that no "L" was present in such an array can, I assume, be justified, and, if so, it is presumably justified by the subject's perceptual experience.[4] The results of such experiments thus cannot simply be dismissed as irrelevant to the question whether the content of (conscious)[5] perceptual experience is conceptual.

That said, however, it is still not clear what the significance of such experiments is. Much of the early part of Fodor's paper is devoted to an attempt to transform the philosopher's question whether perceptual content is conceptual into one on which evidence from psychology can be brought to bear. I wholeheartedly applaud that effort. But why must a philosopher who is committed to the claim that perceptual experience is wholly conceptual deny that the representations that underlie perceptual experience are iconic? As it happens, this issue is related to one that has troubled me for some time.

In the earlier paper already mentioned, I distinguished two forms of the view that perceptual content is non-conceptual, which I called the "state view" and the "content view."[6] The state view is a view about the conditions required if someone is to be in a perceptual state with a given content: It is the view that the content of a subject's perceptual experience is not limited by the concepts she possesses; for example, it would be possible for a subject to be in a perceptual state that represented a surface as being of a particular shade even if she had no concept of that shade. The content view, on the other hand, is stronger: It is the view that perceptual states and cognitive states have different kinds of content.

It should be clear why this distinction is important. The state view is wholly neutral on the question what the contents of perceptual states should be taken to be. It is thus consistent with the state view that perceptual states should have the same kind of content that cognitive states, such as beliefs, have, and so the state view is also consistent with the importation model of perceptual justification. The kinds of arguments McDowell gives, then, in favor of the view that perceptual content is conceptual must have as their target not the state view but the content view. Unless one wishes to abandon the view that perceptual experience does provide us with reasons for our beliefs, a defender of the content view must therefore explain how perception can provide us with reasons for belief if perceptual states do not even have the same kind of content that beliefs do. As said, I think this challenge can be met, but it is nonetheless the case that defenders of the content view have a problem that defenders of the state view do not necessarily have.

So the distinction between the state view and the content view is important, but recognizing it leads first to puzzlement, because one of the central arguments used by proponents of the content view simply does not establish it. The argument in question is the "richness" argument, which begins, and pretty much ends, with the observation that the shades of color one can perceive a surface to have are not limited by the concepts one has available. It is clear that this argument, even if accepted, can establish no more than the state view. But what is worse is that proponents of the content view have not made it at all clear either what it is supposed to mean to say that perceptual states and cognitive states have different sorts of content nor why one should want to make this additional claim.[7]

Proponents of the content view have usually held that the contents of beliefs are conceptual in the very strong sense that they are *composed* of concepts, and they have also typically wanted to deny that perceptual contents are composed of concepts, in this sense. But what is it supposed to mean to say that contents are or are not composed of concepts? For that matter, what are concepts? It is here, I think, that Fodor's reflections have the most to offer the existing literature on non-conceptual content. What I am going to suggest is that the question what kind of content perceptual and cognitive states have is, ultimately, a question about what kinds of representations those states involve. The remainder of the paper will thus concern, primarily, abstract issues about the nature of content.

1 What Is Conceptual Structure?

I have often heard questions of roughly the following form.

> According to the content view, perceptual states and cognitive states have different kinds of content. But these various sorts of content are simply various sorts of abstract entities that we use to characterize the representational properties of states: We have sets of possible worlds, Russellian propositions, Fregean thoughts, and the like. Can't we just use whatever we find convenient? Of what real significance could it be whether we make the same choice in the case of perceptual states and cognitive states or different ones?

It seems to me, however, that the question already contains the seed of an answer.

Let us start a step further back. Why should we attribute content to mental states at all? A common answer might be that mental states are representational: Talk of a state's content is short for talk of its representational properties. That is certainly true. But why trouble ourselves with the representational properties of mental states? What would we lose if we just ignored them? I take it that we would lose the very idea of psychological explanation. We are in the habit of explaining our own behavior, and

120 Richard G. Heck Jr

that of other creatures, in terms of what we believe: We explain why Joe ran across the room in terms of his believing that his stuffed dinosaur was on the other side. These explanations are typically causal and counterfactual supporting, which is to say that there is a law of one sort or another that, if a given explanation is correct, it instantiates. The explanations themselves are formulated not in terms of the neurological features of mental states but in terms of their contents, and the same is true of the laws. And so we might say: The reason we should attribute content to mental states is because there are things we wish to explain in terms of mental states, as individuated by their contents.

That said, it is therefore a condition on what we may take the contents of mental states to be that we should individuate them finely enough for our explanatory purposes. For example, it certainly would not do simply to take the content of a belief to be its truth-value. Beliefs that have the same truth-value need not play the same role in the production of behavior. But before we take the familiar next step to the view that the contents of beliefs are sets of possible worlds, we should pause to ask why that view seems so natural. The problem with the view that the content of a belief is its truth-value would seem to be that it conflates beliefs we need to keep separate. To do that, however, we simply need to make sure that we have enough "contents" to go around. Why not just take the contents of beliefs to be (possibly transfinite) ordinal numbers? There are plenty of them.[8]

There are, I suppose, many different answers one might consider. But the best answer, it seems to me, is that mental states are not just distinguished from one another by their contents: they are also related to one another by their contents. For example, given any two beliefs, there are several other beliefs that are related to them in familiar ways: their negations, their conjunction and disjunction, and so forth. These relations are not just logical but also psychological: Someone who believes two propositions will, *ceteris paribus*, also tend to believe their conjunction, at least when the question arises.

It is not, of course, that one could not state such generalizations if one took the contents of beliefs to be ordinal numbers: Given an assignment of ordinals to psychological states, it will be possible to define relations on the ordinals that mimic logical relations between contents. But the relation so defined is bound to seem arbitrary from a mathematical point of view. Contrast the treatment of belief-contents as sets of possible worlds: it makes it possible to state the sorts of generalizations mentioned above in terms of beliefs' contents because set-theoretic operations on sets of possible worlds correspond in a natural way to logical operations on the contents of the beliefs they represent.[9]

There are arguments of a similar sort against representing the contents of beliefs in terms of sets of possible worlds: Beliefs that are true in the same possible worlds – for example, any two logically equivalent beliefs – need not play the same role in the production of behavior. And again, beliefs are not just distinguished from but related to one another in ways the possible worlds account does not naturally capture. Someone who believes that a is F and also believes that all Fs are G will tend to believe, at least when the question is raised, that a is G. Moreover, beliefs arguably satisfy what Evans called the "generality constraint": A thinker who is capable of entertaining the thought that a is F and is also capable of entertaining the thought that b is G will typically also be capable of entertaining the thoughts that a is G and that b is F (Evans, 1982, pp. 100ff.). Thought, that is to say, is productive and systematic in much the same way that language is.[10]

These sorts of considerations have tended to push people in the direction of the view that the contents of beliefs are structured in some way. It is once again worth pausing to ask why. The answer is that the treatment of contents as structured allows one to state the sorts of generalizations we have been discussing in a natural way, in terms of the contents of psychological states. By contrast, consider again the crazy view that simply takes the contents of beliefs to be ordinals. Given an assignment of ordinals to beliefs, there will be relations on the ordinals that correspond to the relations among structured propositions. The difficulty, however, is again that, from a mathematical point of view, these relations are likely to be quite arbitrary. And we can now see clearly that the concern I am expressing is not just aesthetic. There are *lots* of relations on the ordinals, and one could formulate all sorts of generalizations about beliefs in terms of these various relations. Some of these would be true, but most of them would be false, and there would be nothing in how we were representing the contents of beliefs that so much as suggested a reason for the difference. The generality constraint, for example, would just be one generalization among many, stated in terms of one relation on the ordinals among many, no different in principle from any of the others. If we represent the contents of beliefs as structured propositions, on the other hand, the generality constraint emerges as a natural consequence of the nature of cognitive contents.

Compare the case of temperature, which we measure using real numbers. Here again, there is a sense in which we could just as well measure temperature using ordinals.[11] Well, why don't we? The temperatures of objects are related to one another in an important way: one object can be hotter or colder than another; more precisely, "colder than" is a linear order. This feature of temperature is nicely represented by the natural ordering of the reals. Of course, given a one–one mapping between the reals and the ordinals, it would be easy enough to define a relation on the ordinals that mirrored the natural ordering of the reals: it is just the image of that ordering under the mapping. But this ordering of the ordinals is unlikely to be in any way a natural one. There are ever so many relations on the ordinals: why should that one be of any special significance? Indeed, the ordinals themselves have a natural ordering, but it is very unlikely that it would have any significance at all as regards temperature.

Now, to be honest, I don't know that I have anything to say here that would move someone who was already committed to the view that it is merely *convenient* to measure temperature using the reals rather than the ordinals. But most of us, I hope, don't find this view very appealing. And my point is that, if we are going to reject it, then we should also reject the view that it is merely convenient to represent contents as structured propositions rather than as ordinals or what have you. The representation of contents as structured allows us to state certain generalizations, such as the generality constraint, in a natural way, in terms of beliefs' contents, by representing the relations among contents that figure in those generalizations as essentially syntactic. Moreover, by representing these relations as syntactic, we represent them as different in kind from other relations in which one belief might stand to another.

Richard G. Heck Jr

Such a representation thus points us toward an *explanation* of the generalizations in question.

In the case of the generality constraint, for example, we want not only to observe that there is a certain pattern in people's ability to entertain various thoughts, we also want to explain this fact. The explanation Evans suggests is that the capacity to entertain the thought that *a* is *F* has a structure that corresponds to the structure of the thought itself: Thinking that *a* is *F* involves thinking of the object *a* and thinking of it that it is *F*. The ability to think such a thought thus depends upon and is made possible by one's ability to think of *a* and to think of an arbitrary thing that it is *F*. That someone has these capacities, of course, is something that itself needs to be explained. But what matters at present is not what the correct explanation is: what matters now is just that, if the claim that the contents of beliefs are structured is to be understood as motivated in part by the generality constraint, then the hypothesis that the contents of beliefs are structured must contribute to the explanation of the generality constraint's satisfaction.

I have sometimes encountered a distinction between "weak" and "strong" forms of the generality constraint. In its weak form, the generality constraint simply states that there is a certain kind of pattern in our cognitive capacities. Satisfaction of this weak form of the generality constraint is not sufficient for states of a given kind to have structured contents. One can imagine that a creature's cognitive capacities should exhibit this sort of pattern even though there is no substantial sense in which that creature's ability to entertain the thought that *a* is *F* involved the exercise of distinct abilities to think of *a* and to think of a thing as *F*. Such a creature is empirically implausible. It would be a total mystery why – failing magic or divinely established harmony – such a creature, upon acquiring the ability to entertain the thought that *a* is *G*, should also acquire the ability to think that *b* is *G*, that *c* is *G*, and so forth. And, if a creature's cognitive capacities do not have that sort of structure, then we have no reason to regard the contents of its thoughts as structured, either. For that, the generality constraint must be satisfied in the stronger form to which I've just alluded: The ability to think that *a* is *F* must decompose into the abilities to think of *a* and to think of a thing as *F*, abilities that are sufficiently distinct that one's being able to think that *a* is *F* may be *explained by* one's being able to think of *a* and one's being able to think of a thing as *F*.

What I am suggesting is thus that the claim that beliefs have conceptual content should be understood as the claim that the contents of belief are structured in this sense. Some philosophers will undoubtedly find this construal to be far too strong. Some philosophers, for example, have wanted to say that possessing a concept is just being able to have certain sorts of beliefs: To possess the concept *horse* is to be able to have such beliefs as that Trigger was a horse, that horses have four legs, and so forth. Such a philosopher would regard the claim that the contents of beliefs are conceptual as, in effect, true by definition. There is, of course, little point arguing terminology. My purpose here has been to explain what question the early participants in the debate over non-conceptual content meant to be discussing, and my point is that the claim that the contents of belief are conceptual – as they understood it – is very much *not* a triviality. And it is in part for that reason that the claim that perceptual content is conceptual – as these early participants understood it – is so strong.

Are There Different Kinds of Content?   123

Not all later participants in the debate have appreciated this fact – in part, to be sure, because the distinction that is supposed to be marked by the term "conceptual" is rarely elaborated. In his paper "Perception and Conceptual Content" (Byrne, 2004), Alex Byrne carefully investigates various uses of this term. He notes, for example, that many of the early participants share the assumption that cognitive contents are Fregean, in the sense that the thought that *a* is *F* may have a different content from the thought that *b* is *F*, even if *a* is the very same object as *b*. In the writings of many of these authors – Evans, McDowell, and Peacocke, for example – the claim that the contents of beliefs are conceptual is often treated as equivalent to the claim that these contents are Fregean. But, of course, the assumption that the contents of belief are Fregean is controversial, and it seems irrelevant to the question at issue between Evans and McDowell. As a way of setting that issue aside, then, Byrne uses the term "concept" in a merely "pleonastic" sense that makes that claim that the contents of belief are conceptual all but empty (Byrne, 2004, §1.1). As a result, however, the claim that perceptual content is conceptual becomes correspondingly weak.[12] And so, unsurprisingly, the arguments that have been offered against the claim that perceptual content is conceptual then seem to Byrne to be grossly inadequate (Byrne, 2004, §2.1).

If so little in the debate over non-conceptual content turns upon the assumption that cognitive contents are Fregean, why does setting this assumption aside so distort that debate? Frege and Russell disagreed, of course, about what the constituents of our thoughts are: Frege took them to be senses; Russell, objects and properties. This disagreement is undoubtedly an important one, but, for our purposes, what is much more important is something about which Frege and Russell agreed, namely, that cognitive contents *have constituents* in a sense that is not just pleonastic. The claim that cognitive contents are Fregean thus includes the weaker claim that the contents of belief are significantly structured. We cannot without loss set this claim aside when attempting to understand what is at issue between Evans and McDowell, for it is central to their understanding of the claim that cognitive contents are conceptual. As Evans and McDowell understand it, that claim is very much not a triviality, since it incorporates the generality constraint in its strong form. Their understanding of the term "concept" therefore cannot be the pleonastic one. In particular, for Evans and McDowell, grasping the concept *horse* is not just being able to entertain various beliefs about horses. To grasp that concept is to have a cognitive ability – the ability to think of a thing as a horse – an ability whose possession *partially explains* one's ability to entertain various beliefs about horses. If one had no such ability, then Evans and McDowell would say that one did *not* grasp the concept *horse*.

Now again, one might want to object that we should not understand the term "concept" in this way, perhaps on the ground that, if we do so understand it, it is epistemically possible that no one grasps any concepts. And again, I am not going to argue terminology. My purpose here has simply been to explain what the early participants in the debate over non-conceptual content took to be at issue. What was at issue was, for example, whether the cognitive ability one exercises when one thinks that tomatoes are red – and one's possessing which partially explains one's ability to think that thought – is also exercised when one veridically perceives a ripe tomato, and whether it would be impossible for one to perceive the tomato as one does were

Richard G. Heck Jr

one not able to think as one can. To answer these questions affirmatively is, I hope it is clear, to make a very strong claim indeed.[13] It is, indeed, an empirical claim, or so it would certainly seem, and I am as uncomfortable as Fodor is with the purely a priori arguments that have been offered for it.

I'll return below to the question whether we should understand the distinction between conceptual and non-conceptual content as I have here suggested. First, I want to look at how this distinction, so drawn, might be put to use.

2 What Non-conceptual Content Is: Cognitive Maps

The claim that psychological states of a certain kind have contents that are conceptually structured is defensible, or so I have argued, only if certain sorts of generalizations about states of that kind hold and if the fact that such generalizations hold is explicable in terms of structural features of the states in question: thus, the generality constraint, for example, must hold in its strong form. The general idea behind this suggestion is that the kind of content we should take states of a given sort to have should reflect causally relevant structural features of such states. States that do not satisfy generalizations of the same kind that cognitive states satisfy will then be states whose content is not conceptual. The claim that perceptual content is non-conceptual thus amounts to the claim that there are sorts of relationships that hold among beliefs, and that are partly constitutive of their contents' being conceptual, that do not hold among perceptual states.

Let me illustrate this claim by first discussing an example about which I'm guessing we all have fewer theoretical commitments than we have about the perceptual case.[14] There is strong empirical evidence that our ability to find our way around in the world depends upon our employment of what are known as "cognitive maps." Each of us has a mental map of our surroundings that places locations we encounter relative to other, known locations. Now, cognitive maps are obviously representational, and the term "map" is used here because the representations in question are thought to be very much like more familiar sorts of maps. That is to say: We have and employ a mode of storing information about topographic features of our environment that is very different from storing individual beliefs about the relative locations of objects; it is not, in any sense, *sentential*. Rather, one's cognitive map is a unified and, one might say, organic representation of the environment that does not decompose in any determinate way into parts. Cognitive maps, that is to say, are icons, in Fodor's sense.

Cognitive maps therefore do not have conceptual content: their content is not structured in the way the contents of belief are. That is not to say, of course, that a creature's cognitive map does not interact with its beliefs (and other higher cognitive states): one can come to have beliefs about where certain things are relative to other things because one's cognitive map represents them as so located; one's beliefs can, presumably, also influence one's cognitive map. Nonetheless, having a cognitive map of one's environment is quite different from having a collection of explicit beliefs about it. One manifestation of this fact is that one can "know how to get somewhere" and yet have no idea how to give someone directions for getting there – except, perhaps, by imagining the route one would take, thus putting one's cognitive map to use in imagination. Nor is it to say that explicit beliefs play no role in navigation: In trying to get, say, from my house to the new Institute of Contemporary Art, I might make use both of my cognitive map of the Boston area and of directions I got on the Web. The point, rather, is simply that it is one thing to have a (mental) map of Boston and another thing to have a (mental) description of it, even if all and only the spatial relationships that are indicated on the map are included in the description. If one takes a moment to imagine what a descriptive equivalent of a map of Boston would be like, it will be clear enough how efficient the form of representation maps employ is.

If one wanted to represent the content of a map as a structured proposition, what structured proposition would it be? The only plausible answer would seem to be that the content of the map is given by a complete description of the relationships it indicates.[15] It is no objection to this view that such a description is implausibly long. It is an objection that there is no *unique* such description. At the very least, there will be a question how to order the who-knows-how-many conjuncts that would occur in it. The point, however, is not simply that there is great indeterminacy. Rather, the point is why there is such indeterminacy: There is no unique structured proposition that gives the content of a map because there is no such structure in the map; a map lacks the syntactic structure present in a verbal description of what it represents. Hence, if we were to regard the content of the map as a structured proposition, the structure present in the content would be explanatorily idle. Contrast this case with that of belief: The fact that one of my beliefs has a structured content figures in the explanation of how that belief interacts with other beliefs, for example, in inference.

A second objection derives from the fact that cognitive maps can have only some structured propositions as their contents. One cannot, for example, form arbitrary Boolean combinations of maps: There is no map that is the negation of my cognitive map of Boston; there is no map that is the disjunction of my map and my wife's; and so forth. If the content of a cognitive map is a structured proposition, why shouldn't there be maps with such contents? Why can't the negations of the atomic formulae that figure in the content of a map also figure in its content? Why can't these formulae be disjoined? This objection would also apply, of course, to the proposal that we should take the content of a map to be the set of possible worlds (parts of which) it correctly describes. Here again, there are only some sets of worlds that can be the content of a given map. The intersection of any two such sets can presumably always be the content of a map, but their union cannot. Why not? Or again – and ignoring statues and clay for the moment – no map can have a content that represents two objects as being at the very same location. But of course there is a structured proposition – indeed, just a conjunction of atomic formulae of the very sort that can occur in a description of a map – that represents just such a situation. Why can't it be the content of a map?

One may be inclined to brush such questions aside. But their significance rests upon the fact, noted earlier, that there are both relations and distinctions between contents. These relations are important to our account of the role states with such contents play in reasoning. Suppose, for example, that my cognitive map of

Richard G. Heck Jr

Boston proves faulty: experience has been recalcitrant; the map needs updating. To explain how such updating occurs – or to tell a more normative story about how it ought to occur – we must obviously rely upon a conception of what counts as an alternative to my current map. Suppose, for example, that my map had previously located an object o at location l. Now here I am at l, and o is not to be found; instead, u is there. What to do? It is clear enough what to say if we restrict our attention to the construction of a representation: I should remove the "marker" that indicates o from its position on the map and put a "marker" representing u there; I can then either put the o-marker somewhere else on the map or just leave it off. But if we wish to regard this transformation as a *rational* one – and I for one see no reason to suppose it should not be so regarded – then we must also be able to describe it in terms of *content*, that is, to describe it not just as a change in a representation but as a change in what is represented: previously, I had taken my environment to be thus-and-so; now I take it to be so-and-thus.

The relation between the contents of my maps before and after this change cannot naturally be described in terms of possible worlds or structured propositions. In the case of structured propositions, the problem is that moving the o-marker, for example, does not simply change where o is represented as located; o was also located in relation to other objects, and many of those relations – though not necessarily all of them – will have changed as well. It is thus not as simple as swapping one conjunct for another: the sorts of changes involved will be on a much larger scale, and – or so I am suggesting – the nature of those changes can only seem obscure so long as one insists upon describing them as if one were describing a change in belief. Given these facts, it is therefore hard to see why – absent some strong theoretical commitments that dictated this course – one would care to represent the contents of cognitive maps in terms of structured propositions.

Similar remarks apply to the representation in terms of sets of possible worlds: to make any change to one's cognitive map is to swap one set of possible worlds for another, entirely different set. How are we to capture the relationship between the earlier content and the later one? Actually, that is not hard to do: If a given set of possible worlds is fit to be the content of a map, that must be because each of the worlds in the set contains a part that a single map could correctly describe. These parts must be isomorphic to one another as regards certain features of their topography, namely, those represented on the map.[16] So, the content of the earlier map was a set of worlds containing an isomorphic part; the content of the later map is a different set of worlds containing a different isomorphic part; and the relevant parts are the same, except as regards the locations of o and u. But now it is clear that the possible worlds themselves are playing no significant role: The content of a map is wholly determined by the topography of the isomorphic parts of the sets of worlds in question; its content is what we might call a *spatial distribution*. The spatial distribution determines a set of possible worlds, to be sure, but it is the spatial distribution that is most fundamental.

Now, it is a nice question exactly what we should take spatial distributions to be.[17] Very roughly, they are going to be geometrical entities. But their structure may be quite different from the structure of physical space. I am no expert on the relevant psychological literature – I am ignorant of most of it, in fact – but it is consistent with what I know of that literature that the relations represented on cognitive maps should be *local* in the sense that objects are located on such maps only (or at least primarily) relative to nearby objects and not relative to all the objects the map represents. Suppose, just for example, that one can represent on one's cognitive map only spatial relations between objects that are within some fixed distance of one another, say, 10 yards. Perhaps object *o* is represented as being 10 yards west of object *u*, which is represented as being 10 yards north of object *e*; but no relation between *o* and *e* is explicitly represented. The locality of the explicitly represented relationships may lead to a given map's being, unbeknownst to its possessor, the mental equivalent of an Escher drawing, representing no possible spatial configuration, at least within a (nearly) Euclidean space. On the other hand, it may be that cognitive maps impose a Euclidean structure on the space they represent. I do not know. My point is simply that such questions are ones that would need to be answered before we could claim to have an adequate account of the contents of cognitive maps.

3 What Non-conceptual Content Is: Visual Perception

Many of the points just made about cognitive maps have analogs for visual perception. Consider my current visual experience. There will be no unique structured proposition that might give its content, for my visual experience lacks the kind of articulation that is characteristic of structured propositions. Moreover, only some structured propositions, and some sets of worlds, are suited to be contents of visual experience. Neither of these ways of understanding perceptual contents gives us any purchase on why. In this case, of course, there is no need to speak of "updating" my perception in response to experience. But I take it that we do have, for example, expectations about how our experience will change as we move, and an account of what those expectations are, and why they are rational, will again require an understanding of how perceptual contents are related to one another. The contents of visual experience are plausibly also akin to spatial distributions,[18] though the properties represented in visual experience are of course different from those represented on cognitive maps. So the content of visual perception is also non-conceptual.

These sorts of considerations are obviously quite different from those deployed in the richness argument, mentioned earlier, which turns upon the observation that what colors, shapes, and so forth we can experience in visual perception are not limited by the concepts antecedently available to us. That observation, as noted earlier, has no tendency to show that perceptual contents are spatial distributions rather than structured propositions: regarded as an argument for that conclusion – for the conclusion that perceptual states have a different kind of content than do cognitive states – the argument seems a complete non sequitur. Did Evans just blunder because he was insufficiently sensitive to the distinction between the state view and the content view? Perhaps, but there is another way to understand the significance of his observations.

It is, to be sure, clear enough that the simple observation that the contents of visual experience outrun one's antecedent conceptual capacities cannot by itself show that visual perception has non-conceptual content. But Evans was not, I think, simply observing that we do not have enough concepts adequately to characterize our visual experience. I take him, rather, to have been gesturing toward considerations that suggest that visual experience represents the world in a wholly different way. Evans's point had, I believe, more to do with the *specificity* of visual experience than is usually recognized. His point, that is to say, was not that someone who did not have the concept *magenta* could not experience something as magenta: his point did not concern color concepts of that sort. His point, rather, was that we experience objects as having very specific shades of color. It is, for example, never a complete description of someone's experience of an object to say that it appears blue to her: the object will always appear a specific shade of blue, and it is no help to speak of "light blue" or "Carolina blue." Our color concepts group similar shades, but visual experience does not: one's experience is always of a maximally determinate shade, and it is hard to imagine how that fact could be affected by what concepts one possesses.

Something stronger is arguably true. I have so far been ignoring the question whether the content of visual experience is wholly non-conceptual or only partially so. Evans seems to have held the former view: Concepts *never* figure in the contents of visual perception. Peacocke holds the latter view: according to him, there are always non-conceptual elements present in the contents of visual perception, but conceptual elements may also occur.[19] Now, I am not going to try to resolve this issue here, but I do want to insist that, if there are conceptual elements that occur in perceptual experience, they are not color concepts such as *blue*: I see no reason to suppose that, in the strictest sense, anything ever looks *blue* to anyone.[20] Of course, the key phrase is "in the strictest sense." Certainly, in a less strict sense, objects do sometimes look blue. But an object that looks blue, in that sense, always looks, in the strictest sense, to be some very determinate shade of color, a shade one might reasonably take to be a shade of blue, and what I am denying is that there is anything common to my perceptual experience of the clear blue sky and the deep blue sea. To make this point precise, we must appeal to a distinction between what is explicitly represented and what is only implicitly represented. As I said, I should certainly wish to allow that, in some sense, my perception of the sky represents it as blue. It does so implicitly: The sky is *implicitly* represented as blue insofar as it is *explicitly* represented as being a particular shade that is a shade of blue.

I am not going to attempt here to explain the distinction between implicit and explicit representation, and not for lack of space, but a few words about it are in order. Were I to try to explain it, I should try to ground it in the sort of consideration that motivates the distinction between explicit and implicit belief. This distinction, in the form in which I am interested in it, arises in early discussions of the hypothesis that beliefs are computational relations to sentences in a "language of thought" (Fodor, 1975), sentences stored in the "belief box," in the familiar image. Various people objected that each of us has far too many beliefs for this hypothesis to be true: I believe that Tony Blair is less than 10 feet tall, that he is less than 11 feet tall, and so on and so forth. The response is that we must distinguish between explicit belief and implicit belief: Only explicit beliefs are stored in the belief box; implicit beliefs are those that can be inferred from explicit beliefs via a short enough chain of reasonably obvious inferences (or something of the sort). One might object that the notion of implicit belief, so characterized, is far too vague to be of any scientific use, but that is part of the point: The distinction between implicit and explicit belief is central to any computational conception of cognition, and the notion of explicit belief is the important one. Explicit beliefs are the inputs to reason: implicit beliefs are to be found among its outputs, and where ordinary language draws the line between what one can be said to believe and what one cannot is of no fundamental interest.

The distinction between what is explicitly and implicitly represented in perception has a similar significance. Consider (what I hope will be) an uncontroversial example. On the table in front of me, there are some coasters. I cannot tell how many coasters there are just by looking: I have to count them. So, although my current perceptual experience in some sense represents the number of coasters on the table, it is, or so it seems to me, no part of its content that there are six coasters there: that fact is represented at best implicitly; it is not represented explicitly. The distinction between what is explicitly and implicitly represented in perception is thus, like the distinction between explicit and implicit belief, one between the input to computational processes and the output of them. To answer the question whether the concept *blue* figures in the content of perceptual experience, we would thus need to answer such questions as whether, when I am asked what color the sky is and what color the sea is and answer on the basis of how things look, the perceptual input to these mental processes contains a common element corresponding to the concept *blue*. My suggestion that nothing ever looks blue is based upon the suspicion that there is no such common element: rather, what perception itself provides is different in the two cases; the similarity emerges only at some later stage, as a result of what we call conceptualization.

Many of the alleged counterexamples to Evans's view that perceptual content is wholly non-conceptual can be disarmed with sufficiently careful attention to the distinction between explicit and implicit representation. The ones that most impress me concern language and the way one's linguistic capacities can influence the character of one's perceptual experience. Someone who can read Hebrew, for example – "read" it just in the sense that she can recognize the letters and pronounce them – will experience a page of Hebrew text differently from how I would: the various marks on the page are organized into letters in her perception of it, whereas they are not in mine. But does she, strictly speaking, experience א *as* an aleph – or even *as* a letter? That is obviously an empirical question, and I do not know the answer. In some sense, of course, she does experience the mark as an aleph: she experiences it in such a way that the judgment that it is an aleph could reasonably be made by her wholly on the basis of her then current visual experience. But, unless we simply ignore the distinction between implicit and explicit representation, there is nothing in the mere observation that linguistic abilities *influence* perceptual content that shows that linguistic concepts actually *figure in* the contents of perception. More generally, the question whether what concepts one has can influence the content of one's perceptual experience needs to be kept separate from the question what concepts, if any, actually figure in the contents of perception.

One might object that the specificity of visual experience is no less consistent with the claim that the content of visual perception is conceptually structured than its richness is. I doubt, however, that Evans would have held otherwise. Evans, it is important to remember, shared – indeed, he is to some extent responsible for – the view that I developed in Section 1 of what is required if contents of a certain kind are to be regarded as conceptually structured. I expect that Evans saw in the specificity of visual experience reason to believe that such conditions would not be satisfied, though he did not develop this thought in any detail. One possibility is that he suspected that the specificity of experience would give rise to violations of the generality constraint. There are passages in *Varieties of Reference*, for example, that suggest that Evans wanted to insist that, if a concept of some very particular shade can occur in my perceptual experience, it must also be able to occur in my beliefs and other propositional attitudes: If I can perceive a particular thing as having a particular shade, I must also be able to wonder whether some other thing I encountered last week might have been that same shade, and so forth. If that was Evans's worry, however, then McDowell's response is all but unassailable (McDowell, 1996, pp. 56–8): I can indeed wonder whether that other thing was *that* shade. But whatever Evans's view may have been, I suggest that our view now ought to be that the richness argument – or, perhaps better, the specificity argument – does not demonstrate, or even purport to demonstrate, that the content of visual perception is non-conceptual. Rather, the specificity argument directs our attention to differences between how the world is represented in perception and how it is represented in cognition, differences that are relevant to the question what kind of content visual perception has but that do not of themselves decide it.

Still, reflection on these differences suggests that perceptual content might well fail to satisfy the generality constraint, even within the perceptual realm itself. Now, again, this question is an empirical one, and I remind the reader that I know little of the empirical literature, so I am going to restrict myself to suggesting a couple of ways that perceptual content *could* fail to satisfy the generality constraint. But for some purposes, that will be good enough. As mentioned earlier, most, if not all, of the familiar arguments that perceptual content is conceptual are a priori. If, as I am suggesting, the question whether perceptual content is conceptual is an empirical one, there must be something seriously wrong with those arguments.

Let me begin with a wholly invented example, one I do not claim has any application to human perception. It has, however, the advantage that it is easy to understand. In discussing cognitive maps, I mentioned the prospect that the spatial relations explicitly represented on such a map should be limited to local ones. One can imagine that something similar should have been true of depth perception, that is, that relative distance from the subject should be explicitly represented only for objects that are near one another in the visual field. So one object might be represented as closer than another that was but a short angular distance from it, and that object as farther away than another a short angular distance from it. But no such relationship between the first object and the third might be explicitly represented at all. Such relationships might be implicitly represented, of course: If the second object had been represented as closer than the third, then, in virtue of the transitivity of *closer than*, the first object would be implicitly represented as closer than the third, but there is no contradiction in the supposition that it might not be so represented explicitly: that would be something one could, perhaps, figure out, but it would require figuring out. If it could not be represented explicitly, however, then the generality constraint would not be satisfied: It would not follow from the fact that one could perceive that *a* was closer than *b* and that *b* was closer than *c* that one could also perceive that *a* was closer than *c*.

The feature of perceptual experience I now want to discuss is similar, in that it involves this same kind of locality, but it instead concerns the representation of sameness of color. There is a phenomenon known as *color constancy*: A white piece of paper can continue to look the same color even though the lighting changes in such a way that the light it is reflecting is predominantly red. Something similar is true of perceived surfaces: A paint chip, for example, might look to be uniform in color although different parts of it are reflecting light of different kinds, say, because one part is in shade and another part is partially reflecting a nearby object. (So there is a sense in which the surface looks all to be the same color, and a sense in which it does not.) I am now going to assume that it can be represented *explicitly* in one's visual perception of a surface that it is uniform in color and, further, that only a small, connected surface can be explicitly represented as uniform in color – that is, that neither a large surface occupying, say, half of my visual field nor two small surfaces that make no contact can be explicitly represented as being of the same color. Or maybe small gaps between surfaces are permitted but large ones aren't. It doesn't matter. The point is that, if something along these lines were true, the generality constraint would fail: "*x* is the same color as *y*" would be explicitly representable only under certain circumstances, for example, when *x* and *y* were points on a small, connected surface.

These suppositions – that a surface's being uniform in color can be represented perceptually, but only in certain cases – are again empirical ones, and I am not qualified to make pronouncements concerning them. But they do have a basis in visual phenomenology. If I look now at the wall opposite me, there are certainly no obvious discontinuities in its color. And small regions of the wall do seem to be represented as uniform in color: when I look at a small part of the wall, my eyes themselves seem to be telling me that it's all one color. But the wall as a whole does not seem to be represented as uniform in color nor, for that matter, as not uniform in color: my eyes themselves seem silent on the question. Of course, if I am curious whether the wall as a whole is uniform in color, I can look at it carefully and try to decide. Maybe the right thing to decide, given the perceptual evidence, would be that the wall was uniform in color: in that sense, a large surface can look uniform in color. But it does not follow that such large-scale uniformities even can be explicitly represented in perception.

There is a closely related feature of perception that, to my mind, marks an even more significant difference between it and cognition. I believe both that my laptop is gray and that my car is gray. There is thus something I believe about both my laptop and my car, and that fact is transparent to introspection: it's something I can find out by just examining my beliefs. That I am deploying the concept *gray* when I think that my laptop is gray is something of which I am, or can be, consciously aware, and I can be aware that I am deploying that same concept when I think that my car is gray. Nothing of the sort seems to be true of perception. Imagine a 10×10 array of color patches of various shades of blue. Imagine looking at the patch in the upper left corner and then at the one at the lower right. Suppose that the two patches are in fact the same color and that they are actually represented in one's experience as being of the same color. We may even suppose that the lighting has been carefully controlled, so that the two patches reflect the same spectrum. Even under these ideal conditions, one need not be able to say with any confidence whether the two patches are the same color *nor even whether they look to be.* The content of perceptual experience is thus not "transparent to introspection" in the way the content of belief is. At least to the subject, then, it does not seem as if a single "concept" of a shade is being deployed in the characterization of both patches.[21]

4 Syntax and Semantics

I have argued for two claims. The first is that the question what kind of content we should take perceptual experiences to have should be answered by investigating structural features of the class of perceptual contents. The contents of perception will be conceptual – that is, will be structured – only if the generality constraint, for example, is satisfied. The second claim is then that there are indeed structural differences between perception and cognition that should lead us to reject the claim that perceptual content is conceptual. One might respond, however, that these differences – the failure of the generality constraint, the fact that only certain contents can be the contents of perceptions, and so forth – should be explained not in terms of facts about perceptual *contents* but in terms of facts about perceptual *representations.*[22] That is, suppose that, as Fodor suggests, the mental representations underlying perceptual experience are iconic, whereas those underlying propositional attitudes are discursive, and consider, for example, the fact that cognitive states satisfy the generality constraint. To say that the representations underlying these states are discursive is, roughly, to say that they are sentence-like, that is, that there is a language of thought (Fodor, 1975). So the belief that *a* is *F* comprises a representation of the form $\Phi(\alpha)$, and the belief that *b* is *G* comprises one of the form $\Gamma(\beta)$.[23] It is a fact about these representations that their parts are, normally, freely recombinable, so, normally, someone who can form the two representations $\Phi(\alpha)$ and $\Gamma(\beta)$ will also be able to form the representations $\Phi(\beta)$ and $\Gamma(\alpha)$ and so to think that *b* is *F* and that *a* is *G*. Since perceptual representations do not have this kind of syntactic structure, the corresponding story cannot be told about them, and so it is no surprise that they do not satisfy the generality constraint. The fact that cognitive states satisfy the generality constraint, and perceptual states do not, thus seems to be a consequence not of the kind of *contents* such states have but of facts about cognitive architecture: At no point in the preceding does it seem to matter whether the contents of these states are Fregean thoughts, Russellian propositions, or sets of possible worlds.

There is, I think, something importantly right about this line of thought. In particular, it is, I think, extremely plausible that the sorts of structural facts that determine what kind of content states of a given kind have will supervene on the nature of the representations that underlie such states. Martin Davies has argued, for example, that, if we wish to regard the contents of beliefs as structured for the sorts of reasons sketched above, then we are committed – not on logical grounds, but on broadly empirical grounds – to the claim that the *state* of believing that *a* is *F* is similarly structured, that it too has parts that correspond to one's thinking of the object *a* and to one's thinking of a thing that it is *F* (Davies, 1992, 1998). If it is to be a *law* that the contents of belief are closed under certain sorts of operations – that is, if the generality constraint is to hold in the strong form – and if we wish to explain this law in terms of the structured nature of the contents of these states, then the common elements we claim to find in the contents of different beliefs, the concepts of which they are composed, must have explanatory work to do: The explanation of the fact that I can think both the content that my laptop is gray and the content that my car is gray must turn upon my possessing the concept *gray*. Similarly, the fact that this concept does figure in the contents of both these beliefs should facilitate explanations of why they have similar causal powers: they interact in similar ways, for example, with the desire to acquire gray things. The sort of explanation envisaged here is, of course, causal, so the belief that my laptop is gray must have some causally relevant feature in common with the belief that my car is gray. The existence of this common structural feature is then what explains their common causal powers. And what Davies then observes is essentially just that, given a suitably abstract conception of syntactic structure, the structure we have uncovered in these states can easily be seen to be *syntactic* structure. Thus, the thesis that the contents of belief are conceptual entails (a weak form of) the language of thought hypothesis.

A similar argument could be developed concerning cognitive maps and perceptual content. These states have different sorts of structural features, both from one another and from beliefs. But here too one would suppose that the relations between different such states is susceptible of causal explanation. I noted earlier, for example, that, when a cognitive map is updated in response to recalcitrant experience, the content of the map is, by and large, left unchanged. How one represents the topography of one's environment before such an update has much in common with how one represents it after the update – most objects are still located where they were – and so one acts in similar ways before and after the update, too. The natural explanation of this fact is that the representations that are involved here are structured much like real maps. Updating one's map may involve a marker's being moved from one place on the map to another, so that the map itself is largely unchanged by the update. And so generally: One would expect that the sorts of structural features that determine what kind of content a given sort of state has will supervene on the structure of the underlying representations.

Should we, then, explain the behavioral similarities we notice before and after the update simply in terms of the similarity between the representations before and after the update? Such a move may seem tempting at first, but it should not be tempting for long: We can explain the "behavioral similarities" in terms of the similarity in the representations only if we can explain the behavior itself in terms of facts about the representations. For example, suppose I look for my keys in the kitchen both before and after a particular updating of my cognitive map. If this similarity is to be explained *purely* in terms of facts about the maps – that is, the representations – that can only be because the fact that I look for my keys in the kitchen can itself be explained purely in terms of facts about my representations. This kind of view has been held (Stich, 1983), but few have found it attractive. Most of us suppose instead that my behavior is to be explained not just in terms of facts about representations but in terms of facts about what those representations represent, that is, in terms of facts about their contents. That the representations are similar in certain respects implies that the contents are similar in related respects because the contents of such representations depends in a regular way upon how they are composed of smaller representational parts. That is to say: The similarities in my behavior before and after the update are to be explained in terms of the similarities between my representations, before and after the update, and the fact that their common parts contribute in the same way, before and after the update, to determining the contents of the representations of which they are parts.

The explanation considered above, of why cognitive states satisfy the generality constraint, is incomplete for the same sort of reason. That someone capable of forming the representations $\Phi(\alpha)$ and $\Gamma(\beta)$ can also form the representations $\Phi(\beta)$ and $\Gamma(\alpha)$ is irrelevant unless the presence of the common feature α in $\Phi(\alpha)$ and $\Gamma(\alpha)$ signals some relevant similarity in the contents of these representations: If, that is to say, it is to follow that this person can think that b is F and that a is G, the representations $\Phi(\beta)$ and $\Gamma(\alpha)$ need to have the contents that b is F and that a is G. And to secure that conclusion, we need to regard the parts of these representations as having content in their own right and to regard the parts as contributing their contents to the content of the whole: we need, that is, to regard such representations as compositional. The sorts of structural differences I have suggested distinguish the contents of cognitive states from those of perceptual or topographical ones thus cannot be explained entirely in terms of differences between the representations such states comprise. That is not to say that such syntactic similarities are irrelevant: they are not. But the syntactic similarities are relevant only because of how the syntax is related to the semantics.

To put the point differently: The set of possible worlds with respect to which a given mental state is true and the structure of the representation it comprises do not jointly determine the causal powers of that state.[24] Rather, its causal powers depend upon the semantic properties of the parts of that representation, as well. That does not, of course, imply that one cannot, if one absolutely wishes to insist upon doing so, use the expression "the content of a mental state" to denote the set of possible worlds with respect to which a given state is true. What it implies is that, if one does so use this expression, then one will have to concede that mental states have explanatorily relevant semantic properties that are not determined by their "contents," and that seems to me to be sufficient reason not to use the expression that way. What I am proposing is that we should instead regard the content of a mental state S as encoding not just *what* S represents but also *how*, that is, as encoding S's compositional structure. Different sorts of mental states will then have different kinds of content if the contents of the representations underlying such states are composed in different ways.

And so we can now see quite precisely how Fodor's reflections bear upon the question whether perceptual states have conceptual or non-conceptual content. For what I have argued is that what kind of content states of a given sort have will be determined by how the representations underlying such states compose. And what Fodor has argued is that empirical psychology gives us excellent reason to believe that, while the sorts of representations underlying cognitive states and perceptual states are both compositional, they are structured very differently and so compose very differently, as well. If so, then empirical psychology gives us excellent reason to believe, as well, that cognitive states and perceptual states have different kinds of content.

But if so, then, as I said earlier, we do have a problem we would not have had if perceptual content were conceptual. Part of the problem here is simply to understand how non-conceptual representations are "translated" into conceptual representations. That, of course, is an empirical question, and one in which psychologists have had some interest.[25] But it has a philosophical aspect, too, since – if we wish to regard certain of our beliefs as justified by our perceptual experience – we need also to ask what relationship has to obtain between a state with non-conceptual content and a state with conceptual content if the former is to justify the latter. I do not myself see why this question should not have a sensible answer. But if we are to appreciate what Evans meant when he claimed that perceptual content was non-conceptual, then it is important to see that, if he was right, this question needs asking.

Acknowledgments

Portions of this paper were read at a symposium held at the 2005 meeting of the Pacific Division of the American Philosophical Association. Jerry Fodor also read portions of his contribution to this volume, and Alex Byrne commented. Thanks to Alex for his insightful remarks, which made the paper much better, and to members of the audience for their similarly helpful questions and comments.

Thanks are also due to Alex, as well as to Jake Beck, Michael Rescorla, and Susanna Siegel for comments on drafts of this paper. My views on these topics were substantially shaped by conversations with Jake and Michael, whose work in this area is much better than mine.

Notes

1 Fodor expresses doubt about this view, suggesting that it confuses justifying a claim with justifying one's making the claim, a contrast not unlike that McDowell draws between justification and exculpation. For my part, I think Fodor's criticism itself confuses my believing that it seems to me as if p with its seeming to me as if p. That I *believe* that it seems to me as if p cannot be my reason for the belief that p. But that does not show that its *seeming* to me as if p is not my reason. See Heck (2000, pp. 518–19).

2 Not everyone who has been interested in non-conceptual content has had such motivations. But I am concerned here with one tradition, namely, that originating with Evans, and his motivations are epistemological.

3 So the notion of consciousness that is in play here is *access* consciousness. See Block (1995) for this notion.

4 Or her memory of it (Martin, 1993).

5 Henceforth, I will omit this qualification.

6 I am now somewhat unhappy with how I drew that distinction, and so I shall redraw it here. Do not attempt to reconcile the two versions.

7 This observation has been made by several people. One source is Byrne (2004).

8 Ordinal numbers are numbers such as first, second, and third. There are so many ordinals that (at least in standard set-theories), one cannot consistently suppose they form a set.

9   Something like this is the central insight behind George Boole's revolutionary work on sentential logic (Boole, 1854).

10   The generality constraint is usually stated so as to require unrestricted recombinability. Recent work by Jacob Beck suggests, however, that this condition may be too strong. But I shall not pursue this point here, as I do not believe it affects the discussion to follow.

11   Assuming, of course, that the reals can be well-ordered, which they can be if the Axiom of Choice is true.

12   It is unclear to me whether it is then any stronger than the claim that perceptual content is representational, a claim that is not at issue between Evans and McDowell.

13   And just to be clear: I am not attributing *this* claim to Byrne.

14   The significance of this case was made clear to me by Michael Rescorla, who discusses it in some detail in unpublished work.

15   Or should it be *Fa*, where *F* is a single predicate completely determining the content of the map *a*?

16   They need not be wholly isomorphic, because there may be different objects in different cases that are not represented on the map.

17   If modal realism were true, there might be ontological benefits to regarding spatial distributions as sets of worlds. But modal realism is not true.

18   See Peacocke (1992) for a view with which I'm sympathetic.

19   See Peacocke (1983 and 1992).

20   Austin would have loved that claim. Now, of course, I'll take it back.

21   I suspect this observation bears upon the intransitivity of indiscriminability but have yet to figure out how.

22   Thanks to Alex Byrne for pressing this question in a way that let me finally see how I should answer it.

23   Of course, we are simplifying here by ignoring tense and the like, but not in any way that affects the substance of the discussion.

24   Proof: the belief that water is H_2O and the belief that salt is $NaCl$ are true in the same worlds, and they are of the same structure, but their causal powers are different.

25   One whose importance was first made clear to me by Jerome Kagan.

References

Block, N. (1995). On a confusion about a function of consciousness. *Behavioral and Brain Sciences*, 2, 227–87.

Boole, G. (1854). *The Laws of Thought*. New York: Dover.

Byrne, A. (2004). Perception and conceptual content. In E. Sosa and M. Steup (eds.), *Contemporary Debates in Epistemology*. Oxford: Blackwell.

Davies, M. (1998). Aunty's own argument for the language of thought. In J. Ezquerro and J. M. Larrazabal (eds.), *Cognition, Semantics, and Philosophy*. Boston: Kluwer Academic.

— (1997). Language thought, and the language of thought (Aunty's own argument revisited). In P. Carruthers and J. Boucher (eds.), *Language and Thought*. Cambridge: Cambridge University Press.

Evans, G. (1982). *The Varieties of Reference*. Oxford: Clarendon.

Fodor, J. (1975). *The Language of Thought*. Cambridge, MA: Harvard University Press.

Heck, R. (2000). Non-conceptual content and the "space of reasons." *Philosophical Review*, 109, 483–523.

Martin, M. (1993). The rational role of experience. *Proceedings of the Aristotelian Society*, 93, 71–88.

McDowell, J. (1996). *Mind and World*. Cambridge, MA: Harvard University Press.

Peacocke, C. (1983). *Sense and Content: Experience, Thought, and Their Relations*. Oxford: Clarendon.

— (1992). *A Study of Concepts*. Cambridge, MA: MIT Press.

Stich, S. (1983). *From Folk Psychology to Cognitive Science: The Case Against Belief*. Cambridge, MA: MIT Press.

PART II
PHYSICALISM

IS NON-REDUCTIVE MATERIALISM VIABLE?

Everybody Has Got It: A Defense of Non-Reductive Materialism

Louise Antony

Miss Adelaide: What is? Oh, the book. Yeah. The doctor gave it to me. He said it might help me get rid of my cold.
Nathan Detroit: With a book?
Miss Adelaide: He thinks that my cold might possibly be caused by psychology.
Nathan Detroit: How does he know you got psychology?
Miss Adelaide: Nathan! Everybody has got it.

J. L. Mankiewicz, 1955, Guys and Dolls, screenplay

It is a really striking fact about human beings that we think. Just this morning, for example, I deliberated about what to have for breakfast, wondered if I should let my husband sleep in, noticed the dogs were almost out of food, figured out where my favorite mug was, vowed to write a letter to the editor, imagined how nice a sweater I could make out of that lovely Australian wool, remembered I had to prepare for my seminar today, and wished I didn't have to prepare for my seminar today. That was all before 9 a.m.

Sometimes thinking is more spectacular. Human beings have done amazing things through thinking. They have written epic poetry, discovered laws of nature, navigated seas, composed symphonies, designed buildings, invented machines, and cured disease. Many (if not all) of these accomplishments involved not only thinking, but thinking about thinking, and thinking about what other people were thinking. Also involved was talking, which (at least when some people do it) seems to involve thinking, and, of course, understanding when other people were talking. The invention of a way of capturing talking in a less ephemeral form – writing – was a spectacular use of thinking, and led to even more opportunities for thinking, and for doing all the other things one can do through thinking.

We think that other people think. Thinking this works out really well. By attributing thoughts to other people, we are able to predict and explain their behavior in myriad and immensely useful ways. When I drive my car, for example, I think that the other people driving their cars know much the same things I do about the rules of the road and the basic properties of automobiles. I also think that they, like me, wish to reach their destinations safely. Thinking all this, I drive sanguinely through an intersection marked by a green light. On the car ahead of me to my left, a signal light starts flashing; I take this to mean that the driver intends to pull into my lane ahead of me, and I decelerate slightly to accommodate her.

Of course, sometimes I am wrong about what I think others are thinking. I assume the person to my left knows that I have the right of way at the four-way stop, but when he begins to pull into the intersection out of turn, I revise my view, and come to believe that he believes that he has the right of way instead of me. His believing this would explain his behavior. I honk at him, trusting that he will understand from my honking that I think he is a jerk. He makes a small, conventional gesture with his right hand that I understand to mean that he wishes me to know that the feeling is mutual. And so it goes.

I hope you're finding this a bit boring. What I've been trying to do is hammer home the banality of the claim that human beings possess psychologies and that our psychologies are centrally involved in virtually everything we do, from our most sublime accomplishments to our most ridiculous gaffes. There is, however, no banality so banal that no philosopher will deny it, and many, many philosophers have denied that we have psychologies. Indeed, a cursory survey of the past century's work in the "philosophy of mind" might leave the impression that this is a discipline dedicated to the eradication of its own subject matter. There are two ways to deny that we have psychologies: one can either say "there are no minds," or one can say "there are no minds *as such.*" The first group of naysayers are called "eliminativists," and the second are called "reductionists." It can be a little difficult to tell the difference.

Why would anyone deny the existence of thinking? That is indeed the question. What mind-deniers will tell you is that, one way or another, belief in mental things is incompatible with *materialism*. Materialism, for our purposes, is the doctrine that Descartes was wrong. Descartes, notoriously, argued that the mind, the *res cogitans*, the thing that thinks, was different in its essential nature from the body, and could even exist separately from it. Materialists deny all *that*. Now on the face of it, one should be able to reject a particular *account* of the mind – Descartes's – without having to give up the mind itself. I reject, after all, the view that the moon is made of green cheese, but I'm still pretty confident it's up there. Mind-deniers, however, think the distinction I have in mind cannot be made in this case – that any notion of the mental is bound, one way or another, to implicate us in some problematic form of dualism.

Eliminativists think that belief in mentality is incompatible with a robustly naturalistic view of the human organism. Eliminativists are unimpressed with either the ubiquity or the utility of psychological ascription. According to them, the informal psychologizing bruited above bespeaks what is essentially a pre-scientific "folk" theory, akin to vitalistic theories of life and supernatural theories of disease. Just as biology has obviated entelechies and witches, the maturing sciences of the brain will soon relieve us of the need for beliefs and desires, hopes or fears, pleasures or pains (Churchland, 1981, and EVOLVING FORTUNES OF ELIMINATIVE MATERIALISM). There is no hope, they'll argue, of folk psychology's simply being subsumed by a more precise science, as Newtonian mechanics was subsumed by relativistic physics, because the taxonomy implicit in the folk theory is incommensurable with the taxonomies of the serious, well-established sciences (Stitch, 1983; Bickle, 2003). It may even be incoherent (Quine, 1960).[1]

Reductionists are a bit more charitable than eliminativists are toward the posits of common-sense psychology. Reductionists allow that psychological properties, states, processes, and entities exist, but think that these are all reducible to properties, states, processes, or entities of some other type. They deny, in other words, that there are distinctively psychological phenomena and regularities constituting a proprietary domain for a distinctive science of psychology: psychology can be, for these deniers, nothing more than a branch of human (or animal) biology.

The issues at stake here are more arcane than those that divide the non-reductive materialist from the eliminativist. The dispute here centers on a problem that is as old as Cartesian dualism – the problem of mental causation. For Descartes, as for contemporary dualists, the problem was explaining how two substantially different kinds of substance could interact causally. For contemporary materialists, the problem concerns the causal efficacy of mental *properties*. We begin with a principle generally accepted by materialists, *the causal closure of the physical*; it states that all physical events (that have causes at) all have nomologically sufficient physical causes. Mental events, we assume, sometimes cause physical events. If causal closure is true, then those mentally caused physical events must also have physical causes. But in that case, the putative mental causes look to be otiose. If they are not to be shaved off by Occam's razor, it looks as though they must be identified with the physical events that are doing the actual causal work. But if mental events just *are* physical events, then there are no specifically psychological properties at work, and no need for – indeed, no possibility of – a specifically psychological taxonomy or science (Kim, 1998).

Both eliminativists and reductionists, therefore, deny the possibility of a non-reductive materialist theory of mind, each for their different reasons: eliminativists say it's because there can be no theory of mind, period, and reductionists say it's because a theory of mind must really be a theory of (some non-mental) something else. Eliminativists deny the doctrine of *psychological realism*; reductionists, the doctrine of *the autonomy of psychology*. I'm here to tell you that they are wrong. Both of these doctrines are correct; together they constitute the view of mind called *non-reductive materialism*. This is the view that says that (a) there are mental phenomena; (b) they are material in nature; and (c), notwithstanding (b), they form an autonomous domain.

My defense of this view will proceed as follows: first I'll review the arguments in favor of psychological realism, and defend it against the eliminativist challenge. In the course of doing this, I'll take a look back at the failure of the leading eliminativist program of the twentieth century, behaviorism. Reviewing the reasons for this failure will reinforce my prima facie case for the ineliminability of the psychological, but will also help address the reductionist, by illuminating the reasons why, from a scientific standpoint, psychological phenomena must be treated *as* psychological, and hence, as autonomous. Finally, I'll take up the "new" problem of mental causation, which, I'll argue, is an artifact of residual Cartesian thinking.

But first, two preliminary notes.

The debate about non-reductive materialism is, I acknowledged, esoteric – it is an in-house dispute among committed materialists. But I must warn the reader that there is an even more outré dispute on the horizon. Non-reductive materialists do not all agree with each other about exactly what it means to call the mind material. Some (the philosophers I think of as "Neumanians")[2] are willing to stop arguing once it has been shown that psychology is ineliminable, that the descriptions, predictions, and explanations of folk psychology must be taken at face value (Davidson, 1970; Baker, 1995; Burge, 1993). But others of us (and I am in this camp) think that a full defense of psychology requires more – an account of *how* psychology, with all its distinctive features, could be embodied in material beings. Such an account, we contend, requires providing a *reductive explanation* of psychological phenomena. Thus, I intend to defend a version of non-reductive materialism that insists on ontological autonomy for the entities and properties of psychology, while demanding at the same time an *account* of psychological phenomena in terms of non-psychological phenomena.

In what follows, I'll neglect the views of the Neumanians. I do so for two reasons: first, I think that an adequate answer to the eliminativist requires showing how mentality can be instantiated in a physical system, and how the posits of folk psychology can be integrated into a scientific account of the behavior of the human organism. The Neumanians insist that no such "vindication" is needed – that our ordinary experience suffices to establish the reliability of our folk psychological generalizations and explanations. This, to my mind, evinces a confusion between the *epistemic* ground of our acceptance of folk psychology, and the *ontological* constitution of the psychological realm. As I'll argue myself, the evidence for the truth of our psychological ascriptions is overwhelming: that doesn't obviate the scientific impulse that asks what it is about the world that *makes* them true. In any case, if a reductive explanatory account can be provided, as I think it can, then I can see no cogent argument against providing it.

That, however, brings me to my second reason for setting aside Neumanian non-reductive materialism. Neumanians, deep down, don't believe that it is *possible* to give a reductive explanatory account of the truths of psychology. And the reasons they offer come awfully close to the arguments offered by eliminativists against the possibility of a successor science to folk psychology. Neumanians, like many eliminativists, think that the taxonomy implicit in everyday psychologizing is bound to cross-classify with those of biology, mainly because of the intentionality of psychological types. Much of the inspiration for this line of thought comes from Donald Davidson, who argued that mentalistic ascriptions were "governed" by different "constitutive principles" than were claims about the physical world. In particular, Davidson thought that psychological ascriptions had to conform to *normative* demands that were alien to the physical realm. This disparate set of commitments meant, in his view, that there could be no *lawful* connection between the mental and the physical. In my view, Davidson was trying to ward off a certain possibility: "competition" between rational and non-rational evidence about the content of a mental state. For suppose that we had a well-confirmed theory that said that a person's being in brain state 67 is sufficient for that individual's thinking that Helena is the capital of Montana. Then it might happen that that person could be in brain state 67 without

Louise Antony

satisfying the rational conditions we ordinarily require in order to make such an ascription. But to allow even the possibility of competition of this sort seemed to Davidson to jeopardize our self-conception. Hence, he wrote, "nomological slack between the mental and the physical is essential as long as we conceive of man [sic] as a rational animal" (Davidson, 1980, p. 223).

I think some similar desire to insulate folk psychological practice from certain kinds of empirical risk lies behind Neumanians' insistence that psychology have, as it were, autonomy with a vengeance. I have offered an extended critique of this line of thought in Davidson, and I won't rehearse it here (Antony, 1989, 1995). Suffice to say that we know, thanks to Turing, that it is possible for a physical device to reliably track rational relations. There is no reason, therefore, to think that predictions made from what Dennett (calls "the intentional stance," predictions that exploit rational relations among the presumed contents of mental states, will fail to cohere with predictions made from a lower-level "physical stance" (Dennett, 1971).[3] In any case, we needn't *modus tollens* when we can just as well *modus ponens*. The Neumanians are worried that if we accede to the demand for a reductive explanation of folk psychology, then the failure of such an explanation will jeopardize folk psychology, and they're might-ily skeptical that there'll be a reductive explanation. But in my camp, we reason the other way around: given the abundant evidence for folk psychology, there *must* be a reductive explanation forthcoming.[4]

That's the first preliminary note; the second concerns *qualia*. Qualia are the quali-tative aspects of certain, mainly sensory, mental states – the "what it's like" to smell a rose, taste a lemon, touch velvet, and so forth. There has been a resurgence of interest in states such as these, with some philosophers arguing that they represent an irremovable obstacle to a comprehensive materialism. Few of these philosophers are forthright substance dualists (Swinburne, 1997); most are "property dualists," arguing that the qualitative properties of such states fail to supervene metaphysically on the physical states with which they are lawfully correlated (Jackson, 1982; Chalm-ers, 1996; Nida-Rümelin, 2004). Others argue only that the apparent inexplicability of qualia within materialist constraints presents us with a serious epistemological challenge – how *could* materialism be true if there are qualia (Levine, 2001)? Other materialists, however, are persuaded that materialism can accommodate qualia, and advocate one or another of the following three strategies. One, eliminativism: explain the data about qualia without appealing to qualia themselves (Dennett, 1988; Rey, 1993). Two, functionalism: treat qualitative states as higher-order functional states, in one of the ways propositional attitudes are standardly treated in NRM[5] (Shoemaker, 1975; Lycan, 1987 and 1996; Loar, 1990; Levin, 1991; Dretske, 1995; Tye, 1995; Papineau, 2002; Jackson, 2006). Three, reductionism: identify qualitative states with their neurophysiological correlates (Hill, 1991).

This is not a debate that I can enter into here – not that I want to, anyway. I bring it up only to point out that any one of these materialist options *regarding qualia*, including eliminativism and reductionism, is available to the non-reductive material-ist. NRM is the position that at least *some* psychological states, events, or entities are extant and autonomous, not that *all* such states (or alleged states) are. A successful argument for eliminativism or reductionism about qualia, therefore, does not in itself touch non-reductive materialism about propositional attitude states. For that reason,

I'll be focusing in what follows on states of the second kind, and leave the partisans in the qualia debate to work it out among themselves. The dualists, as always, will be completely ignored.

I turn, then, to the arguments for psychological realism. As I've already indicated, it is folk psychology, that loose system of constructs and platitudes by which we explain and predict the behavior of our con-specifics (as well as many of our *non*-specifics), that provides the strongest prima facie case for psychological realism. So let me be a little more systematic, and draw up the kind of thing Georges Rey has called an "explanatory budget" (Rey, 1991) – a list of mundane features of our (ostensible) mental life that demand explanation, one way or another.

1 *Reasoning and deliberation*: Reflecting on what we want, together with the things we believe, we conceive of and determine on a course of action, which, frequently enough, we pursue. Also, reflecting on things we believe, we often come to believe new things. In both these cases, we seem able to exploit rational relations among propositions that express the states of affairs we want or believe to obtain.

2 *Intentional inexistence*: Wanting something, we imagine the thing that would satisfy us – we have the capacity to conceive of things that do not, or do not yet exist. Sometimes we imagine things just for the fun of it. Sometimes we take other people's imaginings seriously and come to believe in, and possibly even worship, things that don't exist.

3 *Opacity*: The particular actions we undertake appear to be a function of the way we *take* the world to be, rather than just the way the world *is*. When deliberate action is involved, the world's features affect what I do only insofar as I represent those features to myself.[6] The movie may actually begin at 7:25, but the time I leave the house will be determined (alas!) by my belief that it starts at 7:45.

4 *Predictive power*: knowing what people believe and want, we frequently can predict what they are going to do. Understanding what people say gives us a leg up, too, since people often tell us what they are going to do before they do it. "I'll be the one wearing the red carnation." Relying on attributions of mental states, we can often predict things we could never possibly have predicted otherwise. I construct a trivial multiple choice test and administer it to an auditorium full of undergraduates. On the assumption that they know the correct answers to the question, and want to do well on the test, I correctly predict the pattern of graphite marks that will appear on (almost all) of the optical-scan sheets I collect.[7]

Now suppose we simply take all these observations at face value, and ask, openly and naively, what could account for them? I suggest that the following picture emerges quite naturally. The creatures who exemplify these characteristics possess a capacity to generate, store, and manipulate *representations* – states that can carry information about the way the world is, but that can also simply express a way that the world might be. These states, in addition to these representational, or semantic, properties, have *causal* properties – they are affected by things that happen to the creature, and they cause the creature to act in its turn. The causal powers are somehow coordinated, in a law-like way, with the semantic properties.

148 | **Louise Antony**

A good naturalist would make this picture the starting point of scientific investigation – why not? The data are manifest; the picture offers an explanation. The first question to ask would be how to understand the notion of "representation" – what kinds of physical states and mechanisms could implement the information processing posited in the naive picture? Turing, of course, provided an answer, by demonstrating how, in principle, a completely physical and fully automatic representation-processing machine could be built. This would be a machine with structured internal elements that could be construed as symbols and internal states defined partly in relation to those symbols, built in such a way that the principles governing the causal interactions among the states (in conjunction with "inputs" and "outputs") mirror rational relations among the representational contents encoded in the symbols. It is important to the adequacy of Turing's model as a model of mind that the "mirroring" be quite strong, and it is – the physical features of the representational elements to which the machine's causal laws are sensitive are precisely the features that serve to encode the elements of the representational contents that are semantically relevant. The generality of the mirroring – the ability of the mechanism to track all the semantic relations that exist among the contents of the symbols – is due to the compositionality of the symbol system as a whole.

The application of Turing's theory of automatic computation to psychology yields a satisfying precisification of the naive conception of mind: Thinking is fundamentally a matter of the manipulation of symbols – physical items with representational properties. The logically relevant aspects of the representational properties of the symbols are encoded in their syntactic forms, and the compositional structure of the symbol system mirrors the semantic and logical relations in which the representational contents of the symbols participate. Mental states are functional relations to mental symbols, and mental processes are computational processes defined over the mental symbols. The hypothesis that minds are like this is the hypothesis that minds have a "classical" architecture. In the 1970s this hypothesis was first articulated and defended, as the "language of thought" theory, by Jerry Fodor, perhaps the world's foremost champion of intentional realism,[8] but it has received substantial development since then, notably by cognitive scientist Zenon Pylyshyn (Pylyshyn, 1986).

The LOTT explains the central phenomena. The hypothesis that mental representations are syntactically structured explains how psychological processes can respect rational relations during deliberation. The hypothesis that agents' behavior is mediated by representations explains both intentional inexistence and opacity phenomena. And the hypothesis that representations are realized in physical structures whose forms strongly mirror syntactic structure explains how representations can have causal powers that track rational relations. Finally, the entire picture explains the projectibility of mentalistic discourse: it explains how beliefs, desires, and other mental states implicated in perception and action can constitute natural kinds, capable of grounding prediction and explanation.

Not only does computationalism provide a satisfying account of folk psychological data, it has proved immensely fertile when extended beyond the realm of conscious and deliberate thought. Beginning with Chomsky's pioneering approach to language acquisition, and continuing with David Marr's theory of visual processing (Marr, 1982), the computationalist model has offered promising explanations of largely unconscious cognitive feats performed by human beings on a daily basis, such as face recognition. The idea that an innate "theory of mind" underlies our ability to quickly interpret the facial expressions of our con-specifics, and to give intentionalistic construals to characteristically human patterns of behavior, has gained wide acceptance among psychologists: there is serious evidence that absence of such a "psychology module" might be the central deficit in autism. Computationalism has also been extended to the cognitive achievements of infrahuman animals, such as birds' acquisition of their species' songs and insects' spatial navigation, by ethologists such as Peter Marler (1984) and C. R. Gallistel (1990) to account for animal cognition.

So here is the situation: we have available to us an intuitively appealing model of mind, one that explains the central phenomena of mentality and that has generated new and fruitful programs of research within the fields of human psychology and ethology. It is striking, then, that there is so much resistance to this model within philosophy. But what is more striking than the resistance itself is the fact that critics of this picture *have no alternative to offer*. As Georges Rey has pointed out, new paradigms are supposed to recommend themselves by addressing anomalies the old theory cannot explain, but also by "handl[ing] the old one's successes" (Rey, 1991, p. 1).

It is quite true that there are some outstanding problems associated with the computationalist account of mind, the largest of which concerns the notion of "representation." I said that Turing showed that there could be a mechanical device with states that could be *construed* as representations, and I also said that representational properties had to be *encoded* by the posited mental symbols. In the case of artificial minds – computers – we can make sense of all this because *we* create the encodings, and *we* do the construing. But the representational powers of the mind cannot arise in the same way. Partisans of the LOTT must therefore confront the problem of how to *naturalize intentionality*: they must eventually explain how non-intentional processes and relations can give rise to representational relations; how, without the prior activity of minds, some bit of physical reality can come to be "about" something else.

Now the difficulty of this problem may, on its own, frighten some philosophers into mind-denial – surely, they may reason, there's some way to account for human behavior without having to get embroiled in all *that*. But there really isn't. There has been only one serious attempt to develop a non-cognitivist psychology – that is, a psychology that did not posit representational states – and it failed spectacularly. The reasons for that failure are highly instructive. It behooves us, therefore, to remind ourselves why behaviorism didn't work.

Behaviorism was the view that the behavior of all organisms, including human beings, can be predicted and explained without any appeal to independent inner variables (Skinner, 1938, 1957). Behavior was held to be a function of two factors: one, the current stimulus situation of the organism, and two, the organism's past history of environmental interactions. It is not that behaviorists thought that none of the organism's endogenous states were causally relevant to the production of the organism's current behavior. Obviously the organism's history of reinforcement had to leave some kind of mark on the organism in order to affect behavior later on. Moreover, there needed to be a certain number of innate behavioral propensities – there had to be unconditioned reinforcers, and innate "similarity spaces" for example – in order for even classical conditioning to get off the ground. (It is lack of endogenous states of the right kind that explains, in a sense, why houseplants cannot be trained. Cats, of course, are another story.) But these endogenous factors, it was held, could be safely ignored, because the relevant functional relationships were not affected by the nature of the intervening states of the organism. To put the idea somewhat perversely, we could say that behaviorists thought that the internal states and goings-on that (obviously) mediated the connection between stimulus and behavioral response didn't deserve to be called "mental" – they were neurophysiological substrates, not independent psychological variables. But of course, these endogenous states were the best candidates there were for mental states – so if *they* weren't mental, there might as well be no mental states at all!

The case against behaviorism had both conceptual and empirical dimensions. The philosophical version of behaviorism, developed and championed mainly by Gilbert Ryle (1949) was logical behaviorism, the thesis that "mental" states were nothing but patterns of behavior, and, correlatively, that mentalistic expressions could be analyzed in terms of, and hence eliminated in favor of, talk of dispositions to behave. The particularly fine-grained mentalistic ascriptions made to and by human beings could be accounted for, Ryle argued, by the particularly rich behavioral repertoire afforded to us by the capacity to speak. Thus, the "belief" that Helena is the capital of Montana is largely constituted, according to the logical behaviorist, by the disposition to make and to respond to verbal behavior involving sounds such as "What is the capital of Montana?" and "Helena." What *exactly* accounted for this complex dispositional structure – i.e., language – in human beings was presumed to be some purely *quantitative* difference in neurology between us and other reasonably smart primates. (It had to be simply a matter of degree, because the black box approach to the mind offered no other degrees of freedom. But in fact the matter never received serious attention.)

Ryle's eliminativist/reductivist program foundered on the fact that human intentional behavior – the behavior for which we are most apt to give mentalistic explanations – is always a function of at least two independent mental variables: a belief and a desire. There is thus no range of behavioral responses proprietary to any individual mentalistic ascription, even given fixed circumstances. Any piece of behavior can evince any belief whatsoever, provided it is combined with an appropriate desire. So I may evince my belief that Helena is the capital of Montana by saying out loud within your hearing, "Helena is the capital of Montana," *if* I want to inform you about US geography. But if I want instead to mislead you, then I will evince that same belief by saying anything *but* those words. Similarly, one and the same behavioral response can evince contrary beliefs, depending on my other mental states. If I believe that Helena is *not* the capital of Montana, and wish to mislead you, I may say exactly the same words I'd say if I believed it was, but wanted to inform you.

The empirical case against behaviorism included, famously, Chomsky's detailed critique of Skinner's account of human verbal behavior (Chomsky, 1959). Chomsky first showed that the theoretical apparatus of operant conditioning theory was, in one way or another, inadequate for explaining the actual course of human linguistic development. If crucial concepts such as "operant" and "stimulus generalization" were given their strict, technical meanings, the theory failed on grounds of empirical inadequacy. If these concepts were "analogically extended," as Skinner said they must be, then, Chomsky argued, the theory lost empirical content. The second important element of Chomsky's assault was the "poverty of the stimulus" argument, deployed against the associationist element of behaviorist theory. What Chomsky and others demonstrated, in the first instance, was that the amounts and kinds of data that the operant conditioning model predicted would be necessary for the acquisition of language simply did not match the data actually available to successful language learners. Chomsky posited an innate, domain-specific cognitive structure that encoded highly general information about the structure of human languages that sharply constrained the range of grammars a child could hypothesize in response to the linguistic data provided by other speakers.

All this is familiar enough. But there is another line of empirical criticism that may be less well-known, and that is, for my current purposes, more interesting. Although many cognitive scientists and many philosophers were completely convinced, on the basis of the critiques outlined above, that behaviorist theory could not account for *complex* human behavior, such as the acquisition and deployment of language, they were not inclined to doubt that classical and operant conditioning explained at least *some* elements of our behavior. It still seemed reasonable to suppose that the behaviorist story made sense for those relatively unconscious and elementary bits of learning that were investigated in standard behaviorist learning experiments.

William Brewer, however, saw reason to challenge even this bromide (Brewer, 1974). It is important, he argued, to distinguish the phenomenon of conditioning itself from the non-mentalistic *explanation of* conditioning offered by behaviorists. It is one thing to condition a subject to exhibit a high galvanic skin response (GSR) at the sight of a particular apparatus; it is quite another to show that this conditioning is accomplished *automatically*, without any cognitive mediation. It is possible, after all, that the *way* conditioning occurs is entirely cognitive: that the subject *learns that* a certain apparatus is capable of producing a shock, and accordingly becomes fearful in anticipation of receiving the shock. Indeed, as I've been arguing, this is the explanation that common sense suggests. The crucial question for behaviorists, then, is this: What makes the non-mentalistic explanation preferable to the more natural mentalistic one?

What one would need to choose between the non-cognitive and the cognitive explanations of the conditioning effect are experiments that controlled for the putative mental states of the subjects. Permitting ourselves to speak, provisionally, with the vulgar, we would want to ask what would happen, for example, if the subject in a GSR experiment were given reason to think that she would not, in this instance, receive a shock – perhaps by being shown the apparatus being unplugged? Well, as it turns out, Brewer reports, the answer to this very question – together with a wealth of other highly pertinent data – was in fact present in the literature generated by behaviorists themselves. The data clearly supported the mentalistic interpretation. In the case described above, if the subject comes to believe that the conditioned stimulus (the sight of the machine) has been "dissociated" from the unconditioned stimulus (the electric shock), the conditioned behavior is almost instantly extinguished, contrary to the predictions of the behaviorist model. Brewer's extensive review of *behaviorist* experiments involving a variety of such "dissociations" (CS from US, operant from reinforcer, etc.), led him to conclude that "all the results of traditional conditioning literature are due to the operation of higher mental processes, as assumed in cognitive theory, and that there is not and never has been any convincing evidence for unconscious, automatic mechanisms in the conditioning of adult human beings" (Brewer, 1974, p. 27).[9]

I've been arguing that from the point of view of common sense, behaviorism is an extremely radical thesis: it after all denies what appears to be the most salient feature of our psychological lives, namely that it is psychological. Given that, one would have thought it could only have been accepted under irresistible empirical pressure. And yet, as it turns out, the theory was grossly and evidently inadequate in accounting for even the paradigm phenomena in its purported domain. There was, in short, no empirical reason whatsoever to prefer behaviorism to common-sense mentalism. Why did it then flourish for as long as it did?

One reason, surely, was the positivist Zeitgeist of the early twentieth century, which was hostile to theoretical posits. Watson, in his 1915 Presidential Address to the American Philosophical Association (Watson, 1916), made clear that he thought the main argument for behaviorism was the epistemological advantage it afforded over introspectionist psychology. Mental states, per se, were not interpersonally observable, and hence were not fit objects of scientific investigation. No doubt the lingering association of mentalism with dualism – perhaps it was inconceivable to many that one could be a mentalist without being a dualist – inhibited the thought that mental states might earn their way into the realm of genuine science in just the way photons and electrons had, by being ineliminable elements in serious scientific explanations for ordinary observable phenomena.

Quine (1960) offered philosophical reasons for thinking that there could be no science of the mind. But, notoriously, his argument for this conclusion begged the question against the psychological realist. Quine wanted to establish that there were no objective facts about either the meanings of words or the contents of thoughts, by showing that such putative facts would be necessarily underdetermined by the physical facts. Quine began with the explicitly behaviorist premise that human children had to have acquired language on the basis of conditioning to the contingencies of verbal use. On theoretical – that is, empiricist – grounds, he excluded from the child's data set information about general grammatical or semantic structure, as well as any psychological information that (one might have thought, pre-theoretically) would help the child in forming theories of language and language use (information such as: "When Daddy points to something and says a word, he's trying to tell me what that kind of thing is called.")

At the same time, however, Quine liberally idealized *away* the very constraints on amount and type of evidence that in fact make the behavioristic story he told impossible as an account of the acquisition of human language. It matters little whether a child *could* acquire, say, the meanings of common verbs through operant conditioning over many trials with explicit reinforcement, since the child acquires them over few trials and without any explicit reinforcement – because, in other words, the child actually acquires such meanings *without* the kinds and number of experiences that would be required for the behaviorist model to apply. That Quine, the archetypal naturalized epistemologist, could so blithely ignore the real world conditions in which language emerges is testimony to the power of a priori hostility to the mind. The irony is rich – it is Quine himself who taught us that it is bad method to disregard or trade off explanations of known psychological facts for putative gains of a more theoretical – or ideological – nature.[10]

I take it as settled, then, that a good, naturalistic materialist ought to be a psychological realist. But now the reductionist challenge must be faced: Is there an autonomous psychology, or are psychological kinds simply biological kinds spoken of mentalistically? Again, a little history is in order.

In the middle of the twentieth century, U. T. Place (1956) and J. J. C. Smart (1959) advanced and defended the "mind–body identity theory," the view that mental states could be identified with neurological states. Because Place and Smart argued that every *type* of mental state could be identified with a *type* of neurological state, their version of reductionism became known as "type-reductionism." Place and Smart took their view to be simply the natural expression of materialism about the mind, and did not consider the possibility that there might yet be an autonomous, yet materialist, science of the mind. They focused on consciousness and sensations, phenomena that were most amenable to this sort of treatment. It is plausible, at any rate, that a sensation type, such as pain, might at least be reliably correlated with a single type of neurological event or process, such as the firing of C-fibers. What Place and Smart failed to consider, however, were propositional attitude states, such as beliefs and desires. It seemed highly unlikely that these states would be marked by some distinctive kind of neurological cell type or process, and much more likely that they would involve states of great neurological complexity, states that might vary in their details from person to person, or even from one time to another in the same person.

Other materialist philosophers who did pay central attention to these phenomena, notably Putnam, Armstrong, and Lewis, argued that such states needed to be understood in terms of their typical causal profiles, or functional roles (Putnam, 1965 and 1967; Armstrong, 1968; Lewis, 1972). These early functionalists appreciated what the behaviorists did not, namely that behavior crucially implicated complex internal states. But their treatment of mental states did incorporate one important insight of Ryle's, and that was that psychology was a more abstract level of description than was biology. Materialism demanded that every psychological state have *some* physical realization, but because psychological states were functional, the details of that physical realization didn't matter to their identity conditions. Putnam made this view explicit in arguing that mental properties were "higher-order" properties. A higher-order property is the property of having some other ("lower-order") property that meets a certain causal/functional specification. The lower-order properties are called "realizer" properties. The view that mental properties are higher-order, functional properties that could be realized in a variety of distinct lower-order properties became known as the thesis of *multiple realizability* (MR).

The view that mental states are multiply realized yielded a different picture of the relation between mentalistic types and biological types from the one presumed by the identity theorists. On their view, recall, all psychological types would be correlated and henceforth reduced to types in a lower-level science, presumably biology. Bridge laws, expressing the relations among these types, could then be used to reduce all the generalizations of psychology to biology. According to MR, however, the requisite biconditional bridge laws are unobtainable. Psychological states supervene on the biological: lower-order biological states would be nomologically sufficient for, and

Louise Antony

hence would necessitate, higher-order psychological states, but the converse does not hold. Generalizations describing regularities at higher orders are thus irreducible to laws at lower orders. They are autonomous.

The multiple realizability view not only captures the abstractness of psychological description relative to the biological, but it appears to explain how mental events can be causally efficacious in the physical realm. Although they reject the view that mental *types* are reducible to physical *types*, defenders of MR are, by and large, materialists, and take it as part and parcel of their materialism that mental events, like all concreta, have physical properties. (Some advocates of MR accept the stronger view that every instance of a mental type is identical with an instance of some physical type, the view known as *token*-reductionism.) In any given causal interaction involving mental events, it will be the mental event's lower-order physical realizer properties that account for the particulars of that causal transaction. Mental events can therefore "inherit" the causal powers of their physical realizers. Different instantiations of the same mental type must all display, at an appropriate level of abstraction, the same causal profiles; but the explanation for how those profiles are maintained can vary widely from case to case.

Jaegwon Kim has recently charged that this apparent selling point of the MR view is in fact a fatal liability (Kim, 1993 and 1998). To concede that mental events do not form a causally homogeneous group, he argues, is to concede that mentalistic groupings are not genuine natural kinds, and hence, are unfit for science. But MR supporters must concede this: to do otherwise would be to posit new "emergent" causal powers that would compete with the lower-order physical realizer properties, in a way that should be unacceptable to a materialist. The only way out of this dilemma, Kim argues, is to give up on multiple realization, and return to type reductionism. If mental phenomena are to be integrated into the physical world, they must enter as biological, not psychological phenomena.

But what about considerations of multiple realizability? If mental states can indeed be realized in a variety of distinct physical properties, then how can the identification with lower-order properties go through? The phenomenon of multiple realizability, Kim responds, is so far merely theoretical. Our only actual extant examples of minds involve creatures with brains, and our extant psychological theories are designed to describe them. It is fanciful to expect that there would be nontrivial generalizations subsuming any *possible* mind, and it is only this possibility that sustains the argument against identifying (familiar terrestrial) minds with brains.[11] As for the presumed neurological inter- and intra-personal diversity of the biological realizer states, this is not the kind of diversity that warrants the description "*multiple* realizability." Better to say that these states are multiply *instantiable*. While there will be variety in the microstates that instantiate a given psychological state, all these states will be sufficiently similar in their causal powers to be subsumable under the same causal laws.

Many objectors to Kim's argument charge that his "causal exclusion" argument proves too much; that if successful, it would apply to all non-fundamental domains and sciences, delegitimating geology and biology along with psychology. Kim's initial response to this, the "generalization" objection, involved a distinction between "higher-*order*" from "higher-*level*" properties, and the domains defined in terms of them. A higher-level property is a property that applies to an object at a given level of aggregation, and to no proper part of that object, whereas higher-order properties, by definition, apply to precisely the same objects as do their lower-order realizer properties. But higher-level objects, Kim argues, are associated with genuinely novel causal powers – there are things that can be done by masses of 10 grams that cannot be done by anything smaller. There is therefore no question of causal competition between higher- and lower-level properties; no property of a part of a higher-level object has the same causal potential as the properties of the whole. Because chemistry, biology, and geology are all higher-*level* relative to fundamental physics, they are not subject to the causal exclusion argument.

This reply does not work, for two reasons. The first is that psychology is not the only "special science" to make use of functional properties: in particular, such properties are ubiquitous and ineliminable in biology. Moreover, the functional properties appealed to by biology – properties such as "cell" and "gene" – are not just possibly but actually and manifestly multiply realizable. So if there is a problem about the nomic status of psychological generalizations, then there is an equally grave problem about the laws of genetics, and in that case, who cares about nomic status?

The second reason is this: Multiple instantiability is as good as multiple realizability for generating a causal exclusion problem. Consider a particular instance of biological causation, say an immune cell attacking a virus. The biological properties involved will all supervene on specific "microbased" properties, where a microbased property is the property of having such-and-such a microparticulate structure. But then these microbased properties will be higher-order with respect to the lower-order chemical or physical properties possessed by the biological entities' proper parts, and will be available to causally compete with the biological properties. Kim acknowledges this, but thinks that there is, in such cases, no difficulty in identifying the biological properties with the microbased properties. But there is – it is the same problem that confronted classical strong reductionism in the face of (at least the prospect of) multiple realizability: many different microbased properties can instantiate the same biological property; hence the biological property cannot be identified with any of them.

In general, Kim and other reductionists need to show that there is a compelling difference between biology and psychology, such that we can rest content with a biology that is autonomous from chemistry, but not a psychology that is autonomous from biology. I submit that no such difference will be – or can be – found. Biological theories earn their keep by providing fertile and explanatorily satisfying accounts of the phenomena we pick out under biological description. No one frets about how such theories will be "integrated" into the non-biological realm (although I understand that there have been such worries in the past), for it is presumed that the truth cannot be an enemy to the truth; that if biological phenomena are, as they certainly appear to be, part of the natural material world, that their existence is compatible with their being composed of chemical and ultimately physical stuff. Why cannot the same attitude be taken toward psychological phenomena? It is only if one assumes going into the game that "the mental" is somehow defined in contradistinction to the physical that there can even *appear* to be a problem about "locating" the mind in a physical world. Nonreductive materialists are thoroughgoing naturalists: we want only the same consideration for the psychological data as are according the data in any other domain.

Think about it.

Notes

1   Oddly enough, this is a view also held by many philosophers who regard themselves as realists about the mind, e.g., Davidson, Burge, and Baker. More on this below.

2   In honor of Jaegwon Kim's likening their attitude to the insouciance of the *Mad* magazine cover boy, Alfred E. Neuman. There's a picture here: www.leconcombre.com/alfred/img2/alfred_e_neuman_1.jpg

3   I should not leave the impression that Dennett is a psychological realist in my sense. He probably should be placed in the Neumanian camp, since he is an instrumentalist about mentality. He believes that the display of sufficiently robust rational "patterns" in an entity's behavior is ontologically sufficient for attributing mentality to it.

4   For fuller discussion, see Antony and Levine (1997) and Antony (2001).

5   I am including in this group *representationalists* about qualia – theorists who believe that the qualitative character of qualitative states is determined by their representational content.

6   If you won't take my word for it, how about an economist's? "When making choices in the marketplace, 'People are not responding to the *actual objects* they are choosing between,' says Eric Wanner of the Russell Sage Foundation. 'There is no direct relation of stimulus and response. Neoclassical economics posits a direct relationship between the object and the choice made. But in behavioral economics, the choice depends on *how the decision-maker describes the objects to himself.* Any psychologist knows this, but it is revolutionary when imported into economics'" (Lambert, 2006, pp. 94–5). Any psychologist, maybe, but not any philosopher.

   Mind-denial appears to have been rampant in the field of economics, delaying by decades the official recognition, not to mention the theoretical exploitation, of the mundane fact recorded above. In the same article, author Lambert quotes Eric Wanner, who worked together with Alfred P. Sloan to legitimize and develop the field of behavioral economics: "'The field is misnamed – it should have been called cognitive economics,' says Wanner. 'We weren't brave enough'" (Lambert, 2006, p. 52).

7   This example is due to Georges Rey (1997, pp. 88–94).

8   See Fodor (1975 and 1978a) for the canonical arguments, and Fodor (1978b, 1987, and 1990) for responses to some objections. In all of this, my intellectual debt to Fodor is profound, and, I trust, evident.

9   Georges Rey (1997, pp. 99–103) surveys and describes four types of "anomalies" – findings inconsistent with behaviorist predictions, but fully expected on a cognitivist model: latent learning, passive learning, spontaneous alteration, and improvisation.

10 For further discussion, see Antony (2000).

11 See also Millikan (1986).

References

Antony, L. (1989). Anomalous monism and the problem of explanatory force. *Philosophical Review*, 98, 153–87.

—— (1995). Law and order in psychology. *Philosophical Perspectives*, 9, 1–19.

—— (2000). Naturalizing radical translation. In A. Orenstein and P. Kotatko (eds.), *Knowledge, Language, and Logic*. Boston Studies in the Philosophy of Science. Dordrecht: Kluwer Academic.

— (2001). Brain states, with attitude. In A. Meijers (ed.), *Explaining Beliefs: Lynne Rudder Baker and Her Critics*. Chicago: University of Chicago Press, CSLI.

Antony, L. and Levine, J. (1997). Reduction with autonomy. *Philosophical Perspectives*, 11, 83–105.

Armstrong, D. (1968). *A Materialist Theory of Mind*. London: Routledge.

Baker, L. R. (1995). *Explaining Belief: A Practical Approach to the Mind*. Cambridge: Cambridge University Press.

Bickle, J. (2003). *Philosophy and Neuroscience: A Ruthlessly Reductive Account*. Dordrecht: Kluwer Academic.

Brewer, W. F. (1974). There is no convincing evidence for classical conditioning in adult humans. In W. B. Weiner and D. S. Palermo (eds.), *Cognition and the Symbolic Processes*. Hillsdale, NJ: Erlbaum.

Burge, T. (1993). Mind–body causation and explanatory practice. In J. Heil and A. Mele (eds.), *Mental Causation*. Oxford: Oxford University Press.

Chalmers, D. (1996). *The Conscious Mind: In Search of a Fundamental Theory*. Oxford: Oxford University Press.

Chomsky, N. (1959). Review of B. F. Skinner's *Verbal Behavior. Language*, 35, 26–58.

Churchland, P. (1981). Eliminative materialism and the propositional attitudes. *Journal of Philosophy*, 78, 67–90.

Davidson, D. (1980). Mental events. *Essays on Actions and Events*. Oxford: Oxford University Press. Originally published in L. Foster and J. W. Swanson (eds.), *Experience and Theory*. London: Duckworth, 1970, 79–91.

Dennett, D. (1971). Intentional systems. *Journal of Philosophy*, 68, 87–106.

— (1988). Quining qualia. In A. Marcel and E. Bisiach (eds.), *Consciousness in Contemporary Science*. Oxford: Clarendon.

Dretske, F. (1995). *Naturalizing the Mind*. Cambridge, MA: MIT Press.

Fodor, J. (1975). *The Language of Thought*. Cambridge, MA: Harvard University Press.

— (1978a). Propositional attitudes. *The Monist*, 61, 501–23.

— (1978b). Three cheers for propositional attitudes. In E. Cooper and E. Walker (eds.), *Sentence Processing*. Hillsdale, NJ: Erlbaum.

— (1987). The persistence of the attitudes. *Psychosemantics*. Cambridge, MA: Bradford/MIT Press.

— (1990). Why there still has to be a language of thought. In D. Partridge and Y. Wilks (eds.), *The Foundations of Artificial Intelligence: A Sourcebook*. Cambridge: Cambridge University Press.

Gallistel, C. R. (1990). *The Organization of Learning*. Cambridge, MA: MIT Press.

Hill, C. S. (1991). *Sensations: A Defense of Type Materialism*. Cambridge: Cambridge University Press.

Jackson, F. (1982). Epiphenomenal qualia. *Philosophical Quarterly*, 32, 127–36.

— (2006). The knowledge argument, diaphanousness, representationalism. In T. Alter and S. Walter (eds.), *Phenomenal Concepts and Phenomenal Knowledge: New Essays on Consciousness and Physicalism*. Oxford: Oxford University Press.

Kim, J. (1993). Multiple realization and the metaphysics of reduction. *Supervenience and Mind*. Cambridge: Cambridge University Press.

— (1998). *Mind in a Physical World*. Cambridge, MA: MIT Press.

Lambert, C. (2006). The marketplace of perceptions. *Harvard Magazine*, March–April 2006, pp. 50–7, 93–5.

Levin, J. (1991). Analytic functionalism and the reduction of phenomenal states. *Philosophical Studies*, 61, 211–38.

Levine, J. (2001). *Purple Haze: The Puzzle of Consciousness*. Oxford: Oxford University Press.

Lewis, D. (1972). Psychophysical and theoretical identifications. *Australasian Journal of Philosophy*, 50, 249–58.

Loar, B. (1990). Phenomenal states. *Philosophical Perspectives*, 4, 81–108.

Lycan, W. G. (1987). *Consciousness*. Cambridge, MA: MIT Press.

— (1996). *Consciousness and Experience*. Cambridge, MA: MIT Press.

Marler, P. (1984). Song learning: innate species differences in the learning process. In P. Marler and H. S. Terrace (eds.), *The Biology of Learning*. Berlin: Springer.

Marr, D. (1982). *Vision*. San Francisco: W. H. Freeman.

Millikan, R. (1986). Thoughts without laws. *Philosophical Review*, 95, 47–80. Reprinted in R. Millikan, *White Queen Psychology and Other Essays for Alice*. Cambridge, MA: MIT Press, 1993.

Nida-Rümelin, M. (2004). Phenomenal essentialism: a problem for identity theorists. *Philosophy and Phenomenological Research*, 58, 51–73.

Papineau, D. (2002). *Thinking about Consciousness*. Oxford: Oxford University Press.

Place, U. T. (1956). Is consciousness a brain process? *British Journal of Psychology*, 47, 44–50.

Putnam, H. (1965). Brains and behavior. In R. Butler (ed.), *Analytical Philosophy*, 1–20.

— (1967). The mental life of some machines. In S. Hook (ed.), *Dimensions of Mind*. New York: Collier.

Pylyshyn, Z. (1986). *Computation and Cognition: Toward a Foundation for Cognitive Science*. Cambridge, MA: MIT Press.

Quine, W. (1960). *Word and Object*. Cambridge, MA: Technology Press of MIT.

Rey, G. (1991). An explanatory budget for connectionism and eliminativism. In J. Tienson and T. Horgan (eds.), *Connectionism and the Philosophy of Mind*. Dordrecht: Kluwer.

— (1993). Sensational sentences. In M. Davies and G. W. Humphreys (eds.), *Consciousness: Philosophical and Psychological Essays*. Oxford: Blackwell.

— (1997). *Contemporary Philosophy of Mind*. Oxford: Blackwell.

Ryle, G. (1949). *The Concept of Mind*. London: Hutcheson.

Shoemaker, S. (1975). Functionalism and qualia. *Philosophical Studies*, 27, 291–315.

Skinner, B. F. (1938). *The Behavior of Organisms*. New York: Appleton-Century-Crofts.

— (1957). *Verbal Behavior*. New York: Appleton-Century-Crofts.

Smart, J. J. C. (1959). Sensations and brain processes. *Philosophical Review*, 68, 141–56.

Stich, S. (1983). *From Folk Psychology to Cognitive Science*. Cambridge, MA: MIT Press.

Swinburne, R. (1997). *The Evolution of the Soul*. Oxford: Oxford University Press.

Tye, M. (1995). *Ten Problems of Consciousness: A Representational Theory of the Phenomenal Mind*. Cambridge, MA: Bradford Books of MIT Press.

Watson, J. B. (1916). The place of the conditioned-reflex in psychology. *Psychological Review*, 23, 89–116.

The Evolving Fortunes of Eliminative Materialism

Paul M. Churchland

Of the several major positions in the philosophy of mind, eliminative materialism is the focus of the least attention, if measured by the sheer mass of journal pages devoted to its discussion. Perhaps because its central claim involves an extremely long-term *prediction* about the fate of our folk-psychological vocabulary, and about the fate of our current explanatory, predictive, and pragmatic practices where human behavior is concerned, philosophers have been mostly content to let the position simply sit on the shelf, there to await the distant verdict that fate no doubt holds in store for it.

The aim of the present paper is to argue that its fate is nowhere near so distant, and that its evolving fortunes, over the *past* 25 years, bear directly and immediately on a number of philosophical issues currently at the focus of fevered philosophical attention. One of them is the problem of subjective phenomenological *qualia*. Another is the integrity of the *propositional attitudes* as the basis for a computational theory of cognition. And a third is the problem of how a physical system such as a brain can embody systematic *representations* of the world, that is, the problem of how its states can have *semantic contents*. Finally, its fortunes are closely tied to the fortunes of modern pragmatism (broadly conceived), and indeed, to the fortunes of those contemporary epistemological positions that reject the idea of a priori knowledge – both the "substantive" variety embraced by Plato and Kant, and the factually empty or "conventional" variety embraced by much of modern analytic philosophy. Specifically, it is tied to the notion that (a) absolutely all "knowledge" is speculative and revisable, and (b) presumptive knowledge earns that status by allowing us to anticipate, to explain, and in general to navigate and to manipulate phenomena within the domain thereby grasped, whether natural or social.

1 An Epistemological Detour

Let me begin my discussion with this last issue, since it has recently begun to intrude anew into discussions about the mind. Since Quine's landmark "Two Dogmas of

Empiricism," half a century ago, most philosophers have become chary of expressing any sympathy for the analytic/synthetic distinction itself, or for the equally important second dogma, the dogma that the credibility of some observation statements stands or falls on the immediate character of sensory experience alone, with no dependence on the relations those statements bear to an enveloping web of presumed background knowledge. Despite that emerging orthodoxy, a significant minority of the profession, for whatever reasons, retained a covert sympathy for both of these traditional empiricist positions, and in recent years one finds both dogmas peeking out, once more, from behind discussions in the philosophy of mind.

A prominent example is David Chalmers's *Conscious Mind*, which begins with an ostentatiously unmotivated replacement of the familiar identity-relation, as the principal element in any intertheoretic reduction, by the supposed relation of "logical supervenience." This latter relation is said to obtain when the facts-as-described by the reducing theory logically guarantee the facts-as-described by the reduced theory. But the sense of the term "logically" in this formula is not the well-behaved sense of "formally" or "syntactically" guarantee. It is – it slowly emerges – the old Oxfordian sense of "semantically" or "*analytically*" guarantee. The entire history of science, with its wealth of successful reductions, is thereby yoked to a contrived conception of intertheoretic reduction based on a wholly nonexistent relation. Chalmers, of course, sees things otherwise, and he provides, later in the book, a brief (and unprepossessing) critique of Quine's celebrated position.

However lightly motivated, Chalmers's heterodox account of intertheoretic reduction is strategically important. As his story unfolds, the purely "psychological" sense of our folk-psychological terms emerges as eminently subject to a neuroscientific reduction, for their purely "psychological" meanings are said by him to be *defined by* the peculiar set of causal relations in which the extension of each term figures, and neuroscience is entirely capable, in principle, of reconstructing the relevant family of causal relations definitive for each term. Indeed, Chalmers fully expects neuroscience to succeed in this particular endeavor. But there is *another* sense to many of those terms, he avers, a non-causal or non-functional sense. Specifically, many of those terms have a *phenomenological* or non-relational *qualitative* sense, which sense is (alas) forever beyond the reach of the kind of intertheoretic reduction that neuroscience, or indeed, *any* physical science, is capable of providing, at least as Chalmers construes intertheoretic reduction. Thus does Chalmers argue for the irreducibility of phenomenological qualia. Thus also, we should note, does he firmly re-embrace the *second* dogma of empiricism as well, the dogma that at least some "observation sentences" have a meaning and a credibility that is wholly independent of any logical relations they might bear to an enveloping web of presumed background knowledge. The relevant observation sentences are precisely those that deploy the alleged set of non-relational qualia terms identified in the first half of this paragraph.

Chalmers is not alone in this twofold epistemological backsliding. In a recent book, curiously entitled *The Philosophical Foundations of Neuroscience*, R. Bennett and P. Hacker (2003) re-embrace the analytic/synthetic distinction, resurrect the logical behaviorist claim that psychological terms are ascribed on the basis of "logically adequate" criteria, and reaffirm the epistemological incorrigibility of first-person phenomenological reports. Here, too, their background commitments in epistemology play a decisive role in driving their foreground interests in the philosophy of mind. And here, too, those background commitments are clearly both anti- and ante-Quinean, if not quite antediluvian.

We need to do better. Trying to do decent philosophy of mind on the assumption of any sort of foundationalist epistemology is the rough equivalent to trying to do decent astronomy and cosmology on the assumption of a flat, immobile Earth. I make this charge not to insult, but to engage my reader's attention: in fact, the parallels between these two positions are more extensive and more instructive than one might have expected, right down to the historical arguments that have been raised in their defense.

Consider first the argument that runs as follows: What "*x* moves" *means* is precisely "*x* changes its position relative to the Earth." Now consider substituting "The Earth" for "*x*" in the right-hand side of this formula. Since the Earth *cannot* change its position relative to itself, the claim that the Earth itself moves must be sheer nonsense, a conceptual confusion. By the same token, the claim that *everything* in the universe is in motion must be similarly, and even more obviously, incoherent. Motion is and must be a comparatively *occasional and peripheral* feature of the world. A few things do indeed display motion – the clouds, birds, animals, river waters, the sun and moon – but the overwhelmingly greater portion of reality stands fast. Indeed, without it, claims of motion for the occasional item could have no basis.

Interestingly, the meaning analysis on which this geocentric argument rests was probably accurate for most speakers from Ptolemy through Newton. Even so, the lessons of modern astronomy invite us to embrace both of the revolutionary claims so urgently resisted above, and they invite us to adopt a new and more enlightened conception of motion, one in which the notion of a uniquely preferred reference frame at absolute rest is dismissed as both unspecifiable and wholly unnecessary in any case.

Compare now the following epistemological analog: What "*s* is theoretical" *means* is "*s* is speculative; *s* is about something that cannot be directly observed to be true, either by reason of its being a general statement, or by reason of its being about phenomena that lie beyond human perception, or both." Now, if one substitutes for "*s*," in the right-hand part of this formula, a singular observation statement such as "This is an apple," the result is something that apparently *cannot* be true, for the substituted sentence is neither speculative in any familiar sense, nor general, nor beyond our direct perceptual evaluation. For similar reasons, the claim that *all* statements are theoretical leads to comparable contradictions and to even more widespread chaos. Accordingly, being theoretical must be a comparatively *occasional* and *peripheral* aspect of our knowledge. Some statements are indeed theoretical – those about atoms, or electric and magnetic fields, or about the most basic laws of nature – but the overwhelmingly greater part of human knowledge stands fast against such speculative musings. Indeed, it forms the inevitable foundation against which such speculations are and must ever be evaluated.

Interestingly, the meaning analysis on which this foundational argument depends is, once more, probably accurate for most contemporary speakers, and even for most philosophers. But the lessons of modern epistemology – from Quine, Popper, Rorty, Kuhn, Sellars, Feyerabend, and I hope the present author – invite us to embrace the

Paul M. Churchland

idea, however "revolutionary," that singular observation statements (all of them) might indeed be theoretical, and to embrace a new and more enlightened conception of what it is to be theoretical, one in which the notion of a theory-neutral epistemological foundation is dismissed as both unspecifiable and wholly unnecessary in any case.

Pursuing the parallels a step further, note that a common objection to the Copernican/Galilean/Newtonian claim that we humans, and the ground we stand on, are constantly moving eastwards at something close to 1,000 miles per hour[1] was that our subjective impressions are wholly incompatible with our being engaged in any motion of such an extreme and unprecedented character. The idea is ridiculous on its face.

This reaction is entirely understandable, given the default or domain-central prototypes of motion common among people at the time. Riding a galloping horse, rafting a raging river, running full tilt, or falling off a cliff were the sorts of paradigmatic cases of motion to which the Copernican claim was reflexively referred for evaluation, and one's experience while sitting quietly in a chair was not remotely like the experience of any of those prototypes. The thrill of the initial acceleration, the typically bouncing ride, the wind in your teeth, and feelings of vertigo are all utterly absent. And the prototypes listed, note well, are all legitimate examples of genuine motion.

Similarly, the suggestion that all of one's accumulated common-sense knowledge, and one's unfolding perceptual judgments as well, is uniformly *theoretical* seems wholly incompatible with the default conviction that, in such familiar domains, one is mostly dealing with the frankly obvious, and not with issues that are speculative, problematic, and intellectually ambitious. The idea, once again, seems ridiculous on its face.

This reaction, too, is understandable, given the prototypes most people have for identifying things as theories. Theories are typically proposed, at a specific historical time, by someone in a toga, a white lab-coat, or a tweed jacket sporting a frizzy white hairdo. They typically involve strange vocabularies that address abstruse phenomena beyond common experience. You usually can't tell for certain whether theories are true, and evaluating them for truth depends on the deployment of sophisticated measuring devices, often several at once. Moreover, they are typically difficult to understand, and require years of training to master.

Their many real instances notwithstanding, these are profoundly misleading prototypes, for they are drawn from the drama-filled cutting edge of cognition, from its ever-turbulent outer edges, and not from its only rarely questioned core. A better prototype would be our common-sense conceptual framework for three-dimensional, mutually impenetrable physical objects lasting through time. A second prototype would be our common-sense conceptual framework for understanding the motions and transformations of those 3-D objects, and the forces and factors that govern those changes. A third prototype would be the magnificently complex conceptual framework we all use for understanding, anticipating, and influencing the internal cognitive and emotional states of animals, and most especially, of other humans: folk psychology. All of these conceptual frameworks, as we know, take the developing infant years to master. And let me also note that the various *human* sensory systems are, each and every one of them, extremely sophisticated measuring and detection devices, without which none of our sophisticated common-sense frameworks could be applied to the world at all. The various physiological outputs of these biological measuring instruments cause, yield, or otherwise motivate singular judgments expressed in the appropriate common-sense theoretical framework (e.g., "There is a red apple"), from which world-portraying background framework those singular judgments draw their meaning in the first place. Each human is thus a walking, talking *measuring instrument* making constant use of background theories either imbibed or developed in early childhood.

The speculative and revisable character of these common-sense conceptual frameworks is plainly evident from the lessons of history. The distinction between space, on the one hand, and time, on the other – a framework principle of our basic ontology of 3-D objects lasting through time – turns out to be an illusion born of the low relative velocities that most perceptible objects display. As special relativity has taught us, we live in a unified *four*-dimensional universe, and what presents itself as a spatial interval, and what as a temporal interval, varies systematically across reference frames in motion relative to one another. The differences are negligible at low velocities – and so the inadequacies of our folk theory remain hidden – but they become dramatic in cases where the velocities involved approach the speed of light.

The common-sense conceptual framework for understanding the nature and causes of *motion* is no less clearly speculative, since that framework is Aristotelian through and through,[2] and it has already been displaced, for anyone with a freshman physics course behind them, by the quite different Newtonian framework. Here, too, the inadequacies of our folk theory are hidden by the parochial nature of the environment in which the theory is asked to perform. First of all, we, and all of the objects around us, are stuck at the bottom of a deep gravitational well, a cosmically unusual situation. And second, all of the objects in our local environment are doomed to encounter frictional resistance when they move against the (invisible) air – also a cosmically unusual situation. It is no wonder, then, that our folk theory of motion is so badly mistaken: it was tailored to comprehend motion within a uniformly atypical environment, cosmically speaking.

2 The Independent Case for Theoreticity

This brings us, naturally enough, back to the status of folk psychology, that other great edifice in the metropolis of common-sense theory. Its characterization as a theory has been casually dismissed as "bizarre" by no less a figure than Charles Taylor (2005, p. 204), himself no stranger to the idea that conceptual frameworks evolve over time, and, more belligerently, is dismissed as "a disastrous conceptual confusion" by Bennett and Hacker (2003, p. 232). (One is reminded here of Ptolemy's famous dismissal of Aristarchos' heliocentric account of the heavens. It was, he said, "absurd." Well done, Ptolemy!)

But in fact, it is entirely possible to make a decisive case for the theoretical character of folk psychology without first making the larger epistemological case that *all* conceptual frameworks are theoretical. One can start by making explicit the many implicit generalizations or *laws* that collectively give meaning to our psychological vocabulary (cf. Churchland, 1979, 1986). One can display the quotidian role those generalizations play in funding covering-law *explanations* of the full range of

Paul M. Churchland

common-sense psychological phenomena (cf. Churchland, 1979, 1986). One can point to the detailed *contents* of those generalizations so as to account for the specific ways in which such explanations are occasionally contradicted or *defeated* in common conversations (cf. Churchland, 1970). One can point to the role they play in funding the ongoing flow of *singular explanatory hypotheses* ("She's jealous, but doesn't realize it") that give us insight into one another's ongoing mental lives (Churchland, 1979, 1986). One can show how the classical problem of other minds finds a robust and stable solution in the fact that such singular psychological hypotheses supply what are easily the most reasonable and systematic *explanations* currently available for ongoing human behaviors (Churchland, 1979, 1986). One can also point to the underlying *logical structure* of our many predicates for the so-called propositional attitudes: they are one and all predicate-forming functors that take abstract entities (viz., *propositions*) as arguments. This parallels precisely the underlying logical structure of most scientific predicates, such as "has a mass$_{kg}$ of 10." These *also* are predicate-forming functors that take abstract entities (viz., *numbers*, or *vectors*, or *matrices*) as arguments. And in both cases, the *empirical* relations between the properties expressed by those predicates reflect the *abstract* relations that hold originally between the abstract entities thus deployed Churchland (1979, 1986). And one can do all of this *without* first rejecting the analytic/synthetic distinction and the Myth of the Given, and then relaxing into the antecedent idea that all knowledge is theoretical in any case. Indeed, if you wish, the crashingly obvious independent case for the theoreticity of folk psychology can be seen as a (small) part of the case for the theoreticity of conceptual frameworks in general, rather than the other way around.

In either case, we have an arguably overdetermined case for the claim that our common-sense conceptual framework for psychological phenomena is a theoretical framework in all of its salient dimensions – functionally, semantically, structurally, and epistemologically. Which brings us, finally, to the point of our opening epistemological excursion. If folk psychology is a theory, then it is at least a logical possibility that it is radically *false*, either in whole or in part. And this is the opening premise for eliminative materialism. If folk psychology is indeed radically false in some important respects, then it must fail to find a successful intertheoretic reduction in terms of the deeper neuroscientific account of human mental activity that is already under active and accelerating construction, and our folk psychological ontology will thus be a candidate for outright elimination – much like the caloric fluid of early thermodynamics, the phlogiston of late alchemical chemistry, and the crystal spheres of Aristotelian astronomy. There, too, the older theories surrounding such notions proved to be so severely flawed that their ontologies were simply eliminated, rather than smoothly reduced to the displacing ontology of the new theoretical framework. Those historical lessons are still relevant, and much has happened in the several neurosciences (neuroanatomy, neurophysiology, developmental neurobiology, neuropathology, cognitive neurobiology, neural network theory) since eliminative materialism was first mentioned as a possibility in the early 1960s (Feyerabend, 1963; Rorty, 1965) and then articulated as a probability in the early 1980s (Churchland, 1981). Let us now ask: what are the reductive prospects – for folk psychology – as they currently present themselves? And how do these unfolding developments bear on the thesis of eliminative materialism?

3 Totting up the Prospects: Sensory Qualia

Unlike the uniform indications concerning the literal theoreticity of folk psychology, the indications concerning its truth or falsity are decidedly mixed, as we shall see in the pages to come. However, in one important area, a *blanket* eliminative materialism bids fair to be just plain wrong. The reason is simple: The portion of folk psychology concerned with the various *sensations* to which we are subject is in the process of finding a moderately smooth and highly illuminating *reduction* at the hands of unfolding neuroscience. This claim may occasion surprise in some readers, specifically, those still inclined toward the family of convictions epitomized by Chalmers, as discussed several pages ago. That reactionary view is quite prepared to see the relational, causal, or functional features of sensations fall into the explanatory embrace of a neuroscientific reduction. But their *qualitative* features? Never.

And yet, those very qualitative features are beginning to yield to neuroanatomical and neurophysiological explanations. Indeed, the explanatory machinery already in the journals and textbooks not only explains the internal similarity-structure of our familiar phenomenological color space, for example: it also predicts the existence of entirely *new* color qualia, qualia outside the range we have all encountered, qualia whose descriptions in common-sense terms (e.g., "a vivid blue that is fully as dark as the darkest possible black") strike one as semantically self-contradictory. Nonetheless, those descriptions are accurate and the predicted qualia are real.

Figure 10.1a portrays the Hurvich–Jameson neural network model (Hurvich, 1981) of how external color information (i.e., object reflectance profiles) is processed by, and represented in, the human visual system. The basic idea is that the color experienced at a given point in one's visual field is identical with the ordered triplet of excitation values across the three "opponent-process neurons" receiving information about the stimulation levels across the three types of cone cells at the relevant point on one's retina. (These latter are the cells selectively sensitive to specific wavelengths of incoming light, as displayed in Figure 10.1b.)

The three opponent-process neurons at that second-story population embody a three-dimensional code for distinct colors, as displayed in the cubical "activation space" of Figure 10.2. With all three of those neurons at their default or "resting" level of 50 percent possible activation, they are representing a *middle gray* external stimulus. Any other triplet of activation levels constitutes a color-sensation other than middle-gray: a triplet at the top center of the cube-shaped space of possible positions – <50%, 50%, 100%> – constitutes a sensation of white; a triplet at the bottom center – <50%, 50%, 0%> – constitutes a sensation of black; and any triplet around the indicated "equator" of the enclosed spindle constitutes a sensation of one of the saturated hues so familiar to all of us.

As a glance at the network of Figure 10.1a will reveal, the activation-levels of the three second-story neurons are not independent of each other, since they are variously subject to stimulations and inhibitions from the very same family of light-sensitive cone cells. Given the distribution and polarity of the several synaptic connections that drive the second-story neurons, the only activation-triplets possible for that population, when functioning normally, are those confined to the bulgy spindle-shaped solid that takes up the central volume of our cubical activation space, as displayed

Paul M. Churchland

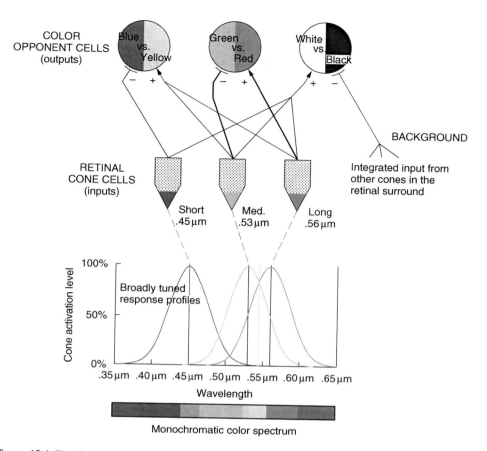

Figure 10.1 The Hurvich–Jameson neural network model (Hurvich, 1981).

in Figure 10.2. The activation-triplets within that subspace represent the full range of objective colors possible for any external object. And their relative positions within that subspace reconstruct very accurately the antecedently known similarity-structure of the range of possible objective colors, and, for that matter, the antecedently known similarity-structure of the range of possible subjective color-sensations. That is, the network at issue explains the peculiar *shape* and internal *organization* of the traditional "color spindle." Note further, it also reconstructs correctly the family of causal relations by which the world's external colors *produce* our internal sensations. For example, a white object – which reflects light more or less uniformly across the visible spectrum – will normally cause a second-story activation triplet of <50%, 50%, 100%>, i.e., a sensation of white. All told, we have a gathering case that human color-sensations simply *are* activation triplets of the kind on display.[3]

Further motivation for proposing a literal identity between human color sensations, on the one hand, and the activation triplets across some neural realization of the second-story neurons of the Hurvich–Jameson network on the other, arises from the model's systematic success in predicting and explaining the qualitative character

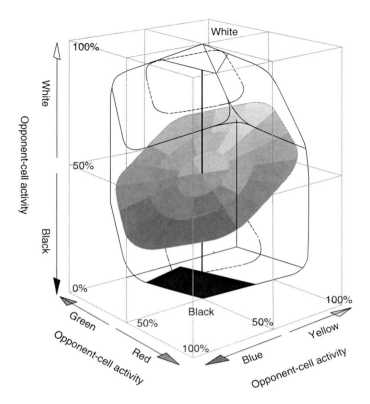

Figure 10.2 Three opponent-process neurons.

of literally thousands of fatigue-induced colored *after-images*, and in its explanation of why the six landmark colors – namely: red, green, blue, yellow, black, and white – strike humans as being uniquely *pure* or "unmixed," while all other colors present as phenomenological "compounds," somehow, of two or more of the colors on this preferred list.[4] But I mention these successes only to acknowledge them. We need to move on to a still more striking success.

An only recently appreciated virtue of the Hurvich–Jameson account is its predictive and explanatory power concerning the possible activation triplets located in the substantial volume remaining *outside* the traditional color spindle for possible external colors, but still *inside* the cubical activation space for the second-story opponent-process neurons. As noted earlier, under normal operation, the H-J net will never produce an activation triplet outside of the spindle. But if the opponent cells are coerced into *abnormal* behavior – via some artful fatigue and/or potentiation, plus some extremal color stimuli – we can briefly produce activation triplets well outside the traditional spindle: on the bottom floor of the activation-cube, for example, but well away from its central axis, as indicated at the lower left of Figure 10.2.

That activation-triplet constitutes a sensation of a "color" you will never see as the objective color of a physical object. That triplet is a representation of something that does not exist in the external world, a representation of a *chimerical* color, a

168 | **Paul M. Churchland**

color that is an "impossible" compound of familiar features. Specifically, it is a sensation of a color that is absolutely as dark as the darkest possible black (after all, it is on the *floor* of the activation-cube, fully as far down as is the triplet for maximal black). But it is not remotely black (after all, it is a long way from the cube's hue-less central axis). In fact, it is a highly vivid but decidedly unfamiliar cousin of *blue* (after all, it is closer to the coding-triplet for a standard blue than to any other color around the spindle's equator).

You can produce this weirdly colored after-image for yourself by placing a nickel-sized yellow paper circle, with a small × drawn at its center, against a middle-gray background; fixate steadily on the × for fully 45 seconds; and then look at any deep *black* surface. A circular after-image, of the impossibly stygian "blue" described above, will appear before your eyes, there to fade, gradually, as your severely fatigued opponent-process neurons gradually recover from their protracted ordeal. You have just succeeded in producing an activation-triplet across those neurons that they have probably never enjoyed before. More to the point, you have just been the subject of a sensation-of-color that you have never had before. And the Hurvich–Jameson theory of human color processing that suggested how to produce it both predicts and explains its novel and deeply implausible qualitative character.

The theory predicts a similarly "impossible" result for each and every one of the diverse colors around the spindle's equator. Fixate at length on any isolated color sample of a determinate shape, then look at a black surface, and an impossibly stygian version of the sample's color-complement (i.e., the color at the antipodal position across the spindle) will briefly appear against the black background. There are hundreds of such experiments you can perform, and in each case, the theory both predicts and explains the novel (and presumptively impossible!) qualitative characters of the after-images thereby produced.

A parallel suite of experiments involves directing your color-fatigued gaze, in each case, to a white surface instead of a black one. Here the after-images that result are impossibly *bright* versions of the color-complement of the original stimulus: they present as positively self-*luminous*. This is no surprise: these triplets are all on the *ceiling* of the activation-cube, but far away from the triplet for maximally bright white at its geometrical center. Here, too, the wealth of predictions derived from the H-J theory test out nicely.[5]

So much for the supposed inaccessibility of phenomenological qualia to the predictive and explanatory reach of neurophysiological theory. Those color qualia are not "metaphysical simples" after all. They have a systematic substructure with three salient neuro-activational dimensions, each of which is essential to the rest of the brain's responding to them in an appropriately discriminatory or recognitional way. The time-honored philosophical view that the "conscious mind" simply apprehends "directly" our unanalyzably "simple" subjective qualia is starting to look like the fairy tale that it always has been. And yet, the common-sense view that there exist color sensations with a range of qualitative characters, characters that are introspectively discriminable, characters whose diversity usefully reflects the diversity of a range of features displayed by external physical objects, here emerges as free of any serious ontological or doctrinal failing. In other words, we are here confronting a fairly clean intertheoretic *reduction* of the class of sensations-of-color as conceived within folk psychology with the class of opponent-cell activation-triplets as conceived within the Hurvich–Jameson theory of how the human brain processes color information. The space of *possible* opponent-cell triplets is somewhat larger than the space of the familiar common-sense color-sensations, as we saw, but the latter finds its place quite neatly, and quite explicably, within the former.

Other kinds of sensations – auditory, gustatory, olfactory, somatosensory, visceral, and so on – will have to earn their own peculiar reductions to their own peculiar neurophysiological mechanisms. But nothing in principle stands in the way of such outcomes. The case of our color sensations provides a deeply instructive existence-proof of how such reductions can be achieved. The other cases can try to follow its example.

I close this section by addressing the old saw that the psychoneural identities claimed above cannot be genuine, since it is possible to know something like the H-J theory in exhaustive detail, and yet still not know what it is like to actually have a sensation of red.[6] Sundry refutations of this inference have been in the textbooks for decades (Nemirow, 1980; also Churchland, 1986, pp. 29–34, and 1998), but I here pass them by to offer a somewhat different take on why the inference is foolish. What is required to have a sensation-of-red, on the view defended above, is that the H-J theory be *true of* oneself: that one have a normally functioning neural network of the kind portrayed in Figure 10.1, and, moreover, that one have an activation-triplet across one's opponent-process neurons of <50%, 100%, 50%>. Whether or not one happens to *know* the H-J theory is, of course, utterly irrelevant to whether or not one has a sensation of red. And knowing the H-J theory would no more *give you* the sensation-of-red than knowing the theory of pregnancy would *make you* pregnant.

Furthermore, "*knowing* what it is like" to have a sensation-of-red requires, *additionally*, that the rest of one's brain, downstream from one's opponent-process neurons, be synaptically configured so as to respond automatically to the activities of one's opponent-process neurons in an appropriately discriminatory way. Without that learned discriminatory capacity – slowly acquired by one's synapse-adjusting color experiences during childhood – one's appreciation of the range and character of human color sensations must remain purely "theoretical," as opposed to "observational." This vital requirement, however, is precisely what is not met in all of the color-blind or color-naive subjects – such as Jackson's celebrated Mary – deployed in the traditional thought-experiments. Their nonstandard anatomies, or their nonstandard life histories, preclude their possessing the relevant downstream neural mechanisms, which require months and even years to organize themselves. And so, of course, these deprived subjects do not, they cannot, "know what it is like" to have a sensation-of-red (and this is true even on the materialists' own story), however much book-learned neuroscience they may have mastered.

But this fact does not entail that sensations-of-red are nonphysical. To see this clearly, note that, for the same suite of reasons, a color-deprived Mary would be equally ignorant of "what it is like" to actually have *an opponent-cell activation triplet of <50%, 100%, 50%>*! No amount of book learning will repair *that* deficit either. But that would hardly entail that such *activation triplets* are nonphysical. Evidently,

Paul M. Churchland

Mary's deficit with respect to sensations is entirely matched by her deficit with respect to opponent-cell activation triplets. That deficit, accordingly, entails nothing one way or the other about the physical/nonphysical status of either. That issue must be decided by our unfolding science, and not by any judo-flip arguments a priori. As we have seen in the preceding pages, the relevant science currently indicates that our sensations-of-color are indeed identical with our opponent-cell activation triplets. Which means that the former are just as physical as the latter.

And just as *real* as the latter. Which returns us to eliminative materialism. Where the common-sense ontology of sensations is concerned, eliminative materialism looks to be false. Sensations are not likely to be eliminated from our scientific ontology. They are already in the process of being smoothly reduced thereto.

4 Totting up the Prospects: The Propositional Attitudes

By contrast with the domain of sensations, a nontrivial case for the failings of folk psychology in the domain of the propositional attitudes has been in the textbooks for almost 25 years (Churchland, 1981).[7] I commend those arguments to the reader's attention, but will here pursue some more recent arguments, based on considerations that were still mostly hidden in 1981.

I begin with human language. A striking feature of the human command of the recursively generative structures of spoken and written language is its apparent uniqueness. Other animals do not seem able to master any but the most rudimentary aspects of this very powerful structure-producing engine. The problem is not so much that animals cannot speak. After all, speechless humans master the recursive complexities of sign language, which are (at least) equal to that of spoken language. And magnetic boards with moveable lexical items provide another avenue of combinatorial expression. Chimpanzees, notably, can learn some marginal skills in these other media, but their maximal adult performance is pitiful compared to an average two-year-old human infant, whose maturational profile is much slower than a chimpanzee's in any case. Humans clearly have some cognitive capacity that the ape lacks. The difference may indeed be only one of degree, but apparently it is a large difference in degree, at least in its effects on human versus ape linguistic behavior.

Other creatures perform even more poorly than the apes. All of this is intriguing since one of the central functions of language, perhaps *the* central function, is widely thought to be the public expression of *propositions*. These abstract entities have a complex but well-behaved combinatorial structure, a structure reflected in the grammatical structure of the sentences used to express them. Now, by the lights of folk psychology, animal cognition, no less than human cognition, consists in large part in the appropriate occurrence and administration of the various propositional attitudes. Dogs, lions, and apes, no less than humans, are thought to perceive that P, believe that Q, desire that R, fear that S, intend that T, and so on. And like us, their unfolding flux of propositional attitudes reflects the various abstract logical relations that variously obtain between the abstract propositions P, Q, R, S, and T (that is to say, they are, to a degree, *rational*). At least, that is how all of us reflexively presume to understand, explain, and anticipate animal behavior. We apprehend it in the same ways we apprehend human behavior: as a further instance of our beloved folk psychology. Animals may not be quite as smart as we are, but their cognition operates by the same basic principles as our own. So says common sense.

But there is a problem here. If animal cognition, like human cognition, consists in large measure in the production and manipulation of propositional attitudes, then animals, too, must have at least an implicit command of the recursive principles by which the logical structure of the propositions in such attitudes (the complex P in "believes that P," for example) is generated. That command may not equal our own command, but it will have to be highly sophisticated nonetheless, because animal perception, practical reasoning, causal insight, and even their social cognition is extremely penetrating. Think of a lion pride organizing a hunt whereby one subgroup skillfully drives the gazelle herd into a waiting ambush prepared by another subgroup. Think of a beaver family building a dam so as to sustain, behind it, a moat-surrounded house with an underwater entryway. Think of a mother pheasant repeatedly feigning a broken wing to lure a predator ever farther away from the chicks in her ground-level nest. Or think of a dog, with entreaty in its unblinking eye-contact, bringing its leash in its mouth and dropping it at the feet of its master when it needs to go for a walk. If the master is napping upstairs, the dog will even seek him out and wake him up with a probing paw, thence to present the request just described. Evidently, animals are smart. Smart enough that, if their sophisticated cognitive states and practical reasonings are to be represented by the propositional attitudes of folk psychology, those animals must possess a command of the recursively generated combinatorial structures displayed in the complex propositional attitudes we so naturally ascribe to them.

But if they do, then why are they so utterly incapable of learning a straightforward system – a language of some sort – for expressing precisely the sorts of combinatorial and structural intricacies that our default explanatory strategies plainly require of them? That is, if they already *think* within the medium of propositional attitudes, then why can't they learn a manipulable system that would allow them to *express* the propositions they are supposed to be already generating and manipulating? Perhaps – just perhaps – the reason is that their cognition does not consist of a logic-governed dance of propositional attitudes at all. Perhaps our common-sense folk-explanatory practices are a whopping case of anthropomorphism, a wanton projection, onto the animal kingdom at large, of categories that are appropriate to language-using humans, but not to creatures incapable of acquiring our highly idiosyncratic linguistic skills. Perhaps the cognition of nonhuman animals ultimately and properly requires an explanatory framework quite different from that provided by our current folk psychology.

That would not be too surprising. Pictures aside, language was the only example of a systematic medium of world-representation available to prehistoric humans (and perhaps to most contemporary humans too, for that matter). And so, it would be entirely natural for them to try to deploy it as a model for the internal-world-representing activities of other creatures, as well as for the internal-world-representing activities of their fellow humans. What else could they do? They had no access to whatever mysterious form of representational activity it is that shapes the inner life of nonhuman animals.

We contemporary humans, by contrast, *do* have some nontrivial access to the form of representational activity that shapes the inner life of every creature throughout the animal kingdom. For modern technology has given us access to the details of both the brain's microanatomy and its micro- and macro-behaviors. Research in these areas has pieced together a highly general portrait of cognitive activity, a portrait that bears little or no resemblance to that contained in folk psychology. And in contrast to folk psychology, this newer portrait does not suggest, even for a moment, that animals in general have a command of the abstract space of propositional attitudes. On this newer view, it is no surprise that nonhuman animals are utterly unable to learn a language. If anything, there is a minor mystery how *humans*, whose brains are architecturally similar to the brains of animals in general, manage to master this species-specific skill.

The elements of this newer portrait are easily outlined, although it will require some time and familiarity with it to fully appreciate the truly extraordinary representational and computational virtues of the biological machinery involved. We begin with the idea of a specific population of sensory neurons, such as those on the retina of the eye, those in the cochlea of the inner ear, those under the surface of the skin, those near the surface of the tongue, those contraction-sensitive neurons inside one's muscles, and so on. These sensory populations are typically very large. There are perhaps 100 million rods and cones in the retina, tens of thousands of frequency-sensitive "hair cells" in the cochlea, hundreds of thousands of mechano-receptors in the skin, and so forth. Collectively, each such population can provide a highly detailed portrayal of the particular aspect of local reality to which it is sensitive, just as a TV screen (which has roughly 200,000 pixels) can provide a detailed portrayal of a football game. (Notice, however, how much poorer is the TV screen compared to the human retina: 2×10^5 pixels for the TV versus fully 10^8 "pixels" for the human eye.)

We should be careful not to be too narrowly impressed by the examples of the retina and the TV screen. While good examples of what is called "population coding" (because a *single* representation uses the *entire population* of active elements), their specifically *picture*-like character is not typical of the genre. The many neurons in the cochlea of the inner ear, to provide a contrasting example, are arranged in a one-dimensional *line* rather than on a two-dimensional surface, and the pattern of activations across them represents the one-dimensional profile of energy levels across the range of wavelengths of incoming sound. The activation-patterns across one's *color*-coding neurons, as we saw earlier in this essay, represent a *three*-dimensional reality. The patterns of excitation across the taste neurons in one's tongue, to take a further example, represent a *five*-dimensional reality, since there are exactly five dimensions of chemical variation to which the five types of taste receptors on the tongue are sensitive: sweetness, sourness, saltiness, bitterness, and fattiness. The patterns of activation across the contraction-sensitive neurons inside one's body muscles represent an even higher-dimensional space: there are perhaps a thousand distinct muscles in one's body, and their collective state of contraction or relaxation specifies a unique posture for one's body and limbs. The momentary activation-pattern across one's contraction-sensitive neurons is thus the nervous system's opening portrayal of one's current overall posture, and as one's posture changes, so does the activation-profile across those neurons.

The Evolving Fortunes of Eliminative Materialism | 173 |

Of course, there is no point to having these high-dimensional sensory representations unless the information they currently contain is somehow sent forward to be exploited in some fashion. And so it is. Each of these myriad sensory neurons has a special extended filament, called an *axon*, that swiftly conveys the neuron's current level of excitation, along its often considerable length, to a largish family of *synaptic connections* at the several tips of its branching far end. Each of those synaptic connections makes a physical contact, as a baby's palm makes contact with a basketball, with some receiving neuron in a second population elsewhere in the brain. Collectively, and via their assembled axonal projections forward, the sensory neurons produce a secondary pattern of activation across that secondary population of neurons. But the pattern across the second population is typically an importantly *modified* version of the pattern sent to it by the first. This modification is owed to the hundreds of thousands, or even millions, of synaptic connections that intervene between the two populations. Some of those connections are excitatory; some are inhibitory; some are strong connections; others are weak. The consequence of forcing the original sensory activation-pattern through this intervening matrix of nonuniform synaptic connections is to *transform* the original sensory pattern into a *new* pattern, an activation-pattern now embodied in the second or receiving population of neurons.

What is the point of transforming it in this fashion? The point is to filter out, highlight, or discriminate aspects of the original sensory input that are of special relevance or interest to the creature that has it. The second neuronal population does not respond equally or indiscriminately to every possible sensory input. The peculiar arrangement of the synaptic connections bridging the two populations has been shaped by *learning* so that the receiving population responds vividly and selectively to certain patterns of sensory inputs, and hardly at all to most others. For example, the auditory input from a noisy downtown street constitutes a background din that the neurons in the auditory cortex mostly ignore. But a sensory input that contains the voice of one's own child against that background is an input that produces a large and highly distinctive response across the neurons in one's auditory cortex. Your child's voice is just an undistinguished part of the background hubbub, so far as your ear's ground-floor *cochlear* neurons are concerned: they passively represent everything faithfully and indiscriminately. But your child's voice is *selectively* represented within the population of second-story neurons at your *auditory* cortex. Most other information, while present at the first stage, simply doesn't make it through the intervening matrix of learned synaptic connections. Thanks to that learned synaptic matrix, the receiving neurons have thus acquired a special concern for, and an appreciation of, a specific dimension of possible auditory experience.

Nor is your child's voice the only possible input to have acquired such a preferred status. A mature auditory cortex has become selectively sensitive, in the same fashion, to a dog's bark, a cat's meow, a car's horn, the sound of breaking glass, screeching tires, musical instruments, and human voices in general. And within each such broad category, there will often be specific and distinct sensitivities to salient instances thereof, such as the voice of one's wife, one's child, one's best friend, and other individuals well known to one; or to guitars, pianos, harps, and other musical instruments with which one has become familiar.

All told, the space of possible activation-patterns across the neurons of one's auditory cortex has been sculpted, by learning, into an abstract and high-dimensional *map* of the "space" of *possible sounds*, a map that contains distinct and especially active locations for what past experience has presented as salient, important, and frequently repeated aspects of one's auditory environment. Closely *similar* objective sounds are represented by closely *proximate* locations within the space of possible activation-profiles across the relevant neurons, and dissimilar sounds are represented by activation-profiles at very distant locations within that activation space. That auditory map is not two-dimensional, as is a familiar fold-out highway map. Indeed, it may have as many distinct dimensions as there are distinct neurons in the auditory cortex! But it remains a map nonetheless, a map of the salient features of objective auditory space, and of the many similarity-relations and difference-relations that collectively configure them within that space.

Such a map embodies one's acquired *understanding* of a systematic family of *universals*, a background understanding or conceptual framework that is deployed each time one encounters an instance of any one of those universals in one's unfolding sensory experience. For that sensory input, thanks to its almost instantaneous transformation at the hands of the synaptic matrix through which it must pass, produces a specialized activation-pattern, within the space of the high-dimensional map, at one of its acquired landmark locations – a location for your child's voice, or for a piano, perhaps – that past training has made selectively sensitive. Such sensory-induced activations of learned activation-profiles are analogous to a laser-pointer's punctate illumination of some landmark location on a two-dimensional highway map, an illumination that indicates "You are *here*" within the space of possible geographical positions. In our brains, however, the "maps" are typically very high-dimensional, and the landmark "locations" within them represent various abstract *categories* or *properties*, rather than geographical places. But here, too, a sensory-induced activation at a particular point within that categorial map indicates that one is currently confronting an instance of the property therein represented.

The several distinct neuronal populations in the primary *visual* pathway display the same functional strategy, but this time the brain's concern is not with sounds, but rather with the space of possible shapes and spatial positions, the space of possible physical objects, and the space of possible motions, behaviors, and causal processes that physical objects may display over time, such as falling, bouncing, running, flying, throwing, and so forth. Here, too, the neuronal populations in the various areas of visual cortex gradually become, through learning, selectively responsive to a comparatively small range of salient, important, and frequently encountered kinds of sensory stimuli. Such stimuli produce signature activation-patterns across the higher-level cortical populations, as those populations also develop into *maps* of the range of important visual phenomena, and of the similarities and differences that unite and divide them. Thus does the brain develop, through learning, a conceptual framework for comprehending the visual world as well as the auditory world.

Beyond the primary visual and auditory pathways, there are, as you might expect, *polymodal* neuronal populations – that is, representational activation spaces that receive input from both of these sensory pathways, and from the tactile pathways as well. The various sensory tributaries, as it were, flow into a common and more voluminous informational river. These further populations slowly come to embody still more penetrating and perspective-neutral portrayals of the abstract categorial and causal structure of the world. Sensory inputs thereto can thus activate a very penetrating activation-pattern across such a downstream population, a pattern that provides a highly informed indication of one's actual here-and-now physical circumstance, as expressed within the conceptual framework or map embodied in that population.

Notice that, just as a current activation-*point* in such a background conceptual space represents a here-and-now instance of some *feature* or other, a continuous *sequence* of such activation-points represents an unfolding *process* of some sort in the world. Thus, a given neuronal population can slowly acquire a heightened sensitivity to special kinds of objective causal processes, to certain kinds of salient behaviors that unfold in time. Thus do the brain's many neuronal populations come to embody a library of prototypical trajectories in their activation spaces, in addition to a library of prototypical points. To undergo such a trajectory is (presumptively) to recognize the corresponding objective process.

Notice also that the mechanism here outlined embodies a general account of how the brain is always and inevitably *interpreting* its peripheral sensory input, interpreting it automatically and almost instantaneously, in terms of the waiting categories that prior learning has imposed (in the form of high-dimensional maps) on the many neuronal populations downstream from the sensory periphery. The theoretical picture here presented assigns an important priority to the brain's acquired grasp of the universe's categorial background structure, for it is only by means of that background structure that the brain is able to make specific and discriminative *sense* of the unfolding flux of its sensory inputs. The picture here is decidedly Platonic, in that knowledge of the general and timeless features of the universe is absolutely essential to making sense of its specific and ephemeral aspects.

So where does that general knowledge of the world's background structure come from? We certainly don't want to embrace Plato's own story: of an ideal world of perfect objects grasped by the immaterial mind before birth. But nor can we embrace the traditional empiricist alternative: that the senses grasp universals all by themselves, and then leave behind faint copies thereof to serve as the mind's ideas. For our sensory organs do no such thing. They simply respond to an endless variety of high-dimensional profiles of punctate causal activity from the objective world. It isn't until that teeming sensory chaos is selectively registered in one or more of the brain's higher-level cognitive maps that such input is interpreted in terms of general categories. Which leaves us re-posing the question: How does the brain acquire those categories? How are its maps of the domain of universals formed in the first place?

It must be by a process that operates prior to, and independently of, the familiar processes of induction, or hypothetico-deduction, or Bayesian learning. The reason is that these familiar processes are all "category-dependent." They all require a determinate conceptual framework already in place, within which hypotheses can be proposed, evidence can be stated, probabilities can be evaluated, and conclusions reached. The learning process that concerns us here, by contrast, is that process by which such categorial frameworks are formed in the first place. They must be formed by some other process entirely. And to be consistent with the positive cognitive story told so far, it must be a process that slowly *sculpts* the many matrices of *synaptic connections*

Paul M. Churchland

that transform the input activation-profiles into a series of progressively transformed activation-profiles across the brain's downstream neuronal population, for it is those very matrices that embody the brain's acquired categorial wisdom. It is they that dictate the acquired categorial structure of the activation-space of the specific neuronal population to which they connect.

The process has been known to neuroscientists for half a century, but it has been revealing its secrets only very slowly. It is called *Hebbian learning.* Present in all species, it is a mechanism of synaptic strengthening and/or weakening as a function of the axonal activity that flows through the synapses over protracted periods of time. Ultimately, of course, that axonal activity arises primarily from the brain's sensory neurons, and over time it embodies the *patterns* of activity – both spatial and temporal – that the external world displays. Hebbian learning is a mindless process by which the brain's synaptic connections are made selectively sensitive to *temporal coincidences* in the arrival of axonal activations to the diverse synaptic connections onto a shared non-sensory neuron. Any such neuron, of course, is likely to be in receipt of more than a thousand distinct synaptic connections arriving from a comparable number of distinct neurons from some upstream population. But if a specific subset of those synapses chronically brings an axonal excitation to the receiving neuron *always at exactly the same time,* the biochemical mechanisms inside the synapses gradually make those synapses, and only those synapses, larger and more effective in activating their common target. In sum, synapses that sing *together* have their individual voices gradually made "louder."

This is a process that slowly discovers order, structure, and repeating patterns in a flux of sensory inputs that must appear, at least at first, to be sheer unstructured chaos. The Hebbian process of synapse adjustment is a process that is deliberately blind to genuine noise and real chaos, but is selectively and constructively sensitive to real structure and to mutual information, especially if it is regularly repeated in the creature's unfolding experience. How this apparently simple process results in the sophisticated activation-space maps of complex domains of interrelated universals discussed above is a pretty question at which theorists and experimentalists are still hard at work, and will be for some time. But this seems to be the hand that Nature has dealt us: the creation of world-portraying categorial frameworks requires a *sub-conceptual* process of synaptic modification, and Hebbian learning would appear to be it, or at least a part of it.

A final virtue of the general cognitive story here outlined is its account of motor behavior and acquired skills, such as running, walking, throwing a baseball, or playing the piano. We here appeal again to the development of learned *trajectories* through a neuronal activation space, as briefly discussed above. But here we locate them in a population of *motor* neurons, neurons whose axons project to, and activate, the many muscles placed throughout the creature's body. Distinct activational trajectories will produce distinct orchestrations of muscle contractions and relaxations, and will thus produce distinct bodily behaviors extended in time. Such neuronal populations have been explored experimentally, and they, too, embody abstract maps, but this time they are maps of salient kinds of motor outputs.

Enough sketching. You now have an opening grasp of a systematic account of human and animal cognition – of perception, of learning, of the nature of conceptual frameworks, of the grasp of salient causal processes, and of the possession and deployment of motor skills – an account that makes detailed contact with the known neuroanatomy and neurophysiological behavior of terrestrial nervous systems. That account is not "behaviorist" in the least. To the contrary, it finds a rich economy of internal representational states interacting with one another, and with sensory inputs, to produce sophisticated motor behavior. Let us suppose, if only for the sake of argument, that it is basically correct. And let us ask, what are we now to make of the propositional attitudes, as presumed causal agents in the ebb and flow of animal cognition?

To this point, they don't appear at all, at least in our first-pass sketch. The fundamental unit of representation for *timeless* features of the universe appears to be the sculpted activation-space or abstract feature map, one produced by Hebbian learning, rather than the universally quantified sentence, a sentence produced by induction. And the fundamental unit of representation for *ephemeral* features of the universe appears to be the ephemeral activation-profile at a specific point within such an abstract map, rather than a singular observation sentence. Moreover, *computation* over those very powerful forms of representation appears to be a matter of the exceedingly swift transformation of one activation-profile into another profile, as performed by the brain's many matrices of synaptic connections. It does *not* appear to be a matter of drawing rule-governed inferences from one propositional attitude to another, a laboriously slow and narrowly informed process in any case, as the poor performance of classical AI research has gradually revealed to everyone's disappointment.

This last point is worth emphasizing, for there certainly do exist electronic "cognitive" systems specifically built so as to embody vast numbers of "propositional attitudes," expressed, of course, in some computer language, rather than in English. These internal "attitudes" are then processed by literal *rules* of inference and transformation, namely, the specific program that the computer is running. Here we have an undoubted informational economy of the same general kind as characterized by our beloved folk psychology: such electronic machines were deliberately built so as to instantiate the style of informational economy here at issue. But their cognitive performance has proved to be pitiful, compared to that of biological brains, and this despite the fact that a computer processes its data a billion times faster than the brain. (Axons conduct their action-potentials at roughly 10 m/s; copper wire conducts an EMF at roughly 10^7 m/s. Neurons can fire at perhaps 10^2 Hz; computer chips have a clock-speed of better than 10^5 Hz. A difference of 10^6 times a difference of 10^3 = a difference of 10^9.) In sum, machines that undoubtedly *do* conduct their cognitive affairs in the style of rule-governed inferences drawn over various propositional attitudes are, once we correct for the blistering speed advantage provided by their electronic components, *at least* a billion times dumber than their biological counterparts. I say, "at least," because, even *with* that artificial speed advantage, they fail to equal the cognitive achievements of their biological counterparts, for all but a few narrowly defined tasks, such as chess-playing and bookkeeping.

Once more, all of this is intriguing. When we look inside the brains of intelligent creatures widely supposed to manipulate propositional attitudes, we find nothing of the sort. Rather, we find a very different system of representation and computation,

Paul M. Churchland

one with many powerful and intriguing features of its own, one that is uniform in its basic rationale across the entire animal kingdom. And when we do construct artificial cognitive systems to perform the problematic manipulations of propositional attitudes supposed common in biological creatures, the artificial systems do not perform at anything like the levels displayed by their biological cousins. Apparently, the *fundamental* apparatus of biological cognition – the apparatus we share with all of our nonlinguistic fellow creatures – has nothing to do with propositional attitudes, or with rule-governed manipulations thereof. At bottom, it would seem, cognition is not a matter of propositional attitudes at all. It is a matter of vector coding (recall the high-dimensional activation-profiles) and vector-matrix processing (recall the transformation of activation-profiles at the hands of well-tuned cadres of synaptic connections). And those synaptic matrices are tuned by a process – Hebbian learning – that has nothing to do with discursive inferences of any kind. Where the propositional attitudes are concerned, and for animals in general, eliminative materialism looks like a good horse to bet on.

5 Is There a Residual Case for Propositional Attitudes in Humans?

"But surely," we may be inclined to respond, "humans must constitute a special case." In some respects, no doubt we are. I have already commented on the apparent fact that humans are unique in being able to learn the combinatorial system – language – necessary to express propositions publicly. What are we to make of this uniqueness?

We might suppose that it indicates a fundamental difference in the ways that human brains conduct their cognitive affairs. But a look at the neuroanatomy and neurophysiology of the adult human brain reveals an information-processing system continuous in its operations with those of the other primates, and indeed, with those of mammals in general. And adult humans stricken with *global aphasia* – with the destruction of the language-specialized cortical areas known as Broca's area and Wernicke's area – show a complete loss of the ability to comprehend or to produce language, in every medium or modality. (This is not a sensory or a motor deficit: those input and output pathways remain entirely undamaged. It is the higher machinery for representing and manipulating propositional structures that has been destroyed.) But such people remain cognitively competent and highly intelligent in most other respects. Even in humans, it seems, the basic machinery of cognition is no different from that found in animals.

What allows humans to acquire the skills involved in mastering a language appears to be a significant advantage we have in producing and in recognizing iterated sequences of elements, sequences that meet the structural demands of some non-random background complexity. This advantage – an advantage of degree – shows itself not just in our language skills, but also in other cognitive areas. Think of Euclid, compass and ruler in hand, spinning out diagrammatic geometrical proofs of theorem after theorem, all of them *valid*, potentially without end. Or think of Bach, hands at the keyboard, spinning out variations on a background chordal theme, all of them *harmonically coherent*, again potentially without end. Or think of a structural engineer, designing skyscrapers one after another, all of them *structurally sound*, again without limit. Like language skills, these other skills are both principled and productive. And incidentally, they, too, appear to be unique to humans. In light of this, the grammaticality of a sentence no longer appears to be so magically and portentously unique as is often believed.

Nor need be the brains that command all these skills. For what gives cognitive creatures a grip on any structured process that unfolds in time – such as chewing, swimming, walking, flying, playing the piano, or talking – is the recurrent axonal pathways that characterize every terrestrial nervous system, from the brainless leech on up. Learned trajectories in neuronal activation space require such recurrent pathways. Humans simply have more of them, and with larger neuronal populations than other creatures, we make better use of them. We also make *novel* use of them, as listed in the preceding paragraph. But none of this changes the basic elements and character of human cognition. They remain, humming away in the background, sustaining a host of motor and manipulative skills, most of them geologically old, some of them geologically quite new, but all of them dependent on the antecedent cognitive machinery of a massively parallel, vector-coding, matrix-processing computer.

In ascribing propositional attitudes to ourselves as our basic cognitive states, and in explaining our behavior in their terms, we are evidently trying to characterize a truly amazing cognitive machine – the brain – in terms of the idiosyncratic features of exactly one parochial game that only one species of animal has recently learned to play: language. From this perspective, why should we expect, even for a moment, that human language would reflect the basic elements and structure of the brain's cognition? Especially after we have looked inside the biological brain, and seen how it really works. The so-called propositional attitudes must be, at best, the occasional and ridiculously low-dimensional "projections" of the mega-dimensional elements of the brain's true representational vehicles. And even on that possibility, they are not the dynamically relevant elements that drive our cognitive activity. More likely still, they don't exist at all, even in humans. Folk psychology looks increasingly like another old friend: Ptolemaic astronomy. It serves moderately well for predicting a very narrow range of phenomena as seen from an extremely parochial perspective, but it badly misrepresents what is really going on. There is no crystal sphere that turns about us daily; we are not the center of the universe, neither astronomically nor cognitively; and human cognition does not consist in the crunching of sentence-like states according to structure-sensitive rules.

Notes

1   As a reminder: the Earth's diameter at its equator is roughly 25,000 miles, and anyone on the equator traverses that distance once every day, as the Earth turns on its axis. Such a person, then, has a constant velocity (eastwards) of 25,000 miles/24 h = 1,042 mph. As one moves northwards, the circle traversed in 24 hours gets smaller, but folks in Europe and the US are still moving at roughly 900 mph.

2   More accurately, Aristotle's dynamics was a more-or-less straightforward *codification* of our pre-existing common-sense dynamics, one that antedated Aristotle by many millennia.

3   For the classic philosophical discussions on these matters, see Hardin (1988) and Clark (1993).
4   For the explanation of this latter phenomenon, note that these are the only six color-sensations in the entire spindle that display a coding-triplet that is both (1) at maximum or extremal value – 0% or 100% – on exactly one of its three dimensions, and (2) at resting, neutral, or default level – 50% – on the other two dimensions. These six colors *center* the six faces of the opponent-cell activation-cube. For the explanation of the former phenomenon, see Churchland (2005).
5   For the full story on these particular matters, see again Churchland (2005).
6   For the contemporary *loci classici* of this worry, see Nagel (1982); also Jackson (1982) and Levine (1983). But in fact, this worry goes back to Nagel (1961), and even to Leibniz (1714).
7   This early paper has since been reprinted some 25 times, mostly, I fear, as an example of a just barely conceivable but plainly lunatic position.

References

Bennett, M. R. and Hacker, P. M. S. (2003). *Philosophical Foundations of Neuroscience.* Oxford: Blackwell.

Churchland, P. M. (1970). The logical character of action-explanations. *Philosophical Review,* 79, 214–36.

— (1979). *Scientific Realism and the Plasticity of Mind.* Cambridge: Cambridge University Press.

— (1981). Eliminative materialism and propositional attitudes. *Journal of Philosophy,* 78, 67–90.

— (1986). *Matter and Consciousness,* rev. edn. Cambridge, MA: MIT Press.

— (1998). Knowing qualia: a reply to Jackson. In P. M. Churchland and P. S. Churchland (eds.), *On the Contrary.* Cambridge, MA: MIT Press.

— (2005). Chimerical colors: some phenomenological predictions from cognitive neuroscience. *Philosophical Psychology,* 18, 527–60.

Clark, A. (1993). *Sensory Qualities.* Oxford: Oxford University Press.

Feyerabend, P. K. (1963). Materialism and the mind–body problem. *Review of Metaphysics,* 17, 49–66.

Hardin, C. L. (1988). *Color for Philosophers: Unweaving the Rainbow.* Indianapolis: Hackett.

Hurvich, L. M. (1981). *Color Vision.* Sunderland, MA: Sinauer.

Jackson, F. (1982). Epiphenomenal qualia. *Philosophical Quarterly,* 32, 127–36.

Leibniz, G. (1714). *The Monadology,* trans. G. R. Montgomery (1992). Buffalo, NY: Prometheus.

Levine, J. (1983). Materialism and qualia: the explanatory gap. *Pacific Philosophical Quarterly,* 64, 354–61.

Nagel, E. (1961). *The Structure of Science: Problems in the Logic of Scientific Explanation.* New York: Harcourt Brace World.

Nagel, T. (1982). What is it like to be a bat? *Philosophical Review,* 83, 435–50.

Nemirow, L. (1980). Review of *Mortal Questions,* by Thomas Nagel. *Philosophical Review,* 89, 473–7.

Rorty, R. (1965). Mind–body identity, privacy, and categories. *Review of Metaphysics,* 19, 24–54.

Taylor, C. (2005). Descombes' critique of cognitivism. *Inquiry,* 47, 203–18.

SHOULD PHYSICALISTS BE A PRIORI PHYSICALISTS?

A Priori Physicalism

Frank Jackson

Physicalism and the Mind–Brain Identity Theory

Mental states play causal roles. Bodily damage causes pain, which in turn causes writhing. Turning on the lights causes perceptions of a burglar, which in turn causes dialing the police. Work on the brain and the way it processes information from the environment, and on the way this information induces movements in bodies, strongly supports the view that the causal roles played by mental states are in fact played by brain states. These reflections lead us to the famous schematic argument for the mind–brain identity theory:

Mental state M = the state that plays causal role R

The state that plays causal role R = brain state B

Therefore, $M = B$.[1]

We distinguish dual attribute and physicalist versions of identity theory. The physicalist version of the view that mental states are brain states – physicalism – is a view about the *properties* of these brain states to the effect that their properties are one and all the kinds of properties that appear in the physical sciences: physics, chemistry, and the biological sciences, including especially neuroscience. They are one and all physical properties. By contrast, the dual attribute version of the view that mental states are brain states holds that these brain states – the ones that are mental states – have special properties that are outside the ken of the physical sciences. It is these properties that constitute the *hurtfulness* of a pain, or that constitute *consciousness*, or the distinctive *sensory nature* of perceptual experience.[2]

A lot has been said about the notion of a physical property that appears in the above account of physicalism. But our debate is independent of the controversial details.[3] We can think of physicalism as holding that sentience does not need radically new properties. Suitable complexity of organization of that which has the kinds of properties that figure in the physical sciences is enough.

Physicalism, then, is a no extra properties doctrine. In some sense – more on the sense below – mental properties are physical properties; psychological kinds are physical kinds. In addition, physicalism is typically a doctrine about the world at large as well as about the mind. The impetus behind it is the conviction that there is nothing "spooky" about the mind, the conviction that we minded creatures are highly complex but physically explicable parts of our world. From this perspective it would be strange to insist that consciousness and the mind fall within the purview of the physical sciences but that a table, or Germany, or the American economy do not. (An obvious question is how one might argue that an economy has only physical properties: economics is not one of the physical sciences listed above. We address this question below.)

The Disagreement between A Priori and A Posteriori Physicalism

If mental nature is not an addition to physical nature, then the physical way things are necessitates the mental way things are. Fix the physical way things are and you have done enough to fix the mental way things are. There is no more to do. The necessitation is not causal – there would not be a small time lag between fixing the physical way things are and fixing the mental way things are, and there would be no transfer of energy. The necessitation is logical.

Everything in philosophy is controversial (just about), but it is widely agreed that physicalists are committed to the determination of the mental by the physical in something (*something*) like the above sense. What divides a priori physicalists from a posteriori physicalists is the nature of the determination. Is it a priori, or is it a posteriori? Is it like the determination of X's shape by the location of the points that make up X's exterior, or is it like the determination of where water is by where H_2O is? A priori physicalists say it belongs in the first category; a posteriori physicalists say that it belongs in the second. They agree that the determination is logical but disagree over whether it is a case of the necessary a priori or the necessary a posteriori. (Some who hold the second position prefer to call the necessity *metaphysical* rather than logical.)

It has always been clear that the concepts of necessity and apriority differ: There is a conceptual difference between, on the one hand, having to be true, being true in every possible world, and, on the other, being knowable in principle without recourse to experience. But until recently it has not been so clear that there is a difference in extension, that there are many examples of truths that are necessary and a posteriori (and truths that are contingent and a priori). Now that this is clear – "Any water is H_2O" is necessarily true while being a posteriori, for famous example – we have two live ways of being a physicalist.[4]

This essay is concerned to make a case for a priori physicalism, or, better, a case for holding that physicalists should be a priori physicalists. Someone who is not a physicalist may hold that physicalists should be a priori physicalists, perhaps adding "So much the worse for physicalism" (as I did before I converted to physicalism, and,

Frank Jackson

e. g., David Chalmers still does).[5] However, it makes the discussion simpler if we presume physicalism, and we will do this in what follows.

De Re versus De Dicto Versions of the Debate

When we say above that the debate is over the nature of the determination of the mental by the physical, we might have in mind the nature of the relation between certain linguistic expressions that stand for the mental and the physical – that's the *de dicto* version of the debate – or we might have in mind the nature of the relation between the features, the ways things might be, and not the words we use for them (that's the *de re* version of the debate); or we might be fudging.

Although my description above of the debate between a priori and a posteriori physicalism is naturally read as describing the *de re* issue (and my description is not atypical) and although we physicalists might well think that the *de re* issue is the one of most interest because physicalism is a doctrine in metaphysics, the debate in the literature is, when one digs into it, mostly focused on the *de dicto* issue. The focus is on whether or not physicalists must hold that one can in principle deduce the mental from enough detailed information about the physical, where deduction is thought of as akin to what happens in the *lines* of a proof – lines in the sense of sentences or anyway in the sense of something in the region covered by the term "*de dicto.*" However, it is important to note that the claim concerns what is possible in principle. There is no suggestion that anyone with less than godlike powers could actually carry out the deduction of the mental from the physical. Consider the very complex sentence that gives the location of every molecule in the universe at some given point in time (we can suppose that there is a finite number for our purposes here). The shape of each and every molecular array in the universe at that time follows a priori from this sentence. One could in principle deduce the shape of every array, but *only* in principle. In practice the deduction of shape from locations is only possible in cases involving a relatively small number of accessible molecules. And even there it is often better to look: it is often easier to *see* that some set of molecules form a circular array than it is to calculate the fact from, say, their coordinates.

We will start by looking at the debate understood *de dicto*. For now, our discussion should be read as directed to the debate *de dicto* even when there is no explicit flagging one way or the other.

I will offer two reasons for holding a priori physicalism to be the physicalism of choice. One is epistemological, and the other is a semantic argument that turns on a certain view about what we do with words when we use them to describe our world. The discussion of the second leads naturally into a discussion of a priori physicalism understood *de re*.

The Epistemological Argument from Zombies for A Priori Physicalism

It is a reasonably recent discovery that water is H_2O. For a long time, water was believed to be a basic constituent of our world, not a compound of more basic constituents, and even after it was suspected that water is a compound of oxygen and hydrogen, there was for a time debate over the ratio of hydrogen to oxygen. Although it is necessarily true that water is H_2O, it is epistemically possibility that water is not H_2O, and until the key experiments by Lavoisier in the 1700s, that possibility received significant credence.

The above paragraph is a reminder that when we are dealing with the necessary a posteriori, there are *two* epistemic possibilities: that we have a truth and that we have a falsehood. This makes a posteriori physicalism vulnerable to a version of the famous zombie argument against physicalism in general, as we now see. I have in mind the following version of the zombie argument.

Perhaps it is impossible to have two worlds exactly alike physically while differing in cognitive mental states such as belief and desire. States like these, states that lack a distinctive phenomenology, do seem to be intimately tied to functional roles of a kind that must be in common between the physically exactly alike. However, the situation with those mental states for which there is something it is like to be in them – conscious pain, perceptions of red, and all the rest – is completely different. It clearly is possible that I be physically exactly like a *zombie*. Being physical duplicates, we writhe alike, but only I have pain, real pain, accompanying the writhing. He *feels* nothing. But if I differ from my zombie twin in having consciousness, my consciousness must be something more than my physical nature, for that is something we share. It follows that physicalism is false.[6]

A posteriori physicalists often pride themselves on having a good reply to this argument: zombie twins aren't possible but they seem to be possible because their impossibility is a posteriori. The conditional that goes from physical nature to my conscious nature is necessary a posteriori.

The irony is that their very granting of the epistemic possibility of zombies makes serious trouble for them. There are two epistemic possibilities according to a posteriori physicalists: (i) I and my zombie twin are exactly alike physically but differ in that I alone have phenomenal consciousness; (ii) I and my zombie twin are exactly alike physically *and* alike in lacking phenomenal consciousness. How can a posteriori physicalists consistently argue that we know or have any reason to believe that it is the second epistemic possibility that is realized? When physicalists of either stripe discuss the use by dualists of the zombie argument, they often point out that dualists must admit that the unconscious zombie that they argue is possible would have the very same cognitive states as we conscious creatures do; would produce the very same sentences, including ones like "It is immediately introspectively obvious to me that I am conscious and that this is something over and above anything to be found in my physical makeup"; would have the very same putative memories of pain; and so on. The zombies would be convinced that they were not zombies. The reason is that the conviction in question is determined by the physical alone, and we and our zombie twins are exactly alike physically. But what is sauce for the goose is sauce for the gander. A posteriori physicalists must admit that they could not tell the difference between the epistemic possibility that, as they fervently believe, they are not zombies and have conscious experiences, and the epistemic possibility that they are themselves zombies.

Moreover, there is nothing they can point to that is well explained by the first epistemic possibility but not by the second. Of the two epistemic possibilities – that water is H_2O and that water is not H_2O – the first alone explains a host of experiment results, which is why we are certain it obtains. By contrast, there is nothing that the a posteriori physicalist can point to as being well explained by the hypothesis that we are not zombies that is not explained equally well by the hypothesis that we are zombies. Moreover, there is no gain in simplicity or ontological austerity in adopting the hypothesis that we are not zombies.

The key point here applies more generally to scientific reductions, including the famous reduction of the thermodynamic theory of gases to statistical mechanics. When it was discovered that the functional roles played by pressure, temperature, and volume in gases, as given in idealized form in the ideal gas law, were played by various molecular-statistical properties, we had a choice: identify or eliminate. We could have said that we had discovered what temperature, for example, *is*, or we could have said that gases lack temperature and that the explanatory role that we once needed temperature for has been handed across to a certain energy property of gas molecules. I think the reason for saying the second can only be that the functional roles played by pressure, temperature, and volume are, near enough, definitive of those properties. In consequence, it is a priori that finding that which plays the roles is finding what pressure, temperature, and volume *are*; it is not finding out that we need no longer have reason to believe that gases have such properties.[7] For suppose that no matter how great our knowledge of gases were, as expressed in terms of molecular-statistical properties, it always remained an epistemic possibility that gases lacked, say, temperature – and that will be the case if the passage from molecular-statistical knowledge, no matter how exhaustive, to gases having temperature is irremovably a posteriori – what reason could we give for putting our money on the epistemic possibility that gases are at such-and-such a temperature as opposed to the epistemic possibility that they lack temperature properties but have certain molecular-statistical properties?

We can now put the problem for a posteriori physicalism more directly. A posteriori physicalists (but not a priori physicalists) must allow that there are two epistemic possibilities: that things are physically exactly as they actually are and there is sentience, and that things are physically exactly as they actually are and there is no sentience. There seems no reason they can give for favoring the first over the second. The first has no explanatory advantage and no advantage in terms of simplicity over the second.

I now turn to our second argument.

The Semantic Argument for A Priori Physicalism

Words are useful in the same way as flags and maps. They represent how things are; they carry putative information. We know what a red dot on a shopping center map represents about how things are, the putative information it provides. It is the same information as is carried by the words "You are here." Indeed often those very words are placed next to the red dot on shopping mall maps as a bit of overkill. Likewise, a red flag may signal danger, as does the word "danger" suitably deployed. The ability of maps, flags, words, and sentences to represent how things are in a way that allows them to be sources of information rests on there being a function from the physical structures – the flags, sentence tokens, marks on maps, and so on – to one or another way things might be, *plus* our knowing what that function is. The existence of the function in ignorance of what it was would be useless. It would be like having a map with symbols you do not understand, or trying to find your way around in a city whose language you do not understand.

As the representationalist-cum-source-of-information view of language is sometimes denied,[8] let me labor it with a simple "hands on" example. If I produce the words "There are exactly four chairs in this room" at a seminar, anyone with a grasp of English knows how things in the room would have to be in order for that sentence to be true, and what to do to the chairs to make the sentence true should that be necessary. How so unless there is a function from the sentence to the relevant aspect of how things are being represented to be, and moreover one we grasp?

Psychological terms and the sentences employing them represent things as being a certain way, and we know what that way is, or at least we do when the sentences are in a language we understand. The alternative is to hold that we don't know what we are saying when we say that someone is in pain (why then do we care on hearing or seeing the words?), or believes in God, or likes chocolate. What property then is being ascribed by our use of the phrase "believes that snow is white"? There are a number of possible answers but physicalists must insist that the answers are restricted to physical properties. The instantiation of what is being ascribed is what makes the ascription true but, for physicalists, the only properties instantiated are physical ones. It follows that they had better be the properties being ascribed. On pain of making all psychological ascriptions false, physicalists must allow that their very understanding of psychological predicates delivers to them the physical properties ascribed by those predicates. Our very understanding of, for example, the sentence "x believes that snow is white" tells us how things have to be if that sentence is to be true, but that "how things have to be" had better be physical if physicalism is to be true. But then the passage from the physical to descriptions of how things are in psychological terms is accessible from understanding alone. That's tantamount to a priori physicalism understood *de dicto*.

Some (Substantial) Tidying Up

I have given the bare bones of the semantic argument. Now for the needed qualifications and clarifications.

First, I assumed that psychological ascriptions are often true. That is why it had to be the case that they ascribed physical properties if physicalism is true. But many physicalists hold that our mental language embodies a degree of error consequent on the fact that the folk conception of sensory states attributes to them intrinsic *qualia*-type properties, or perhaps a strong kind of privacy property that physicalism tells us is nowhere instantiated, or in the case of intentional states, propositional modularity.[9] If this is the case, the properties the folk ascribe are nowhere instantiated and, if we go by the strictest standards, the only viable form of physicalism is the eliminative version. In that case I cannot insist that the physicalist must allow that our

Frank Jackson

understanding of the language of psychology reveals the physical properties ascribed by that language.[10] Nevertheless, unless we are prepared to embrace the idea that when we talk, think, and write about the mind, we folk are talking, thinking, and writing about *nothing*, there needs to be an understanding of our psychological language that is close to the folk one and that ascribes properties, physical ones as physicalists must hold, that we grasp and that are, on the relevant occasions, actually possessed. It is psychological predicates and sentences – or a good number thereof – so understood that I hold follow a priori from a suitable conjunction of physical ones. There had better be some kind of tidying up of our ordinary psychological language and concepts that is close enough to count as a tidying up and not an elimination, which is such that understanding the language amounts to grasping the psychological properties ascribed by that language and which allows us to see how the properties picked out by that language follow a priori from the physical.

Second, it might be objected that we do not need to know what psychological terms stand for in order to use them fruitfully. It might be held that we do not know what "pain," say, stands for, but we know enough to make sense of its role in debate over the mind and enough to feel sorry for someone who we are told in words is in pain. There is a deal of opacity connected with the term but it is much less than that associated with words in languages we do not understand. This might be part of a view that holds out the promise of one day knowing precisely what the property is.

We need, however, to know *something* about the property "pain" stands for. We do not do much by way of anchoring debate on the mind and accounting for the communicative value of psychological language if we know merely that psychological terms stand for *some* property or other. But suppose we know that "pain" stands for the property, whatever it is, that is K. Our degree of ignorance is over which property it is that is K. If this is correct, under what circumstances will we use the word "pain" to describe something? Obviously, when we think it has the property of *having* the property that is K. But this means that what we are saying about something when we say it is in pain is that it has the property of having the property that is K. But then "pain" stands for the property of having the property that is K, and we do, after all, know what it stands for. Perhaps one day "pain" will stand for the property that is K, whatever that property is, but that is another question.

The key point is that to apply a word to x just when it has some property or other that meets condition K, in ignorance of what that property might be, is not to use the word to ascribe an unknown property: it is to use it to ascribe the property of having whatever it is that meets condition K.

Third, it might be objected that the terms "water" and "H_2O" stand for the same property and, though it is a priori that any property is self-identical, it would be wrong to infer that "Any water is H_2O" is a priori. It is famously a posteriori.

This objection misunderstands the sense we are giving to a predicate standing for a property. What makes it true in English that the word "round" stands for the shape that "$\bigcirc$" exemplifies is that one who understands English knows that "round" is a word to use to convey the information that something has that shape. Now the word "water" is not a word we learn to use to convey the information that something is H_2O. If it were, "Any water is H_2O" would be a priori; what makes "Any water is H_2O" a posteriori is precisely that we do not use the word "water" for H_2O. Rather, we learn to use the word "water" for the kind that is watery: the potable, normally but not always clear kind that falls from the sky, fills the oceans, was baptized with the word "water" by English-speakers, and all that, and that roughly is the information about how things are that we use the word "water" to pass around.

In discussion I have met the following objection. "Water" *is* a word for conveying putative information about, say, where H_2O is. When people said, even before it was known that water is H_2O, that lakes contain water, they were giving out the information that lakes contain H_2O. The reason is that to give out putative information is to say what you believe, and the belief that lakes contain water is one and the same as the belief that lakes contain H_2O. Surprising but true, in much the way that it is surprising but true according to many that the belief that Hesperus is Phosphorous is the belief that Hesperus is Hesperus (so we must not say that the second is a priori true and the first is a posteriori true). This position is of a piece with the view that when you look at a glass of water and your visual experience represents that there is water in the glass, it equally represents that there is H_2O in the glass. I have to say that positions like these seem to me to be exercises in "bullet biting," but let me try to bring out their implausibility with an argument rather than a phrase.

Surely the following epistemic state is a possible one to be in. You believe there is a unified kind that manifests itself to you in various ways, but you have no belief as to what that kind is. You can, that is to say, believe that there is a kind that is in fact of type K without believing that it is of type K. But creating a word, say, "water," for that kind would not in itself change what you believe about how things are – introducing a word does not make for new belief (except for the belief that there's a new word around). Words *per se* are not belief-makers. Ergo, the belief that x is water is not the belief that x is H_2O.

Of course we are left with the problem of what to say about the fact that the word "water" refers to H_2O at all possible worlds, and this fact's connection with what one believes when one believes that x is water. Isn't reference across possible worlds how we capture how things are being represented to be? Representation *is* dividing how things might be, possible worlds, into those in accord, versus those not in accord, with how things are being represented to be? This is a controversial issue but the answer I favor draws on some ideas that come to us from two-dimensional modal logic.[11]

There are two ways to think of the reference of a word at different possible worlds: on one way we track the reference of the word at w, for every w; on the other, we track the reference of the word at w under the supposition that w is actual, for every w. Often it makes no difference: an example is the word "round." Often it does make a difference: an example is the word "water." When it does make a difference, the reference that captures what a word stands for in our sense is the reference at w under the supposition that w is actual and, in my view, the reference of "water" at w under the supposition that w is actual is to the kind that is watery, which is H_2O at our world but not at all worlds.[12]

Finally and perhaps most importantly, the schematic version of the semantic argument would seem to contradict something that is close to common ground among physicalists, namely, that physicalism is a contingent truth. There are possible worlds where it is false. Mentality might have been realized in "nonphysical" stuff. But if

Frank Jackson

this is right, it seems that what we say about how x is when we use the word "pain" or the phrase "believes that snow is white" to describe it cannot be that x has such-and-such a physical nature. For how then could the truth of physicalism be contingent?

At this point we need to address a matter scooted over early on. We said that we would use "physical properties" for properties that appear in the physical sciences – physics, chemistry, and biology. Many have pointed out that the reference to physical sciences had better not be to physical sciences as they are as of now, for then physicalism would require a commitment to the bold (too bold) doctrine that the properties that appear in physical sciences as they are now will not need emendation in the future. But if it is physical sciences at the end of inquiry, isn't the resulting notion of a physical property too vague? It gives too much of a hostage to fortune.

One's attitude to this objection partly depends on how confident one is that the properties that appear in current physical science will still be there at the end of the day. But we can sidestep the issue. For us, the reference to the physical sciences can be thought of as a reference to those sciences concerned to give an account of the non-sentient items of our world: water molecules, cells, nerve fibers, force fields, the big bang, the sun, and so on. Physicalism is then the doctrine that the properties needed for those parts of our world are enough for all of our world including, for example, the humans and the cats.

However, there is still a problem. Call the properties that count as physical by the criterion just given physical$_1$ properties. Physicalism as a metaphysical doctrine about the fundamental nature of our world, and not just the mental part of it, holds that our world is a huge aggregation of things with physical$_1$ properties (in the wide sense that includes relations). I am a very complex medium-sized aggregation of cells, nerves, fluids, hairs, skin, bones, and so on, whose nature is given in full by the physical sciences. Canada is a complex, much larger aggregation of rocks, rivers, and so on, again whose nature is given in full by the physical sciences. The world in its entirety is an even bigger and even more complex aggregation of me, you, Canada, the sun, and so on and so forth. However, we cannot say that the huge aggregation that is our world has only physical$_1$ properties, and the same goes for bits of our world like you and me and Canada.[13]

The reason is that aggregation creates new properties in the sense of creating new patterns in nature. Three straight lines arranged in a certain way make a triangle. None of the lines has the property of being triangular: it is the aggregation that has that property. A house is an aggregation of items none of which is itself a house. Aggregations of items with only physical$_1$ properties will exemplify patterns that do not match up with any physical$_1$ properties. This means that when we say that physicalism is the view that minds, and everything on the wide reading of physicalism, have only physical properties, that physicalism is explicitly not a species of dual attribute theory, we must give the notion of a physical property a wider reading. A physical property is any property possessed by items that are, and that are set in a world that itself is, nothing more than an aggregation of items having physical$_1$ properties only. Every property that is instantiated is either a physical$_1$ property or is a property one can get by aggregation of the physical$_1$ by modes of aggregation that are themselves physical$_1$. This connects with a familiar way of characterizing physicalism in terms of what can be created from a given set of ingredients. Give God enough physical₁ ingredients and physical₁ modes of composition, and She can make minds, pain, and inflation – that is the essential idea behind physicalism.[14] And we can now answer the question posed near the beginning of how physicalism might plausibly claim that an economy has only physical properties. What is false is that an economy has only physical₁ properties; what is true, according to physicalism, is that an economy has only the properties that one can get by aggregating enough items with physical₁ properties alone.

We can now return to the point that launched this discussion of what counts as a physical property. The sense in which physicalists are committed to holding that psychological predicates ascribe physical properties is the wide sense, and in that sense items made of stuff that has properties quite foreign to those found in the physical sciences, that is, properties that are not physical₁ properties, can have physical properties. Physicalism insists that mental properties are patterns in the physical₁ properties, but those patterns might be patterns in aggregations of items that have properties quite distinct from the physical₁ properties. The mental properties are patterns in the physical₁ – that's what makes physicalism true – but what makes the truth of physicalism *contingent* is that they might have been patterns in properties other than the physical₁ properties. Physicalists say that God might have made consciousness from physical₁ ingredients alone, suitably arranged. This is consistent with holding that God might also have made consciousness from quite different ingredients, suitably arranged. Indeed functionalists about the mind will go on to explain that all that is required is that the suitable arrangements in both cases preserve the key functional roles. The functional roles are the patterns in reality that are the mental properties.

The Analogy with Shapes and the Relevance of Functionalism

We have just said – speaking as good physicalists but independently of the disagreement between a priori and a posteriori versions – that mental properties are physical properties in the sense of being patterns in the physical₁. This means that the claim above in support of a priori physicalism – that physicalists had better allow that our understanding of mental predicates delivers the physical property ascribed by the predicate – amounts to the claim that our understanding of mental predicates had better deliver the relevant patterns in the physical₁. How could that possibly be true? Our *understanding* tells us *that* much?

Our ability to recognize shapes suggests a way of thinking about the problem.

People can learn to recognize and name the shapes of closed figures without knowing the formulae that gives the commonality among the points that make up their boundaries. All the same, the locations of those points a priori determine the shapes, and there will be a formula that shows this. This is because finding the formulae satisfied by the points that make up any given shape is an exercise in mathematics and mathematics is an a priori discipline. In the case of circles it is an easy exercise; in the case of shape recognition of handwritten words, it is a very hard one tackled by those who write programs to turn handwriting into *Times New Roman*. We are able to recognize the pattern, the commonality, that unites the written a's. We cannot write down the formula that gives it but there must be one, and it will express the a priori way that the locations of the points of something with the "a" shape make it "a"-shaped. That is to say, if α is a name for that shape – where α is *not* the name of the response that prompts the judgment that something is an "a," but is the name of the *shape* that is shared between all the "a"-shaped and that prompts the judgment – there is a complex sentence giving location of the boundary points of X that a priori entails "X is α." What is more, we folk know this. We know that α is nothing more than a pattern among point locations.

A priori physicalists have to say that the language of psychology is like this but in a much more complex way – and one way to put a bit of detail on these bones draws on a functionalist picture of the mind. But let's introduce the key point with a simpler example: inflation. Inflation is a pattern among facts concerning the role of money in securing goods. No one can write down some neat formula that says "There is inflation in an economy" is true if and only if such-and-such is happening to the amount of money required to secure a house or a car or.... But we know a priori that if two economies differ in regard to inflation, they differ somewhere or other in matters to do with securing goods using money. This bit of a priori knowledge reveals the fact that we use the word "inflation" for a pattern *in* the role of money in securing goods. Now consider two people who differ in their mental makeup. There is some plausibility – of course the matter is debatable in a way that does not obtain in the inflation example – that *somewhere* this difference will show up in the actual or possible ways they interact with, and store information about, the world. If one wants candy more than the other, she will reach for candy that little bit faster; if one fears tigers more than the other, were they each to be confronted with a tiger, one would run that bit faster; if one itches that bit more than the other, the disposition to scratch will be that much stronger; if one knows the answer to a problem that the other does not, there will be a possible way this will manifest itself in behavior; if one is conscious of a pain to a greater extent than the other, this will, in some possible circumstances, show up in a difference in reactions to their surroundings; and so on. Moreover, there are folk maxims connecting behavior and mental states that are arguably part of our understanding of what it is to be in those states. Examples are: belief is a state that seeks to fit the world, whereas desire is a state that seeks to change the world; subjects act so as to realize their desires if their beliefs are true; subjects act so as to prolong pleasures and curtail pains; perceptions are responses to our surroundings that enable us to navigate those surroundings; and so on.

If difference in mental nature implies functional difference, then sameness in functional nature implies sameness in mental nature. The language of psychology will be a language for picking out functional patterns. This implies that enough detailed knowledge of our worlds in physical$_1$ terms delivers a priori the account of our world in mental terms, for it delivers a priori all the functional and information-storage facts, and the language of psychology is a language for those latter facts. In this picture there is no suggestion that we might be able to write down sentences framed in physical$_1$ terms that a priori entail sentences about seeing red or believing in God, but we cannot write down sentences about point locations that a priori imply that X is α. In both cases, we have a mastery of a language for patterns – in one case in the functional, in the other case in point locations – a mastery that involves substantial recognitional capacities, and in both there must be certain a priori true conditionals, in one case from location to shape, and in the other from physical$_1$ to functional to mental, but in neither is there an ability to write down the antecedents of those a priori true conditionals.

De Re A Posteriori Physicalism and the Problem of Distancing *De Re* A Posteriori Physicalism from Dual Attribute Theories

We have focused on the debate read *de dicto*. I will close with a short discussion of the debate read *de re*.[15] What should physicalists say about the determination of the mental way things are by the physical way things are, read not as a claim about words for those ways but as about the ways, the properties, themselves?[16] They should say that this determination is a priori, otherwise they cannot distance themselves from a necessitarian version of dual attribute theories.

Necessitarian versions of dual attribute theories of mind agree with physicalism in holding that the physical way things are necessitates the mental while insisting that the mental is distinct from the physical. They sometimes use an interesting theory of laws as an illustrative analogy. On this theory, the law in the special theory of relativity that light is a first signal is a necessary a posteriori truth, because the properties of being light and being a first signal, while being distinct, are such that the first a posteriori necessitates the second.[17] How can we physicalists distance ourselves from this position?

One way is to say that it is fundamentally confused: it violates the Humean principle that distinctness implies separability. I have some sympathy with this position but it involves holding that the interesting theory of lawhood just mentioned is fundamentally confused. Also, I would be more comfortable in making the allegation of fundamental confusion if I had in my back pocket a neat statement, immune from counterexamples, of the Humean distinctness doctrine. I don't. The secure way for physicalists to distance themselves from necessitarian dual attribute theories is to *say* that mental properties are *identical* to uncontroversially physical ones. They need to add to physicalism's claim that the mental supervenes on and is necessitated by the physical, an identity claim that for each mental property M something of the form

M = the property of being so-and-so

is true, where being so-and-so is beyond question physical, though of course they may not know exactly which value to give "so-and-so" for any given M.

What is it to be beyond question physical? It is to be such that it is transparent that it is a priori determined by the physical$_1$. Indeed most often the claim is that being so-and-so is one or another physical$_1$ property, and so it is trivial that it is a priori determined by the physical$_1$.[18] The claim is, for instance, that something like the following holds

pain, the type = having C-fibers' firing

where this is a necessary a posteriori truth, and having C-fibers' firing is a priori determined by the physical$_1$ because it is physical$_1$. An alternative identity strategy affirms identities of the form

pain, the type = being in functional state such-and-such

where it is transparent that being in functional state such-and-such is a priori determined by the physical$_1$.[19]

But physicalists who distance themselves from necessitarian dual attribute theories by affirming identities of either kind are, by Leibniz's law, committed to a priori physicalism read in the *de re* sense. If mental properties are identical to properties a priori determined by the physical$_1$ way things are, then mental properties are a priori determined by the physical$_1$ way things are, whatever may be the case for one or another linguistic representation of the relation between the mental and the physical.

Acknowledgments

The seeds for this volume were sown in a debate with Brian McLaughlin at the Fifth International Congress of the Society for Analytical Philosophy, in Bielefeld. My side is given in Jackson (2005). The essay here draws on, while being a substantial development of that paper. I am indebted to discussion at that congress, with Brian McLaughlin especially, despite our failing to convince each other. I am also indebted to decades of discussions of physicalism with friends and colleagues.

Notes

1   See, e.g., Lewis (1966) and Armstrong (1968).
2   See, e.g., Campbell (1970).
3   Though this claim is itself controversial; for more argument and references see Jackson (1998).
4   I take it for granted, with the majority, that the work of (especially) Kripke (1980) and Putnam (1975) make a decisive case that there is a difference in extension. What is more controversial is whether the difference in extension is true for propositions as well as for sentences.
5   See Jackson (1994) and Chalmers (1996).
6   See Campbell (1970) and Chalmers (1996) for arguments of this style.
7   This is the picture of reduction that informs Armstrong's and Lewis's approach to the identity theory in, respectively, Armstrong (1968) and Lewis (1966).
8   See, e.g., Davidson (2001).

9   See, e.g., Churchland (1981); Lewis (1995); Jackson (2003).
10 As Rorty said for these kinds of reasons in the early days of the debate over materialism: see Rorty (1965).
11 As understood in the manner of Tichy (1983).
12 For more on this, see Jackson (2004) and Chalmers (1996, ch. 2, section 4).
13 There is an issue in fundamental metaphysics over whether we should think of the "is" in a claim such as our world is a vast aggregation of items with only physical₁ properties as the "is" of identity or the "is" of constitution. The same question arises for the view that a table is an aggregation of molecules. We can afford to fudge this interesting issue.
14 See, e.g., Kripke (1980, p. 153).
15 There is much more to be said here: see Jackson (2006).
16 In discussion, some have said that being a priori true (false) is a property of words and sentences and there is no *de re* issue to be addressed. To debate the a priori as such would take us too far afield, but I note that very many interesting theses in metaphysics often said to be a priori true (or false) are very obviously not about words – for example, that to be is to be determinate, that there exist temporal parts, that free will is incompatible with determinism, and that unrestricted fusion is true.
17 See the introduction and references in Carroll (2004).
18 For a theory of this kind, see Hill (1984). Hill holds that the identities are necessary a posteriori truths.
19 Analytical functionalists hold these identities to be analytic for the right choices of "such-and-such": see Braddon–Mitchell and Jackson (1996). Incidentally, some physicalists hold that the best version of their view holds that mental properties can be divided into two groups. One group is identical to functional properties, the other group to the neurological state types that play the functional roles; see Lewis (1966).

References

Armstrong, D. M. (1968). *A Materialist Theory of the Mind.* London: Routledge & Kegan Paul.

Braddon–Mitchell, D. and Jackson, F. (1996). *Philosophy of Mind and Cognition.* Oxford: Basil Blackwell.

Campbell, K. (1970). *Body and Mind.* London: Macmillan.

Carroll, J. W. (ed.) (2004). *Readings on Laws of Nature.* Pittsburgh: University of Pittsburgh Press.

Chalmers, D. J. (1996). *The Conscious Mind.* New York: Oxford University Press.

Churchland, P. M. (1981). Eliminative materialism and the propositional attitudes. *Journal of Philosophy,* 78, 67–90.

Davidson, D. (2001). Epistemology and Truth. *Subjective, Intersubjective, Objective.* Oxford: Clarendon.

Hill, C. S. (1984). In defence of type materialism. *Synthese,* 59, 295–320.

Jackson, F. (1994). Finding the mind in the natural world. In R. Cassati, B. Smith, and G. White (eds.), *Philosophy and the Cognitive Sciences.* Vienna: Holder-Pichler-Tempsky. Reprinted in D. J. Chalmers (ed.), *Philosophy of Mind: Classical and Contemporary Readings.* New York: Oxford University Press, 2002.

— (1998). *From Metaphysics to Ethics.* Oxford: Clarendon.

— (2003). Mind and illusion. In A. O'Hear (ed.), *Minds and Persons.* Cambridge: Cambridge University Press.

Frank Jackson

— (2004). Why we need A-intensions. *Philosophical Studies*, 118, 257–77.

— (2005). The case for *a priori* physicalism. In C. Nimtz and A. Beckermann (eds.), *Philosophy–Science–Scientific Philosophy, Main Lectures and Colloquia of GAP.5, Fifth International Congress of the Society for Analytical Philosophy*, 22–6 Sept. 2003. Paderborn: Mentis.

— (2006). On ensuring that physicalism is not a dual attribute theory in sheep's clothing. *Philosophical Studies*, 131, 227–49.

Kripke, S. (1980). *Naming and Necessity*, rev. edn. Oxford: Basil Blackwell.

Lewis, D. (1966). An argument for the identity theory. *Journal of Philosophy*, 63, 17–25. Reprinted in D. M. Rosenthal (ed.), *Materialism and the Mind–Body Problem*. New Jersey: Prentice-Hall, 1971.

— (1995). Should a materialist believe in qualia? *Australasian Journal of Philosophy*, 73, 140–4.

Putnam, H. (1975). The meaning of "meaning." In K. Gunderson (ed.), *Language, Mind and Knowledge*. Minneapolis: University of Minnesota Press.

Rorty, R. (1965). Mind–body identity, privacy and categories. *Review of Metaphysics*, 19, 24–54.

Tichy, P. (1983). Kripke on necessity a posteriori. *Philosophical Studies*, 43, 225–41.

CHAPTER TWELVE

On the Limits of
A Priori Physicalism

Brian P. McLaughlin

Physicalists hold that, all things considered, physicalism is more reasonable than any of its competitors (dualism, panpsychism, neutral monism, etc.), and indeed reasonable enough for acceptance. There is, however, disagreement among physicalists over whether the plausibility of physicalism depends on whether certain kinds of truths are knowable in principle a priori.[1] This disagreement will be my main topic. I will first present what I think should be common ground among the parties to the dispute – so-called "a priori physicalists" and "a posteriori physicalists."[2] Then, I will try to make some progress toward adjudicating the central dispute.

1 Common Ground

There is no consensus about how, exactly, the doctrine of physicalism should be formulated. But, as we will see in due course, the dispute between a priori and a posteriori physicalists can be addressed without settling that issue.

By "physical truths" let us mean truths of the physics that is true or our world – hereafter, "completed-physics."[3] Let P be the conjunction of all of such physical truths, both general and particular; thus, P will be a complete characterization of our world in each and every physical detail. And call any possible world in which P holds a P-world. Following David Chalmers and Frank Jackson, then, let us say that "world W1 outstrips world W2 if W1 contains a qualitative duplicate of W2 as a proper part and the reverse is not the case . . . [and that] a minimal P-world is a P-world that outstrips no other P-world" (2001, p. 317). I will take it as common ground among a priori and a posteriori physicalists that any doctrine deserving of the name "physicalism" will imply the thesis that our world is a minimal P-world.[4] And I will call the thesis "the physical minimality thesis."[5]

Let us say that Φ semantically implies Ψ if and only if it is impossible that Φ and $\sim\Psi$.[6] And let us call the conjunction of P and the physical minimality thesis "the Grand Conjunction."[7] With the notion of semantic implication in mind, Chalmers and Jackson state that the thesis that our world is a minimal P-world "intuitively . . . says that our world contains what is implied by P, and *only* what is implied by P" (ibid., emphasis theirs). That, however, is not what the thesis says, even intuitively. But it is equivalent to that claim given certain (not entirely uncontroversial) assumptions that are common ground to a priori and a posteriori physicalists. One such assumption is that haecceitism is false, where haecceitism is understood to be the doctrine that two worlds can differ either *only* in what objects they contain or *only* in which objects have which complete qualitative profiles.[8] It will be assumed here that all truths globally supervene on qualitative truths, and so that haecceitism is false. I won't pause to consider whether further assumptions are required to maintain that the Grand Conjunction will semantically imply all truths. For present purposes, it suffices to note that it is common ground that physicalism requires no less.

Not all semantics implications are a priori. The reason is that there are necessary truths that are knowable only a posteriori.[9] Water is H_2O; the "is" here (we will assume) is the "is" of identity: water $= H_2O$. That water $= H_2O$ is knowable only a posteriori. But if water $= H_2O$, then necessarily water $= H_2O$.[10] As Saul Kripke (1980) pointed out, if $A = B$, then necessarily $A = B$. This necessity of identity principle is an a priori truth that is derivable from two other a priori truths: the indiscernibility of identicals ($A = B$ only if whatever is true of A is true of B) and the thesis that everything is such that it is necessarily identical with itself. Of course, there are contingent statements of identity such as "Benjamin Franklin is the inventor of bifocals." They are not counterexamples to the necessity of identity principle since in such statements one of the singular terms[11] flanking "is" is not a rigid designator: that is to say, it is not a term that refers to the same thing in every world in which it refers to anything.[12] Thus, in our example, although the proper name "Benjamin Franklin" is a rigid designator, the description "the inventor of bifocals" is not. Benjamin Franklin is the inventor of bifocals, but he might not have been; in some worlds Newton invented bifocals. Both the term "water" and the description "H_2O," however, are rigid designators: each rigidly designates a kind of stuff; indeed, on the evidence, the same kind of stuff.[13] Thus, given the necessity of identity principle, if water is H_2O, then necessarily water is H_2O, and so it is also necessary that something is water if and only if it is H_2O.[14] Given that it is necessary that water is H_2O, the truth, for instance, that there is water on the Earth semantically implies that there is H_2O on the Earth. But the implication fails to be a priori.

There is also a purely epistemic notion of implication: Φ epistemically implies Ψ if and only if the material conditional truth $\Phi \rightarrow \Psi$ is a priori.[15] As has in effect already been noted, not every semantic implication is an epistemic implication. It is also the case that not every epistemic implication is a semantic implication. The reason is that there are contingent a priori truths.[16] Secretariat won the 1973 Kentucky Derby. That is a contingent truth since Secretariat might not have been the winner. The name "Secretariat" is a rigid designator; the description "the winner of the 1973 Kentucky Derby" is not: in some worlds Seattle Slew is the winner of the 1973 Kentucky Derby. It is, however, both a priori and necessary that if Secretariat is the winner of the 1973

Kentucky Derby, then Secretariat is the actual winner of the 1973 Kentucky Derby.[17] But consider the converse claim: If Secretariat is the actual winner of the 1973 Kentucky Derby, then Secretariat is the winner of the 1973 Kentucky Derby. That is a priori, but it is not necessary. The description "the actual winner...," unlike the description "the winner...," is a rigid designator.[18] If it is true that Secretariat is the *actual* winner of the 1973 Kentucky Derby, then it is necessarily true that Secretariat is the actual winner of the 1973 Kentucky Derby; and if it is false, then it is necessarily false. It is contingently true that Secretariat is the winner of the 1973 Kentucky Derby. So, the conditional "If Secretariat is the actual winner of the 1973 Kentucky Derby, then Secretariat is the winner of the 1973 Kentucky Derby" has a necessarily true antecedent and a contingently true consequent. Thus, it is only contingently true. Still it is a priori. In the epistemic sense of implication, that Secretariat is the actual winner of 1973 Kentucky Derby implies that Secretariat is the winner of the 1973 Kentucky Derby. Indeed they are epistemically equivalent. But they fail to be semantically equivalent since the former is necessary and the latter contingent.

There is thus semantic implication and epistemic implication, and neither ensures the other. Every necessary truth is of course trivially semantically implied by any claim whatsoever. The reason is that for any claim C and any necessary truth T, it is impossible that C and not T, for the simple reason that it is impossible that not T. Also, every a priori truth is trivially epistemically implied by any claim whatsoever, for a material conditional is a priori if its consequent is.

The notion of epistemic implication is defined by appeal to the notion of a priority. But what is a priority? It is common ground that although there is a distinction between a priori and a posteriori truths, the a priori/a posteriori distinction is, in the first instance, a distinction between two kinds of epistemic justification or warrant for belief.[19] There is no received view of what it is for a warrant to be a priori. But the intended notion is stronger than the notion of what we may count as being able to come to know from the armchair, so to speak, by supra-empirical considerations such as simplicity, and the like.[20] Also, being warranted otherwise than on the basis of empirical evidence does not suffice for being warranted a priori in the intended sense, for the latter can be a contextual matter; in certain epistemic contexts, one might simply be entitled to presuppose that p, and so in that way warranted in believing that p otherwise than on the basis of empirical evidence; but that would not suffice for being a priori warranted in the intended sense. I will take it that an a priori warrant for a belief is a warrant that is empirically indefeasible.[21] Thus, the belief that p is a priori if and only if it can have an empirically indefeasible warrant.[22]

Some contingent truths (or beliefs) are, arguably, "subject-relative a priori."[23] It is arguable that these include certain contingent first-person indexical truths such as that I exist, and that I am here now.[24] If such truths are indeed a priori for a subject (an issue I will leave open), then of course the Grand Conjunction trivially epistemically implies them for the subject in question. The relevant material conditionals will then be subject-relative a priori since their consequents are.

The conjunction P will contain no indexicals. Thus, the Grand Conjunction won't, for instance, epistemically imply that it is now noon here; that there is water here; that this is water; that I am Brian McLaughlin; that I speak English; and so on and so forth. If physicalism is true, then these indexical claims will be semantically implied by the Grand Conjunction. But it is common ground that they won't be epistemically implied by it.

The Grand Conjunction, however, can be supplemented in each of our own cases by conjoining it with certain indexical information ID, information that Chalmers and Jackson (2001) call "locating information." They characterize ID as follows:

> I[D] can be thought of as a "you are here" marker ... I[D] can consist of the conjunction of any two truths "I am A" and "now is B," where A is an identifying description of myself (or the subject in question) and B is an identifying description of the current time. An identifying description is a description such that [the Grand Conjunction epistemically] implies that there is a unique individual or time satisfying the description. (p. 318)

They stipulate that the identifying descriptions A and B are to be in the vocabulary of completed-physics. Let the Grand Conjunction henceforth be understood to be supplemented with ID in each of our own cases. Thus, on this usage, the Grand Conjunction for me now is the conjunction of P, the minimality thesis, and ID. There will be a different such Grand Conjunction for each of us at each moment, but to avoid prolixity and awkward notation, I will often write as if there were only one Grand Conjunction. To elaborate on Chalmers and Jackson's metaphor, then, the idea is that someone provided with the information in the Grand Conjunction would have a complete physical map of our world – one that represents it in each and every physical detail however minute – and the information that the map is complete. The person would also have a "you are here" marker by which to locate themselves, namely ID (I am A and that now is B).[25]

The central disputes that divide a priori and a posteriori physicalists concern the sorts of a posteriori truths the Grand Conjunction (for a subject at a time) epistemically implies (for the subject at that time), and so concern what material conditional truths with the Grand Conjunction in their antecedents and a posteriori truths in their consequents are (subject-relative) a priori.[26] Disputes thus center on what are called "a priori entailment theses."

2 Disputed Territory

2.1 All truths

The default a priori physicalist position is that the following unrestricted a priori entailment thesis is true:

> *The A Priori Universal Entailment Thesis.* The Grand Conjunction epistemically implies all truths.

It is worth pausing for a moment to reflect on just what a truly breathtaking thesis this is, even for someone who embraces the thesis that the Grand Conjunction semantically implies all truths. If the a priori universal entailment thesis is true, then, provided one had the requisite concepts, one would be able in principle to deduce a priori from the Grand Conjunction not only, say, that water = H_2O and that it boils at sea level at 212 °F, but also that over 80 percent of the population of the United States in 2006 professes belief in God or a higher power, that US interest rates were raised in 2006, that there are more shopping malls in the state of New Jersey than there are in the state of Montana, what anyone has ever thought or felt about one, indeed what any being in the universe has or will ever think or feel about anything (provided of course that one have the requisite concepts to understand): all that just from the conjunction of P, the minimality thesis, and ID.

I am uncertain whether any a priori physicalist actually holds the universal entailment thesis.[27] But before turning to a priori entailment theses that have been debated in the literature, I will mention four worries about the universal entailment thesis that generalize.

First, even setting asides concerns about non-indexical and non-demonstrative terms, it is very much an open question whether the locating information ID will ensure that the Grand Conjunction will epistemically imply every indexical and demonstrative truth.[28] But I will pass by this issue. Given that instances of "I am A" and "B is now" are included as conjuncts of the Grand Conjunction, it would not be a significant further compromise should it turn out that some additional indexical information would have to be included for the universal entailment thesis to be true.

Second, there are truths to which all known species save our own are cognitively closed.[29] Even chimps and dolphins, for instance, are cognitively closed to the truth that 3 is the square root of 9. Might there be truths to which all human beings are cognitively closed even in the idealized situations relevant to in principle apriority? If there are, then the universal a priori entailment thesis is false *if* in-principle apriority is supposed to be in-principle apriority *for us*. I will pass by this issue too.

Third, T-sentences, sentences that follow the paradigm "'Snow is white' is true in my language as I am now using it if and only if snow is white," are often presupposed in the relevant literature. But with T-sentences, bivalence can be derived even in Kleene weak three-valued logic. Arguably, then, if T-sentences are assumed, there will be bivalence. But if bivalence is assumed, then the a priori universal entailment thesis will have to be restricted to *semantically determinate* truths. The reason is that only semantically determinate truths are knowable. Given bivalence, it is either true that Harry is bald or it is false that Harry is bald. But if Harry is a borderline bald person, then it is unknowable whether Harry is bald, even on the basis of all the information in the Grand Conjunction.[30] To maintain the a priori universal entailment thesis either bivalence must be rejected or else the thesis must be restricted to semantically determinate truths.[31]

Fourth, there are non-analytic, yet non-contingent claims whose truth or falsehood would not, it seems, be settled by the Grand Conjunction unless the claims are a priori despite not being analytic. Consider the claim that there is a necessarily existing God.[32] Assuming bivalence, proponents of the a priori universal entailment thesis must maintain that the negation of this hypothesis is a priori implied by the Grand Conjunction. If, however, it is not a priori false that there is a necessarily existing God, then it seems that the claim that there is no necessarily existing God will fail to be epistemically implied by the Grand Conjunction, for every necessary being exists in a minimal P-world. Thus, if the Grand Conjunction epistemically implies that there is no necessarily existing God, then it seems that that will have to be because it is a priori false that there is such a God. But is it a priori false? And does the truth or even the plausibility of physicalism turn on whether it is? In answer to the second question, a posteriori physicalists say "no." A posteriori physicalists are content to maintain simply that they have no need of this God-hypothesis.

Many paradigmatic metaphysical claims raise the same sort of issue. Consider the claim that there are Platonic universals, and the mereological thesis that for every set of things there is a unique fusion of the members of the set. Assuming bivalence, these claims are either necessarily true or necessarily false. But they are neither analytically true nor analytically false. Moreover, there seems no reason to think that completed-physics will settle whether they are true. It is common for both a priori and a posteriori physicalists to posit Aristotelian universals and reject Platonic universals. Such a posteriori physicalists need not argue that it is a priori false that there are Platonic universals; they need only defend the claim that they have no need of the hypothesis that there are such universals. In contrast, proponents of the a priori universal entailment thesis must maintain that it is a priori false that there are Platonic universals. But is it a priori false? Is it, for instance, a priori false that fire engines are instances of the Platonic universal redness?

The same kind of issue arises for some mathematical claims. Neither the continuum hypothesis nor its negation is implied by the axioms of set theory, and although completed-physics may settle the issue of whether the continuum hypothesis is true, it also may very well not. Whether the claims in question are epistemically implied by the Grand Conjunction seems to turn on whether they are a priori.

For all that I have said, the claims in question may be a priori true or a priori false. But a case for that would have to be made. Rather than being a priori, they may instead be matters that are to be settled by considerations of overall coherence and simplicity, where not all of the coherence relations are a priori.[33]

In any case, all these issues aside, questions remain about a priori entailment theses restricted to truths in one or another of the special sciences: economics, sociology, psychology, biology, and even chemistry.[34] Consider chemistry. The a priori chemical entailment thesis is directly relevant to the ongoing debate in the foundations of chemistry over in what sense, if any, *ex nihilo* chemistry is possible. Schrödinger's equation has an analytical solution only for the hydrogen atom; in other cases, there is a many-body problem, and so approximation techniques must be used. All extant ones rely on explicitly chemical knowledge. There is, however, no reason to doubt that all chemical truths are semantically implied by physical truths. There are, for instance, existence proofs of unique solutions to Schrödinger's equation for each of the chemical elements. But whether all chemical truths are a priori deducible in principle from physical truths is an issue that is unresolved. One would think that this would be a good place for a priori physicalists to start in trying to make the case that all special science truths are epistemically implied by the Grand Conjunction: they might try to make the case that all chemical truths are epistemically implied by the Grand Conjunction. But there is, to my knowledge, no discussion of this issue in the a priori physicalist literature.

In any case, there are two a priori entailment theses that have been the main focus in the literature. They will be our exclusive focus in what remains. I turn now to the first of them.

2.2 Vernacular-physical truths

As I have defined "P," P, if such there be, will be (or be expressible) in a minimal vocabulary of completed-physics and will epistemically imply every truth couched (or expressible) in that vocabulary.[35] The reason is that it will contain every such truth as a conjunct. There are, however, also truths that are couched in our vernacular-physical vocabulary – truths that I will call "vernacular-physical truths." These include truths such as that water freezes at 32 °F, that salt tends to raise the boiling point of water, that over 60 percent of the surface of the Earth is covered with water, that the main source of water in rivers is water that has flowed down from mountains, that salt is water soluble, that steel is fragile at very cold temperatures, that short circuits can cause fires, and that gases tend to expand as they rise in temperature. A priori physicalists maintain the following:

> *The A Priori Vernacular-Physical Entailment Thesis.* The Grand Conjunction epistemically implies all vernacular-physical truths.

It is open to an a posteriori physicalist to accept this entailment thesis. As we will see, the main case against a priori physicalism is independent of whether this entailment is true. Nevertheless, it seems to me very much an open question whether it is true.

Let "O" stand in for a vernacular-physical property or kind term, and let "S" stand in for a property or kind term in a minimal vocabulary of completed-physics. A central part of the defense of the a priori vernacular-physical entailment thesis is that the Grand Conjunction will epistemically imply every a posteriori true instance of "O = S" and every a posteriori true instance of "O does not exist." This twofold contention will be our main focus in this section.

In order that the discussion not be devoid of examples, I will follow the practice in the literature of letting terms of current physics and chemistry do duty for the as yet largely unknown terms of completed-physics. Most of the main philosophical issues concerning true instances of "O = S" can be addressed treating such a posteriori identity claims as "Water = H_2O" and "Temperature in gases = mean molecular kinetic energy in gases" as if they were instances.[36]

Given that water = H_2O, water-truths will be semantically equivalent to H_2O-truths; similarly, for temperature-in-gas truths and mean-molecular-kinetic-energy-in-gas truths. But the implications will fail to be epistemic in either direction. That is common ground. A priori physicalists contend nevertheless that such a posteriori identity claims – indeed all true identity claims – will be epistemically implied by the Grand Conjunction. (That claim is, of course, compatible with the identity claims being only a posteriori knowable; for the Grand Conjunction is knowable only a posteriori.)

What would ensure that an a posteriori property or kind identity claim is epistemically implied by the Grand Conjunction? Consider the following schema:

(A)   O is the F.
(B)   S is the F.
(C)   O = S.

If (A) and (B) are both true, then (C) follows.[37] Suppose, then, that (A) is a priori and (B) is epistemically implied by the Grand Conjunction. It would follow that the Grand Conjunction epistemically implies that O = S. Thus, suppose that it is a priori that water is the kind such that so-and-so, and that the Grand Conjunction epistemically implies that H_2O is the kind such that so-and-so. Then, the Grand Conjunction will epistemically imply that water = H_2O.[38]

One problem with the above answer is that instances of (A) will typically fail to be a priori. The reason is that they imply that O exists, and it will typically be an a posteriori issue whether O exists.[39]

One might, then, try to appeal to instances of this schema:

(A′)   If O exists, then O is the F.

But one problem is that even if an instance of (A′) is a priori, and the corresponding instance of (B) – the instance of (B) that involves the same F-term as the instance of (A′) – is epistemically implied by the Grand Conjunction, it would not in general follow that O = S. What would follow in general is only that either (i) O = S or (ii) O does not exist.

Of course, a priori physicalists maintain that the Grand Conjunction epistemically implies all true instance of (i) and all true instances of (ii), including the a posteriori ones. But the question we are now pursuing is what a priori truths would ensure that. Let us consider first the case of true instances of (i) and then the case of true instances of (ii).

Consider the following schema:

(A″)   If there is a unique F, then O is the F.[40]

Suppose that an instance of (A″) is a priori. Then, if the corresponding instance of (B) is epistemically implied by the Grand Conjunction, the Grand Conjunction will epistemically imply that O = S. Thus, if whenever an instance of "O = S" is true some instance of (A″) is a priori and some corresponding instance of (B) is epistemically implied by the Grand Conjunction, then all true instances of "O = S" will be epistemically implied by the Grand Conjunction. The leading a priori physicalist view is that all true instances of "O = S" will meet this condition.[41]

Let us turn to (ii)-cases. Consider:

(D)   If O exists, then O is a G.
(E)   Nothing is a G.

If an instance of (D) is a priori and the Grand Conjunction epistemically implies the corresponding instance of (E), then the Grand Conjunction epistemically implies that O does not exist. If whenever an instance of "O does not exist" is true there is some instance of (D) that is a priori and a corresponding instance of (E) that is epistemically implied by the Grand Conjunction, then the Grand Conjunction will epistemically imply every true instance of "O does not exist." A priori physicalists maintain that whenever an instance of "O does not exist" is true, this condition will be met.

Consider some cases of *elimination* from the history of science for would-be illustrations. *Suppose* that it is a priori that if there is unnatural motion then it is motion that is in a direction away from the proper place of an object in the universe, a priori that if entelechies exist they are immaterial entities that guide the development of organisms and sustain their life, a priori that if phlogiston exists then it is a substance responsible for combustion and calcination that is emitted during burning, and a priori that if ether exists then it is a uniform and absolutely stationary substance that pervades space serving as an absolute reference frame for inertial systems. Then, *if* the Grand Conjunction epistemically implies that nothing is motion in a direction away from a proper place of an object in the universe, that nothing is an immaterial entity that guides the development of organisms and sustains their life, that nothing is a substance mainly responsible for combustion and calcination that is emitted during burning, and that nothing is a uniform and absolutely stationary substance that pervades space serving as an absolute reference frame for inertial systems, it would follow that the Grand Conjunction epistemically implies that unnatural motion, entelechies, phlogiston, and ether do not exist.

Now, to be sure, that nothing is movement away from a proper place of an object in the universe, that nothing is an immaterial entity that guides the development of organisms and sustains their life, that nothing is a substance mainly responsible for combustion and calcination that is emitted during burning, and that nothing is a uniform and absolutely stationary substance that pervades space serving as an absolute reference frame for inertial systems are all good and sufficient reasons for believing, respectively, that unnatural motion, entelechies, phlogiston, and ether do not exist. Still it is another matter whether the instances of (D) listed above are all a priori. That matter is, I believe, complicated by the fact that when we come to the conclusion that a kind term or name is vacuous or empty – that it fails to refer – we typically then use a description that fails to be satisfied to say what someone using the term had in mind by it.

In any case, I won't attempt to determine whether all (or any) of these instances of (D) are a priori. For the moment, suffice it to note that the fact that nothing is a G can be a good and sufficient reason in an epistemic context for believing that O does not exist without its being the case that it is a priori that if O exists then O is a G. That nothing is a G could rebut any warrant we had for believing that O exists, even if it is not a priori that if O exists then O is a G. For instance, if nothing responsible for combustion is emitted during burning, then the would-be explanation of combustion in terms of phlogiston is hopelessly wrong, and that rebuts the warrant eighteenth-century theorists such as J. J. Becher and Georg Ernst Stahl had for positing phlogiston. The point is that this is so even if it is not a priori that if phlogiston exists, then it is emitted during burning (a matter I leave open). Similarly, in an epistemic context, that S is the F and if there is a unique F then O is the F can be a good and sufficient reason for believing that O = S, even if it is not a priori that if there is a unique F then O is F.

Brian P. McLaughlin

The leading a priori physicalist view, however, is that the following twofold thesis is true: first, whenever an instance of "O = S" is true, there will be some instance of (A″) that is a priori and a corresponding instance of (B) that is epistemically implied by the Grand Conjunction; and, second, whenever an instance of "O does not exist" is true, there will be some instance of (D) that is a priori and a corresponding instance of (E) that is epistemically implied by the Grand Conjunction. What is at issue is whether that is true. The Grand Conjunction can epistemically imply instances of (B) and (E), for it includes the minimality thesis as a conjunct. Moreover, it is not in question whether there are any a priori instances of (A″) or any a priori instance of (D). Still there is an issue of whether all vernacular-physical cases of identification and of elimination fit the respective models.

Of course, if vernacular-physical property and kind terms could be defined in a minimal vocabulary of completed-physics, then there would always be the sorts of a priori truths required by the models. But no one thinks that all vernacular-physical terms can be so defined – or even defined in such a vocabulary supplemented with the several additional words in which the minimality thesis and ID are couched. Indeed a priori physicalists readily acknowledge that it may very well be that no vernacular-physical property or kind term can be so defined. They maintain, however, that such definitions are not required for the truths in question to be epistemically implied by the Grand Conjunction.[42] They appeal to the distinction between meaning-giving analyses – non-circular statements of conditions that are individually analytically necessary for and jointly analytically sufficient for the analysandum – and contingent a priori reference-fixing analyses. They count them both as kinds of conceptual analysis on the grounds that they spell out what property or kind the term purports to be used for.[43] An a priori reference-fixing analysis for a term "O" will yield an a priori instance of (A″) and an a priori instance of (D). A priori physicalists maintain that every ordinary physical kind or property term will have an a priori reference-fixing analysis, even if typically only a contingent a priori one.[44]

It is, however, very much an open question whether every vernacular-physical term has either a meaning-giving or contingent a priori reference-fixing analysis. It seems that precious few such terms have meaning-giving analyses. And I know of no adequate defense of the claim that all vernacular-physical terms that lack meaning-giving analyses nevertheless have contingent a priori reference-fixing ones. It is sometimes suggested that to fully understand such a term, one must have (at least implicit) knowledge either of a definition of it or of a contingent a priori reference-fixing analysis for it. But that looks to be an empirical hypothesis about understanding such terms. Suffice it to note that it cries out for defense.

Suppose, though, for the sake of argument, that it is indeed the case that every vernacular-physical term has either a meaning-giving or a contingent a priori reference-fixing analysis. As noted above, the latter are supposed to epistemically imply a priori instances of (A″) and a priori instances of (D). If all vernacular-physical kind and property terms have contingent a priori reference-fixing analyses couched in the vocabulary of the Grand Conjunction, then there will always be the kinds of a priori truths required by the models. No one, however, thinks that we know such analyses for any vernacular-physical kind or property terms. Indeed descriptions couched in the vocabulary of completed-physics play no role in our current reference-fixing practices since, among other things, we know so very little about what that vocabulary will be.

Unfortunately, a priori physicalists provide no spelled-out examples of contingent a priori reference-fixing analyses for any vernacular-physical property or kind terms. We are told such things as that "water" has a reference-fixing analysis such that it is contingent yet nevertheless a priori that if there is a unique "waterish stuff of our acquaintance" then water is the waterish stuff of our acquaintance, and such that it is contingent yet a priori that if water exists, then water is a waterish stuff of our acquaintance. The F-term here is "waterish stuff of our acquaintance." We are told that the description "the waterish stuff" is an abbreviation of a description of a role (mainly causal), and similarly that "our acquaintance" is an abbreviation of a role. These abbreviations are, to my knowledge, nowhere adequately spelled out. Partial spellings-out of "waterish stuff" have included in various places in the literature terms such as "cause," "rain," "ocean," "lake," "river," "stream," "potable," "transparent," "colorless," "tasteless," "odorless," and "our acquaintance" has been partly unpacked using terms of perception, and sometimes in social terms such as deference to experts.[45] The Grand Conjunction will not be couched in any of these terms. But it is supposed to epistemically imply that H_2O is the waterish stuff of our acquaintance. Even granting that it will epistemically imply that there is H_2O, the issue remains then whether it will epistemically imply that H_2O is the waterish stuff of our acquaintance, for the issue remains whether it will even epistemically imply that there is waterish stuff of our acquaintance, or even that there is waterish stuff, or indeed that we are acquainted with anything.

A priori physicalists readily acknowledge that in a typical contingent a priori reference-fixing analysis, the F-term – the reference-fixing term – will be a complex term couched entirely in words that, with the exception of logical vocabulary, will not be part of any minimal vocabulary of completed-physics or of such a vocabulary supplemented with the few additional words in which the mininality thesis and ID are couched, or even definable in such terms. The F-term is, however, supposed to provide an a priori link between the terms "O" and "S". But a priori physicalists point out that that does not require that the F-term be in the vocabulary of the Grand Conjunction, or definable in such a vocabulary, or even that it have an a priori reference-fixing analysis couched in such a vocabulary. It requires only that an instance of (A″) be a priori and the corresponding instance of (B) be epistemically implied by the Grand Conjunction, and analogously for (D), (E), and elimination. The term "cause" (or one of its cognates), for instance, will appear in a typical reference-fixing analysis. But it will not appear in the Grand Conjunction, nor will it be definable in the vocabulary of the Grand Conjunction, nor will it have an a priori reference-fixing analysis in such terms. Still, arguably, one may be able to determine a priori what physical events are causally related if the world is as P depicts it. A truth can be epistemically implied by the Grand Conjunction even if it is not couched in vocabulary of the Grand Conjunction, or definable in such terms, or even couched in terms that have a contingent a priori reference-fixing analysis in such terms. All that is required is that the material conditional with the Grand Conjunction in its antecedent and the truth in question in its consequent be a priori.[46]

Fair enough. Nevertheless, the point remains that even if every vernacular-physical property or kind term has either a meaning-giving or a contingent a priori reference-fixing analysis, that is no guarantee that there will always be the F-terms and G-terms required by the models for identification and elimination, respectively. It is compatible with the thesis that every vernacular-physical property or kind term has one or the other such analysis that there fail to be the requisite a priori links between the terms in which the analysans are couched and the vocabulary of the Grand Conjunction. And if there are any cases in which there fail to be the requisite a priori links, then the a priori vernacular-physical entailment thesis is false. Whether there are any such cases is an open question. Thus, it is an open question whether the a priori vernacular-physical entailment thesis is true.

Let us say that it is epistemically possible that P and Q if and only if it fails to be a priori that not-(P and Q).[47] If the a priori vernacular-physical entailment thesis is false, then there is at least one (non-borderline) case such that it is both epistemically possible that the Grand Conjunction and O = S, and also epistemically possible that the Grand Conjunction and O does not exist. Suppose, then, that one is in an idealized situation, rationally reflecting on the Grand Conjunction in its entirety. The Grand Conjunction includes the minimality thesis, a kind of ontological simplicity thesis, as a conjunct. But, by hypothesis, both O = S and O does not exist are epistemically compatible with the actual world being a minimal P-world. What, then, could make one but not the other of the beliefs warranted in the idealized situation?[48] Keep in mind that we want an answer that a physicalist can accept.

The answer is: considerations of overall coherence and simplicity with respect to total worldview. The belief that O = S may better cohere with the Grand Conjunction and what else one believes than does the belief that O does not exist; or instead the belief that O does not exist may better cohere with the Grand Conjunction and what else one believes.

The a priori physicalist would agree, but insist that the coherence relations will all be a priori. A posteriori physicalists who reject the a priori vernacular-physical entailment thesis will maintain that they will not all be a priori. They will insist that the coherence relations will involve implicit or explicit a posteriori theories that we hold. The dispute is thus over whether all the relevant coherence relations will be a priori.

A posteriori physicalists maintain that a posteriori elimination and identification beliefs must be warranted, ultimately, only on grounds of overall coherence and overall simplicity, where some of the coherence relations are a posteriori. But that view is actually common ground with a priori physicalists. The Grand Conjunction is a posteriori. It must be warranted, ultimately, on grounds of overall coherence and overall simplicity, where some of the coherence relations are a posteriori. Moreover, it is common ground that given P and ID, whether to accept the minimality thesis will turn on what one must then be an eliminativist about and on what one can identify with something characterized in P. The disagreement is over whether such matters can always be determined a priori.

A posteriori physicalists deny that such matters can always be determined a priori. But they are by no means committed to the view that such matters cannot be rationally decided. They can maintain that even when both O = S and O does not exist are epistemically compatible with the Grand Conjunction, it is nevertheless the case that were one warranted in believing the Grand Conjunction, then one would either be in a position to be warranted in believing that $O = S$ or else in a position to be warranted in believing that O does not exist. The reason is that the Grand Conjunction can provide warrant for a belief without a priori ensuring that the belief is true. Knowledge of the Grand Conjunction could, for instance, provide warrant for the belief that there is no necessarily existing God without a priori entailing that there is no necessarily existing God. It could render the hypothesis otiose. The same may be true of certain contingent elimination beliefs. The warrant for believing that O does not exist may just be that one has no need of the hypothesis that O exists. Moreover, given the Grand Conjunction, the best explanation – best on grounds of overall coherence and overall simplicity – of various apparent correlations might be that $O = S$, even though there is no a priori instance of (A″) such that the corresponding instance of (B) is epistemically implied by the Grand Conjunction. Physicalists maintain that the Grand Conjunction can in principle provide warrants for all true a posteriori beliefs, where the warrants are such that they would not be defeated in the sense of rebutted. But to maintain that, they need not maintain that such warrants will always or even typically be empirically indefeasible – be such that they could not be rebutted. It is one thing for a warrant to be such that it would not be rebutted; another for it to be such that it could not be rebutted. It is common ground that for a warrant for believing that p to be adequate for knowledge that p, it is not required that the warrant epistemically imply p; for it is common ground that there is a posteriori knowledge.

It remains whether the a priori vernacular-physical entailment thesis is true. I have not of course shown it to be false. I hope, however, that I have succeeded in making a case that it is by no means obvious that it is true, indeed that there is reason to doubt its truth. In any case, though, what is important for present purposes is that the truth of physicalism does not turn on whether that entailment thesis is true. Whether or not the Grand Conjunction epistemically implies all vernacular-physical truths, the most reasonable position, all things considered, is that it semantically implies them.

2.3 Truths of phenomenal consciousness

A priori and a posteriori physicalists divide over whether the Grand Conjunction epistemically implies all a posteriori mental truths. A priori physicalists maintain that it does. A posteriori physicalists deny that it does. It is, however, open to a posteriori physicalists to maintain that some a posteriori mental truths are epistemically implied by the Grand Conjunction. An a posteriori physicalist might embrace analytical behaviorism for propositional attitude types such as belief, preference, intention, and the like, or its more plausible (though nevertheless controversial) progeny, analytically functionalism for such attitude types, and maintain, for example, that a posteriori truths of the form "X has beliefs" will be epistemically implied by the Grand Conjunction.

The primary divide between a priori and a posteriori physicalists is over the following thesis:

Brian P. McLaughlin

The A Priori Phenomenal Entailment Thesis. The Grand Conjunction epistemically implies all phenomenal truths.

By "phenomenal truths" I mean truths concerning states and events of phenomenal consciousness as such. Phenomenal states are states such that it is like something for the subject of the state to be in the state. They include such states as feeling pain, and sense experiences within each sense modality (visual, aural, etc.). The what-it-is-like-for-the-subject aspect of a state is its phenomenal character. In one of the many senses of the term "qualia," qualia are phenomenal characters. I will use "qualia" in that sense.[49] All a priori physicalists accept the a priori phenomenal entailment thesis. All a posteriori physicalists reject it on the grounds that no a posteriori phenomenal truth is so implied. It thus marks the great divide. This entailment thesis will occupy us for the remainder of this essay.

In reflecting on the thesis, the well-known knowledge argument naturally springs to mind. That is not a single argument, but rather a family of arguments that has a long history, tracing back to C. D. Broad (1925), and even further back to Samuel Alexander (1920), both of whom recognized that it turns on features special to consciousness. Here is Bertrand Russell's elegant version of it: "It is obvious that a man who can see knows things which a blind man cannot know; but a blind man can know the whole of physics. Thus the knowledge which other men have and he has not is not a part of physics" (1927, p. 389). It does not diminish the force of the argument to understand by "the whole of physics" the whole of completed-physics, rather than the whole of current physics. Nor does it diminish the force of the argument to suppose that a congenitally profoundly blind person has the locating information ID, and knows (somehow) that our world is a minimal P-world. Indeed it does not diminish the force of the argument to assume that the Grand Conjunction will epistemically imply all chemical truths, all vernacular-physical truths, all biological truths, all neuroscientific truths, and all truths of computational psychology. Such a blind person could (ideally) know the whole of the Grand Conjunction. And even if all such truths were epistemically implied by it, there would still be knowledge that a normal sighted adult human has that such a blind person would not be in a position to have: namely, knowledge of what it is like to see, of what it is like to have a visual experience, and so on. If it is a consequence of the a priori phenomenal entailment thesis that there is no knowledge that the sighted have that such a blind person would nevertheless lack, then the dispute is settled: the a priori phenomenal entailment thesis is false, and so a priori physicalism must be rejected.

The leading a priori physicalist response is that there are indeed things the sighted know that even such a blind person would not know, but that that is compatible with the a priori phenomenal entailment thesis. The sighted know what it is like to see; the congenitally profoundly blind do not, and even learning the whole of the Grand Conjunction would not enable them to know. But knowledge of what an experience is like is know-how, not knowledge-that, not factual knowledge. This is the well-known "ability response."[50] There are things that Nadia Comaneci knows that I do not; among them is how to do a backflip. Similarly, there are things the sighted know that the blind do not; among them are how to imagine themselves having a visual experience (in a sense of imagination that involves having visual images), and how to recognize visual experiences when they are having them. But there is no truth that the sighted know that a blind person would be unable in principle to deduce a priori from the Grand Conjunction. Even a blind person could in principle deduce all truths of visual phenomenal consciousness from it. Similarly, someone who suffers from CAD (congenital autonomic dysfunction), and thus who does not know what it is like to feel pain,[51] could nevertheless in principle a priori deduce all truths about the feel of pain just from the Grand Conjunction. Likewise, Frank Jackson's Mary could deduce all truths about colors and color experience while in her black and white room, never having had (chromatic) color experiences (Jackson, 1982).

To many philosophers, including me, the ability response has seemed too clever by half. In counter-response, it has been argued that such know-how requires knowledge-that since the ability to recognize experiences of a certain type (e.g., visual) requires the ability to have knowledge-that an experience is of that type.[52] But whether or not there is any such knowledge-that requirement on such know-how, it is nevertheless the case that those of us who are sighted have in fact had knowledge-that that even a blind person who knew the whole of the Grand Conjunction could not have; and it is nevertheless the case that those of us who have felt pain have in fact had knowledge-that that even a CAD victim who knew the whole of the Grand Conjunction could not have. The knowledge in question is demonstrative knowledge, where what is demonstrated is an experience. To illustrate from my own case (Moore-style), as I sit here at my desk, I know that this is what it is like to have a visual experience, and that this is what it is like to see red, and (attending now to my right shoulder) that this is what is it like to have a dull ache.

According to a posteriori physicalists, such demonstrative knowledge involves the exercise of a *phenomenal concept* of the kind of experience in question (the kind of quale in question).[53] The profoundly congenitally blind lack phenomenal concepts of visual experiences; CAD victims lack a phenomenal concept of pain; and Mary (before leaving the room) lacks phenomenal concepts of any color experiences.[54] That explains why they cannot have the knowledge-that in question. What Mary acquires after she leaves her black and white room are phenomenal concepts of color experiences.

I think that this view is correct. However, a point that has gone largely unappreciated in the literature is that if it is correct, then the knowledge argument poses no threat whatsoever to a priori physicalism. It is no challenge to the claim that it is a priori that if A then B, that someone who lacked the concepts required to understand B could not a priori deduce B from A. I thus think that the knowledge-argument, in all of its manifestations, is inconclusive against the a priori phenomenal entailment thesis. The a priori physicalist can, and indeed should, concede that there is knowledge-that which the blind, CAD victims, and Mary (before she leaves the room) could not acquire on the basis of knowledge of the Grand Conjunction. But the reason they cannot is that they lack the requisite phenomenal concepts to have such knowledge-that. The fact that knowledge of the Grand Conjunction would not suffice to ensure that they satisfy the possession conditions for the phenomenal concepts in question does not entail that the relevant phenomenal truths fail to be epistemically implied by the Grand Conjunction.

Of course, a posteriori physicalists will insist that even someone in possession of the requisite phenomenal concepts would be unable to a priori deduce any a posteriori phenomenal truths from the Grand Conjunction. But their argument will be different from the knowledge argument. There are other lines of objection to the a priori phenomenal entailment thesis, lines that have historical roots that go even further back in the empiricist tradition than the knowledge argument. I have in mind inverted qualia arguments, which have their roots in John Locke, and absent qualia arguments, which have their roots in John Stuart Mill – in his discussion of the problem of other minds. It seems coherently conceivable that two individuals who are physical duplicates could nevertheless be such that the one has qualia that are inverted with respect to the qualia of the other. Indeed it seems coherently conceivable that two individuals who are physical duplicates could nevertheless be such that the one is phenomenally conscious and the other entirely devoid of phenomenal consciousness – a zombie.[55] Zombies do not seem to be a priori impossible; the idea of a zombie seems to harbor no contradiction that can be discovered solely by a priori reasoning.

On these matters, a posteriori physicalists agree with Cartesian property dualists. They also agree about the core explanation of why these matters are coherently conceivable. The reason that absent and inverted qualia cases are coherently conceivable is that phenomenal concepts lack either meaning-giving or contingent a priori reference-fixing analyses in even broadly physical or topic-neutral/functional terms, and indeed there fail to be the sorts of a priori links between phenomenal concepts and physical or functional concepts that would be required to render such would-be possibilities a priori incoherent. A posteriori physicalists and Cartesian property dualists are thus united in rejecting the a priori phenomenal entailment thesis. They are, moreover, united in holding that there is a kind of unbridgeable explanatory gap between phenomenal consciousness as such and the physical/functional as such: types of states of phenomenal consciousness as such cannot be reduced to types of physical or functional states as such via either meaning-giving or contingent a priori reference-fixing analyses.[56] The disagreement between Cartesian property dualists and a posteriori physicalists is over whether this explanatory gap entails an ontological gap, in particular whether it entails property or type dualism. A posteriori physicalists deny that it does. They claim that despite the absence of such a priori links between the concepts in question, phenomenal concepts nevertheless denote (broadly) physical or functional properties.[57]

2.4 Self-knowledge and a posteriori physicalism

I will close with a brief response to a would-be problem that Jackson poses for a posteriori physicalism. He says:

> We can now put the problem for a posteriori physicalism more directly. A posteriori physicalists (but not a priori physicalists) must allow that there are two epistemic possibilities: that things are physically exactly as they actually are and there is sentience, and that things are physically exactly as they actually are and there is no sentience. There seems no reason they can give for favoring the first over the second. The first has no explanatory advantage and no advantage in terms of simplicity over the second. (Jackson, A PRIORI PHYSICALISM, p. 255.)

But there is a reason. We each know in our own case that we are sentient – that we are phenomenally conscious. That the world is devoid of sentience is not an epistemic possibility for me since I know that I am now in pain; that I am in pain epistemically implies that there is sentience. Of course, there is no consensus as to the nature of our first-person knowledge of our current states of phenomenal consciousness. But one thing is perfectly clear: such knowledge is not based on our knowing that we satisfy some physical-topic neutral condition. It is open to an a posteriori physicalist to maintain that such first-person knowledge is based on direct awareness that we are in a certain state of phenomenal consciousness.[58]

Of course, there remains an issue of whether others are sentient, and whether we were sentient in the past. A posteriori physicalists face the problem of other minds. But given the falsity of analytical behaviorism and analytical functionalism for phenomenal consciousness, we all face that problem. Any a posteriori physicalist theory of phenomenal consciousness, however, will be committed to some solution to it. We can each know in our own case that we are phenomenally conscious. A posteriori physicalists are committed to the view that if others are like us in the relevant physical-functional respects, then they too are phenomenally conscious. And a posteriori physicalists will be committed, by their particular brand of a posteriori physicalism, to a view as to what those relevant physical-functional respects are. Thus, type materialists will hold that a type of state of phenomenal consciousness is identical with a certain type of neuroscientific state, and psycho-functionalists will hold that a type of state of phenomenal consciousness is identical with a certain type of psycho-functional state.

Now a priori physicalists also hold either that types of states of phenomenal consciousness are identical with certain types of neuroscientific states or else that they are identical with certain types of psycho-functional states. Type materialists and psycho-functionalists hold that the type identities will be warranted on grounds of overall coherence and theoretical simplicity, where the coherence relations include a posteriori ones. But a priori physicalists hold that too. What a priori and a posteriori physicalists disagree about is whether the type identities will be epistemically implied by the Grand Conjunction. A priori physicalists maintain that such psycho-physical identities will be so implied. A posteriori physicalists deny that.

Acknowledgments

I would like to thank Alex Byrne, Janet Levin, and Ted Sider for helpful comments on an early draft of this paper. Also I would like to thank David Chalmers, John Hawthorne, and Frank Jackson for many helpful discussions of the issues addressed in this paper.

Notes

1   I use "truths" to wade across the surface of some deep and murky waters. I will assume that truths have logico-syntactic and constituent structures. For present purposes, they

216   Brian P. McLaughlin

may be taken to be true sentences or instead to be true pleonastic propositions (Schiffer, 2003). I will use "claims" as neutral between truths and falsehoods.

   In principle a priori knowability is a priori knowability upon rational reflection under certain idealized conditions. The idealizations include the sorts standardly presupposed by proponents of the view that all mathematical truths are knowable a priori: idealizations away from our limitations in memory capacity, attention span, and so on (and so from our limited life span). Some a posteriori physicalists are skeptical about in principle a priori knowability, and some are skeptical even about a prior knowability. Suffice it to note that such skepticism will not be an issue here.

2   These labels are misleading since they suggest that what is at issue is whether physicalism is a priori, and that it is not what is at issue. But they have caught on in the literature, and so are used here.

3   More specifically, physical truths will be truths couched in (or expressible in, dependingon one's view of truths) a minimal vocabulary of a language adequate to express completed-physics. A set of words is a minimal vocabulary of such a language if and only if it is a vocabulary of such a language, and no proper subset of it is. To give content to the notionof physicality, physicalists typically maintain that completed-physics will be a suc-cessor theory to current physics, even if not an immediate successor theory. I will pass by the complications of spelling out the relevant notion of succession since they arise for both a priori and a posteriori physicalists. But one requirement on appropriate succession is worth mentioning explicitly: like current physics, completed-physics will not posit mental substances or properties as such, and so will not be a Cartesian physics.

4   Chalmers and Jackson (2001) is a reply to the case against a priori physicalism that is made in Block and Stalnaker (1999). It should be mentioned that while Jackson is an a priori physicalist, Chalmers is not a physicalist at all. Chalmers (1996) denies that our world is a minimal P-world. He maintains that some possible world is a zombie world: a world that is an exact physical duplicate of our world, but that is devoid of phenomenal consciousness. All physicalists that are realists about phenomenal consciousness deny that any possible world is a zombie world. Realism about phenomenal consciousness will be assumed here. Of phenomenal consciousness, more in due course.

5   Two points should be noted. First, the truth of the physical minimality thesis fails to be sufficient for physicalism since, for one thing, the minimality thesis is compatible with the existence of a necessarily existing God, and physicalism is not. (Also see Hawthorne, 2002, for a more interesting kind of case.) Nevertheless, it is a non-trivial necessary condi-tion for physicalism that will serve our purposes. Second, Chalmers and Jackson (2001, p. 316) use "P" for the conjunction of all microphysical truths. I intend P to include as conjuncts not only all microphysical truths, but also all macrophysical truths (at any scale), and thus truths such as those expressible in the solid state physics true of our world and in the astrophysics true of our world. There are a posteriori compositional principles that bridge the microphysical and macrophysical – principles such as, e.g., the principle of the additivity of mass as well as some non-additive, indeed non-linear, principles (see McLaughlin, 1992). But I will pass by these issues in this essay and will write as if my P is theirs. This will not affect any of the points below. Indeed, my broader use of P will, if anything, only make it easier to make a case for a priori physicalism.

6   "Impossible" is used here in its broadest sense: Γ is impossible if and only if not-Γ holds in (literally) every possible world. Similarly, "necessary" will be used in this essay in its strongest modal sense: Γ is necessary if and only if it holds in (literally) every possible world. (Even though not all metaphysically necessary truths are logical truths, I take it that the metaphysically possible worlds are the logically possible worlds: they are one and the same space of possibilities.)

7   Later I will add additional conjuncts to the Grand Conjunction.

8   See the discussion of haecceitism in Lewis (1986); haecceitists need not assume there are "thisness" properties.

9   Kripke (1980).

10 More precisely, what is necessarily true is that if there is water, then water $= H_2O$. I will omit this qualification.

11 I use "singular term" in the Quinean sense of a noun or noun phrase that purports singularity of reference; thus definite descriptions count as singular terms.

12 Kripke (1980).

13 It is assumed here that kinds are Aristotelian universals.

14 In the last claim, the "is" is that of "is an instance of."

15 Cf. Chalmers and Jackson (2001, p. 316). This characterization of epistemic implication, like the earlier characterization of semantic implication, is a stipulation.

16 Kripke (1980).

17 More precisely, what is a priori and necessary is that if Secretariat exists (or existed), then if Secretariat is the winner of the 1973 Kentucky Derby, Secretariat is the actual winner of the 1973 Kentucky Derby. I will continue to omit this qualification.

18 Here I use "actual" in the sense that is explicated by modal logic, where "the actual Φ" is explicated as "the Φ in the actual world." If X is the Φ in the actual world, then it is true in every possible world that X is the Φ in the actual world.

19 I use "justification" and "warrant" interchangeably. Epistemic warrant (or justification) is the kind of warrant for belief that is relevant to knowledge. It contrasts with pragmatic justification or warrant for belief – justification of the sort that, for instance, Pascal's Wager was intended to provide for belief in God. Hereafter, I will omit the qualifier "epistemic," but by "warrant" I will always mean epistemic warrant.

20 See Chalmers and Jackson (2001, pp. 345–9).

21 Elsewhere I have called empirically indefeasible warrant "strong a priori warrant" to contrast it with warrant that is simply otherwise than on the basis of empirical evidence (McLaughlin 2000, 2003a). In explicating the idea of empirical indefeasibility, it is important to note that in the intended sense this indefeasibility is not contextually cancelable. It is also important to distinguish two kinds of defeaters: rebutting and undercutting defeaters (Pollock, 1974, 1986). A rebutting defeater of a warrant for believing that p is empirical evidence for not-p that outweighs the warrant for believing p. ("Evidence" is used here in such a way that one can have evidence for something that is not true, and so evidence can be misleading. Also defeaters, in the intended sense, can be false.) My visual observation that not-p might outweigh the warrant provided by Tom's testimony that p, and so be a rebutting defeater of it. An undercutting defeater of a would-be warrant w for believing that p is empirical evidence that w fails to be warrant for believing that p. Evidence that Tom is an inveterate liar is an undercutting defeater in this case: it is evidence that his testimony fails to be (or provide) warrant for believing that p. The notion of defeat invoked in the definition of a priori warrant is defeat by a rebutting defeater. If the kind of defeat at issue were to include defeat by an undercutting defeater, then there would be no a priori warrant; for warrant for any belief can be undercut (Field, 1996). The warrant provided for a belief in a mathematical theorem by working carefully, with full understanding, and without mistake, through a proof of the theorem could be undercut by the (mistaken) testimony of leading mathematical experts that there is a subtle flaw in the proof. By empirical defeat, then, is meant defeat by a rebutting defeater. (One source of skepticism about apriority, I believe, has been failure to distinguish undercutting defeaters from rebutting defeaters; another is failure to distinguish pure mathematics from applied mathematics. But I cannot pursue these issues here.)

Brian P. McLaughlin

22 Chalmers and Jackson say: "apriority is a matter of non-empirical justification" (2001, p. 349). Their discussion of this idea indicates that they regard empirical indefeasibility as required for non-empirical justification, and thus that they do not just mean that the justification is otherwise than on the basis of empirical evidence. (But see note 24.)

I should mention that Jackson (2005 and A PRIORI PHYSICALISM) has introduced a notion of *de re* apriority. I won't discuss it since I think that it should be common ground between a priori and a posteriori physicalists that *de re* a priori physicalism (in his sense) is true.

23 I lift this expression from Chalmers and Jackson (2001).

24 Kaplan (1989a, 1989b) maintains that these are examples of the contingent a priori. It is arguable that a belief that is warranted by direct awareness of one's own current experience as such and a priori reasoning can be immune from rebutting defeaters, and so can be subject-relative a priori. Perhaps, then, the belief that I exist can be a priori for me in the sense defined above. It should be noted, however, that the belief that I exist will not be a priori for me if a priori warrant must be independent of experience in the sense of never including experience. Chalmers and Jackson (2001) characterize a priori knowledge as knowledge with justification that is independent of experience. It is uncertain whether their notion of justification independent of experience is supposed to require that the justification be independent even of the experience of understanding a thought. But, in any case, my notion of apriority may be weaker than theirs since it may be possible for experience to be part of an empirically indefeasible warrant, and thus for a warrant to be empirically indefeasible yet not independent of experience. I leave the issue open here. If my notion of a priority is indeed weaker than theirs, that should only make the case for a priori physicalism that much easier.

25 Because of vagueness, no such "identifying" indexical truths as "I am A" and "now is B" will be semantically determinately true. Nevertheless, it will be semantically determinately true that there are such identifying indexical truths. (For discussion, see McGee and McLaughlin, 1994, 2000, and 2003, in which a semantically determinate operator is introduced that does not commute with existential generalization.) Although I will recur to issues of vagueness below, such issues will be largely ignored here.

26 Hereafter, I will typically drop the parenthetical qualifications.

27 Frank Jackson has informed me that he does not hold the a priori universal entailment thesis.

28 Despite their optimism that the addition of ID to the Grand Conjunction will yield epistemic entailments of truths expressed by such sentences as "I am Australian" and "There is water on this planet," even Chalmers and Jackson acknowledge that ID may fail to be sufficient to capture all indexical and demonstrative truths (2001, p. 318, n. 4).

29 For discussion of the notion of cognitive closure, see Chomsky (1980) and McGinn (1993, 2001).

30 Issues arising from vagueness are briefly discussed in Jackson (1998) and Chalmers and Jackson (2001).

31 No such restriction is needed, however, for the thesis that the Grand Conjunction semantically implies all truths. The reason is that even non-contingent truths can be semantically indeterminate. (For discussion, see McGee and McLaughlin, 2003.)

Timothy Williamson (1994) denies that there is semantic indeterminacy, maintaining that the indeterminacy of borderline cases is entirely epistemic. (For a response to Williamson, see McGee and McLaughlin, 2003.) Suffice it to note that if a priori physicalists embrace his epistemic theory of vagueness, then they will regard the issue of whether vagueness poses an obstacle to embracing the a priori universal entailment thesis as turning on whether the kinds of idealizations relevant to in principle a priori knowability are to include ones such that our cognitive faculties will leave no margin for error.

32 Chalmers and Jackson (2001) mention this claim; see also Jackson (1998).

33 Of course, the claims in question are special in that they are non-contingent. But identity claims in which the identity sign is flanked by rigid designators are also non-contingent: If they are true, they are necessarily true.

34 Questions also arise concerning any truth that contains a proper name. Moreover, questions arise concerning normative truths. But space forbids examination of those questions.

35 A minimal vocabulary of completed-physics, you will recall, is a set of terms that is such that it is the vocabulary of completed-physics in a language in which the theory can be completely expressed, but no proper subset of it is.

36 Moreover, in appealing to an example such as "Water is H_2O," one can view the a priori physicalist as defending the conditional claim that if the Grand Conjunction epistemically implies a true instance of "H_2O is S," then it will epistemically imply the corresponding instance of "Water is S."

37 The "is" in (A) and (B) is that of identity. The descriptions in instances of these schemata will have the logical form: "the K such that K is L, where K is a second-order variable that ranges over kinds or properties of individuals (see Linsky, 2006). Kinds can be motley kinds such as jade (or even more motley kinds such as air) or natural kinds such as water (gold, etc.).

38 It seems that precious few instances of "$O = S$" will be semantically determinate. The term "O" will be vague. Although the language of the completed-physics will no doubt be vague too, it seems wildly optimistic to think that there will always be a term "S" in a vocabulary of completed-physics such that it is semantically determinate that "$O = S$". I regard this as a matter of referential indeterminacy (see McGee and McLaughlin, 2000). But, again, I pass by issues of vagueness.

39 If properties and kinds are Platonic universals, this issue won't arise. It is typically assumed in the a priori physicalist literature, however, that they are Aristotelian universals, and so not necessary existents, and, you will recall, we are making that assumption here.

40 An instance of (A″) can be a priori even if the corresponding instance of (A′) is not. An instance of (A′) can fail to be a priori even when it is a priori that if O exists then O is an F, for there may be no a priori guarantee that there is a unique F. But it is not required for an instance of (A″) to be a priori that it be a priori that there is a unique F. Notice also that an instance of (A′) can be a priori even if the corresponding instance of (A″) is not: it can be a priori that if O exists then O is the F, even though it is not a priori that if there is a unique F then O is the F. Even if it were a priori that if phlogiston exists then phlogiston is the substance mainly responsible for combustion and calcination, it would not follow that it is a priori that if there is a unique substance that is mainly responsible for combustion and calcination, then phlogiston is the unique substance that is responsible for combustion and calcination. Indeed the latter claim is false. There is such a unique substance and it is not phlogiston; it is oxygen. (Georg Ernest Stahl made the mistaken assumption that rusting is a kind of combustion, and thus took phlogiston to be responsible for calcination. As it happens, oxygen, which is responsible for combustion, is also responsible for calcination.)

41 See Jackson (2005 and A PRIORI PHYSICALISM).

42 See, for example, Chalmers and Jackson (2001).

43 If the reference-fixing description in a contingent a priori reference-fixing analysis is rigidified using "actual" (as in "the actual F"), the result will be an a priori claim that is also metaphysically necessary. But the resulting claim may nevertheless fail to be a meaning-giving analysis since the a priori, metaphysically necessary truth may fail to be analytic. (It should be mentioned that the notion of apriority invoked in this essay does

Brian P. McLaughlin

not presuppose the notion of analyticity. Thus, the claim that there are a priori truths does not entail that there are analytic truths.)

44 This idea of a contingent a priori reference-fixing analysis is inspired not only by Kripke's idea of contingent a priori reference fixing, but also by Gareth Evans's well-known discussion of the Julius example (Evans, 1982). Someone might stipulate, "Let 'Julius' name the inventor of the zip." The idea, then, is that given the stipulation, it would be a priori, despite being contingent, that if Julius exists, then Julius invented the zip; and a priori that if there is a unique inventor of the zip, then the inventor of the zip is Julius. Whitcomb L. Judson is the inventor of the zip. It follows that Julius is Whitcomb L. Judson. Similarly, Urbain Le Verrier stipulated "Let 'Vulcan' name the planet between Mercury and the sun." Given the stipulation, it is a priori that if Vulcan exists, then Vulcan is a planet between Mercury and the sun. Of course, nothing is a planet between Mercury and the sun. Hence, Vulcan does not exist. These examples raise a host of complex issues. I won't pause to examine them.

45 The use of some of these terms raises the crucial issue of whether all phenomenal truths are epistemically implied by the Grand Conjunction; but of that, more later. Chalmers (1996) has claimed that phenomenal terms are not required to specify contingent a priori reference-fixing analyses for vernacular-physical and kind terms, and thus, for example, that "transparent," "colorless," "tasteless," and "odorless" need not be used to spell out the notion of waterish stuff. I won't pursue that issue here. Suffice it to note that a case would also have to be made that "our acquaintance" could be unpacked without even implicit appeal to terms of phenomenal consciousness.

46 Chalmers and Jackson (2001) defend this claim at length.

47 We should add the requirement that the instance of (P and Q) is semantically determinate; let that be assumed.

48 A similar question is raised, rhetorically, by Jackson (A PRIORI PHYSICALISM) in his defense of the a priori physicalist models of identification and elimination.

49 It is thus not assumed here that qualia are essentially private or that they are ineffable. Those are substantive claims about qualia that are made by dualists. They are denied by physicalists who are realists about qualia.

50 See Nemirow (1980); Lewis (1990).

51 CAD suffers feel no pain whatsoever.

52 Williamson and Stanley (2001) argue that *all* know-how requires knowledge-that. I will remain neutral on that issue here, and indeed even on whether the sort of know-how in question requires knowledge-that.

53 See, e.g., Loar (1997); McLaughlin (2001, 2003b); and Levin (2006).

54 This is not to say that the congenitally blind lack the concept of visual experience, that CAD victims lack the concept of pain, or that Mary lacks (say) the concept of the experience of red. They have such concepts. Phenomenal concepts are recognitional concepts (see Loar, 1997; Levin, 2006).

55 Chalmers (1996).

56 Levine (2001).

57 For further discussion, see Hill (1997), Hill and McLaughlin (1999), Papineau (2002), and McLaughlin (2003c).

58 I lack the space to discuss whether it is possible for one to have subject-relative a priori warrant for one's present-tense first-person belief that one is in a certain state of phenomenal consciousness. (See note 24 in this connection.) If one can have such subject-relative a priori knowledge (an issue I leave open), then that one is in the conscious state in question will of course be trivially epistemically implied by the Grand Conjunction, and so the Grand Conjunction will trivially epistemically imply that there is sentience. Still,

though, the Grand Conjunction will not epistemically imply any a posteriori phenomenal truth; it won't, for instance, epistemically imply that I was in pain yesterday, or that many people are suffering.

References

Alexander, S. (1920). *Space, Time, and Deity*, 2 vols. London: Macmillan.
Block, N. and Stalnaker, R. (1999). Conceptual analysis, dualism, and the explanatory gap. *Philosophical Review*, 108, 497–528.
Broad, C. D. (1925). *The Mind and Its Place in Nature*. London: Routledge and Kegan Paul.
Chalmers, D. (1996). *The Conscious Mind*. New York: Oxford University Press.
— and Jackson, F. (2001). Conceptual analysis and reductive explanation. *Philosophical Review*, 110, 315–60.
Chomsky, N. (1980). *Rules and Representations*. New York: Columbia University Press.
Evans, G. (1982). *Varieties of Reference*. Oxford: Clarendon.
Field, H. (1996). The *a prioricity* of logic. *Proceedings of the Aristotelian Society*, 359–76.
Hawthorne, J. (2002). Blocking definitions of materialism. *Philosophical Studies*, 110, 103–13.
Hill, C. (1997). Imaginability, conceivability, possibility, and the mind–body problem. *Philosophical Studies*, 87, 61–85.
— and McLaughlin, B. P. (1999). There are fewer things than are dreamt of in Chalmers's philosophy. *Philosophy and Phenomenological Research*, 2, 445–54.
Jackson, F. (1982). Epiphenomenal qualia. *Philosophical Quarterly*, 32, 127–36.
— (1998). *From Metaphysics to Ethics: A Defense of Conceptual Analysis*. Oxford and New York: Oxford University Press.
— (2005). The case for a priori physicalism. In C. Nimtz and A. Beckermann (eds.), *Philosophy, Science, and Scientific Philosophy, Main Lectures and Colloquia of GAP.5, International Congress for the Society for Analytical Philosophy*. Paderborn: Mentis.
Kaplan, D. (1989a). Afterthoughts. In J. Almog, J. Perry, and H. Wettstein (eds.), *Themes from Kaplan*. Oxford: Oxford University Press.
— (1989b). Demonstratives. In J. Almog, J. Perry, and H. Wettstein (eds.), *Themes from Kaplan*. Oxford: Oxford University Press.
Kripke, S. (1980). *Naming and Necessity*. Cambridge, MA: Harvard University Press.
Levin, J. (2006). What is a phenomenal concept? In T. Alter and S. Walter (eds.), *Phenomenal Concepts and Phenomenal Knowledge: New Essays on Consciousness and Physicalism*. Oxford: Oxford University Press.
Levine, J. (2001). *Purple Haze* (Oxford: Oxford University Press).
Lewis, D. (1986). *On the Plurality of Worlds*. Oxford: Basil Blackwell.
— (1990). What experience teaches us. In W. Lycan (ed.), *Mind and Cognition: A Reader*. Oxford: Basil Blackwell.
Linsky, B. (2006). General terms as rigid designators. *Philosophical Studies*, 128, 655–67.
Loar, B. (1997). Phenomenal states. In N. Block, O. Flanagan, and G. Güzeldere (eds.), *The Nature of Consciousness*. Cambridge, MA: MIT Press. Originally published 1990.
McGee V. and McLaughlin, B. P. (1994). Distinctions without a difference. *Southern Journal of Philosophy*, 33, 203–53.
— (2000). Lessons of the many. *Philosophical Topics*, 28, 129–50.
— (2003). Logical commitment and semantic indeterminacy: a reply to Williamson. *Linguistics and Philosophy*, 26, 637–50.

McGinn, C. (1993). *Problems in Philosophy: The Limits of Inquiry.* Oxford: Basil Blackwell.

— (2001). How not to solve the mind–body problem. In C. Gillett and B. Loewer (eds.), *Physicalism and Its Discontents.* Cambridge: Cambridge University Press.

McLaughlin, B. P. (1992). The rise and fall of British emergentism. In A. Beckermann, H. Flohr, and J. Kim (eds.), *Emergence or Reduction?* Berlin: Walter de Gruyter.

— (2000). Self-knowledge, externalism, and skepticism. *Proceedings of the Joint Session of the Aristotelian Society,* 74 (suppl.), 93–118.

— (2001). In defense of new wave materialism. In B. Loewer (ed.), *Physicalism and Its Discontents.* Cambridge: Cambridge University Press.

— (2003a). McKinsey's challenge, warrant transmission, and skepticism. In S. Nuccetelli (ed.), *New Essays on Semantic Externalism and Self-Knowledge.* Cambridge: Cambridge University Press.

— (2003b). Colour, consciousness, and colour consciousness. In Q. Smith and A. Jokic (eds.), *Consciousness: New Philosophical Perspectives.* Oxford: Oxford University Press.

— (2003c). A naturalist-phenomenal realist response to Block's harder problem. *Philosophical Issues,* 13, 163–204.

Nemirow, L. (1980). Review of *Mortal Questions,* by Thomas Nagel. *Philosophical Review,* 89, 473–7.

Papineau, D. (2002). *Thinking about Consciousness.* Oxford: Oxford University Press.

Pollock, J. (1974). *Knowledge and Justification.* Princeton: Princeton University Press.

— (1986). *Contemporary Theories of Knowledge.* Towota, NJ: Rowman and Littlefield.

Russell, B. (1927). *Outline of Philosophy.* London: Routledge.

Schiffer, S. (2003). *The Things We Mean.* Oxford: Clarendon.

Williamson, T. (1994). *Vagueness.* London: Routledge.

— and Stanley, J. (2001). Knowing how. *Journal of Philosophy,* 98, 411–44.

IS THERE AN UNRESOLVED PROBLEM OF MENTAL CAUSATION?

Causation and Mental Causation

Jaegwon Kim

1

An epistolary event occurred in 1643 that will live in the history of the debate on mental causation. In the May of that year, Princess Elisabeth of Bohemia dispatched to Descartes what must be one of the most celebrated philosophical letters, challenging him to explain:

> How the mind of a human being can determine the bodily spirits [i.e., the fluids in the nerves, muscles, etc.] in producing voluntary actions, being only a thinking substance. For it appears that all determination of movement is produced by the pushing of the thing being moved, by the manner in which it is pushed by that which moves it, or else by the qualification and figure of the surface of the latter. Contact is required for the first two conditions, and extension for the third. [But] you entirely exclude the latter from the notion you have of the body, and the former seems incompatible with an immaterial thing.[1]

A need for explanation arises for Elisabeth because she takes contact as a necessary condition for physical causation: the cause – at least, the proximate cause – of the motion of a material body must be in spatial contact with that body, a condition that plainly cannot be met by an immaterial causal agent outside physical space. The idea that causation requires contact survives even in Hume, a philosopher who is commonly thought to have held a deflationary view of causation as consisting solely in de facto regularities. One of the conditions Hume laid down for causation is that of contiguity in "space and time" between cause and effect, either direct or mediated by a chain of contiguous cause–effect pairs. (We will recur to the contiguity condition below.)

Elisabeth's challenge is intelligible and surely reasonable, both in commonsensical terms as well as in light of what Descartes had written, in *Meditation* II, about bodies and causes of their motions:

> By a body I understand whatever has determinate shape and a definable location and can occupy a space in such a way as to exclude any other body; it can be perceived by touch, sight, hearing, taste or smell, and can be moved in various ways, not by itself but by whatever else comes into contact with it. (Descartes, [1641] 1985, p. 17)

To be sure, Descartes doesn't say that is the only way to set bodies in motion; however, if the mind's causation of bodily motion is an exception, we are in need of an explanation. There may well have been earlier philosophical concerns about the powers of the mind to bring about changes in the physical world,[2] but, for many of us, the exchanges between Descartes and Elisabeth are the first episode we encounter in the mental causation debate during the early modern period. Descartes continues to loom large in contemporary discussions of many central issues in the philosophy of mind, and our current concerns with mental causation are no exception.

What is of interest to us here is Elisabeth's appeal to a specific feature of causation in her challenge to Descartes, the requirement that to cause a material body to move, physical contact with the body is necessary. Such contact, in more modern terms, represents the imparting of energy, or transfer of momentum, from one body to another, and this fact constitutes the causal action. Elisabeth's simple complaint, which still resonates with us, is that such a conception of causation leaves no room for mental causation within Cartesian dualism. Minds, being essentially extensionless and without location in physical space, cannot meet Descartes's contact requirement for causation of bodily motion: in fact, the idea of contact between an immaterial mind and a material body lacks a coherent sense. It appears, therefore, that on Cartesian terms, mental causation is a metaphysical impossibility, or the very idea is unintelligible.

2

Mental causation has been a flash point of debates in the contemporary philosophy of mind for well over three decades, ever since the publication of Donald Davidson's "Mental Events" (1970). In this paper Davidson put forward what was then considered a startling thesis to the effect that there are no "strict" laws about mental phenomena – neither mental-physical laws nor mental-mental laws. Strict laws, if they exist, are found only in "developed physics" (Davidson, 1993). Further, he claimed that strict laws are required to underwrite causal relations. The two claims together appear at first blush to entail the impossibility of mental causation. However, Davidson had a deft reply: All that his two principles imply is that any causal relation must instantiate a strict *physical* law, and that what is required for a mental event to enter into a causal relation is for it to have an appropriate physical description under which it instantiates a physical law. From this Davidson derived his "anomalous monism": All individual mental events – in fact, all individual events[3] – that enter into any causal relations are physical events. The only events that escape Davidson's argument are those that are both causeless and effectless – entities hardly worth worrying about.

This ingenious solution was the spark that brought back the problem of mental causation to contemporary philosophy. It all began when several philosophers noticed (Stoutland, 1980; Honderich, 1982; Kim, 1984; Sosa, 1984; McLaughlin, 1989), apparently independently, that although Davidson's anomalous monism allowed individual (or "token") mental events to be causes and effects, it failed to give any role to mental properties, or mental descriptions, of these events in determining what causal relations they enter into. The reason is simple: since, on Davidson's view, all strict laws are physical laws and they apply to individual events solely in virtue of their physical properties, the mental properties they may have – or the mental kinds (e.g., pain, desire, thought) under which they may fall – are rendered irrelevant to the events' causal relations, or so it seemed to his critics. Though Davidson's anomalous monism is not a form of "token" epiphenomenalism, it was generally perceived as a form of "type" epiphenomenalism (a distinction due to McLaughlin, 1989), the view that psychological characteristics and features contribute nothing to the causal powers of objects and events that have them. The position has the consequence that if we were to redistribute psychological, and other nonphysical, properties over the events and objects of this world – even if these properties were entirely removed – that would not change a single causal relation as long as the distribution of physical properties (and relations) remains the same. Davidson (1993) tried to defend anomalous monism against the epiphenomenalist charges; however, few seem to have found his efforts persuasive.

It did not escape philosophers' attention that Davidson's troubles with mental causation crucially depended on his conception of causation – in particular, the condition that causally related events must instantiate "strict" laws. There has been some controversy about how to understand the strictness of strict laws, or what Davidson intended with the term. Strict laws of course must be laws – that is, as Davidson (1970) explicitly notes, they must be capable of supporting counterfactuals and subjunctives and also be capable of confirmation by observation of positive instances (that is, inductively projectible). There seem two further features that make for strictness: first, strict laws are totally exceptionless (in this regard, they contrast with laws or generalizations hedged with *ceteris paribus* clauses), and, second, they are often (always?) found as part of a theory that is in some sense "complete" and gives comprehensive coverage over its domain. (Paradigm cases of such theories will include physical theories such as classical mechanics, electromagnetic theory, and quantum mechanics.) It is not easy to spell out this second condition in precise terms, something that Davidson himself seems never to have done. In practice, however, exceptionlessness is what does most of the work, and for most purposes this has seemed sufficient. In any case, a natural question to raise, when we are faced with Davidson's epiphenomenalist predicament, is why we should tie causation to strict laws. Why can't there be causation where there are no strict laws in Davidson's sense? This question is especially appropriate given the fact that Davidson never stated a clear reason, much less a detailed argument, for his requirement of strict laws for causal relations.

3

One strategy that will naturally occur to many is to abandon Davidson's strict law requirement, or relax it by allowing non-strict laws, or laws with *ceteris paribus* hedges, to ground causal relations. Jerry Fodor is one such philosopher. He admits that "even the best psychological laws are very likely to be hedged," and then continues "it [is] no longer clear why hedged psychological laws can't ground mental causes; and, presumably, if hedged psychological laws can, then strict physical laws needn't" (Fodor, 1989, p. 72). But how can a *ceteris paribus* law, a law whose antecedent, say F-events, does not necessitate its consequent, G-events, ground a causal relation between F-events and a G-events? Given the law, it is amply possible for an F-event to occur without being followed by a G-event. Being qualified by a *ceteris paribus* clause, the law is immune to falsification by such counter-instances; that is exactly the point of *ceteris paribus* hedges.

Fodor's argument is based on a special construal of "*ceteris paribus*" clauses. He proposes:

> The first – and crucial – step in getting what a robust construal of the causal responsibility of mental requires is to square the idea that Ms [mental events of kind M] are nomologically sufficient for Bs [bodily events of kind B] with the fact that psychological laws are hedged . . . [If] it's a law that M → B ceteris paribus, then it follows that you get Bs whenever you get Ms *and* the ceteris paribus conditions are satisfied. This shows us how ceteris paribus laws can do serious scientific business since it captures the difference between the (substantive) claim that Fs cause Gs ceteris paribus and the (empty) claim that Fs cause Gs except when they don't. (Fodor, 1989, p. 73)

The heart of Fodor's strategy, then, appears to be the thought that whenever we have a serious *ceteris paribus* law "Ms cause (or are followed by) Bs, *ceteris paribus*," there is a set C of conditions (as yet not fully identified) such that "Whenever C obtains, Ms cause (or are followed by) Bs" is a strict, exceptionless law. The reader will have noticed the alternate formulations, "cause (or are followed by)," in the preceding sentence. This was to reflect Fodor's unexplained move, in the quoted passage, from "M → B ceteris paribus," which presumably states only that M is (nomologically) sufficient for B *ceteris paribus*, to "Ms cause B *ceteris paribus*." This slide between nomological sufficiency and causality occurs throughout Fodor (1989), and it is indicative of the fact that Fodor's operative conception of causality is straightforwardly based on nomological regularity.[4] In any case, on Fodor's view, *ceteris paribus* hedges represent only our ignorance of the details of causal/nomological regularities, nothing metaphysical about the regularities. So, for him, wherever there is a *ceteris paribus* law, there is a strict law waiting to be discovered. A *ceteris paribus* law connecting M-events with B-events can support the hedged causal claim "This M-event caused this B-event *ceteris paribus*," and if the unspecified *ceteris paribus* conditions are in fact satisfied (whether or not we know it), we have the true unhedged causal judgment "This M-event caused this B-event."[5]

But this, to my mind, is to mislocate the real problem. What one should worry about in this context is not *ceteris paribus* clauses but a more fundamental question about causation and regularities. This question concerns whether or not we can get causation out of regularities, whether these are strict or hedged, or whether they are mere *de facto* regularities (Humean "constant conjunctions") or given a suitable modal force ("physical/nomological necessity," "lawlikeness," "projectibility," and the like). As early as 1925, C. D. Broad made the following simple observation: "Again, if causation be nothing but regular sequence and concomitance, as some philosophers have held, it is ridiculous to regard psycho-neural parallelism and interaction to be mutually exclusive alternatives. For interaction will mean no more than parallelism, and parallelism will mean no less than interaction" (Broad, 1925, p. 96).[6]

Actually, the situation is not quite as simple as Broad describes, for causation, or causal interaction, has directionality, whereas psychoneural correlations under a strict parallelism are entirely symmetrical, and it would be difficult to determine which of the two symmetrically correlated events, one mental and one physical, is the cause and which the effect. But that is the least of the problems faced by the regularist, or nomological, approach to causation.

First, there is the much discussed situation in which two phenomena are correlated, with nomological necessity, because they are collateral effects of a single cause.[7] One of the two effects may always occur a little earlier than the other so that we may mistakenly think that the first is the cause of the second. There must be many such cases in medicine where a single underlying pathological state gives rise to two distinct symptoms, one occurring earlier than the other. The regularity connecting the two symptoms may be projectible and law-like, and there seems no reason to deny that it holds with nomological necessity (we could even suppose it strict and exceptionless, though this is unlikely). The regularity, though it arises from underlying causal processes, clearly does not constitute causation – a relation in which one event brings about another.

Situations with the following structure present an analogous difficulty. We observe a regular connection between two events, A and B, with A preceding B, and we may be tempted to postulate a causal connection between them, with A as cause and B as effect. A believer in a purely regularist-nomological conception of causation would be committed to this conclusion. However, it may well turn out that the observed correlation between A and B is due to A's regular correlation with event C and B's regular correlation with event D, where C causes D. The correlation from A to B is only a superficial manifestation of an underlying causal process involving C and D. It will be easy enough to find instances exemplifying this situation in medicine in which an underlying pathological process gives rise to regular connections between symptoms caused by the various stages in the progression of the pathology. Closer to home, where mental causation is concerned, regular sequences of mental events may well be cases of this kind. If so, the impression that we are observing mental-to-mental causation would only be an impression. The fact would be that the observed sequence of mental events is grounded in, and is explained by, an underlying causal process between the neural substrates of the mental events. There is no direct causal relationship between the successive mental events in the sequence; the only genuine causal relations present are those between the neural substrates underlying the mental sequence. Thus, the relationship between the two successive mental events is like that between a series of shadows cast by a moving car at successive instants. The moving shadows do not constitute a causal sequence; nor would a sequence of mental events grounded in (or supervenient upon or realized by) a series of causally connected neural substrates.[8] It should be clear that the issues about *ceteris paribus* laws do not touch these difficulties with the regularist-nomological conception of causality.

Trying to soothe our fear of epiphenomenalism (or "epiphobia," as he calls it), Fodor tells us:

> According to the present view, the properties projected in the laws of basic science are causally responsible, and so too are the properties projected in the laws of the special sciences. Notice, in particular, that even if the properties that the special sciences talk about are supervenient upon the properties that the basic sciences talk about, that does *not* argue that the properties that the special sciences talk about are epiphenomenal. (Fodor, 1989, p. 66)

But this is no cure for epiphobia. Our discussion shows that though there may be projectible special-science properties and there may be special-science laws, that does not guarantee that there is causation in the special sciences. Fodor continues as follows: "Not, at least, if there are causal laws of the special sciences. The causal laws of the special sciences and causal laws of basic sciences have in common that they *both* license ascriptions of causal responsibility" (Fodor, 1989, p. 66).

To be sure, if there are *causal* laws in psychology, they will license ascription of causal responsibility to psychological properties and ground psychological causal relations. The crucial question unaddressed by Fodor is whether psychological laws *are* causal laws – that is, whether the regularities we observe in the psychological domain are causal regularities, or mere reflections of the causal regularities at a more fundamental level. Fodor's neglect of this question is evident in his seemingly unconscious slide between regularities and causal regularities, and between laws and causal laws. All this seems to be an outcome of his unreflective assumption of a regularist-nomological conception of causation.

4

So the issue of mental causation cannot be resolved by simply invoking the regularist or nomological approach to causation. In saying this, I don't mean to say that the nomological model of causation doesn't work anywhere; it is possible that it is the right account of causation at the fundamental physical level. Precisely because it is the bottom level with nothing below, regularities, or "constant conjunctions," may be all we can get: it makes no sense to speak of "underlying" mechanisms, or "real" causal processes at a lower level. Or we can perhaps take this to mean that, although only "constant conjunctions," but no causation, exist at the fundamental level (the textbook Hume was right about this level), causal relations can, and do, exist (or "emerge") at higher levels. These are interesting and intriguing issues but we set them aside and move on.

The nomological conception, which once was the reigning approach to causation and scientific explanation, seems to have lost favor with a significant number of philosophers. The tide now seems to have turned in favor of a broadly sine-qua-non

Jaegwon Kim

conception of causation whose most influential modern version is due to David Lewis's seminal account of causation in terms of counterfactual dependence (Lewis, 1973a). This approach has recently attracted a lot of attention from an active and energetic group of philosophers, and there appear to be numerous ongoing research projects attempting to develop a satisfactory version based on Lewis's basic insights. The idea of counterfactual dependence is this: e is counterfactually dependent on c just in case if c had not occurred, e would not have occurred. Since counterfactual dependence as defined is not transitive whereas causation is, Lewis explained "c causes e" as the ancestral of counterfactual dependence, that is, in terms of there being a series of events linking c with e such that any event in this series is counterfactually dependent on its predecessor. There are numerous outstanding difficulties with the counterfactual approach, among them the problems of overdetermination and preemption – problems that seem highly resistant to solution. The current literature is rife with increasingly complex and clever counterexamples and equally complex and ingenious remedies to evade them.[9] The impression one gets from looking in from outside is that we are still very far from achieving the desired end, and that a reasonably simple and intuitively well-motivated counterfactual account of causation is not yet in sight. The increasing number of epicycles being piled on top of the epicycles already there reminds one of the ultimately fruitless search for the "fourth condition" of knowledge prompted by the Gettier problem. I don't want to say that the ongoing research on the counterfactual analysis of causation is without value; far from it, it may yield – I believe it has already yielded – some valuable insights into our causal talk, just as the Gettier-inspired work in epistemology has contributed much to our understanding of knowledge and justification. Our present concern is not with the ultimate viability of the counterfactual approach to causation; it is a more restricted one of assessing the prospect of explaining mental causation in terms of counterfactuals, although in doing this our discussion will inevitably involve some general issues about causation and counterfactuals.

One such general issue concerns the apparent dependence of counterfactuals, at least those involved in causal attributions, on laws and regularities, and if this is the case, embracing the counterfactual approach to causation will have no advantages over the regularist-nomological approach we considered earlier. Consider the causal claim: The striking of the match caused it to light. On a simple counterfactual analysis, this amounts to the assertion of the following counterfactual:

C If this match had not been struck, it would not have lighted.

Almost all current counterfactual theorists of causation use the semantics of counterfactuals developed by Robert Stalnaker (1968) and David Lewis (1973b), based on comparative similarity among possible worlds. According to this scheme, (C) is true just in case the consequent of the conditional "the match did not light" is true in the world that, apart from the fact that the match was not struck in that world, is the closest – that is, the most similar – to the actual world (we use this somewhat simplified formulation; this will make no difference). Assume (C) is true. That means that in the closest world in which the match was not struck, it did not light. How do we know that this world is closer to the actual world than is the closest world in which the match was not struck but it nonetheless lighted? The obvious, and the only possible, answer seems to be that, in the actual world, dry matches struck in the presence of oxygen usually and reliably ignite, and that it is our knowledge of this regularity, or law, combined with knowledge of the actual circumstances in which the match was struck (e.g., it was dry, oxygen was present, etc.), that accounts for the judgment that the world in which the match that was not struck does not light is closer to the actual world than is the world in which the unstruck match lights. Perhaps the laws involved might be more theoretical and concern the chemical composition of the match head, its combustibility, the characteristics of the surface against which the match was struck, and so forth. In any case, one crucial respect in which the comparative similarity of worlds is to be determined evidently involves the similarity of laws holding in them. It is difficult to see how evaluations of conditionals such as (C) could avoid adverting to laws and regularities.

Let us see how this affects the use of counterfactuals to account for mental causation. Consider the claim that a sudden attack of migraine headache caused Susan a frightful sense of anxiety. For the counterfactualist, this amounts to the truth of:

D   If Susan had not had the sudden migraine headache, she would not have experienced frightful anxiety.

We can concede that our common-sense "knowledge," or assumption, that counterfactuals like (D) are often true grounds our belief in the reality of mental causation. Our job as philosophers is to see what makes the likes of (D) true and whether this justifies the claim that Susan's migraine headache caused her anxiety. If our observations relating to (C) are correct, the truth of (D) must depend on the regularity connecting sudden attacks of migraine headaches and feelings of anxiety. This regularity could be limited to Susan and others like her in relevant (presumably neurophysiological) respects, or it could be a (*ceteris paribus*) law for all people with migraine headaches. It seems to me that even an epiphenomenalist such as T. H. Huxley (1901) can, with consistency, accept a regularity of this kind and acknowledge it to be lawlike (surely, the connection isn't accidental or coincidental – not even for an epiphenomenalist). However, the epiphenomenalist will deny that (D) warrants the causal claim that the attack of migraine headache caused the sense of fearful anxiety. The observed regularity arises out of a genuine causal process connecting two neural substrates on which the headache and the anxiety respectively causally depend. The situation is fundamentally the same if you believe that the dependence relation between mental states and their neural substrates is better described in terms of supervenience or realization than causation.[10] And these observed psychological regularities may very well underwrite the corresponding counterfactuals. As we saw with Fodor, however, there is no guarantee that they are causal regularities, and if they are not, there is no reason to think that the counterfactual dependencies they ground yield genuine causal relations.

5

In spite of these and possibly other difficulties, the counterfactual approach to causality remains popular – among philosophers working on issues about causation

Jaegwon Kim

(especially the analysis of the concept) and among philosophers who aim to defend mental causation against various epiphenomenalist threats.[11] The intuition that supports the counterfactual approach, I believe, is the close association we form between a cause of an event and a sine qua non condition of its occurrence. A cause is the condition but for which the effect would not have occurred. We can grant the legitimacy of this intuition, without necessarily wedding it to any particular way of making it precise and exact – without, that is, necessarily explicating it in terms of counterfactuals with a Stalnaker/Lewis-style semantics, or any other special semantics of conditionals.

But there is another strong intuitive conception of causation that contrasts sharply with the conception tied to counterfactual dependency, or the sine qua non condition. It is a *productive* or *generative* conception of what causing consists in. On this conception, a cause is something that produces, or generates, or brings about its effects, something from which the effects derive their existence or occurrence. This idea was given its classic expression when Elizabeth Anscombe wrote:

> There is something to observe here, that lies under our noses. It is little attended to, and yet still so obvious as to seem trite. It is this: causality consists in the derivativeness of an effect from its cause. This is the core, the common feature, of causality in its various kinds. Effects derive from, arise out of, come of, their causes. For example, everyone will grant that physical parenthood is a causal relation. (Anscombe, 1993, pp. 91–2)

Indeed, in a recent article, Ned Hall (2004) makes a plausible case for the thesis that there are two fundamentally distinct notions of causation:

> Causation, understood as a relation between events, comes in at least two basic and fundamentally different varieties. One of these, which I call "dependence," is simply that: counterfactual dependence between wholly distinct events. In this sense, event c is a cause of (distinct) event e just in case e depends on c. That is, just in case, had c not occurred, e would not have occurred. The second variety is rather more difficult to characterize, but we evoke it when we say of event c that it helps to *generate* or *bring about* or *produce* another event e, and for that reason I call it "production." (Hall, 2004, p. 225)

According to Hall, three characteristics are central to productive/generative causation: transitivity, locality, and intrinsicness. Of these what is relevant to our present concerns is locality, which Hall states as follows: "Causes are connected to their effects via spatiotemporally continuous sequences of causal intermediaries" (Hall, 2004, p. 225). This seems equivalent to Hume's contiguity condition alluded to earlier. Hume's own statement is this:

> I find in the first place, that whatever objects are consider'd as causes or effects, are *contiguous*; and that nothing can operate in a time or place, which is ever so little remov'd from those of its existence. Tho' distant objects may sometimes seem productive of each other, they are commonly found upon examination to be link'd by a chain of causes, which are contiguous among themselves, and to the distant objects; and when in any particular instance we cannot discover this connexion, we still presume it to exist. (Hume, [1739] 1888, p. 75)

As Hall notes, causal relations conforming to the dependence idea need not meet the locality condition; we will see some examples below.

What we have seen in earlier sections is that neither the nomological nor the dependency conception of causation can properly ground mental causation. I argued that nomological relationships do not deliver the kind of causal efficacy, or productivity, we want for mentality, and that the counterfactual approach seems to presuppose, or collapse to, the nomological conception and thereby inherit the latter's shortcomings. Many counterfactualists will dispute this claim. We need not concern ourselves with this general issue about causation. In this section, I will try to argue that the relation of causation as dependence, or counterfactual dependence, even if it is a proper and useful causal relation, is not the source of our worries about mental causation. That is, even if we succeed in showing that mental causation, with causation construed as dependence, is real, that would not suffice to vindicate mental causal efficacy and thereby dissipate our epiphenomenalist worries. Fundamentally these worries arise, I believe, from the question whether mentality has the power to bring about its effects in a continuous process of generation and production – or the question whether we can show that this is so.

Why should we resort to this "thick" variety of causation in thinking about mental causation? My answer is pretty simple: We care about mental causation because we care about *human agency*, and agency requires the productive/generative conception of causation.[12] I don't have a knockdown argument to prove that agency requires productive causation; I hope what I will say here makes my claim at least plausible. It seems to me that mere counterfactual dependence is not enough to sustain the causal relation involved in our idea of acting upon the natural course of events and bringing about changes so as to actualize what we desire and intend. An agent is someone who, on account of her beliefs, desires, emotions, intentions, and the like, has the capacity to perform actions in the physical world: that is, to cause her limbs and other bodily parts (e.g., the vocal cords) to move in appropriate ways so as to bring about changes in the arrangement of objects and events around her – open a door, pick up the morning paper, and make a cup of coffee. It seems to me that without productive causation, which respects the locality/contiguity condition, such causal processes are not possible. These causal processes all involve *real connectedness* between cause and effect, and the connection is constituted by phenomena such as energy flow and momentum transfer, an actual movement of some (conserved) physical quantity.[13] In saying this we need not impugn the dependency conception of causation: all we need is the point that agency requires productive causation.[14] Note, further, that we need not claim that dependency is not involved in actions; it may well be that the dependency involved, say between a limb movement and a desire, has an explanation in terms of the productive/generative relations between them.[15]

Consider the component of mental-to-physical causation involved in action, namely the causation of bodily movements by our desires, beliefs, intentions, and the like. To endow our mental states with causal powers to move our limbs (or, more proximately, the powers to bring about changes in our neural states), would it be enough to show that counterfactuals such as the following are true – and that we have reason to believe them true?

If Susan had not wanted to open the window, neural state N would not have occurred in her brain (where we suppose N triggers an appropriate sequence of bodily movements).

If Susan had not experienced the sudden migraine headache, neural state N* would not have occurred (where we assume N* to be the neural substrate of anxiety attacks).

We earlier argued that counterfactuals like these ultimately involve reference to psychological or psychophysical regularities, and that their significance for mental causation depends on the question whether these regularities are *causal* regularities. Apart from this issue, there are reasons to be suspicious about relying on counterfactuals alone to defend mental causation – what such a strategy could show.

Friends of the counterfactual approach often tout its ability to handle omissions and absences as causes and the productive/generative approach's inability to account for them. We are inclined to take the truth of a counterfactual such as:

If Mary had watered my plants, the plants would not have died

as showing that Mary's not watering, an omission, caused the plants' death and take that as a basis for blaming Mary for killing the plants. But obviously there was no flow of energy from Mary to the plants during my absence (that exactly was the problem!); nor was there any other physical connection, or any spatiotemporally contiguous chain of causally connected events.

One issue with regarding Mary's omission as a cause of the plants' death on the strength of the foregoing counterfactual is that there are indefinitely many other counterfactuals like it inappropriately certifying an indefinitely large number of other omissions as causes of the plants' death:[16]

If George W. Bush had watered my plants, the plants would not have died.

If Laura Bush had watered my plants, the plants would not have died.

If Hillary Clinton had watered my plants, the plants would not have died.

Well, you get the idea. I blame Mary for not watering the plants: we may blame agents for their omissions. But we don't have to say that the omissions are causes. We need not say that I am blaming Mary for killing my plants (she would have killed them if she had sprayed them with a herbicide): the fact is that she didn't do anything to them while I was away. I am blaming her for breaking a promise – her promise to water the plants.

If omissions should count as actions, something we *do*, then by staying in my room "doing nothing" (I could be taking a long nap), I would be performing countless actions, such as not watering my plants, not writing an email to my niece, not doing the MS walk, not space-walking out of the shuttle *Discovery* . . . Of course these are not intentional omissions (at least they don't have to be), but it is difficult to see how intentional omissions and mere omissions could differ metaphysically, in particular, with respect to their causal powers. At any rate, it is by no means clear that its apparent ability to handle omissions as causes is something that the dependency theorist should celebrate. Not thinking, not believing, not desiring, and so on are mental omissions. If causation by mental omissions count as mental causation, that would make mental causation easy – too easy. My not believing (or disbelieving) that a chest of treasures is buried in my backyard is a cause of my not digging in my backyard; my not believing treasures are buried in your backyard causes my not digging in your backyard, and so on ad infinitum. This doesn't look like a causation worth having.

6

But if we understand causation in mental causation in the productive/generative sense, wouldn't that rule out mental causation – in particular mental-physical causation – too quickly, without any need for an argument? Especially if we require that causation requires energy flow or momentum transfer, how could there be such a process from a mental entity to a physical entity, or in the converse direction? Remember Elisabeth's challenge to Descartes: the causation of physical motion requires spatial contact, but how could an immaterial mind outside physical space be in such contact with a material body? Notice that this problem is not special to Cartesian physics: it arises even under Hume's concept of causation, which, as we saw, requires a spatially contiguous chain of causally connected events. Don't all such conceptions of causation, conceptions that require some "real" connections between cause and effect, automatically rule out mental-physical causation (and hence human agency)? Further, what could "contiguity" mean unless it meant spatial contiguity? Further, what "real" connection can there be between two immaterial and non-spatial substances? Wouldn't the productive/generative conception of causation preclude, without much ado, mind-to-mind causation as well as mind-to-body causation – that is, all mental causation?[17]

An answer – the right answer, in my opinion – is contained in a follow-up letter Elisabeth sent to Descartes in June 1643: "And I admit that it would be easier for me to concede matter and extension to the mind than it would be for me to concede the capacity to move a body and be moved by one to an immaterial thing" (Garber, 2001, p. 172).

This, I believe, is a remarkable statement attesting to the philosophical astuteness of Elisabeth. She is saying what some of us have been saying for the past two decades – namely that to make sense of mental causation, she would rather physicalize the mind ("concede matter and extension to the mind") than acquiesce in the unworkable idea that immaterial minds can be in causal commerce with material bodies. Elisabeth is voicing the thought that we would now express by saying that mental causation is possible only if mentality is physically reducible. Her avowal may well have been the first causal argument ever for physicalism.

The dominant strain of physicalism on the contemporary scene has been the non-reductive kind. Non-reductive physicalists, while rejecting Cartesian immaterial minds or any nonphysical object, nonetheless resist the idea that mental properties are reducible to physical properties. Beliefs, desires, intentions, pains, visual images, and the rest, though they may be supervenient on neural/biological processes, are irreducible to them; nonetheless, these mental states are claimed to be causally efficacious. But how can the idea of productive/generative causation be applied to them in relation to neural/physical states? How can there be energy flow or momentum transfer from a desire, as an irreducible mental state, to the firing of a group of neurons? In his characterization of non-reductive physicalism, Terence Horgan, a leading proponent of the position, writes:

> First, mental properties and facts are determined by, or supervenient upon, physical properties and facts. Second (and contrary to emergentism), physics is a causally complete science; the only fundamental force-generating properties are physical properties. More specifically, the human body does not instantiate any fundamental force-generating properties other than physical ones. Third, mental properties nonetheless have genuine causal/explanatory efficacy, via the physical properties that "realize" mental properties on particular occasions of instantiation. (Horgan, 1996, p. 498)

So, on Horgan's anti-reductionist view, a desire (as an individual "token" event) has "genuine" causal efficacy, say the power to move my arm to reach for a glass of water, in virtue of the fact that its neural realizer, an instance of a neural property on which the desire supervenes, has this causal power.

Horgan's suggestion, I believe, is fundamentally right: mental events and states have the causal efficacy that they have because their neural/physical realizers have causal efficacy. In fact, a mental state, occurring on a given occasion, in virtue of being realized by a certain neural/physical state, has exactly the causal powers of that physical state (Kim, 1992). Where I differ from Horgan is that once we are prepared to say what we have just said, the next natural step to take – in my view, a step we are compelled to take – is to reductively identify this particular mental state with its neural/physical realizer (Kim, 1993, 1998). This of course is to jettison the "non-reductive" part of non-reductive physicalism. To say what Horgan says, namely that the belief is a distinct state from its neural realizer, and yet consider each a sufficient cause of the arm rising, is to walk smack into the problem of overdetermination. And to say that the mental state has causal efficacy "via" the causal efficacy of its neural realizer carries an apparent epiphenomenal implication: Given that the neural realizer is a full cause of the arm rising, what causal work is left for the mental state to contribute? Or, to put the question another way, what could "via" mean here? What is it for an event to cause something "via" another event that presumably does the real causing?

So the idea of causation as production and generation, or causation as requiring a "real" connection between cause and effect, can be applied to mentality as long as, and presumably only so long as, mental states have physical realizers. Whether an approach of this kind leads to reductionism, as I just claimed, or it is compatible with a non-reductive view of mentality is a further, currently much debated, issue (Kim, 2005).

Notes

1   Elisabeth to Descartes, May 1643. This quotation is taken from Garber (2001, 172).
2   See Caston (1997).
3   Here we assume that the mental–physical dichotomy is both exhaustive and exclusive. Also, Davidson believes that strict laws (if there are any) can be found only in physics.
4   Fodor (1989, p. 65) briefly considers the possibility of non-causal laws, that is, nomological regularities that do not constitute causal relations, but waves it off in his typically light-hearted way.
5   It is a bit of a mystery how we can ever know these "unknown" conditions are satisfied and hence how on Fodor's account we can know a causal relation exists on the basis of a "*ceteris paribus*" law.
6   Thanks to Brian McLaughlin for bringing this paragraph to my attention.
7   For extensive discussions of "causal forks," see Wesley C. Salmon (1984). Broad (1925, esp. pp. 115–17) notes such cases.
8   This is the gist of what I have called the "supervenience argument": see Kim (1998, 2005).
9   A good place to sample some of this is Collins et al. (2004).
10 I doubt that Huxley would have cared one way or the other. Obviously the idioms of supervenience and realization were not available to him.
11 For example, LePore and Loewer (1987), Horgan (1989), Loewer (2002 and MENTAL CAUSA-TION, OR SOMETHING NEAR ENOUGH).
12 In correspondence Barry Loewer has challenged this claim. According to him, "thin" causa-tion, or dependence, is sufficient to ground agency. See Loewer (MENTAL CAUSATION, OR SOMETHING NEAR ENOUGH).
13 I am of course referring to the so-called conservative quantity approach to causation. See Dowe (1992, 2000), Salmon (1994); for an early statement, see Fair (1979). See also the exchange between Dowe (2004) and the dependence theorist Schaffer (2004).
14 For our purposes we need not claim that all cases of action involve productive causation; perhaps we are willing to regard certain cases of omissions as actions and consider omis-sions as eligible as causes. See later for further discussion of omissions.
15 Sometimes in terms of the absence of such relations, e.g., in cases of causation by omis-sions and absences; see later. Can there be any causation– any dependency causation – without there being at least some productive causation? I don't know the answer.
16 I saw examples like these in Abbott (1974) for the first time. This paper is recommended to those interested in the counterfactual approach to causation. See also McGrath (2005).
17 For an argument for an affirmative answer to this question based on spatial considerations, see Kim (2005, ch. 3).

References

Abbott, B. (1974). Some problems in giving an adequate mode-theoretical account of cause. In C. Filmore, G. Lakoff and R. Lakoff (eds.), *Berkeley Studies in Syntax and Semantics*, vol. 1. Berkeley: University of California Press.
Anscombe, E. (1993). Causality and determination. In M. Tooley and E. Sosa (eds.), *Causation*. Oxford: Oxford University Press. Original edition, Cambridge: Cambridge University Press, 1971.

Broad, C. D. (1925). *The Mind and Its Place in Nature*. London: Routledge and Kegan Paul.

Caston, V. (1997). Epiphenomenalisms, ancient and modern. *Philosophical Review*, 106, 309–63.

Collins, J., Hall, N. and Paul, L. A. (eds.) (2004). *Causation and Counterfactuals*. Cambridge, MA: MIT Press.

Davidson, D. (1970). Mental events. In L. Foster and J. W. Swanson (eds.), *Experience and Theory*. London: Duckworth, 79–91. Reprinted in D. Davidson, *Essays on Actions and Events*. New York and Oxford: Oxford University Press, 1980.

— (1993). Thinking causes. In J. Heil and A. Mele (eds.), *Mental Causation*. Oxford: Oxford University Press.

Descartes, R. ([1641] 1985). *Meditations on First Philosophy: The Philosophical Writings of Descartes*, vol. 2, trans. J. Cottingham, R. Stoothoff, and D. Murdoch. Cambridge: Cambridge University Press.

Dowe, P. (1992). Wesley Salmon's process theory of causality and the conserved quantity theory. *Philosophy of Science*, 59, 195–216.

— (2000). *Physical Causation*. Cambridge: Cambridge University Press.

— (2004). Causes are physically connected to their effects. In C. Hitchcock (ed.), *Contemporary Debates in Philosophy of Science*. Oxford: Blackwell.

Fair, D. (1979). Causation and the flow of energy. *Erkenntnis*, 14, 219–50.

Fodor, J. A. (1989). Making mind matter more. *Philosophical Topics*, 17, 59–79.

Garber, D. (2001). *Descartes Embodied*. Cambridge: Cambridge University Press.

Hall, N. (2004). Two concepts of causation. In J. Collins, N. Hall and L. A. Paul (eds.), *Causation and Counterfactuals*. Cambridge, MA: MIT Press.

Honderich, T. (1982). The argument for anomalous monism. *Analysis*, 42, 59–64.

Horgan, T. (1989). Mental quausation. *Philosophical Perspectives*, 3, 47–76.

— (1996). Reduction, reductionism. In D. M. Borchert (ed.), *The Encyclopedia of Philosophy: Supplement*. New York: Simon & Schuster Macmillan.

Hume, D. ([1739] 1888). *A Treatise of Human Nature*, ed. L. A. Selby-Bigge. Oxford: Clarendon.

Huxley, T. H. (1901). *Methods and Results: Essays*. New York: D. Appleton. [A useful excerpted version can be found in D. J. Chalmers (ed.) (2002). *Philosophy of Mind: Classical and Contemporary Readings*. Oxford: Oxford University Press.]

Kim, J. (1984). Epiphenomenal and supervenient causation. *Midwest Studies in Philosophy*, 9, 257–70.

— (1992). Multiple realization and the metaphysics of reduction. *Philosophy and Phenomenological Research*, 52, 1–26.

— (1993). Postscripts on mental causation. In J. Kim (ed.), *Supervenience and Mind*. Cambridge: Cambridge University Press.

— (1998). *Mind in a Physical World*. Cambridge, MA: MIT Press.

— (2005). *Physicalism, or Something Near Enough*. Princeton: Princeton University Press.

LePore, E. and Loewer, B. (1987). Mind matters. *Journal of Philosophy*, 93, 630–42.

Lewis, D. (1973a). Causation. *Journal of Philosophy*, 70, 556–67. Reprinted in D. Lewis (ed.), *Philosophical Papers*, vol. 2. Oxford: Oxford University Press, 1986.

— (1973b). *Counterfactuals*. Cambridge: Harvard University Press.

Loewer, B. (2002). Comments on Jaegwon Kim's *Mind in a Physical World*. *Philosophy and Phenomenological Research*, 65, 655–62.

McGrath, S. (2005). Causation by omission: a dilemma. *Philosophical Studies*, 123, 125–48.

McLaughlin, B. (1989). Type epiphenomenalism, type dualism, and the causal priority of the physical. *Philosophical Perspectives*, 3, 109–36.

Salmon, W. C. (1984). *Scientific Explanation and the Causal Structure of the World*. Princeton: Princeton University Press.

— (1994). Causality without counterfactuals. *Philosophy of Science*, 61, 297–312.

Schaffer, J. (2004). Causes need not be physically connected to their effects: the case for negative causation. In C. Hitchcock (ed.), *Contemporary Debates in Philosophy of Science*. Oxford: Blackwell.

Sosa, E. (1984). Mind–body interaction and supervenient causation. *Midwest Studies in Philosophy*, 9, 271–81.

Stalnaker, R. (1968). A theory of conditionals. In N. Rescher (ed.), *Studies in Logical Theory*. Oxford: Blackwell.

Stoutland, F. (1980). Oblique causation and reasons for action. *Synthese*, 43, 351–67.

Mental Causation, or Something Near Enough

Barry Loewer

Ever since Descartes proposed the pineal gland as the locus of mind–body interaction the problem of mental causation has been at the center of philosophy of mind. Descartes and his contemporaries were worried about how events involving a non-spatial immaterial substance can causally interact with events involving an extended material substance. Subsequent advances in the physical and biological sciences made it very plausible that physics is causally and nomologically closed: that is that all motions of material bodies can be accounted for – to the extent they can be accounted for – in terms of physical events and laws. So not only is it incomprehensible how a non-material mind can move a material body but it looks like it isn't needed to do so.[1] These and other problems ultimately killed off Cartesian substance dualism. Nevertheless the Cartesian intuition of distinctness remains very much alive. The conventional view in contemporary philosophy of mind is that even though all *things* are materially constituted, mental *properties* and *events* are distinct from and in some sense irreducible to physical ones. It is not surprising then that the problem of mental causation is still with us now as the question of how mental and physical *properties* and *events* can causally interact.

It would be nice then to find a metaphysical framework that is compatible with the causal completeness of physics, explains the distinctness intuitions, and also provides a place for mental causation. Without the latter it is arguably impossible to make sense of experience, rationality, and action since they inextricably involve causal or cause-like relations. Perceptual beliefs *causally* depend on phenomenal experience, intentions *causally* depend on preferences and beliefs, reasons *cause* actions, and so on. Non-reductive physicalism (NRP) is claimed to be the metaphysical framework that fits the bill. Proponents of NRP, among whom I count myself, want to eat our cake and still have it. On the one hand, we endorse physicalism and thus claim our view to be compatible with the scientific account of the world. On the other hand, we claim it is also compatible with the pre-scientific and Cartesian intuitions that the mental is distinct from the physical and yet participates in the causal order.

During the last few decades Jaegwon Kim has been telling philosophers of mind that when it comes to the mind body problem "you can't both eat and have your cake" and that when it comes to mental causation there are "no free lunches."[2] He has developed a line of argument – the "supervenience" or "exclusion" argument – that he thinks shows that no version of NRP can properly accommodate mental causation and for this reason NRP is not acceptable. My aim here is to articulate and defend a particular version of NRP against Kim's exclusion argument and to make a proposal for how mental causation – or something near enough – can find a home within this version of NRP.

1 What is "Non-Reductive Physicalism?"

The guiding idea behind physicalism is that once the physical facts and laws of the world are fixed, so are all other facts and laws (and causal relations, and explanations, and so on). Here is a more precise formulation:

> Physicalism: Every positive truth and every truth concerning laws and causation is meta-physically necessitated by truths concerning the spatiotemporal distribution of instantiations of fundamental physical properties and relations and the fundamental physical laws.[3]

In terms of an oft-used metaphor, physicalism requires that once God created the totality of physical facts and laws he created the whole world. He didn't have to add mental (or any other) properties or bridge laws connecting them with physical properties or special-science laws connecting them with each other or extra causal relations or anything else.

Physicalism comes in two varieties; reductive physicalism (RP) and non-reductive physicalism.[4] The best way to explain NRP is to begin with RP since NRP was proposed to replace it. RP, as it is usually understood, includes the view that every *real* or as I will say "*genuine*" property (G-property) that has instances in our world (or any physically possible world) is identical to a *physical* G-property, and that every individual is composed out of fundamental physical individuals. NRP agrees with RP about individuals but claims that there are G-properties, in particular mental properties, that are not identical to any physical G-properties.

RP (like physicalism itself) is a contingent claim of empirical metaphysics. It is metaphysical since it is a very general claim about the nature of the properties that are instantiated and the individuals that exist in physically possible worlds. RP (like physicalism) is contingent and empirical since there are possible worlds whose G-properties include nonphysical ones, and empirical investigation is relevant to finding out whether or not it is true of our world.

All philosophers engaged in discussions of RP and NRP who are willing to speak of properties at all employ a "thick" notion of property on which it is possible for predicates that differ in meaning to correspond to the same property. For example, "is a puddle of H_2O" and "is a puddle of water" differ in meaning but correspond to

Barry Loewer

the same property.[5] The meanings of RP and NRP depend on what counts as a G-property and what counts as a *physical* G-property. To explain how I will employ these notions I will adopt a framework devised by David Lewis although without all of his metaphysical commitments.[6] Lewis calls the conception on which every predicate corresponds to a property the "abundant conception" of properties. Philosophers who are engaged in the discussion of RP and NRP think of G-properties in a more restrictive way. Roughly, the idea is that G-properties are those "that cut nature at its joints." At one extreme is the view that only fundamental properties and relations – what Lewis calls "the perfectly natural properties" – count as G-properties.[7] Since Lewis thinks physicalism is true his example of plausible candidates for natural properties instantiated at our world – *mass, charge, spin* – are all properties that occur in proposals for the most fundamental laws of physics.[8] Nonphysicalist philosophers might include properties involving phenomenal consciousness and intentionality – pain, acquaintance, reference, and so on – among the fundamental G-properties.

Our discussion of NRP involves a more liberal account of G-properties than Lewis's In addition to the fundamental properties any property that corresponds to a kind term of any science is a G-property. Kind terms are predicates or concepts involved in the appropriate way in laws.[9] By "law" I mean a simple true generalization or equation that is counterfactual supporting and projectible.[10] This includes fundamental laws of physics and also *ceteris paribus* laws of the special sciences.[11] I will discuss causation in the last section of the paper. For now it suffices to say that any property (except perhaps spatiotemporal relations) that figures in any dynamical law is a causal property in that it can ground a causal relation between events. So if there is some reason to think that a certain property cannot ground causal relations then that is some reason to think that it cannot figure in laws and so is not a G-property.

On this view properties such as *positive charge, being a gas, mutation rate, episodic memory*, and *being a monetary exchange* plausibly count as G-properties, while *being gruesome, being post-modern*, and *being a gas or a mutation* don't count as G-properties.[12]

Here are a bit of terminology and some abbreviations that will be useful. A *mental* property, M-property, is any property that corresponds to an intentional predicate or to a qualia predicate. A *physical* property, P-property, is any property that is picked out by a kind predicate of a natural science. By "natural science" I intend to include physics, chemistry, biology, and so on but not intentional/consciousness psychology. So every P-property is a G-property but it is left open whether M-properties are G-properties and if so are P-properties. There are two important questions for physicalists about M-properties.

1   Are M-properties G-properties?
2   Are M-properties P-properties?

RP says that if any M-property is a G-property then it is a P-property. NRP says there are M-properties that are G-properties and that are not identical to any P-property.

RP and NRP are *metaphysical* not *epistemological* theses. Even if RP or a particular property identity is true, it may be very difficult or even impossible to discover that it is true. It could turn out that even though "thinking about snow" corresponds to a neurophysiological property, the natural science expression that denotes that property is so complicated that it is virtually impossible to discover the identity. Of course if RP is false then that would provide an explanation of why we don't find, if we don't, property identities connecting mental and physical predicates.

2 Why NRP Replaced RP

In the 1950s advocates of "the identity theory of mind" suggested that neurophysiologists would soon discover neural correlates of various mental properties: for example, that PAIN is correlated with C-FIBER FIRING. Some philosophers thought that such correlations are backed by fundamental "bridge laws" connecting the two properties. But this view is incompatible with physicalism since it posits mental properties and laws *over and above* physical properties and laws. Real reduction requires the correlations to be grounded in identities as RP claims: for example that PAIN = C-FIBER FIRING. Some proponents of the "identity theory of mind" argued that the best explanation of why PAIN and C-FIBER FIRING are always found together is that they are in fact one and the same.[13] In this way they thought that RP, at least as it concerns certain mental properties, could be established. But by the early 1970s a consensus began forming that the identity theory, and more generally RP, is not correct. There were a number of reasons for this. One was, as Fodor (1974) observed, the property identities that RP claimed to exist failed to be found. Aside from this many philosophers became convinced that certain features of mentality – features that seem essential to intentionality and consciousness – establish that mental properties are not identical to neurophysiological or any other P-properties. These features are quite familiar to philosophers of mind, but a brief discussion of them will be useful as a reminder why they motivated rejecting RP.

The features are (1) multiple realizability, (2) externalism, and (3) the existence of an "explanatory gap" between mental and physical facts.

    1   Multiple realization: Certain predicates seem to apply not because their instances possess a particular physical constitution but rather in virtue of their instances satisfying a particular causal or functional specification. For example, "is a computer of simple arithmetical functions" applies to a system when it is so configured that, when it is in its ready-to-compute state and is given appropriate representation of numbers and a simple arithmetical function as input, it yields a representation of the function's value. It is striking that there are mechanisms that satisfy this general specification that are physically *heterogeneous*. It even seems possible for there to be computers in possible worlds whose physics is very different from the physics of our world. That is, it is possible for there to be computers even though they are made out of *alien* substances following *alien* laws as long as this alien physics implements the causal/nomological profile of a computer. Functionalism about the mind is the view that many psychological predicates are similarly associated with functional specifications.

Despite there being no persuasive *complete* functional analyses of any psychological predicate, the view that many psychological predicates denote functional properties became and still is the mainstream view.[14] A functional property is a property that something possesses in virtue of its satisfying a certain causal/nomological/structural specification.[15] If a functional property F is instantiated by X, and F is itself not a fundamental property,[16] then X satisfies some more fundamental property P (or X is composed of parts that satisfy more fundamental properties and are configured in a particular way) that satisfies F's causal/nomological profile. P is said to *realize* F.

If a functional property is involved in a law it is a G-property and if it is involved in a natural science law it counts as a P-property. The question is whether mental functional properties are also P-properties (i.e. appear in natural science laws) and it seems that they are not. The reason is that the various possible physical realizers of a mental property are *heterogeneous*. So if there are mental properties that are functional G-properties then RP is false. One response to this would be to broaden the conception of Ps to include configurations of G-property instantiations and arbitrary conjunctions and disjunctions of such configurations. But even then functional properties of psychology may not be identical to any physical properties. The reason is that psychological functional properties may be realized by *alien* fundamental properties that conform to alien laws.[17] It is at least prima facie plausible that there could be creatures composed not of molecules but gunk whose behaviors and dispositions to behave are caused in ways that qualify them as having minds. So if mental properties are functional properties then it is quite plausible that RP is false.

2   Externalism: Putnam's Twin Earth thought experiments, Burge's arthritis/tharthritis example, Davidson's swamp man, and related examples persuaded a substantial part of the philosophical community that intentional states fail to supervene on a subject's intrinsic physical condition. The intentional contents of one's beliefs and other attitudes are constituted also by environmental, social, and historical factors. Externalist content-constituting features seem to be very complicated and gerrymandered from the point of view of any natural science, and so it is quite implausible that any such property is a property that occurs in any natural science law.

3   Explanatory gap: Joe Levine and others have persuasively argued that there is an *explanatory gap* between the physical description of a person, no matter how complete, and descriptions of that person's conscious experience employing phenomenal concepts.[18] Even if we were to be sure that pain is perfectly correlated with C-fiber firing it seems that we would have no account of *why* C-fiber firing feels *painful* instead of being associated with different qualia or with none. The situation seems quite different with respect to other macroscopic properties. For example, there is an explanation or explanation sketch in terms of quantum mechanics of why certain configurations of microparticles constitute a pane of transparent glass. The difference is that in the latter case it is plausible that there is a functional characterization of what it is to be a pane of transparent glass, i.e. a characterization in terms of allowing the passage of light and so on. If it can be shown that a certain microconfiguration of molecules satisfies the functional specification then we have a constitutive explanation of why that microconfiguration is a transparent pain of glass. But it seems that there is no complete functional specification of phenomenal experience that can play a similar role in accounting for why a certain physical configuration is painful. The point is made vivid by the fact that we can conceive of beings that are

functionally and physically identical to us with inverted qualia or with none at all. It is tempting to conclude from this that no physical property or configurations of physical property instances is identical to or even is metaphysically sufficient for the instantiation of any qualia property.

There may also be an explanatory gap between the physical and the intentional. Donald Davidson (1980) sketched an argument that has been as influential as it is obscure to this conclusion. Davidson claims that the constitutive principles of physical attributions and the constitutive principles of intentional attribution are so different as to prevent there being any law-like connections between vocabularies from the two domains. At one point he glosses this by saying that there are "no tight connections" between the mental and the physical. The lack of such connections apparently rules out, in his view, explaining propositional attitudes (belief, intention, and so on) in terms of physical phenomena along the lines of functional explanations we discussed earlier. I don't want to get into the details of Davidson's argument here, except to say one way of understanding Davidson is as arguing that no intentional property is *either* identical to or even realized by any genuine physical property.[19]

These features persuaded many philosophers of mind that there are M-properties that are not identical to P-properties and perhaps not even to any construct out of configurations of P-properties. One response to this "discovery" is to reject physicalism. This is the line taken by those who think that the explanatory-gap considerations rule out there being physical realizations of mental properties.[20] I will have a few words to say about how a physicalist might respond to explanatory gaps later. Another response is elimitivism. Elimitivism can take the relatively mild form of denying that M-properties are G-properties, or the much tougher view that mental properties are not instantiated or even that mental predicates don't denote properties at all.[21] A third response, the one that interests me here, is NRP.

Here is the version of NRP that I think is most plausible:

> NRP: Some M-properties are functional G-properties and are not identical to any P-property. Each (physically possible) instantiation of a mental property is metaphysically necessitated by (i.e. realized by) configurations of instances of P-properties.[22]

NRP is both non-reductive and physicalist. It is non-reductive since according to it there are G-properties – specifically mental properties – that are not identical to P-properties. It is physicalist since it says that every instance of any G-property is realized by configurations of instances of genuine physical properties and so is compatible with physicalism.

NRP is a form of *functionalism* since it says that among the G-properties are mental properties that are individuated in terms of causal/nomological relations. But it does not say that mental predicates can be *functionalized*. Kim says that a predicate or concept is "functionalizable" when it can be associated with a functional analysis. It may be that some mental predicates correspond to functional properties even thought they don't have a functional analysis. This point is essential to whether NRP can accommodate the explanatory gaps that we noted earlier. We can understand how NRP might accommodate the multiple realizability and externalist considerations since we can see how there may be configurations of P-property instantiations that realize functionalist and externalist specifications. But, as we saw, the most natural way of accommodating the explanatory-gap considerations is to say that mental properties are not metaphysically necessitated by or realized by physical properties or constructs out of physical properties. Since physicalism requires that every property instantiation is metaphysically necessitated by physical facts and laws, this account of the explanatory gap is incompatible with physicalism and so incompatible with NRP.[23] A defender of NRP (and any other version of physicalism) must argue either that there are no genuine explanatory gaps or that they result from the fact that phenomenal (and perhaps intentional) predicates and concepts while not functionalizable still correspond to functional or physical properties.[24]

NRP is committed to the existence of mental laws. In particular, it is committed to laws connecting intentional and conscious phenomena (characterized as such) with each other, with external phenomena, and with behavior. I won't attempt to make the case of there being such laws here since that case is amply made elsewhere (Fodor, 1974, 1992, 1998). However, the existence of such laws looks as though it may present a problem for NRP. Fodor points out the problem in the course of defending his view of the relation between the special sciences and physics from Jaegwon Kim's objections:

> So then, *why is there anything except physics?* That, I think, is what is *really* bugging Kim. Well, I admit that I don't know why. I don't even know how to *think about* why. I expect to figure out why there is anything except physics the day before I figure out why there is anything at all, another (and presumably related) metaphysical conundrum that I find perplexing. (Fodor, 1998, p. 161)

I am not sure that this is what is "*really* bugging Kim" but I do think that Fodor is asking an excellent question. If the laws of physics are causally complete and closed, how is there room for additional laws? How can there be laws other than the laws of physics? For a physicalist the answer must be that the laws of physics *together* with additional physical facts entail what special-science laws there are. The story of what additional facts are needed and why it is plausible that they do entail special science laws that are not reducible to laws of physics (in the sense of reduction at issue in the dispute between RP and NRP) is a complicated issue that I address elsewhere (Loewer, forthcoming-a). But even without an answer to Fodor's question one can see that there is no contradiction between Physicalism and the existence of laws involving nonphysical mental properties. We can see this because we know that there are laws of, e.g., meteorology that are *ceteris paribus laws*, and that the dynamical laws of physics are exceptionless and so cannot on their own entail *ceteris paribus laws*, and that meteorology doesn't conflict with physicalism.

Before looking at Kim's exclusion argument I want to discuss and then dismiss another line of thought (suggested by some of Kim's discussion) that threatens to show that NRP is unstable and make my criticisms of the exclusion argument moot. Suppose that M is a mental property and occurs in some law, say M → R (the law may be a *ceteris paribus* law) and so is a G-property. Suppose also that physicalism is true. Won't there be some property physical property Q constructed out of physical genuine properties – i.e. a disjunction of physical properties or configurations of physical properties – that is coextensive with M in all physically possible worlds? But then won't it be the case that $Q \rightarrow R$ is also a law? If so it follows that Q is a G-property since it figures in a law. If this is correct then NRP comes very close to collapsing into RP since either $M = Q$ or $M^* = Q$ where M^* is the property M restricted to the class of physically possible worlds. In the first case RP holds; in the second case it is close enough to make the difference between RP and NRP look awfully trivial.

There are two responses to this argument. One is to say that if any construct out of physical properties that is coextensive (or coextensive in every physically possible world) with a G-property counts as a P-property then indeed NRP and RP come to much the same. This maneuver for RP looks a lot like "declaring victory and withdrawing" since it amounts to R is a G-property in virtue of satisfying a *psychological* law. But if one wants to keep the argument going (as I think was intended by the sides of this debate) then one should resist this argument by denying that $Q \rightarrow R$ is a law. If laws are thought of as generalizations or equations (i.e. as *proposition*-like) then this is a natural response. The considerations involving functionalism and externalism show that Q will have an enormously complex characterization in terms of physics and plausibly has no characterization in terms of any of the special sciences. As Fodor (1998) indicates, discussing a point similar to this one, "is a law" is an intensional context. This is obvious on any account of laws on which laws are projectible since projectibility is an epistemic notion.[25] I conclude that this line of thought doesn't work to undermine NRP. Let's see if the exclusion argument is more successful.

2.1 The supervenience/exclusion argument

Kim's supervenience/exclusion argument has received a lot of discussion so I will be going over some well- (in some cases *very* well) trodden ground. Here is how Kim recently formulated the exclusion argument (2005, p. 39).

Let M and M^* be mental properties and m and m^* be the events of M's instantiation at some location and time t and the event of M^*'s instantiation at some place and time t^*, and suppose that

1   m causes m^*.[26]

In saying that m causes m^*, Kim is supposing that m is causally sufficient in the circumstances for m^*. Since physicalism holds there will be some physical property P^* whose instantiation p^* at time t^* is such that

2   m^* has p^* as its supervenience base.[27]

Kim argues that (1) and (2) support

3   m caused m^* by causing p^*.

Since physicalism holds

4   m also has a physical supervenience base p.

Kim then appeals to a principle he calls "Closure":

Closure: If a physical event has a cause that occurs at t, it has a (sufficient)[28] physical cause that occurs at t.

It follows that

5   m causes p* and p causes p*.

Since we are assuming NRP, i.e. non-identity:

6   M ≠ P and so m ≠ p.

At this point in the argument Kim appeals to a principle that he calls "Exclusion":

Exclusion: No single event can have more than one sufficient cause occurring at any given time – unless it is a case of causal overdetermination.

But according to Kim this isn't a case of causal overdetermination. By causal over-determination Kim means the kind of case in which there are two shooters, each of which kills the victim. That seems right.

7   p* is not causally overdetermined by m and p.

It follows that either p or m does not cause p*. By closure it must be that

8   The putative mental cause m is excluded by the physical cause p. That is, p not m, is a cause of p.

As Kim observes, supervenience isn't needed for the argument. The conflict is among M ≠ P, Closure, and Exclusion. It appears then that the argument works equally well against NRP and against non-physicalist views.[29]

3 The Exclusion Argument Defanged

At this point it may be useful to remind ourselves what is at stake in the exclusion argument. Various considerations (functionalism, externalism, explanatory gap) argue for M ≠ P. There are scientifically compelling reasons to accept physicalism. Epiphe-nomenalism is uncomfortably near to elimitivism and that hardly seems an option. And given the connection between causation and laws the argument seems to rule out mental laws. So Kim's argument is a paradox. Each of M ≠ P, Closure, and Exclusion is plausible, but together they are inconsistent. We proponents of NRP accept M ≠ P and Closure, so we have to reject Exclusion.

Kim's exclusion principle says that "no single event can have more than one sufficient cause occurring at any given time – unless it is a case of causal overdetermination." By "causal overdetermination" I think Kim has in mind the type of situation in which two assassins fire simultaneously at the victim causing his death. In this kind of situation the two events (the two firings) are *metaphysically* independent and each involves its own causal process that culminates in the death of the victim. Causal overdetermination like this may be rare but it is not metaphysically problematic. Kim observes that the putative situation in which a nonphysical genuine property instantiation $M(y,t)$ and its physical realizer $P(y,t)$ are said both to cause $Q(z,t')$ is not a case of ordinary causal overdetermination. He is certainly correct about this since $P(y,t)$ and $M(y,t)$ are not metaphysically independent. Let's call the kind of overdetermination involved in mental/physical causation M-overdetermination and understand Kim as ruling it out by the exclusion principle. It follows that the two putative causes of $Q(z,t')$ compete, and so one is not really a cause of $Q(z,t')$. Since NRP assumes that the physical realm is causally closed, $P(y,t)$ wins the competition and $M(y,t)$ is not a cause of $Q(z,t')$ or anything else. The question we need to address is whether there is an option of accepting that M-overdetermination occurs and is as pervasive as NRP says. But before that we need to make an adjustment to Exclusion that will be important for our criticism of Kim's argument.

If $M(y,t)$ and $P(y,t)$ are ordinary macro events then, contrary to Kim's supposition, they are certainly *not causally sufficient* for $Q(z,t')$. It is a commonplace among philosophers of science, but perhaps not as recognized as it should be outside of philosophy of science, that for any small region R of space at time t nothing much short of the state of the universe in a sphere with center R and whose radius is one light second (i.e. 186,000 miles) at $t - 1$ second is causally sufficient for determining what will occur (or the chances at $t - 1$ of what will occur) in R.[30] Because of this I suggest that we interpret Kim's exclusion principle not as involving causes that are literally sufficient for their effects but as follows:

> Exclusion*: There can't be two distinct causes of $Q(z,t')$ that occupy the same space–time region.

Exclusion* would be trivial if there can't be distinct events that occupy the same region at all. But if we understand events (as Kim does) as having properties as constituents then there seems to be no reason why two events with different constitutive properties can't occupy the same regions.[31] So the question is why can't distinct events – a mental event and its realizer – that occupy the same space–time region both be causes of another event?

Does Kim have an argument for Exclusion or Exclusion*? In *Mind in a Physical World* he argued that over-M-determination would be a violation of Closure (Kim, 1998). Of course, if this could be shown then NRP would be shown to be incoherent since it entails Closure. But it is not difficult to see that without some further assumptions Closure and overdetermination are consistent with each other and also consistent

Barry Loewer

with physicalism.[32] Kim's current view is that causal exclusion "is virtually an analytic truth without much content" (2005, p. 51). But it is sufficiently contentful to play an essential role in the argument that NRP – the proper formulation of non-reductive physicalism – is incoherent. And philosophers who deny it, I myself among them, don't think that we are denying an analytic truth. So what is going on?

Ned Hall (2004) has recently argued that causation comes in two varieties, "production" and "dependence." Production is the relation that supposedly obtains when one billiard ball hits another and thus *produces* motion in the second. Dependence is the relation that holds between two events when features of the second (including whether or not it occurs) counterfactually depends on features of the first (including whether or not it occurs). Hall thinks that the two kinds often go together but are different. It is possible to have dependence without production. For example, the kitchen fire may depend on my forgetting to turn off the heat under a pot, but my forgetting does not produce the fire. And Billy's throw may produce the broken window even though dependence is absent since Billy's rock arrived a moment before Sally's, which would have broken the window.

My diagnosis of what is going on in discussions of the exclusion argument is this: if causation is understood as *production* then it does seem that causal exclusion is, as Kim says, "virtually analytic." If P(y,t) produces Q(z,t') how can a *distinct* event M(y,t) also produce Q(z,t')? As Kim likes to put it, there is "no work for a distinct mental event to do." Kim seems to think of causal production as an intrinsic relation between relatively local events. So, for example, a brain event *produces* a bodily motion by transferring some kind of causal energy, or, as Hartry Field (2003) says, "causal liquid," from the cause to the effect.[33] It seems obvious that if the brain event produces the bodily motion, a distinct mental event has nothing more to do.

The trouble is that there is no relation of causal production in nature that works quite like this. Bertrand Russell noted almost 100 years ago that the notion of *causation* makes no appearance in the fundamental dynamical laws of physics.[34] He observed that these laws are differential equations that specify the rate of change of certain quantities (e.g., velocity, field-intensity wave function amplitude, and so on). Russell concluded, correctly in my view, that *causation* (whether of the productive or the dependence kind) is not among the fundamental furniture of the universe. Causal claims must supervene on more basic facts. This is true of both causation as production and causation as dependence. For a physicalist the basic facts are the fundamental laws of physics and the totality of fundamental physical property instantiations.

If we understand "production" literally as the producer being sufficient for its product, then for an event E occurring at time t only a vast part of the physical situation at time t − 1 can be said to "produce" E. A consequence is that relatively local macroscopic events that occur a second apart are not literally related by production. If production is understood less literally then we might be able to characterize a relation of production that relates relatively local macroscopic events, but this relation doesn't support the denial of overdetermination required by the exclusion argument.

Suppose we consider an event, say the acceleration of a billiard ball B located at point R at time t. Suppose we ask what event or events occurring at a second prior to t produced this change in motion? If we assume classical physics but with the addition that no causal influence propagate faster than the speed of light then it is a feature of the fundamental laws that we will need to specify the state of the universe on the surface of a sphere with a radius of 186,000 miles centered on R to specify what will happen at R. So if we are asking what at $t-1$ second literally produces the motion of the ball then nothing short (or much short) of the complete microphysical state of the universe on the surface of this sphere will do.

Of course, there is a less demanding way of talking about production. If there is a ball C moving on a straight path toward B at $t-1$ that then strikes B at t, it is natural to say that C's motion produced B's acceleration. This works given the assumptions that there are no other balls headed toward R and that the effects of the motions of air molecules and fields around B cancel out. We are treating the system of two balls as an isolated system as far as application of the fundamental laws are concerned. Our world does contain many almost isolated systems that for all practical purposes we can treat as isolated. Underlying this are the fact that gravitational fields are generally fairly uniform and the gravitational effects of distant bodies very weak, that electromagnetic forces generally cancel, and that statistical mechanical probabilities make it overwhelmingly likely that the forces due to motions of matter in the environment of a system cancel out.[35] But of course the two balls do not really constitute an isolated system, and a great deal more than the motion of ball B goes into producing the motion of ball C. Literally it is the totality of events in the 186,000 mile region around R that is responsible for B's acceleration. If we want to specify what it is at $t-1$ that literally *produces* an event E at t in the sense that "there is no more work to do," then we need to specify nothing less than the situation on the whole slice off the back light cone of E.

I don't know of any good analysis of this less demanding notion of production, which we can call "local production" (Hall, 2004). But Kim may think that the notion is clear enough for us it to be undeniable that distinct events that occupy the same spatiotemporal regions cannot both be "local productive" causes of some other events. One remark to make about this is that it is not clear that an intentional event and its core realizer do occupy the same region since the mental event supervenes on other features of the environment. But even if the two events occupy the same regions I see no temptation to think that one of these excludes the other. Once we realize that local production is not a basic relation but supervenes on the total state that literally produces subsequent states, we can think of the mental and the physical event as picking out features of that state that are involved in, though not completely, the production of the effect. On this way of thinking it may be that an event in my brain locally produces my hand waving and that my decision to wave my hand (which is realized by the brain event) *also* locally produces my hand waving. It is not at all like two pushes where one would do. The complete state does whatever pushing is involved in causation. Macro-physical and mental events and relations of local production supervene on the evolution of the complete microstate.

The upshot of this discussion is that if production is understood literally then perhaps Exclusion holds, but neither brain events nor mental events are producers of bodily movements. But if production is understood as local production it is compatible with an event having multiple distinct producers. The intuitive force of Kim's argument derives from the fact that we tend to think, mistakenly, that causation is a

Barry Loewer

fundamental relation of production that connects relatively local events. Rejecting the existence of such a relation may do damage to our intuitive notion of causation but I don't see that it undermines the central aspects of our notion of mental causation that are involved in mentality since I think that these aspects can be underwritten by causation as dependence, to which we now turn.

The dependence conception of causation: Counterfactuals are notoriously vague and context dependent. The way they should be understood for the purposes of characterizing causation as dependence is along the lines of David Lewis's famous account. On that account A > B is true if either there are worlds at which A&B are true that are more similar to the actual world than any world at which A & − B is true. Lewis specifies a particular account of world similarity that he thinks has the consequence that in evaluating A > B one looks at worlds that are identical to the actual world from the world's initial condition and then diverges from the actual world (perhaps this requires a violation of actual laws in a small region for a short time) and then evolves in accord with the laws of the actual world so that A is true. If all these worlds are all worlds at which B is true then A > B is true. For example, "if at noon Terry had wanted a beer he would have opened the refrigerator" is true if the worlds that are identical to the actual world, up until a moment prior to noon when a small miracle occurs so that Terry is in a brain state that realizes wanting a beer, are also worlds where he opens the refrigerator.[36]

Lewis says that E depends on C iff C and E are non-overlapping events, and if C had not occurred then E would not have occurred. His original account of causation was that C causes E iff C and E occur and E depends on C or there is a chain of events connected by dependence from C to E. This account is vulnerable to cases of preemption in which C causes E but E doesn't depend on C because there is another event C* waiting in the wings to cause E if C didn't occur. His most recent account of causation as dependence handles some of these preemption worries. Lewis says that an event E *influences* an event C if E and C don't overlap and if there are suitable variations in C that are counterfactually correlated with variations in E. C causes E iff C and E occur and there is a chain of events connected by influence from C to E. For example, the height of mercury in a thermometer depends on the ambient temperature since the counterfactuals "if the temperature had been (or were to be) x the height of the thermometer would have been (would be) y" are true for a range of x and y.

Given this account of counterfactuals, dependence, and influence it is very plausible that typically a person's bodily movements (and more distal events) depend on her mental states. My proposal is that this much mental causation is near enough to our folk conception of mental causation to underwrite the role of causation in folk psychology, rational deliberation, action theory, and so on. Further, properties involved in special-science laws are causal in the dependence sense, not in the production sense. Finally, causation as dependence is impervious to Kim's exclusion argument.

The first thing to note is that there is no problem of overdetermination if causation is understood as dependence. On Lewis's account of counterfactuals a particular event (or the value of a range of possible events) can depend on many co-occurring events. The motions of one's body, for example, the motions of a person's arms and hands when reaching into the refrigerator, depend counterfactually both on her mental states (which snacks she wants) and on her brain (and other bodily) states and on a myriad of other states and events. Also, the kind of "overdetermination" involved in B depending on both M and P is like neither the two assassins kind nor the production kind. In particular there is no temptation to say that if B depends on P it can't also depend on M since "there is no work for M to do." So the question we need to examine is whether causation as dependence is causation enough to ground mental causation as we need it in making sense of reasoning, action, and so on.

Kim (1998, p. 43) expresses his worries about counterfactual accounts in this passage:

> To summarize our discussion of the counterfactual approach then, what the counterfactual theorists need to do is to give an *account* of just what makes those mind–body counterfactuals we want for mental causation true and show that on that account those counterfactuals we don't want, for example epiphenomenalist counterfactuals, turn out to be false. Merely to point to the apparent truth, and acceptability of certain mind–body counterfactuals as a vindication of mind body causation is to misconstrue the philosophical task at hand . . . what we want – at least what some of us are looking for – is a philosophical account of *how* it (mental causation and the corresponding counterfactuals) can be real in light of other principles and truths that seem to be forced upon us.

I have already pointed at an answer to Kim's question of "what makes those mind–body counterfactuals we want for mental causation true." They are made true by the fundamental laws and facts of physics.[37] "If I were to decide to get a beer I would walk over to the refrigerator" (and similarly for the battery of other counterfactuals that ground causation as dependence) is true when the worlds most similar to the actual world in which I decide to get a beer are worlds in which I walk over to the refrigerator. Whether that is so depends on the actual laws of physics (since what they are determines what counts as a "small violation") and on the actual physical facts. So it is clear that this account of counterfactuals is compatible with physicalism. Also, we have seen that there is no problem about overdetermination so the account is compatible with M ≠ P. So the issue remains whether the account of counterfactuals really underwrites "those counterfactuals we want" and not "those we don't want." Fully establishing these claims is not something that I can do since it would involve establishing the truth values of many counterfactuals and that can literally be done only by knowing the physical realizers of mental states and the fundamental laws. But I think I can go some distance toward making the claim plausible and replying to Kim's arguments that causation as dependence cannot do the work we want mental causation to do.

Kim suggests that there may be dependence where there is no mind–body causation. If so then dependence is too weak to ground genuine mind–body causation. He mentions three kinds of situations, common causes, omissions, and epiphenomenalism, where dependence holds but there is no causation.

C is a common cause of A and B when C causes both A and B but there is no causal relation between A and B. For example, a rock thrown into the center of a pool (C) causes a wave to hit at point *a* and at point *b* at time t. The worry is that the counterfactual "if A had not occurred then B would not have occurred" may appear to be true. In fact I think that in ordinary language this counterfactual is plausibly true in the situation I described. But recall that the characterization of causation as dependence involves a very particular way of evaluating counterfactuals. On that way this counterfactual is false since the world in which a small violation of law occurs just before t that leads to A not occurring but leaves all else the same including B is a more similar world to the actual world than the world that also leads to the wave not hitting *b* at t.

An interesting example of a possible common-cause situation concerns the relationship between conscious decisions to act. There is evidence that at least in some cases the decision and the act are related as the common effects of a brain event that is the common cause of both (Daniel and Wegner, 2002). Whether or not this is so, it is clear that causation as dependence has no trouble distinguishing between the decision being the cause of the act or the two being common causes of an unconscious brain event.

Kim raises another worry about dependence that is related to the common cause objection. He argues that causal dependence cannot distinguish epiphenomenalism from mental causation. Kim pictures the situation involving mental causation as shown in Figure 14.1.

An epiphenomenalist like T. H. Huxley holds that P1 and P2 are events that are sufficient – in senses to be specified – respectively for the events M1 and M2, and that there is a genuine causal relation between P1 and P2 but not between M1 and P2 (or M2). Kim claims that this is completely compatible with P2 counterfactually depending on both P1 and M1. The response to this claim depends on the strength of the relation between the Ps and the Ms depicted by the *vertical* lines. Epiphenomenalists generally think of this relation as *weaker* than metaphysical necessitation. Perhaps it is nomological. Kim likes to illustrate epiphenomenalism with the example of the positions of a shadow cast by a moving ball that *seem* to be causally connected. The positions of the shadow are nomologically connected to the positions of the ball that casts the shadow but are not causally related to each other. Kim seems to think that the counterfactual account fails to count this as epiphenomenalism since −M1 > −P2 will be true. But I think he is wrong about this if we evaluate counterfactuals along Lewisian lines. −M1 > −P2 fails since the most similar world in which −M1 holds is one in which the vertical law connecting P1 to M1 is broken while the horizontal law connecting P1 to P2 continues to hold.[38] On the other hand, −P1 > −P2 may be true. In contrast to this NRP holds that the connection between P1 and M1 is one of metaphysical not merely nomological necessitation. In the most similar worlds at which −M1 it is also −P1 since there is no question of "breaking" the metaphysical connection. So in this situation −M1 > −P2 may well be true. But it would

Figure 14.1 Kim's favorite diagram.

be question-begging to say that M1 isn't *really* a cause of P2 in this case, say because it doesn't produce or transfer causal liquid to P2.

The last problem is that Kim points out that dependence can connect omissions with events. Kim says:

> Friends of the counterfactual approach often tout its ability to handle omissions and absences as causes and the productive/generative approach's inability to account for them. We are inclined to take the truth of a counterfactual such as
>
>> If Mary had watered my plants, the plants would not have died
>
> as showing that Mary's not watering, an omission, caused the plants' death and take that as a basis for blaming Mary for killing the plants. But obviously there was no flow of energy from Mary to the plants during my absence (that exactly was the problem!); nor was there any other physical connection, or any spatiotemporally contiguous chain of causally connected events.

Kim's objection seems to be that since dependence can connect an omission (Mary's not watering the plants) with an event (the plant's dying) even though there is no transfer of energy from Mary to the plants, dependence cannot really be what we want by mental causation. He says of it "This is not causation worth having." But, in the first place unless Mary is outside of the back light cone of the plant's death there will almost certainly be some energy transferred from her to the plants, just not in the right way to save the plants. In any case, omissions are not events. It doesn't follow from the fact that there is dependence on omissions that dependence on commissions, and specifically the counterfactual sensitivity of the positions of one's body (and fingers, and so on) to one's volitions and the counterfactual sensitivity of one's volitions on one's intentions, beliefs (and so on), is "not causation worth having." Indeed, these relations of dependence and influence are absolutely essential to mentality and action. If the transfer of energy is involved in any case of genuine mental causation it is also likely involved in any case of mental causation as influence. But the *mere* transfer of energy certainly isn't what we want for mental causation. Exactly how (certainly not how much) energy is transferred is essential to our minds controlling our bodies (and other kinds of mental causation).

Suppose in fact that the batteries of counterfactuals that are associated with volitional control of bodily movement, with stimuli and perceptual belief, with rational thinking, and so on obtain but without the transfer of energy and without productive causation connecting individual events.[39] Perhaps this would be the situation, if, as Jonathan Edwards seemed to think, one state of the universe doesn't *produce* the next via law but rather the states are produced one after another by God in the manner of a movie projector producing the moving image on a screen. I am not sure that this fantasy is coherent but if it is then I think we would say that in this world there is dependence but no production (the production comes from outside the world). If we were to come to believe this is the way things are, should we really miss causation as production? Would we stop taking aspirin for headaches, cease taking seriously the readings on thermometers, and so on? Would we think that causation as dependence (without production) is not worth having?

I want to conclude with a few sketchy and perhaps surprising remarks about the connection between Lewisian accounts of counterfactuals and mental causation. We have appealed to Lewis's account of causation as dependence to ground mental causation. But there is a way in which mental causation, or more precisely, our neural/cognitive structure, grounds Lewis's account of counterfactuals.

On Lewis's account the candidates for most similar worlds in which the counterfactual antecedent A(t) is true are those whose pasts match the actual past until a short (or as short as can be) time prior to t and then diverges by a small local violation of law (or, as Jonathan Bennett says, "diverges in a way that macroscopically appears unextraordinary") and then evolves in accordance with the actual laws. But why, we may ask, are we interested in *this* notion of similarity among the infinity of possible similarity relations that can be used to characterize conditionals?[40] One might think that the answer is that this relation is or at any rate is close to tracking the causal relation and we are interested in that relation because it is a fundamental relation between events. But I think this has things backwards. My view is that we are interested in the causal relation not because it is a fundamental relation – we saw that there is no fundamental causal relation to be found in physics that connects local events in the way causation is alleged to – but rather because of its connection to our ability to influence the likelihoods of events depending on the decisions we make. Here is what I have in mind. We truly assume that the alternative decisions that we might make in the next few moments correspond to very small local physical differences in our brains. That is, different decisions that one might make are realized in differential brain phenomena that can result via the laws from tiny microscopic immediately prior physical differences. If the laws are deterministic then these small differences from actuality involve small localized violations of law.

Naturally we are interested in what will happen on the alternative hypotheses of each decision. Of course, that depends not only on the decision but also on many other matters in the environment. For example, suppose RR is deciding whether to press the button marked "Nurse" or the button marked "Launch." Assuming that RR's body, hand, fingers, and so on are appropriately connected to his brain, then what will happen depends on the buttons being hooked up to various further devices. The interesting point for us is that what will happen (or, if we allow probabilities over microhistories, the probabilities of what will happen) is given by adding one or the other decision – or rather the physical phenomena that realize them – to the rest of the state at t. So the reason we are interested in evaluating counterfactuals along Lewisian lines (or rather along the lines that he thought his proposal yields) is that conditionals so evaluated contain information that is enormously important to our getting what we want. If this is on the right track then it is tempting to think that the notion of causation as dependence has its origin and is most at home in mental causation.

My conclusion then is that distinctness (M ≠ P) and physicalism are compatible with mental causation, or something near enough.

Notes

1 Papineau (2001) contains an excellent discussion of how the idea that physics is causally/ nomologically closed (or causally complete) became so persuasive and the problems this poses for various forms of dualism. See also Kim (2005) for the problem of making sense of causal interactions between mental and material substances. A quite different line of criticism of dualism was pursued by philosophical behaviorists (e.g., Ryle, 1949) who emphasized what they took to be epistemological and semantic problems with dualism. While these arguments were quite influential 50 years ago they have now been mostly rejected along with the behaviorism they were thought to support.

2 Kim at first seemed to express sympathy with some version of NRP and the hope that the concept of supervenience could provide the key to formulating it (Kim, 1993) but he seems to have soon come to the conclusion that NRP cannot properly handle mental causation (Kim, 1993) and has been arguing against it for the past quarter-century.

3 Frank Jackson (1998) and David Chalmers (1996) characterize physicalism as the claim that every truth is necessitated by the totality of truths in the complete language of ideal fundamental physics and the laws of fundamental physics, and a statement to the effect that this is the totality of fundamental truths and laws. (The latter can be avoided by restricting the characterization to positive truths). They hold additionally that the entail- ments required by physicalism are a priori. I do not assume that here. David Lewis (1983) earlier provided a similar characterization of physicalism. There are issues concerning how to define "fundamental physical property or ideal physics" and whether this account is sufficient for physicalism (it is surely necessary). I discuss these issues in Loewer (2001).

4 Some philosophers call themselves (or are called by others) "physicalists" because they hold that all things are materially constituted even though they reject physicalism. Perhaps Davidson (1980) is an example.

5 Needless to say, except in a footnote, that the view that predicates with non-analytically connected meanings may correspond to the same property depends on a Fregean-like notion of meaning.

6 Lewis thinks that any class of possible individuals is a property (the "abundant" con- ception) and that certain of these classes are, or correspond to, perfectly natural pro- perties (the "sparse" conception) and that naturalness comes in degrees. He also holds that the degree of naturalness of a property is a matter of metaphysical necessity, that the perfectly natural properties instantiated at our world are all intrinsic to space-time points (or small regions) except for space-time relations, and that all truths – including the laws – supervene on the distribution of perfectly natural properties. The latter two comprise his doctrine of Humean supervenience. I make none of these assumptions in this paper.

7 Perhaps there are worlds with no absolutely fundamental properties but I assume with Lewis that the actual world is not like that.

8 Lewis holds both that physics makes the best estimates of the natural properties and that what properties are natural is a matter of necessity. There is a tension between these commitments.

9 Armstrong (1978) holds this view concerning universals. Of course exactly what this view comes to depends on what laws there are and what it is to enter into a law or causal relation in "an appropriate way." Fodor says that *natural kinds* (i.e. genuine properties) are properties that appear in laws, and then explains laws by saying that laws are gener- alizations connecting *natural kinds*. Well, explanation has to end somewhere.

10 These are the usual criteria for lawhood. Their exact characterization is a bit tricky. Some- thing along the following lines is what I have in mind. If $F \rightarrow G$ is a law and Fa is logically

Barry Loewer

compatible with its being a law then Fa > Gi (Gi is an appropriate instance of the law) is true, and a positive instance of F → G provides confirmation for further positive instances.

11   The main kinds of metaphysical views about laws are Humean and non-Humean. On Lewis's Humean account laws are generalizations entailed by the true theory of the world that best combines simplicity and informativeness (Lewis, 1986; Loewer, 1996). Non-Humeans (e.g., Armstrong, 1983) think of laws not as generalizations but as items (for Armstrong they are relations between properties and for Maudlin they are *sui generis*) that "back" or entail generalizations or equations. Where I speak of laws they would likely speak of "law-backed generalizations and equations." Although I favor Humean views, nothing in this paper depends on adopting Humeanism about either laws or causation.

12   Of course the instances of any "gruesome" property fall under laws and can be causes. The claim is that the gruesome property does not itself occur in a law or ground a causal relation.

13   Kim (2005, ch. 5) argues that identities don't explain correlations. For an effective reply see McLaughlin (2004).

14   There are a number of versions of functionalism. According to analytic functionalism there is an analytic connection between a psychological predicate and a functional specification. Some analytic functionalists think that the reference of the predicate is the functional property associated with the specification, but others think that there are no functional properties as such, but the predicate applies if there is a genuine property that satisfies the specification. According to psycho-functionalism there need be no analytic connection between psychological predicates and functional properties, but psychological predicates (or certain of them) refer to functional properties.

15   A different view is that a functional property is a "second-order property" – the property of having a first-order property that satisfies a certain functional profile.

16   Some philosophers, e.g., Shoemaker (1980), think that fundamental properties are themselves individuated in terms of their nomological/causal relations. Others, e.g., Lewis (1983), think that fundamental properties are *categorical* and it is an entirely contingent matter what laws/causal relations they are involved in. I don't take a stand on this very interesting issue in this paper.

17   It is not implausible that there are worlds whose ultimate constituents are Newtonian particles conforming to Newtonian-like laws, worlds whose ultimate constituents are gunky fluids obeying classical fluid mechanics, worlds whose ontology and laws are those of Bohmian quantum mechanics, all of which contain configurations that realize the nomological/causal specifications associated with at least some mental properties.

18   The phrase "explanatory gap" is due to Joe Levine (2001), but the point that there is a problem with understanding how physical phenomena can constitute consciousness is as old as the philosophy of mind.

19   The claim that there are not sufficient conditions in physical vocabulary for intentional predicates has also been taken to be supported by Quine's indeterminacy argument, Kripkenstein considerations, and the failure to come up with such physical conditions.

20   In particular this is the view of Chalmers (1996). It seems that Kim also takes this view (2005, ch. 6).

21   The mild form allows that mental predicates correspond to abundant properties. Kim's view is that a token of an intentional predicate that refers in a particular instance refers to whatever physical property realizes it in that instance.

22   Fodor (1974) and Putnam (1975) are among the prominent proponents of NRP. An excellent recent exposition and defense of a version of NRP is in Melnyk (2003).

23 Chalmers (1996) argues that the existence of an irremediable explanatory gap between physical facts and facts about phenomenal consciousness entails that physicalism is false.

24 The most promising approach for a physicalist is to attempt to explain explanatory gaps in terms of the special nature of first person consciousness concepts. See Loar (1990), Papineau (2002), and Balog (forthcoming).

25 If confirmation is understood in Bayesian terms, then this point is obvious. A subjective probability distribution on which $M->R$ is confirmable but $Q->R$ is not is perfectly coherent and given the complexity of R is quite reasonable.

26 Kim talks of properties being in causal relations and also property instances being in causal relations. He identifies events with property instances so the latter involves event causation.

27 That is, there is some physical fact that is metaphysically sufficient for M*. We can think of P* as the property of this fact obtaining at some region of space–time. Although Kim doesn't emphasize the point, P* may be enormously complicated and may involve events in a temporal region. It may not be a *genuine* physical property.

28 Kim (2005, p. 43) doesn't say "sufficient cause," but that is what he must mean since otherwise Closure doesn't engage Exclusion.

29 Actually, as I will argue in the next section, the argument doesn't work against NRP but has some bite against nonphysicalist emergentism.

30 Or if the fundamental laws are deterministic as determining the chance at t of $Q(z,t')$. This point is made by Latham, Field, Loewer, and Elga among others. It often appears that philosophers of mind are not aware that this is so. For example, Davidson and Fodor both seem to think that the strict causal laws of physics connect relatively local events at distinct times. More exactly, for any event E at t' there will be a physical proposition K that holds at time t that is a minimal sufficient condition for the occurrence of E (given the physical laws) which is typically a partial description of the complete state at t (or state on a hyper-surface intersecting t), but this proposition will involve values of physical parameters throughout the hyper-surface. This point is made by Latham, Field, Loewer, and Elga among others.

31 David Lewis's account of events as inter-world space–time regions also allows for different events to occupy the same actual space–time region.

32 Kim (2005, p. 49) grants that criticisms by Crisp and Warfield (2001) effectively undermine the claim that Closure is incompatible with M/P overdetermination.

33 Field of course is making fun of the production view of causation.

34 "All philosophers, of every school, imagine that *causation* is one of the fundamental axioms or postulates of science, yet, oddly enough, in advanced sciences such as gravitational astronomy, the word 'cause' never appears. Dr. James Ward . . . makes this a ground of complaint against physics . . . To me, it seems that . . . the reason why physics has ceased to look for causes is that, in fact, there are no such things. . . . The law of causality, I believe, like much that passes muster among philosophers, is a relic of a bygone age, surviving, like the monarchy, only because it is erroneously supposed to do no harm." Russell (1913, p. 1) had in mind classical mechanics and electromagnetic theory. His point applies (perhaps even more so) as well to quantum mechanics and relativity (special and general) and is almost sure to apply as well to whatever theory ultimately unifies the two.

35 See Elga (forthcoming) and Loewer (forthcoming-b) for discussions of why we can treat many systems in our world as isolated and why there are lawful regularities involving relative local macroscopic properties.

36 Unfortunately, Lewis's account of world similarity doesn't have the consequence he thinks it has. The heart of the problem is that his account of similarity involves laws and other

considerations that are temporally symmetrical, while the similarity he thinks he gets out of these considerations is temporally asymmetrical, as it must be if it is going to get the truth values connected with causation as dependence correct since these counterfactuals are temporally asymmetrical. See Elga (2001). Jonathan Bennett (2003) characterizes truth conditions of counterfactuals by simply counting past perfect match and not future match as making for similarity. It is possible to fix this all up by adding a bit to Lewis's account so that one gets more or less the similarity relation Lewis was aiming at, but it would take us too far afield to do it here. See Loewer (forthcoming-b) for the fix-up.

37   Kim (CAUSATION AND MENTAL CAUSATION) suggests that the truth-makers of counterfactuals or the counterfactuals that go along with mental causation involve causation as production. This is correct if one has in mind the fundamental physical laws evolving fundamental physical states. But Kim is more likely thinking of what I called "local production." Relations of local production are not the truth-makers of counterfactuals on Lewis's account. The fundamental laws and fundamental physical state are the ultimate truth-makers of both kinds of causal relations.

38   Of course there are contexts in which the counterfactual "if the shadow had not been at position x at time t the ball would not have been at position y at time t+," but it is important to keep in mind that the relevant account is Lewis's. On that account the counterfactual is evaluated as false since small violations in law that change the position of the shadow leave the position of the ball as it was.

39   Of course this would involve very different physical laws than the actual laws. I have argued that in our world nothing exactly like causation as production (where the cause is sufficient for the effect) is instantiated between local events.

40   This question is asked by Horwich (1987) and answered more fully than I have here in Loewer (forthcoming-b).

References

Armstrong, D. (1978). *A Theory of Universals*, vol. 2. Cambridge: Cambridge University Press.
— (1983). *What Is a Law of Nature?* Cambridge: Cambridge University Press.
Balog, K. (forthcoming). Mental quotation.
Bennett, J. (2003). *A Philosophical Guide to Conditionals*. Oxford: Clarendon.
Bennett, K. (2003). Why the exclusion problem seems intractable, and how, just maybe, to tract it. *Noûs*, 37, 471–97.
— (forthcoming). Exclusion again.
Block, N. (1994). Functionalism. In S. Guttenplan (ed.), *A Companion to the Philosophy of Mind*. Oxford: Blackwell.
Chalmers, D. (1996). *The Conscious Mind*. Oxford: Oxford University Press.
Crisp, T. and Warfield, T. (2001). Kim's master argument. *Noûs*, 35, 304–16.
Daniel, R. and Wegner, D. M. (2002). *The Illusion of Conscious Will*. Cambridge, MA: MIT Press.
Davidson, D. (1980). Mental events. *Essays on Actions and Events*. Oxford: Oxford University Press.
Elga A. (2001). Statistical mechanics and the asymmetry of counterfactual dependence. *Philosophy of Science*, 68, proceedings.
— (forthcoming). Isolation and folk causation. In H. Price and R. Corry (eds.), *Russell's Republic: The Place of Causation in the Constitution of Reality*. Oxford: Oxford University Press.
Field, H. (2003). Causation in a physical world. In M. Loux and D. Zimmerman (eds.), *Oxford Handbook of Metaphysics*. Oxford: Oxford University Press.

Fodor, J. (1974). Special sciences, or, The disunity of science as a working hypothesis. *Synthese*, 27, 97–115.

— (1976). *The Language of Thought*. Hassocks: Harvester.

— (1992). *Psychosemantics*. Cambridge, MA: MIT Press.

— (1998). Special sciences: still autonomous after all these years. *Philosophical Perspectives*, 11, *Mind, Causation, and World*, 149–63.

Hall, N. (2004). Two concepts of causation. In J. Collins, N. Hall, and L. Paul (eds.), *Causation and Counterfactuals*. Cambridge, MA: MIT Press.

Horwich, P. (1987). *Asymmetries in Time*. Cambridge, MA: MIT Press.

Jackson, F. (1998). *From Metaphysics to Ethics: A Defense of Conceptual Analysis*. New York: Oxford University Press.

Kim, J. (1998). *Mind in a Physical World*. Cambridge: Cambridge University Press.

— (2005). *Physicalism, or Something Near Enough*. Princeton: Princeton University Press.

Levine, J. (2001). *Purple Haze*. Oxford: Oxford University Press.

Lewis. D. (1983). New work for a theory of universals. *Australasian Journal of Philosophy*, 61, 343–77.

— (1986). *Philosophical Papers*, vol. 2. Oxford: Oxford University Press.

Loar, B. (1990). Phenomenal states. *Philosophical Perspectives*, 4, 81–108.

Loewer, B. (1996). Humean supervenience. *Philosophical Topics*, 24, 101–26.

— (2001). From physics to physicalism. In C. Gillett and B. Loewer (eds.), *Physicalism and Its Discontents*. Cambridge: Cambridge University Press.

— (2001). Review of Jaegwon Kim's *Mind in a Physical World*. *Journal of Philosophy*.

— (2002). Comments on Jaegwon Kim's *Mind in a Physical World*. *Philosophy and Phenomenological Research*, 65, 655–62.

— (forthcoming-a). Why there is anything except physics. In J. Hohwy and J. Kallestrup (eds.), *On Being Reduced*. Oxford: Oxford University Press.

— (forthcoming-b). Counterfactuals and the second law. In H. Price and R. Corry (eds.), *Russell's Republic: The Place of Causation in the Constitution of Reality*. Oxford: Oxford University Press.

McLaughlin, B. (2004). Identity, explanation, and consciousness: a reply to Kim. Talk delivered at the Pacific APA, March.

Melnyk, A. (2003). *A Physicalist Manifesto*. Cambridge: Cambridge University Press.

— (2005). Review of Jaegwon Kim's *Physicalism, or Something Near Enough*. *Notre Dame Philosophical Reviews*.

Papineau, D. (2001). The rise of physicalism. In C. Gillett and B. Loewer (eds.), *Physicalism and Its Discontents*. Cambridge: Cambridge University Press.

— (2002). *Thinking about Consciousness*. Oxford: Oxford University Press.

Putnam, H. (1975). The nature of mental states. *Philosophical Papers*, vol. 2. Cambridge: Cambridge University Press.

Russell, B. (1913). On the notion of cause. *Proceedings of the Aristotelian Society*, 13, 1–26.

Ryle, G. (1949). *The Concept of Mind*. Chicago: University of Chicago Press.

Shoemaker, S. (1980). Causality and properties. In P. van Inwagen (ed.), *Time and Cause*. Dordrecht: D. Reidel.

Barry Loewer

PART III
THE PLACE OF CONSCIOUSNESS IN NATURE

IS CONSCIOUSNESS ONTOLOGICALLY EMERGENT FROM THE PHYSICAL?

Dualist Emergentism

Martine Nida-Rümelin

When consciousness arises in the phylogenetic or in the ontogenetic evolution of a biological system, something fundamentally new comes into existence. Once it has arisen, consciousness causally influences the functioning of the biological system that gave rise to it. These are typical emergentist ideas about consciousness. There are dualist versions as well as materialist versions of emergentism. I will focus in this paper on a dualist version of emergentism.[1] I will describe its intuitive motivation and sketch some arguments in its favor.

1 Conscious Individuals and Consciousness Properties

The term "conscious" is used in many different ways. In one of its senses we can use the term to mark the fundamental distinction between those concrete individual things that have experiences (that have "an inner life," "a point of view," that are such that it is something like to be them) and the rest of concrete things or matter.[2] Thus, the notion of "consciousness," or, to be more precise, the notion expressed by the adjective "conscious" as it will be used in this text, is applicable to individual things only. It marks a distinction between, e.g., humans, dolphins, and many other animals on this and hopefully some other planets, on the one side, and tables, stones, mountains, etc., on the other. The term will not be used here to mark a difference between states of individuals or between processes or events. Furthermore, in the sense at issue a dolphin is a conscious being even while in dreamless sleep.[3] The capability of having experiences is necessary and sufficient for an individual to be a conscious being.

Conscious beings have properties that no individual without consciousness could possibly have. I will call these properties *consciousness properties*. I cannot use the common term "mental properties" instead since it is controversial whether all mental properties require consciousness. Having a propositional attitude (having beliefs, desires, intentions, and the like) is an example. If propositional attitudes can be defined in functional terms, and if any property that can thus be reduced to its causal role does not require consciousness for its instantiation, then having a propositional attitude is not a consciousness property.[4] Neither can I use the term "phenomenal properties" to replace the term "consciousness properties." As will be explained below (see section 5), the property of being active by doing something is a consciousness property in the sense just explained. Only conscious individuals can be active in the relevant sense. But it is quite clear that properties that consist in being active in a particular way (e.g., the property of running or the property of taking a decision) are not phenomenal properties.[5]

2 The Evolution of Consciousness

At some point in the evolution of life some specific pieces of matter got arranged in a way that led to the occurrence of consciousness. At some point in the development of individual humans and other conscious animals the same kind of change takes place. This radical change may be interpreted in two ways. According to the first interpretation, the change involves new individuals, conscious beings, coming into existence (this is the view I favor and the one the substance dualist accepts). According to the second interpretation, no new individuals come into being. Rather the organism at issue acquires qualitatively new properties, consciousness properties. The emergentist believes that this change occurs as a result of physical conditions satisfied by the biological system. A certain arrangement of matter leads with nomological necessity to the existence of conscious individuals with qualitatively new properties. The following two claims partially characterize a substance dualist version of emergentism:

> *Claim 1 (Emergence of new individuals):* There are specific physical conditions C such that the following holds: at any time t, if t is the time at which a particular material system M (e.g., a biological organism) first satisfies C, then with nomological necessity a subject of experience (a conscious being that belongs to an ontological category different form the one of material objects) comes into existence at t and starts at t to have M as its body.

> *Claim 2 (Emergence of consciousness properties):* A subject cannot have consciousness properties unless the subject's body has corresponding physical properties. No change in consciousness properties is nomologically possible without a simultaneous change in corresponding physical properties of the subject's body. No two nomologically possible individuals (whether in the same world or in different worlds) can differ in their consciousness properties without a difference in the physical properties of their respective bodies.

Both of these claims need some explanation and additional remarks.

Nomologically possible worlds are worlds with the same laws of nature as the actual world. These laws include psychophysical laws that are – according to the emergentist view here presented – fundamental laws of nature.

Martine Nida-Rümelin

According to claim 1, subjects of experience are a product of nature. The existence of a subject without a body that satisfies the physical conditions C is nomologically excluded. Subjects of experience come into existence when their body satisfies certain physical conditions. This implies that the conscious being at issue has not existed before: reincarnation is nomologically excluded.[6]

Claim 1 is a substance dualist claim: the conscious being that comes into existence at t1 is not identical to the system that gives rise to its occurrence. According to this view the occurrence of consciousness is more than the instantiation of qualitatively new properties. The occurrence of consciousness requires the coming into being of individuals belonging to the special ontological category of experiencing subjects.

To call the view "substance dualist" is not meant to imply that there are two kinds of stuff involved (see section 3). It is, however, meant to imply that the subject is something over and above its body in a sense in which a statue is *not* something over and above the corresponding lump of clay.

These new individuals have the system at issue as their body. What is it for a subject S to have the organism O as its body? This means, roughly, that (a) the consciousness properties of S causally depend in the right way on the physical properties of O (e.g., if O is damaged, S feels pain) and that (b) S does what it does with the organism O (e.g., O's hand goes up, if S raises its hand).[7]

According to claim 1, the occurrence of a conscious being is nomologically necessitated by the conditions C. An emergentist might however consider the possibility that there is – within limits – a certain amount of real chance involved: it might not be nomologically determined at what point exactly the individual at issue comes into existence. The claim could be reformulated accordingly (but for simplicity I will not include this complication here).

Talk of "physical" conditions should be understood in a broad sense. Biological and chemical as well as functional properties are included. Claim 1 is compatible with the idea that the occurrence of consciousness depends only on functional properties of the system. It is thus compatible with the claim that conscious individuals might occur on the basis of a non-biological system made up of some non-biological stuff.[8]

Claim 2 states a close dependence between consciousness properties and physical properties. It is impossible, e.g., to take a decision without a simultaneous change taking place in the body (presumably the brain). Mental events need a physical basis. However, claim 2 does not imply that consciousness is in any sense causally inert. Claim 2 is compatible with causal influence in both directions: physical changes cause changes in consciousness properties. Claim 2 allows for the possibility that the subject itself influences via simultaneous causality the processes in its brain by taking decisions, considering hypotheses, directing its attention, and moving its body (see section 5 below).

The ideas formulated in claim 2 can be captured in part by stating a thesis of strong nomological supervenience: there are no nomologically possible worlds w1 and w2, and subjects s1 and s2 and times t1 and t2, such that there is no physical difference between s1 at t1 in w1 and s2 at t2 in w2 but yet there is a difference between the two subjects at the times in these two worlds with respect to their consciousness properties.[9]

3 Substance Dualism

With the emergence of consciousness, new individuals of a special ontological category, conscious beings or subjects of experience (I will use these terms interchangeably), come into existence. A philosopher who accepts this claim (formulated above as claim 1) endorses some version of substance dualism. Substance dualism is often presented in a way that makes the view appear clearly unacceptable and quite ridiculous. It is therefore necessary to make a few remarks to avoid possible misunderstandings.

Substance dualism – as I use the term – is characterized by the claim that the subject of experience (the thing that has consciousness properties, the thing a person refers to using the first person pronoun, the thing people refer to using a name of a person or a name of an animal) is not composed of matter. The experiencing subject, according to this view, is not a body or a brain or a system composed of anything; nor is it an abstract entity. What a subject of experience is can best be positively characterized by saying that it is capable of having consciousness properties and by describing the special ontological status of its identity across time and of its identity across possible worlds.[10]

For contingent historical reasons substance dualism is often associated with the view that animals are mere automata (mechanically functioning bodies) while the human animal alone has a different ontological status. There is no systematic reason for a substance dualist to be tempted by this idea. We know that we are not alone in the animal kingdom in being conscious.[11] But it is the mere fact of the existence of consciousness in a particular given individual A that justifies a substance dualist view with regard to A. So a reasonable substance dualist will not restrict his or her claim to the human case.

The present version of substance dualism does not imply that the human person is composed of a material and a non-material part, a body and a soul. According to the present version of substance dualism there is no need to talk of composition in this context. The person *is* the subject of experience and he or she *has* a body. A given agglomeration of molecules A is the body of the subject of experience S if and only if there is the right kind of relation between the experiences and the activities of S and physical changes and/or movements within/of A. (If, for instance, A is damaged, then S feels pain, and if S is engaged in running, then A moves in a "running way.")

According to a traditional religious view a person *has* a body and *has* a soul. According to the present view a person has a body but no person *has* a soul. At best persons *are* souls. However it would be misleading to use the term "soul" in the description of the kind of emergentist dualism I have in mind. The soul is supposed to be able to exist without a body. The emergentist dualist does not endorse the claim that subjects can exist without having a body. The soul is supposed to be immortal. The emergentist dualist view does not include the claim that subjects of experience cannot cease to exist. The soul is often thought of as being composed of some thin non-material stuff. The emergentist substance dualist does not postulate the existence of thin immaterial stuff. The soul is often thought of as being able to be located in space (people think of the soul as something that can leave the body and fly away).

Martine Nida-Rümelin

The emergentist dualist should resist these ideas with respect to subjects of experience. Subjects of experience are located only in the sense of having a body with a spatial location.

The emergentist substance dualist claims that Peter, a subject of experience (a person), is not identical to his body. This claim, however, does not imply that Peter is in any sense "hidden" in his body. The substance dualist can endorse the natural view that you see *me* when you look at my body. The substance dualist can justify this claim in the following way. When looking at my body (e.g., into my face) you can see non-inferentially that I have certain properties. This is why it is appropriate to say that you see me by looking at my body. You can see non-inferentially that I am laughing by looking into my face while I am laughing. When you look into my face while I am laughing you see *me* laughing.

Another misleading term often used in this context is the term "the Self." Here again it is sometimes said that a person *has* a self. The emergentist substance dualist position I wish to defend rejects this idea. The referent of the term "the Self" is the referent of the first person pronoun used by some person. But the referent of the first person pronoun used by a person P is simply P. So "the Self" (in a given case) is simply the person (or the subject of experience).

Talking of "the Self" in this context invites another idea that we should reject. Some philosophers argue that selves are somehow constituted by their capacity to refer to themselves in "I-thoughts."[12] But subjects of experience may and do exist without having the capability of entertaining I-thoughts.

The idea of subject causation developed below does not make sense if the subject is numerically identical to its body or a part of the body. Therefore, every argument for subject causation is also an argument for substance dualism. The most powerful arguments for substance dualism are related to the philosophical problem of identity across time.[13]

4 Qualitatively New Properties

According to the view defended in this paper, new *individuals* come into existence when consciousness arises. But contemporary discussions about emergentism focus on a different idea of novelty. As emergentism is commonly understood the novelty brought about by the occurrence of consciousness consists in the instantiation of qualitatively new properties by individuals that already existed before. According to widespread opinion, conscious individuals are biological organisms; consciousness properties thus are properties of a complex material thing that is composed of smaller parts (e.g., of cells that stand in a great variety of causal interactions). With this in mind the question about the relation between consciousness and its physical basis becomes a question about the relation between properties of the whole organism and properties and relations instantiated by the smaller parts that make it up. The emergentist is portrayed as saying that consciousness properties are emergent in this sense: they are properties of a whole that cannot be reduced to the properties of its parts and the relations between them but they "emerge" on the basis of (because of) the properties of the parts and the relations obtaining between them. The intuitive idea is that the instantiation of emergent properties of a whole *consists in more than* in the instantiation of the property of being composed of parts that satisfy certain conditions. The shape of an object and its weight are examples of properties of a whole that are *not* emergent. The functional properties of a biological system provide further examples of non-emergent properties of a whole.

It is not a trivial task to account in a precise manner for the distinction between emergent properties of a whole and non-emergent properties of a whole (relative to certain microproperties and microrelations of microparts that make up the object).[14] An emergentist who accepts that conscious individuals are biological organisms must, however, rely on some account of this distinction in order to give a precise meaning to his claim that consciousness properties are qualitatively new properties.

But this approach to the emergentist idea of novelty is erroneous according to the view defended in this paper. One reason is that – according to this view – subjects of experience are not composed. So the sense in which some of their properties are qualitatively new or emergent cannot be understood according to the model of emergent properties of composed wholes.[15] Another and maybe more important reason is this: to explain the novelty intuition along these lines misconstrues the character of the change that takes place when consciousness arises. Let me try to explain.

Suppose consciousness arose for the first time on our planet in the moment in which a particular quite primitive organism somewhere in some ocean began to feel comfortable warmth when it moved by chance into warmer water. According to the emergentist an astonishing and radical change took place in this moment. But let us ask what exactly it is that makes the change a radical change and a change that deserves amazement. It is not the instantiation of the particular phenomenal property of feeling warmth. What makes the change amazing has nothing to do with this special phenomenal character. Rather, the astonishing fact is this: since, as we assumed, a feeling of warmth has occurred, there is "someone" who feels the warmth. The fact that "someone" came into existence is the astonishing aspect of the change and the aspect that makes the change a radical change. Before the first occurrence of a faint feeling, no one was on our planet to experience the world. In that moment, a subject capable of experience came into existence.

According to this view any justification of the emergentist claim that a radical change has taken place when consciousness occurred must be based on the fact that the first instantiation of consciousness properties requires the coming into being of subjects of experience. It is this coming into being of conscious individuals that deserves astonishment. If this is correct then an appropriate formulation of the emergentist intuition of novelty does not require, contrary to what is commonly assumed, any general theory about reduction. We need not define what it would be for a property to be irreducible to other properties or relations in order to explicate what makes consciousness properties qualitatively new and radically different from physical properties. We can understand what makes these properties qualitatively new by taking into account the following two elements: (a) the instantiation of consciousness properties requires that the instantiating being is a subject of experience and (b) subjects of experience are radically different in kind from all other kinds of entities. The main task if we wish to get a clear understanding of the novelty of consciousness is then to get clear about the special ontological status of conscious individuals.[16]

Martine Nida-Rümelin

Given what has been said in this section we can add the following claim to the characterization of dualist emergentism:

Claim 3 (Qualitatively new properties): Consciousness properties are qualitatively new properties. The instantiation of consciousness properties does not consist in the instantiation of physical properties of parts of the organism at issue and/or relations between them. The novelty of consciousness properties is due to the fact that they are instantiated by subjects of experience that are not identical with any physical thing.

5 Subject Causation

One important characteristic of conscious individuals is their capacity to have experiences such as the feeling of warmth, the visual experience of an approaching object, the complex experience of listening to a piece of music, and the like. To have a particular experience sometimes involves being active in a specific way. Listening to a piece of music attentively and with the intention to enjoy its particular musical qualities involves, e.g., directing one's attention toward aspects of the piece. In this sense many experiences are not passive. The subject of experience is itself active in the experiencing. The same holds for thinking. To think about a philosophical puzzle involves actively considering different theoretical possibilities and actively directing one's attention upon a specific subpart of the problem. Subjects *do* something in their experiencing and in their thinking. Subjects of experience are even more obviously and more visibly active in their bodily doings. Only some of our doings are actions but all actions are doings. Doings can be "mental" (e.g., the forming of an intention, the direction of attention in thought or perception) or they can involve bodily movements (e.g., turning one's head, smiling, walking). Not all our movements and bodily changes are doings (breathing can be automatic; digestion involves movements but is not a doing). There might not be a sharp line between doings and non-doings and there might not be a sharp line between actions and other doings. I will not presuppose any particular view about the difference between actions and mere doings. Although actions are (on our planet) probably restricted to the human case, doings are not. Many animals (maybe even all animals) are active in their doings too.[17]

With these preparations a further characteristic of conscious individuals can be described. Doing something requires a subject of experience who does the doing. Only conscious individuals can be active in the relevant way. To be active in the relevant way means – according to the view here proposed – that the subject is itself a causal origin of what happens. The subject is a causal origin of changes in the brain when it directs its attention to a particular aspect of a problem and it is a causal origin of changes in the brain that initiate and that uphold a movement when the subject does something involving a bodily movement. I will call this kind of causation *subject causation*.

A similar idea is known under the heading "agent causation." Some incompatibilists with respect to determinism and human freedom defend the view that in acting the person is itself the cause of some event.[18] According to their view, agent causation is not to be confused with event causation. The person is not an event, but the person is a (or the) causal origin of her action (or of some event preceding or accompanying her action). So the causal relation does not obtain in this case between two events. The view here proposed has some similarity to these theories. Like agent causation theorists, I claim a causal relation between subjects and events that are caused by the subject and I subscribe to the view that the causal relation at issue is different from event causation. However, there are also several important differences.

First, the idea of agent causality is normally assumed to be restricted to the human case and it is assumed to occur only in the context of human action. The view here proposed is in a sense more radical than this. It includes the claim that conscious individuals in general are active in all their doings. The claim is thus neither restricted to action nor to the human case.[19] According to the view I advocate, the jump of a squirrel or the barking of a dog is an example where "someone" is active in the sense of subject causation.

Second, agent causation theorists normally think of the person as intervening at a given isolated moment t. Up to that moment t several options are open (it is causally underdetermined which of them will be realized). The intervention of the person results in a realization of one of these options. After t things develop in the normal causally determined manner. According to this picture, agent causation is a temporally quite local phenomenon. The agent intervenes at specific points in time while leaving the rest of the causal chains intact. This is not the picture I wish to propose. I think of subject causation as *continuously* and *simultaneously* influencing some of those physiological events in the brain that are the basis of mental doings (such as considering a hypothesis or directing one's attention) or of bodily expressed doings (such as jumping for joy or playing a piece of Mozart on a piano). According to this view the events resulting from subject causation are not to be thought of like exceptional isolated miraculous "little bangs." Rather, subject causation is present virtually all the time while a conscious being is awake and it continuously influences in a complex way what happens in the brain and in the subject's body. When at some point in its development a brain brings it about that a subject of experience comes into existence, then the brain itself thereby undergoes a fundamental change. It ceases to be a physically determined system and a great variety of processes underlying the many activities of the subject develop in a way in which they could not develop without the subject's causal influence.

Third, libertarians (who believe in human freedom and in the incompatibility of freedom with determinism) sometimes seem to think that in the case of free action a *preceding* mental event (e.g., a decision) causes a *later* physical event. Agent causation theorists (who are libertarians of a special sort) sometimes seem to endorse this view too (adding that the person herself causes the mental event that in turn causes the physical event). If this idea of a preceding mental event causing a later physical event is combined with the dualist claim that the mental event is nonphysical then the following picture emerges: there are nonphysical mental events that happen without any physical basis. The corresponding physical change happens only a bit later. The present view does not imply this problematic result. The result is avoided by the idea of simultaneous causation. In taking, e.g., a decision the person simultaneously causes changes in her brain. In general, the person cannot cause anything without thereby *simultaneously* causing a change in her brain.[20]

Martine Nida-Rümelin

Fourth, if the problematic picture just sketched were correct, then consciousness properties would not supervene on the physical. There could be two individuals at some time t with the same physical properties that differ with respect to the decision they make at t. Some libertarians and some agent causation theorists therefore seem to be forced to deny the claim of nomological supervenience of consciousness properties on physical properties. The present view about subject causation does not exclude nomological supervenience. To the contrary, the overall view here proposed explicitly endorses nomological supervenience of consciousness properties on physical properties or more precisely on neurophysiological properties of the brain (compare claim 2 above). This claim of nomological supervenience is well motivated within the present approach: (a) all differences with respect to phenomenal properties are brought about by differences in physiological properties of the brain (brain processes cause the instantation of phenomenal properties), and (b) the subject's activities are always accompanied by corresponding physiological processes since the subject cannot cause anything without causally influencing processes in its own brain.[21]

According to the emergentist view here proposed the subject can causally influence physical events happening in its own brain. These physical events would not occur if the subject were not active in the relevant way. It follows that these events are not causally determined by preceding physical events. There is no overdetermination involved here. Subject causation is incompatible with the claim that every brain event has sufficient physical causes and it is also incompatible with the claim that all brain events have only physical causes. Since brain events are physical events, the thesis of the existence of subject causation here proposed is incompatible with the principle of the causal closure of the physical.[22]

6 Causal Relevance of Consciousness Properties

The causal relevance of consciousness properties is an empirical question to be treated in psychology and in neurophysiology. The philosopher, however, can and should contribute by describing various ways in which consciousness properties could in principle be causally relevant to the behavior of the subject and to the development of brain processes. A philosopher who accepts the version of dualist emergentism proposed in this paper has the additional task to explain how he or she can account for the obvious causal relevance of consciousness properties in a way that fits into his or her overall view and that in addition does not contradict and is in the best case already supported by available empirical data. In this section, I will only mention a few elements that would have to be developed in a more comprehensive presentation of dualist emergentism.[23]

In some cases the causal relevance of given instantiations of consciousness properties is due to subject causation. In these cases the instantiations of consciousness properties owe their causal relevance to the fact that the subject is active in a particular way.

Example 1: I see an apple in front of me and I desire to eat it. I reach out for the apple.

In this case I act on the basis of a conscious perception with a particular content and on the basis of a conscious desire. My conscious perception and my desire do not directly cause my act. But they are both causally relevant: I would not have acted in the way that I acted if I did not have these consciousness properties. It is I who make the arm movement by causing specific changes in the brain. But I would not cause these changes if I did not have those consciousness properties.

To say that in this case the perception and the desire are both causally relevant might invite the idea that there are three partial causes: the subject (who causally influences certain processes by way of subject causation), and the perception and the desire (which causally influence the result by way of event causation). If we think of partial causes as cooperating to bring about a result, as several fires may "cooperate" to warm up a room, then this picture is quite clearly inappropriate. The perception and the desire do not do any causal work in addition to motivating me to act in a particular way.[24]

But this way of describing what happens in example 1 may cause still another possible misunderstanding. If the desire and the perception do not have any causal impact by themselves but owe, as I said, their causal relevance entirely to subject causation, then one might be tempted to conclude that the present view implies the following claim: the subject brings it about all by itself that the processes in the brain responsible for the triggering of the movement occur and develop in the way they do. But this cannot be so. Learned motor programs realized in the brain are obviously necessary for me to be able to reach out for the apple. I do not cause the brain process that triggers the movement out of nothing. The present view does not imply the denial of the following obvious truth: complex physiological processes have to occur in the preparation of any bodily movements and these complex physiological processes are in great part predetermined by the "programs" realized in the motor cortex. The present view implies only that subject causation is a necessary condition for the occurrence of these brain processes in a given case.

Another way in which consciousness properties can be causally relevant has to do with the programming of motor programs and other programs in the brain.

Example 2: While practicing, Anna, a pianist, carefully listens to the sounds she produces with her fingers. The way the piece sounds to Anna will influence in a complex manner the way Anna moves her fingers. After a few months Anna will be able to play the piece in a way that conforms to her musical judgment.

We sometimes say that a pianist plays a piece "automatically," which is in a sense partially correct. It is impossible to have the movements of the fingers in all musically relevant aspects under conscious control while playing a complex piece rapidly. Often the pianist would not know how to play on without "letting the fingers decide" what to do next. (This is why in order to remember the movements you go back a few bars in the piece and "let the fingers do it.") But still the movements are not automatic in this sense: the pianist does the playing. Anna is herself causally relevant for the physical events that bring about the movements. She causes the movements by way of continuous and simultaneous subject causation. But, of course, she has no conscious control over all the relevant details. She causes the movements of her fingers,

Martine Nida-Rümelin

but the way the fingers move depends in great part on a learned program. The learned program, and this is what the example is supposed to illustrate, depends itself on consciousness properties. The learned program would be different if Anna had played the piece differently in the past. And she would have played the piece differently in the past if it had not sounded to her the way it did while she played. We may say that the way the piece sounded to her motivated Anna to move her fingers in a specific way. But the case is quite different from example 1. In example 1, the agent decides to reach out for the apple on the basis of what she sees and wants. There is no time for taking decisions about finger movements in the piano-playing case. You just listen carefully, attend to the musical qualities you are interested in, and try to make it sound a particular way. Often you do not know what exactly you do when it begins to sound all right.[25] But the fact that it begins to sound all right is causally relevant: you will try to do it again this way next time and if you succeed then a new detail of the program is beginning to be implemented in your brain.[26]

We often say that we did something automatically when there was no time to think.

> *Example 3:* John is lost in his daydreaming while driving a car. He almost overlooks a red light. He sees it just in time to jump on the brake. There is no time for reflection. He jumps on the brake without any thought intervening between the seeing and the jumping.

If John had not seen the red light he would not have jumped on the brake. His seeing of the red light is causally relevant for his jumping. Still, even in this case, we should not say, or so I claim, that the seeing caused the jumping all by itself.[27] Even in a case of a rapid reaction it is still the person (or subject) who does the doing. Jumping on the brake is a doing (even if one doubts that it is an action). If it is a doing, then the person causally brings it about that the body makes the movement. The fact, however, that John can react so quickly and without reflection in the right way is due to a program developed in a previous process of learning.[28]

The three examples considered so far seem to suggest that the causal relevance of the instantiation of a consciousness property is either due to subject causation (in this case a consciousness property or event inherits its "causal powers" from subject causation) or it is due to the physiological processes underlying the consciousness properties (in this case a consciousness property inherits its causal powers from the causal powers of the underlying physical process). This naturally raises the question of whether consciousness properties can have causal powers of their own, causal powers that are not inherited (either from subject causation or from physical event causation). A potential example might be the case of an insight on the basis of thinking.

> *Example 4:* Elisabeth has been thinking about a philosophical puzzle again and again for many weeks. One morning suddenly a simple solution pops up in her mind. Elisabeth carefully considers this way to solve the puzzle and finds it intuitively highly attractive. Elisabeth forms the belief that this is the correct solution.

The fact that the solution appears intuitively correct to Elisabeth is causally relevant for the formation of the belief. This claim should be true according to any acceptable theory about thinking and believing. If we exclude (as I think we should) that this is a case of overdetermination then either the instantiation of the consciousness property (being an intuition with a specific content) has its own causal powers (over and above the causal powers of the instantiation of physical properties by the underlying brain processes) or its causal power is entirely due to subject causation (as in at least some of the other cases considered before). But the latter possibility is excluded: the formation of belief (maybe in contrast to acceptance) is not an action and it is not a doing. So the causal relevance of intuitions for the formation of belief cannot be due to subject causation. But intuition should not be epiphenomenal. I therefore tend to think that consciousness properties in some cases have causal powers of their own.

Let me summarize the theses developed in the last two sections:

Claim 4 (Subject causation): Whenever a conscious individual does something then it is itself a causal origin of the doing. This causation (subject causation) is not a case of event causation. Subject causation is continuous and simultaneous causation.[29] Subject causation is incompatible with the causal closure of the physical.

Claim 5 (Causal powers of consciousness properties): In many cases consciousness properties are causally relevant. They often (but not always) owe their causal powers to subject causation and/or to the underlying physiological processes.[30]

7 Why Believe in Subject Causation?

If you observe a squirrel jumping from one branch of a tree to another, then the squirrel does not look to you like a mechanism that jumps as the result of some inner "mechanical" process. It looks to you as though the squirrel itself, the subject of experience, does the jumping. When you see a conscious individual that looks around, sits down, turns its head in the direction of a noise, then you do not see these events as the result of a mechanical process. We see the movements of biological organisms that we implicitly accept to be conscious as being done by the conscious individual itself. A related claim is true for the way we experience our own doings. We experience our doings as brought about by ourselves. To assume that some inner processes cause our doings is incompatible with the content of the phenomenology of our experience.[31] If these experiences of ourselves when we are active and our perceptions of others as being active are not illusory, then conscious individuals *are* active in their doings. They are not, in that sense, biological "automata." We should not be ready to accept a philosophical theory that implies that our way to perceive the world (ourselves and other conscious beings) is fundamentally mistaken in a radical way. This is, in a nutshell, the most powerful argument, I claim, for the acceptance of subject causation.

There is no room here to defend the view in detail. But let me mention the elements that would have to be present in an elaborated version of the argument. (a) The content of the experiences at issue must be further analyzed. It has to be shown that the experiences just mentioned really have the representational content that I just claimed they have: they represent the other subject (or ourselves) to us as being active in the sense of subject causation and thus in a way that is incompatible with the assumption of causal determination. If this is the correct analysis of the content of our experiences then it follows that our daily experiences cannot be veridical unless conscious individuals really are active in the sense of subject causation. (b) The experience of others as active and of ourselves as active is deeply entrenched in our worldview and in our emotional and intellectual life. In a second step it has to be shown that this fact justifies us in taking the corresponding conviction (the conviction that subject causation is real) as epistemically central in this sense: we should not be ready to abandon the claim of subject causation unless we are forced to do so by extremely powerful counter-evidence. (c) In a third step the argument has to show that there is no such extremely powerful counter-evidence. In particular it has to be argued that, contrary to what many people assume, there is no powerful *empirical* evidence for the nonexistence of subject causation.

8 The Adequacy of Amazement

For the emergentist, consciousness is an astonishing phenomenon. There is a puzzle about how nature is capable of "producing" this "new" phenomenon on the basis of something quite different: the arrangement of molecules in a particular way and their causal interaction. Many philosophers accept that there is prima facie an explanatory gap. We do not seem to be able to *understand* why a certain complex arrangement of molecules leads to the occurrence of consciousness (*general explanatory gap thesis*) and why a certain complex arrangement of molecules leads to the occurrence of a particular kind of experience (*specific explanatory gap thesis*).[32] Most philosophers who accept these "gaps" argue, however, that the puzzlement dissolves once we understand what it is about our cognitive makeup that makes it difficult or even impossible to understand why consciousness occurs (given a certain physical basis) and why specific conscious states (or events) are correlated with specific physical states (or events). A number of proposals have been made to explain the existence the so-called explanatory gap thereby providing an illusion theory: they explain why consciousness *appears* mysterious to us given our cognitive architecture although there really *is* no mystery about consciousness.[33] According to these philosophers, from an objective point of view, there is nothing to be puzzled about.

The emergentist rejects the idea that our natural puzzlement about consciousness is illusory. It is an essential part of the emergentist position to insist on the *adequacy* of our amazement when we reflect about the phenomenon of consciousness. The emergentist understood in this way not only subscribes to the explanatory-gap claims just mentioned. These claims merely *describe* our cognitive situation. The emergentist adds a normative claim: Consciousness *deserves* astonishment. According to that view, consciousness is *objectively* an astonishing phenomenon and it is therefore a mistake to think that our puzzlement is the result of some kind of illusion. To the contrary, our amazement about the occurrence of consciousness is a symptom of our grasp of the phenomenon. A person who understands what consciousness consists in will see upon reflection how amazing it is that consciousness arises on the basis of some arrangement of matter. The emergentist so understood insists that it is perfectly *appropriate* to be puzzled about the occurrence of consciousness and that a person who does not see any puzzle here thereby shows a lack of understanding of what it is for an individual to be conscious.

Acknowledgments

I am grateful to Terence Horgan, Brian McLaughlin, and Barry Loewer for very helpful comments on an earlier version of this paper that motivated a number of changes and saved me from several mistakes.

Notes

1   David Braddon-Mitchell (AGAINST ONTOLOGICALLY EMERGENT CONSCIOUSNESS) argues against any emergentist view that tries to avoid dualism and yet to incorporate its intuitive merits. The present version of emergentism is not among the views he attacks since it implicitly endorses a dualist ontology. Contrary to Braddon-Mitchell I claim that the present dualist proposal does deserve the label "emergentism" for reasons that will, I hope, become apparent in my description of the view.

2   It is hard to explain this general notion of consciousness non-metaphorically. This may invite the conclusion that we need a clear definition or at least some explication before we may use the term in philosophical theory. Of course it is in order to ask for clarifications in some sense, e.g., to ask for an analysis of how the term is conceptually related to other notions and of how it is distinct from similar concepts. But we should not expect too much. When we attribute some specific experience to an individual we thereby already presuppose that "it is something like to be that individual." (The locution has been introduced by Thomas Nagel, 1974, in his famous paper.) Arguably, the general notion of consciousness at issue here is *conceptually prior* to any specific notion of any kind of experience. If this is so, then it should not be expected that someone would ever come up with any illuminating, noncircular definition of what it is to be conscious. But this does not mean that the term is in any sense obscure. To the contrary, or so I claim, we do have – upon reflection – an intuitive notion of what it is for an individual to be a conscious being that is quite clear and easy to grasp. Any proposed definition would have to be tested on the basis of this pre-theoretic intuitive understanding.

3   This needs to be pointed out since "conscious" is sometimes used in the sense of "awake."

4   In my opinion the first claim is wrong and the second true.

5   This is not to deny that having these properties is accompanied or even requires some specific phenomenology – I use the term "running" as a description of an activity and not as the description of a kind of bodily movement. In this sense, no non-conscious robot can run, only subjects of experience can run or swim or do anything (see section 5).

6   A weaker claim that one might still call emergentist would be silent about whether subjects can change their body and about whether subjects can exist without a body. This weaker claim would state only that certain physical conditions C are nomologically sufficient for there being a subject that starts at t to have the system as its body.

7   It is tempting to say that S's activities cause certain changes in O. But this would not be quite right at least in many cases. My raising my hand does not cause my hand to go up; rather it is partially constituted by my hand's going up.

8　　Claim 1 thus allows for the possibility that future robots will give rise to the occurrence of consciousness. However, once the subject of experience at issue had become active (see section 5) its body would cease to be a mechanically functioning system.

9　　Emergentism is often characterized by the combination of a thesis of metaphysical supervenience with an anti-reductionist claim. The dualist emergentist, however, has no reason to endorse metaphysical supervenience. It is often assumed that dualism can be partially characterized by the denial of metaphysical supervenience. But while it is obvious that the denial of metaphysical supervenience implies dualism, I doubt the reverse implication. The issue of metaphysical supervenience is therefore left open in the present characterization of emergentist dualism. For the role of supervenience in an explication of emergentism see Beckermann (1992), Stephan (1997, 2002), and Kim (1999).

10　　The special ontological status of identity across time of conscious individuals is the topic of my book *Der Blick von Innen* (Nida-Rümelin, 2006).

11　　I am leaving it open how far "down" in the animal kingdom there are conscious beings. Of course there is an interesting philosophical problem about how the claim of the existence of consciousness in other individuals can be justified. But there is also an interesting philosophical problem about how our belief in the existence of the external world can be justified. It would be inappropriate and irrational if someone withheld opinion about the existence of the external world as long as no generally accepted justification has been explicitly developed. The same is true for the case at issue.

12　　A view of this kind may be found in Jonathan Lowe (1996) and in Lynn Rudder Baker (2000).

13　　For reasons of space these arguments cannot be presented in the present paper. Some of these arguments are developed and discussed in detail in Nida-Rümelin (2006).

14　　See, e.g., Ansgar Beckermann (1992).

15　　According to the view I have in mind here, subjects of experience are not composed of matter but also they are not temporally extended (they do not have temporal parts although they persist through time).

16　　At this point someone might reply in the following way: The difference is simply that the former but not the latter can instantiate consciousness properties. So the task is quite trivial. We can make a list of consciousness properties and say that a being is conscious if and only if it is capable of instantiating at least one of these properties. The list will be an open list and we might want to add something like "or properties similar to those on the list." There will be a certain amount of arbitrariness, so the reply might go on, in this procedure. There simply might not be any fact of the matter about whether a given property deserves to be added to the list. Accordingly in many cases there is no fact of the matter as to whether a given being is a conscious being. According to this view, to understand the difference between conscious individuals and other concrete individuals is to have an appropriate list of this kind in mind and to know that a being is conscious if and only if it is capable of instantiating some of these properties.

　　This proposal is fundamentally misguided according to the view I propose. For each property it is a substantial factual question whether it should be added to the list. The answer depends on whether the property requires a subject of experience for its instantiation. Furthermore, the list cannot be used to clarify what it is to be a subject of experience. If there are only consciousness properties on the list (as it should be) then to understand what having one of the properties on the list consists in already requires a grasp of what it is to be a subject of experience.

17　　Actions are normally (but maybe not always) done for some reason. Doings are often done without any reason. While sitting in a train a person may turn her head from time to time. These movements are doings (it is the person who does them, the movements are not in that sense automatic) but they can be done without any reason. In actions we are normally in some way aware of what we do. We need not be aware of our doings. While giving a talk a person might move her hands without being aware of the fact that she does. I leave it open here whether the capability of having an experience can occur without the capability of being active and vice versa. I also leave it open how far down in the evolution animals are active in the sense at issue.

18 Agent causation theorists disagree about the kind of event that is directly caused by the agent. For a brief survey see section 2.4 in Timothy O'Connor (2002). Roderick M. Chisholm famously held an agent causation view at some point (see Chisholm, 1976). More recently a new, detailed elaboration of a version of the view has been developed by O'Connor (see O'Connor, 2000).

19 It could be claimed that all conscious individuals are in fact or even necessarily active. This claim is plausible but I cannot see how the speculation could be justified in a convincing way.

20 The term "change" might invite misunderstandings. The person can cause that a certain state continues; she then causes (in a sense) that no change takes place. (Of course the upholding of a particular state involves neural activities that again involve a great variety of changes.)

21 The theoretical motivation for the acceptance of some supervenience claim is normally quite different. Philosophers hope to express some form of dependence of the mental upon the physical without thereby endorsing any causal relation between the mental and the physical. Contrary to this, the claim of nomological supervenience is combined in the present view with a form of interactionism: the subject itself causes physical changes and physical changes cause the instantiation of certain consciousness properties by the subject. Compare for the discussion of supervenience Kim (1993) and McLaughlin (1995).

22 The principle of the causal closure of the physical as I understand it here states the following: For every physical event E, if X is a cause of E, then X is physical too. Subject causation is, however, compatible with the following principle of causal closure: For every physical event E1, if the event E2 is a cause of E1, then E2 is physical too.

23 I hope to develop some of this in my paper "Doings and Subject Causation," in preparation for a special volume of *Erkenntnis* edited by Michael Esfeld, Albert Newen, and Vera Hofmann (Nida-Rümelin, forthcoming).

24 Motivation cannot be explicated in terms of causation. That certain psychological preconditions motivate a person to act in a particular way does not mean that they cause the person to act in that way.

25 To say that you do not know exactly what you do is to say that you would not be able to give an independent description of the movements. Of course this is the case too in virtually all our daily actions. We have to do some reflection in order to describe the movements we execute when we pour water in a glass or open a window.

26 Something like this happens in most cases of acquisition of motor skills. The joy of a child that learns to walk when it realizes "now it works!" is causally relevant for the learning, just as the phenomenal character of the sounds is in Anna's case.

27 One might think that the seeing is nonetheless a cause of the jumping since it causes a reaction in the subject. But I hesitate to agree. The subject's causal influence is not caused by any preceding event, not even "in part." The subject does the doing *on the basis* of the perception where – even in this case – the "on the basis"-relation is not to be confused with being caused.

28 I am not claiming that every such program that we "rely on" in our doings is due to learning. There may be a great variety of innate motor programs that still require an active subject to be "executed."

Martine Nida-Rümelin

29   By calling subject causation "continuous and simultaneous" I mean to express the idea that subject causation is not to be thought of as an initial cause of a physical process but rather as an influence stretched out in time while the physical process is happening. Subject causation is "continuous" in the sense that a whole physical process between t1 and t2 is brought about by a subject who is active between t1 and t2 and it is simultaneous in the sense that details about the physical process realized at t′ (between t1 and t2) are caused by the subject at t′.

30   It should be added here that causal powers owed to the underlying processes are not genuinely causal powers of the consciousness properties at issue. I am convinced by the reasoning developed by Jaegwon Kim according to which consciousness properties would be epiphenomenal if all their causal powers were "inherited" from the causal powers of the physical. A parallel reasoning however does not apply to causal powers that are due to subject causation.

31   A similar point is made by Terence Horgan (forthcoming-a, forthcoming-b).

32   Levine argues forcefully for the explanatory-gap thesis (compare Levine, 1993 and 2001).

33   As an example see Papineau (2002), chapter 5.

References

Baker, L. R. (2000). *Persons and Bodies: A Constitution View*. Cambridge: Cambridge University Press.

Beckermann, A. (1992). Supervenience, emergence, and reduction. In A. Beckermann, H. Flohr, and J. Kim (eds.), *Emergence or Reduction? Essays on the Prospects of Nonreductive Physicalism*. Berlin: Walter de Gruyter.

Chisholm, R. M. (1976). *Person and Object*. Dordrecht: D. Reidel.

Horgan, T. (forthcoming-a). Causal compatibilism about agentive phenomenology. In M. Sabates, D. Sosa, and T. Horgan (eds.), *Supervenience and Mind*. Cambridge: MA: MIT Press.

— (forthcoming-b). Is agentive experience veridical?

Kim, J. (1993). *Supervenience and Mind: Selected Philosophical Essays*. Cambridge: Cambridge University Press.

— (1999). Making sense of emergence. *Philosophical Studies*, 95, 3–36.

Levine, J. (1993). On leaving out what it's like. In M. Davies and G. W. Humphreys (eds.), *Consciousness: Psychological and Philosophical Essays*. Oxford: Blackwell. Reprinted in N. J. Block, O. Flanagan, and G. Güzeldere (eds.), *The Nature of Consciousness: Philosophical Debates*. Cambridge, MA: MIT Press, 1997.

— (2001). *Purple Haze: The Puzzle of Consciousness*. Oxford: Oxford University Press.

Lowe, J. E. (1996). *Subjects of Experience*. Cambridge: Cambridge University Press.

McLaughlin, B. P. (1995). Varieties of supervenience. In E. Savellos and U. Yalcin (eds.), *Supervenience: New Essays*. Cambridge: Cambridge University Press, 16–59.

Nagel, T. (1974). What is it like to be a bat? *Philosophical Review*, 83, 435–50.

Nida-Rümelin, M. (2006). *Der Blick von Innen. Zur transtemporalen Identität bewusstseinsfähiger Wesen*. Frankfurt am Main: Suhrkamp. [English translation in preparation: *The View from Inside: Transtemporal Identity of Conscious Individuals*.]

— (forthcoming). Doings and subject causation. *Erkenntnis*.

O'Connor, T. (2000). *Persons and Causes: The Metaphysics of Free Will*. Oxford: Oxford University Press.

O'Connor, T. (2002). Libertarian views: dualist and agent-causal theories. In R. Kane (ed.), *The Oxford Handbook of Free Will*. Oxford: Oxford University Press.

Papineau, D. (2002). *Thinking about Consciousness.* Oxford: Oxford University Press.

Stephan, A. (1997). Armchair arguments against emergentism. *Erkenntnis, 4,* 305–14.

— (2002). Emergentism, irreducibility, and downward causation. *Grazer Philosophische Studien,* 65, 55–93.

Against Ontologically Emergent Consciousness

David Braddon-Mitchell

Introduction

There's no doubt that dualism about the mind – especially about consciousness – is appealing. Even when physicalism has won almost complete victory in the arena of professional philosophy of mind, dualism perennially gains converts. Frank Jackson's knowledge argument (Jackson, 1982, 1986), the Zombie argument,[1] various other respects in which we might need to revise our commonsense picture of consciousness if dualism is false (Lewis, 1995) all ensure that the debate between physicalists and dualists never dies down. My own preferred diagnosis of dualism's appeal is that of David Lewis. It is a fairly deep feature of our conception of consciousness (or at least of qualia) that we can identify its essential intrinsic features in experience. If physicalism is true, that part of our conception is untrue of our minds. So there is a big intuitive cost in accepting physicalism. I accept it nonetheless.

For all that dualism gains converts, there's not much sign of it converting the majority. Explaining the causal interaction between the physical and the nonphysical taxes our philosophical resources. Epiphenomenalism is unacceptable to many on familiar grounds. Perhaps, above all, it is the argument from dualistic properties as "nomological danglers" in Jack Smart's phrase (Smart, 1959) that is the barrier to its widespread acceptance. We have come to accept that a coherent picture of the world, united by an account of its fundamental properties and the laws of nature, is both what we want and what the Occamist method that has served us so well in the natural sciences mandates. To accept dualism is to accept things beyond the ken of our best methodology. It is to accept a realm of substances or properties that are scientifically unacceptable.

Whenever there are jointly inconsistent views, each of which has much appeal, the temptation to have your cake and eat it too arises. The temptation has been especially strong in the case of dualism and physicalism about consciousness. A successful reconciliation of what is desirable about each would be a major achievement.

That is the achievement that ontological emergentists like to think that they have managed. But exactly what emergence is supposed to be has never been clear, and many doctrines have gone by that rubric.

One strategy for a piece in a collection like this would be to exhaustively enumerate every doctrine about consciousness that has been described as emergent, and argue against it. Instead I will do something close: I'll try to see what the *point* of labeling a position an emergent one is, and evaluate emergentist views about consciousness according to whether they both are plausible and meet the standard of doing what you need to do to fulfill the purpose of an (ontologically) emergentist view. That is, that they coherently fill a middle ground that reconciles in a particular way the appealing features of both physicalism and dualism. I'll conclude that nothing I know of meets both these desiderata. If I'm right we should set aside ontologically emergent views about consciousness, for they are either incoherent, or they are straightforwardly dualist or physicalist pictures misleadingly described.

The Emergentist Idea

A common strand to much emergentism is the intuitive idea that whatever is emergent *emerges from* the base. So emergentism about consciousness is the idea that consciousness emerges from the physical base. Whatever that exactly means, it is the part that is meant to give you most of what it desirable about physicalism – it attacks the nomological dangler argument. For it is the operations of the laws of nature on the fundamental properties and substances that consciousness emerges from.

On the other hand, what is supposed to give us the benefit of dualism is that the emergent is *novel*. Something genuinely new is what emerges: either new properties (in the usual way of understanding emergentism) or new substances. But this novelty is one that is tightly integrated with the physical. Another feature that adds to the idea that the best of the physical is being preserved here is that while consciousness is genuinely novel, the ingredients are not. It emerges from a physicalistically kosher base. So we get a marvelous trick: nothing *fundamental* is nonphysical, but consciousness is genuinely novel, and nonphysical, even though it is nomologically tied to the physical base. This is the standard I'll be holding emergentism to, and which I doubt it can meet.

Some Non-Starters

Some doctrines called emergentism don't really even aim to meet this standard. In particular, there is a range of essentially epistemological positions that are labeled as emergent. According to some views, emergence is the view that we cannot explain macroscopic laws or properties in terms of fundamental physical ones. To the extent that explanation is an epistemological notion, or at least a psychological one, this may well be true, but has no bearing on the ontological issue. If it is merely a question of the limitations of human thought, or even of finite thought, then this (if it is

David Braddon-Mitchell

true) provides an important typing of levels of analysis of the natural world on epistemological grounds, but need not detain us much further.

It is even plausible that there are certain kinds of macroscopic patterns that cannot in principle be predicted from the physical base. Extreme chaotic systems, for example, display a sensitivity to the accuracy of measurement of initial conditions, which means that, in effect, no matter how accurately we measure them, if there is any error in the measurement, then massive differences in the macroscopic patterns that emerge will be found. Since there is no way in principle to get zero error, there is no way in principle to get prediction of macroscopic patterns from this base. But this is all on the assumption that the underlying dynamical equations that govern the base are deterministic, and their actual values do determine the patterns. It doesn't give us any additional reason to hold that the macroscopic is ontologically novel, for the difficulty is with prediction, not determination.

All of this can be accepted while setting aside the issue of ontological emergentism: for it is consistent with failure of prediction or explanation that we are talking about a single ontology, with epistemological barriers between moving from one level of description of the ontology to another. Theoretical biologists almost routinely talk of emergent process, patterns, properties, and descriptions – and none of that commits them to a genuinely ontological emergence (though of course some may hold that it exists).

Anodyne Novelty

There is, though, another sense of novelty that is not epistemological, but is also not what we are looking for, and so we should get it out of the way immediately. In one sense of "novel" there are certainly many properties that are what we might call "emergent," and are novel in the sense of coming to be instantiated when physical systems are organized in certain ways. These, then, are properties that were not instantiated before, and that are clearly in *some* sense nonphysical.

Suppose that no sphere has been created in the history of some physical world. And then, physical substances come together in such a manner that, in three dimensions, they are all equidistant from some point. We now have the first sphere, and the property of sphericality is instantiated for the first time. So in one sense the property is novel. It is not even clear that in some good sense of "physical" it is a physical property. The sphere itself is physical, but what of the property? Whatever else a property is, it is a respect in which things can resemble each other. Whenever there is a distinctive pattern, there is the property of instantiating that pattern. Now let us suppose that there are logically possible worlds in which there are only non-physical substances. And let us suppose that some of these are arranged so that, spatially or in some other way that maps onto the geometry of spheres, some of these nonphysical substances are arranged in a more or less dense way such that they are all equidistant from some point. We thus have a sphere in this nonphysical world. So being spherical is a property that can be instantiated in a nonphysical world. In some sense then, it can't be called a physical property. Nonetheless this is an anodyne sense of nonphysical. Geometrical and mathematical properties are ones we need to do the very natural sciences that define the physical properties, and their presence is no threat to physicalism, unless construed in a rabid way.

This is the very same sense in which functionalists about the mind who hold that physicalism is contingently true admit that functional properties are not physical properties. There are worlds that contain nonphysical substances. What these worlds are like depends, of course, on your account of what it takes for a property to be physical. If you have one of the accounts according to which to be a physical basic property is to be one of the properties in the completed science of the actual world, or one suitably similar, then one of these nonphysical worlds will simply be one where the fundamental properties are all or mainly alien to the actual world. But whatever the account is, so long as the nonphysical substances (or property instances) in a world are able to stand in causal relations (something dualists usually imagine that they can) then there exists a world in which these nonphysical substances stand in the right causal relations to each other so as to play the roles specified in your favorite functionalist theory. In which case, we have in those worlds whatever mental states are specified by that favorite functionalist theory. So there is a pattern of mental similarity, which holds between worlds that are fundamentally entirely physical and entirely nonphysical. In some sense or other, mental properties are not physical properties. But this is the very same sense as that in which geometrical properties are not physical properties.

None of this should be news, but I rehearse it to emphasize one sense of emergence that cannot be the interesting halfway house between physicalism and dualism. The sense in which the properties of both being a sphere and being a pain are novel just because they are patterns that can be instantiated physically and nonphysically is surely not what this interesting halfway house amounts to. It is a point that the most diehard physicalist should accept. Exactly what to say about the relation that has to obtain between the fundamental physical properties and the macroscopic properties in a world for physicalism to obtain in it is outside the scope of this paper – but the idea that it is a kind of a priori metaphysical entailment (see Jackson, A PRIORI PHYSICALISM, and Jackson, forthcoming) is the one that most persuades me.

The Role of Ontological Emergence

So what makes for ontological emergence, or how can we capture the idea that emergent properties are genuinely novel or distinct, and yet still keep some distance between emergent and traditional dualism? I think the idea that underlies most of the proposals, including Broad's (1925) and those that vary greatly in detail from his, is that while the emergent properties or substances are genuinely novel, they come out of a base of fundamental ontology that is naturalistic. This is how we genuflect to naturalism, while holding a kind of dualism about consciousness. But we can get a little more precise without descending to the detail of a particular proposal. The idea is that fundamental ontology is physicalist, but the physical produces nonphysical consciousness (where nonphysical is meant in some stronger sense than the anodyne sense of the previous section). So to make it into a recipe: "no fundamental non-physical ontology, but genuinely distinct nonphysical products of the fundamental

David Braddon-Mitchell

ontology." In the case of consciousness, if the claim that consciousness is produced by the physical is true, there will be a kind of supervenience of consciousness on the physical, but not a supervenience that exists in virtue of reducibility (Bacon, 1986).

How to Implement the Role of Emergence

So the general idea of ontological emergence will be that consciousness supervenes on the physical. But what is the domain of this supervenience, and what explains it? A very natural proposal, and one that is in keeping with the role of emergence as a kind of dualism for those who want integration with the laws of nature, is to suppose that the supervenience is limited to the nomologically possible worlds: those ways things could be that share the actual laws of nature. So there are ways things could be in which the fundamental physical properties are instantiated just as they are in the actual world, but in which there fails to be any consciousness. This proposal has the merit of making it very clear how consciousness is ontologically distinct from the distribution of physical properties, for their correlation is logically contingent. Since there are physical duplicates of the actual world that fail to be consciousness duplicates, we can be sure that the consciousness is a distinct property (or substance) from the matrix of instantiated physical properties that give rise to it actually.

But why does consciousness arise in the actual world? We need to know what the difference is between the worlds in which it fails to arise from the same physical components, and the worlds in which it does.

The standard answer is the laws of nature. It is something about the actual laws of nature that guarantees the emergence of consciousness. Now presumably, on a contingent account of laws of nature,[2] there are worlds that at least share the same distribution of physical properties at a time but fail to share our laws of nature. Of course that difference in laws must show up in some way. If the world shares the distribution of properties at a time, the difference in laws might show up in different distributions of properties in the past or future. If the pattern of property instantiation is identical across all time, the difference might show up in different counterfactuals. These worlds have different laws of nature from ours in a very straightforward sense, and if they were the only ones we had to consider, then we would be able to explain the emergence of consciousness by our laws of nature. We could then point to obvious differences in the laws that are present in those worlds that share chunks of distributions of physical properties (or all the distributions but different counterfactuals about them) to explain the lack of consciousness in some of them.

But such worlds are not the only ones we must consider. If emergent consciousness is genuinely distinct from its productive base, then presumably there are logically possible worlds that share *throughout time* the distribution of physical property instances, and share all the counterfactuals about them, but in addition lack the emergent properties.

Here things begin to depend on your account of the physical laws of nature. But certainly on Humean accounts, Ramsey–Carnap–Lewis accounts, and others that take into account counterfactuals, these worlds share the very same *physical* laws of nature as the actual world. So it cannot be the laws of nature that explain the supervenience of consciousness on the physical in the actual world.

The solution is of course straightforward, but not good news for the spirit of emergentism. The solution is to add psychophysical laws to the actual world, and explain the lack of consciousness in other physically identical worlds to different or absent psychophysical laws in those worlds. The reason this is not good news for the spirit of emergentism is that what was most appealing about the nomological supervenience picture is lost. The appeal was that while there was nothing fundamentally nonphysical in the actual world, the laws of nature together with the distribution of physical properties produced nonphysical consciousness. But now we have added something fundamental to the actual world: basic psychophysical laws. The emergentist picture has become a brand of traditional dualism. Perhaps there are no fundamental substances of a nonphysical kind in the world, but there certainly are laws with a nonphysical component (and presumably there are nonphysical properties as well, since they must appear as *relata* in the psychophysical laws).

There is a move that can be made here by the emergentist. That is to deny that the world that contains the same physical property distribution and counterfactuals does indeed contain the very same physical laws as our world. The emergentist might insist that the physical laws in the actual world are the very laws that produce ontologically emergent consciousness; they cannot be separated into a set of physical laws and psychophysical laws.

It is hard, though, to know what this claim amounts to. It will certainly require a different conception of laws of nature to the mainstream ones. Exactly what is it in metaphysics that makes for the distinction between, on the one hand, a world that contains a set of physical laws of the kind ours does, and a set of psychophysical laws that produce emergent consciousness, and, on the other, a world with a "unified" set of laws that explains both the distribution of physical properties and emergent consciousness? There is the threat of this amounting to no more than a terminological distinction.

In any case it isn't clear that it helps. For we still have something fundamental in the actual world: a big set of integrated psychophysical causal laws that puts us squarely in the terrain of traditional dualism. The nonphysical properties are present as *relata* in laws.[3] Consciousness doesn't emerge; the property was latent in the laws that govern it.

More than Merely Nomological Supervenience

One way to parry the charge of mere terminological maneuvering that was levied against the integrated laws is to give bite to the distinctness of the two sets of laws v. one set of laws claim. And one way to do that is to deny that there can be two logically separable sets of laws. The reason, this response would run, that we don't have to address the question of what to say about worlds that are physical duplicates (property for property and counterfactual) of ours that lack emergent consciousness is that there are no such worlds.

David Braddon-Mitchell

Of course it had better not be that there are no such worlds because consciousness is just reducible to the physical. It had better be because of the laws of nature.

There is a way for the emergentist to achieve this. So far I have been assuming a version of quidditism[4] – the view that there is trans-world identity of properties – according to which the nature of the properties is intrinsic, and the nomic profiles of the properties is fixed by the laws of nature in which they feature from world to world. On such a view, we can, for example, suppose that there is a world in which electrons have slightly less mass, or in which the Higgs field has a different effect on inflation.

But there is an alternative view: the so-called necessitarian view of laws[5] in which properties have their nomic profiles essentially. On this view if an electron enters into certain laws actually, then they do so necessarily. So all possible instances of the property of being an electron enter into those laws, and so on for all the basic properties. Now on this view, if actually the physical properties play a role in producing emergent consciousness, then they do so necessarily. So if the physical properties instanced in the actual world enter into laws that guarantee the production of emergent consciousness, they do so in every possible world. There will, therefore, be no world in which we find the same pattern of distribution of physical properties or substances, but which lacks emergent consciousness. Thus the embarrassment of being able to distinguish the genuinely physical laws from the psychophysical laws will not arise. Necessitarianism comes in different flavors, however, and the consequences for an account of consciousness as ontologically emergent vary with them.

Analytic Necessitarianism

One version of necessitarianism admits that a kind of weak quidditism is true: there is an intrinsic component to the nature of property instances. But it denies that this component exhausts what it is to be a physical property. The physical properties are instead identified by the conjunction of these intrinsic natures and their nomic roles. On the other hand, according to this version, there is no logical necessity connecting the intrinsic natures with their nomic roles. On this view there is no world that contains the same distribution of physical property instances as our world but that fails to contain emergent consciousness. This is because in order to make the claim that some world contains exactly the same property instances as ours, they must play the same nomic roles, and among those roles is the production of emergent consciousness.

There are, however, worlds that fail to contain the same physical property instances as our world, but nonetheless exhibit the same pattern of instancing of intrinsic natures, and which fails to count as containing the same physical property instances only because they fail to exhibit the same nomic profile. Some of these worlds will contain the very same pattern of intrinsic natures, but different counterfactuals will be true of the pattern.[6] Others may contain the same pattern of intrinsic natures, and the same pattern of counterfactuals about the intrinsic natures, but differ in the pattern of the extra ontologically emergent properties that our world possesses.

Consider the extreme case: the world that contains the same pattern of intrinsic natures as ours, but lacks the consciousness properties entirely. Such a world is of course no counterexample on this view to the claim that it is a necessary truth that the consciousness properties are produced by this distribution of physical properties. This is because the intrinsic natures on this view do not exhaust what it is to be an instance of a physical property. But it seems that this is, again, more or less a terminological feature. The question arises as to what makes the actual world differ from the world that contains exactly the same intrinsic natures, but in virtue of the different nomic profiles, different physical properties. What do we need to add to the pattern of intrinsic properties to upgrade them to the same full-fledged physical properties? Something metaphysically very much like a set of fundamental psychophysical laws that guarantee the production of emergent consciousness.

The concern, then, is that this view does not seem to achieve the desideratum of having no fundamental components of ontology that are nonphysical in nature. This is perhaps because it is not clear that the view differs in a substantial way from the picture that has fundamental physical laws, and sets of physical-physical laws, as well as psychophysical laws. For it is hard to see that there is more to this proposal than using the *label* "fundamental physical properties" for the conjunction of the actual intrinsic properties when they play their actual nomic roles.

An Ontology of Powers

That is not, of course, the only necessitarian approach that can be taken, and that would make it a necessary truth that physical duplicates of the actual world would be psychological duplicates. Some deny that there are any intrinsic or categorical natures, and have an ontology only of powers. In which case, property instances become bundles of powers. In this case physical properties could be re-identified by their nomic roles, but this would be a much better motivated idea than in the previous proposal, since there are no intrinsic natures to do the job.

In this picture, things might look better for the emergentist, for it seems at least coherent that the fundamental things identified in the physical sciences – the fundamental particles or fields or strings or whatever they turn out to be – are bundles of powers, some of which are powers to produce emergent consciousness. The bundles then get to count as fundamental and physical, and the bundles turn out to be necessarily consciousness-involving. So the fundamental things are just the physical power-bundles, and they necessarily produce consciousness.

But there are a number of difficulties with this proposal. For one, the traditional problem with the binding of bundles that appears in bundle theories arises with a special force here. Let us suppose that there is some successful account of how the bundles are actually co-instantiated. There does not seem to be any logical constraint on there being worlds that contain all and only the powers that correspond to the purely physical roles that the actual bundles of powers play. If these bundles constitute part of the bundle of the actual bundle of powers, then the remainder of the actual bundle must be special, fundamental psychophysical powers. So the view won't pass the no fundamental nonphysical component test for ontological emergentism. If this is not the case, we must somehow be able to deny that the world that contains only the purely physical powers contains the same bundle as the hypothetical purely physical component of the actual bundle. But since this is an ontology of powers, there is nothing to their identity or distinctness other than their roles, so this will be hard to do.

There is a general problem for ontologies that posit only powers that seems to be of particular concern when these ontologies are used as a base for ontologically emergent conceptions of consciousness. In addition to the binding problem (solved if there is something that possesses the powers) there is also the issue of what it is that the powers are supposed to affect. Suppose that in general this is solved, and somehow it is fine for powers to affect only each other. An emergentist view seems to require that something comes out of the base. It requires that the consciousness properties or substances are novel in some strong sense, and that they are brought into being by the operation of natural law. But if natural law is a bundle of powers to affect things, prima facie there is a worry if the nonphysical realm is not already there to be affected. Perhaps there are special creative powers. But in a pure ontology of powers, all that could be created is yet more powers. So the difference between an emergentist inter-actionist and a physicalist picture would be that in the physicalist picture there are physicalist powers that affect other physical powers; in the emergentist picture the physical powers will bring about nonphysical powers that then affect the same physi-cal powers that would have been directly affected by the physical powers in the physicalist pictures. In this conception the emergentist layer seems more like an idle cog even than traditional substance dualism with overdetermination. If there were some nonphysical categorical substances, then things might proceed this way. First, the physical powers exert their influence on the nonphysical substances. Then the nonphysical substances exert powers back on the physical realm. This would be dis-tinguished from the physical powers directly affecting the physical realm by the change in the categorical nature of the nonphysical substance. But if the only non-physical element is nonphysical powers, and these powers influence the physical in a way that is isomorphic to the physical influencing the physical, then it is difficult to see what basis we have for believing in the psychophysical powers. For they make no difference to what happens, and powers, unlike categorical natures, are just indi-viduated by tendencies to make things happen.

Necessitarianism with Strong Necessity

The final way to get a necessitarian result is to accept that there are categorical physi-cal natures, but insist that the connection between then and the laws they enter in is (logically) necessary. So it's not just a restricted realm of nomologically possible worlds in which the actual physical natures play the roles they actually do. The natures play these roles in all the worlds in which they are instantiated. (The view could be a strong version in which it is logically impossible for there to be any natures other than the physical ones that are actually instantiated, and thus in no sense could there be counter-nomic worlds. Alternatively it could come in a more moderate version that accepts counter-nomic possible worlds, but only if the properties connected by the laws are so-called alien properties, properties not instantiated in the actual world.)

So let's see how the view looks in this version. There are actual physical natures, and they produce as a matter of natural law emergent consciousness when they are organized in various ways, of which our physical structure is a very salient example. The benefit of emergence (as I am characterizing it) over traditional dualism is supposed to be that there is no *fundamental* nonphysical stuff or properties required, even though novel properties and substances are produced. In this picture the fundamental substances and properties are purely physical. The laws that guarantee the production of the novel conscious states, because they are logically necessary, cannot be distinguished from the mundane physical laws, since they are necessarily coextensive. Remember every nomic role that is played by an actual substance or property is played necessarily on these necessitarian views. So by accepting that there is no necessary connection between distinct laws, we get to claim that the psychophysical laws are not distinct from the physical laws. Then we have the novel conscious states produced by the purely physical property instances or substances together with the physical laws. So we get a result consistent with our slogan: no fundamental nonphysical substances or laws, but with novelty emerging.

But unfortunately, it won't work. For consider the following argument by dilemma. Suppose that we accept (as I do) the Humean dictate that there are no necessary connections between distinct existences. I accept it because I take it to be analytic. A lot of talk is bandied about in philosophy about distinct and non-distinct properties, and failure of necessary coextension seems to me to be what captures the very idea of distinctness.[7] In any case suppose it is true. Then we get the desirable result for the emergentist that there are no fundamental nonphysical laws. This is because according to the Humean dictate, things are distinct only if logically distinct. But the psychophysical laws necessarily co-vary with the fundamental physical laws, so they cannot be distinct from them.

The bad news for the emergentist, though, is that allegedly emergent consciousness that is produced does not get to be novel in the right way! For these allegedly emergent conscious states will, with logical necessity, correlate with the compounds of physical states that produce them. And given the Humean doctrine that there are no necessary connections between distinct existences, they too are not distinct from their physical correlates. The laws are necessary, so whenever in some world things are the way they are actually and there is actually consciousness, so is there consciousness in that world. Perhaps this is not really surprising; if the laws are not really distinct from the physical laws, we might expect that they don't have what it takes to produce distinct substances or properties.

Now let me turn to the second half of the argument by dilemma. Suppose that there can be necessary connections between distinct existences. In this case, we can't rule out the possibility that the allegedly emergent conscious states are distinct from the physical states that give rise to them – we just have to suppose that they are primitively distinct. But then, we have lost our guarantee that the psychophysical laws and the physical-physical laws are not ontologically distinct! For the fact that the fundamental physical natures enter into the same purely physical relations and psychophysical relations in every possible world could easily be just another case of

David Braddon-Mitchell

distinct existences (in this case laws) necessarily connected. And since what they produce are distinct existences, and there are at least conceptually possible worlds that contain only the physical-physical laws, the claims of emergentism on this view seem to rest on a bald claim about the non-distinctness of the laws coupled with the distinctness of the produced states, with no obvious way to settle what this means, or how to determine if it is true.

Other Roles for Ontological Emergence

Before concluding, I'll look at two other ways we might make a distinction between traditional dualism and ontological emergentism about consciousness. The first of these is to note that, supposing that there are fundamental psychophysical laws that determine what novel properties are produced, we might limit the domain of the dualistic to all and only that which is produced by these laws. Further we might limit those laws to producing only emergent consciousness that could be predicted by observing the purely physical configuration of the world. This then would guarantee a supervenience of emergent consciousness on the physical, even though it is explained by there being at least partly nonphysical basic psychophysical laws.

This would amount to a kind of minimal dualism. It would be a kind of dualism that denied that there were any nonphysical substances or properties in the world prior to the correct configuration of physical properties and substances. It would also deny that the realm of consciousness ever had any effects on other aspects of consciousness that had no impact on the physical or were impacted by the physical. There would be no psycho-psychological laws, as it were, that were not mirrored by common causes in the physical.

There is a certain ontological economy in such a view, even though I don't think it fully meets what I've been describing as the point of an emergentist view – since it depends on fundamental nonphysical components. But worse, I think it is not well motivated. If one believes in psychophysical laws that are ontologically distinct from the physical laws, then we have admitted into consideration a nonphysical realm that may or may not have some variation independently of the physical. We have good reason to believe empirically in *rough* supervenience of the psychological on the physical. We know that dramatic psychological changes correlate with changes in brain activity, and so on. The reason to believe that this supervenience is *complete* is that a good explanation of the rough supervenience is physicalism, which itself entails complete supervenience. If there were a kind of genuine emergentism that worked, where the purely physical properties and laws produced the nonphysical, that too would explain the rough supervenience, and give us a reason to believe that it was complete. But if we have some fundamental nonphysical elements in the laws, then whether the rough supervenience is complete is an empirical matter (or perhaps a phenomenological one) that should not be settled by building it into the theory.

One last attempt at an ontologically emergent account of consciousness: some have suggested (Stoljar, 2001) that we might suppose that the intrinsic nature of physical things has a kind of proto-psychological nature. The idea is that the natural sciences tell us only the causal roles of what is fundamental in the universe (Lewis, 1995).

There is in addition the nature of the things that play those roles. One account of consciousness is that the aggregate intrinsic nature that comprises our brains is what consciousness is. Some think of this as a kind of physicalism (Stoljar calls such properties 0-physical). Others think of it as a kind of dualism – these natures are proto-conscious nonphysical properties possessed by the bearers of the physical properties. Probably the debate is terminological. But if good philosophers can't decide if a view is a species of dualism or of physicalism, then perhaps that is a sign that it's the halfway house we have been looking for: emergentism.

I think not. Whether this view is physicalist or dualist, it does not involve the production of anything ontologically novel by the recombination of the basic components. It is a fully reductive view: Consciousness is nothing over and above the combination of the intrinsic natures that were there to begin with, whether they were physical or nonphysical.

Conclusion

So I don't think there is a role for ontological emergence. One reason to add to the more substantive ones is that emergence as a term is pretty much co-opted by the special sciences to refer to those patterns and laws that are epistemologically inaccessible from fundamental science. So to use it in an ontological way creates confusion. However, the substantive reasons seem to me to be quite compelling. The emergentist wanted to be a dualist while somehow respecting the primacy of the physical sciences. That can't be done, I've argued. A view according to which there are strongly novel nonphysical states or properties requires the strongly non-physical to appear in the fundamental properties or laws. That is not a reason to suppose that dualism must be false. It is just to point out that dualism really is at odds with the picture that says that the physical sciences are roughly right about what there fundamentally is. Dualists would be better to admit that, and stop talking about emergence, much as my fellow physicalists would be better off admitting that there are some fundamentally counterintuitive elements to physicalism, even if it's worth paying that price.

Acknowledgments

Thanks to Denis Robinson, Frank Jackson, and Kristie Miller for valuable comments and suggestions.

Notes

1 The source of the current popularity of the Zombie arguments is Chalmers (1996). Keith Campbell (1970) also has a nice version of the argument. The term seems to enter philosophy via Kirk (1974).
2 Contingent v. necessitarian laws.

3   According to some views, uninstantiated properties cannot exist in a world (see, e.g., Armstrong, 1989). Of course we are discussing here cases where such properties become instantiated, but there were laws about them prior to their instantiation. But it is hard to see why this case should be treated differently from cases where the properties are never instantiated for purely contingent reasons but feature in laws.

4   See Lewis (forthcoming).

5   Examples include Swoyer (1982), Shoemaker (1998).

6   Except, of course, on radically Humean views that make the counterfactuals depend on the actual pattern.

7   If I can preempt the obvious response, of course plenty of distinct *concepts* apply to all and only the same things in every possible world, but that's another matter.

References

Armstrong, D. M. (1989). *Universals: An Opinionated Introduction.* Boulder: Westview.

Bacon, J. (1986). Supervenience, necessary coextension, and reducibility. *Philosophical Studies,* 49, 163–76.

Broad, C. D. (1925). *The Mind and Its Place in Nature.* London: Routledge & Kegan Paul.

Campbell, K. (1970). *Body and Mind.* New York: Doubleday.

Chalmers, D. (1996). *The Conscious Mind.* New York: Oxford University Press.

Jackson, F. (1982). Epiphenomenal qualia. *Philosophical Quarterly,* 32, 127–36.

— (1986). What Mary didn't know. *Journal of Philosophy,* 83, 291–5.

— (forthcoming). On ensuring that physicalism is not a dual attribute theory in sheep's clothing. *Philosophical Studies.*

Kirk, R. (1974). Zombies versus materialists. *Proceedings of the Aristotelian Society,* 48 (suppl.), 135–52.

Lewis, D. (1995). Should a materialist believe in qualia? *Australasian Journal of Philosophy,* 73, 140–4.

— (forthcoming). Ramseyan humility. In D. Braddon-Mitchell and R. Nola (eds.), *Naturalism and Analysis.* Cambridge, MA: MIT Press.

Shoemaker, S. (1998). Causal and metaphysical necessity. *Pacific Philosophical Quarterly,* 79, 59–77.

Smart, J. J. C. (1959). Sensations and brain processes. *Philosophical Review,* 68, 141–56.

Stoljar, D. (2001). Two conceptions of the physical. *Philosophy and Phenomenological Research,* 62, 253–81.

Swoyer, C. (1982). The nature of natural laws. *Australasian Journal of Philosophy,* 60, 203–23.

ARE PHENOMENAL CHARACTERS AND INTENTIONAL CONTENTS OF EXPERIENCES IDENTICAL?

New Troubles for the Qualia Freak

Michael Tye

The phenomenal character of an experience is what it is like subjectively to undergo the experience. Experiences vary in their phenomenal character, in what it is like to undergo them. Think, for example of the subjective differences between feeling a burning pain in a toe, experiencing an itch in an arm, smelling rotten eggs, tasting Marmite, having a visual experience of bright purple, running one's fingers over rough sandpaper, feeling hungry, experiencing anger, feeling elated. Insofar as what it is like to undergo each of these experiences is different, their phenomenal character is different.

Experiences not only have phenomenal character. In many cases, it is uncontroversial that they also carry information, that they tell us things about ourselves or the world around us. Visual experiences purport to inform us as to the colors and shapes of things in our environments; pain experiences signal bodily damage. The informational aspect of experiences is something that many philosophers suppose is entirely separable from their phenomenal character, as indeed is anything external to the experience itself. On this view, what matters to the phenomenal "feel" of an experience is only how it is intrinsically. Duplicate the causal relations the experience stands in, the cognitive responses the experience generates, the informational links between the experience and other things outside it, and you need not thereby have duplicated the experience. It is in principle possible that all these external things are present and yet there is no internal state with phenomenal character at all. This is the so-called absent qualia hypothesis (Block, 1980).

Another way to help explain the notion of phenomenal character is to reflect on the famous inverted spectrum hypothesis – the hypothesis, that is, that what it is like for you when you see red things is the same as what it is like for me when I see green things and vice-versa, with corresponding inversions for the other color experiences, even though you and I function in the same ways in color tests and in our everyday behavior toward colored things (Shoemaker, 1975). Whether or not this hypothesis is true, it can be used to focus our attention on the phenomenal character of an experience just as the description "the man drinking champagne" can be used to single out a person who in actual fact is female and drinking water (Donnellan, 1966).

A further way to fix the referent of the term "phenomenal character" is to say that it is what gives rise to the explanatory gap (Levine, 1983). Tell me everything you like about what goes on physically and functionally in someone who is experiencing red and, it seems, you still won't have told me what it is *like* to experience red. For even after I have all the relevant physical and functional information, I can still intelligibly ask, "Why do those physical and functional goings-on generate *that* phenomenal character (the phenomenal character of the experience of red)? Why *couldn't* another phenomenal character be present?"

Reflections of the above sort have tended to foster a picture of the basic phenomenal "feels" (or qualia) as irreducibly nonphysical properties of experiences with no hidden nature – simple, nonrepresentational properties that are intrinsic to experiences. Since the usual view of experiences has been that they are wholly internal states, a widely accepted correlative thesis has been that of qualia internalism: necessarily, intrinsic duplicates do not differ with respect to their qualia. I shall call philosophers who think of phenomenal character in this way "unrepentant qualia freaks." It is these philosophers and their brethren who are my target in this essay.

My aim is to create trouble for each component of the view of the unrepentant qualia freak and to do so with largely new arguments. These arguments will point us toward what is by now a reasonably familiar conclusion, however, namely that the phenomenal character of an experience is one and the same as a certain sort of representational (or intentional) content the experience has.

I begin with a new argument against phenomenal dualism. I then argue against the view that the phenomenal character of an experience is, by its nature, an intrinsic property. Section 3 is devoted to attacking the view that phenomenal character is nonrepresentational. In sections 4 and 5, a thought experiment is developed in support of phenomenal externalism. Section 6 draws some general conclusions about qualia and phenomenal character.

1 Against Phenomenal Dualism

Zombies have played a prominent role in some recent arguments for dualism with respect to phenomenal character (e.g., Chalmers, 1996). The zombie is a dangerous creature, however. As we are about to see, *partial* zombies can be used to mount an argument against phenomenal dualism.

Let me begin by distinguishing between the specific phenomenal character of a particular experience, the specific phenomenal character of my knee pain now, for example, and phenomenal character as a feature common to all experiences. The latter is the property of phenomenality or phenomenal consciousness, assuming that phenomenal character is properly classifiable as a property at all. It is shared by my knee pain, auntie's itch, NN's experience of bright red, and so on. The unrepentant qualia freak holds that the property of phenomenality is a simple, irreducibly nonphysical property, as is each basic individual quale (the overall phenomenal character of each experience being a compound of such properties).

Suppose that the qualia freak is right: phenomenality is indeed a simple, irreducibly nonphysical property. Then connections between the physical and phenomenality take the form of laws that fail to obtain in some metaphysically possible worlds.[1] Accordingly, there are metaphysically possible worlds in which I have a microphysical duplicate and everything in any way physically connected to me presently and historically is physically the same as it is in the actual world (as are all the physical laws) but in which my duplicate has no phenomenal states at all. In this case, I have a full-fledged zombie replica.

Equally, however, if phenomenality is a simple, irreducibly nonphysical property, then there are metaphysically possible worlds in which I have a microphysical duplicate and everything in any way physically connected to me presently and historically is the same (as again are all the physical laws) but in which my duplicate is without phenomenal states on *some* (but not all) of the occasions on which I have them. Here I have a partial zombie replica.[2]

Consider then my lunchtime zombie replica. This being is a microphysical duplicate of me who duplicates my phenomenal states in the mornings and in the afternoons but for whom at exactly midday everyday he becomes a zombie for a short period of time. Suppose that my lunchtime zombie replica is situated physically as in the general partial zombie case above. Suppose further that at noon on Tuesday, I am drinking some beer and commenting to my companion on the fine taste of Newcastle brown ale. In these circumstances, for me, there is no sudden dramatic change in my taste experience at noon. For my zombie replica, there is such a dramatic change, however. His taste experience suddenly disappears altogether.

Now one standard view on phenomenal change is that it is always manifest to its subject. For example, Sydney Shoemaker (1998) has remarked that it is constitutive of the notion of phenomenal character that one does have introspective sensitivity to changes in it, whatever the source of the changes" (p. 667). This view is not one that would be universally accepted, however. Can one really *always* tell such changes? What if one is extremely tired and the difference is very small? What if the difference comes about gradually? What if the change is between the phenomenal character of my mental state now and the phenomenal character of my mental state at the same time yesterday? In this case, the change is one to which I have no *introspective* sensitivity, only sensitivity through memory, and memory may go astray.

One more cautious claim, similar in spirit to that of Shoemaker, which sidesteps these difficulties is made by Ned Block in a discussion of some of my own earlier views concerning his Inverted Earth example (1990). Block comments:

> NC "it is a necessary feature of phenomenal character that if a change in it is big enough and happens fast enough, we can notice it." (1998, p. 668)

(NC) seems to me very plausible, so long as the subject has the general ability to introspect and her cognitive mechanisms are operating normally.[3] Given (NC), my zombie replica must be *able* to notice the sudden change in phenomenal character (that is, its total disappearance) at noon. But if he and I are both paying careful attention to the way the beer tastes, then if he is able to notice the change in taste, he will notice it. Why, then, does he behave just as I do? Why does he continue to sip his beer and make the very same remarks about taste as me? Why are his behavioral dispositions the same? Surely, given the global microphysical duplication, there *cannot* be a difference in cognitive abilities as striking as the one being supposed to obtain here between myself and my replica. It seems, then, that I cannot have a lunchtime zombie replica in exactly the same physical setting. But if this is not metaphysically possible then the thesis that phenomenality is a simple, irreducibly nonphysical property is in trouble.

The conclusion we have reached thus far leads to another. Suppose that individual qualia are both simple and irreducibly nonphysical. Then if phenomenality is not a simple, irreducibly nonphysical property, as I have argued, it cannot be metaphysically necessary that, for any given individual quale *Q*, whenever *Q* is tokened, phenomenality is tokened. Clearly, however, this *is* metaphysically necessary: there is no metaphysically possible world in which someone feels pain, for example, without feeling anything at all. So, the claim that the basic, individual qualia are simple, irreducibly nonphysical properties is in trouble too.

Opposition to dualism about phenomenal character has been urged by many philosophers, typically by appeal to the causal efficacy of phenomenal character and the hypothesis that there are no nonphysical causes of physical goings-on. I am in full agreement with the causal considerations that lead us to reject dualism for phenomenal character. What is striking about the present argument is that it appeals to a case very similar to that of the full-fledged zombie. In so doing, the present argument, unlike the causal one, hoists the unrepentant qualia freak on his own petard.

2 Why the Phenomenal Character of an Experience Is Not One of Its Intrinsic Properties

The term "intrinsic" sometimes means *essential*. Consider the visual experience I am undergoing now, as I view the page before me. It is not implausible to hold that this experience could not have had a different phenomenal character. If I had been having a visual experience with a different phenomenal character, then it would not have been *this* very experience.[4] If the phenomenal character of my experience is essential to it, then its phenomenal character is intrinsic to it in the above sense. There is another sense of "intrinsic," however, that contrasts with extrinsic, and it is over whether the phenomenal character of an experience is an intrinsic property in this sense that the qualia freak and I disagree.

The recent literature on the metaphysics of intrinsic properties shows that it is not easy to say in full detail just what an intrinsic property is in the second sense.[5] But, at least for our purposes, the following remarks will suffice.

> An intrinsic property is "a property a thing has (or lacks) regardless of what is going on outside of itself" (Yablo, 1990).
> "The intrinsic properties of something depend only on that thing; whereas the extrinsic properties may depend, wholly or partly, on something else" (Lewis, 1983).

| **Michael Tye**

"If some thing has an intrinsic property, then so does any perfect duplicate of that thing; whereas duplicates situated in different surroundings will differ in their extrinsic properties" (Lewis, 1983).

Thus, being a sister is extrinsic, as is being 3 feet from a table. By contrast, having mass is intrinsic as is being round (unless the shape of a thing can be made to vary with the curvature of the space in which it is located).

Given the above understanding of an intrinsic property, it follows that microphysical duplicates situated in different surroundings do not differ in their intrinsic, microphysical properties or in any other intrinsic properties that are metaphysically necessitated by their intrinsic, microphysical properties. Let us call all such intrinsic properties of a thing, be they microphysical or microphysically necessitated, "P-properties" of that thing. With these preliminaries out of the way, we are ready to turn to the main argument.

Consider a very simple *token* visual experience v – the experience of a flash of light at time t, say. I begin with something that is undeniably true:

1   If the phenomenal character of v is an intrinsic property of v then either it is a P-property of v or it is an intrinsic, irreducibly nonphysical property of v.

From the definition of an intrinsic property, we have

2   Microphysical duplicates situated in different surroundings do not differ in their P-properties.

Next, I assume token physicalism with respect to v:

3   v is a neural event (or state token).

(3) will have its opponents, of course, but qualia freaks need not be among them; for qualia freaks insist only on attribute dualism for phenomenal properties. So, it cannot be said that this premise begs the question against the qualia freak. And, of course, there are independent reasons to accept token physicalism anyway.

My final premise is as follows:

4   A microphysical duplicate of v in a Petri dish has no phenomenal character.

The reasoning behind (4) is simply this. Suppose that there is a microphysical duplicate of v in a Petri dish. This duplicate will be a certain connected structure of firing patterns in an appropriate group of neurons in the dish. However, there won't be any token experience in the Petri dish. For patently there is no subject in the dish to have an experience and experiences cannot exist unowned, any more than laughs can exist unlaughed. But if there is no experience in the dish then there is no entity in the dish having phenomenal character. And if this is true, then (4) follows.

One objection to this reasoning is that the relevant structure of neuron firings will be widely scattered, bringing in events from many different regions of the brain, and thus it will not obviously be the sort of event that could occur in a Petri dish (even an oversized one) or without a subject for that matter. This seems a very implausible view, however, for such a simple visual experience as that of a sudden flash of light. Further, it confuses the question of which token physical event is the token experience v with the question of which overall physical setting must be present for that physical event to have the phenomenal character of v or to be an experience at all.

Here is a parallel. Suppose I launch the rocket by pressing the red button at time t in mission control. My launching the rocket at t just is my pressing the button at t.[6] But what makes my pressing the button a rocket launching is something involving many other events. This is why a microphysical duplicate of my button pressing located against a different background need not be a rocket launching.

Correspondingly, it is certainly the case that without many brain events occurring at t, including activity in the brain stem, there would be no visual experience with the phenomenal character of v. But MEG scans reveal sudden localized activity in the mesial occipital cortex temporally coinciding with v. *This* token physical activity, the physicalist should say, is v. It has the right temporal length and it plays the right causal role. The other events form part of the background without which this activity would not have the psychological character of v.

One possible reply to this is to say that v is not an event at all, but rather a state token and that the best candidate brain state token for identification with v (or for constituting v) is a global one – that of the given brain's having such-and-such activity in the brain stem and so-and-so activity elsewhere, including activity in the mesial occipital cortex. This seems ad hoc, however. Why suppose that there is such a complex state token? To be sure, there is a relevant, very complex neural property the subject instantiates at t, that of having a brain with activity in regions X, Y, Z, etc. And there is also a corresponding complex neural property the brain instantiates. But what reason is there to hold that there is a state *token* that lasts just as long as v and has its causal powers? None that I can see.

From (1)–(4), we may conclude

5   The phenomenal character of v is not a P-property of v.

So,

6   If the phenomenal character of v is an intrinsic property of v, then it is irreducibly nonphysical.

However,

7   The phenomenal character of v is not irreducibly nonphysical.

This premise would be denied by the qualia freak; but it is not assumed here without any supporting argument (given the previous section's conclusion that phenomenal character is not a simple, irreducibly nonphysical property). Furthermore, it is independently plausible for the usual causal reasons. From (6) and (7), we reach the conclusion:

Michael Tye

8   The phenomenal character of v is not an intrinsic property of v.

So, phenomenal character is not, by its nature, an intrinsic property.

3 Why the Phenomenal Character of an Experience Is Not One of Its Nonrepresentational Properties

The many-property problem was a problem Frank Jackson (1975) raised some 30 years ago for adverbial theories of visual experience. In this section, I am going to raise a version of this problem for theories that take the phenomenal character of a visual experience to be a nonrepresentational property of the experience. I shall call the new problem "the phenomenal many property problem."[7]

Consider first the following claim:

9   What it is like for me to have an experience of a red square has something in common with what is it is like for me to have an experience of a red, round thing.

This surely is true. There is a phenomenal overlap between my experience of a red square and my experience of something red and round. Another obvious phenomeno-logical truth is the following:

10   What it is like for me to have an experience of a red square and a green triangle is different from what it is like for me to have an experience of a green square and a red triangle.

These claims are unproblematic for those who hold that the phenomenal character of an experience is a structured representational content the experience has into which the experienced qualities enter. In the case of (9), the representational content that there is a red square is a content into which the color, red, enters, as is the representational content that there is something red and round. In the case of (10), the representational content that there is a red square and a green triangle is a different content from the content that there is a green square and a red triangle, even though the two contents include the same color and shape properties.

(9) and (10) are also unproblematic for those who hold that the phenomenal character of an experience is the property of being a sensing of so-and-so sense-datum or sense-data. In the case of (9), the property of being a sensing of a red', square' sensum clearly includes the property of being a sensing of a red' sensum. I use the prime notation here to indicate a phenomenal property – for (9), phenomenal redness and phenomenal squareness. I might add that I do not myself have any clear grasp on what these phenomenal properties might be if they are not just plain old colors and shapes, but I take it that at least some of those who appeal to sense-data would want to distinguish between sensed properties of sensa and properties of material surfaces.

In the case of (10), the property of being a sensing of a red', square' sensum together with a green', triangular' sensum clearly is not the same as the property of being a sensing of a green', square' sensum together with a red', triangular' sensum.

There is, however, a *big* problem here for those who hold that the phenomenal character of an experience is a nonrepresentational property of the experience and who also eschew the sense-datum theory. To see this, consider my experience of a red square, and suppose that it has the nonrepresentational color and shape qualia, Q_r and Q_s. This handles (9) well enough, since my experience of something red will have the quale, Q_r, whatever other shape quale it has. But what now grounds the phenomenal difference in (10)? After all, each experience has the *same* color and shape qualia, Q_r, Q_s, Q_g, and Q_t.

A possible way out for the philosopher who holds that phenomenal character is nonrepresentational and who wishes to avoid the obvious dead-end provided by the sense-datum theory is to embrace the adverbial theory. On this view, or at any rate on any version of this view that does not try to eliminate token experiences altogether in favor of sensing properties of subjects, one who has an experience of red senses redly and one who senses redly undergoes an event having the property of being a red' sensing (just as one who walks slowly undergoes an event that has the property of being a slow walking). Unfortunately, the adverbial theory also encounters immediate difficulty. That was the point of the original many-property problem.

Consider again (10). Clearly, it won't do to try to account for the phenomenal character of the experience of a red square and a green triangle by appeal to the experience having the properties of being a red' sensing, being a square' sensing, being a green' sensing, and being a triangular' sensing. For these properties are possessed by the experience of a green square and a red triangle. So, (10) now comes out false.

Nor will it do to appeal to the experience having the property of being a red' and square' and green' and triangular' sensing in the case of the former experience, and to the property of being a green' and square' and red' and triangular' sensing in the case of the second experience. For the predicate modifiers here commute.

It seems, then, that on an adverbial account, in the case of (9) we need to appeal to the property of being a red-square-thing sensing, where this includes the property of a red-thing sensing. For (10), we need the properties of being a ((red-square-thing) and (green-triangular-thing)) sensing and being a ((green-square-thing) and (red-triangular-thing)) sensing.

This gets very unattractive and highly complicated. How exactly are we to understand such adverbial operators as (red-square-thing)-ly? What are the relevant detachment rules? And the complications created by the above example are just the tip of the iceberg.[8]

A final response the qualia freak might make is to propose that experiences have qualia in something like the way that a person who is touching a table has the property of touching a table. Here the person has the property via his having a part (his hand) that has that property. Correspondingly, an experience has the quale Q by its having a part that has that Q.

This does not help, however. To see this, consider again the experiences to which (10) adverts. On the above view, the experience of a red square and a green triangle has a part with the conjunctive property Q_r and Q_s, and a part with the conjunctive property Q_g and Q_t. Similarly, the experience of a green square and a red triangle has a part with the conjunctive property Q_g and Q_s, and a part with the conjunctive

Michael Tye

property Q_r and Q_t. The former experience, then, has the conjunctive property Q_r and Q_s, and also the conjunctive property Q_g and Q_t. The latter experience has the conjunctive properties Q_g and Q_s, and Q_r and Q_t. But an item has a conjunctive property just in case it has the properties that are its conjuncts. So, both experiences to which (10) adverts have the very same qualia.

Furthermore, qualia are now being attributed to parts of experiences as well as to experiences themselves, so that parts of experiences must now be counted as experiences. Thus, it will no longer be true that in undergoing an experience of a red square and a green triangle, I undergo a single token experience. This seems very counterintuitive. There is also the question of just how many experiences I do then undergo.

So, assuming that we are not prepared to make the retrograde move of buying into the sense-datum theory, with all of its well known problems and objections, we are left with the view that the phenomenal character of a visual experience is *not* a non-representational property of the experience.

What about experiences that do not represent anything, however? What about *their* phenomenal character? My view is that all experiences have representational content, so the case does not arise. I cannot defend this claim properly here. I merely note that I (and others) have made a case for emotional experiences and mood experiences having representational content; likewise for bodily sensations, of which more in the next section. So, there is no obvious bar to generalizing the conclusion reached for the phenomenal character of visual experiences.

4 Phenomenal Externalism

If physicalism is true, then the thesis of phenomenal internalism reduces to the thesis that it is metaphysically impossible for microphysical duplicates to differ with respect to the phenomenal character of their internal states. To refute this thesis, it suffices to produce an example of two entities that are microphysical duplicates in some possible world W without the two entities being phenomenal duplicates in W.

Here is the example. On the planet Xenon, there are massive trees. These trees produce many very large, hanging pods every four years. The pods grow gradually and depend for their development upon the copious rainfall that is found on Xenon. When the contents of the pods are ready for harvesting, their shells begin to crack open. This process is hastened by the many electrical storms that occur. Lightning often strikes the trees and the electricity is conducted throughout the tree limbs and into the bodies of the pods, thereby causing them to split apart once they have grown to a certain size. The contents of the pods are eaten by the people who live on Xenon (Xenonites, as I shall call them). Sometimes, the Xenonites are so anxious to eat the pod contents that they go out during the storms and devour them straight from the trees as the pods split open. Xenonites are very different from us. Their physiology is not brain- and spine-based as ours is. They do not have any neurons inside their bodies. Instead, their minds function hydraulically.

The pods themselves are each large enough to contain a human brain and remarkably their contents, just before harvesting, are chemically very like human brains in which there is no activity. Even more remarkably, one particular pod (call it "XP1"), during an electrical storm that infuses it with electricity for 15 minutes, is actually a microphysical *duplicate* of an active brain – one belonging to a human being named "Lolita" who for the same period of time on Earth initially is having sexual intercourse, and then (after 8 minutes) smoking a cigarette and drinking green chartreuse.

I take it to be obvious that the pod contents are not themselves genuine brains. Upon rare occasion, they may briefly be microphysically identical to live human brains, as with XP1 for 15 minutes, but brains they are not. In making this assertion I am not supposing that there cannot be brains without bodies. Clearly, there can be brains in vats or brains removed from bodies that are subsequently destroyed. However, in these cases, it is at least true that the brains were *designed* to control the bodies of the creatures to which they belong or did belong, even if those creatures no longer exist or have had their usual bodies taken from them. Nor do I wish to deny that swamp brains are possible; intuitively, a molecule by molecule duplicate of my brain that is functioning for a sufficient period of time *as* a brain inside a human body is a brain even if it was accidentally created by a chemical reaction that took place in a swamp.

What I am denying is that something becomes a brain *simply* by replicating a brain microphysically. We don't suppose that something becomes a key just by replicating a key microphysically. Think, for example, of a plastic card that happens to replicate a card key, but is actually designed for use as a credit card for xeroxing articles at a library. Nor do we suppose that something becomes a tiger just by being a microphysical duplicate of a tiger. If the thing has the wrong evolutionary history, it isn't a tiger no matter how closely it resembles one. A voltmeter, as all will agree, doesn't become a speedometer unless it is designed (or at least used) to measure speed. An intrinsically identical voltmeter used to measure volume may be a fuel gauge instead. Similarly, a microphysical duplicate of my little finger that is actually a toe on a three-headed Martian is not also a finger. The same points apply *mutatis mutandis* to microphysical duplicates of human brains.

XP1, then, is not a brain. It was not designed by nature to function as a brain; nor has it become a brain by taking on the appropriate control role with respect to a body. By pure accident, XP1 briefly replicates a brain microphysically, but that is not enough to make it a brain.

Does XP1, for the period of time during the storm in which it is microphysically identical to a particular human brain, undergo experiences, all of which are phenomenally identical to the experiences of the relevant human on Earth? I say *no*.

5 Lolita, XP1, and Bodily Sensations

Consider the bodily sensations Lolita undergoes. There is a locational component to these sensations. When she feels a pleasurable tickling sensation in her upper arm, say, the bodily location she experiences for the tickle contributes to, or is at least fixed by, the overall phenomenal character of her sensation. This is not to imply that bodily experiences that have the same phenomenal character must represent the same bodily part. There is no obvious reason to deny that a creature might feel a pain

Michael Tye

in a finger that is shaped just as one of my toes is and that feels to the creature, location-wise, just as a pain in a toe does to me. This seems possible since the fingers of such a creature might bear the same torso-relative bodily locations as my toes. Even so, in such a case, there is a commonality in represented torso-relative bodily location notwithstanding the difference in objective, bodily part location; it is the former that, I claim, contributes to, or is at least fixed by, phenomenal character. The relevant location is *represented* location, since one can feel a pain in a given bodily location even though one has no bodily part in that location (as, for example, if the appropriate bodily part has been amputated).

Here is another way to make the point. Suppose I feel a pain in a finger and I move my finger to a different location relative to my torso. Then my pain feels to be in a different location and this entails that there is a difference in phenomenal character before and after the movement. By contraposition, then, sameness in phenomenal character entails sameness in felt torso-relative location. Since sameness in felt location necessitates sameness in represented location, sameness in phenomenal character in this case necessitates sameness in represented torso-relative location.

In making these remarks, I am not assuming the truth of representationalism either with respect to phenomenal character generally or more narrowly with respect to the phenomenal character that attaches to the experience of bodily location. According to representationalism in its weakest form, necessarily experiences that have the same representational content have the same phenomenal character. This is not assumed above even for the special case of bodily location phenomenal character; nor is it a consequence of what I say.[9] As just noted, what my comments entail is only that bodily sensations that feel alike with respect to bodily location (and thus have the same locational phenomenal character) must represent the same torso-relative bodily location.[10]

Consider now XP1. If XP1's bodily sensations, if any it has, feel to it just as Lolita's bodily sensations feel to her, then XP1 must have an internal state representing a bodily part with the same boundaries and torso-relative location as an arm, given that Lolita has a tickle in her arm. But this seems *very* implausible. XP1 does not belong to a species of creatures with arms (or bodily parts that resemble arms). It is not a brain belonging to such a species. Indeed, as we saw earlier, XP1 is not a brain at all. Further, XP1 does not have any internal states that are *supposed* to indicate arms or disturbances in arms (or arm-like parts).[11] Nor does XP1 have any internal states that causally co-vary with disturbances in, or on the surface of, arms; for XP1 is hanging in a pod on a tree. Also, XP1 has no internal states that lead to arm-rubbing or arm-moving behavior. To be sure, XP1 has internal states that *would* causally co-vary with arm disturbances (or would lead to arm-related behavior), *were* XP1 connected in a certain complicated way to an appropriate human body for the crucial 15 minutes. But why suppose that this is relevant to what, if anything, the internal states of XP1 represent, as it hangs on the tree in a pod? After all, there are many other possible bodies XP1 could be connected to in complicated ways so that the same internal states of XP1 would then causally co-vary with disturbances in regions of XP1's torso.

What, then, could make it the case that XP1 has any internal states representing arms (or bodily parts spatially related to torsos as arms are)? The physicalist has no satisfying answer to this question. Admittedly, she might insist that there is an answer, but not one that we can grasp or, at any rate, yet formulate. But this seems very unsatisfying. Prima facie, in the case of XP1, there simply isn't any physical fact that can ground the relevant representational relations.

Of course, the dualist might respond that there are *primitive* representational relations that XP1's internal states bear to arms or arm-like bodily parts. These relations are nonphysical and it is just a brute fact that they obtain for any intrinsic duplicate of a being with internal states representing arms or arm-like parts. This view seems to me extremely implausible but, as noted in the opening part of the essay, my aim here is not to refute the dualist.

Given physicalism, then, the conclusion to which we are led is that XP1's internal states do *not* represent arms (or bodily parts spatially related to torsos as arms are). XP1's bodily sensations, if any it has, do not feel to it just as Lolita's bodily sensations feel to her. It follows that what it is like for XP1 is not overall the same as what it is like for Lolita.

Compare the Xenon tree case with the case in which a mad neurophysiologist of the future probes the brain of Lolita while doing neurosurgery and causes her to go into just the brain states she would have gone into had she been engaging in sex, and then drinking green chartreuse and smoking a cigarette. In this case, I have no hesitation in saying that Lolita is experiencing just what she would have experienced, had she really been doing these things. What is the difference between this case and the Xenon one? At the most general level, the difference is one of background context. In this case, there is a normal setting, relative to which the given situation counts as abnormal, and this setting can be used to justify the attribution of experiences of just the phenomenal type that would have been present in the normal case. In the Xenon tree case, there is no normal setting that can play this role.

But what if some visiting Earth scientists had placed XP1 in an appropriate human body for the crucial 15 minutes? With the right connections, XP1's behavior, both verbal and nonverbal, would have mirrored that of Lolita. Isn't that evidence that XP1 is psychologically like Lolita?

My reply is that XP1 could have been hooked up to many other possible nonhuman bodies and thereby have produced very different narrow verbal and nonverbal behavior. This being so, there is no clear reason to hold that the scenario in which XP1 is suitably connected to a brainless human body shows anything about the psychological life of XP1, as it hangs from the tree in a pod. Consider a card designed for use as a credit card for xeroxing (to return to the earlier example). It could have been used for all sorts of things. For example, it could have been used by a thief to open hotel room doors. It hardly follows from this possibility that the card is, in actual fact, a key card.

Suppose now that the original scenario had been different and that just as the crucial 15 minute period was ending, XP1 had been placed in a live human body and connected to it just as our brains are standardly connected to our bodies. Would not the embodied individual remember immediately afterwards having had just the very sensations Lolita had? If so, then isn't the best explanation of these memories that XP1 in this case really did have the relevant experiences? And if this is correct, then shouldn't we agree that XP1 in the original case had those experiences too, especially

Michael Tye

since the difference between the two cases occurs only *after* the 15 minutes during which XP1 is infused with electricity? How can a later difference make a difference to what occurs before?

Let us grant for the moment that the being with a human body has apparent memories of some earlier experiences. Then we should also grant that this being has other apparent memories. For example, she seems to remember lying on a bed, smoking a cigarette, talking to another person, drinking chartreuse, having her arm tickled. In reality, none of these things took place. Her beliefs about her past real-world life are false, as are her beliefs as to who she is. Furthermore, her beliefs about experiences she had prior to the crucial 15 minute period are false too. Given all this, it is not in the least obvious that the best explanation of her beliefs about her most recent experiences are in any better shape. There seems no obvious rationale, other than a blind adherence to phenomenal internalism, for treating these beliefs as any different from her other beliefs about her past. After all, there is no privileged access to past psychological states any more than there is privileged access to past, objective goings on. Surely, the simplest, most coherent view is that her beliefs about the past stand or fall together.

It is also worth noting briefly that it is not *obvious* that a real psychological subject exists immediately after XP1 and the human body are joined together. Of course, it appears to others that there is such a subject, but appearances can be deceptive. Something can appear to be a key without being one; something can appear to be a tiger and be something else; something can appear to be a finger when it is actually a toe; something can appear to be a brain and not be a brain. Why cannot the same be true of psychological subjects? Given the complexity of the resulting structure, and the physical similarity between its parts and those of real psychological subjects, it is tempting to assume that the structure *must* be a psychological subject. But this would be hasty. Some further argument is needed.

I shall not pursue this point here. I merely observe that *if* the combined structure is not a psychological subject, or at least is not such a subject *initially*, then XP1 prior to embodiment is not a subject either.[12] But if XP1 is not a subject, then XP1 cannot have *any* experiences prior to embodiment. Experiences cannot exist unowned any more than laughs can exist unlaughed or screams can exist unscreamed. For each experience, there must be an experiencer – someone for whom there is something it is like. But if XP1 has no experiences, then there is *nothing* it is like for XP1 at all.

In my view, then, the Xenon example provides us with a possible case in which a standardly embodied creature with a brain and a microphysical duplicate of that brain differ phenomenally. It does not yet show that microphysical duplicates can differ phenomenally. However, there is a simple extension of the thought experiment that does. Let the subject on Earth be some human being whose body has been destroyed and whose brain has been envatted and subsequently is supplied by inputs from a supercomputer, so that XP1 is now a microphysical duplicate of a person who is systematically hallucinating the act of sexual intercourse followed by smoking a cigarette and drinking green chartreuse. Here we really do have microphysical duplicates that differ phenomenally. The case thus supports phenomenal externalism.[13]

This view will not be shared by everyone. Some will no doubt dig in their heels and insist that XP1 is a brain and that it does have phenomenally identical experiences for the 15 minute period, however strange that initially seems. Still at a minimum, even those philosophers who react in this way should agree that the example raises a serious doubt as to whether any two microphysical duplicates must be alike phenomenally. Thus, the Xenon tree example *at least* shows that phenomenal internalism is not a position that is self-evidently true or one that cannot reasonably be disputed.

6 An Alternative Proposal and Some Final Thoughts on Qualia

If, as I have argued, the phenomenal character of an experience is not, by its nature, an intrinsic property of the experience and neither is it a nonrepresentational property, then what is it? My proposal, mooted above in connection with the discussion of the phenomenal many-property problem, is that phenomenal character is a certain sort of representational content. Furthermore, it is externalist content. Here is not the place to try to develop the further conditions on content that must be met for it to be phenomenal. Instead, let me close by making some general remarks about qualia.

What does the above discussion tell us about qualia? Well, if qualia are any of the following:

1 intrinsic, introspectible properties of experiences
2 nonrepresentational, introspectible properties of experiences
3 irreducibly nonphysical properties of experiences

then my view is that there are no qualia. In this sense, qualia should be quined, as Dennett (1988) put it (though not for the right reasons) some time ago. If, however, qualia are nonrepresentational properties of which we are aware when we introspect experiences, then I accept that there are qualia. But qualia, so understood, are not properties of experiences. They are properties experiences represent – in the visual case, properties like squareness and redness. These are the properties of which we are aware when we introspect, or so says the thesis of transparency that I accept (Harman, 1990; Tye 2000, 2002).[14] Transparency, then, as I understand it, does not eliminate qualia altogether. But it does eliminate them in any interesting sense of the term that applies to properties. Does transparency eliminate phenomenal character? Of course, it does not. But phenomenal character, in my view, is not a *property* at all, mental or otherwise, any more than is the meaning of a word or the content of a belief.

Acknowledgments

I would like to thank Jonathan Cohen and Fred Dretske for helpful comments. I am also indebted to members of the audience at a University of Maryland colloquium for their remarks on an ancestor of this essay, and to the audience at a Pacific APA symposium on the intrinsic qualities of experience.

Michael Tye

Notes

1   Some qualia freaks might insist here that phenomenality, as they conceive of it, is a simple quality with no hidden nature that is nonetheless metaphysically necessitated by the microphysical. I deny that there are any such qualities, since I deny that there are brute supervenience laws of the sort needed by this view. (For more here, see Tye, 1995, ch. 2.) But leaving this to one side, the argument of the present section assumes an understanding of "irreducibly nonphysical" under which phenomenality, so conceived, does not count as irreducibly nonphysical.

2   For other uses to which part-time zombies may be put, see Hawthorne (in press).

3   Note that (NC) does not require that sudden and big changes in phenomenal character always be *noticed*. So, (NC) is not threatened by the results of recent psychological experiments on change blindness.

4   I myself am disinclined to accept this claim. See Tye (2003, ch. 4).

5   A summary of this literature is provided by Brian Weatherson (2002).

6   This assumes a sparse view of token events of the sort persuasively argued for by Davidson (1970). The claim that my pressing the button at t just is my launching the rocket at t is not undermined by the thought that I could have pressed the button without the rocket being launched whereas I couldn't have launched the rocket without the rocket being launched. What this shows is that the property of being a rocket launching is only an accidental property of that particular button pressing (the very event that is, in fact, a rocket launching). This is on a par with the claim that inventing bifocals is only a contingent property of Benjamin Franklin (the man who, in fact, invented bifocals).

    Another way of dealing with this point that is in the general spirit of Davidson is to say that my pressing the button at t is my launching the rocket at t, even though the relationship is not one of strict identity. The former event *constitutes* the latter, and constitution does not require possession of all the same modal properties. This is my preferred view of the relationship between token visual experience, v, and the relevant neural event.

7   Variants of this problem are to be found also in Clark (2000) and Byrne (2004).

8   For more here as well as a detailed presentation of a version of the adverbial theory that tries to handle the above difficulties, see Tye (1984).

9   For a detailed discussion of bodily sensations (and pain in particular) from a representationalist perspective, see my Tye (forthcoming).

10 I shall not press the point here since it is not needed for present purposes, but, in my view, our experiences generally have what might be called a "presentational phenomenology." For the appropriate external aspects, experiences with the same phenomenal character present the same aspects of the world to us or the same aspects of our bodies (or sometimes both). I focus on the case of phenomenal location, since it seems especially clear-cut and compelling.

11 For ease of exposition, for the rest of this paragraph, I leave out the parenthetical qualification.

12 Here is more food for thought on the question of whether XP1 is a psychological subject. Suppose that the Xenonites in their zeal to taste the pod contents had pulled XP1's pod from the tree before the final electrical storm ended and had eaten XP1. Would they have been doing a *bad* thing? It is tempting to suppose that, even if consequentialism is true, no question of goodness and badness arises here. However, if XP1 is a psychological subject, the Xenonites' behavior is open to moral assessment.

13 For more on internalism versus externalism with respect to phenomenal character, see Byrne and Tye (2006) and Tye (forthcoming).

14 Not everyone who accepts transparency agrees that these are the relevant properties. See here Shoemaker (1994) and Thau (2002).

References

Block, N. (1980). Troubles with functionalism. In *Readings in the Philosophy of Psychology*, vol. 1. Cambridge, MA: MIT Press.

—— (1998). Is experiencing just representing? *Philosophy and Phenomenological Research*, 59, 663–70.

Byrne, A. (2004). Inverted qualia. In E. Zalta (ed.), *Stanford Encyclopedia of Philosophy*. Stanford, CA: Metaphysics Research Lab/Stanford University.

—— and Tye, M. (2006). Qualia ain't in the head. *Noûs*, 40, 241–55.

Chalmers, D. (1996). *The Conscious Mind*. New York: Oxford University Press.

Clark, A. (2000). *A Theory of Sentience*. Oxford: Oxford University Press.

Davidson, D. (1970). The individuation of events. In N. Rescher (ed.), *Essays in Honor of Carl G. Hempel*. Dordrecht: D. Reidel.

Dennett, D. C. (1988). Quining qualia. In A. Marcel and E. Bisiach (eds.), *Consciousness and Contemporary Science*. Oxford: Oxford University Press.

Donnellan, K. (1966). Reference and definite descriptions. *Philosophical Review*, 75, 281–304.

Harman, G. (1990). The intrinsic quality of experience. In J. Tomberlin (ed.), *Philosophical Perspectives*, vol. 4. Atascadero, CA: Ridgeview.

Hawthorne, J. (in press). Dancing qualia and direct reference. In T. Alter and S. Walter (eds.), *Phenomenal Concepts and Phenomenal Knowledge: New Essays on Consciousness and Physicalism*. Oxford: Oxford University Press.

Jackson, F. (1975). On the adverbial analysis of visual experience. *Metaphilosophy*, 6, 127–35.

Levine, J. (1983). Materialism and qualia: the explanatory gap. *Pacific Philosophical Quarterly*, 64, 354–61.

Lewis, D. (1983). Extrinsic properties. *Philosophical Studies*, 44, 197–200.

Shoemaker, S. (1975). Functionalism and qualia. *Philosophical Studies*, 27, 291–315.

—— (1994). Phenomenal character. *Noûs*, 28, 21–38.

—— (1998). Two cheers for representationalism. *Philosophy and Phenomenological Research*, 58, 671–8.

Thau, M. (2002). *Consciousness and Cognition*. Oxford: Oxford University Press.

Tye, M. (1984). The adverbial approach to visual experience. *Philosophical Review*, 93, 195–225.

—— (1995). *Ten Problems of Consciousness*. Cambridge, MA: MIT Press.

—— (2000). *Consciousness, Color, and Content*. Cambridge, MA: MIT Press.

—— (2002). Representationalism and the transparency of experience. *Noûs*, 36, 137–51.

—— (2003). *Consciousness and Persons: Unity and Identity*. Cambridge, MA: MIT Press.

—— (forthcoming). Phenomenal externalism, Lolita, and the planet Xenon. In D. Sosa and T. Horgan (eds.), *A Collection of Essays for Jaegwon Kim*. Cambridge, MA: MIT Press.

Weatherson, B. (2002). Intrinsic versus extrinsic properties. In E. Zalta (ed.), *Stanford Encyclopedia of Philosophy*. Stanford, CA: Metaphysics Research Lab/Stanford University.

Yablo, S. (1999). Intrinsicness. *Philosophical Topics*, 26, 479–505.

A Case for Qualia

Sydney Shoemaker

1

The term "qualia" has been used in a variety of ways, but I think that the dominant usage is one on which qualia are the features of experiences or sensory states that determine their phenomenal character, or "what it is like" to have them. Understood one way this would allow even standard representationalists about the phenomenal character of experience to accept qualia: on their view, qualia would be representational features of experiences, such as being "as of red."[1] On this understanding the existence of qualia is not in question: what is in question is their nature.

But the claim that there are qualia is often regarded as controversial. One way to make it controversial is to build into the specification of qualia that they are *nonrepresentational* features of experiences. Certainly some defenders of qualia have thought of them in this way (I did so myself at one time), and plainly representationalists deny the existence of qualia on this understanding of them. But I will focus on a different way of making the existence of qualia controversial, namely by building into their specification that they are *internally determined* features of experiences. On this conception, their existence is denied by standard representationalists about phenomenal character, those who hold that the phenomenal character of experiences is determined by their externally determined representational content, i.e., by what objective properties they represent as being instantiated in the perceiver's environment (see Harman, 1990; Dretske, 1995; Tye, 1995 and 2000; Lycan, 1996). But this conception would allow qualia to be aspects of representational content, as long as the representational content they figure in is internally determined. I will discuss later what form such a view might take. For now I just want to state what I take to be the central issue between those who affirm the existence of qualia and those who deny it: the issue is between internalist and externalist views about what determines the "what it is like" of sensory states.

Belief in qualia often goes with belief in the possibility of "inverted qualia" – e.g., in the possibility of spectrum inversion. On one conception of spectrum inversion, it involves different perceivers perceiving the same colors by means of experiences that differ in what qualia they instantiate (differ in "phenomenal character"), and perceiving different colors by means of experiences that instantiate the same qualia. This goes with a conception of colors as objective properties of things in the environment, and with an externalist conception of the color content of perceptual experiences. It also goes with the view that the phenomenal character of color experiences is only contingently connected with what colors they represent – so that different perceivers who mean the same by "red" can report phenomenally different experiences when they say "It looks red." If one accepts this, but also thinks that qualia are representational features of experience, one must hold that there is more to the representational content of color experiences than its externalist content – one must hold that the content has an internalist component.

But one can be an internalist about phenomenal character without accepting the possibility of spectrum inversion on this conception of it. There are internalist views on which those who mean the same by "red" necessarily report phenomenally similar experiences when they say "It looks red." Those who hold an error theory about color experience – a "projectivist" view about it – will be internalists about the phenomenal character of color experience, but they will be likely to hold that the connection between phenomenal character and representational content is necessary rather than contingent (see Boghossian and Velleman, 1989 and 1991). They can hold, indeed, that having a certain phenomenal character – instantiating a certain quale – just is representing the instantiation of a certain color, and they can therefore be representationalists about phenomenal character. But of course they think that the representational content of color experiences is always false.

Likewise, proponents of the view that color attributions are relative will be internalists about the phenomenal character of color experiences, but can hold that the connection between phenomenal character and representational content is necessary rather than contingent.[2] For them, there is no such thing as being red *simpliciter*; there is only being red for such-and-such a sort of perceiver in such-and-such circumstances, and this is a matter of being such as to produce in such a perceiver a color experience having a certain phenomenal character.

But both the error theorist and the proponent of relativized colors will accept the possibility of something that might be called spectrum inversion – that the color experiences of different observers in the same objective circumstances might differ in qualitative character, and that the color experiences of different observers in different objective circumstances can be the same in qualitative character, without the different observers differing with respect to the veridicality of their color experiences. The error theorist, of course, will say that the experiences of both are nonveridical, since, according to her, all color experience is illusory. The proponent of relativized colors will say that what is red for one sort of observer is green for another, and vice versa.

My own view is the first of the internalist views just sketched, that which shares with standard representationalism the assumption that colors are objective properties of external things and that the color content of experiences is externally determined.

And it is a version of this which holds that the phenomenal character of color experiences is an aspect of their representational content, an aspect that is internally determined and can vary independently of the externally determined part of the content. I hold much the same about the phenomenal character of experiences involved in the perception of properties other than colors. But the difference between this and the other internalist views is not really about the nature of qualia – it is about the nature of colors and color representation, or, more generally, about the nature of sensible qualities and the perceptual representation of them. So despite my disagreement with error theorists and proponents of relativized colors, we are on the same side of what is the crucial issue here – the issue of whether phenomenal character is internally or externally determined.

2

Why should we think that the phenomenal character of experiences is internally determined? An important part of the answer is that there are very good reasons for holding that the similarity and difference relations among phenomenal characters are internally determined. As Quine emphasized, any creature that perceives has an innate quality space. The structure of this space can be mapped by determining what discriminations the creature can make, what sorts of recognitional capacities it has, and what sorts of inductions it is naturally prone to make. This structure is determined by the way the creature's perceptual system is wired. In the case of color perception, the currently favored theory is that it is determined by an opponent processing system.[3] It is this that determines what combinations of wavelengths are metamers for a given perceiver, and so indistinguishable by it, what combinations produce experiences of unique hues and what combinations produce experiences of binary hues, and what the similarity and difference relations are among experiences produced by lights involving particular combinations of wavelengths. Other parts of our perceptual system will determine similarities and differences in how things taste, smell, and feel.

It seems out of the question that similarities and differences in what it is like to experience certain things is constituted by similarities and differences in what properties are represented by the experiences. There are lots of cases in which phenomenal samenesses and differences in experiences do not correspond to perceived samenesses and differences: a mineralogist may perceive similarities in the chemical contents of different minerals by means of phenomenally very different experiences, and may perceive differences in chemical content in minerals by means of phenomenally very similar experiences. It is of course characteristic of what have traditionally been classified as "secondary qualities" that perceived samenesses and differences among instantiations of such qualities go with samenesses and differences in the phenomenal character of the perceptual experiences involved in their perception. But this can only be because in one way or another the similarity and difference relations among the experiences determine what count as similarities and differences among the items perceived. This of course will be true on a dispositionalist account of secondary qualities; if secondary qualities are just dispositions to produce experiences having certain phenomenal characters, it is to be expected that similarity (difference) with respect to such qualities will go with phenomenal similarity (difference) in the experiences of them. But it will also be true on the view, suggested by Hilbert and Kalderon in a recent paper, that our visual system "selects" certain objective properties to be colors, and certain relations among these properties to be relations of color similarity and difference (see Hilbert and Kalderon, 2000, and Shoemaker, 2003a). Here the internally determined relations of phenomenal similarity and difference partly determine what properties and relations in the world are represented by experiences among which these relations hold – they determine this in such a way as to guarantee that there will be, normally, a correspondence between phenomenal similarity (difference) and similarity (difference) in what is represented.

Could it be that the relations of phenomenal similarity and difference among experiences are internally determined but that the phenomenal character of the experiences is externally determined? I cannot make any sense of that. It is not that I think that the structure of the quality space determines the phenomenal character of the experiences. (That does seem to be the view of Hilbert and Kalderon, 2000, and of Austen Clark, 2000.) I think that we can make sense of the idea that different creatures might have structurally identical quality spaces and yet differ systematically in the phenomenal character of their experiences. What I cannot make sense of is the idea that it might be that the quality spaces are identically structured but that there is a difference in the phenomenal character of the experiences *because of* a difference in what properties are represented.

Perhaps it will be suggested that the "selection" view mentioned above gives us a way of making sense of this. Mightn't there be two different sets of properties and relations either of which could be selected by a certain sort of perceptual system to be the colors and color similarity relations? One of these is instantiated in one possible world, and is there selected by a perceptual system of that sort, while the other is instantiated in a different possible world, and is there selected by a perceptual system of the same sort. And the experiences of the perceivers in the two worlds (the possessors of the perceptual systems) differ in phenomenal character because of the different properties they represent.

One problem with this is that it suggests that the experiences could have the similarity and difference relations they do without having any phenomenal character at all. The view allows that the phenomenal similarity and difference relations are internally determined, and so are independent of what sort of environment the creature is embedded in, while holding that the phenomenal character is determined by the creature's being embedded in an environment in such a way as to make the experiences representations of particular properties. But that suggests the possibility that a creature with experiences having such relations of phenomenal similarity and difference might not be embedded in *any* environment in a way that makes the experiences representations of properties instantiated in that environment. An example of such a creature would be Joe Levine's "Swampbrain-in-a-vat" (see Levine, 2003). This would be a brain in a vat that originated in the manner of Donald Davidson's swampman – it "coalesces out of swamp gas inside a vat" (ibid., p. 66), and is molecularly identical to the brain of one of us.[4] If there being experiences standing in relations of phenomenal similarity and difference is internally determined, presumably Swampbrain will have such experiences. And presumably Swampbrain's experiences will not represent any properties instantiated in his environment. On the view sketched above, his experiences would stand to one another in relations of phenomenal similarity and difference, but would lack phenomenal character. And that, I think, is manifestly impossible.

The Swampbrain example is of course far-fetched. But so, I think, is the proposal I have used it to counter. Let me mention one additional problem with that proposal. The proposal drew on the idea that our visual system selects certain objective properties and relations to be the colors and relations of color similarity and difference. It is important to note that the selection has to be of relations as well as properties. For it is easily conceivable that visual systems having different color quality spaces might select the same properties but represent them as standing to one another in different relations of similarity and difference (see Shoemaker, 2003a). Clearly in that case it could not generally be the case that an experience of a property in one of these systems has the same phenomenal character as an experience of the same property in a system having a differently structured color quality space. So what property is represented won't be sufficient to determine the phenomenal character of the experience. But a large part of what motivates standard representationalism, with its view of phenomenal character as externally determined, is the Moorean transparency intuition – the intuition that what we are introspectively aware of when we introspect the phenomenal character of our experience is the property represented. That intuition is not respected by a view that takes the property represented to be an objective property whose representation does not by itself determine the phenomenal character of the experience.

3

I have long held that the relations of qualitative (phenomenal) similarity among experiences are functionally definable (see Shoemaker, 1975, 1982, 1996, and 2003a). What Quine says about the similarity and different relations imposed on stimuli by a quality space will apply to the experiences produced by these stimuli. Experiences that are qualitatively different will contribute to discriminatory behavior on the part of the subject, while ones that are qualitatively alike will contribute to recognitional behavior. What inductions a creature is disposed to make on the basis of its experiences will depend crucially on the similarity and difference relations holding among them. Qualitatively similar experiences will tend to give rise to beliefs in objective similarities in the environment, while qualitatively different experiences will tend to give rise to beliefs in objective differences in the environment. And the holding of these relations among experiences will also give rise to introspective beliefs to the effect that there are experiences so related.

Qualia I see as the properties of experiences in virtue of which they stand in the relations of qualitative similarity and difference. There is thus a sense in which qualia are functionally definable: we can say in functional terms what it is for a property to be a quale, drawing on the functional account of the qualitative similarity and difference relations. A property will be a quale if it belongs to a family of properties such that experiences that are alike with respect to which properties in this family they instantiate will be qualitatively identical, and such that all of the similarity and difference relations among experiences are determined by what properties in this family they instantiate. Of course, to say that we can say in functional terms what it is to be a quale is not to say that that individual qualia can be functionally defined. Whether that is so is a question I shall return to in section 4.

Although the sketch just given of the functional roles of qualitative similarity and difference stresses the effect of the holding of these relations on the subject's beliefs, I think that it is better to put the stress on the effect on the subject's perceptual representations. Normally, of course, our perceptual representations issue in beliefs. But they don't always do so, and there are creatures who have perceptual representations but do not have states that clearly count as beliefs. So let's say that part of the functional role of qualitative similarities and differences among experiences is to give those experiences contents that represent similarities and differences in the environment or in the subject's body. If we put the matter this way, then it seems that there is a case for saying that the qualia, the features of experiences that determine their relations of qualitative similarity and difference, are intentional or representational properties.

In a recent paper Brian Loar (2003) rejects a conception of qualia as what he calls "raw qualia" in favor of a conception of qualia as "property-directed," and calls the latter "intentional qualia." Raw qualia, I take it, would be entirely nonrepresentational – which is how I once thought of them. In speaking of qualia as "property directed" Loar does not mean that for each quale there is some one property of which it is constitutively a representation: he thinks that in different circumstances the same quale could be involved in the representation of different properties, and that there are possible circumstances, e.g., that of an "isolated brain in a vat," in which qualia-laden experiences would represent no properties at all. Nevertheless, he holds that qualia "present themselves on reflection as purporting-to-refer," though "they are conceivable quite independently of all referential properties" (p. 84).

My current view is similar to Loar's, although there are differences. For some time I have been trying to develop a view that does justice to the Moorean transparency intuition but is compatible with an internalist view of phenomenal character. Such a view must hold that what we are aware of when we introspect the phenomenal character of an experience is an aspect of its representational content, but that this aspect is independent of what objective properties, if any, the experience represents. Initially I suggested that the phenomenal character of the experience consists in its representing what I first called "phenomenal properties" of external things and more recently have called "appearance properties" (see Shoemaker, 1994 and 2000). These are properties things have in virtue of producing, or being disposed to produce, experiences of certain sorts. The view was that, for example, one perceives a color by perceiving an appearance property that things with that color present to creatures of the sort one is. The view was designed to allow for the possibility of spectrum inversion: owing to differences in their perceptual systems, different creatures may perceive the same appearance property when viewing things of different colors, and may perceive different appearance properties when viewing things of the same color. Although I think there undoubtedly are appearance properties, I have come to doubt whether

Sydney Shoemaker

they are represented in our experience, and this has led to a different version of the view (see Shoemaker, 2006). On the current version, the claim is that each color has a variety of different "qualitative characters," and presents different ones of these in different viewing conditions (e.g., different lighting conditions), and also presents different ones to creatures with different sorts of perceptual systems. So instead of perceiving the color of an object by perceiving a different property of that same object (an appearance property), we perceive it as presenting one of its qualitative characters. The same qualitative character can be presented, in different circumstances or to different sorts of perceivers, by different colors, and different qualitative characters can be presented to different sorts of perceivers, or in different circumstances, by the same color: so on this version of the view, as on the earlier one, spectrum inversion is possible.

My view differs from Loar's in holding that each quale has, constitutively and independently of context, a representational content of its own – it represents a particular qualitative character, an aspect of a perceived property. On Loar's view, as I understand it, what is represented by a particular quale can vary with context, and there may, as in the case of the isolated brain in a vat, be nothing that is represented by it. I think my view fits better with the phenomenology, and does a better job of respecting the Moorean transparency intuition. Loar tells us that "The technique of qualia spotting is fairly simple. One attends to or imagines a visual experience, and conceives of it as lacking some or all of its actual references, whether objects, properties, or relations, and then attends to what phenomenally remains" (p. 84). Conceiving of the experience as lacking its actual references cannot be just conceiving of it as illusory, for even illusory experiences have representational content. I think that I can conceive of my current color experiences as not referring to the colors they actually refer to, and referring to different ones instead – as in a case of spectrum inversion. And, with more difficulty, I can conceive of them as not referring to any colors at all; I can conceive of experiences like them being had by an isolated brain in a vat where the properties they represent are properties of states of the computer that provides the brain in a vat with its sensory input. And I can even conceive of the experiences as being had by Joe Levine's Swampbrain-in-a-vat, where there are in fact no actually instantiated properties they refer to. But even in this last case, I think, if the experiences are phenomenally like mine it would seem to their subject that he was perceiving something having properties that present a certain phenomenal character. Loar says that qualia "present themselves on reflection as purporting-to-refer," and I think he would say that this would be true of the qualia of the experiences of Swampbrain-in-a-vat. On my view, this purporting-to-refer has to consist in its seeming to the subject of the experiences that he is appeared to in a certain way, and this consists in the experiences representing there being properties that are presenting certain qualitative characters to him.

4

As a physicalist I think that whatever properties are instantiated in the world must be physically realized. So I hold that this must be true of qualia.

We can see how qualia can be physically realized by taking note of my earlier point that the relations of qualitative similarity and difference among experiences are functionally definable, and that qualia can be defined as the properties of experiences in virtue of which these relations hold. I said earlier that a property will be a quale if it belongs to a family of properties such that (1) experiences that are alike with respect to which properties in this family they instantiate will be qualitatively identical, (2) experiences that differ with respect to which properties in this family they instantiate will be qualitatively different, and (3) all of the similarity and difference relations among experiences are determined by what properties in this family they instantiate. For a physical property to realize a quale it must belong to a family of physical properties that satisfy (1) and (3). But assuming that qualia are multiply realizable, the family of physical realizers that satisfies (1) and (3) will not satisfy (2); for the family of all qualia realizers will include pairs of properties whose co-instantiation does not contribute to qualitative difference. What we can require of any physical property that is a quale realizer is that it belongs to a subset of the set of properties that satisfy (1) and (3) that also satisfies (2). This subset will not satisfy (3) without qualification, for there will be cases in which properties not belonging to this subset will contribute to the determination of qualitative similarities and differences among experiences. But it will satisfy it in cases in which only properties belonging to this subset belong to the experiences in question.

It remains to say what it is for two different physical properties to be realizers of the same quale. This will be true when the result of replacing an instantiation of one of these properties with an instantiation of the other, leaving the experience otherwise the same, results in an experience qualitatively identical to the initial experience.

Assuming that we can explain in some such way what it is for a physical property to be a qualia realizer, and what it is for different qualia realizers to be realizers of the same quale, we can easily say what it is for experiences of different subjects to be qualitatively alike or different. My experience of red things will be qualitatively like yours just in case yours and mine instantiate the same qualia, which will be true just in case either yours and mine instantiate the same physical qualia realizers or they instantiate different physical realizers of the same qualia. This makes it in principle discoverable empirically whether different subjects have qualitatively identical color experiences in the same objective circumstances, or whether they are spectrum inverted relative to each other. For it is in principle discoverable empirically what the physical realizers of qualia are, and whether different ones of these are realizers of the same quale, and it is in principle discoverable empirically whether qualia realizers that are instantiated in the experiences of different persons are realizers of the same quale. This is of course compatible with the claim that no behavioral test could establish whether different subjects are spectrum inverted relative to each other.[5]

I said earlier that my claim that we can say in functional terms what it is to be a quale does not mean that individual qualia are functionally definable. The question whether they are functionally definable is a tangled issue. In earlier work I maintained that they are not, basing this on the claim of Block and Fodor that two creatures could be "qualia inverted" relative to each other despite being functional isomorphs (see Block and Fodor, 1972, and Shoemaker, 1975 and 1982). The sort of qualia

Sydney Shoemaker

inversion on which I rested my case was spectrum inversion. This met with the objection that spectrum inversion between functional isomorphs would require symmetrical color quality spaces, and that in fact our own color quality spaces are not symmetrical – there is no mapping of determinate shade of color onto other shades that both preserves the similarity and difference relations between the shades, and maps unique hues onto unique hues. I replied that there could be creatures with symmetrical color quality spaces that could be spectrum inverted relative to each other, and that this is enough to preclude qualia from being functionally definable. But while this might preclude the qualia of such creatures from being functionally definable, it does not follow without further argument (which I shall not attempt to give here) that it precludes *our* qualia from being functionally definable.

It is worth asking at this point just what sort of functional definability is in question. I think it would be agreed by everyone that individual qualia do not have functional definitions *á la* analytical functionalism – definitions that express a priori knowable conceptual truths. That leaves open the possibility that they have scientifically discoverable functional definitions *á la* psychofunctionalism (see Block, 1978a). That would require that each quale occupy, as a matter of nomological and perhaps metaphysical necessity, a unique functional role having to do with its causal relations to sensory inputs, behavioral outputs, and other psychological states. This is ruled out if there can be qualia inversion between functional isomorphs – for functional isomorphs will be exactly alike in what functional roles of this sort are occupied by their states and the properties of their states. But suppose that we drop the requirement that functional roles have to do with relations to sensory inputs, behavioral outputs, and other psychological states, and allow them to include all of the causal relations a state or property instantiation can have to anything at all. So, for example, such a functional role of a quale would include its causal relations to the neural states that can cause or be caused by its instantiation. On this fine-grained conception of a functional role, functional isomorphs will have to be such that their properties can be put in one–one correspondence in such away that corresponding properties have identical causal profiles. To suppose that qualia inversion is possible between creatures that are functional isomorphs in this sense is to suppose, in effect, that qualia are epiphenomenal.

I take it that the view that qualia are epiphenomenal is unacceptable. It is, of course, a consequence of my functional account of qualitative similarity and difference, and my use of this to say what makes a property a quale, that qualia play a distinctive causal role in discrimination, recognition, and belief fixation. And if we have introspective knowledge of our own qualia, and if such knowledge involves qualia instantiations generating awarenesses of themselves, then qualia must have causal profiles containing at least the propensity to produce this sort of effect.

I believe that properties that can be possessed contingently by concrete things are individuated by their causal profiles – by what contribution their instantiation can make to causing various effects (their forward-looking causal features) and by what sorts of states of affairs can cause their instantiation (their backward-looking causal features). In the actual world, and worlds nomologically like it, properties having the same causal profiles are identical.[6] To hold that different properties can have the same causal profile is, I believe, to put properties beyond our semantic and epistemic reach.

Supposing there to be sets of properties whose members have the same causal profile, there is no way in which we could refer to one of the properties in such a set rather than the others, and there is no way in which we could know specific ones of them to be instantiated. And supposing that there can be such sets, there would seem to be no way in which we could know that they are not ubiquitous, and so no way in which we could ever know that we have a handle on a single property rather than on a set of causally equivalent ones.

If qualia are properties, and properties are individuated by causal profiles, then qualia must be individuated by causal profiles. This is not to say that qualia are "definable" in terms of causal profiles, for I think there is no prospect of there being a finite and noncircular specification of the causal profile of a quale. So we probably should not say that qualia are functional properties, even on the most generous notion of what it is to be a functional property.

Still, if qualia are individuated by causal profiles, then there is available a simpler account than what was given above of what it is for a physical property to be a realizer of a particular quale. We can say that one property realizes another just in case the forward-looking causal features of the realized property are a subset of the forward-looking causal features of the realizer, and the backward-looking causal features of the realizer are a subset of the backward-looking causal features of the realized properties (see Shoemaker, 2003b). And so it will be with qualia.

5

It is likely to be objected that the view of qualia just sketched shares a defect that is thought to be damaging or fatal to the view that qualia are functional properties or that that they are identical with physical properties, namely that of making it totally mysterious how qualia can do what they are supposed to do, that is, account for the what-it-is-like of the experiences or sensory states that instantiate them. How can the causal features that individuate qualia constitute the "Technicolor phenomenology" of our experience of the world?

It has been objected to the view that qualia are functional properties that this makes them relational and non-intrinsic – whereas, it is thought, qualia are paradigmatically intrinsic qualities (see Levine, 1995, and Kim, 1998). And the same objection might be leveled against the view that qualia are individuated by causal profiles. But I think that it is a mistake to think that a property's being a functional property makes it relational and non-intrinsic, and it is certainly a mistake to think that a property's being individuated by a causal profile makes it relational and non-intrinsic. Causing is of course relational. But being apt to cause (or to contribute to causing) certain effects is not a relational feature of something, even though reference to a relation (causing) enters into its description. To insist that properties individuated by causal profiles cannot be intrinsic would be to stipulate that intrinsic properties are epiphenomenal. And it cannot be part of the phenomenology of experiences that their phenomenal character is epiphenomenal. Supposing that a property is epiphenomenal, what it is like to be in a state having that property could be no different from what it is like to be in an otherwise similar state that lacks it.

It should be noted also that the claim that qualia are individuated by causal profiles is not itself a physicalist claim. Even if qualia are nonphysical, their instantiation will have causes and effects, which means that they will have causal profiles. And their being nonphysical could not make it the case that there is more to being a particular quale than having a certain causal profile, in such a way that it could be the case that one property having that profile is that quale while another having the same causal profile is not. If there were such a pair of properties, then if someone's experience changed from instantiating the one that is a quale to instantiating the one that isn't, the person would not notice a difference (for of course, his noticing a difference would require that the properties differ in their causal profiles).

We are not of course aware of qualia *as* properties having certain causal profiles, The introspection of a quale is itself an exercise of its causal features but usually provides little or no information about what these causal features are. In this respect introspection is like perception. What is common to the ability to introspect a property and the ability to perceive a property is the ability to detect the property's presence or absence, to be aware of similarities and differences between its instantiations and the instantiations of other properties, and to refer to it demonstratively.

Given transparency, demonstrative reference to a quale is hard to distinguish from demonstrative reference to what the quale represents, which according to me is a qualitative character, i.e., an aspect of a perceived property. And puzzlement about how the phenomenal character of experience can be constituted by causally individuated properties is equally puzzlement about how the qualitative character of colors and other perceived properties can be so constituted. One asks, focusing on the way something looks to one, "How can *this* be a property, or a feature of a property, that is individuated by a causal profile?" and it can easily seem that nothing could count as an answer.

One component of the puzzle is the thought that knowledge of the causal profile of the quale, supposing it were possible, could not possibly amount to knowledge of what it is like to have an experience in which that quale is instantiated – and it is the latter, it is natural to suppose, that would constitute knowing the nature of the quale. Here a version of Frank Jackson's Mary argument comes into play (see Jackson, 1982 and 1986). Mary knows all of the physical and functional facts relevant to perceptual experience, and so, we will suppose, knows the full causal profile of the physical property that is the best physical candidate for being the quale involved in experiencing red. But she has spent her entire life in a black and white room, and until she is released does not know what it is like to see red. The argument concludes that the quale cannot be any such physical property. One much discussed, and widely rejected, response to the argument is the Nemirow–Lewis view that the knowledge Mary acquires when she leaves her room is not *knowledge that* but a kind of *knowledge how*, that she does not learn any new fact, and so that there is no relevant fact of which she was ignorant when she knew all of the physical facts but did not know what it is like to see red (see Nemirow, 1980, and Lewis, 1990). What she acquires is a set of abilities – to recognize experiences of red, to imagine them, and so on. Critics rightly claim that it is implausible to say that Mary does not learn any new facts. But one doesn't need to accept that in order to accept that what Mary crucially lacked before leaving her black and white room were certain abilities. And these include the ability to refer demonstratively to the quale instantiation – or, better, to the qualitative character it represents.[7] The functional role of the quale includes its being such that its being instantiated in an experience of a creature bestows, or contributes to bestowing, such abilities. And the ability to refer demonstratively to the quale, or to the associated qualitative character, is one that is available only to creatures in whose experience the quale is instantiated. Mary's ignorance, before she leaves her room, is not ignorance of the nature of the quale: it is basically the lack of a particular way of referring to it, and knowing about its instantiation. This lack will bring with it an inability to make factual judgments about it that involve that way of referring to it – e.g., the judgment that after her release Mary can express by saying (P1), "This is the quale having causal profile C." But note that this is an identity judgment. In one sense the fact it expresses was already known to Mary, since she already knew the truth of (P2), "The quale having causal profile C is the quale having causal profile C." If we individuate the facts expressed by judgments by the modes of presentation involved in their expression, P1 and P2 express different facts. But if we individuate facts by the things and properties involved in them, they are the same fact.

There is said to be an "explanatory gap" between the physical and the phenomenal facts (see Levine, 1983, and 1993). What is supposed to cry out for explanation, and yet be incapable of it, is the fact that when someone's perceptual system is in a certain physical condition, that person has an experience with a certain phenomenal character. But if physicalism is true, and if qualia are properties of experiences, then for any quale Q there will be a physically realized property P whose causal profile is such that anything we might want to explain in terms of an experience's instantiating Q (discriminative and recognitional abilities, introspective judgments, etc.) is explained by its instantiating P. The obvious explanation of this – the only one that is compatible with qualia not being epiphenomenal – is that Q is identical with P. And there is no call for an explanation of this; identities are not the kinds of facts that require, or can have, explanations (see Block, 1978b, and Papineau, 2002). What we can ask for an explanation of is how it can be, in a particular case, that different modes of presentation pick out the same thing. Applied to the present case, this might be the question of how an introspective-demonstrative mode of presentation of a quale can pick out the same thing as a description of it in terms of causal profile. And the answer to this was sketched in the preceding paragraph – the causal profile of a quale includes its making itself available to introspection and for demonstrative reference.

Notes

1 This is Michael Tye's use of the term (1997).
2 See Tye (1994) and McLaughlin (2003). Tye later abandoned internalism about phenomenal character. He says that "*phenomenology ain't in the head*" (1995, p. 151).
3 See Hardin (1993) for an account of this.
4 For Swampman, see Davidson (1987).
5 For spectrum inversion to be behaviorally undetectable the color quality spaces of the creatures in question would have to have a symmetrical structure, which is arguably not

true of the color quality spaces of actual human beings – see next paragraph in text. But creatures with asymmetrical color quality spaces could be spectrum inverted relative to other creatures with identically structured quality spaces in a way that is behaviorally detectable – see Shoemaker (2003a).

6 I also hold that the causal profiles of properties are essential to them, and that having the causal profile it has is metaphysically necessary and sufficient for being that property – but I needn't insist on this stronger claim here. Both claims are defended in Shoemaker (1980 and 1998).

7 I say "better" because it goes with the Moorean transparency intuition that demonstrative reference in introspection is to what is ostensibly represented by the experience rather than to the experience itself.

References

Block, N. (1978a). Troubles with functionalism. In W. Savage (ed.), *Perception and Cognition: Minnesota Studies in the Philosophy of Science*, vol. 9. Minneapolis: University of Minnesota Press.

— (1978b). Reductionism: philosophical analysis. In W. T. Reich (ed.), *Encyclopedia of Bioethics*. London: Macmillan.

— and Fodor, J. (1972). What psychological states are not. *Philosophical Review*, 81, 159–81.

Boghossian, P. and Velleman, D. (1989). Color as a secondary quality. *Mind*, 98, 81–103.

— and — (1991). Physicalist theories of color. *Philosophical Review*, 100, 67–106.

Clark, A. (2000). *A Theory of Sentience*. Oxford: Oxford University Press.

Davidson, D. (1987). Knowing one's own mind. *Proceedings and Addresses of the American Philosophical Association*, 60, 441–58.

Dretske, F. (1995). *Naturalizing the Mind*. Cambridge, MA: MIT Press.

Hardin, L. (1993). *Color For Philosophers: Unweaving the Rainbow*. Indianapolis: Hackett.

Harman, G. (1990). The intrinsic quality of experience. *Philosophical Perspectives*, 4, 31–52.

Hilbert, D. and Kalderon, M. (2000). Color and the inverted spectrum. In S. Davis (ed.), *Color Perception: Philosophical, Psychological, Artistic and Computational Perspectives*. Oxford: Oxford University Press.

Jackson, F. (1982). Epiphenomenal qualia. *Philosophical Quarterly*, 32, 127–36.

— (1986). What Mary didn't know. *Journal of Philosophy*, 80, 291–5.

Kim, J. (1998). *Mind in a Physical World*. Cambridge, MA: MIT Press.

Levine, J. (1983). Materialism and qualia: the explanatory gap. *Pacific Philosophical Quarterly*, 64, 354–61.

— (1993). On leaving out what it's like. In M. Davies and G. W. Humphreys (eds.), *Consciousness: Psychological and Philosophical Essays*. Oxford: Blackwell.

— (1995). Qualia: intrinsic, relational or what? In T. Metzinger (ed.), *Conscious Experience*. Lawrence, KS: Allen.

— (2003). Experience and representation. In Q. Smith and A. Jokic (eds.), *Consciousness: New Philosophical Perspectives*. Oxford: Oxford University Press.

Lewis, D. (1990). What experience teaches. In W. Lycan (ed.), *Mind and Cognition*. Oxford: Blackwell.

Loar, B. (2003). Transparent experience and the availability of qualia. In Q. Smith and A. Jokic (eds.), *Consciousness: New Philosophical Perspectives*. Oxford: Clarendon.

Lycan, W. (1996). *Consciousness and Experience*. Cambridge, MA: MIT Press.

McLaughlin, B. (2003). Color, consciousness, and color consciousness. In Q. Smith and A. Jokic (eds.), *Consciousness: New Philosophical Perspectives*. Oxford: Oxford University Press.

Nemirow, L. (1980). Review of *Mortal Questions*, by Thomas Nagel. *Philosophical Review*, 89, 473–7.

Papineau, D. (2002). *Thinking about Consciousness*. Oxford: Clarendon.

Shoemaker, S. (1975). Functionalism and qualia. *Philosophical Studies*, 27, 292–315.

—— (1980). Causality and properties. In P. van Inwagen (ed.), *Time and Cause*. Dordrecht: D. Reidel.

—— (1982). The inverted spectrum. *Journal of Philosophy*, 74, 357–81.

—— (1994). Phenomenal character. *Noûs*, 28, 21–38.

—— (1996). Intrasubjective/innersubjective. In *The First-Person Perspective and Other Essays*. Cambridge: Cambridge University Press.

—— (1998). Causal and metaphysical necessity. *Pacific Philosophical Quarterly*, 79, 59–77.

—— (2000). Introspection and phenomenal character. *Philosophical Topics*, 28, 247–73.

—— (2003a). Content, character, and color. *Philosophical Issues*, 13, 253–78.

—— (2003b). Realization and mental causation. In C. Gillett and B. Loewer (eds.), *Physicalism and Its Discontents*. Cambridge: Cambridge University Press.

—— (2006). On the ways things appear. In T. Gendler and J. Hawthorne (eds.), *Perceptual Experience*. Oxford: Oxford University Press.

Tye, M. (1994). Qualia, content, and the inverted spectrum. *Noûs*, 28, 159–83.

—— (1995). *Ten Problems of Consciousness*. Cambridge, MA: MIT Press.

—— (1997). Qualia. In E. Zalta (ed.), *The Stanford Encyclopedia of Philosophy*. Stanford, CA: Metaphysics Research Lab/Stanford University.

—— (2000). *Consciousness, Color and Content*. Cambridge, MA: MIT Press.

Sydney Shoemaker

IS AWARENESS OF OUR MENTAL ACTS A KIND OF PERCEPTUAL CONSCIOUSNESS?

All Consciousness
Is Perceptual

Jesse Prinz

When it comes to consciousness, many researchers like to divide and conquer. They distinguish different species of consciousness and then explain these separately. The taxonomies vary, of course, but the preference for distinctions is widespread. If there are many species of consciousness, then for each putatively conscious mental episode there will be a question about what category it belongs to. In this spirit, Christopher Peacocke (MENTAL ACTION AND SELF-AWARENESS (I)) inquires into the nature of conscious thoughts. One possible view is that we are never conscious of our thoughts. Another possible view is that consciousness of thoughts is a distinctive species of consciousness in its own right. A third possibility is that conscious thoughts are a special case of another species of consciousness – a species not obviously associated with thinking. Peacocke opts for the third strategy, and offers arguments for the conclusion that conscious thoughts are a case of conscious actions. He contrasts this proposal with the idea that conscious thoughts can be characterized as a species of conscious perception. Peacocke believes in perceptual consciousness, but he thinks that that action consciousness is different, and that conscious thoughts fall on the action side of this divide. I want to resist this picture. I want to suggest that there is just one species of consciousness, and it is perceptual consciousness. Any conscious state is a perceptual state, and appearances to the contrary can be explained away. Accordingly, I claim that conscious thoughts, insofar as such things exist, are perceptually represented. I will not discuss all of the rich and interesting ideas developed in Peacocke's paper. Instead, I will present an alternative picture. I will discuss forms of consciousness, including conscious thoughts, that seem to resist explanation in perceptual terms, and I will argue that perceptual accounts are actually quite plausible on closer analysis. If I am right, all consciousness is perceptual consciousness. In a final section, I will summarize some of the ways in which this thesis differs from the views defended by Peacocke.

1 Perceptual Consciousness

Let's begin with some definitions. Throughout this discussion, I will use the term consciousness to refer to phenomenal consciousness. Phenomenally conscious states are mental states that have phenomenal character: it is like something to have such states (Block, 1995). It is sometimes suggested that the term consciousness can also be applied to mental states that lack phenomenal qualities. In ordinary usage, there are two obvious examples. We sometimes seem to use "conscious" to refer to a kind of information access, as in, "Are you conscious of the fact that Jones voted for Bush?" And we sometimes use "conscious" as a synonym for "awake." These uses lead some to conclude that "conscious" is ambiguous (Block, 1995). I'm not so sure. I think these uses are parasitic on phenomenal consciousness. Information access is cheap. Any search engine has access to information stored on the World Wide Web, but we don't say that Google is conscious of anything. When we talk about consciousness of information we seem to always have in mind episodes of information access that are also phenomenal in character. Likewise, when we say that being conscious is being awake, we seem to presuppose that being awake correlates with having phenomenal states. Once it is pointed out that dreams are phenomenal states, it no longer seems natural to say people are unconscious when they are asleep, and if we were to discover that people had conscious states when they were comatose, we would hesitate to refer to such people as unconscious. Likewise, when we consider someone who is undergoing a petit mal seizure, we are inclined to say she is awake but not conscious. These linguistic intuitions lead me to conclude that phenomenal consciousness is an essential thread uniting all mental states that we refer to using the word "conscious" in English. Nothing much rides on this assessment. I will be content to prove that all phenomenal consciousness is perceptual, even if I can't establish the stronger thesis that all consciousness is perceptual.

I will define a perceptually conscious mental state as a mental state that is couched in a perceptual format. A perceptual format is a representational system that is proprietary to a sense modality. To say that phenomenal states are perceptual is to say that their representational vehicles always belong to one of the senses: touch, vision, audition, olfaction, and so on. This assumes that conscious states comprise mental representations, but notice that it does not entail representationalism, the thesis that every difference in phenomenal qualities is a difference in representational content. Perceptual formats may have a kind of content that is not representational, such that two perceptual representations can represent the same thing even though they are phenomenally distinct. With Peacocke (1983), I suspect that this is right. For example, I think we can phenomenally represent the feature of being located to the left of us, by vision, audition, touch, and probably smell. There is very good evidence that there are multiple modality-specific spatial maps in the brain (e.g., Gross and Graziano, 1995), and these may underwrite distinct phenomenal qualities even if they sometimes represent the same spatial features. So, in my definition on perceptual consciousness, I am committing only to the thesis that perceptually conscious states comprise mental entities that are in the business of representing. This definition would need to be amended only if we discovered that perceptual format includes components that are not representational in nature. It is sometimes suggested that there are words in languages that don't serve a referential function. Some expletives, particles, and logical operators may fall into this category. Perhaps perceptual symbol systems contain such things as well, and perhaps these things can contribute to the phenomenal quality of an experience. I am willing to accept that possibility. The key point about perceptual consciousness is the claim that perceptually conscious states have a perceptual format.

Perceptually conscious states include conscious sensory states, such as smelling cinnamon or hearing the sound of a harmonica, and they also include mental images, such as an image of a pink rhinoceros or a recollection of the feeling of walking around in wet socks. This much isn't especially controversial. The main thesis I want to defend here is that every phenomenally conscious mental state is perceptually conscious. We do not have conscious states couched in non-perceptual formats. If I am right, we never have conscious states in our motor systems, and no conscious experiences are constituted by amodal representations, such as the representations postulated by people who believe in a language of thought. This means that if we are ever conscious of thoughts and actions, it is by means of associated perceptual states. All phenomenally conscious mental states are perceptually encoded. I will call this the perceptual consciousness hypothesis, or PC.

There are two general arguments for PC. One is an argument from parsimony. If all phenomenally conscious states are perceptually conscious and there is a unified theory of perceptual consciousness, then there is a unified theory of phenomenal consciousness. Having a single unified theory is, all things being equal, better than having a family of different theories for each kind of phenomenal state that we experience. Some parsimony arguments are very weak. For example, suppose a syntactician were to argue that her theory of grammar is simpler than a competing theory, and hence more likely to be true. Her opponent could reply that we have little reason to think that the human mind has evolved to acquire rules that are maximally simple. Psychological mechanisms are not necessarily as elegant as they could be. But, the argument that I am putting forward is not based on the assumption that consciousness involves simple mechanisms. Rather, I am arguing that the same kinds of mechanisms may underwrite all forms of phenomenal consciousness if PC is true. This would be an attractive outcome because all phenomenally conscious states share something in common: they have qualitative character. There may be other commonalities as well. Here are three functional similarities: under ordinary conditions, phenomenal states are available for reporting; all phenomenal states can be intensified by increasing the allocation of attention; and having phenomenal states seems to be a precondition for laying down an episodic memory (we do not have episodic memories of things we perceived unconsciously). The functional and phenomenal similarities shared by all phenomenal states suggest that phenomenal consciousness arises in the same way in every case. A theory that postulated one kind of mechanism for giving rise to consciousness would do better than a heterogeneous theory. PC offers hope for a unified account. If PC delivers a unified theory, then that gives us a good (though non-demonstrative) reason for thinking that PC is true.

This parsimony arguments rests on two hidden premises. The first is that we have a unified theory of perceptual consciousness. If different sense modalities generate conscious states in different ways, then our hopes for a unified theory are dashed.

Fortunately, I think there is a good unified theory of perceptual consciousness on offer. I have defended such a theory elsewhere (e.g., Prinz, 2000, 2001, 2005, 2007, forthcoming-a). Here, I offer a statement of the theory rather than a defense. The theory has two parts. The first is a hypothesis about where in information-processing perceptual consciousness arises. This hypothesis was originally defended by Ray Jackendoff (1987). All perceptual systems are hierarchically organized. Low-level subsystems sample local features of the environment, such as edges, in the case of vision, or individual tones, in the case of audition. At the intermediate level, these features are integrated into coherent forms: edges become contours, and tones become melodies or words. At the high level, invariant features are abstracted: an object seen from different vantage points generates the exact same high-level visual representation, and a word spoken by different people with different accents produces the same high-level auditory representation. Given this general story about how sensory systems are organized, it seems overwhelmingly likely that conscious perceptual states always reside at the intermediate level. When we see an object, we see a coherent contour from a particular point of view, and when we hear a word or a melody, we experience its specific acoustic properties. The low level is too piecemeal and the high level is too abstract. This observation led Jackendoff to conclude that conscious perceptual states are always composed of intermediate-level perceptual representations. I think Jackendoff is right, but notice that mere activity in intermediate-level subsystems is not sufficient for consciousness. In subliminal perception, we represent stimuli throughout our perceptual hierarchies, but there is no conscious experience of those stimuli. Consciousness requires something more, and I think the missing ingredient is attention. Consciousness arises when and only when we are attending. Mack and Rock (1998) have shown that visual consciousness of a stimulus is lost when we are not paying attention, and the same seems to be true in other modalities. So I think conscious perceptual states are all attended intermediate-level representations, or AIRs for short. The AIR theory is a unified theory of perceptual consciousness. If all consciousness is perceptual then all consciousness arises in the same way.

The argument from parsimony has another hidden presupposition. To be convincing, it must be the case that theories that do not reduce all consciousness to perceptual consciousness either lack unity or suffer from other serious defects. I am assuming that there cannot be a unified theory of consciousness unless all conscious states are perceptual (or at least that unity is unlikely to be achieved if we go another route). On the face of it, there seem to be some unified theories of consciousness that do not assume that all consciousness is perceptual. For example, consider the higher-order thought theory (Rosenthal, 2005). On this view, a mental state becomes conscious when and only when it is the object of a non-inferential self-inscriptive higher-order thought. The experience of seeing red becomes conscious when a red perceptual state directly leads me to the thought that I am seeing red. The very same mechanism underwrites consciousness of non-perceptual states. I become aware of an action by thinking that I am acting, and I become aware of a thought by thinking that I am thinking. This is an extremely elegant account and it promises to deliver a unified theory of consciousness without presupposing PC. Strictly speaking, then, the argument from parsimony for PC is weaker than I initially implied. If PC provides a unified theory, that lends support to PC, but only to the extent that PC is superior to other unified theories. Someone like Peacocke who thinks that conscious actions and conscious thoughts are not explicable in terms of conscious perceptions could achieve unity by embracing a higher-order thought theory, or some other theory of consciousness that doesn't abide by PC.

To rebut this weakening of the argument from parsimony, I would have to show that the AIR theory is better than other non-PC theories, and that is beyond the scope of the present discussion. Elsewhere, however, I have argued on the basis of empirical evidence that the AIR theory is the correct theory of perceptual consciousness (Prinz, 2005), and, if I am right, the parsimony argument that I have offered here is very strong indeed. If perceptual consciousness is AIR consciousness, then parsimony suggests that all consciousness is AIR consciousness. For present purposes I am content with the argument that PC is attractive because it is one *of several possible* ways of achieving unity, but, for the record, I submit that it is the best way to achieve unity, because the AIR theory has advantages over other theories. Here let me just mention one advantage.

Recall the functional features shared by all phenomenal states: they are available for reporting, they are intensified by attention, and they are a precondition for episodic memory. I submit that the AIR theory offers direct explanation of all of these. The bit about attention is built into the theory. If consciousness arises with attention, then intensification of attention should lead to intensification of consciousness. The higher-order thought theory has no ready explanation of the link between consciousness and attention, nor even of the fact that consciousness comes in degrees. The AIR theory also explains the link between consciousness and reporting because there is a link between attention and reportability. I think "attention" is a natural kind term, and the best scientific analysis of what is going on when we attend is that information-processing systems are modulating activity in a way that makes their representations available to working memory. Items in working memory are reportable. Therefore, if consciousness requires attention and attention is the gateway to working memory, then consciousness will usually lead to reportability. (I say "usually" because, under some circumstances, language systems are occupied or not functioning or too slow to verbalize the steady flow of attended inputs.) Higher-order thought theory can explain reportability only by building in the ad hoc assumption that mental states are reportable whenever we think about them. Finally, the link between consciousness and episodic memory is explained because there is good empirical evidence that working memory encoding is a prerequisite to episodic encoding. If attention is needed for working memory, and working memory is needed for episodic memory, then attention is needed for episodic memory. If consciousness requires attention, then so does episodic memory. These considerations suggest that AIR has explanatory advantages over the higher-order thought theory and over any theory that doesn't implicate attention. If I am right, the only way to offer a non-PC theory that has any hope of competing with the AIR theory is to admit that consciousness requires attention and drop the claim that consciousness always requires perceptual representations. I don't think there is much hope for such a theory since everything we know about attention suggests that attention is a perceptual phenomenon. Attention mechanisms seem to operate on perceptual systems. Those who want to challenge this claim have the burden of establishing non-perceptual attention, and that is a tall order. These are some of the considerations that lead me to think that the AIR theory is the best unified theory of phenomenal consciousness in town. Moreover, if I am right that all attention is perceptual and all conscious states have the functional properties adduced earlier, then this is a strong reason for thinking that all consciousness is perceptual consciousness. PC coupled with AIR may be not merely *a* parsimonious theory but *the best* available parsimonious theory. One could abandon parsimony, but only on pain of losing explanatory purchase on functional and phenomenal similarities shared by all conscious states.

For these reasons, I think the parsimony argument is quite powerful. It's not just an argument to the effect that PC would lead to a simpler theory of consciousness, but also that the unity afforded by PC, when combined with an attention-based theory of perceptual consciousness, has important explanatory virtues that are lacking in other accounts. There is, however, one important caveat. Above I said that the parsimony argument has two hidden assumptions. First, we have seen, the most plausible way to achieve unity is to explain all consciousness in terms of perceptual consciousness. The second assumption is that such a reduction is even plausible. If there is a fundamental obstacle to explaining all consciousness in perceptual terms, then the parsimony argument can't get off the ground.

This brings me to a second general argument for PC. I think PC is prima facie plausible. I think that, whenever we examine the contents of conscious experience, all the phenomenal qualities we encounter seem to be perceptual in nature. Introspection suggests that all consciousness is perceptual. There is no difference between conscious episodes that cannot be chalked up to a perceptual difference. Consciousness just seems to be perceptual in nature. Call this the argument from perceptual sufficiency. I find the perceptual sufficiency claim introspectively obvious, but others do not. Many researchers seem to find it obvious that there are examples of conscious experience that cannot be explained perceptually. To defend the argument from perceptual sufficiency, I need to consider these alleged counterexamples. That is the task I turn to in the next section.

The interim moral is that there are two arguments that could be used to defend PC. PC would provide a unified theory of consciousness, and there is good reason to think a unified theory would be much better than a disunified theory. This argument can be weak or strong. On the week formulation, PC offers one of several possible strategies for attaining unity, and on the strong formulation, PC offers the most plausible strategy, because the functional features that are shared by all conscious states are most likely to be explained by mechanisms that operate only within perceptual systems, namely mechanisms of attention. The second argument says that all phenomenal qualities just seem to be perceptual: they can be sufficiently explained by appeal to perceptual representations. The two arguments work in concert. The argument from parsimony suggests we should explain all consciousness in perceptual terms if we can, and the argument from perceptual sufficiency suggests that we can. By *modus ponens*, we have a powerful case for PC. But this case depends on whether I am right about perceptual sufficiency. Some people argue that there are conscious states that cannot be explained in perceptual terms.

To identify apparent counterexamples to PC, recall that perceiving is only one aspect of mental life. Traditionally, the mind is partitioned into three broad classes of information-processing systems. In addition to perceptual systems, which receive inputs from the mind-external world, there are systems and output systems. Central systems are in charge of cognition or thinking. They are the control centers for judgment, planning, and deliberation. Output systems control behavior. They orchestrate the movements in our bodies when we execute decisions to act. If thinking and acting have phenomenal qualities that outstrip perception, then PC is false.

My strategy here will be to argue that PC is possible, even plausible, by explaining how consciousness of action and thought might turn out to be perceptual. My proposals can be taken as empirical hypotheses in need of further investigation, but, even if they are wrong in detail, they serve to show that PC is worth taking seriously.

2 Action

To begin with, consider action. There are conscious feelings associated with action. When we walk, leap, reach, or grasp, we experience what we are doing. On the face of it, the experiences in question are not perceptual. They are, instead, motoric. Within the brain some information-processing centers are dedicated to the planning and execution of motor responses. These centers are active when we move our bodies, and activations in these centers are often presumed to be the neural correlates of the experience that we have when we move. If this presumption is right, then action is a counterexample to PC.

There is an obvious alternative explanation for the awareness of action. Rather than experiencing the motor commands that cause us to act, we may be experiencing the changes in our bodies that result from the execution of those commands. The experience of action may be somatosensory. We have several ways of sensing the body: kinesthesia conveys information about the tension in our muscles, proprioception conveys information about posture and the position of our extremities, and touch conveys information about those things that make contact with our skin as we move through space. Just as we have nerves sending signals to our bodies, there are nerves coming back in. We may be experiencing the outputs rather than the inputs. If you wiggle your finger, you will have a kinesthetic experience. See if you find anything else in your experience. When I introspect, I do not. We know from neuroimaging that movement causes activation in the somatosensory cortex and it is possible that the neural correlates of sensory experience reside there.

This proposal could also be applied to cases in which we merely imagine acting. Imagine hopping up and down. On the motor theory of action consciousness, your experience as you imagine hopping supervenes on activity in your motor cortices. But it is equally plausible, I submit, that you are also imagining sensory changes in your body. When we imagine hopping, we imagine what it's like to feel our weight shift as we rise into the air, and we imagine the impact as our feet hit the ground. Such experiences may exhaust the conscious qualities of imagined actions.

Against this proposal, the opponent of PC might point out that there is a phenomenal difference between acting and being acted upon. It feels different to raise your arm and to have your arm lifted. In the former case, there is a feeling of agency. Yet, in both cases, you will be receiving sensory feedback from your arm. Therefore, it is natural to suppose that the difference in active and passive movement is explained by a difference in the contribution of motor plans. We feel as though we are the cause of our movements when our movements are caused by states in our motor systems, and that may be taken as evidence for the claim that motor states are constituent parts of our experiences of agency.

This story is tempting but not compulsory. The feeling of agency could be explained by a kind of prediction that the brain makes when we are about to act. If you elect to move your arm, you will be able to anticipate its movement. According to some leading neurobiological theories, when a plan is generated in the premotor cortex, a representation is sent to the somatosensory cortex corresponding to what the bodily senses should perceive when that action is executed. That representation is called a "forward model." A forward model is an anticipatory somatosensory image. When our bodies carry out motor plans, the forward model is compared with the actual changes that take place in our body as we move. The feeling of agency may arise from this matching process. If a match occurs, we feel we are in control. If a match doesn't occur, it's because our bodies didn't move as we predicted they would, and that results in an experience of being passively moved by an external source.

This proposal is consistent with a large and growing body of neuroscientific evidence. We know that somatosensory areas are active when people plan and execute actions, and we know that abnormalities in neural processing in somatosensory areas can give rise to illusions of passivity. In alien hand syndrome, for example, patients report that their limbs are moving against their will. This syndrome is sometimes caused by damage in the parietal cortex. In these cases, there may be a malfunction in the matching process. The patients may be able to form action plans that project forward models to somatosensory systems, but those models cannot be accurately matched against incoming information. Forward models may also be compromised in schizophrenia, leading to motivation disorders and misperceptions of control.

Let me consider several objections to this account of experienced agency. First, one might worry that it is phenomenologically implausible that we are forming anticipatory images of our actions whenever we act. The model implies that just before a voluntary movement, there will be a sensory image of that movement, and then, as we move, there will be a match made between the image and the actual movement. But, introspectively, it may not seem that we form such anticipatory images. Arguably, we do not have sensory experiences of the movements in our bodies before we act, and we are not aware of any matching process.

I think this objection rests on a questionable introspective premise. It is perfectly plausible that we form conscious anticipatory images of our actions before executing them. These images may be generated just a few milliseconds before movement, so they are quickly succeeded by the perception of our bodies in motion. The matching process may consist in the fact that there is no significant change in the image that immediately precedes the movement and the one that follows, so we don't have any experience of two representations being compared, but only one experience of our bodies in motion, which begins just before acting and continues on after initiating movement.

There is a second worry facing the forward model story. I suggested that active and passive movement can be distinguished by the presence or absence of anticipatory images that match the experiences we have when our bodies move. But, on the face of it, this proposal is easy to refute. If I know you are about to lift my arm at a specific speed in a specific direction, I can form an anticipatory image of what that will feel like, but my movement will still seem passive. Anticipatory imagery cannot distinguish the experience of active and passive movement.

In response, it is important to point out merely predicting how your body is going to move is not sufficient for a sense of agency on the forward model view. It's not enough to know that my arm is about to be lifted upward. The forward model is likely to be much more specific than that. It is triggered from within by the systems that control action and, consequently, it may include very specific information about what muscles will be engaged, how fast they will move, and when the movement will begin. Timing may be crucial here. If the movement does not start at a particular time interval after the forward model has been generated, the system may send out a mismatch signal, and the agent will feel surprised. She might think: I knew my arm was about to be lifted, but I didn't know *exactly* how it would feel. This story is confirmed by studies of tickling. Notoriously, you can't tickle yourself. On the forward model view, this is explained by the fact that the tickle response requires unexpected movements. Blakemore et al. (1998) developed a robotic hand that a subject can use to tickle herself. The hand is controlled by the subject's own finger movements. If it moves in sync with the subject's fingers, tickling does not occur, but if a slight delay is introduced between the subject's finger movements and the movements of the robotic hand, tickling does occur. Agency is sensitive to subtle differences in timing.

This account predicts that temporally accurate anticipatory bodily images will lead to illusions of control. That is just what happens. Wegner and Wheatley (1999) conducted an experiment in which two participants held a computer mouse and collectively controlled an arrow that moved across an array of objects depicted on the screen. Both participants also wore headphones and listened to words corresponding to objects on the screen, but they were told to move the mouse around randomly. One of these participants was an accomplice of the experimenters, and, in one condition, she deliberately moved the mouse so that the arrow would align with the object whose name had just been played on the headphones. Afterwards, the other participant reported that she had intentionally moved the arrow to the named object. This illusory feeling of control occurred only when the experimenters' accomplice moved the mouse within a small time window after the word was heard. If the movement came too soon or too late, the other participant did not feel any sense of control. One explanation is that every word automatically triggered a body image of movement toward the named object, and when these anticipatory images were followed by externally caused movements in the right direction, there was a match of anticipated movement and actual movement, giving rise to a sense of agency. If you are not convinced, try to bend one of your own fingers forward using your other hand. It will feel as though you are bending your finger willfully in sync with your other hand. You will lose this sense of agency only if you bend your finger in a direction that it cannot move on its own, and, in this case, I think it is background knowledge together with felt discomfort that leads you to recognize that the movement is not being controlled from within.

All Consciousness Is Perceptual | 343

A third objection to the forward model account comes from research on individuals who suffer from deficits in their capacity to perceive changes in their bodies. This disorder is very rare, but there are several known cases, and they have been extensively studied. Consider Ian Waterman (Cole, 1995). He has no sense of kinesthesia or proprioception. He cannot receive direct sensory feedback from his body. To coordinate movement, Waterman must use vision. He must look to see where his limbs are located. Using visual feedback, Waterman can walk and reach and perform other successful behaviors, but, if the lights are shut off, he will fall down. He relies on vision to do what kinesthesia and proprioception do in the rest of us. Waterman puts pressure on the forward model theory for the following reason. He does not suffer from a profound deficit in a sense of agency. When he decides to execute an action, he knows that he has made the decision, and he know that the action is his. If somatosensory states were essential for a sense of agency, we should expect Waterman to feel that he is entirely passive with respect to his movements. A similar objection stems from experiments on healthy individuals with anesthetized limbs. When our limbs are anaesthetized we can still move them voluntarily, and presumably we feel a sense of control when we do so. Consider too the experience of smiling after an oral injection of a local anesthetic. Without seeing a reflection in the mirror, it's difficult to know whether the command to smile was successful, but we feel a sense of control when we succeed. We don't think someone else moved our lips!

On closer analysis, Ian Waterman may not pose a threat to the forward model theory. Waterman suffers from a deficit in sensory inputs, but he may not lack the ability to form somatosensory images. That is, when Waterman decides to move, he may form kinesthetic or proprioceptive images of the movement he is about to make. He can't match these against his actual movements, but he may derive a sense of agency from the generation of forward models. The same explanation can account for the sense of agency in healthy subjects under local anesthesia. We feel that we are commanding our bodies to move even though we can't feel the movement, because we experience somatosensory imagery. In addition, there is good evidence that forward models are not restricted to somatosensory representations. Just before acting, we may form anticipatory *visual* representations corresponding to how our bodies will look once the action is initiated. It is quite clear that Waterman uses vision in this way, and neuroimaging studies of healthy subjects show activation in visual areas when action intentions are formed. If you have received an oral anesthetic, you won't know if your command to smile was successful unless you can see your reflection in the mirror.

Let me consider one final objection to the forward model story. On that story, we feel like the agentic source of an action if an anticipatory image matches the outcome we produce. That explains our sense of agency when we act. But what about when we don't act? What happens when we have a conscious experience of the intention to act but we don't execute the act? What is a conscious experience of intention? In line with my remarks about Ian Waterman, I think a conscious experience of intention is constituted by a forward model. We form the image of how we are going act, and we experience that image as an intention. This proposal is a natural corollary of the forward model story, and it fits nicely with neurophysiological results. In particular, it makes sense of the fact that the felt decision to move occurs 250 milliseconds after a readiness potential in motor areas of the brain. If the conscious experience of intention supervened on motor representations, we might expect the felt intention to co-occur with the onset of the motor response. Unfortunately, the forward model theory of conscious intentions faces a serious objection. I can form an image of how my body is about to move without forming an intention, and surely when I do so it doesn't feel as though I am intending to move. If I know you are about to lift my arm, I may imagine what the movement would feel like, but, in so doing, I won't think that I just intended to move my arm. I may even have the opposite intention. If this objection succeeds, it casts doubt on the forward model story.

I think the best response to this objection is to bite the bullet and say there is no phenomenological difference between intending a movement and expecting one. If phenomenology were all one had to go on, one wouldn't be able to tell these two apart. This response seems introspectively plausible to me. To test it on yourself, try to form a decision to move your finger at a random point in time. See if you can tell by phenomenology alone whether this decision is an intention that your finger move or merely an expectation that it will move. Would the two states *feel* any different? I don't think so. Of course, there is an important difference. In the case where you make the decision to move rather than merely expecting movement, you know that you are the author of the decision. You *believe* that you intend to move. If beliefs can be conscious (see below), this belief will be part of your total phenomenal state at the time, but, I submit, it will not be a component of your intention or a component of the feeling of intending. Rather it will be a contingent accompaniment to that feeling. In principle, one could intend to move, experience that intention, and yet not know that you intended to move. I think we are actually in exactly this state much of the time. We anticipate our intentional actions without forming conscious beliefs to the effect that we intended them. This is what happens, for example, when we walk down the street avoiding collisions with other people. We know which way we are going to move, but this knowledge is not phenomenally marked as an intention or as a mere expectation. We have no thought one way or the other; we just move. To have conscious awareness of an intention as such seem to require an extra bit of thinking, and the formation of a conscious belief, which is about the intention but not constitutive of it. Of course, in some cases an intention may be accompanied by a conscious urge or desire, in which case an affective state will accompany the anticipated action, but for many of our most typical movements through the world, there is no more to the feeling of intending than the feeling of expecting. This may sound surprising at first, but I find no introspective reason to doubt it.

In sum, I think the forward model account of how we come to have feelings of agency is very plausible, and objections to that account can be rejected. If I am right, then the defender of PC has a perfectly good story to tell about this aspect of conscious experience.

Before resting my case, I must briefly consider one final objection to the claim that consciousness of action can be explained in perceptual terms. From the outset, I assumed that perceiving and acting are separate cognitive abilities, served by independent neural systems. This assumption is widespread in cognitive science, but it has recently come under attack. A number of authors have been defending an "enactive" view of perception and perceptual consciousness (e.g., Cotterill, 1998; Hurley,

1998; O'Regan and Noë, 2001; Noë, 2005). On this approach, action and perception are inextricably bound. There is no physical or functional division between action and perception systems, and perception always involves the detection of sensorimotor contingencies: actions afforded by features of a perceived stimulus. On the enactive view, every difference between sensory qualities is a difference in potential for behavioral interaction, and if our capacity to represent behavioral implications of stimuli were lost, we would have no perceptual experience of the external world. If this approach is right, then it makes no sense to reduce consciousness of action to perceptual states, because perceptual states are intrinsically action-oriented.

This is not the place for a full-scale critique of the enactive view (see Prinz, 2006a, forthcoming-b). Let me just register that I think the evidence against enactive perception is extremely strong. First of all, damage to areas of the brain that are known to be used in motor control does not result in perceptual impairments, and damage to perceptual areas does not result in motor impairments: there is a double dissociation. Second of all, there are many qualitative differences between perceptual states that have no obvious motor implications. If you look at a colored surface occupying your entire visual field and then shift to an equally encompassing surface of another hue, there will be no obvious changes in motor affordances, but the color will chance. Conversely, one can learn new affordances without changing perceptual qualities. If you were to move to a country where red lights meant go and green lights meant stop, you could learn to cross the street safely, and doing so would not, we can presume, change the spectral appearance of these colors. I do not deny that under special circumstances, motor responses can influence perception (this may occur when we acclimate to inverting lenses), but I am aware of no compelling evidence for the claim that motor responses are necessary for perception or constitutive of perceived qualities. I am unpersuaded by the enactive view. Indeed, I am advocating the opposite: Where defenders of the enactive view say that every phenomenal quality associated with perception can be explained in terms of a motor response, I claim that every phenomenal quality associated with a motor response can be explained in terms of a co-occurring perceptual state.

3 Thinking

I have been arguing that our experience of action can be explained in perceptual terms. That conclusion adds support to PC, the thesis that all phenomenal consciousness is perceptual consciousness. But action is not the only domain that poses a threat to PC. There are other examples of conscious states that may seem to resist perceptual analysis. Arguably, we have conscious experiences associated with thinking, and it is difficult to see how these experiences can be fully captured by appeal to perceptual episodes. My goal in this section is to argue that this difficulty is merely apparent. There are many plausible strategies for accommodating cognitive phenomenology without violating the strictures of PC.

The term "thinking" probably doesn't refer to a psychological natural kind. There are many distinct processes and capacities that fall under that broad umbrella. Certain forms of conscious thinking may be unproblematically perceptual. Visual problem-solving is one example. Imagine trying to decide whether one can fit another pair of shoes into a suitcase: a natural strategy is to visualize the size of the shoes in relation to the remaining space. Likewise, when adding ice to a beverage, one might visualize the resulting displacement of liquid to determine when to stop. These are examples of conscious thought, and there is little reason to doubt that they are experienced in a perceptual format. More problematic are cases of conscious propositional attitudes, especially when those attitudes have abstract contents. I can consciously entertain the thought that liberals will win the next federal election. I can also believe that this is the case, and desire that it be the case. Each of these attitudes is available to consciousness. It feels like something to have thoughts about the next election. Can such feelings be explained in perceptual terms?

To address this question, let's distinguish between two components comprising a propositional attitude. There is a proposition, and an attitude toward that proposition (entertaining, believing, desiring, and so on). Presumably, both components contribute to the phenomenology, and both must be explained perceptually if PC is right. The propositional content of a propositional attitude is not literally in the head: it is rather, the semantic content of a mental representation. To explain the phenomenology of propositional attitudes, we should ask what are the representational vehicles of propositional attitudes. One answer to this question is that propositional attitudes are mediated by sentences in a language of thought. I don't find this answer compelling, but, in any case, it won't help here. Defenders of the language of thought admit that it is entirely unconscious (Fodor, 1975). There is no phenomenology associated with items in Mentalese. Therefore, even if there is a language of thought, the conscious experiences associated with propositional attitudes must have another source.

It seems to me that there are exactly two ways in which we might have conscious experiences associated with thought contents. First, we can experience silent speech in a natural language. Mentalese has no phenomenology, but English does. Most people experience an incessant inner narrative in their native tongue. This is a vivid and pervasive component of conscious experience. Such inner narratives are perfectly consistent with PC. They are auditory representations. We literally hear sentences in our heads. (I would guess that people who are deaf experience images of gestures or moving lips.)

It would be a mistake to assume that the phenomenology of thought is exhausted by verbal imagery. We know, for example, that people with aphasia continue to think, and there is no reason to deny that some of their thoughts have phenomenal qualities. Lecours and Joanette (1980) describe a person with transient bouts of aphasia who managed to check himself into a hotel and order food at a restaurant during one episode. The desire to check into a hotel can, it would seem, occur without language, and the testimony of this patient would suggest that, in his case, it was a conscious desire. To explain this kind of case, we need to suppose that the phenomenology of thought extends beyond language, and includes other forms of imagery. In particular, it is plausible that thoughts are sometimes experienced via mental images of what they represent. We can certainly recognize hotels without using language. If you were visiting Uzbekistan and didn't know the language, you could find a hotel and check yourself in, by looking for prototypical features – a conspicuously signed residential building, people with luggage, porters, etc. Thoughts about hotels can enter into consciousness by imagining things like that, or by imagining the interior of a hotel room.

Some thought contents are difficult to imagine, of course. It's unlikely that any particular image comes to mind whenever you have the thought that the liberals will win the next election. Of course, if there is a particular liberal candidate running for office, you might form an image of that candidate, and the conscious experience of that image may exhaust the conscious experience you have when entertaining the thought that the liberals will win. Suppose someone asks you whether the liberals will win, and you know who is running. In consciousness, you may experience nothing more than an image of the candidate's face, and the word "yes" in your mind's ear. I don't need to insist that these images represent the proposition that a liberal will win (though I think very simple images can temporarily take on such complex contents: Prinz, 2006b). I need only say that such images may co-occur with the thought that the liberals will win, and, on some occasions, they may be the only conscious manifestations of that thought. When this occurs, the thought itself might be unconscious, but it casts an imagistic shadow on consciousness.

I claim that perceptual images exhaust the conscious experiences associated with propositional contents. There are different ways to argue for this thesis. One strategy would be to argue that all mental representations are perceptual in nature, and hence all thoughts have perceptual phenomenology. That view has been defended by traditional empiricists, such as Hume, and I happen to think it is correct (Prinz, 2002). But it is sufficiently anachronistic these days that I cannot rely on it for the purposes of this discussion. Instead, I want to rely on a combination of introspection and burden-shifting. Everyone admits that there are phenomenal qualities associated with perceptual imagery, and, when I introspect, I find nothing more. For those who think that the phenomenology of thought outstrips perceptual imagery, I offer a challenge: come up with a case of two mental episodes that are phenomenologically distinct, yet alike in all their perceptual qualities.

There is a standard way of meeting this challenge (Block, 1995; Siewert, 1998). Opponents of PC might be impressed by the fact that there is a phenomenological difference between hearing a word in a language that one understands and hearing a word in a language one does not understand. If you are a monolingual English speaker, the word *hujambo* won't have any significance to you; you will hear it as a mere sound. If you speak Swahili, you will recognize the very same sound as a greeting, and, arguably, that difference in comprehension makes a phenomenal difference. Does this show that there are non-perceptual components of phenomenology? I don't think so. Defenders of PC have several compatible strategies for dealing with cases such as this. In some cases, comprehending a word triggers images of what the word represents. The word *hujambo* is not likely to be associated with any image of an object or property, but a Swahili speaker might visualize a greeting situation or attend to aspects of the scene that are relevant to greetings. Second, when one understands a word, other related words immediately come to mind. We know language games or "scripts" for greeting people. The Swahili speaker knows how to continue to the greeting dialog. Third, there are behavioral sequelae when a word is understood. A greeting might warrant a warm smile, a wave, or a handshake. Each of these behaviors can be imagined. Fourth, there are emotions associated with comprehension and with failure to comprehend. A familiar word feels familiar, and there may be emotions associated with the meaning of that word. A greeting from a stranger may elicit a feeling of standoffishness or skeptical curiosity. A greeting from a friend might elicit delight. If the word were unfamiliar, there might be a feeling of puzzlement or a felt urge for clarification. Finally, when we hear familiar words, our experience of the speech sounds may be affected. Ambiguous phonemes may be corrected for via top-down auditory imagery, and breaks between words might be salient. If you know a word it is easier to hold it in working memory, and that can extend the duration of the auditory experience as you rehearse the word in your head. In sum, there are many phenomenal differences associated with hearing words you understand and words you fail to understand, and all of these can be explained in terms of perceptual imagery.

I don't think the *hujambo* case or any other like it can be used to establish that phenomenal differences outstrip perceptual qualities. The defender of PC has many resources to explain what goes on in consciousness when we understand words. Beyond this, I know of no plausible argument for thinking that the phenomenology associated with mental contents is ever non-perceptual. But this leaves one issue unsettled. Even if opponents of PC grant the perceptual character of the conscious mental representations corresponding to the propositional contents of propositional attitudes, they might deny that the attitudes themselves have a perceptual character. It feels different, they will say, to believe something, to desire something, and to entertain something. These attitudes are phenomenally different, but, the objection goes, they cannot be distinguished perceptually. Beliefs and desires feel different, but they don't taste, smell, or look different.

A defender of PC might respond to this worry by simply denying the phenomenon. According to the most plausible theory of propositional attitudes, the difference between believing, entertaining, and wanting is a difference in functional role. If you believe the liberals will win the next election, you act as if that were true (e.g., by placing bets on a liberal victory), and if you want them to win you try to make it true (e.g., by voting liberal), and if you are merely entertaining the thought, you draw the inferences that would follow without acting as if any of them were true (e.g., you might imagine that more money will be invested in environmental causes). These differences in functional role can have an indirect impact on phenomenology. They result in different behavior, and therefore, the experiences you have *after* coming to believe, desire, or entertain thoughts about a liberal victory will differ depending on the attitude. But, if we freeze time and focus on what it is like to consciously experience these different attitudes at the moment they arise, there may, on some occasions, be no difference. Phenomenologically, conscious experienced beliefs may be indistinguishable from entertained thoughts and even desires. We usually *know* if a current mental state is a belief or a desire, but this knowledge may be inferred from unconscious recognition of the functional role, rather than any overt mark on phenomenology.

This reply may work in many instances, but it is difficult to deny that different propositional attitudes can feel different on some occasions. These feelings must be explained. I think that propositional attitudes have an affective phenomenology. When attitudes feel a certain way, it is in virtue of emotions that they elicit in us. There are trivial cases of this. If you fear that the liberals may win, that thought will trigger a feeling of fear or anxiety. If you are delighted that they may win, the thought will trigger joy. The term "desire" probably covers a range of affective states. There are sexual urges, gustatory cravings, personal aspirations, and political preferences, and each of these may have its own affective landscape. These feelings are united by the fact that they involve anticipatory awards. We assign positive value, and hence positive affect, to most of the things that we desire, and anticipating positive affect presumably gives rise to feelings that are at once positive (we revel when we reflect on achieving our goals), but also uncomfortable insofar as they have yet to be realized (like an itch that needs scratching). The itch of hunger may feel different from the itch of career goals, but both have a phenomenology and both involve a kind of fetching discomfort that prods us forward.

I think believing often has an affective phenomenology too, and like desiring it can be highly variable. Belief comes in degrees: we can feel certain, we can feel confident, or we can feel that something just might be true. Each of these feelings seems to be different. I would call each an epistemic emotion. Epistemic emotions have not been extensively investigated, but they should be. They would make a fine dissertation topic. Other examples include doubting, curiosity, surprise, wonder, affirmation, agreement, trust, familiarity, ambivalence, conflict, and what psychologists call "the feeling of knowing." Most of these phenomena can be distinguished by their functional roles, but each also has an emotional character. Perhaps some of the emotions are overlapping, or too close to easily distinguish phenomenologically, but broad phenomenological distinctions are easy to make. Skepticism feels different than enthusiastic endorsement. Epistemic emotions may allow us to phenomenologically differentiate certain propositional attitudes, such as believing and desiring. There may be propositional attitudes that have no concomitant emotions (such as entertaining), but we can identify these by this fact. If someone asks whether I really believe that the liberals will win or if I am just entertaining that possibility, I can answer by seeing whether any feeling of confidence attaches to the thought.

I conclude that, when propositional attitude types have a distinctive phenomenological character, it is typically in virtue of associated emotions. This conclusion is consistent with PC, because emotions are perceptual states. Elsewhere I argue at length that emotions are perceptions of patterned changes in the body (Prinz, 2004a). This view was defended by William James (1884), and has come back into vogue with recent advances in neuroscience (Damasio, 1994). For present purposes, I can settle for a thesis somewhat weaker than James's. What matters here is that emotional *feelings* derive from perceptions of the body. Perhaps, in addition to such feelings, emotions involve unconscious processes, such as automatic appraisal judgments. I don't endorse this hypothesis, but nothing rides on it here. I need only borrow James's account of what emotional feelings are, not his stronger hypothesis that emotions are exhausted by feelings. If emotions also have an unconscious appraisal component, that's irrelevant. I have argued that propositional attitudes can be phenomenologically distinguished by emotional feelings, and I claim that such feelings are perceptions of changes in the body. If I am right about those two claims, then I can defend PC.

In this section, I have argued that the phenomenology of propositional attitudes can be explained in perceptual terms. Attitude contents are represented in consciousness by perceptual images, and attitude types are experienced by means of characteristic emotions. I think the phenomenology of propositional attitudes can be fully explained in perceptual terms, and therefore PC is defensible.

4 Why Peacocke's View Isn't PC

PC contrasts with Peacocke's discussion of "Mental Action and Self-Awareness." Here I will briefly indicate some of the points of content. As I understand him, Peacocke is advancing three central conjectures:

1 Many of our thoughts are mental actions.
2 Consciousness of such thoughts is a special case of action-awareness.
3 Action-awareness is different from perceptual awareness.

I am not sure whether Peacocke wants to treat "consciousness" and "awareness" as synonyms, and I'm not sure whether he means "phenomenal consciousness" by "consciousness." I will assume that these constructs are, at least, intimately related. As a first pass, let's say that we become aware of something if and only if that thing is a conscious mental state or represented by a conscious mental state, and all conscious mental states are phenomenally conscious. If so, Peacocke is committed to the following theses:

1 Many of our thoughts are mental actions.
2′ Consciousness of such thoughts is a special case of conscious action.
3′ Conscious action is different from conscious perception.

I am inclined to accept (1), but with a caveat. I suspect that the term "action" can be defined so broadly as to include both intentional behaviors and certain thoughts, but this does not entail that mental and behavioral actions involve the same processes. The fact that one term can be used in both cases should not be taken as strong evidence for share mechanisms. "Action" is a general term. Peacocke's suggestion that there may be psychological affinities between mental and behavioral actions is certainly intriguing, and not implausible. My caveat is simply that we should exercise caution in drawing such an inference from the fact that the term "action" seems applicable in both cases. If there are mechanisms in common, they must be established empirically.

My more serious disagreements with Peacocke concern his other conjectures. I reject (2′) and (3′). I don't think consciousness of thoughts is a special case of conscious action. Rather, I think both are a special case of conscious perception. I don't think that conscious actions are metaphysically or explanatorily prior to conscious thoughts. The relation is not one of genus to species. In both cases, forward models may give us a sense of authorship, but the actual states constituting conscious experiences of thoughts and actions are quite different. My analysis of conscious thoughts primarily involved conscious experiences of images of words, images of things, and emotions. I think it is wrong to say conscious thoughts can be assimilated to the model of conscious actions. I reject (3'), because it is at odds with PC. Actions become conscious through our experiences of real or anticipated perceptions of the body in motion. All consciousness is perceptual.

I haven't argued directly against Peacocke. I simply presented an alternative picture. Let me briefly consider whether there is anything in his discussion that might pose a serious threat to PC. Peacocke argues that action-awareness is "distinctive," and by that I assume he means it differs from perceptual awareness (what I am equating with perceptual consciousness). Let's consider his five marks of distinction. First, he says that "you can be aware that you are doing something without perceiving that you are doing it." This is a claim that I want to deny. I think, at least, that when you are consciously experiencing yourself acting that is in virtue of perceiving or imagining your body moving. Who is right? Peacocke supports his view by considering the case of opening your mouth after receiving a local anesthetic at the dentist. He says you will be aware that your mouth is open even though you can't feel it. I disagree. In the case of opening your mouth, the muscles in your face and jaw that have not been anesthetized can sense the movement. So we need to consider a subtler facial gesture, such as smiling. Above I noted that you precisely can't tell whether you are smiling after an oral anesthetic preparation without looking in the mirror. You can experience the intention to smile, because your capacity to form sensory images is intact, but you won't know whether you have succeeded.

Peacocke's second mark of distinction is equally open to doubt. He says that action-awareness is awareness that you are doing something, not merely awareness that something is happening. There may be a sense in which this is true. It is in virtue of doing something – of being the author of an action – that one has an experience of that action. Perhaps, then, conscious experiences of actions represent doings. But there is another sense in which Peacocke's claim may be false. On the model that I propose, action-awareness is an awareness of something happening to one's body. We are not directly aware of authoring the action, we are aware of the acting body. Peacocke could show that action-awareness differs from perceptual awareness only if he could refute this interpretation.

Peacocke's three remaining marks of distinction do not actually distinguish action-awareness from perceptual awareness. First, he says that action-awareness is representational, but does not depend on concepts of beliefs. This is famously true of conscious perception. Second, he says that action-awareness is first-personal and present-tensed. This seems to be true of perceptual awareness as well. When you look at a tulip, it is always from a point of view, and there is a sense of ownership that seems to come along with that experience. Accounting for the sense of ownership is a notoriously difficult problem. For present purposes, I need point out only that it is as much a part of perceptual consciousness as action consciousness. Third, Peacocke says that action-awareness makes available demonstrative ways of thinking: we can think about "this movement." Of course, the same is true of perception, as Peacocke himself acknowledges.

In discussing action demonstratives, Peacocke notes that the reference of "this movement" is determined by the movements we actually bring about, not by one's perceptions of those movements, which may be erroneous. To use Peacocke's example, if you intentionally produce a movement that you know to be Churchill's victory gesture, but, by some accident of wiring, misperceive it, your phrase "this gesture" will refer to the movement you make, not the one you perceive. This may look like evidence against the perceptual account of action consciousness. If conscious experiences of actions were perceptual, and if demonstratives were semantically fixed by those perceptual states, then, in the Churchill example, you would refer to the movement you experienced, not the one you made. Peacocke would claim that this is a fatal consequence for the theory. I disagree. I think the phrase "this movement" can be used in two ways. In public discourse it can be used to pick out the most salient, visible movement. That is not a case of a phenomenal demonstrative. Internally, I submit that a phenomenal demonstrative refers to the movement you represent in experience, not the one you make. In the Churchill case, you might anticipate the correct movement through somatic imagery, and, in that case, if you think "this movement" just prior to acting, you will refer correctly to the movement you actually make. But suppose you think "this movement" just after acting, and suppose, as in Peacocke's case, your experience differs from the movement you actually make. My intuition is that you refer to the experienced movement. If you had this experience in a dark room, so that you could not see the gesture you produced, you would think, "Damn! I intended to make Churchill's victory gesture, but *this movement* is different." Were this a public demonstrative, your thought would be false, because "this movement" would refer to the actual gesture, which was just like Churchill's. But if you are really using a phenomenal demonstrative, then your thought is true. In fact, the frustration arises precisely because you experientially recognize a movement that differs from your intentions. You think, "this movement that I am experiencing now is not what I intended." Fortunately, the movement you are experiencing now is not the one you actually made. You might discover that when the lights go on, at which point you'll say, "this movement that I am experiencing from the inside differs from this movement that I am observing with my eyes." The fact that we can form informative identities using the phrase "this movement" suggests that two different kinds of demonstratives are at work.

In sum, I don't think that Peacocke identifies any features that distinguish conscious experiences of actions from conscious experiences of perceptions. And therefore he leaves PC unscathed.

Let me mention just one more point of contention. I have been focusing on action, and have said little about Peacocke's account of conscious thought. Is there any reason to favor his theory, according to which many conscious thoughts are conscious actions, over mine, according to which conscious thoughts are conscious perceptions of words, images, and emotions? There is one relevant argument in Peacocke's discussion, which parallels my *hujambo* example above. He notes that the same words can be associated with different thoughts. But Peacocke's example adds a new twist. In the *hujambo* case, I sought to explain how perceptual features can distinguish the experience of a word one understands from a word one doesn't understand. Peacocke gives an example in which the words are fully understood, but the kind of thought they express differs from occasion to occasion. Here's his case. The words: "Meeting tomorrow!" can be experienced as an unbidden imagination, as a judgment based on memory, or as a decision. It is implausible that any different imagery, verbal or otherwise, can distinguish these three cases. That raises doubts about my account of how we phenomenally experience thoughts.

I think this is a nice case, but it can readily be accommodated on my view. Here again, I appeal to emotions. Imagining, judging, and deciding feel different because they are associated with different affective states. Imagining may be the most affectively neutral of the three. In unbidden imagination, the words "meeting tomorrow" might just appear in auditory consciousness. But if I am making a judgment from memory, there will be a feeling of affirmation, and perhaps also a feeling of recollection ("Come to think of it, I have a meeting tomorrow"). The decision to hold a meeting tomorrow will feel different. Emotions of an imperative nature will arise. This may sound far-fetched. We don't ordinarily talk about feelings of judgment or feelings of decision. But it is easy to prove that such emotions exist. Notice that unbidden imagination, judgment based on recollection, and decision are all associated with different intonation. A decent actor could say "meeting tomorrow" in three ways, and it would be immediately obvious whether he was imagining, judging, or deciding. Intonation is a verbal expression of affect. It conveys the diverse feelings that accompany different propositional attitudes toward the same content. Just as interrogative intonation expresses a feeling of uncertainty, certain kinds of assertoric intonation can reflect decisions or recollections. Indeed, differences in intonation are enough to phenomenally distinguish these three ways of thinking about the meeting in question. Even if one doesn't have the corresponding emotions, one might intone the words "meeting tomorrow" differently in silent speech.

The argument from intonation is intended to prove that the very same phrase could be experienced differently depending on one's propositional attitude, and that is enough to show that Peacocke's example can be accommodated without giving up on PC. I mention for the record, however, that I think we often use subvocal speech without special intonation or accompanying emotions. In such cases, we could not tell phenomenologically whether we were recalling or deciding. This is important because it may correspond to a difference between my view and Peacocke's. It may be a feature of his view that different propositional attitudes are always phenomenally discernable when we have conscious thoughts. I doubt that this is true. While reading a philosophy paper I might spontaneously think "the author is mistaken" without knowing whether I just decided that, whether I recalled from an earlier point when I was thinking about the same issues, or whether I even really believe it. Attitudes may not always reveal themselves in phenomenology. PC has an explanation of this phenomenon, because the affective states that phenomenally differentiate our attitudes need not be felt on every occasion.

Perhaps Peacocke can find a way to explain cases where we are conscious of thinking, but unaware of what attitude we are having. I don't mean to imply that such cases pose a serious objection to his proposal. Perhaps, when fully spelled out, our competing theories offer equally good explanations of all aspects of phenomenology. When I introspect my thoughts and actions, I seem to experience nothing but perceptual images, but perhaps I'm a bad introspector. Perhaps my interpretation of my inner states is theory-laden and flawed. How then can we adjudicate between my proposals and the one advanced by Peacocke? What if both are phenomenologically adequate? Let me mention three reasons for preferring my account.

First, I think my version of the forward model theory of experienced agency enjoys more empirical support. Peacocke invokes forward models in his discussion of schizophrenia, using Helmholtz's old term "corollary discharge." But Peacocke assumes that these forward models are copies of motor commands rather than predictions of the sensory states that those commands will bring about. I think the neurobiological evidence supports the conjecture that we are generating anticipatory sensory states. Delusions of control have been associated with abnormal processing in the parietal cortex, which is the main locus of bodily experience. We also know that the parietal cortex is activated just before people act. This is consistent with the sensory interpretation of forward models. Motor areas of the brain also increase activations before people act, but that is no surprise to anyone. The fact that the parietal cortex is involved is predicted by the sensory approach to feelings of agency, but not predicted by the purely motoric approach.

Second, Libet's studies suggest that the experience of agency comes after the generation of a motor plan. If motor responses were the correlates of experienced agency, then there should not be a temporal lag.

Third, if there is an available explanation of conscious thoughts and actions in perceptual terms, it should be preferred on reasons of parsimony. The overarching argument of this paper is that PC offers a unified theory of consciousness and, consequently, should be preferred to other theories, all things being equal. If both Peacocke and I have phenomenologically adequate accounts, then mine should be preferred because it is more parsimonious.

I don't think any of these arguments is conclusive, but collectively they may tip the balance toward PC.

5 Conclusion

Everyone agrees that there is perceptual phenomenology. Defenders of PC argue that this is the only kind of phenomenology there is. If all species of experience can be plausibly explained in perceptual terms, then we should embrace PC. Postulating non-perceptual aspects of conscious experience is unparsimonious. Opponents of PC have the burden of proving that something more is needed. I have not shown here that every phenomenal quality is perceptual, but I hope to have shown that the thesis is plausible, and, given that plausibility, it should be our default hypothesis.

Ultimately, the debate over PC must be resolved empirically. For every alleged non-perceptual phenomenal quality, the defender of PC will propose a possible perceptual state that might explain the experience. That has been my strategy here. But these proposals must be tested using the full resources of experimental psychology and cognitive neuroscience. Otherwise, the debate over PC will collapse into an irresolvable battle of intuitions. History teaches a sober lesson here. During the heyday of introspectionist psychology, Wundt and Titchener insisted that every conscious thought is constituted by perceptual imagery. Their critics, such as Külpe and Woodworth, denied this, arguing that some thoughts are imageless. For example, Woodworth (1906) argued that action intentions have no associated perceptual imagery, and Titchener (1917) argued that conscious intentions are constituted by images of the body in motion. Unfortunately, neither side could convince the other, and this cast introspectionist methods into doubt. Introspection can reveal that action intentions have a distinctive feeling, but the identity of that feeling is very difficult to discern. Progress comes when we combine introspection with other methods. We now have evidence from neuroimaging that bodily imagery probably does occur when people form intentions (see Prinz, 2004b). This kind of research can help adjudicate between competing hypotheses. It supports Titchener's intuitions, and would not have been predicted on Woodworth's theory. Thus, we now have tools that allow us to make progress on a debate that once looked intractable. My assessment of the current literature is that there is no evidence for conscious states in the absence of perceptual imagery; there are no uncontroversial examples of imageless thoughts. One might regard Peacocke's chapter as an attempt to show that conscious experience outstrips perception. I have argued that his evidence is inconclusive, and that the perceptual theory may have some empirical advantages over his account, in addition to being more parsimonious. But I don't take my arguments to be conclusive. Like all empirical claims, PC is provisional, and I would welcome any effort to refute it. In the interim, I place my bets on PC. Conscious experience seems to be a realm of the senses.

References

Blakemore, S.-J., Wolpert, D. M., and Frith, C. D. (1998). Central cancellation of self-produced tickle sensation. *Nature Neuroscience*, 1, 635–40.

Block, N. (1995). On a confusion about a function of consciousness. *Behavioral and Brain Sciences*, 18, 227–47.

Cole, J. (1995). *Pride and a Daily Marathon*. Cambridge, MA: MIT Press.

Cotterill, R. (1998). *Enchanted Looms: Conscious Networks in Brains and Computers*. Cambridge: Cambridge University Press.

Damasio, A. R. (1994). *Descartes' Error: Emotion, Reason, and the Human Brain*. New York: Gossett/Putnam.

Fodor, J. A. (1975). *The Language of Thought*. New York: Cromwell.

Gross, C. G. and Graziano, M. S. A. (1995). Multiple representations of space in the brain. *Neuroscientist*, 1, 43–50.

Hurley, S. (1998). *Consciousness in Action*. Cambridge, MA: Harvard University Press.

Jackendoff, R. (1987). *Consciousness and the Computational Mind*. Cambridge, MA: MIT Press.

James, W. (1884). What is an emotion? *Mind*, 9, 188–205.

Lecours, A. R. and Joanette, Y. (1980). Linguistic and other psychological aspects of paroxysmal aphasia. *Brain and Language*, 10, 1–23.

Mack, A., and Rock, I. (1998). *Inattentional Blindness*. Cambridge, MA: MIT Press.

Noë, A. (2005). *Action in Perception*. Cambridge, MA: MIT Press.

O'Regan, J. K. and Noë, A. (2001). A sensorimotor account of vision and visual consciousness. *Behavioral and Brain Sciences*, 24, 939–1103.

Peacocke, C. (1983). *Sense and Content*. Oxford: Oxford University Press.

Prinz, J. J. (2000). A neurofunctional theory of visual consciousness. *Consciousness and Cognition*, 9, 243–59.

—— (2001). Functionalism, dualism and the neural correlates of consciousness. In W. Bechtel, P. Mandik, J. Mundale, and R. Stufflebeam (eds.), *Philosophy and the Neurosciences: A Reader.* Oxford: Blackwell.

—— (2002). *Furnishing the Mind: Concepts and Their Perceptual Basis.* Cambridge, MA: MIT Press.

—— (2004a). *Gut Reactions: A Perceptual Theory of Emotion.* New York: Oxford University Press.

—— (2004b). The fractionation of introspection. *Journal of Consciousness Studies,* 11, 40–57.

—— (2005). A neurofunctional theory of consciousness. In A. Brook and K. Akins (eds.), *Cognition and the Brain: The Philosophy and Neuroscience Movement.* Cambridge: Cambridge University Press.

—— (2006a). Putting the brakes on enactive perception. *Psyche,* 12 (http://psyche.cs.monash. edu.au/symposia/noe/Prinz.pdf).

—— (2006b). Beyond appearances: the content of perception and sensation. In T. S. Gendler and J. Hawthorne (eds.), *Perceptual Experience.* Oxford: Oxford University Press.

—— (2007). The intermediate-level theory of consciousness. In S. Schneider and M. Velmans (eds.), *Blackwell Companion to Consciousness.* Oxford: Blackwell.

—— (forthcoming-a). *The Conscious Brain.* New York: Oxford University Press.

—— (forthcoming-b). Is consciousness embodied? In P. Robbins and. M. Aydede (eds.), *Cambridge Handbook of Situated Cognition.* Cambridge: Cambridge University Press.

Rosenthal, D. M. (2005). *Consciousness and Mind.* Oxford: Oxford University Press.

Siewert, C. (1998). *The Significance of Consciousness.* Princeton: Princeton University Press.

Titchener, E. B. (1917). *A Text-Book of Psychology.* New York: Macmillan.

Wegner, D. M. and Wheatley, T. P. (1999). Apparent mental causation: sources of the experience of will. *American Psychologist,* 54, 480–92.

Woodworth, R. S. (1906). Imageless thought. *Journal of Philosophy, Psychology, and Scientific Methods,* 3, 701–8.

Mental Action and
Self-Awareness (I)

Christopher Peacocke

This paper is built around a single, simple idea. It is widely agreed that there is a distinctive kind of awareness each of us has of his own bodily actions. This action-awareness is different from any perceptual awareness a subject may have of his own actions; it can exist in the absence of such perceptual awareness. The single, simple idea around which this paper is built is that the distinctive awareness that subjects have of their own mental actions is a form of action-awareness. Subjects' awareness of their own mental actions is a species of the same genus that also includes the distinctive awareness of bodily actions. More specifically, I claim:

1   Much conscious thought consists of mental actions.
2   A thinker's awareness of those of his mental events that are mental actions is a species of action-awareness. This I call "The Principal Hypothesis."
3   The Principal Hypothesis can provide a clarification and explanation of a range of features and phenomena present in conscious thought.
4   The Principal Hypothesis is a resource that can be used in addressing various classical philosophical issues about the mental, self-knowledge, and the first person.

Gilbert Ryle once asked: "What is Rodin's *Le Penseur* doing?" (Ryle, 1971a). My answer in this paper is that he is literally doing something, is engaged in mental actions; and our task is to say more about what this involves.

My strategy will be first to articulate some distinctive features of bodily action-awareness; then to characterize the range of mental actions; and to argue that all of these distinctive features of action-awareness in the bodily case are present also for mental actions. I will go on to consider some of the attractions and consequences of the Principal Hypothesis; to apply it in the characterization of some pathological states; and to consider some aspects of its significance for the nature of first-person thought. There are many other issues raised by the Principal Hypothesis besides those discussed here. This applies especially to its epistemological ramifications. I attempt to address them in a further paper, "Mental Action and Self-Awareness (II)" (Peacocke, forthcoming).

1 The Distinctive Features of Action-Awareness

(a) You can be aware that you are doing something without perceiving that you are doing it. If you have a strong injection in preparation for a root canal operation at the dentist, you may have no sensation in and around your mouth and your jaw. If you are asked to open your mouth, you can do so, and you will be aware that you are opening your mouth. This awareness exists even though you do not perceive your mouth or your lower face at all. You can be aware that you are opening your mouth without seeing or feeling your mouth, and without any of the sensations or perceptions of your own body from the inside (that is, without any proprioception). A person whose afferent nerves have been severed or have suffered decay may still be aware that he is extending his arm and pointing to the right, even though he is looking the other way, and does not perceive his own arm at all.

The same kind of action-awareness that is present in these exceptional circumstances is also something we enjoy in normal bodily action in more ordinary circumstances. Your everyday awareness that you are moving your hands, turning your head, or opening your mouth is not purely perceptual.[1] Even if it is true that action-awareness requires some general capacity to perceive, action-awareness on a particular occasion that you are doing something does not require you to perceive, on that occasion, that you are doing it.

(b) The content of your action-awareness is that you are doing something. It is not merely a consciousness that something is happening (though of course that is implied by the content). This fact arguably parallels a corresponding truth about the content of perceptual states. Perception is as of states of affairs in the objective world, states of affairs of a sort that cause perceptions. If action-awareness is caused by tryings, this awareness is as of what's the case when those tryings successfully cause events in the objective world. What is then the case is that one is doing something.

(c) The content of the action-awareness is representational in the sense that in enjoying action-awareness, it seems to the subject that the world is a certain way. This seeming is belief-independent. It may seem to the unfortunate person whose arm is, unbeknownst to him, severed in a car accident that he is moving his arm, even though he has no sensation in it. This seeming has a false content. The seeming, just like a visual illusion, can persist after the subject knows his unhappy situation. In my view, action-awareness should not be identified with any kind of belief, whether first- or second-order.

Bodily action-awareness is to be distinguished from mere awareness of trying to do something. Suppose you are trying, but failing, to unscrew a tight lid on a jar. You are aware that you are trying to unscrew it. You have no awareness, either real or apparent, of the bodily action of unscrewing it. It may be that in certain circumstances, when there is no information to the contrary, tryings cause apparent action-awareness. That does not make apparent action-awareness identical with awareness of trying. It means only that what the latter kind of awareness is awareness of can itself cause apparent awareness of bodily action. Apparent awareness of successfully doing something is distinct from apparent awareness of trying to do it.

Those who hold that there is non-conceptual content at the personal, conscious level will be attracted to the idea that some awareness of bodily action may have an at least partially non-conceptual content. I myself see nothing intrinsically problematic in the idea that an animal without concepts, but with non-conceptual mental representations of the world, may have a form of non-conceptual awareness of its bodily actions. The content of the awareness should be captured in a form that specifies the change in location or properties of the bodily parts that are involved in the apparent action. Such contents could be integrated into the scenario content possessed by perceptual states that I used in earlier work (Peacocke, 1992). Such a conception is not essential to the main theses of the present paper, however. Thinkers like John McDowell, who hold that all personal-level conscious content is conceptual, could also recognize the existence of belief-independent action-awareness (McDowell, 1994). They would simply insist that its content is conceptual too.

(d) The content of the action-awareness is both first-personal and present-tensed. The content is of the form "I am doing such and such now." When you take such an awareness at face value, and judge "I am doing such-and-such now," your judgment is identification-free in a familiar sense. It is not the case that you are making this judgment only because, for some mode of presentation m other than the first person, you judge that m is doing such-and-such now, and you also accept that you are m. There are further distinctions to be drawn here, and I will return to them.

(e) (i) Action-awareness makes available demonstrative ways of thinking of particular actions. You can think of a movement demonstratively, as "this movement," a way of thinking of a movement made available by your action-awareness of the movement.

(e) (ii) The reference of such demonstratives is determined by which movement is caused by one's trying. It is not determined by its relations to one's perception of the movement, if indeed any such perception exists. Nor is the reference determined by which movement one believes it to be. There may be no such movement, even though one believes there is; or one may be wrong about which movement it is one has made. You can think to yourself, while making a certain gesture with your hand, "*This* is the victory gesture Churchill made," where the demonstrative is made available by apparent action-awareness on this particular occasion. The demonstrative refers to the movement (type) you actually make. If your efferent nerves have been rerouted, your thought that this is the victory gesture Churchill made may be false, even though you know perfectly well which type of movement it was that Churchill used as a victory gesture. You are just wrong in thinking that *this* movement (action-demonstrative) is an instance of that movement-type you know so well.

(e) (iii) There is a distinction in the case of action-based modes of presentation which parallels that between the demonstrative and recognitional in the case of perceptual modes of presentation. The action-awareness based demonstrative "this movement" requires that one enjoy at least an apparent action-awareness at the time of thinking. Otherwise it is not even available for use, just as a perceptual demonstrative

Christopher Peacocke

is not available for use in the absence of perceptual experience. But there is also a way of thinking of a certain type of movement, made available by the fact that one can reliably make the movement. One can use this type of way of thinking even when one is not trying to make the movement so thought of. "I could make such-and-such gesture," one may think, in the process of deciding how to act.

2 The Nature and Range of Mental Actions

Events that are mental actions include instances of the following kinds:

decidings
judgings
acceptings
attendings to something or other
calculatings
reasonings
tryings.

Some types of mental event are such that instances of the type may or may not be mental actions. Such is the case with imagining. Imagining in your mind's ear Beethoven's "Hammerklavier Sonata" may on a particular occasion be a mental action. On another occasion, that sonata may equally come to your auditory imagination unbidden – your imagining may be a hindrance to what you are trying to do. In this respect, imagining as a type is like the bodily type of making marks on the carpet. When someone is making marks on the carpet, that may or may not be something she is trying to do.

Within the class of mental events, what makes an event a mental action? For a mental event to be a mental action, it must consist of an event that either is, or constitutively involves, a trying. If "constitutively involves" is allowed to count as a reflexive relation, this criterion can be simplified. To be a mental action, a mental event must constitutively involve a trying.

Every mental action involves success in something at which one may in principle fail. You may find that you cannot bring yourself to believe that p (for instance, that your friend is lying to you); you may find that you cannot bring yourself to try to do something; you may find that you cannot bring yourself even to decide to do something. Sometimes lack of success is obvious to the would-be agent himself. In other cases, an agent may have an illusion of success. A subject may think he has formed the belief that p when in fact he has not. No amount of affirming to himself that p will guarantee that he has succeeded in storing the content that p among his beliefs. This fact is the ground of possibility of one sort of self-deception.

The success or failure of our attempts at mental action depends upon all sorts of sub-personal conditions to which we do not have independent access, in the way in which perception gives us independent information on whether our attempts at bodily action have been successful. The real possibilities of continuing, ordinary error about some of our mental states are in this respect far more extensive than the real possibilities of such error about our bodily actions. To describe a situation in which someone is self-deceived on the issue of whether he has really unscrewed the lid off the jar would take Monty Python–like resources.

The condition I have offered for a mental event to be a mental action is the same condition that I would offer for a bodily event to be a bodily action: it must constitutively involve a trying. Mental actions and bodily actions are actions in exactly the same sense. The differences between them are the differences between the bodily and the mental.[2]

Tryings themselves featured on the above list of mental actions. This does not involve a vicious regress (nor a non-vicious one either). An unacceptable regress would be generated by the conjunction of the following propositions: tryings are actions, and for an event to be an action, it must be caused by a prior trying. That last proposition is false, however, which is why there is no regress of that sort. Tryings themselves are one of the best counterexamples to the thesis that for an event to be an action, it must be caused by a prior trying.

Though the main concern of this paper is action-awareness, the recognition that there is a range of mental action-types that includes both judgment and decision already has consequences for a range of philosophical and psychological issues, independently of theses about action-awareness. I give four examples, which should help to locate this position about mental actions in a wider philosophical and psychological landscape.

Outright judgment, something that seems not to be a matter of degree, has often seemed to play a special role in the formation of propositional attitudes.[3] This appearance is both understandable and correct if judgments are mental actions. A mental action involves a trying, and whether you are trying to do something is not itself a matter of degree. You are either trying or you are not. What it is you are trying to do may vary in degree: you may be trying to write a long letter or a short letter, to make a lot of money or a modest sum. But whether you are trying or not is not a matter of degree. Since trying involves the occurrence of an event, an initiating event that produces an effect, it is not surprising that it should not be a matter of degree. It is not a matter of degree whether such an initiating event occurs.

There is such a thing as trying harder or less hard to do something, and this distinction does get a grip in the mental realm as well as in the bodily. But no one who advocates the importance of degrees of belief would be tempted to identify greater degree of belief with (say) lower degree of effort in trying to make an outright judgment. Such theorists would want to contrast degrees of belief with outright judgments, however the members of each of these categories may be reached.

These points about judgment apply also to decision and to the other mental action-types. Deciding to do something cannot be a matter of degree. Again, there can be variation in degree in respect of what it is that one is deciding to do; but that is a different matter.

Not every case in which you come to believe something involves mental action. By default, we take many experiences, memories and utterances of other people at face value. What they represent as correct goes straight into our store of beliefs

Christopher Peacocke

without any mental action. So I am not saying that every time we form a belief, even a conscious belief, there is mental action. It is however characteristic of beliefs, as opposed to more primitive representational states, that they can be assessed and reviewed. Such assessment and review does involve mental action.

A second consequence of acknowledging the existence of mental actions that include judgments concerns the idea of concepts as individuated by norms for making judgments in which those concepts are applied. These concept-individuating norms can then be seen as norms of rational action. They are norms of action applying in the special case in which the action is a mental action, that of judgment. The case is also arguably special in that the applicability of the norms is what makes something a judgment with a given content.

A third consequence concerns the philosophy of mind and action more generally, and it bears upon the existence of the phenomenon of akratic judgment. Knowing or having evidence about what it is rational to think, all things considered, or having information about what is most likely to be the case, never entails that the thinker will perform a certain *action*.

We know this very well from the case of bodily action. If judgments and decisions are mental actions, exactly the same point applies to them too. Akratic belief, and other akratic mental actions, are just as possible as akratic bodily actions. They are possible for the same reasons as in the bodily case. Mental action has all the frailties of subjection to desire, self-deception, and wishful thinking that bodily action also suffers. Mental agency is not in a privileged position vis-á-vis bodily agency. This may be humbling, but it also puts us in a much better position to explain the range of phenomena that actually occur.

A fourth consequence concerns the unified theoretical treatment of areas that have not always been considered instances of a single kind. Daniel Kahneman writes of his own and Amos Tversky's work on the two topics of intuitive thinking and of choice that it "highlights commonalities between lines of research that are usually studied separately" (Kahneman, 2003, p. 717). If both judgments and choices are mental actions, we should be ready for the possibility that, as mental actions, some of the characteristics of the mechanisms producing them are the same. In deliberating what to think, our deliberation is about a mental action, what to judge; in deliberating between options, we are deliberating about what to choose, equally a mental action.

Kahneman summarizes his views by saying that "In particular, the psychology of judgement and the psychology of choice share their basic principles and differ mainly in content." Kahneman draws a distinction between what he calls "System 1" and "System 2." This distinction maps onto, and can help explain empirically, some of the distinctions I have drawn. His System 1 is "fast, parallel, automatic, effortless" and it delivers what Kahneman calls "impressions." These "impressions" are not mental actions. In this respect his comparison of them with perceptions is wholly apt. Like perceptions, they just occur to the thinker. Judgments are the output of Kahneman's System 2 and of them he writes: "In contrast, judgements are always intentional and explicit even when they are not overtly expressed" (pp. 698ff.). This is a clear classification of judgments as actions. We will later make use of Kahneman's distinction between Systems 1 and 2.

3 The Principal Hypothesis and Its Consequences

The Principal Hypothesis, as I formulated it, states that a thinker's awareness of those of his mental events that are mental actions is a species of action-awareness. If mental actions are literally actions, it should not be surprising that a subject's awareness of them is of the same kind as other examples of action-awareness.

All the distinctive features of action-awareness we noted for bodily actions are also present for mental actions. We can run briefly through them, with the same lettering as above.

(a) Since you do not have perceptual experiences of your mental actions at all, and you have a distinctive awareness of them, you can certainly have this awareness without perception of them.

(b) Your awareness of your mental actions, such as your awareness that you are deciding, that you are calculating, and the like, is not merely an awareness that something is happening. It is an awareness that you are doing something, an awareness of agency from the inside.

(c) The awareness is representational: it seems to you that you are deciding, calculating, and so forth. Correspondingly there is such a thing as taking the world to be as this awareness represents it as being.

(d) The content of your awareness of your mental actions is first-personal and present-tensed: you are aware for instance that you are calculating now. An expression of this awareness with the first-person pronoun would be counted by Wittgenstein as a use of "I" as subject. Your belief that you are calculating now does not rest on two beliefs, for some mode of presentation m other than the first person, that m is calculating now and that you are identical with m.

(e) (i) Mental action-awareness makes available to the thinker particular demonstrative ways of thinking of those mental actions. One can think "this judgment," "this calculation," and these demonstratives in thought refer to the particular mental actions awareness of which makes the demonstratives available in thought. This action-awareness makes available to a thinker ways of thinking of her own mental actions. These ways of thinking are essential to self-scrutiny and critical reflection on her own mental actions.

(e) (ii) One may have an apparent awareness of a mental action that misrepresents the mental action. When, for instance, there is a sufficiently complex structure of desires and/or emotions leading to self-deception, one may think one is judging something when one is not, and may be judging something entirely different, or nothing at all.

(e) (iii) We noted an analog, in the case of bodily action, of the distinction between demonstrative and recognitional modes of presentation in the perceptual case. There is a corresponding distinction between two ways of thinking of mental actions. "This deciding," "this calculation," "this judgment" are all demonstratives in thought that refer to particular mental actions. But there is also a way of thinking of a type of mental action, for example the action-type of judging that London is burning, that is individuated by its connections with one's ability to engage in mental actions of that type. It is that way of thinking of a type that one employs when one thinks "If it is reported on the news that London is burning, of course I will judge that London is burning; but not otherwise." In normal cases, when one tries to perform a mental action of this type, one succeeds. One does not normally perform mental actions of these types by doing something else. These are the analogs in the mental case of a species of basic action.[4]

4 The Principal Hypothesis: Attractions and Possibilities

I now turn to some attractions of the Principal Hypothesis, and some theoretical possibilities and reflections that it suggests.

One of the attractions of the Principal Hypothesis is that it assimilates those conscious events that are mental actions to a wider class whose members equally share some of the distinctive features of conscious mental actions. One of the most distinctive features is that such mental actions as judging, deciding, and the rest have the phenomenology of doing something, rather than involving the phenomenology of something being *presented* as being the case, as in perception, or as of something occurring to one, as in unintended imagination, in which cases the subject is passive. This active phenomenology is present for bodily action too. The action-awareness of raising one's arm is equally not that of being presented with some fact, but is rather a phenomenology of one's doing something. The position I am developing is, then, in head-on disagreement with the view that the character of conscious thought involves only states that are sensory or, like imagination, individuated by their relations to sensory states. That opposing view is well formulated (though not fully endorsed) by Jesse Prinz, who writes "When we introspect during thought, all we find are mental images, including auditory images of natural-language sentences (subvocal speech). With no phenomenal traces of non-sensory representations, it is tempting to conclude that all thought is couched in perceptual imagery" (Prinz, 2002, p. 103).

Here are three cases, subjectively different, in which exactly the same words – for instance, "Meeting tomorrow!" – may occur in your mind's ear:

1   The words may just passively occur to you; this could be memory or unbidden imagination.
2   You may be judging that the meeting is tomorrow, on the basis of remembered evidence.
3   You may be making a decision to convene the meeting tomorrow.

The difference between these three – imagining or remembering, judging, and deciding – is certainly not something within the phenomenology of passive imagination or presentation. Nonetheless, it is a feature of your consciousness that you are, for instance, judging something rather than forming an intention. It is equally a feature of your consciousness if you are merely passive in this respect. Action-awareness is given as action-awareness, and is subjectively different from merely passive states. Any description of your conscious state is incomplete if it omits the characteristics of action-awareness. "No difference in imagistic or presentational phenomenology" does not imply "No difference in phenomenology at all."

The point applies even when there are no mental images or perceptions involved at all. Someone, Rodin's *Penseur* with his eyes closed, may be passively drifting in thought, and nothing may come to his mind; or he may be thinking hard about how to solve some theoretical or practical problem – and equally nothing may come to mind. These are very different total subjective states. The person who is concentrating on finding a solution to a problem is actively trying to do something in thought, and this contributes to the phenomenology of his state.

Correspondingly there is a difference in imagining being in these two states. This is what one would expect if imagining, from the inside, being in a certain state is subjectively imagining what it is like to be in that state. Imagining drifting aimlessly in thought is different from imagining concentrating on solving a problem.

Recognition that there is a distinctive category of mental action-awareness can account for many of the features of conscious thought that so engaged Gilbert Ryle in his late writings on the topic.[5] Someone so inclined could devote a whole paper (or more) to this topic. Here I just give two examples.

Ryle repeatedly emphasized that neither the occurrence of any one particular event involving the imagined uttering of words, or visualizing of scenes, or anything else of the sort, or any disjunction thereof, is what constitutes judging, when out on a drive, that the petrol (gas) station at the next village may be closed on Sunday (see Ryle, 1971b, pp. 393ff.). In my view, Ryle is right about this. Under the Principal Hypothesis, his point is just what one would expect. None of the things Ryle rightly cites as insufficient for judgment involves action-awareness of judging, which is something additional to, and not ensured by, any amount of word-imagining, picturing in one's mind's eye, and the like.

The other example involves Ryle's long-standing (perhaps even fatal) attraction to "adverbial" theories of mental phenomena. He notes that in the case of bodily events, some of them have "thick" as well as thin descriptions. His example is that a hitting of a ball with a golf club may also be a "practice approach shot," and "a piece of self-training" (p. 474). He says these thick descriptions involve "intention-parasitism," and that the same phenomenon is found among mental events, which may, in the case of a composer, be tryings-out, modifications, assemblies, and in the case of other projects in thought, may be serving many other purposes. He rightly concludes that descriptions of mental events involving intentionality on the part of the thinker will not be determined by neutral characterizations of the subjective contents of imaginings and visualizings; and that the intentional characterizations may be correct for many different kinds of imaginings and visualizings (pp. 476–9). What Ryle call intention-parasitism is possible only where there is mental action. From the standpoint of the present paper, there is nothing either adverbial (or higher-order, for that matter) in a mental event's being a mental action. To be a mental action, the event must have the additional property of having been produced in the right way by the subject of the event. When it is so, it is then possible for the "thick" descriptions that Ryle mentions to get a grip. (The "intention-parasitism," insofar as I understand it, is

Christopher Peacocke

also not necessary for an event to be a mental action: I may actively imagine the Hammerklavier on a whim, and not in pursuit of some further purpose.)

In current philosophy of mind, there is a range of kind of states each of which is recognized as having representational content, in the sense that in being in one of these states, it thereby seems to the subject as if that content is correct. This seeming may be overruled by judgment, or it may be taken at face value. In either case, the state's possession of a representational content should not be identified with the subject's judging that content (or a corresponding content) to be correct. States currently recognized to possess such representational content include at least the following three kinds. There are perceptual states in which, in having an experience in a particular sense modality, it seems to the subject that the world is a certain way. There are states of pure thought, in which it strikes one as the case that (say) the American Declaration of Independence was signed in 1776, where this purely propositional impression does not need to correspond to any personal memory. There are representational states of personal memory, in which one has a memory of, say, walking on the beach at Big Sur, and it thereby seems to one that one was there. To this list of kinds I suggest that we should add action-awareness. Your apparent action-awarenesses of raising your arm, of judging that it is time to leave, of calculating the sum of two numbers each represent you as doing these very things. And just as a memory-impression may be a memory of your perceiving something in the past, and that represents you as so perceiving, a memory may also be of your doing something, and represent you as having done that thing. A memory of walking along a beach will commonly do both. To give a correct account of the relation between these states and the kinds of content they can contain, and to do so in way that provides a philosophical resource, is a general challenge. I will return to it in the particular case of action-awareness and its contents.

When a subject has an action-awareness that he is φ-ing, for example, that he is turning the left-hand knob, all the contents of the that-clause contribute to the character of his awareness. There is the action-type of turning, different from that of pushing or pulling, and which he is aware of performing. Similarly action-awareness of judging is different from action-awareness of coming to a decision. But the intentional objects of the action also contribute to the awareness too. One is aware that one is turning this knob rather than that one (both demonstratively given in thought). Similarly one is aware that one is judging one complete propositional intentional content rather than another; and that one is coming to one decision rather than another.

In earlier writing I drew a distinction between being the object of attention, and occupying attention (see Peacocke, 1998). In conscious thought, your attention is occupied, but there need not be anything that is the object or event to which you are attending (not even an apparent object). The Principal Hypothesis contributes to an explanation of this difference. In ordinary action-awareness of bodily action, such as your awareness of raising your arm, your action-awareness need not involve your attending to your arm, or to its rising, even though your conscious action can certainly occupy your attention. If conscious thought is action-awareness, we would expect the same. The action of which you are aware in a distinctive way – making a judgment, forming an intention – does not involve the making of the judgment, or the formation of the intention, being the object of your attention. Rather, as in the case of bodily action, making the judgment, or forming the intention, *occupies* your attention.

5 Describing and Explaining Schizophrenic Experience

Our Principal Hypothesis states that a thinker's awareness of those of his mental events that are mental actions is a species of action-awareness, with all the distinctive characteristics of action-awareness. The Principal Hypothesis bears upon our understanding of the phenomenon of schizophrenia. The hypothesis contributes to a correct characterization of what it is that the schizophrenic subject lacks. It is equally essential to providing a deeper unification of some of the symptoms of schizophrenia. The distinctions drawn upon in elaborating the hypothesis are also important to current psychological theories in their explanation of the occurrence of schizophrenia.

I divide the significance of the Principal Hypothesis for schizophrenia into five different headings.

1   What the schizophrenic subject lacks in the area of conscious thought is action-awareness of the thoughts that occur to him. To enjoy action-awareness of a particular event of thinking is to be aware, non-perceptually, of that thinking as something one is doing oneself. The awareness of one's own agency that exists in normal subjects is missing in, for example, the schizophrenic experience of "thought insertion." One schizophrenic subject famously reported: "The thoughts of Eamonn Andrews [a UK television presenter in the 1960s] come into my mind. He treats my mind like a screen and flashes his thoughts on to it like you flash a picture" (Frith and Johnstone, 2003, p. 36).

It is important to characterize the schizophrenic's consciousness as lacking action-awareness. It is not merely that these subjects report that their conscious mental events are caused by external, intervening agents. Even when they no longer report that they are so caused, because they are persuaded of the non-veridicality of these conscious events, these subjects' experience of passivity persists. Action-awareness is still absent, whatever the schizophrenic subject's own beliefs, if any, about why he is having mental events from which the action-awareness is absent. Precisely because action-awareness is, like perception, belief-independent, it cannot be restored simply by altering someone's beliefs.

The schizophrenic condition is also sometimes characterized as a "failure to distinguish between ideas and impulses arising from within the subject's own mind and perceptions arising from stimuli in the external world" (Frith and Johnstone, 2003, p. 37). But subjects do draw the distinction. The ability to draw the distinction is implied by the subject's own description of thought-insertion just quoted. It is in part because the distinction is drawn that the conscious states of schizophrenia are so alarming to their unfortunate subjects. The right way to formulate the point about the distinction rather involves action-awareness. The schizophrenic subjects lack the action-awareness in thought present in normal subjects, an awareness that, in its representational content, draws the distinction between events produced by oneself and events produced by others in the right place.

368 | **Christopher Peacocke**

2   The Principal Hypothesis provides a straightforward unification of some of the symptoms of schizophrenia in thought and some of its symptoms in bodily action. Some schizophrenic subjects experience delusions of control of their body by an external agency. "It is my hand and arm that move, and my fingers pick up the pen, but I don't control them. What they do is nothing to do with me" (Frith and Johnstone, 2003, p. 37). Sean Spence asked subjects with delusions of control to perform a simple bodily task of holding a lever and producing a random sequence of movements. They performed this task normally, but still reported that their movements were controlled by alien forces (ibid., p. 137; Spence et al., 1997).

The Principal Hypothesis states that awareness of mental actions is action-awareness of the same sort as occurs in bodily-action-awareness. Subjects who lack action-awareness of the thoughts they are in fact producing must have some kind of impairment of the mechanism that, in healthy subjects, produces action-awareness. But if action-awareness in the bodily case is awareness of exactly the same kind as in the case of conscious mental actions, it is to be expected that some cases of impairment of the mechanism producing action-awareness would affect awareness of bodily actions too. This is just what one finds. Symptoms that might otherwise seem somewhat diverse, and might even raise doubts about whether there is a single underlying condition of which they are both manifestations, are in fact unified by the Principal Hypothesis.

3   Some of the phenomena of schizophrenia highlight, and cannot be properly characterized without, the distinction between action-awareness and awareness of goals and intentions. The idea of a defect in awareness of goals and intentions has sometimes played a large role in some earlier theorists' explanation of schizophrenia. It played such a role in Christopher Frith's 1992 account in *The Cognitive Neuropsychology of Schizophrenia*.[6] But we should remember the subjects in the Spence study just mentioned, in which subjects succeeded at simple bodily tasks they were instructed to carry out, but who still experienced delusions of control. These subjects knew their goal and their intention – it was to perform the task the experimenter had requested. Their abnormality is not in failing to represent their goal or intention correctly, but in their lack of action-awareness of their bodily actions as their own.

4   There is a theory proposed by Irwin Feinberg, and developed further by Frith and Johnstone, which proposes for schizophrenia an analog of Helmholtz's famous "corollary discharge" in visual perception (see Helmholtz, 1962; Feinberg, 1978; Frith and Johnstone, 2003). Helmholtz offered an explanation of why the world does not seem to move when you move your eyes, even though the image of objects moves on the retina as your eye moves. According to Helmholtz, just prior to a movement of your eyes there is a corollary discharge caused by the attempt to move the eyes, and this discharge permits a computation of the location of objects in the environment that takes into account the movement of the eyes. Frith and Johnstone write that "Patients with delusions of control and related symptoms have problems that suggest that they cannot monitor their own movements in the normal way" (p. 133). When we regard consciousness of mental actions as a species of action-awareness, such awareness can be accounted for in this explanatory structure. The natural conjecture, given all the evidence to date, is that:

Mental Action and Self-Awareness (I)   369

(a) When there is no corollary discharge, there is no action-awareness of the movement in question as one of your own actions, and this applies quite generally, both in bodily and mental cases. If the corollary discharge theory is correct, this hypothesis would explain the absence of action-awareness in schizophrenic subjects, again both in bodily and in mental cases.

(b) If the corollary discharge is caused by trying to perform the action in question, in normal subjects, that explains why, when there is no evidence to the contrary, trying itself causes an (apparent) action-awareness. Computationally, it is for the agent exactly as one would expect it to be when there is action. This would also explain the apparent action-awareness in trying to move a severed limb. It may also explain some illusions of having formed a belief.

5   There is a syndrome of symptoms in schizophrenia having to do with a loss of will, an absence of spontaneous action and thought, and blunted emotional responses. Action-awareness is the most obvious and fundamental manifestation in conscious life of oneself as a successful agent. When this awareness is lacking, it is not surprising that a subject's sense of himself as an agent should suffer, and that he should be less motivated to action and spontaneity. When your actions, however extensive, are experienced only passively, it is hard to conceive of yourself as a successful agent. Absence of action-awareness is not an isolated phenomenon of consciousness, but has ramifying effects, both for the emotions of the schizophrenic subject and for his self-conception.

Obviously there is much about schizophrenia that the Principal Hypothesis does not explain. A full understanding has to explain the prevalence of the impression of control by alien agencies and forces. Why an absence of action-awareness should lead to this specific kind of illusion needs an empirical explanation by resources going far beyond those of the Principal Hypothesis. My position is only that we need the distinctions I have been drawing to characterize and unify the schizophrenic phenomena. We will not have a proper empirical explanation of the phenomena without an accurate characterization of what it is that has to be explained.

6 The First Person in Action Self-Ascriptions

I now turn to the role of the first person in action-awareness. I define a use, on a particular occasion, of the first person in thought as a *use of "I" as agent* as one in which that use occurs in a first-person judgment made simply by taking the representational content of an apparent action-awareness at face value. The uses of the first person in the judgments "I am pressing the button" and "I judge that Bush will be re-elected" will be uses of "I" as agent when made by taking the corresponding action-awarenesses at face value.

Uses of "I" as agent are uses of "I" as subject, in the sense employed by Wittgenstein in *The Blue and Brown Books*, and later so well elucidated in Sydney Shoemaker's important papers (Shoemaker, 1984a, 1984b). As we noted, in ordinary circumstances, when a thinker uses "I" as agent in a judgment "I am φ-ing," his judgment does not rest on a pair of beliefs that m is φ-ing, for some m distinct from the first person, together with an identity belief "I am m." I do not have first to judge "that person is pressing the button," or "CP is pressing the button," before I am in a position to judge "I am pressing the button." Action-awareness already has a first-person component in its intentional content. If the thinker is taking that awareness at face value, no such identity belief is needed for the thinker to be in a position to make a self-ascription of the action in question. The case quite unlike that in which my belief "My car alarm is sounding" is based on the two beliefs "That car's alarm is sounding" and "I am the owner of that car." In Shoemaker's terminology, judgments "I am φ-ing" involving the use of "I" as agent are immune to error through misidentification relative to (the first occurrence of) the first person.

For enthusiasts about these distinctions, this is arguably a case of what Shoemaker calls *de facto* immunity (1984a). In a world in which devices or Wilder Penfield–like persons intervene after one's tryings, and, by means of some randomizing mechanism, may or may not make their intended bodily and mental effects come about, there could regularly be incorrect apparent action-awarenesses. In such a world a thinker could introduce a demonstrative "That $_A$ agent" that refers to whoever is the agent of the event of which the subject has a token action-awareness A. This is the action-analog of the demonstratives for times and places I imagined in *Sense and Content* for cases in which there are massive time-lags in perception, or perceptions as from places other than one's current location (Peacocke, 1983, pp. 125ff.). In those circumstances, one could reasonably wonder "Am I identical with that $_A$ agent?" But this is no more our actual situation with respect to agency than is the corresponding situation for the invented temporal and spatial demonstratives. Whatever the correct explanation of the phenomenon, contingent features of our actual circumstances can have a bearing on what is required for coming to make a judgment reasonably.

The existence of a use of "I" as agent and the nature of the conscious states on which these uses are based can help explain some of the illusions, in the history of philosophy, to the effect that there exists a transcendent subject whose transcendent operations affect the spatial world, and the mental world. In the apparent action-awareness "I am φ-ing" itself, the subject is not given as having a location in the spatial world, nor as having spatial or material properties. This applies to predications of bodily actions of φ-ing, as well as to mental actions. The apparent action is bodily, but the subject who is represented as doing it is not represented in the awareness as a spatial object, or as having spatial properties, itself.

It would be a terrible fallacy – one of those non sequiturs of "numbing grossness" – to conclude from this fact that the subject referred to in such thoughts and awarenesses does not have a spatiotemporal location and does not have spatiotemporal and material properties. It would be a fallacy even to conclude that the subject referred to does not need to have such properties. But it would be a brave person who, on reading the works of those who have postulated a transcendental subject, concludes that no such fallacious transition is hovering over their writings. This is particularly so in the case of those writers who have placed some species of agency in a noumenal realm.

As is often the case with the postulation of transcendental subject-matters, the motivation for the postulation involves a genuine insight, misapplied. It is right to

Mental Action and Self-Awareness (I) | 371 |

hold that much thought is mental action, and so must be explained in the same general way that other action is. It is wrong to think that a transcendent subject is either necessary or possible in explaining these distinctive phenomena.

The case of action-awareness is a distinctive one among the range of phenomena that can generate illusions of transcendence, in that the intentional content of the awareness itself contains the first person. A wide range of other cases that generate the illusion have the property that in *Being Known* I called "representational in-depen-dence" (Peacocke, 1999, section 6.1). When self-ascribing a perception, or an occur-rence of a passive occurrence of a conscious thought to oneself, one does not rely on a conscious state that represents oneself as enjoying that mental state. Rather, one moves rationally from that mental state itself to a self-ascription. There are thus two rather different ways in which it may come to seem that "I" refers to something without spatial or material properties. One way is for the transition to a judgment to move from a state that does not contain the first person in its intentional content (or not as stand-ing in the relation self-ascribed). The other is for the rationalizing state to contain the first person in its intentional content, but for that content not to represent the subject as having spatial and material properties. Described in the abstract, this case might seem to be of questionable possibility, but it is this possibility that action-awareness realizes. (It also follows that a different explanation of the entitlement to the transition must be given in the case of action-awareness than in the representationally indepen-dent cases. In *Being Known*, I offered what I called "the delta account" (Peacocke, 1999, sections 6.2, 6.3). The account in Peacocke (forthcoming) of entitlement for the case of action-awareness, which in abstract structure more closely parallels that for perceptual judgments, is quite different from the delta account.)

While all uses of "I" as agent are uses of "I" as subject in our ordinary circum-stances, the converse is not true. There are uses of "I" as subject, even uses in the self-ascription of attitudes, that are not uses of "I" as agent. An example of Richard Moran's illustrates the possibility (see Moran, 2001). You may come to the conclusion that you believe that someone has betrayed you on the basis of information about your feelings, emotions, and other judgments. As Moran writes:

> insofar as it is possible for one to adopt an empirical or explanatory stance on one's own beliefs, and thus to bracket the issue of what their possession commits one to, it will be possible for one to adopt this stance to anything theoretically knowable, including private events or attitudes that one may be somehow aware of immediately, without inference . . . We may allow any manner of inner events of consciousness, any exclusivity and privacy, any degree of privilege and special reliability, and their combination would not add up to the ordinary capacity for self-knowledge. (pp. 92–3)

Suppose you come to the conclusion that you believe that a certain person has betrayed you, and your evidence for this self-ascription consists of your other mental states that, in self-ascribing, you use "I" as subject. The evidence might, for instance, include your emotions of anger or irritation at the person, and your self-ascriptions can involve uses of "I" as subject. Your inferential judgment "I believe that person has betrayed me" would, in these circumstances, not be reached by some identity inference from two premises of the form "*m* believes that that person has betrayed

Christopher Peacocke

him" and "I am *m*." So the self-ascription does, in ordinary circumstances, involve a use of "I" as subject. But it is not a use of "I" as agent based on an action-awareness of judging that that person has betrayed you. There is, in the example, no such action-awareness, and no such judgment for there to be an action-awareness of.

In this example, the self-ascription in "I believe that that person has betrayed me" uses "I" as subject because the premises from which it is reached also use "I" as subject. But the same propositional evidence about some person given in a third-person way *m* could equally, and in normal circumstances, support the conclusion "*m* believes that that person has betrayed him." By contrast, when one self-ascribes a belief on the basis of action-awareness, such awareness involves the first-person essentially. Reliance on action-awareness is a way of coming to ascribe an attitude that one can, in ordinary circumstances, use only in ascribing attitudes to oneself. In this respect, it is unique to the first person.

7 Concluding Remarks: Rational Agency and Action-Awareness

Rational agency and action-awareness are coordinate elements in being a rational subject. Neither element seems to be definable in terms of features of the other.

The idea that the nature of action-awareness is explicable without reference to rational agency is immediately puzzling. As we emphasized, an apparent action-awareness has a representational content whose correctness requires that the subject of the awareness be the agent of the event that the awareness represents the subject as producing. The correctness of the apparent awareness requires rational agency. If the apparent action-awareness is correct, there will be rational agency. Further, if the apparent awareness is apparent awareness of some state of affairs whose existence is independent of the apparent awareness, as it seems to be, the prospects for reducing rational agency to features of action-awareness are poor.

What of the converse direction? Can action-awareness be reduced to other features of rational agency? Perhaps the most salient candidate for reduction is a philosophical explanation of facts about action-awareness in terms of a thinker's knowledge of his intentions. Is a thinker's knowledge of what he is doing really explained by his knowledge of his intentions in acting?

There are at least two problems with this idea. The first is that a thinker can intend to act at a given time; may know that that time is now; but may yet fail even to try to act. When the thinker does try to act, how does he know that he is trying? It is no defense of this position to say that he is aware that he is trying. Trying itself is a mental action, and awareness of it is a case of action-awareness, the phenomenon that this account was trying to explain in terms of knowledge of intentions.

The other problem is that even if we grant that the subject knows that he is acting, his knowing that he is intending to φ does not imply that he has an action-awareness of φ-ing. In operating the photocopying machine, I know that I am intending to make a good copy of a document. I do not have an action-awareness of making a good copy of the document. I have only an action-awareness of moving my hands and, possibly, of pressing the button. Only by opening the lid of the machine and perceiving the result do I become aware that I have made a good copy, if I have. The same applies even when it is not a question of operating machines whose results are not immediately open to view. If I am novice at Greek, then whether I have successfully written a Greek letter zeta, or traced its shape correctly in the air, may not be something I know or am aware of simply by having an operative intention to do so. It is not true that you know what you are really doing simply by knowing your intentions in acting.[7]

As we stand back from the details of these issues, the deep question that emerges is why there is a connection between rational agency and awareness. It is an instance of a more general connection of which we need a better understanding. In the case of the non-mental world, we know that a rational subject can judge and act only on what he is aware of. We do not expect the informational states of the blindsight subject, however reliable, to explain his rational decisions and actions. If they do explain his decisions and actions, it is not by rational transitions of thought. What applies to the non-mental world holds here equally for the mental world. A rational subject can make decisions and mental self-ascriptions, and keep track of his own mental events and states, only if he is aware of them. The awareness may be of a distinctive kind, as I have been arguing that it is, but the general principle still holds. Further investigation of this territory should include exploration and explanation of the internal connections between awareness and the rationality of thinkers.

Acknowledgments

Earlier versions of this paper were presented in 2004 to the Language and Mind Seminar at NYU and to the Santa Barbara Conference on Content and Concepts, and in 2005 to the Conference on Mental Action at the School of Advanced Studies, University of London, and to my seminar at Columbia University. I have been helped by the comments of Ned Block, David Chalmers, Jerry Fodor, James Pryor, Michael Rescorla, Nathan Salmon, Stephen Schiffer, Sydney Shoemaker, Susanna Siegel, and Aaron Zimmerman.

Notes

1   This kind of awareness is the subject of Marcel (2003) and Peacocke (2003).
2   I have unified mental and bodily actions by their common relation to tryings, but someone skeptical that this is the right account of action could still accept the other main claims of this paper. That skeptic could still agree that mental action-awareness is a species of the same genus of action-awareness that includes bodily awareness of bodily actions. The skeptic would just be offering a different account of what makes something an action, whether bodily or mental.
3   For one good statement of this position, see Harman (1986, pp. 22–4).
4   On basic actions, see originally Danto (1963) and for refinements (Goldman, 1970, chs. 1–2).
5   See especially Ryle (1971b, 1971c, 1971d).
6   Frith (1992). See the summary on pp. 133–4, and earlier in the same chapter.

Christopher Peacocke

7 Some of these cases appear to be counterexamples to what Richard Moran calls "Anscombe's Condition": "If he can only know what he is doing by observing himself, that would be because, described in *these* terms (e.g. clicking out the rhythm [while pumping water]) his action is *not* determined by his primary reason, is not undertaken by him as the pursuit of some aim. Otherwise, he would know what he is doing in knowing his practical reasons for adopting this aim." See Moran (2001, pp. 126–7). My own view is that Moran's fundamental insights on the role of agency in a range of cases of self-knowledge can be reconciled with, and may be strengthened by, an account of action-awareness in self-knowledge. The relation of Moran's fertile discussion to the theses of the present paper merits extensive independent consideration.

References

Danto, A. (1963). What we can do. *Journal of Philosophy*, 60, 435–45.

Feinberg, I. (1978). Efference copy and corollary discharge: implication for thinking and its disorders. *Schizophrenia Bulletin*, 4, 636–40.

Frith, C. (1992). *The Cognitive Neuropsychology of Schizophrenia*. Hove, East Sussex: Erlbaum.

— and Johnstone, F. (2003). *Schizophrenia: A Very Short Introduction*. Oxford: Oxford University Press.

Goldman, A. (1970). *A Theory of Human Action*. Princeton, NJ: Princeton University Press.

Harman, G. (1986). *Change in View: Principles of Reasoning*. Cambridge, MA: MIT Press.

Helmholtz, H. von (1962). *Treatise on Physiological Optics*. New York: Dover.

Kahneman, D. (2003). A perspective on judgement and choice: mapping bounded rationality. *American Psychologist*, 58, 697–720.

Marcel, A. (2003). The sense of agency: awareness and ownership of action. In J. Roessler and N. Eilan (eds.), *Agency and Self-Awareness: Issues in Philosophy and Psychology*. Oxford: Oxford University Press.

McDowell, J. (1994). *Mind and World*. Cambridge, MA: Harvard University Press.

Moran, R. (2001). *Authority and Estrangement: An Essay on Self-Knowledge*. Princeton: Princeton University Press.

Peacocke, C. (1983). *Sense and Content: Experience, Thought and Their Relations*. Oxford: Oxford University Press.

— (1992). *A Study of Concepts*. Cambridge, MA: MIT Press.

— (1998). Conscious attitudes, attention, and self-knowledge. In C. Wright, B. Smith, and C. MacDonald (eds.), *Knowing Our Own Minds*. Oxford: Oxford University Press.

— (1999). *Being Known*. Oxford: Oxford University Press.

— (2003). Action: awareness, ownership, and knowledge. In J. Roessler and N. Eilan (eds.), *Agency and Self-Awareness: Issues in Philosophy and Psychology*. Oxford: Oxford University Press.

— (forthcoming). Mental action and self-awareness (II): epistemology. In L. O'Brien and M. Soteriou (eds.), *Mental Actions*. Oxford: Oxford University Press.

Prinz, J. (2002). *Furnishing the Mind: Concepts and Their Perceptual Basis*. Cambridge, MA: MIT Press.

Ryle, G. (1971a). The thinking of thoughts: what is *Le Penseur* doing? In *Collected Papers*, vol. 2, *Collected Essays, 1929–1968*. London: Hutchinson.

— (1971b). A puzzling element in the notion of thinking. In *Collected Papers*, vol. 2, *Collected Essays, 1929–1968*. London: Hutchinson.

— (1971c). Thinking and reflecting. In *Collected Papers*, vol. 2, *Collected Essays, 1929–1968*. London: Hutchinson.

— (1971d). The thinking of thoughts. In *Collected Papers*, vol. 2, *Collected Essays, 1929–1968*. London: Hutchinson.

Shoemaker, S. (1984a). Persons and their pasts. *Identity, Cause and Mind: Philosophical Essays*. Cambridge: Cambridge University Press.

— (1984b). Self-reference and self-awareness. *Identity, Cause and Mind: Philosophical Essays*. Cambridge: Cambridge University Press.

Spence, S. A., Brooks, D. J., Hirsch, S. R., Liddle, P. F., Meehan, J., and Grasby, P. M. (1997). A PET study of voluntary movement in schizophrenic patients experiencing passivity phenomena (delusions of alien control). *Brain*, 120, 1997–2011.

Index

content (*cont'd*)
cognitive, xiii, 5–10, 14–18, 122, 124
color, 320
complete, 367
conceptual, xv, 62, 113, 119, 123, 125, 136
conceptualized, 115
empirical, 151
epistemic, 27
externalist, 316, 320
intentional, 37, 72, 247, 371–2
logically wide, 59, 61–2
mental, xii, xiii, xv, 106, 349
metaphysically wide, 61–2
narrow, xiii, 14, 20, 23–33
non-conceptual, xiv, xv, 118–20, 123–5, 128, 135–6, 360
non-rational, 146
of conscious experience, 340, 360
of propositional attitudes, 6
of visual experience, 128
perceptual, xv, xvi, 119, 120, 123–5, 128, 130–1, 133–4, 136–7
psychological, xiii, 24, 28
public, 6–7
representational, 106, 309
semantic, 107, 160, 347
sentences, 5
thought, 347–8
content view, 119, 120, 128
contentful concept(s), xiv, 50
contiguity, 227, 235–6, 238
continuum hypothesis, 205
corollary discharge theory, 355, 369, 370
counterfactual(s), xvii, 17, 20–9, 31, 55, 70, 96, 121, 229, 233–7, 240, 245, 255–9, 263, 291–3, 299
covering-law explanations, 164

Davidson, Donald, 15, 69–70, 72, 73–5, 79–82, 99–100, 114, 146, 147, 157, 197, 228–30, 240, 247–8, 260, 262, 317, 322, 330
Davies, Martin, 39, 51, 63, 133–4
decision theory, 70
defeasibility argument(s), 78, 91–2
deliberation, 72, 148–9, 255, 341, 363
delta account, 372
Dennett, Daniel, 33, 70, 74–5, 81, 147, 157, 316
dependence *see* causation, causality

dependency, 55, 57–8, 61, 235–6, 238, 240
metaphysical, 55
necessary relation, 55
thesis, 57–8, 238
Descartes, 48–9, 51, 144–5, 227–8, 238, 240, 243
dualism, 145, 228; property, 215; substance, 243
intuition(s), 243
physics, 217, 238
privileged access, 54
skeptical possibility, 48
traditional view, 53
determinism, 198, 275–6
Dilthey, W., 69
directionality, 231
dispositionalism, 90, 100, 321
dream argument, 48
dual attribute theory, 185, 193, 196–7
dualism, xviii, 144, 148, 153, 188, 200, 215, 221, 260, 272–3, 282, 283, 287–8, 290–1, 297–8, 304, 306–7; *see also* Descartes and emergentism
consciousness, 290
contemporary, 145
distinctness intuitions, 243
emergentist, 272–3, 283
minimal, 297
phenomenal, 304
property, 147, 215, 287
substance, 147, 243, 270–3, 295
traditional, 290, 292, 296–7

Earth, 5–6, 26, 61–2, 162, 180, 201, 206, 312, 314–15
inverted, 305
lolita, 312
twin, 5–8, 37, 62, 247
Edwards, Jonathan, 258
Einstein, 74
Eklund, Matti, 100
electromagnetic theory, 229, 262
emergentism, xviii, 239, 273, 277, 282–3, 288–91, 292, 294, 297–8 *see also* Descartes and dualism
astonishment, xviii, 274, 281
consciousness, 272, 282, 291–4, 296–7
dualism, 269, 270, 272–3, 275, 277, 283
genuine, 297
interactionist, 295

H^{2}O, 37, 40, 61, 137, 186–9, 191–2, 201, 204, 206–7, 210, 218, 220, 244
Hacker, P., 161, 164
haecceitism, 201, 218
Hall, Ned, 235–6, 253, 254
Harman, Gilbert, 71, 81, 316, 319, 374
Hawthorne, John, 99, 216, 217, 317
Hebbian learning, 177–9
Heck, Richard, xv, xvi, 117, 119, 136
hedged causal claim, 230
hedged psychological laws, 230
Helmholtz, H. von, 355, 369
Higgs field, 293
higher-order thought theory, 338–9
Hilbert, D., 322
H-J net, 168
Horgan, Terrence, 239, 240, 282, 285
Hornsby, Jennifer, 74
Horwich, Paul, 76–7, 92, 263
hujambo case, 349, 353
human foibles, 75
Hume, David, 77, 227, 232, 235, 238, 348
    distinctness doctrine, 196
    Humeanism, 261
    principle, 196
    supervenience, 260
Humpty Dumpty, 81
Hursthouse, Rosalind, 72, 94
Hurvich, L. M., 166
Huxley, T. H., 234, 240, 257

iconicity, 111 *see also* representation(s), iconic
identification, 155, 209, 211, 221, 308
identity, xvii, 23, 106, 154, 167, 196–8, 201, 206, 220, 245, 246, 272, 283, 293, 295, 330, 356, 371–2
identity claims, a posteriori, 206
illusion theory, 281
illusions of control, 343
illusions of passivity, 342
imagining, 12, 126, 341, 348, 352, 354, 361, 365–6
immaterial mind(s), 176, 228, 238
importation model of perceptual justification, 119
incompatibilism, 275
incorrigibility, 161
independent theories, 82

indeterminacy, 69, 81, 100, 126, 219, 220, 261
    argument, 261
    translation, 69
indexical information, or ID, 203–4
indiscernibility of identicals, 201
individualistic properties, 20, 24, 37
innate theory of mind, 150
inner life, 172–3, 269
intention, xiii, 54, 78, 90, 97, 100, 212, 248, 275, 344–5, 352, 365, 367–9, 374
intentional realism, 149
intentional theory, 70
intentionality, 72, 106, 115, 146, 245–6, 366
intention-parasitism, 366
interactionism, 284
internalism, 60, 317, 330
    logical, 60, 62
    phenomenal, 311, 315–16
    qualia, 304
interpersonal relation(s), 77
interpretivism, 99
intertheoretic reduction, 161, 165, 169
intransitivity of indiscriminability, 137
introspection, 54, 114, 132–3, 329, 330–1, 348, 356
inverted spectrum hypothesis, 303
item effect, 111–13

Jackson, Frank, xvii, 147, 170, 181, 185, 197–8, 200–1, 203, 214–21, 260, 287, 290, 298, 309, 329
James, William, 105, 262, 350, 374
Joanette, Y., 347
Johnstone, F., 368–9
judgment
    akratic, 363
    appraisal, 350
    causal, 230
    factual, 330
    first-person, 370
    identity, 330
    inferential, 372
    introspective, 330
    musical, 278
    outright, 362
    perceptual, 106, 114–15, 163, 372
Judson, Whitcomb L., 221
justification and exculpation, 114–15, 136

affective, 349, 350
distinctive, 188
of propositional attitudes, 347, 350-1
perceptual, 348, 355
presentational, 317, 366
technicolor, 328
visual, 132
physicalism, xvi, xvii, xviii, 185-8, 190, 192-
    4, 196-7, 200-2, 205, 212, 215-17, 219,
    238, 243-6, 248-51, 253, 256, 259, 260,
    262, 287-8, 290, 297-8, 311, 314, 330
  a posteriori, xvii, 186-9, 200-1, 203, 205,
    212-17, 219
  a priori, xvii, 186-7, 189, 190, 194, 197,
    200, 205-7, 209-17, 219-21, 290
  eliminative, 190
  non-reductive, 239, 244, 253
  reductive, 244
  theory of identity, 185
  token, 307
picture principle, 108-9
Pietroski, P., 82, 99
Place, U. T., xviii, 154
Plantinga, Alvin, 63
Plato, 160, 176, 205, 220
possible world, 27-8, 33, 121, 126-7, 135,
    192, 217, 244, 246, 250, 270, 272, 289,
    291, 297, 305
  canonical descriptions of, 27
  closest, 233
  counter-nomic, 295
  crack, 49
  empty, 49
  nomological, 271, 291, 295
  sets of, 120, 121, 127, 133
  shadow, 49
  similarity, 233-4, 255, 262
pragmatism, 160
preemption, 233, 255
Princess Elisabeth of Bohemia, 227
principal hypothesis, 358, 364-5, 367-9
principle
  of charity, 69, 79, 99
  of correctness, 87
  of identity, 201
  of individuation, 10, 62, 109, 110
  of necessity of identity, 201
  of privileged access, 54
  of rationality, xiv, 80, 86-7, 91, 95
  of the additivity of mass, 217

of the causal closure of the physical, 277,
    284
Prinz, Jesse, xx, 335, 338-9, 346, 348, 350,
    356, 365
privileged access, xiii, 38-41, 48, 50, 53, 54,
    56, 58-9, 60, 62-3, 315
  to content, 41, 54-8, 62
  to individuating properties, 59, 60, 62
  to the world, 39, 50
  unproblematic, 40, 48, 50
  unrestricted, 56
problem
  of identity, 273
  of intentionality, 150
  of mental causation, 145, 229, 243
  of other minds, 165, 215, 216
  of overdetermination, 233, 239, 255
  of qualia, 160
production
  behavior, 121, 150
  propositional attitudes, 172
  causation, causality, 235-6, 239, 240,
    253-6, 258-9, 262-3
  emergent consciousness, 293-4, 296, 298
projectibility, 149, 231, 250
proprioception, 341, 344, 359
psychology, xvi, 14, 16, 25-6, 28, 30, 70-2,
    74, 78, 80, 91-2, 97-8, 105, 111, 115,
    119, 143, 145-7, 149, 150, 154-6,
    165-6, 170, 173, 180, 195, 205, 213,
    247, 277, 355, 363
  autonomy of, xvi, 145, 154
  causal laws in, 232
  child, 30
  cognitive, 25
  computational, 106
  consciousness, 245
  dispositions, 97
  empirical, xv, 79, 85, 97, 99, 135-6
  folk, 70, 74, 144-8, 163-6, 171-3, 178,
    190, 255
  introspectionist, 153, 355
  language of, 191, 195
  realism, xvi, 145, 148, 153, 154, 157
  scientific, 14, 16, 17, 24-5, 28-30
psycho-neural parallelism, 231
Ptolemy, 162, 164, 180
Putnam, Hilary, xiii, 32, 37, 51, 62, 79, 154,
    197, 247, 261
Pylyshyn, Zenon, 79, 149

CPSIA information can be obtained at www.ICGtesting.com
Printed in the USA
BVOW061714160712

295357BV00009B/4/P